Always,
Rachel

Always,
Rachel

The Letters of

Rachel Carson and Dorothy Freeman,

1952–1964

Edited by Martha Freeman

BEACON PRESS
Boston

BEACON PRESS

25 Beacon Street

Boston, Massachusetts 02108-2892

Beacon Press Books

are published under the auspices of

the Unitarian Universalist Association

of Congregations.

Library of Congress Cataloging-in-Publication Data

Carson, Rachel, 1907–1964.

Always, Rachel: the letters of Rachel Carson and

Dorothy Freeman, 1952–1964 / edited by Martha

Freeman.

p.   cm. — (Concord library)

Includes bibliographical references (p.   ) and

index.

ISBN 0-8070-7010-6

1. Carson, Rachel, 1907–1964—Correspondence.

2. Freeman, Dorothy, 1898–1978—

Correspondence.

3. Biologists—Correspondence.

4. Environmentalists—Correspondence.

5. Women biologists—Correspondence.

6. Women environmentalists—Correspondence.

I. Freeman, Dorothy, 1898–1978.

II. Freeman, Martha E.

III. Title.

IV. Series.

QH31.C33A4   1994

574'.092—dc20

[B]

94-25849

CIP

In memory of Dorothy,

with love and gratitude

All I am certain of is this:

that it is quite necessary for me

to know that there is someone

who is deeply devoted to

me as a person, and who also

has the capacity and the

depth of understanding to share,

vicariously, the sometimes

crushing burden of creative effort.

RACHEL CARSON

Contents

This book could not have been accomplished without the support of many people. The encouragement of Paul Brooks, Shirley Briggs, Jeanne Davis, and Roger Christie, all of whom knew both Rachel Carson and Dorothy Freeman, helped me to go forward. Especially, I thank Paul Brooks, Rachel Carson's editor at Houghton Mifflin, for his active interest and kind intercessions and for his introduction to this book.

Rachel Carson's letters would not have been published now without the permission of Frances Collin on behalf of the Carson estate. I wish to thank Fran for making this project possible.

I am grateful to Wendy Strothman and all of her excellent staff at and associated with Beacon Press for their enthusiasm for this book. Deanne Urmy's delight in these letters, her diligence, good judgment, and gentle initiation of me into the publishing world, were a boon to me. I cannot imagine a better editorial partner. Lydia Howarth's sensitive copy editing was also of great help.

Many people in Maine are responsible for this book coming into being. Without the understanding of my staff in the Maine Legislature's Office of Policy and Legal Analysis, and the support of Sally Tubbesing, I could not have undertaken this work. Without the wise legal counsel of Gordon Scott I could not have completed this book on time or with an easy mind. To all of these friends and colleagues go my heartfelt thanks.

The contributions to this book by two groups of Maine people were critical to its creation. Kristin, Shanna, and Jay Wheelock, Shirley McIntosh, and Jo Anne Erving painstakingly handled thousands of pages of stationery to produce a copy of the letters from which I could work. For their care and interest I am grateful. Linda Weston, Carolin Hanoian, Sharon Dunn, Shelley Cox, Lisa Rollins, and Tami Merry typed and proofread hundreds of thousands of words. Their tirelessness and enjoyment of the project contributed immeasurably to this book, and they have my everlasting appreciation. Linda Weston's computer skills, organization of this work, and attention to detail kept us all moving ahead. I was blessed by her intelligence, care, concern, and pleasure in these letters; I cannot thank Linda enough.

The Maine State Library's reference librarians and Doreen Christianson assisted me in my research for which I thank them. I am also grateful to Linda

Lear for her review of my footnotes. Stanley Freeman, Jr., my father, helped with the task of searching through his father's photographs to select the ones that appear here; for this I thank him.

I am grateful to many friends who over the years believed in this book and in my ability to bring it about. To name all my friends whose kind inquiries spurred me on would consume too much space; but I wish to name a few whose love and support I could not have done without. Thank you for your friendship to Linda Harvell, Frank O'Hara, Jane O'Rourke, Tim Glidden, Michael Higgins, Janice Abarbanel, Ellen Baum, Jeff Fischer, John and Jean Cole, Susan Wittenberg, Carol Stein, Elizabeth Malone, and Margaret Vaughan.

My family has lived with me and these letters for many years. I am forever grateful to my parents, Stanley and Madeleine Freeman, and to my brother, Richard Freeman, for their constant support, both practical and spiritual. I wish to extend my thanks to Sean Meehan, too. My stepsons and daughter-in-law—Sam, Adam, Greg, and Ian Barringer and Jill Cioffi—have displayed an interest in my doings with these letters that has been of great help. The interest of Christopher Morin and Dana Duquette has helped, too. Last, my husband, Richard Barringer, has given me love, time, space, understanding, and advice. His steadfast support for this book has been a lovely gift for which I am deeply grateful.

Rachel Carson has always been in my life. Although by the time I was born she was a best-selling author, who later caused a worldwide uproar when she warned in *Silent Spring* (1962) about the dangers of the indiscriminate use of pesticides, I knew her first and always as my grandmother's friend, and as someone who shared with me her love of low-tide explorations, walks in the woods, and sunsets over the sea. In recent years, she and my grandmother, Dorothy Freeman, have been with me through their correspondence.

Rachel and Dorothy met in the summer of 1953, a few months after my birth, when Rachel was forty-six and Dorothy fifty-five. The prelude to their meeting was an exchange of letters during the 1952 winter holiday season. Dorothy had written Rachel when she had learned that the author of *The Sea Around Us* (1951) was building a cottage on Southport Island, Maine, near that of my grandparents. My grandfather, Stanley Freeman, Sr., had received Rachel's book as a birthday gift in the summer of 1952; he and Dorothy had loved reading it together at their seaside cottage.

When Rachel and Dorothy first met in Maine in July of 1953, the two women's intense and delighted interest in sea life served as an early basis for friendship. Rachel and Dorothy's correspondence began in earnest that fall, and quickly gained in intimacy and in volume. For the first year alone, the collection contains ninety letters. The letters continued for eleven years, during the autumns, winters, and springs of their separations, Rachel at home in Maryland and Dorothy in Massachusetts, until Rachel's death in 1964.

Although my childhood memories of Rachel Carson are ones I treasure, I have come to know her too as an internationally best-selling author and to understand her role as one of our first ecologists. The biographical introduction of Rachel Carson contributed to this book by Paul Brooks, her editor at Houghton Mifflin, supplies important information about her concern for nature from her childhood through her career as a scientist and renowned writer. Paul Brooks recreates the publishing history of two of her best-sellers, *The Edge of the Sea* (1955) and *Silent Spring*; these are the two writing projects, along with a magazine article first published in 1956 and later published posthumously as *The Sense of Wonder* (1965), that consumed Rachel's time during the years of her correspondence with Dorothy Freeman. Part of the value of these letters is the light they shed on Rachel's writing process; on the staggering familial and health burdens she sustained as she wrote; on her sense of destiny as a creative writer; on her moments of despair and then of calm assurance that she had done what she imagined doing.

These letters offer even more of value, however, than a window on the creative process. They give us new writing from Rachel Carson, writing that, as in her books and articles, helps us feel our kinship with plants and animals of the sea, marsh, thicket, field, and sky. The writing and sharing of natural descriptions is a mainstay of the correspondence. Dorothy's descriptions within her letters of the natural world at her beloved Southport became, over the years, an increasingly important gift to Rachel.

Born on June 15, 1898, Dorothy Murdoch Freeman spent most of her childhood in the seafaring town of Marblehead, Massachusetts, and for every summer of her life resided at her family's cottage on Southport Island, Maine. When she graduated from Framingham (Massachusetts) Normal School (now Framingham State College) in 1919, after three years of training to be a home economics teacher, she taught at the high school level in New York state. Two years later she became an assistant director of the Massachusetts Department of Agriculture's Extension Service, where she was in charge of a program for teaching girls and women homemaking skills. At the age of twenty-six, while managing this program in Amherst, Massachusetts, she met Stanley Freeman, who was studying agriculture at the Massachusetts Agricultural College (now the University of Massachusetts) in Amherst. They married in 1924, soon settled in West Bridgewater, Massachusetts, and had one child, my father.

After their marriage, Stanley Freeman began a career in agricultural services, which was to include twenty years' work as an executive for a large animal feed company in Boston. Dorothy left her Department of Agriculture job. She was now a mother and homemaker and eventually was able to compose a life as an avid reader, fan of opera and classical music, gardener, and prolific writer, although an unpublished one. While at times writing daily letters to Rachel, Dorothy also kept a daily diary, wrote to other friends, and corresponded every few months with a group of women who had been her college classmates. She also attempted a few essays, and dreamed of authoring a book, but, as this correspondence illuminates, was never confident in her nonletter writing. All she had to offer as a writer Dorothy put into her correspondence.

While the seeds of the correspondence and friendship between Rachel Carson and Dorothy Freeman lay in their mutual love of the natural world, their letters lead us rapidly into the private world of their shared recognitions. The letters express the quickly developed deep friendship between Rachel and Dorothy and take us along the paths of their loving twelve-year relationship. The rush of warmth appearing early in the letters is breathtaking, and, to me, understandable. Only a short while after they had met for the first time, Rachel was able to write to Dorothy: "It seems as though I had known you for years instead of weeks, for time doesn't matter when two people think and feel in the same way about so many things."

When Rachel and Dorothy became friends, they were mature women, neither of them lacking in self-knowledge, and they easily recognized in each other sympathetic souls. Within five months of the beginning of their correspondence, Rachel wrote: "And I do know that the fact that we are, to an incredible degree 'kindred spirits,' and that for many reasons we need all that we mean to each other, probably lie at the heart of our love." Rachel and Dorothy did not see their love as replacing others in their lives, but as nourishing all they cared for. Rachel wrote of this love that is "poured out:" "You wrote so beautifully, weeks ago, of how one's capacity to give love grows with the exercise of it, so perhaps the more love we have received, the more we are able to absorb and in that sense no one ever has enough." Ultimately, Rachel was able to write that she and Dorothy had happily accepted the wonder of their relationship: "I am glad to remember we decided long ago that there was something beyond the sum of all the 'reasons' we could put forth—a mystery beyond all the explainable mysteries."

Rachel and Dorothy understood, also, the impact on their relationship of writing. Early in the correspondence, Rachel reflected:

You suggest, too, another thought that I believe has been drifting about at least in my subconscious mind—that perhaps if we could have arranged our lives as we would have chosen—to be in daily association—we might have defeated ourselves by so doing, for it may well be that the enforced separation, and the necessity of writing instead of speaking, have contributed to the depth of love and understanding that have developed.

A year later, looking back on the previous year's correspondence, Dorothy added to the thought: "But what amazed me was the depth to which our love had gone in that time for after all we had been together exactly the 6½ hours at Southport in the summer plus the 13 hours here in December. What magic letters can work!"

During the period of their correspondence, each woman experienced her share of burdens, of responsibilities for work and family, of concerns for health, all of which are reflected in the letters presented here. Rachel was not only breadwinner but caretaker for an extended family. In 1952, when these letters begin, Rachel lived with her mother, Maria Carson. Nearby lived Rachel's niece, Marjorie Williams, stricken with diabetes and arthritis, and Marjie's young son, Roger, both of whom Rachel supported financially and emotionally. Rachel's brother, Robert Carson, and another niece, Virginia King, also lived near Rachel's home in Maryland and appear in these letters. (In the mid-1930s, Rachel's father and her older sister, Marian Williams, had died. Marian's two young daughters, Marjorie and Virginia, had come to live with Rachel and her mother. Thus by 1952, Rachel had headed a household for many years.)

In the years of her correspondence with Rachel, Dorothy tended to the health problems of her husband and her mother, Vira Murdoch, who lived with Dorothy and Stanley. She traveled to Maine year-round to visit the home of her son, Stanley Freeman, Jr., his wife, Madeleine, and their children, my brother Richard and me. Eventually, as Rachel struggled with cancer, Dorothy strove to tend to her friend in Maryland and Maine. Throughout the vicissitudes of their work and their personal and family lives, however, the joy of Rachel and Dorothy's spiritual and artistic connection with each other was always present; each always preserved time for beautifully written, caring conversation with the other in letters.

These letters are in my hands because Rachel directed in her will that at the time of her death her collection of Dorothy's letters be returned to Dorothy. By Dorothy's wish, all letters in her possession, hers and Rachel's, were given to me at her death. In the mid-1970s, Dorothy began talking with me about her correspondence with Rachel. She told me then that she and Rachel had discussed destroying the letters, and that they had each chosen to destroy some; these discussions are reflected in the correspondence. A few preserved letters are labeled by the correspondents as destined for "the strong box," a term Rachel and Dorothy used to single out a letter for immediate destruction. The correspondence also contains a few references to the possibility of destroying or burning letters wholesale. Dorothy told me of only one time when such an event occurred. During one of Dorothy's visits to Rachel's Maryland home in the early years of their friendship, Dorothy and Rachel together burned packets of Dorothy's letters in Rachel's fireplace. I believe that this event explains why the first preserved letter written by Dorothy in this correspondence does not appear until December of 1954. Dorothy's 1957 diary also states that she burned some of Rachel's letters in that year.

A few comments in early letters indicate that Rachel and Dorothy were initially cautious about the romantic tone and terminology of their correspondence. I believe this caution prompted their destruction of some letters within the first two years of their friendship, but that in later years the letters they culled from their collection pertained primarily to health or family reports or personal reflections written in the depths of a dark mood; each woman emphasizes in several letters her desire to dwell in happy times despite the family and health problems that entered their lives. Over the years, Rachel also made a greater effort than Dorothy simply to reduce the volume of collected letters. Because of this, of the 750 letters in the collection I possess, three-fourths are Rachel's.

I helped Dorothy to organize this collection in preparation for its possible future publication. She realized that she was unlikely to live to see this project through, and said she hoped I might find an interest in pursuing it. Finding that interest has been easy. Dorothy understood that the letters contain beautiful writing from Rachel Carson and that they should be shared with posterity. I believe also that others will benefit from the story of Rachel and Dorothy's friendship as it unfolds in both of their letters.

I have considered how Rachel would feel about the publication of this correspondence. If Rachel had felt certain that the letters should never be published, she could, and I believe would, have done more during her lifetime, by herself and with Dorothy, to prevent publication, by actual destruction of the letters and through legal instructions about their disposition at the time of her death. Instead, by her actions and the terms of her will, Rachel left the decision about physical preservation of these letters to Dorothy, and the decision about publication of preserved letters to Dorothy regarding her own letters and to Rachel's literary trustee regarding Rachel's letters. The support I have received for the publication of this correspondence from others who knew Rachel, and the reaction I have received from those who have read these letters in preparation for their publication, have buttressed my own feeling that, if Rachel could comment today, she would be happy with this book. I believe Rachel would understand the potential value to others these letters carry.

The physical condition of the letters, as well as the words themselves, speak to me of the care Dorothy and Rachel applied to their friendship. They chose delicate and attractive stationery for their letters, pale shades of blue, cream, or green. Their notecards always pictured a scene or sign of nature. Only a few of the letters are typewritten; each woman possessed strong and distinctive handwriting clearly applied to the pages of her letters. On occasion, when I unfold a letter I discover a dried flower from one woman's garden or a sprig from a woods plant tucked within. At times, the fragrance of my grandmother even drifts up to me from the pages of some letters.

There are two types of letters in this correspondence, and a single envelope sometimes contains both. Rachel and Dorothy wrote public and private letters. Frequently they signaled that the letter was public or private through the salutation: the public letters are often to "Dearest" while the private letters are usually addressed to "Darling" (the use of these differing salutations is not perfectly consistent, however). The public letters, which Rachel and Dorothy refer to as "family" or "sharing" letters, were intended to be read by family and friends. The private letters, which Dorothy and Rachel term letters "for you" or "apples," were written by each woman solely for the other. Dorothy explained to me that the "apple" designation derived from a toy, a small wooden apple that, when the top was removed, contained a smaller apple inside.

The apple image is especially apt for letters containing two parts, one public and one private. Within an envelope containing a public letter sometimes appears a private letter folded doubly so as to fit within the other, or contained within a separate envelope inside the first. Many of the private letters in this collection stand alone. Where a public letter and its companion "apple" are presented, I have called the reader's attention to their relationship by placing the public letter first and by omitting the date in the heading of the private letter or "apple" that follows it.

Although the public letters at times carry more news, they often are not strikingly different in tone or content from the private letters. The private letters do seem to have been reserved for more extensive expressions of endearment and for the more complete sharing of troubles, but they were not always intended to be hidden from others. Early in their correspondence Rachel wrote that she did not object to Dorothy's desire to share a private letter with her husband Stanley: "And darling, I hope I made it clear in my little note that I was so glad you read him the letter—or parts of it. I *want* him to know what you mean to me. Whenever there is something in 'your' letters that you want to share, please remember that you are to decide that, and that I shall be happy in your decision."

This episode in the correspondence reflects an important aspect of Rachel and Dorothy's love for each other: much of its extent was not kept from Dorothy's husband. Instead, their correspondence reveals that Stanley Freeman recognized and supported their love and was supported in turn by their friendship. Stanley, too, had a life-long interest in nature, expressed not only in a career that involved him with farming, but in his expertise as a sailor and his amateur's love of nature photography. Rachel and Stanley developed their own relationship around photography of seashore life. Guided by Rachel, Stanley produced slides of Southport shore and underwater plants, animals, and settings that Rachel used to illustrate her lectures on *The Edge of the Sea*. "Uncle Stan" also provided Rachel's grandnephew Roger with male companionship in outings and letters. Fortunately for this book, Stanley, as the family photographer, created the photographic record that appears here.

I have added footnotes to the text to identify many of the people, places, and events mentioned in the letters. I have sought to provide helpful information, but not to overburden the reader with detail. In the footnotes, Rachel and Dorothy are referred to by the abbreviations RC and DF. The information given in the footnotes derives from several principal sources, in addition to all I could glean from library research. Three books about Rachel Carson helped me considerably in my search for facts: Paul Brooks's *The House of Life: Rachel Carson at Work* (1972) was my primary resource, but Philip Sterling's *Sea and Earth: The Life of Rachel Carson* (1970) and Virginia Wadsworth's *Rachel Carson: Voice for the Earth* (1992) supplied important details.

I have also drawn at times from materials about Rachel Carson saved by Dorothy Freeman, referred to in this correspondence as her "Rachel file": magazine articles by and about the author, newspaper clippings, copies of speeches given by Rachel, a few letters from others about Rachel, Dorothy's own notes about her friend's activities, and other miscellaneous documents. Dorothy's diaries, for 1952 through 1958 and half of 1960, and Stanley's diaries for 1961, 1963, and a short period in 1964, supplied some footnote information. In a few other instances, my memory of conversations with Dorothy about her friendship and correspondence with Rachel provided the clue needed for a footnote. In more instances, the memories of my parents about the happenings and people mentioned in these letters provided the footnote information. The reminiscences of Rachel's colleagues and friends Paul Brooks, Shirley Briggs, and Jeanne Davis also aided my research.

In editing this correspondence, I felt that the letters themselves did the best job possible of narration. I did not excise portions of letters, except in a single case: Dorothy's first letter of January 1960, written over three days, contained material important to the story but also one day's worth of inconsequential writing, which I deleted and noted. Most of the letters that I chose not to include are from the period between 1954 and 1956 because of the disproportionate number of letters (over 300) from these years in the collection. I employed two criteria to guide my selection of letters: I sought to include letters that best advanced the narrative and that touched on all subjects and themes contained in the entire correspondence. For the former reason, I also did not include some long letters of Dorothy's from the later years of the correspondence that provided extensive detail about domestic life or forays into the natural world. These are poignant letters, for they were penned to provide Rachel with greater contact with everyday activities, and with the nature she loved, as her life became filled with illness, doctors, hospitals, and the never-ending demands generated by *Silent Spring*. Although these letters contain some lovely descriptive passages, on balance they slowed the pace of the story.

From 1957 through 1964, and especially during the 1957 through 1960 period, I selected out relatively few letters from the correspondence. Rachel and Dorothy both experienced difficult family circumstances in the years 1957 through 1960, trying situations that reduced the number of letters written or preserved. During these years, too, as seen in the letters preserved, they turned more often to the telephone for their connection. As family situations settled into new patterns, as Rachel undertook the difficult but exhilarating research and writing that produced *Silent Spring*, and as Dorothy and Rachel began to acknowledge that Rachel would lose her battle with cancer, their correspondence blossomed again. Only a few letters have been left out of this collection for the last three years, and these were omitted only to bow to book length limitations. Throughout all the years of the correspondence the reader will notice the dearth of letters in the summer months, a pattern easily explained by Dorothy and Rachel's proximity at Southport.

I have made very few corrections or changes in the letters. I have added a date in the letter heading if the correspondents did not provide one (except at the letters that were private enclosures in envelopes with dated public letters) and have standardized the dates they did provide. The salutations in the letters rarely contain the name of the recipient; I have added names in brackets to eliminate any possible confusion. I have also italicized all book and journal titles. (Rachel and Dorothy variously used underlining, quotation marks, and no special treatment of titles.) Rachel and Dorothy generally spelled and used grammar well; on only a few occasions have I corrected a verb tense or a clear misspelling, revised for consistency between a plural or singular subject and verb, or created a correct compound word where the handwriting did not clearly do so. The idiosyncratic use of hyphens and capitalizations, especially by Dorothy, is for the most part retained. If the correspondents' use of hyphens or capitalization varied with regard to certain words, I made the treatment more consistent. Rachel's infrequent misspellings occurred almost always in relation to the names of the significant numbers of doctors and domestics with whom she was associated in the last years of her life. These misspellings are preserved and noted. A distinctive trait of Rachel's penmanship was her dropping of apostrophes in contractions and plurals; I have silently corrected these. I have made very few other punctuation changes in the letters of both women when not doing so impeded reading. Both Rachel's and Dorothy's letters are sprinkled with marginal insertions, some quite charmingly draped around the letter. I have not attempted to reproduce their placement but have inserted them in the letters as parentheticals. I have not done any other rewriting, restructuring, or recomposition of these letters.

As much as possible, I have included in this book any letter that is referred to in another letter. If a letter that Rachel or Dorothy refers to does not appear, it is usually because the letter was not preserved, but occasionally it has been omitted because the sense of the missing letter is clear or could be provided in a footnote and to include it would have been unnecessarily repetitious. Occasionally, a letter refers to a clipping or other enclosed item. If the enclosure is preserved I have described it in a footnote; if the enclosure does not exist, I have noted that.

These letters, then, come to you as they are, essentially unfiltered by me. Over the fifteen years of my solitary travels through these letters, from the first dipping of my toe into them when I received them from my grandmother to my full immersion in editing this book, I have learned anew lessons of love from Rachel and Dorothy. It was important to me as editor of this book to make no choice which would diminish or obscure these lessons because, as Rachel wrote, they were important to Rachel and Dorothy:

. . . what I feel most clearly is that we must never again for a moment forget what a precious possession we have in our love and understanding, and in that constant and sometimes almost puzzling longing to share with each other every thought and experience. . . . If ever I have seemed to forget the wonder and fragile beauty of it, darling, know that I won't forget again.

The threads of all the words in Rachel and Dorothy's correspondence come together for me on Southport Island, the place each loved the best. Southport is another character you will come to know in this book, for Rachel and Dorothy's tie to that bit of Maine coast was a spiritual touchstone for both women. Whenever I travel the winding, spruce-lined road to their Southport shore, I feel a delightful cord reeling me in. My journey ends when I sit down on a granite rock at the edge of the sea and breathe salt air, gaze at the moving ocean and neighboring islands, watch sea ducks bob and fly, and feel the wind. I know that the cord that tethers me to this place is love. It is the love of beauty and for one another that I knew from Rachel and Dorothy years ago, and that I have found, again, in Rachel and Dorothy's letters.

PAUL BROOKS

The publication of Rachel Carson's correspondence with Dorothy Freeman is a major event, putting the reader on intimate terms with one of the most widely read, most influential, but least known women of our time. The letters begin in 1952, when Rachel was forty-five years old, having recently achieved worldwide fame with the publication of a record-breaking best-seller, *The Sea Around Us*. They conclude twelve years later when she has finished writing *Silent Spring*, in the face of what she called "a catalogue of illnesses" that would have defeated a less courageous woman. To appreciate what this friendship with Dorothy Freeman meant to them both—almost from the very start—one needs to look back on Rachel's astonishing career up to that time.

Born on May 27, 1907, the youngest of three children, Rachel Louise Carson (she later dropped the middle name) grew up in a rural area of the lower Allegheny Valley of Pennsylvania. Thanks to her mother, who read to her from early childhood, she acquired a deep appreciation of the beauty and mystery of the natural world. As she remarked many years later: "I can remember no time when I wasn't interested in the out-of-doors and the whole world of nature." And from earliest childhood she assumed that she was going to be a writer. Beginning at age ten she wrote stories and essays for *St. Nicholas* magazine. Her dedication to writing continued through high school and on into college— Pennsylvania College for Women (later Chatham College)—where she started out as an English major but later, thanks to a brilliant teacher, became fascinated with zoology, and changed to that field. At the time she believed that she had abandoned her dream of a literary career; only later did she realize that, on the contrary, she had discovered what she wanted to write about. The merging of these two powerful currents—the imagination and insight of a creative writer with a scientist's passion for fact—goes far to explain the blend of beauty and authority that was to make her books—and even her letters while writing her books—unique.

After graduating from college with honors, Rachel went on to get a degree in zoology at Johns Hopkins University, and to teach there and at the University of Maryland. Most important for her future career were the summers she spent studying at the Woods Hole Marine Biological Laboratory in Massachusetts. Here she would learn about the sea, for which she had a childhood yearning but had known only from books by such writers as Joseph Conrad, John Masefield, Henry Williamson, and, nearer home, Henry Beston, whose *The Outermost House* she read again and again.

When I first met Rachel Carson she was chief of publications for the Fish and Wildlife Service in Washington, where she was working to support the family after her father's death. In addition to the writing she had done for the service, she had contributed articles on marine subjects to the local papers and—most important to her future career—an article in the *Atlantic Monthly* magazine entitled *Undersea*. This had caught the attention of book editors, and resulted four years later in the publication of her first book, *Under the Sea-Wind*. Unfortunately the timing could not have been worse: it came on the market a few weeks before Pearl Harbor and failed to get the attention it deserved. Reviews were very good, but few; sales were disappointing. Rachel, however, was not easily discouraged—as her future career was to testify so splendidly.

Although the first edition of *Under the Sea-Wind* did not enjoy a wide readership, it did lead directly to Rachel's next enterprise. She was soon launched on a far more ambitious book project, which would bring into focus both the emotional ties with the sea that she had felt since childhood and the wealth of knowledge she had acquired since she chose marine biology as a career. Entitled *The Sea Around Us*, it would reflect the vast strides in oceanography made during the war, which her position with the government gave her a rare opportunity to appreciate. But it was an overwhelming job. "More than once I asked myself why I should have even undertaken such a task."

When *The Sea Around Us* was published in 1951—a decade after *Under the Sea-Wind*—it was an instant success, rising rapidly to the top of the best-seller lists. Rachel Carson became a national celebrity overnight. Translations were soon being published throughout the world. Rachel herself—a modest, quiet, albeit determined woman—found this sudden fame somewhat overwhelming. She wrote to Dorothy in February 1954,

The publicity-type references of course affect me very negatively—I don't want to see or hear them. . . . Ordinarily—and this sounds ridiculous but it's true—I have no sense that they are really talking about *me*—it's quite impersonal, and doesn't get below the surface of my mind. But if the awareness ever does penetrate, there is a frightened and lonely feeling. . . . The heart of it is something very complex, that has to do with ideas of destiny, and with an almost inexpressible feeling that I am merely the instrument through which something has happened.

The Sea Around Us set a record by remaining on the best-seller lists for eighteen months. One side effect of this remarkable achievement must have been very gratifying to the author: when her first book, *Under the Sea-Wind*, was reissued in a new edition, it too became a best-seller, though on a more modest scale. (I myself feel that it contains some of her best writing. It has that rare quality: the freshness and the "sense of wonder"—one of her favorite concepts—that is sometimes found in a writer's first book.)

Thanks to the royalties earned by *The Sea Around Us*, Rachel achieved financial independence for the first time in her life. She was able to give up her government job, to realize her long-held dream of acquiring land on the coast of Maine, and to build a cottage near the tide pools that were her joy to explore. And most important of all, she could now devote her working hours to her own research and writing.

Early in June 1951—two weeks before the publication of *The Sea Around Us*—Rachel had escaped for a brief rest to her favorite beach in Beaufort, North Carolina, where she happily wore out the seat of her pants on barnacle-covered rocks, "getting acquainted with a whole village of sea anemones, crabs and so on. . . . I spent the morning on a shoal near here, wading in water up to my knees, not a human soul in sight." She was already looking forward to her next book, which she had contracted to write when she was still a government employee, and *The Sea Around Us* not yet published. Like most creative writers, she had her eye constantly fixed on the future. "I am always more interested in what I am about to do than in what I have already done." She saw the new book, to be entitled *The Edge of the Sea*, as a biological counterpart to its predecessor. Research would be largely outdoors, rather than in libraries and laboratories. (She had experienced only one sea voyage while she was writing *The Sea Around Us*.) Now she would be studying marine life largely within arm's reach, from the rocky coast of Maine to the sand beaches of the Atlantic coastal plain and the "mangrove ghost forests" bordering the Florida coast. With her would be her indispensable companion, Fish and Wildlife Service artist Bob Hines. Thanks to Rachel's genius as a creative writer, the original idea that I had given her for a guide to seashore life evolved into something far more interesting. In her own words, her aim was "to take the seashore out of the category of scenery and make it come alive—an ecological concept will dominate the book." She was hard at work on it when she first met the woman who would play a vital role in the last—and historically most significant—decade of her life.

In the fall of 1952, while Rachel's cottage was still being built on the shore of Southport Island in Maine, she received a welcoming letter from her future summer neighbor, Dorothy Freeman, who spent every summer on Southport and was deeply interested in the surrounding life of birds, woods, and sea. After Rachel's first summer there, the letters continued. Dorothy wrote to her son: "It is a revelation to study the development of the friendship from 'Mrs. Freeman' to 'Dorothy' and all by letters." When they finally met in the summer of 1953, it was to explore together the local tide pools at low tide. Soon thereafter they came to realize they shared interests which clearly ranged far beyond the pleasure they both felt, not only in the sea, but in the whole world of nature. Rachel wrote to Dorothy, "I think that the rapid flowering of our friendship, the head-long pace of our correspondence, reflects a feeling, whether consciously recognized or not, for the 'lost' years and a desire to make up for all the time we might have enjoyed this, had something brought us together earlier."

The period covered by these letters includes the completion of *The Edge of the Sea*. But they are largely concerned with the creation of *Silent Spring*. As one reads them, the importance to Rachel of this friendship becomes increasingly clear. Some years earlier, replying to a fan letter from a college girl determined to have a literary career, she concluded with a note of warning: "A writer's occupation is one of the loneliest in the world." As she would now write to Dorothy Freeman, it was necessary for her to have someone who has "the depth of understanding to share, vicariously, the sometimes crushing burden of creative effort." Dorothy, who was enamored of the creative process, and who never ceased to feel protective of Rachel's physical and creative self, supplied this sustaining understanding to Rachel throughout.

During the early period of her friendship with Dorothy, Rachel was hard at work completing *The Edge of the Sea*: "I'm still so far from the end that at times I feel pretty desperate about it in spite of my publisher's understanding indulgence." Dorothy's love and support had already become essential. She read each chapter as it was finished. "I couldn't do without you," wrote Rachel as she finally approached the end of a highly rewarding but difficult task. As publication day came near, the tension vanished. She was actually looking forward to the party her publishers planned to give in New York, for "friends of theirs and mine who will be happy about the book. In other words, a real celebration. (In still other words, to say 'Thank God, she did finish it at last!')" *The Edge of the Sea* is dedicated to "Dorothy and Stanley Freeman: who have gone down with me into the low-tide world and have felt its beauty and its mystery." Reviews were all that she and her publishers could have hoped for, and her book was soon at the top of the best-seller list.

In the years immediately following the publication of *The Edge of the Sea*, Rachel was actively considering plans for her next project. "No writer," she believed, "can stand still. He continues to create or he perishes. Each task completed carries its own obligation to go on to something new."

Meanwhile, however, her family situation was becoming more and more troublesome and demanding. Her aging mother needed constant attention. Her niece Marjorie Williams, who was living with her, had become seriously ill. Her responsibilities for Marjorie's young son Roger (whom Rachel would soon adopt after her niece's death) compromised the time she needed to devote to writing. Rachel almost never complained. But she finally did let herself go in a letter to Dorothy: "When I feel, as I do now, the pressure of all the things that seem worth doing in the years that are left, it seems so silly to be spending my time being a nurse and housemaid." She had several literary projects in mind. Her reputation virtually ensured the success of anything she wrote or edited.

In January 1958, an event occurred that would eclipse all these considerations. Back in the days when she was a government employee, Rachel had been deeply troubled by the reckless use of deadly poisons such as DDT for insect control. She had tried in vain to publish a warning in the press. Now, many years later, she was moved to act by a letter to the *Boston Herald* from her friend Olga Owens Huckins whose home and private bird sanctuary had been sprayed from the air with DDT, killing both birds and harmless insects. Rachel was shocked. "The more I learned about the use of pesticides, the more appalled I became. I realized that here was material for a book. What I discovered was that everything which meant most to me as a naturalist was being threatened, and that nothing I could do would be more important." She did not take on the burden gladly, but only when she realized that there was no alternative.

Research for such a book was a formidable task: a far cry from those days spent along the beaches and among the tide pools while working on *The Edge of the Sea*. But Rachel was excited and happy with what she was doing. "For all its unpleasant features," she wrote to Dorothy, "it is something with so many complexities scientifically that it is mentally stimulating, as are the contacts with many of the people I talk or write to." For a year and a half all went well. But in the spring of 1960 she had to undergo an operation for breast cancer. Such was the beginning of the "catalogue of illnesses" which would plague her throughout the writing of the book that would become *Silent Spring*—obstacles that would make its successful conclusion seem almost like a miracle.

Inevitably, the scientific research necessary for the new book project was demanding, often cheerless work. She was well aware that Dorothy was not happy about her project. "I know you dread the unpleasantness that will inevitably be associated with its publication. . . . But knowing what I do, there would be no future peace for me if I kept silent." By the autumn of 1958 she was "excited and happy about the book": stimulated by its scientific complexities and by the interesting people with whom she was in contact. Among them was the world-famous ornithologist Robert Cushman Murphy, who had brought suit against the federal and New York government for needless and destructive spraying with DDT of his own and adjoining properties on Long Island, which had resulted—together with other devastation—in the death of a neighbor's horse. Although the suit was eventually dismissed on technical grounds, the scientific evidence on which it was based, collected from experts in America and abroad, became the basis of the research for *Silent Spring*.

The year 1958 ended sadly with the death of Rachel's mother, the person most responsible for setting her on her remarkable career. "My mind," Dorothy wrote to Rachel, "dwelt on all that I know of her life, of the wonderful person she has been, of her great love for all living things. . . . Do you know when I think I shall miss her most?—When we shall sit down together and she will not be there to say Grace."

During the spring and summer of 1959 Rachel had little time for writing to Dorothy. She was working hard on the book which would become *Silent Spring*.[1] She was, in her own words, "riding the crest of a wave of enthusiasm and creativity." But all too soon she was in the hospital. She looked back with nostalgia to the early, more leisurely, years with Dorothy. Now she had become aware that "life is not only uncertain but short at best." She was also aware of the importance of what she was doing: she had, in her own words, "no time for anything unless it is somehow related to the great projects that are uncompleted." At one point she felt for a moment that "life had burned down to a very tiny flame, that might so easily flicker out." For months thereafter she was in and out of the hospital. But she kept writing late into the night. Dorothy could hardly believe it. "Darling, you amaze me at the nonchalance with which you say 'two more chapters off to Paul.' How incredibly wonderful!" By January of 1962 (the year of publication) Rachel had, in her own words, "almost reached the end of the long road." She was able to send a virtually complete manuscript to William Shawn, editor of the *New Yorker*, which would print three installments during the summer, and to Houghton Mifflin, which would publish the complete book in September.

The first installment of *Silent Spring* appeared in the *New Yorker* for June 15, 1962. It caused an immediate sensation throughout the country and became the target of a savage and relentless attack by the pesticides industry. Rachel had been warned of the storm her book would create, but she could hardly have foreseen its extent and its ferocity, which included personal attacks on this "hysterical woman." Pesticide manufacturers were unable to refute her allegations (she had source references for every statement she had made) so they treated the whole matter as a publicity problem. The National Agricultural Chemicals Association appropriated a quarter of a million dollars "to improve the image of the industry" (an action that backfired by giving *Silent Spring* publicity on a scale that no book publisher could afford).

The fury with which the book and its author were attacked had, I believe, deeper roots than the chemical companies' concern for profits. After all, DDT and other pesticides were not a vital part of their business. Her attackers must have realized that she was questioning not simply the use of poisons, but the basic irresponsibility of our industrial society toward the natural world: the belief that damage to nature was an inevitable cost of "progress." That was her heresy.

Although the attacks on *Silent Spring* and its author came as no surprise to Rachel, its immediate impact certainly did: "I never predicted the book would have a smashing success. I doubted it would, so all this is unexpected and wonderful to me." What's more, it promised to get results: "The tremendous response that has come in letters to me and to the *New Yorker* Editor has been beyond all expectations and seems to indicate a strong desire on the part of the public to bring about some improvement in the situation." An immediate result of the controversy was the appointment, by President Kennedy, of a Pesticides Committee, to make a scientific study of the whole matter. The Committee's report not only vindicated Rachel in her statements about the dangers of pesticides, but gave her credit for making the public aware of them. One of Rachel's staunchest supporters was Secretary of the Interior, Stewart L. Udall, a dedicated conservationist who understood the worldwide importance of her protest against reckless use of poisons that were contaminating the entire environment.

In his excellent book *Since Silent Spring* (1970), Frank Graham comments on the wider significance of what Rachel Carson was saying:

What was this book which created such an uproar? *Silent Spring* is, essentially, an ecological book. Almost everything that had been said about chemical pesticides before this time had been phrased in *economic* terms: we need more and better pesticides to grow bigger and better crops to make agriculture more profitable and more convenient for the farmer. . . . Rachel Carson approached the subject from a different direction—from the breadth of her experience in the biological sciences and the depth of her sympathy for all living things.

In other words, she was acutely aware that all forms of life on earth are interrelated. When she began writing, the word "environment" had few of the connotations that it has today. "Ecology" (derived from the Greek for "habitation") was an unfamiliar scientific term. While no one person or one book can be credited with launching the so-called environmental movement of the 1960s, *Silent Spring* obviously played a lead role, not only in America, but throughout the industrial world.

Rachel herself did not live to see more than the initial impact of her now classic book. Early in 1963—less than six months after publication of *Silent Spring*—she was suffering from heart trouble as well as cancer. She knew that her time was limited. But as she wrote to Dorothy, "We are not going to get bogged down in unhappiness about all this. We are going to be happy, and go on enjoying all the lovely things that give life meaning."

Meanwhile, her book was being translated and published all over Europe, and in Japan (where her reputation continues to grow and a Japanese edition of her biography has long been in print). Soon after publication *Silent Spring* was being read in South Africa and Australia. In England Prince Philip, a notable conservationist, said, "I strongly recommend Rachel Carson's *Silent Spring* if you want to see what is going on." The idea of "biological" control, as opposed to use of poisons, was beginning to be taken seriously.

No conventional scientific study, however hair-raising its conclusions, could be expected to arouse such widespread interest. Rachel's genius lay in her ability to make a formidable subject like chlorinated hydrocarbons into a work of literature. As she wrote to a friend: "I myself never thought the ugly facts would dominate, and I hope they don't. The beauty of the world I was trying to save has always been uppermost in my mind—that, and anger at the senseless, brutish things that were being done. I have felt bound by a solemn obligation to do what I could—if I didn't at least try I could never again be happy in nature."

As Rachel's worldwide influence continued to grow, her own health continued to decline. "So many ironic things," she wrote to Dorothy, less than a year after publication of *Silent Spring*. "Now all the 'honors' have to be received for me by someone else. And all the opportunities to travel to foreign lands—all expenses paid—have to be passed up. Sweden is the latest." (Having to forgo the trip to Sweden was a particularly bitter disappointment.) She did manage to fulfill one long-held desire: a visit to the California redwoods. And she was able to get to New York City in early December to receive personally two awards that she treasured most of all: one from the American Geographical Society (of which her friend Robert Cushman Murphy was a prominent member), the other from the National Audubon Society, which gave her their annual gold medal.

By the spring of 1964, Rachel realized that the end was near. She urged Dorothy Freeman—who had recently lost her husband—to "remember the joys we have shared." Rachel Carson died on April 14, 1964.

The Rachel Carson Council, established soon after her death, continues to carry on her work, until recently under the firm and skillful direction of Shirley Briggs, Rachel's close friend from the day they first shared office space in the Bureau of Fisheries in Washington. The Council has long been the recognized center for current information about pesticides and a powerful force in maintaining their regulation.

As she was completing the manuscript of *Silent Spring*, Rachel wrote to a friend, "Now I can believe that I have at least helped a little. I would be unrealistic to believe one book could bring a complete change."

True. But in the words of a newspaper editorial eight years after publication of *Silent Spring*: "A few thousand words from her, and the world took a new direction."

Always,
Rachel

Part One: The Sea Around Us

. The odd thing
that, in writing
little. I was
a publisher

DECEMBER 15

Dear Mrs. Freeman:

What a charming and thoughtful greeting from our Southport[1] neighbors—to be! We do hope the cottage will be ready early in June. It is a lovely
spot which you probably know—a little north of Hendrick's Head and south of
Deep Cove. I have loved the Boothbay Harbor area for years and do look forward to having a summer place to write in such beautiful surroundings.

Yes I'm sure we have the bunchberry, and how pretty it is.

Do come to see us. We look forward to knowing you, and I do appreciate
your gracious welcome.

Sincerely,

Rachel L. Carson

[1] Southport Island,
Maine, site of the
Freeman and
Carson summer
cottages.

SEPTEMBER 3

Dear Mrs. Freeman:

It was sweet of you to take time out of your Canadian holiday to write me.[1]
We too, are looking forward to Sunday. Mr. Freeman thought you would both
enjoy going down into the low tide world, so here are a few suggestions—I'm
taking it for granted you haven't done quite this sort of thing before! Bring
along a pair of old sneakers for wading. Out here no deep wading is necessary,
and I just roll up my jeans. If anyone need go in beyond the knees, it can be I,
for I'll have a change at hand. I'm sorry it won't be one of the really low tides—
as you know, they will come later in the week—but since Mr. Freeman is leaving
soon we'll just make the best of this. And we can bring up a few things to see under the microscope. And have a cup of tea after we dry off!

[1] The Carsons and
Freemans had
first met in
Southport on
July 12.

I believe Sunday's low will come between four and four-thirty. Can you be here by 3:15 or 3:30 at the latest, for it is best to follow it out?

Both my mother and I do appreciate your sympathy, for the understanding of friends who have really loved cats themselves helps as much as anything can. But the heartbreak of Muffie's death seems never to grow any easier to bear, and there are always tears in our hearts, and sometime in our eyes. He was our loved and constant companion for two years—still young enough to be fun-loving and gay, but old enough to be loving, understanding, and devoted in the way that only a cat can be. Some time after I get home I must send you his picture.

It will be such fun to have you Sunday. Marie Rodell, who is my literary agent, will be here for the week-end, and I know she will enjoy meeting you, too.

Sincerely,

Rachel L. Carson

I do have the copy of *Punch*, and had a laugh out of it. Fortunately, "Sea Wind" is a sufficiently old "brainchild" that I can feel quite detached about it. And remind me to tell you about the movie—no child of mine at all![2]

[2] *Under the Sea-Wind*, RC's first book, published in 1941. RC had not been pleased with an RKO film based on *The Sea Around Us* in 1951, the year of that book's publication.

[3] The Freemans were leaving Southport for their home in West Bridge-water, Massachusetts.

THURSDAY, SEPTEMBER 10

Dear Mrs. Freeman:

Just a note to say goodbye and to wish you a good trip home[3]—also to tell you how very much we enjoyed having you with us on Sunday. We both wish we might have seen more of you this year, but as you say, there will be another summer, and we look forward to knowing others of your family, too.

Wasn't the surf beautiful on Monday? We couldn't go to Ocean Point or Pemaquid because of expected visitors, but it was exciting here.

Do tell Mr. Freeman that the picture of the gulls is on the little table under the lamp where we can enjoy it every day!

Our very best to you both—

Rachel Carson

P.S.—in the Post Office—And here is your sweet letter, so I have opened this note to thank you for that and to say again how happy we are that you took the trouble to write me last winter and start this very pleasant friendship. I, too, feel a strong bond of common interests—and that we have the same feeling about many things. So let's drop formality—and when I send you darling Muffie's picture it will be to "Dear Dorothy" if that is all right with you, and I think it is!

Goodbye again—

Rachel

Dear Dorothy,

This is the letter I wasn't supposed to write (you said) but I'm writing it anyway for what seems to me a very good reason—I really want to!

The big September tides have come and gone, and every time I was down there exploring I wished you were there, too—you would have enjoyed it so. Of course wind and surf made each day quite unpredictable; what should have been the lowest tide wasn't, and one day the surf was so heavy that just being down within reach of it was an adventure. I'm sending you a snapshot taken from the "edge of the edge" on September 22, to show what I mean—you know it's not supposed to look like that at low tide! (By the way, I think I see Dogfish Head in this picture. The near points are, of course, the entrance to Deep Cove, but I thought the dimly seen bit on the horizon might be yours. If so, I can wave to you at low water of springs, anyway.) I am so sorry we didn't have a good tide the day you were here. When it is really low, it is nothing to see as many as thirty anemones under one ledge—big things six to eight inches long. And there are so many urchins right out on the flat rock surfaces where the tide falls down below all the Irish moss, and there is nothing but the rose-colored coralline algae encrusting the rock. And then all the Laminarias and other deep-water plants begin to show themselves, and somehow everything seems so very different.

I think the things you might have enjoyed most (as I believe I did) were these. The first day, when the tide was only "0.0" and so not as exciting as the later ones promised to be, I was poking around a big rock that had thick crusts of the coralline algae that looked as though they could be broken off. I found they could be—because the pink coating was covering some very large barnacles, or rather barnacle shells, for they were empty. So I took a small mass of the stuff to the house, and spent the evening being entertained by all the creatures that were living in and on that little world that wasn't more than two inches across in any direction. Among other things, there were tiny anemones living inside the empty barnacle shells. And on the outside of the shells there was attached a whole new generation of baby barnacles. When they fed (as they did, madly, all the time I was watching) I could see that the inside of their shells, and their own little feathery appendages, were for some odd reason colored the same deep pink as the algae that were cementing their world together. The whole catalogue of creatures would be too long to list, but there were many different species and literally hundreds of individuals. (They all went home on the next low tide.)

The other especially choice thing (and I really got excited about this, because I didn't know it at all and have never seen any report of it) was the discovery that, where the pink crust of corallines over the rock has become thick and heavy enough that pieces can be chipped off, there is a whole community of creatures living in it and under it. That, again, was a whole evening's work and entertainment at the microscope, the high point of which was the discovery of an exquisitely beautiful worm (don't laugh, and don't shiver—it is the most beautiful worm in the world!) that I had never personally collected before, though of course I've seen it. The whole algal crust is riddled with the borings of things that have made a home in it, and with winding tunnels going off in all directions; sometimes one of those very tiny crustaceans that has a single, glowing eye would come up out of the darkness of such a tunnel, always reminding me of a miner with his head lamp. Well, you see I had a good time.

And the high tides, too, were something to enjoy, and on the moonlight nights we didn't go to bed till "all hours"—for we could sit by the living room window and enjoy the water without even being cold. On one of those nights there was really a tremendous surf—I don't know why, but there were real, open-ocean rollers. And almost every night, after we'd gone to bed, we could hear the surf trampling in over our ledges, and then I would think about all the creatures I knew were down there, and wonder how they were getting along.

At one point, I thought I'd ration these good tides—maybe go to your shore for one, to Ocean Point, and to Pemaquid; but finally I decided it made more sense to get to know my own shore really well this year, at all the various tidal levels. Maybe we can do yours together, on a really good tide, next year. And that reminds me to say that when you decide when to take your 1954 vacation, you really must plan it with a tide table in hand. No coming on any old neap tides!

I always like fall better than summer, and we stay on and hate to think of going. One day there was a school of porpoises over on the far shore; we have had loons just offshore several different days; and yesterday a big seal put his head out several times and swam in toward the rocks in front of the Mahard place. And the *Register*'s[4] society notes this week contain items about a whale, a moose, and three deer. I seriously doubt that we shall be able to send ourselves home until they come to turn the water off, October 20th. Besides, I have certain manuscript goals[5] that I want to reach before that break comes, and progress is—well, I may as well admit it—SLOW.

I was interested in your note about the movie, and if you go, and like it, I am quite prepared to forgive you. Of course I was terribly prejudiced, and perhaps a person going to see it just for itself, without particular reference to the book, would find it enjoyable. Anyway, please tell me. It has just opened at home (how glad I am that I'm not in Washington) and the *Washington Post*, while liking some of the photography, roasted the script, for which I was duly grateful.

May I tell you that every one of your letters has given me a great deal of pleasure. It seems as though I had known you for years instead of weeks, for time doesn't matter when two people think and feel in the same way about so many things. I, too, am looking forward to lazy hours when we can sit on our beach next summer and just talk! That will be one of the great pleasures of the

[4] The *Boothbay Register*, the weekly newspaper for the Southport area.

[5] RC was at work on *The Edge of the Sea*.

summer. In the meantime, if I steal time from this tyrant manuscript now and then to write you, you must realize that I am doing it chiefly from selfish motives, because I like writing to friends almost as much as I like hearing from them!

And I'm glad that the books (and I) stood the test of rereading after you had met the author. Now that I know you, I value your devotion to what I've written all the more. I doubt that I could explain how any particular feeling or effect is achieved (you know the story of the centipede) but if there is any simple explanation I think it is that my sensory impressions of, and emotional response to, the world of nature date from earliest childhood, and that the factual knowledge was acquired much later. I had no formal training in biology, for example, until my second year of college, yet I had felt at home with wild creatures all my life. And I loved the ocean with a purely vicarious love long before I had seen it.

Thanks for the suggestion of a book for Roger;[6] he is already showing great delight in being read to. He has four of the Beatrix Potter books (I grew up on them—did you?) and brings them to his mother one after another to have them read.

If I don't stop you will feel that you have read another book! I have just thought of about ten other things I meant to tell you but for once I shall take myself in hand and go back to the manuscript!

My best to all the Freemans, and to you my affectionate regard—

Sincerely,
Rachel

[6] Roger Christie, RC's grand-nephew, son of her niece, Marjie Williams, who lived near RC in Silver Spring, Maryland, and often visited Southport with her.

OCTOBER 5

Dear Dorothy,

I'm both glad and sorry to say that I don't expect to be home until quite near the end of the month. It would have been such fun to see you there, but you understand perfectly the reluctance to leave here a minute before we must! October 20 seems to be the zero hour as far as water is concerned, and how perfectly maddening it is to look at the tide table and see what will be happening the 22nd and 23rd! In any event, we may possibly stop over in Amherst a day or so, delaying our return still further. However, there are one or two family matters that might possibly make us feel we should go sooner; in that case I'll certainly call you.

This is not a reply to your letter, which gave me as great pleasure as all the rest. But please don't start not-writing, when you think of something you want to tell me—for fear I'll think I have to rush to the typewriter and answer. I'll promise to try to think of the manuscript first, but just remember that it is a joy to write to you, for I, too, have that feeling of all the thoughts I'd like to share!

One reason the book is so far behind is that I have put aside a whole section of it, because it didn't please me at all, and now I'm writing a replacement.

It is the part on the rocky coast, and doing it with the subject at my elbow is a much happier experience.

Incidentally, I'll be in Boston for a couple of days around December 29th, attending some scientific meetings. It would be fun if you could come up for lunch—or does your Christmas date take you to Maine?[7]

And for October 9th,[8] my love and congratulations, and many, many happy returns.

Affectionately yours,

Rachel

Something you said in an earlier letter, about music, made me want to send you this quotation from the book I spoke of.[9]

[7] To Orono, where the Freemans' only child, Stanley Freeman, Jr., lived with his family. In these letters Stanley, Jr., is "Stanley," and Stanley, Sr., is "Stan." References to father and son in the footnotes refer to "Stanley" and "Stanley, Jr."

[8] Dorothy and Stanley Freeman's twenty-ninth wedding anniversary.

[9] Quotation not preserved with this letter.

MYRTLE BEACH, S.C., NOVEMBER 5

Dear Dorothy,

Because of the change of scene and activities, I suppose, it seems almost months since I wrote you last from Southport; in the interval there have been so many things I've wanted to say to you, but have been unable to put on paper, that I feel quite frustrated, and now it seems almost hopeless to begin!

Perhaps the beginning is now, in the midst of a drenching northeaster that has brought the rain all this area needs so badly—but also, I'm afraid, the end of our warm, sunny days on the beach. But we shall have to go out tomorrow regardless of weather to see what this storm surf has brought in. Someday—next summer?—perhaps I can tell you what an exciting beach this is, and the reasons. I keep returning to it and always learn something new. One of my finds here turned out to be something never before reported from the Atlantic coast.

Roger has had a part in all our adventures. Tonight we took him down to the beach in all the wind and rain to see the surf; another night he went with us to hunt ghost crabs with a flashlight. I hasten to add that he also gets to the beach at hours more seemly for a baby, and is becoming an avid shell collector. He used to gather periwinkles at Southport, and amazingly the memory carried over in his little mind, for his first day on this beach he handed me a shell (of quite a different sort, of course) and said "winkie."

I am so glad you had even a short visit with your baby Martha[10] now to bridge the gap till Christmas, and I'm glad, too, that you used some of your traveling hours to write me. You must have been told many times before, but may I add my own comment—that you have an unusual ability to put yourself into your letters. And that is something that is all too rare. When I'm away from certain friends who really are quite dear to me, I feel so cut off from them just because the qualities I love are so dimly reflected in their letters. But not so with you—which is one of several reasons why I welcome your letters so gladly. An-

[10] Dorothy and Stanley Freeman's granddaughter, and this book's editor.

other, which perhaps needs no elaboration but I think must be said once, for you still don't seem quite sure of it, is that getting to know you and to count you among my friends is one of the nicest things that has happened to me in a very long time; and it happened, too, when I needed all that you have come to mean to me very much. Please believe me that if you are happy in our friendship, I am at least equally so.

As I think back over your letters there is much in every one of them that I'd like to comment on (what do I do with time, that there is so little of it, and so little to show for it?) and while feeling frustrated by the impossibility of doing so, I suddenly remember the prospect of seeing you next month and talking instead of writing! Perhaps we should carry forward our plans now, for if it is convenient for you to be in Boston I do want to see you, and I'd like our plans to be definite before other things begin to nibble away my brief store of time there. If you could lunch with me on the 30th that would be best. While I'll be there on the 29th, I doubt that I could be free for lunch, and anyway I'd be in no state to enjoy it, for I have to take part in an afternoon symposium on the sea[11]—a very unnerving prospect! I'll probably have to return home the evening of the 30th, so may I mark it up on my calendar that I'm lunching with you that day unless blizzards or something equally beyond control prevent your coming to Boston?

[11] Sponsored by the American Association for the Advancement of Science (A.A.A.S.).

NOVEMBER 6

Our northeaster rained itself out last night, but today's skies have been full of leaden clouds and a bitterly cold wind. Visits to the beach have been very short and uncomfortable, but exciting. This morning there were porpoises in some number just offshore, and the horizon was so jagged with waves that I thought at once of one of Tomlinson's[12] descriptions in *The Sea and the Jungle*— do you like that book as much as I do? This afternoon a number of creatures from the offshore reefs that so fascinate me began to appear on the beach—or rather bits and remnants of them did: pieces of green and orange and yellow sponge, sea squirts, parchment worm tubes, crabs, starfish, urchins . . . and a large horseshoe crab . . . AND a fair-sized octopus, still living but in dire difficulties on the sand. After everyone had braved the freezing wind to see him, I managed to get him back into the water with the aid of a broom, and after several tries was rewarded by having him swim off. (Shades of that movie called *The Sea Around Us* which, to my horror, pictured the octopus as a dreadful "monster of the deep!")

[12] H. M. (Henry Major) Tomlinson, British naturalist and writer. *The Sea and the Jungle* was published in 1928.

You asked about the summer's progress on the manuscript. It was disappointing and I'm still so far from the end that at times I feel pretty desperate about it in spite of my publisher's understanding indulgence. It was a hard summer in more ways than one and perhaps I expected to accomplish too much, but then—life is just too short to spend this much time on one book! The reasons for this dragging progress are of course in myself and I know most of them, but they are better subjects for conversation than for letters, and by the time there is a chance of that—next summer—surely, surely my troubles on this book will be over.

To skip over a few things hurriedly: our visit in Amherst was short, really just one whole day and that a chilly, cloudy one, so we spent almost all of it indoors visiting with our friends. It is beautiful country, isn't it? From Alice's[13] house one can see both the Berkshires and the Pelham Hills. We were so aware, as you were, of the comparative drabness of the foliage in southern and western New England and farther south. Indeed, from the moment we left Maine, the colors dimmed rapidly. I have never seen anything so vivid as the Southport foliage those last days.

And I was so pleased to have you mention *How to Live with a Cat*,[14] which probably is my favorite of cat books. I don't know the author, but do know very well the editor who had much to do with the existence of that book—Maria Lieper at Simon and Schuster, who dearly loves cats herself. Some time I must tell you more about her. And of course I'm happy that you agree with me on *Conversation with the Earth*.[15] I left my copy in Amherst for Alice Mullen to read, but I shall want to return to it again and again. Now I suppose this must be all for now; true to my bad habits, I have written this letter first because I knew I would enjoy writing it, and have left those that are mere chores for later. We shall probably stay on here until Monday, then go up and leave Virginia[16] in Wilmington, and reach home sometime Tuesday. We had planned to go Sunday, but the change of weather interfered with our plan to drive down to Hampton Plantation to see Archibald Rutledge,[17] who is a dear friend, and since he is now quite frail we hate to leave without seeing him. Besides, it is always easy for me to postpone leaving the sea, as you know.

Why don't I stop and do those other letters? Maybe the easiest way for me to write a chapter of my book would be to type "Dear Dorothy" on the first page! As a matter of fact, you and your particular kind of interest and appreciation were in my mind a great deal when I was rewriting parts of the section on rocky shores.

Please give my best to all your dear ones—how nice that you had Stanley Jr. with you for his birthday, and of course I want to meet him and your daughter-in-law and the baby next summer.

My love to you,
Rachel

And thank you for the clipping from Rudolph Elie's column, which meant to me just what it evidently meant to you!

[13] Alice Mullen, a Carson family friend who had lived in Washington, D.C.

[14] By Margaret Cooper, first published in 1946.

[15] Authored by Hans Cloos and first published in America in 1953.

[16] RC's niece, Virginia King, and Marjie Williams's sister.

[17] Author of, among other books, *Peace in the Heart* (1932).

Dorothy, my dear—

This can be only a few lines before I turn out the light—I really should have written "Friday morning" for it's well past midnight. I've been mentally sending you notes all day, especially since your wonderful letter arrived, but I'm afraid few of them are going to take tangible form tonight.

For the present, let's adopt your general outline for the 30th. If it has to be a choice between lunching with you or going to you for part of the afternoon and the evening, I'm sure the latter would give us more time together. I really hope it can be both and perhaps it can. Unless we are lunching in Boston, I *don't* think you ought to come in, but I won't protest at this point, at any rate.

About Jefferies[18]—not many people know him and of course not all would care for him. He was both a prolific and an uneven writer and if you happened to pick up the "wrong" volume you might never find the Jefferies I have loved. Many of his things have been republished in England within recent years (I'll tell you more about all this some day!) and the first I ever owned, or even knew, was a sort of anthology of selected essays called *Jefferies' England*—and I still think it contains the cream of Jefferies' nature writings. If your library doesn't have this particular volume I'd love to lend you mine. I doubt that it is easily come by, now. It was given to me by another Dorothy—the year *Under the Sea-Wind* was first published. I always regard Jefferies as a sort of literary grandfather of mine—the reason being this. I am sure that my own style and thought were deeply influenced, in certain critical years, by Henry Williamson, whose *Tarka the Otter* and *Salar the Salmon* are, I'm convinced, nature writing of the highest order. And Williamson has said that he owes the same sort of debt to Jefferies.

And in line with this—to me at least—fascinating business of tracing literary origins, I have been thinking that since that fog passage in *The Sea* is clearly one of your favorites—you have referred to it several times—perhaps you would like to see its embryonic beginnings as they appear in my *Albatross*[19] notes. So I hunted up the notebook and found them for you. It's odd—I expected to find that bit about the petrels passing through the curtains of fog, for it so impressed me, but evidently I just supplied that from memory. But all the rest is there, in rough form.

I think you would like some of the writings of R. A. Daly, Harvard's great geologist. In almost all his books there are passages that show his awareness of the majesty and grandeur of the processes he is describing. I should refresh my memory, but it seems to me his *Our Changing Earth* (listed in the reading list in *The Sea*) would be the most promising. If I remember correctly, this one while generally descriptive of geologic phenomena, had a good deal of fascinating stuff on Africa. What an exciting continent that must be! And that reminds me to ask whether you read *Venture to the Interior*, by Laurens van der Post published

[18] *Jefferies' England: Nature Essays by Richard Jefferies* was first published in 1937. In March of 1954, RC gave DF a 1943 edition of this book.

[19] In July of 1949, RC had sailed from Woods Hole, Massachusetts, to Georges Bank on a fishing trawler converted to a research vessel named *Albatross III*.

about two years ago—not geology, but giving an unforgettable picture of some of the mountain forest of Africa. It impressed me deeply.

Oh dear—I don't want you to be sick! I do hope it isn't anything much and that you are not leading up to something unpleasant like an operation. Whatever it is, please get well right away!

As usual, I've hardly made a dent in the things I want to say. I can see us sitting on the rocks next summer, each with a mountain of old letters, too busy hunting through them for "things I meant to comment on" even to talk! Now wouldn't that be the height of frustration!

There is bound to be another letter soon for there are some things I just must write, but no more now.

Very much love—

Rachel

DECEMBER 11

My dearest Dorothy,

I would have asked you in this letter for your phone number, if you hadn't had the same thought!

My plans have been to arrive on the Federal the morning of the 29th. Although I'd like nothing better than to step off the train into your arms (much, much better than a publisher's red carpet) it would be foolish to plan it even if you were not busy with your children that day. For the plans also demand an immediate dash to the hotel for a bath and change before the morning session of the sea symposium. I don't have my say until afternoon, but the chairman of the morning is Harvard's Henry Bigelow,[20] whom I think I respect more than any other scientist in the world—and also love as a person. And one of the A.M. speakers is a close friend and former colleague. So I must be there. Besides, I shall spy out the land, and see what sort of hall, microphone, projector, and audience I shall have to cope with! But to return to the time of my arrival—life has now been complicated by a letter today that may make it necessary for me to be in Boston by Monday afternoon. That would mean flying Monday. It's still uncertain—you will hear later how things are working out; and I had planned to phone you Tuesday—late afternoon or evening—to complete our own plans. You may be sure that Wednesday afternoon and evening are inviolate; no matter what is suggested by anyone, I just won't be available! Oh yes—I'll be home for Christmas—I always am! Baby Roger will come the day before, so we'll have the joy of seeing him Christmas morning with his stocking, the tree, and all his presents. He loved it even last year and I suppose he'll just be almost overwhelmed with excitement now.

Right now, at least a million things seem to stand between me and Christmas—and Boston, and I'm going mad! The paper itself is far from finished—then it has to be mimeographed—additional slides have to be made—the chronic feminine problem of "what to wear" has to be dealt with—my Christ-

[20] Dr. Henry B. Bigelow, professor and oceanographer.

mas shopping has to be finished (finished? It's hardly well begun!)—and not a single Christmas note has been written. Maybe it will all be done somehow, but just now I can't imagine it. (Oh yes, and a book has to be read and reviewed for the *New York Herald Tribune*.)

I thought if I'd use this paper I could trap myself into being brief, but here I go spilling over to another sheet. Of course I was happy that you wanted to share with me the letter from your Canadian friends, and the incident itself, was so delightful and so *right*; I'm sure that the Freemans just have a way of attracting kindred spirits—who would naturally do and enjoy doing the same things.

There is so much in your recent long letter that I want to talk about (not a very new remark, is it?) but—the eternal "but"! Let me say, though, that it brought such a sense of your nearness—more, perhaps, than any other letter. But then all of your letters make me feel that we had really been together and talked, as we would like to do. I am touched by your unselfish concern for what you think is best for me. But don't attach too much importance to the "after-midnight" letter writing—a detail I was thoughtless to mention—for I'm just a nocturnal creature by instinct. Anyway, perhaps we have both been "a bit crazy"—for if you have, it applies equally to me—and perhaps we shall have to make some New Year resolutions, cruelly hard as that would be. But I think that the rapid flowering of our friendship, the headlong pace of our correspondence, reflects a feeling, whether consciously recognized or not, for the "lost" years and a desire to make up for all the time we might have enjoyed this, had something brought us together earlier.

And that leads me to say, my very dear one, that all your chain of "ifs" refer (in my mind) just to how it *did* happen; not to *whether* it would have happened. For, given the two essential steps—your Christmas letter and our first meeting—the rest would have followed one way or another. That is—to the extent that I had any control over it, it would.

And, as you must know in your heart, there is such a simple answer for all the "whys" that are sprinkled through your letters: As why do I keep your letters? Why did I come to the Head that last night? Why? Because I love you! Now I could go on and tell you some of the reasons why I do, but that would take quite a while, and I think the simple fact covers everything.

S ATURDAY

Now it is another day, and a dark and dripping one, but I have to go out and I shall take this to the box. Under the growing burden of Christmas mail, Uncle Sam's phenomenal speed seems to be faltering. Your letter mailed Tuesday reached me Thursday, and you obviously had not received mine mailed Sunday. But I hope this may be in your hands Monday.

Because I really am getting a bit desperate, you may not have even a note till almost Christmas, but I know you understand. This Boston occasion is really very important, the auspices are so distinguished, and my own role is a peculiarly difficult one, all of which I can explain when I see you. But the more I am aware of all this, the longer I sit at the typewriter, a helpless dope—busily not-writing this paper that has to accomplish such conflicting things!

Oh dear, I haven't told you anything about our little black Jeffie,[21] who is a perfect darling. But I *won't* take another sheet.

[21] A new kitten.

All my love,
Rachel

DECEMBER 21

My dearest [Dorothy],

It would be a happy thing if the miles were fewer and we could have even a little time together this Christmas Day—the first since we met. But it doesn't matter really, for you seem very close. And I love knowing that you have baby Martha and all the others with you on this day that is like no other of the year.

Christmas brings most of all a sense of rather starry wonder—from the wonder of the first one that still shines through the years, to the miracle of friendship and of the warmth and joy that fill the human hearts when it experiences that rare and beautiful thing, a sense of perfect communication with another. And so tonight I want to say thank you for those precious gifts of friendship and love and understanding, that cannot be bought and could never be replaced.

My dearest love, always,
Rachel

DECEMBER 26

My dearest [Dorothy],

It was so lovely—and only you would have thought it out in all its sweet details. It did bring you to me so clearly—very early Christmas morning—and the warmth and glow linger still. How can those hours Wednesday possibly be enough for all there is to say? But I am so happy that we are to have them now.

All my love—
Rachel

JANUARY 1

My Darling [Dorothy],

Now we have talked, but I shall write this anyway, as I'd planned to do, on this first day of a year from which we hope so much. Besides wanting to write to you on this particular day, I wanted to say a few of the things I've been thinking, before your letter comes, as perhaps it may tomorrow. But I won't mail this till it does.

As I told you, you were always with me when I wakened in the night—and I did often, not being a very good train sleeper—and always the sense of your presence, and of your sweet tenderness, and love was very real to me. And I wondered if perhaps, in the same sense, I stayed in West Bridgewater that night. You don't need to answer that, for I think I know.

And let me say again how truly perfect it all was. Reality can so easily fall short of hopes and expectations, especially where they have been high. I do hope that for you, as they truly are for me, the memories of Wednesday[1] are completely unclouded by any sense of disappointment, or of hopes unrealized. And as for you, my dear one, there is not a single thing about you that I would change if I could! Once written, that seems an odd thing to say; I am trying to express my complete and overflowing happiness in the whole thing!

I have always loved these lines of Keats' and now they keep coming into my mind as describing the feeling that exists between us:

A thing of beauty is a joy forever:
Its loveliness increases; it will never
Pass into nothingness; but still will keep
A bower quiet for us, and a sleep
Full of sweet dreams.

I am certain, my dearest, that it will be forever a joy, of increasing loveliness with the years, and that in the intervals when being separated, we cannot have all the happiness of Wednesday, there will be, in each of our hearts, a little oasis of peace and "sweet dreams" where the other is.

I can see your eyes this minute—bless your dear heart!

My dearest love, always and always,
Rachel

[1] On her first visit to the Freemans' home on December 30, RC had arrived in the afternoon and spent the night.

Dearest [Dorothy],

After this one I'm going to behave—by at least *trying* to write on schedule, and no more! But your note written Tuesday morning needs a prompt reply, not so much because of your question as something else it suggests. Of course I don't mind if you want to inflict me on the Garden Club, though I'm sure they'd rather hear about Martha. Please do whatever you like about it, and know that if you do talk about our first adventure together, and read from the letter, I'll have not the slightest misgivings about the way you would handle it. Now for the other: the fact that you have mentioned this meeting next week makes me want to anticipate something that would have gone into my next "regular" letter—if there is such a thing. There is a critical situation developing about one of the National Monument areas in Colorado and Utah—a plan to build a dam that would submerge an area that is not only beautiful, but of great interest and importance as a geologic record. There seems to be no question that the dam could serve its intended purpose just as well if built somewhere else—so to put it in the Dinosaur Monument, submerging these wonderful formations and fossil beds, is nothing but blind and wilful destructiveness. The issue of the magazine *The Living Wilderness* that reached us yesterday says that the Secretary of the Interior—who is supposed to have such things in his care—has recommended the dam in Dinosaur Monument to the President, in whose hands the thing now is, or will be shortly. They urged everyone interested to write, or better wire, the President urging preservation of the National Parks and Monument, and specifically urging that this project be abandoned. We are wiring, and I felt you and Stan would feel as we do if you knew about it. I have asked that a copy of the magazine be sent you (see pages 26–28, and the hand-written note on p. 29) along with some other literature on the Dinosaur Monument. Remembering Stan's pictures, the feeling you both have for the West, and your appreciation of Mr. Cloos, I don't have any doubt how you'll feel about this. Now, however, I'm wondering if you won't carry it further and try to interest your Garden Club in the situation, if they aren't already. I know so many instances where Garden Clubs have become a strong constructive force for conservation. If this group saw Stan's Grand Canyon pictures, they ought to understand what this means.

This is something we shall talk of much in the years and months ahead, I know. It is part of the general problem that is so close to my heart—the saving of unspoiled, natural areas from senseless destruction. But in this particular case the time is short and perhaps you will find time and inclination to say something about it at your meeting next week.

I have been undergoing a new permanent this afternoon—writing this at possible intervals. Not the best conditions for concentration, but I want to mail this today.

Darling, I do plan to call you Sunday, and since I can tell you are going to hover around the phone, I won't make it person-to-person this time. But the next time (whenever that is) I won't let you be tied down in that way. I'll try to make this between 10:45 and 11:15.

Will you forgive me for laughing when I read your description of waiting for the mailman Monday to see if "It" would be there? Just as if my handwriting hadn't been appearing in your mail practically every day!! We are really awful! Aren't we worse than ever? Now, I guess, no more till—when? By this time I don't even know when it should be.

> But my dearest love, always
> *Rachel*

JANUARY 25

My darling [Dorothy],

This has to be brief—you see there isn't very much space—a situation deliberately contrived for *our* own good! I am glad we can laugh at ourselves. We really are pretty crazy, aren't we—and getting worse by the day. But to me the wonderful thing is that we are both "crazy" in the same way, and at the same time! Wouldn't it be awful if it was only one of us—either one! Your dear and more than satisfying letter is here and as always has brought so much happiness with it. This can hardly be a reply to it; "the" letter must wait until the week-end. Just a few things. I think it is quite possible for you and me and the veeries to be together in some magical time and place next June. It is much less a matter of chance than you might suppose. The hour is after sunset. The place can easily be discovered for the people at the Audubon Camp will know where there are nesting veeries. It is like no bird song I have ever heard. As long as I live I shall never forget my first veery—heard in Rock Creek Park in a green woodland twilight.

I find that when I think of Southport I am assuming that *you* will be there all summer. And when I realize you won't, I have to think of something else, quickly! Please do make it as much time as you possibly can. Perhaps I should telephone (I did so love hearing your voice—and it was so easy it made 500 miles seem as nothing!) you every day. At least it is fun to pretend that is why I got so much done yesterday—pages and pages! When things go reasonably well, as they did then, I feel so hopeful that maybe it *can* be finished, and maybe it is not too bad. As I told you, I think I should know by the end of the week whether there is reasonable hope. If I do have to give up the end-of-March deadline, I must push on anyway to finish before June (and Southport). Please give me no peace if I seem to be weakening from that resolve! Now to show you that I can "scheme," too—how about giving me a letter "for publication" soon? Having in past weeks suppressed volumes of correspondence in what I—probably mistakenly—thought the best interests of all concerned, I now find myself hopelessly trapped in my own duplicity! I have wanted to share some of your recent letters—but visibly to extract only a paragraph here and there out of a fat letter isn't such a good idea, either. I shall not explain more for I know you do understand. Perhaps your next long letter can be in two parts. It occurs to me that if you are writing anything about the Garden Club—or the books—that could go in the general letter. This need not happen often just now and then to take care of the "when have you heard from Dorothy" question. After all, as you know, our brand of "craziness" would be a little hard for anyone but us to understand.

What are margins for, except to be written on? This is the end of the letter, so go inside first! Darling, you are too fearful of misinterpretation. I am too certain of your love and understanding to suppose you would hurt me for anything in the world. If any word or sentence ever requires "between-the-line" interpretation be sure I am capable of supplying it. So think no more about it—of course, I didn't misunderstand.

There is a "why" in a recent letter that you say not to answer; and I won't, except to say that everything is explained by the fact that you are *you*, and I can imagine no substitute for you in my life.

I love you so dearly—
Rachel

THURSDAY, JANUARY 30

Darling [Dorothy],

Probably this letter won't be mailed until Saturday, but I think I'll start now and do it in installments.

I'm stretched out on my bed—it's 9:20 P.M. (almost "Ernie Ford" time)—and Jeffie is taking a bath in the midst of various sheets of notes and manuscript. There—you say you like to have the picture! And I just had to go for my glasses—I'm getting so farsighted I can't even write a letter without holding the paper at arm's length.

It was wonderful to talk last night, dear. In a way I suppose it made me long for you even more, but it did ease my anxiety about you and was at least next best if I couldn't have you.

And then, darling, there was an interruption—I can't even remember what, and after I came back, I was so overwhelmed with sleepiness I couldn't write. That seems often to happen to me now. So here we are—same place, same bath-taking cat, about 24 hours later.

Meanwhile—your sweetest of notes this morning. There had been a letter yesterday—the one you mentioned on the phone—so this morning I kept telling myself there couldn't possibly be another. "*Unless*," the thought only whispered, "she wrote a note after we talked Wednesday night. But of course she didn't, so don't look for anything." But still the same leaping heart when the red, white, and blue truck came in sight, and the same sharply in-drawn breath when the envelope appeared. She did! Darling—I suppose the world would consider us absolutely crazy, but it is wonderful to feel that way, isn't it? Sort of a perpetual springtime in our hearts. And your note was so sweet, dear one, and expressed my own thoughts in so many ways.

It does seem such an eternity since last October—and it's far longer until summer. And how much time will that hold for us? I shouldn't even bring up that thought, I know. But somehow, darling, we have to be together *before* summer. I know I need you terribly. (And I believe you need me, too. Shameless!)

If we could only be near enough to talk often and be together even once each month. I really don't think I'd ever sink into the state of despair that so often comes over me. And it is so much better to talk than to write—for I think in a way writing magnifies things—makes what was perhaps a passing annoyance seem bigger or more lasting than it was. When I said, recently, that I was going to try to stop writing of my troubles, I had all that in mind, dearest. Not that I wouldn't *tell* you if we could be together. But it just doesn't seem fair to unload it all at 500-mile range.

What about those last letters that were so full of woe, darling? Did you put them in the Strong box?[2] If not, please do. And when I slip in the future—as almost certainly I will—please destroy such letters. And darling—it isn't anything you have said that makes me feel I should curb my pen—I know you want me to write my thoughts but *I* think I ought to write facts without being so harrowingly subjective about them!

But that has become such a habit that I'll have trouble breaking it.

Oh, I'm such a dope, dear. Sometimes I think if I had time and energy I should hunt up a psychiatrist for *myself*. If I can't change the facts, I could perhaps at least change my attitude toward them. And as long as family health permits, I should shake myself out of my lethargy and make an effort to see other people more.

[Love, *Rachel*][3]

[2] A term used by RC and DF to refer to letters they wished to be destroyed.

[3] The final page or pages of this letter not preserved.

SATURDAY NIGHT, FEBRUARY 6

Darling [Dorothy]—

Now—I saved this till last—the other letter is done, and I can just relax and say the things that are only for *you*. I really didn't plan to make it so long, and know you wouldn't expect me to—but it was all things I really wanted to tell you. Probably next week *that* part will be very short—just a report that I'm working hard and not much more. But really, dear, this is the part that means so much to me, as I'm sure you do understand, and I couldn't stop writing to you!

Your letter that came yesterday was one of the sweetest and most satisfying ones you have written me, which is saying a good deal. It, and the phone calls, and other letters, bring up so much that I wish I could say to you, but I suppose most of it *must* wait, until the happy day when we can talk about it instead.

Do you remember what someone said to the effect that (I'm quoting very inexactly) if he had two pennies he would use one to buy bread and the other to buy "a white hyacinth for his soul"? You, dearest, are the "white hyacinth" in which I invest part of my time—and I couldn't invest all of my time pennies in the "bread" of the book, even for two months, if it meant giving up all that you do for me.

Probably, just for the sake of disposing once and forever of the doubts in your mind, I should have tried to explain to you, when we were together, just why I need the "particular combination of qualities" that is you. It seemed too time-consuming a thing to bring into that short day—as it is for a letter—and besides I think I had the feeling that since you don't know most of my friends and family, anything I'd say in explanation might seem to imply quite unfair criticism of them. So, my darling, except for the little I say now, just try to accept in your heart and mind that the lovely companionship of your letters has become a necessity to me, and that, just by being you, you are helping me more than you can imagine. Surely you know I wouldn't say this if I didn't mean it! We can talk about it this summer, to our heart's content!

I don't suppose anyone really knows how a creative writer works (he or she least of all, perhaps!) or what sort of nourishment his spirit must have. All I am certain of is this; that it is quite necessary for me to know that there is someone who is deeply devoted to me as a person, and who also has the capacity and the depth of understanding to share, vicariously, the sometimes crushing burden of creative effort, recognizing the heartache, the great weariness of mind and body, the occasional black despair it may involve—someone who cherishes me and what I am trying to create, as well. Last summer I was feeling, as never before, that there was no one who combined all of that. I had always known such understanding of these things from my mother, but that was becoming so dim as you know, and for what reason. The few who understood the creative problem were not people to whom I felt emotionally close; those who loved the non-writer part of me did not, by some strange paradox, understand the writer at all! And then, my dear one, you came into my life! Are you beginning to understand a little better? I knew when first I saw you that I wanted to see much more of you—I loved you before you left Southport—and very early in our correspondence last fall I began to sense that capacity to enter so fully into the intellectual and creative parts of my life as well as to be a dearly loved friend. And day by day all that I sensed in you has been fulfilled, but even more wonderfully than I could have dreamed.

So, my dear, when you say, "Don't you ever wonder at it?"—of course the answer is yes—I feel such a joyous surge of wonder every time I stop to think how in such a dark time and when I least expected it, something so lovely and richly satisfying came into my life.

Darling, if you could only tell me now that you do understand and accept this—you, who understand so much, but have found it so hard to believe all this—because it concerns you! I would feel so much more at peace if I could feel that at last you do understand what you have done for me.

Of course—there is another side to all this. I know so well what this experience means to me—but I can't see that *I* can possibly be giving *you* anything comparable in return! But darling—before you begin to protest—let me say that I, unlike you, simply accept the fact that evidently—in a way I don't understand—I have filled some need in your life. What it is doesn't matter—unless or until you want to tell me. Perhaps you don't even know. That part isn't important—I'm just deeply grateful that I can mean so much to you. There—I was only going to say "a little" about it, wasn't I—and I've gone on for pages! But if I have convinced you it is well worth it.

You will have this Tuesday, I suppose. I wanted to mail it tonight, but couldn't get to it in time. So you will have not only this "double feature" but my letter written last Wednesday to answer. (And I imagine you *wanted* to reply to it sooner!) I'll anticipate a little by saying that I *was* a bit worried over the effect of my call on Monday—but that after talking to you Wednesday and particularly after your letter (of Tuesday-Wednesday-Thursday!) stopped worrying. But this time I'm really sincere in saying I won't call again for a good while. I think we both have ourselves under better control—we don't need to call for a while—and let's not.

I've laughed many times about my poor reception of your telepathy. Before my first reply to your question, "What do you usually do Wednesday evenings?" the thought of a call flitted quickly across my mind—yes, really—but was as quickly dismissed because after all you hadn't said any particular Wednesday—just Wednesday in general! (See how logic can lead you astray.) Then on my retake, I was so sure I knew what you meant! And if you needed proof that neither my senses nor my extra sense were working—you had it in the fact I allowed the line to be tied up so long. If I'd dreamed you'd be calling I would have been having fits about that—and what a strain the busy signals must have been on you! Goodnight dear—but I hope you were asleep a long time ago.

SUNDAY MORNING

Realizing that this Tuesday is one on which you say you are away all day—I'm going to try to get this into an earlier mail than our late-afternoon collection, and hope you may have it tomorrow. I know you are wanting to hear something after that wonderful Wednesday evening call, and perhaps to have a "postscript" to my recent letter.

Although this is growing into quite a volume, I haven't touched several of the things I wanted to talk about but will save them for another time. The chief subject of this letter is something I had to say—I hope you can tell me you do understand.

One thing more—that was a wonderful quotation from Toynbee. (And it is one illustration of your beautifully satisfying responses—I say something, and you reply in a way that shows you understand but also adds a new depth of meaning by your own comment!) But let me quote a line of this back to you— "when he (the creator) has *the good fortune* to enjoy the companionship of a few kindred spirits." So, darling, Mr. Toynbee is expressing what I have tried to tell you—that it is my good fortune—that my wonder is that something so lovely could have come into *my* life. Now this must be all. The next letter will be much shorter I promise you—both parts. And I do think we should give the one-a-week schedule a fair trial—it may be a very good thing for both of us once we get used to it. May I (please) look for yours maybe Thursday or Friday? Then mine will be mailed sometime over the week-end and perhaps usually reach you Tuesdays. Dear, I am so glad your mind is relieved after Stan's clinic check-up. And are you resting a lot for me—and May 11th?

> Darling, I do love you so dearly—
> *Rachel*

SATURDAY AFTERNOON, FEBRUARY 13

My darling [Dorothy]:

When you sit down to write my letters, do you sometimes feel over-whelmed by the impossibility of saying all that is in your heart to say? I think I know that you do, and I have before, but never more than today. And I'm es-pecially overwhelmed because I've set myself a time limit and am going to try to keep within in.

Your perfect valentine with its sweet enclosure came yesterday. And Jeffie was so pleased with his very first valentine (at least he looked pleased) and hopes you liked his. He also sent a picture-valentine to his mother—his cat-mother, that is. Yes, I did love childhood valentines, and there used to be perfectly won-derful sets of materials for making your own—much more elaborate and de-lightful than any they have now. I always liked making them.

Oh darling, it was a beautiful exchange of letters, wasn't it? And so deeply satisfying—perhaps as though something now is established that nothing in the world could take away from us. I am sorry I waited so long to "put it into words" for you. It has all been in my heart so long that perhaps I almost felt I had said, or at least suggested, most of it. Do you remember that this was all brought about by the question in your February 2 letter: "Don't you ever marvel at your-self, finding yourself in such an overpowering emotional experience?" And I have wondered since (not being able to remember all I said) whether I may have forgotten to make it clear that—besides all the intellectual satisfactions I per-haps dwelt on at great length—it truly is for me, as for you, "an overpowering emotional experience." If I didn't, I think I can now trust that your heart knows it. I was thinking today, with what depth of gratitude I hope you know, how won-derfully sustaining is the assurance of your constant, day-and-night devotion and concern. Without it, I truly don't know what I would be doing now, when there are a good many otherwise dark days.

It was because I truly seem to myself to be the one who receives everything, and gives little, that I said something to the effect that I didn't understand how I could be meeting any need in your life, but just had to believe I did. I loved everything you said in reply, although, as I said, no reply was needed unless you really wanted to give it. I especially loved the fact that you felt no need to keep the "awful questions" to yourself, for that in itself says much about the quality of the feeling between us. Of course I understand them! And of course I know even better than you that it isn't pride in a "famous author's" (!!*!) friendship. I say I know that better than you, because the past 2 or 3 years have brought me a good many new experiences, and I'm confident I can recognize *that* sort of interest in me a mile off! And since one of the things about you that impressed me from the beginning was the lovely quality of your family life, I knew, too, that it was not lack of love. No one could be with you and Stan even a short time without realizing how devoted and congenial you are. And I wonder whether the very fact that you have experienced, and have yourself poured out, so much love, has not made you all the more receptive to the devotion offered by this newcomer in your life. You wrote so beautifully, weeks ago, of how one's capacity to give love grows with the exercise of it, so perhaps the more love we have received, the more we are able to absorb and in that sense no one ever has enough. And I do know that the facts that we are, to an incredible degree "kindred spirits," and that for many reasons we need all that we mean to each other, probably lie at the heart of our love. But the more I think about all we both have said, the more I feel that there is also something that perhaps will always remain elusive and intangible — that the whole is something more than the sum of the various "reasons." Henry Beston says in the review[4] I'm sending you today: "the sun — is always more than a gigantic mass of ions, it is a splendor and a mystery, a force and a divinity, it is life and the symbol of life." Our analysis has been beautiful and comforting and satisfying, but probably it will never be quite complete — never encompass the whole "splendor and mystery." That is how I feel about it. Do you agree?

This tyrant clock says I must hurry on to some of the other things I want to say. Oh darling, I, too, feel such terrific impatience for the time we can be together. And I know it is tantalizing always to be saying, "I'll tell you later" — but it just has to be. Largely, of course, it's a matter of time; but also it is so much more satisfactory to *talk* about some things than to write. This, however, I just want to suggest, and "later" we'll talk about it. Please, my dearest, don't ever imagine I regard it as silly or overly emotional when you write of being stirred when you hear or see some reference to me. I have made a real effort to imagine how it would seem to you, and I think I can at least partially understand. Now what I'd like is to have you understand how such things affect *me*! And that's hard to do because I don't think I know — and I think perhaps in talking to you

[4] Of *Under the Sea-Wind*. Henry Beston authored, among others, one of RC's favorite books, *The Outermost House*, first published in 1928.

about it, I could figure it out and then we'd both understand! The publicity-type references of course affect me very negatively — I don't want to see or hear them — I have a definite "avoiding reaction," to use a biologist's term. About things that, because of their source or what they say, are real tributes, I think I have one of two reactions. Ordinarily — and this sounds ridiculous but it's true — I have no sense that they are really talking about *me* — it's quite impersonal, and doesn't get below the surface of my mind. But if the awareness ever does penetrate, there is a frightened and lonely feeling. Frightened because you think — "Could this possibly be true and if so could I ever again live up to it?" Lonely, because there are so very, very few who could understand that sort of experience. That is why I want to talk to you about it — because you could! And I wanted to say even this much before you read Henry Beston's review.

Darling, I do so hope you will have perfect weather for the trip to Orono, and I know it will be such a joy to see Martha, and Martha's parents. (Please *do* send me Stanley's publication sometime soon — I don't promise a profound opinion until later, but would love to read it.) Because I, too, can be something of a worrier, I'll be so anxious to know you are safely at home again; so, without waiting for time for a real letter, won't you just send me a tiny note when you get home? Will that be Tuesday? But of course I'm looking for a letter before you go!

Oh, I *must* stop! This, as you can see, is no 2-part letter; I'll try to do that next time. When you write, darling, tell me whether you have any major engagements between the 15th and 31st of March. *If* I go to Boston it should be sometime in that interval, and I'd plan to avoid any conflicting plans of yours. I'll write more of that next time. Don't count completely on it, but I do so long to be with you even a little while.

> So very, very much love, my dear one —
> *Rachel*

WEDNESDAY NOON, FEBRUARY 17

My darling [Dorothy],

This note was to be sent to you today regardless of whether I heard from you — just to tell you again how very much I hope for perfect week-end weather, and a perfect trip in every way. And now there is added reason, for your letter is here! Like you, I had been prepared to wait another day for it — but how I did watch for the mailman just the same! And there it was. Really amazing, isn't it — stamped in W. Bridgewater at 3 P.M. Tuesday, in my hands at 11:30 today. Usually it is only the Brockton letters that come through in one day — oh, I'm so glad this one did!

First of all my dearest — far from "minding" that you shared the letter with Stan, I am so very glad you did. Although in a way (but only in unimportant ways) I don't know him very well. I would have not the slightest fear of his failing to understand. How dear of him to say what he did. Perhaps this is the little final touch of the perfection in the whole episode. Darling, I wonder if I'll ever get used to the fact that you think my thoughts before I've expressed them? For I, too, was wondering whether we ever would have said the things we've just written. I had meant to try to tell you at Southport (or before, if I see you sooner) but perhaps it wouldn't all have been said. And then the spoken word is ephemeral — the written can be treasured and re-read so many, many times! When I sat down to write that letter (February 6th, was it?) I really intended only to suggest my answer to your question, and put the rest of it off with one of those "sometime I'll tell you" phrases. And then I just went on and on. I am so glad I did, and not only because I know it did bring you happiness and peace, but — selfishly — because the whole exchange of letters has done so much for me.

You suggest, too, another thought that I believe has been drifting about at least in my subconscious mind — that perhaps if we could have arranged our lives as we would have chosen — to be in daily association — we might have defeated ourselves by so doing, for it may well be that the enforced separation, and the necessity of writing instead of speaking, have contributed to the depth of love and understanding that have developed.

Darling, what I said on the phone about coming up soon — that is very soon — was just whimsical nonsense. I said I'd just been looking at the unused half of my railroad ticket and thinking if I went down and got on the Federal, I could see you the next day! Of course I was just expressing what I'd *like* to do — not reality. The March idea is not entirely fantasy, however — but still don't count on it. I'll write more of that in my letter(s) that should be in your hands Tuesday, after your return from Orono. Darling — always and always — I love you so dearly —

Rachel

My precious darling [Dorothy],

What lovely surprises this week! Monday Jeffie had a letter, which he very sweetly shared with me. Wednesday brought your perfectly wonderful two-part letter — the surprise there being the date of its arrival. Friday — and this was a real surprise — your pictures and Stanley's paper. How sweet of you darling, and how dear to send them for "company" while you are away — and I have been as acutely aware that you're away as though I'd seen you drive off! Then today, two: the note written under the drier Thursday, *and* (this will surprise *you*, too) the letter begun Wednesday and mailed yesterday!

And if you knew how wonderful it was to have each one! Friday, I found myself watching for the mailman — habit, do you suppose? — although I told myself firmly that of course there wouldn't be anything from you — there just wouldn't! But the irresponsible half of me answered back that there just *might* be, and kept watching. And was so, so rewarded when there was your dear handwriting after all! Today I wouldn't let myself watch but when I heard the rattle at the mailbox my heart leaped as if it knew. As one little measure of how much those letters meant, I'll tell you that hours later I suddenly realized that the rest of the mail was still lying unopened. Now why have I taken time to write all that — just because it's fun, I guess. But I shouldn't, because there is a staggering list of other things I want to talk about, and the evening is not young.

Darling, why in the world shouldn't you write to Henry Beston if you want to? I'd certainly have neither right nor reason to object, and I don't. So if there are things you'd like to say to him, why don't you? One of these days I may even get around to my own 20-year-overdue letter to him! As to his address, I'd had in mind that he lives near Nobleboro, though now I don't know why I thought so. But it may well be, for the preface of his *Northern Farm* says "Chimney Farm, Lincoln County, Maine." Why don't you try Nobleboro with, of course, your return address? Or you could send it in care of his publisher. I think *Northern Farm* was his most recent book and I'll add the name of the publisher later (Rinehart and Co., New York) — the book is downstairs. By the way — for your Stardust[5] department, did you notice the name of the magazine in which his review was published? You must have. I had forgotten, having received the review in the pre-Freeman era of my life, but when I saw it the other day I loved the symbolic linking of the three names — Freeman, Beston, Carson. The review is for you to keep, of course.

[5] A term the correspondents used for coincidental or serendipitous occurrences or expressions.

My darling, there is no end to the things that might be said now that what you call "The Revelation" has been put on paper. How blind I was not to realize sooner that I should say it! Do you remember now that I did at least skirt around the edge of the subject that day as we were sitting in the car watching the ducks? But so tentatively, I suppose, that you, darling, didn't know what I meant! And while the essence of it all was in my heart then, probably it's true that I hadn't thought it all out. Yes, we were a little shy, weren't we, especially at first — but it was rather sweet that way and perhaps as it should have been for the first time you and I were together! And I'm sure that from now on, anything we want to say will be said.

In the progress of our "discovery" of each other there have been several important milestones already, and it is interesting to see how, following each, there has been a little change in the tone of our letters. Our "thirteen hours,"[6] when we became so much more real to each other, was one. And the letters of early February were another. What will be the next? It is hard to imagine anything that could bring greater joy and deeper satisfactions than we know now.

[6] The duration of RC's visit to DF's West Bridgewater home on December 30 and 31, 1953.

But, oh darling, I want to be with you so terribly that it hurts! And I'm torn between wanting to give in, and make what I long for a reality, (and how easy it would be to do it!) and feeling that I must wait, at least until about the time we'd planned for. You see from this that I've been wanting to come much sooner. There have been days when I wanted to see you so badly I thought I'd have to. In those moods I argue myself into believing it would help me so that I could then settle down and get on faster. In more sensible moments, I am reasonably sure that an interruption now would be very bad — and that very likely it would be unsettling rather than the reverse. (I mean that only in terms of progress on the book — if that were not to be considered, I'd so gladly be "upset" in such a lovely way.) So — I'm going to try to stick it out for another month, and hope that by then I'll have more nearly "earned" the right to see you.

As you must suspect from my recent silence on the subject, I see no real hope now of finishing by the end of March. For various reasons, that is not as tragic as it might be, and at least I'm much nearer the end than I would have been if I hadn't chosen to follow that almost impossible goal. Paul Brooks[7] is saying now that even if they get it in mid-April they could still publish in the fall, but there are two things against that. One (and I've known this ever since I began the mad push to finish) is that fall publication cuts out any chance of a magazine sale. That is a complicated subject that I'd rather save for "later" rather than give time to it now. The other is the April schedule which I'll put into my "Part 2." I plan to work on the book intensively till the end of the month (March) — except for that dash to Boston — then put together the Cranbrook lecture,[8] then the others, and I won't get back to the book till the last week of April. It should be virtually finished by mid-May (you wouldn't mind too much, would you, if there were a couple of chapters that still had to be read over and thought about at Southport then?) and completely so before I settle down there for the summer in June. Those seem, at least, to be the possible realities of the situation now. But oh, I'm so agonizingly slow! This means publication early in '55 — but for me the all-important thing is when I finish, not when it appears.

Now — let's have fun planning my Boston trip, and I really do mean to come sometime in that two-week interval, as I said! Even if I don't have a complete manuscript it will be good to go over what there is with H.M.[9] And I do want to go out to Cambridge to see Henry Bigelow. So darling — you put *this* idea in my head! I never would have thought of such a thing. But you and I know that what we shall both want — and especially after these recent letters — is hours and hours of uninterrupted talk — just you and I! And what a perfectly wonderful opportunity for it if you could come to Boston for the first night! And that would eliminate any possible need to return to Boston after I'd gone home with you. If anything of a business sort was not completed the first day, it could be attended to the next morning. This time there would be no dinner with zoologists, no evening at the Forbes house, no A.A.A.S. (oh joy) — so I'd be yours for at least the end of the afternoon, all evening, all night! Then we could go home the following morning or early afternoon, and I'd have the rest of that day, and the following one, with you at home — to do whatever you want. I don't think I should be away longer — and maybe I should fly home the last day instead of waiting for the train — I'll know better nearer the time.

Now darling, this is planning it the loveliest way I can think of. But if you didn't really mean your suggestion, or it proved hard to carry out at the time, of

[7] Editor-in-chief at Houghton Mifflin Company, publisher of *The Edge of the Sea* and of *Silent Spring*.

[8] Delivered at the Cranbrook Institute of Science in Detroit in early April.

[9] Houghton Mifflin Company.

course I can come to you the first night, as I had originally planned to do. And if there's more to do in Boston I can go back. The really important, really wonderful thing is that I'm going to see you — just where and how is secondary.

My dearest, there are a few thoughts I want to add as postscripts to what has already been said, and I'll try to be brief for it's late. Tomorrow morning, I'll dash off "Part 2" on the typewriter.

One is that at the time you wrote about the music of *Tristan and Isolde* I felt so deeply all you said, you expressed it so beautifully. But now that you have given it this added depth of meaning, I shall never forget it. And perhaps I've been holding out on you. You've told me of shedding tears when you read "Undersea"[10] or the Beston review — maybe you ought to know that I shed some too, when I read that, and about other things in almost every letter for the past several weeks. Not always, for quite the same reasons, but always related to the happy reason that I love you so.

And also I wanted to say that in addition to all my other reactions to our wonderful exchange of thoughts, I have such a feeling of relief. Do you know why? As you think back over my letters, don't you know how hard I have been trying, from the very beginning to destroy a barrier that was between us. That was the "famous author" concept that in the beginning so filled your mind and made you afraid to believe what your heart must have been trying to tell you. I was fighting to have you accept me as a simple human being first, an author second. (You know it makes such a difference which end of a telescope you look through.) After the "13 hours" I knew I had made progress; now, at last, my darling, I think I've won.

And do you realize that until we reached that point I couldn't send you the Beston review — or tell you other things I could tell you now? Not that I would ever have felt you'd think I was trying to impress you — my fear would have been that I'd add to the barrier I was trying to tear down, by strengthening what I shall call the myth of the famous author. The other day I found a delicious remark by T. S. Eliot on how a writer reacts to recognition — I'm enclosing it; think about it and then return it someday.

Now that you seem almost part of me — and you do — I can share with you the things that give me the "frightened, lonely feeling" I told you about, and feel that you will truly understand.

When I tried to explain the frightened reaction of course I was giving only a small part of it in saying I wonder whether I can "do it again." The heart of it is something very complex, that has to do with ideas of destiny, and with an almost inexpressible feeling that I am merely the instrument through which something has happened — that I've had little to do with it myself. Shall we talk about that?

As for the loneliness — you can never fully know how much your love and companionship have eased that. Some of it, however, is an inseparable part of writing (which someone accurately described as "a lonely adventure of the

[10] RC's first literary publication, a magazine article in the *Atlantic Monthly*, September 1937.

mind") but how lovely to come in from the adventure at intervals to the warmth of your understanding and love!

What a wonderful thing for Stan to say after reading the Beston review. That tells me more of his depth of understanding than anything else I can imagine. This might almost sound like a presumptuous thing for me to say, but I don't think you'll consider it so — that it means so very much to me to know that you have such an understanding, loving and wonderful husband. And darling, I hope I made it clear in my little note that I was so glad you read him the letter — or parts of it. I *want* him to know what you mean to me. Whenever there is something in "your" letters that you want to share, please remember that you are to decide that, and that I shall be happy in your decision.

SUNDAY

Jeffie made me stop, and it was high time. This is growing to a volume as thick as your 10-page one. After writing such a letter, I think I've said everything there is to say, and that the next time I can be brief — but the "next time" there is just as much to say!

This morning there are two things in the *Times*, one a review of Virginia Woolf's diary, the other extracts from T. S. Eliot's new play, that in a very curious way illuminate some of the things I've been saying to you about writers and writing. It must be "in the air." I'll save them to show you.

Darling, one more thing and I'll stop. You said there were "other factors" you would tell me about when we are together. That's all right — I'm content to wait. Just tell me one thing. It was not quite clear to me whether you meant the factors concerned you and me, or something unrelated to "us" that had a bearing on our return to a more "normal" pattern of life. Just tell me which it is — no elaboration now, dearest.

About Southport in May — do you think perhaps about the 12th would be better than the 17th? The tides aren't good anyway — and the full moon is so late getting around to the Bay. Of course, if we stay up all night that wouldn't matter!! But would the 12th or 13th be too early?

I love you darling — I don't need to tell you but I shall anyway.

Rachel

WEDNESDAY, FEBRUARY 24, 10 P.M.

Darling [Dorothy],

If I don't mail this tomorrow you might have to "suffer through a week with just one letter" — think of it! So, schedule or no schedule, at least, a small note will go to you tomorrow. This morning the mailman came about an hour earlier than usual, just as if he knew he should, so I didn't have to go downtown without your letter after all. What a wonderful report on the trip you have given us — I feel almost as though I'd been there too. It was lovely to know you had visited our place too — and that it's all there, intact! Of course there was a great deal of silence those last weeks we were there, when everyone else was gone — but I imagine the silence of even a spring-like February day has a different quality.

Isn't it odd how we both felt that your being away from home made such a difference — when we're not together anyway? But it did! And while I was so glad you made the trip, I couldn't help being relieved to know you were back safe. That was the chief reason of my call yesterday — I had to know that!

I am working pretty intensively now and *if* I could hold this pace for a whole month there would be real results. But I won't I guess. Most of these nights Jeffie and I are going to bed about 2:30 or 3:00 — and he says he needs more sleep soon! But of course we don't get up at your awful hour of six! I'm going to go and do some more work now, but first I wanted to say goodnight to my darling and tell her (I wonder if she knows) how much I love her. More tomorrow.

THURSDAY

Forsythia is beginning to bloom in downtown Washington. We are higher and cooler and so about a week later here, but even on ours I've noticed a tentative blossom or two. It makes me feel sort of cheated in a way — spring coming before it should, so much still to do, and so much harder to stay in and work with that softness in the air. We'll be hearing frogs any time now.

Darling, I must save your letters to answer this week-end (and maybe the Letter will be here tomorrow — oh, I do hope so!) I am hurrying to get some more pages to the typist this evening, so mustn't yield to the temptation to say anything more — just remember, dearest, how deeply I mean everything I have said and how much I love you always.

Rachel

MARCH 9

My dearest [Dorothy],

Now may I "talk back" right away? Then I'll try not to again until the week-end; and you see how good I'm being, making them all short now ("all" being about two, I think). Do put your mind at rest, darling, I *am* convinced that you "understand"; I know that even though the long letters have brought you happiness, you are willing and even eager to do without them. And as I've told you, they are my "fault," not yours. If there is another before I see you (meaning a long one) please know it was the result of my own need and nothing else!

Oh, I'm so glad you are to have Stanley this week-end, as you really knew or you wouldn't have written that dear note. Don't even say (or wonder to yourself) "Why do I bother you with this?" You know I'm happy about anything that makes you happy.

Yes, I do remember "your little girl." Do you know how sweet you are? But of course you don't — that's one of the reasons you are. Bless your dear heart!

And then today's letter, in my hands 20 hours after it was postmarked. (Don't you think we should give the Post Office Department a testimonial?) More of your stardust. You said: "talking to you — you must know by now, brings me the most happiness." In the note you'd have today, I'm sure there is an identical thought. And of course about the letters: your note yesterday told of reading from the "13 hours" on (did you stay up all night?) and two of mine you'd have since then told you of similar activities on my part.

My chief reaction to your suggestion on bringing the correspondence together 20 years from now: who is going to provide the horde of slaves necessary to carry the staggering load of letters that will have accumulated by then?

Darling, now it is my turn to regret something carelessly phrased. As soon as that letter had gone I wished I could have it back to change that last page, for I wondered if it could possibly imply that I had felt you lacked understanding of my multiple responsibilities. Now I know it did, and I'm so very sorry, dear. Not only would I not hurt you for the world, but it wasn't so anyway — of course I didn't take you seriously about you, Jeffie, and the book being my whole life! (But they are a very big and important part of it!) Really, I was just a little overwhelmed with the pressure of some of those responsibilities the day I wrote that, and was only using your neat phrase as a springboard to complain about them. If I'd said it (orally that is) you would have known. Please, darling, if there is ever anything in a letter that hurts you, just know it wasn't meant to. And forgive my carelessness this time.

Not long now, darling. It will be that week that's part March, part April, I'm sure. But I can hardly believe it. I love you, ever and ever so much.

Rachel

MARCH 12

My darling [Dorothy],

Let's not stop commenting on the stardust — it's fun, and besides sometimes part of it has to be told or the other wouldn't know. For example, here is one of the shiniest bits yet. This morning while I was still abed, considering getting up and meanwhile entertaining various delightful thoughts, I said to myself (and I swear these were the exact words): "In three weeks I will have seen her." Can you imagine my feelings when, a few hours later, those same words looked up at me from your letter? As I think I've said before, I just don't get used to it; I've never had this experience before.

And this, too, of stardust, but in a different vein. I think you'll get a laugh out of it, as I did. Yesterday, in the midst of having my hair done, my eye fell on a little placard in my operator's booth, making a special offer of some product "plus gift of Stardust." I didn't know what, in the parlance of the beauty salon, "stardust" was, so immediately inquired, and I'm sure the girl thought my interest and amusement quite out of proportion to the subject.

Of course I was charmed by the clipping on narcissus as food for the soul. I realize that I never did see my "quotation" in print — I think I told you it was being quoted very inexactly. My source was Alice Mullen, my Amherst friend, who repeated it as a quotation often used by her mother, a great reader, to justify expenditures for books that seemed out of proportion to the family budget. As she quoted it, it was definitely "a white hyacinth" — I remember that Alice once sent a pot of hyacinths to my mother with a reminder of the thought. I must ask her if she knows where her mother got it. The chances are this is the original, and that it has "evolved" through various repetitions into its final (for us) form expressing so perfectly "What You Mean to Me!"

To think, my dearest, that I'll really be with you in about two and a half weeks! A month ago, I well remember, I had such a terrible sense of urgency about it I thought I *couldn't* wait — but I've lived through all that time and suppose I can endure what's left. Just think, if I had gone in February we wouldn't have it to look forward to. Oh darling, let's be thoroughly "selfish" this time — after all, it's our first real visit. The "thirteen hours" were just a prelude. What I said about meeting your friends was dictated by the thought that maybe you very much wanted something of the sort. Now I think you really do feel as I do — begrudging terribly every moment shared with anyone else. And the time will be so short at best. So why not save friends for another time? Darling, I sound perfectly nasty, don't I? I'm only daring to tell you how I really feel about it because I think you, too, want every moment we can have together. (If you need "excuses," perhaps the uncertainty of my plans for seeing people at Harvard, etc., will serve. [The schemer in action.] Or shall I be sick and have to go to bed for the duration of my visit?)

Sometimes I have to smile at the way you disqualify yourself as an expert when I suggest I'm going to ask your advice. So you know nothing about gardening! Let's say that at least you couldn't know less than I, and I think we'll find you know a whole lot more. Planned or orthodox gardens wouldn't interest me anyway, and if I could get anything to "running wild" at Southport I'd be delighted. And of course I want only things that seem to belong there. Anyway, let's talk about it. Undoubtedly, the "leaning" spruce on the shore is the one my "friend" Mr. Conley[11] put the cable on — and was supposed to have restored it when it broke in December. I'll get after him at once — it won't be necessary to say who told me. This doesn't increase my regard for him!

Oh yes — and you're not really qualified to judge *The Edge of the Sea* — if I'm to believe you! You "don't know my science" — darling, it is written for people who don't! And anyway, you do know more of it than most of my prospective readers. You "know very little about English composition." Now, Mrs. Freeman, you really make me laugh! You don't know "the aim of the book." Nei-

11 A Boothbay Harbor landscaper.

ther does any other reader till he's read it—then if he doesn't, it's the author's fault! But seriously, darling (and I won't tease you anymore about it), you— even aside from my personal feelings about you—could very well represent my "ideal reader"—the kind of person for whom I'm writing. And all I want to know is whether it tells you things you're glad to know, in a way you enjoy. Or to put it another way, does it serve as a passport to that new world of which we've spoken? Sometime before I see you, you'll have a sample to read.

I'm being very lazy tonight—writing propped up in bed, and Jeffie is sound asleep in his basket on the bed beside me. He is so big now it's almost hard to remember he's still a baby (5½ months) but a couple of weeks ago I had a re-minder: I discovered he had lost all four of his baby canine teeth. Now the lower ones are growing up like weeds, and he is very bitey—cutting his new teeth on my poor hands! The "eye teeth" haven't appeared yet—except for big swellings on his gums. He is much better now and is able to play again almost normally. The great joy of his life is to be given a round metal tray with a deep rim, a large marble, and a piece of tissue paper. That last is the touch of perfection that makes the game so delightful.

I'm glad you didn't disqualify yourself on the what-to-wear question, for you've helped me realize that I should find out more about the character of the Cranbrook lecture which is an evening affair. But so much depends on the com-munity, the Institute itself, and so on that it is hard to know, and I've decided on a direct approach to the problem—I'll ask the wife of the Director whether my attire should be formal or otherwise. Fortunately I've already corresponded with her—she wrote to invite me to stay with them that night.

I thought I might bring up a few of my slides for you and Stan and your mother to see, if you'd like to.

Darling, you write so seldom of your "disability"[12] and please don't ever regret it when you do! Don't you know that (as you have said to me) I want to share your sorrows as well as your joys? And although I seldom ask how you are (just because I have felt that usually you'd rather not talk about it) it is always in my mind, with the wish that there was even some tiny thing I could do to make it more bearable. Oh dearest, I hope you will be willing to tell me more about it when we are together if only for my sake. I'm so sorry.

[12] Arthritis.

SATURDAY AFTERNOON

Now a little more and then I'll mail this so you'll be sure to have it Monday. I'd better come to grips with the question of dates without waiting any longer. Perhaps I've been putting it off from page to page because there are still uncer-tainties in my mind, but let's talk about them. I've been thinking that if I flew up sometime Monday (instead of taking the train that night) it would give us at least an extra evening and night, and make little difference at this end because I'd be away that night anyway. But if I should do that darling, I *don't* want you to come to the airport—I know just enough Boston geography to know it's at the other end of nowhere from you. There must be trains to Brockton—tell me about them. Or if I came late in the day couldn't I go home with Stan? Let's have your suggestions on this, just in case. Coming on the train and getting off at your Route 128 station would, I suppose, be easiest, but I begrudge the long hours on the train when I could be with you, instead. And then Tuesday would be unbroken—and Wednesday, too, if I planned to see the Cambridge people Thursday morning, and Paul that afternoon. But even a quick trip to Cambridge another day wouldn't be too bad, would it? We'd be together on the drive there and back.

That is about as definite as I can be now, dear, but it does give us something to go on, doesn't it? And I'm afraid a certain element of uncertainty must remain; the situation here always has disturbing possibilities, as you know in a way, and will understand more fully after we've been together. But I think and do so hope that approximately this plan can stand. Oh darling—could it be true? And somehow my dearest, your ingenuity has to contrive hours and hours for us to be alone—there is so much I want to hear and so much I long to tell you!

As I suggested in the note you would have yesterday or today, I might call you someday next week to discuss all this—quite unnecessarily, I suppose, for really there is time to write about it, so I admit I'm just looking for an excuse to talk to you. Some morning, maybe. If you have meanwhile suggested in a letter replying to my note a good time I'll try to make the call then. Monday is not likely to be a good day—after that I think I'll be here most mornings.

I'm thinking of you as being very happy all this week-end, and I'm so glad for you. Stanley will be with you till Monday morning, won't he?

Well darling, this is a medium-fat letter, isn't it? You see I couldn't stick to the tiny ones very long. But now I shall try to again until I see you—there is so much to be done, somehow, before then.

And suddenly I realize I haven't thanked you for letting me see the "grandmother" picture, which I love. As your intuition tells you, I have mixed emotions about emphasizing the grandmother role—feelings that have nothing to do with you and that sweet baby but are rooted, I suppose, in the old-fashioned and very outmoded concept of a grandmother, and perhaps also in the fact that the only one of my grandparents who survived to know me was, even in my early and only recollections of her, gray-haired and seventyish. However, all that has nothing to do with a grandmother of the 1954 model! And I really believe this picture (especially the glimpse of you in the mirror) is more the You I think of than any other I've seen. So maybe someday I will ask you to get one for me. Meanwhile, I've loved seeing it. And I'm so eager to see the others you tell me about.

Now, no more, my darling, for this time. I love you so dearly—you know I'm sure.

Rachel

My dearest Dorothy,

I'm sure you know, but I must tell you again anyway, how lovely and satisfying and happy those days with you were.[13] Seventy-two hours, you said on the phone; I hadn't then stopped to count up their number, just reckoning them by their happiness, instead. It was all that in the weeks of waiting I hoped it would be—and do I need to say anything more?

As I think I told you on the phone, we had sun and blue skies all the way down, and even the clouds below us were only scattered ones. As seen from nearly three miles up in that air ocean that so intrigues me now, the landscape that lies between us seems not so extensive, after all.

You will be surprised, I think, to know that the freesias are still wonderfully fresh (seeming to be endowed with some special life), that they are still fragrant, and of course full of a lovely meaning for me.

There was a note from Dr. Bigelow this morning, filled with his dear thoughtfulness and delightful humor. It always means so much to me to see him, and I was especially glad that you had a word with him this time, too. And I want you to know (lest you begin to worry that I took my time to come "only" to see you) that as I look back on it the visit with Houghton Mifflin seems a real necessity at this point. And I'm sure it was, from their viewpoint, as resulting in a last frantic effort on my part. It is going to mean a less peaceful summer at Southport, with somewhat less time for things I'd like to do; but the tasks left for then will be more or less routine ones, that *can* be scheduled, for all the creative effort will (she thinks hopefully) be done by that time. And it will be wonderful to have it behind me—the whole heartbreaking effort, I mean.

Someday soon—next week probably—I'll send you a few prints of the more successful pictures that were taken last week. I just thought I'd warn you now. They will at least give you some setting for your thoughts of me at home.

Jeffie has been so sweet. Most of yesterday afternoon he lay on a chair drawn up beside mine at the typewriter—with, I must admit, intervals of getting up to assist directly in the typing process, to mix up my papers, and knock pencils off the table. Very early Friday morning he wakened me, and when I sat up in bed to see what he wanted, he rushed over and threw himself into my lap with such obvious joy that I really knew then how much he had missed me.

The Cranbrook lecture seems to be straightening itself out fairly well; but when I remember that by one week from today I must have completed that, have gone to Detroit and given it, and have finished the sand section—I don't feel exactly relaxed. So I suspect, my dear, that after this you won't hear again until that little group of problems has been solved; in other words, for maybe a whole week!

[13] RC had stayed with the Freemans in West Bridgewater from March 29 to April 1.

Tell Stan I'm still laughing over his sign. I'll be on my guard about him in the future. And thank him for tying up my package, and for all the ways he helped to make the visit so happy. And my love to your mother.

Now I must go back to work. My dearest love to you, as always.

Rachel

WEDNESDAY NIGHT, APRIL 21, 11:50

My darling [Dorothy],

Bless your dear heart for that note! This time I had great self-control and kept it until the evening "ordeal"[14] was over—that was to be my reward, and it was! And darling—this is a completely shameless thing for me to say—but in a way I think it did work out almost like your Fairy Tale. Oh, I can't tell you all about it now—but from the very beginning of the plans for this thing, I have had an odd feeling that there were some things I needed to say—and that perhaps this was the place to say them. So—after the desired light and anecdotal touch in perhaps the first two-thirds of the talk, I drifted into my theme of the place of beauty in our lives, and the tragedy of its destruction. It was so similar in its basic thought to what I read in your letter yesterday—about Tomlinson's "A Lost Woods"[15]—that I, too, caught my breath. The response was really so wonderful that I feel it was worth all the agony—that maybe this was really something very important for me to do. My "thousand dragons" sat through it all with such beautiful attentiveness; afterwards so many said: "Oh, I'm so glad you said that," or "That's just how I feel, but I didn't know how to put it in words." One said—you will love this, I think—"I had such a feeling of calmness and peace while you were speaking." There was one incident that so reminded me of your story of William Lyon Phelps that you must hear it. The audience remained seated while those at the speaker's table filed out when it was over. As I neared one woman seated on the aisle, she looked at me with such a wonderful expression, and made an impulsive little movement of her hand. With perhaps equal impulsiveness, I stopped and took her hand. She said "Thank you, oh, thank you."

Since I've been so completely lacking in modesty, I may as well go on and tell you that the committee members pronounced it "the best, most satisfying speech" in the 30-year history of The Matrix Table. But if it was, it was because of the importance of what I had to say, and my feeling about its importance. That feeling helped, I'm sure, to put me at ease so that I really was quite happy and relaxed during the giving of it.

Darling, how shameless of me to tell you all that—but to how many people do you suppose I'd tell it?

This morning I woke to such a feeling of utter weariness, that I couldn't bear to open my eyes. It was partly physical, but more psychological—for I dreaded the going terribly. Then two things happened that changed the tone of

[14] RC had spoken at a dinner held in Columbus, Ohio, by Theta Sigma Phi, a national sorority for women in journalism.

[15] An essay in H. M. Tomlinson's *Out of Soundings* (1931).

the day. When I did open my eyes, my first action was to look over at baby Jeffie's bed—a soft spread folded and put on the floor, surrounded with cushions. And the baby had gotten up, and for the first time in a whole week had left his bed![16] He was lying on the rug, looking so bright-eyed and happy. Yesterday he had taken two or three tottering little steps—his first. So this is a great gain—though of that, more later.

[16] Jeffie had injured his back.

This was the second thing. When I came downstairs there was a telegram from the "jury of award" for the Limited Editions Club 25th anniversary celebration on May 11th. The jury has nominated me, as one of "ten living American authors who are considered to have written in the quarter-century 1929–54 books which seem most likely to survive as classics." These people will receive the "Silver Jubilee Medals" the club is giving to those "who have rendered the most extraordinary services to the world of books during the past 25 years." (This seems to be Rachel's night to be shameless!) This is the occasion I mentioned as possibly delaying us a day. I'd received an invitation, but didn't then know I was getting an award, though there had been rumors.

I think you will know which of these two events of the morning gave me the greater happiness. But how few people could possibly understand that.

As to our Maytime, darling, if it is possible for me to go on schedule (I mean, that week) I could take the overnight train from New York—I think it becomes part of the Federal. But as to all that, be patient, darling, and we shall see.

I told you in a recent letter that I wouldn't let myself think about the future and Jeffie till this was over. Despite the wonderful improvement, the whole thing still has disturbing possibilities as to its true nature. We are having new tests made and I should know more when I go home. Meanwhile, I'm so thankful he was a little better before I had to leave. He gave me an impish little nip on the cheek when I got down to kiss him goodbye!

Now, my dearest, it's getting late. Breakfast will be brought to my room at 8:30. At ten, two of my transformed dragons will arrive to take me on a tour of the Ohio State campus. Then luncheon at 12:30, when I'll show a few of my slides—then home.

So much I want to say about your wonderful Easter letter and Tomlinson. But that must be later.

My dearest love, always
Rachel

WEDNESDAY, APRIL 28

Darling [Dorothy],

Wasn't that wonderful news from Stanley![17] That is real achievement for one of his years, I know. I am so happy for you. And how nice the news came before Stan left on his trip.

[17] DF's son had received a promotion from instructor to assistant professor of education at the University of Maine.

And Martha always seems to be far ahead of her age—it must be inherited!

You will have had mail every day this week—and so have I to this point. We're an incorrigible pair, aren't we?

The next time you write, how about telling me something of your visit to the clinic Monday? Any change in your treatment? And are you doing your exercises??

Oh darling, day after tomorrow (I mean the day after that!) it will be *May*. How wonderful.

I love you.
Rachel

MAY 3–4

Darling [Dorothy],

This letter must be started, at least, before I sleep tonight, though I admit it's late.

At this moment two weeks hence, I hope we shall be in the little house at Southport, perhaps asleep, perhaps talking before the fire, perhaps watching the moon if it hasn't already set. It seems like one of your fairy tales about to come true, but now I really believe it will.

Housekeeping? A minimum, I imagine, but what fun. Will you bring a thermos—I can't remember whether we left any there, but probably not. And we might want to eat lunch on the shore someday.

[18] A Southport building contractor.

I talked to Mr. Delano[18] tonight, and he is going out someday probably this week to attend to everything—the installing of the heater, laying the linoleum, taking off the storm windows, and having electricity, water, and phone restored. He is so satisfactory. I forgot to ask him how the weather is. Do you suppose *we'll* wear our hats?

About May 11—yes, I am going to wear the navy dress. This is a "black tie" affair and I think it will be just right. So far I've worn it only for Columbus and the New York Zoological Society affair, and I'm Scotch enough to feel I haven't had my money's worth out of it. Anyway, I doubt I'd find anything I'd like as well. I am staying at the Hotel Pierre, where the dinner is, provided

[19] Marie Rodell, RC's literary agent.

Marie[19] was able to reserve a room there—I asked her to last night. That will simplify things—I won't have to take an evening wrap. Of course I'll let you know definitely later.

Darling, I'd dearly love to wear your flowers. It is barely possible that the Limited Editions Club expects to provide them, though since I'm the only woman it may never occur to them. Otherwise, Oxford would presumably do so, but I'm certain they would rejoice in not having to—they are very thrifty, shall I say. And they wouldn't without consulting Marie, and I could tell her to decline, if that is your wish. If you can do it without a lot of trouble, darling, know that I should be deeply happy to have you so tangibly part of it—if not—know that you will be intangibly just as much a part of it, and that I love your thought anyway. Just let me know.

Mr. Macy (the director of the club) writes happily that apparently all the recipients of the awards "who aren't in Europe" will be present. I don't know who is in Europe. I'd told him I wanted to be forewarned if there was to be any speech making, however brief. This was his answer: "Probably more than 700 people will be there. I think it safe to say that the announcement of the Award for you will receive some kind of ovation. The gathering would of course be disappointed if you were not prepared to utter a few graceful sentences." Oh dear! They will certainly be few—but it is difficult to say anything very memorable in a minute or so. I had hoped they would skip speech making since there are 25 awards: the 10 writers, as you know, but also artists ("the best book illustrators of the past quarter-century") and the typographers and printers "who have produced the finest books."

The plan is for a "a classic dinner from Homer to Dickens; there will be wine courses equally classic."

This, I think, is all I know at present!

Yes I did try to think what women might have been possibilities—one I thought of was Pearl Buck, and my "nomination" was based chiefly on the fact that she received the Nobel Prize (probably the only American woman to do so, isn't she?) and is the only woman member of the American Academy of Arts and Letters. (I'm in the Institute, the larger, associated organization.) I wonder how diligently the judges really tried to think back through the 25 years. Perhaps they let the light of recent success blind them to earlier work!

I think I may send you (I am sending it today—regular mail) my notebook containing the Columbus talk and, in rather rough form, the Cranbrook Lecture, though of course the latter isn't fully intelligible without the slides. In spite of saying I was only going to make notes for Columbus, I finally sat down and typed it out in as conversational a style as possible, about as I intended to give it. I know by now that having done that gives me greater assurance than I'd have otherwise. When the moment came, however, I'd read it over often enough that I was able just to talk, with only an occasional glance at the script. But this is substantially what I said. I thought I'd send it in advance, as interim bed-time entertainment, because I don't want to allot too much precious Southport time to reading speeches!! Just bring the notebook with you dear, instead of mailing it back.

During the week before Columbus the whole situation seemed so intolerable that I promised myself to agree to no more such engagements, ever! It came at such a disastrous moment in relation to the book. I was having to prepare the material while suffering such anguish over Jeffie, and over it all was the specter of perhaps having to go at a moment when things were even worse in relation to him, for I could scarcely believe he'd survive. It all amounted to almost more than I could take—and then turned out so happily in the end. What I meant to be leading up to was the fact that what to do about the various invitations to go here and there is a very difficult problem—much against it and at least some arguments for it. I'd like to talk about it when we are together. There is one now — about giving the "Clark Lectures" at Scripps College in California next March. I don't have to decide until the end of the month, when the President will be in the east and wants to come to Washington to see me. But oh dear, how can I know in May what I'll be doing in March? (Working on *The Edge of the Sea*, most likely!!!)

Oh my darling — these days we are about to have at Southport will be so, so wonderful. There should be much happiness during the summer too, but it can't be the same, as we both know. How little I dreamed, when we closed the door last October, *who* would be with me when I should open it again!

One of the reasons I didn't want to continue on to Southport after the big night in New York was that I do hope to be reasonably fresh and not tired. That was my one regret about my visit with you, darling; I was more exhausted than I wanted to admit and as a result was not exactly the kind of guest I'd like to have been. That, I knew, you understood. What I regretted was that I was just too weary to make the effort to talk about some things I really wanted to say to you. However, there was also the feeling that Southport was really the place for some of it, where for long, satisfying hours we can talk with no interruption. Darling, I think I should say this now — that I wish every one of our moments there could be completely happy, but I am afraid, for a little while at least, we must talk of things that aren't happy. There are stresses and worries in my general situation that I feel I must talk about with you — if I don't do it then, I don't know when I ever can or will. But that will be as brief as possible; then we'll shut the door on it and just be happy — so very happy, my dearest.

I'll bring my bird glasses — the warblers we used to watch in October while we ate breakfast may be coming through again, northbound. And there will be others, of course.

You spoke — many letters back — of bringing a record player. Did you mean this time, or in the summer? Of course I'd love it, if it's feasible.

When shall I see the "secret" Kodachrome? I think I know what it is.

Darling, lest you think I wrote all this in the middle of the night, I said goodnight many pages back (Jeffie wanted to go to sleep) and it is now Tuesday morning. I want to go on, but I mustn't. Later in the week I'll let you know where I'll be in New York. I should hear from Marie by tomorrow.

Are you resting any this week, darling? Please do. You will have this Thursday, I suppose. Then only one week and a tiny fragment of one until — the 17th.

My dearest love always
Rachel

I just asked about the Federal, assuming there may have been a change with the switch to Daylight time. It reaches the Rt. 128 station at 7:50 Daylight Saving Time. (Or did you know?)

And I've been wanting to say this — I don't know how you feel about letting other people drive your car (I'm very fussy about who drives mine!)—but I want you to know that I'll be more than glad to drive any or all of the distance, if you're willing and it will make it easier for you.

I love you. R.

MAY 23

Darling [Dorothy]—

Your train note was so sweet—especially your musical analogy and your likening the visit to a symphony. A thought so typical of you and one I shall always remember.

As I shall remember every one of the Hundred Hours.[20]

All my love, dear one,
Rachel

SUNDAY AFTERNOON, MAY 23

My dearest [Dorothy],

Does it seem to you a long time since I said goodbye to you and Stan and disappeared into "The City of Trenton" (the same car that brought me to you)? It does to me, already. And I wanted to write you yesterday, so that you might have this Monday. But there was a little sleep to be made up ("You know I don't sleep well on trains," I explained to everybody interested) and a few necessary chores, besides much talk, of course, so the letter just didn't get written. And even now I'm watching the clock for that 4:30 collection, so this must be shorter than I'd like.

Darling, I can't remember when I've had such a relaxed and happy time, and if perhaps we did talk more than we slept, the hours with you meant far more to me, and did me more good, than any amount of sleep. The memory of those days and nights—each and every one of them—will always be precious to me. How wonderful that our dream, begun so tentatively in December, could come true!

Already I've begun to make a pile of books to send up later for us to enjoy together this summer. The *Beagle* Diary,[21] *Northern Farm*,[22] John Mason Brown's *As They Appear*, one or two of Edwin Teale's,[23] and Peterson's *Birds Over America*. In another month the list will have grown enormously, no doubt, and beyond all possibility of reading them. The summer is beginning to seem short and crowded already!

Did I carry away your Fisherman's Wharf tide calendar? I have one that doesn't look as dog-eared as mine, and suspect I may have taken both—mine may be in the laundry case.

Jeffie left no doubt in my mind that he was glad to have me back—the darling. He had stayed upstairs all week, you know, but came down very shortly after our reunion. He seems in pretty good shape, as far as surface appearances go, at least.

[20] RC and DF had just concluded a visit from May 17 to May 21 at RC's Southport cottage and had visited Henry Beston and his wife, Elizabeth Coatsworth, at their home in Nobleboro, Maine. RC and DF often exchanged notes—DF's here termed a "train note"—when they parted.

[21] Charles Darwin's *Journal of Researches into the Natural History and Geology of the Countries Visited during the Voyage of H.M.S. "Beagle" Round the World, under the Command of Capt. Fitz Roy R.N.* (1891).

[22] By Henry Beston, first published in 1948.

[23] Edwin Way Teale, author of, among many other books, *North with the Spring* (1951), and friend of RC.

No doubt you, too, have discovered that "rote" is a perfectly good dictionary word, though I still think it is an unusual one. If ever you see it in print, try to remember to tell me, for I'm sure I haven't. But I'm delighted to have made its acquaintance.

I've just received copies of the Yugoslavian translation of *The Sea*, and am interested to discover that my name has become Carsonova!

Last night I read a chapter of my new Tomlinson just before I turned out the light—it is a delight, and wonderful to have it from you.

Now I'm sitting out in the back yard under a clear blue sky, the air filled with the fragrance of roses, and every tree and bush alive with baby birds. And I wish you were here, darling; but the days will fly and time for Southport will soon be here. I do hope your week-end will be a comfortable and happy one, and that you can wait until Tuesday to return.

Now I suppose this must be all for now, but I'll write again before you go. When do you leave? Friday morning? I can't remember.

I'll decide by tomorrow night whether I'm going to New York Wednesday. I think probably I won't.

My dearest love, always
Rachel

TUESDAY AFTERNOON, JUNE 1

Darling [Dorothy]—

How I did wish you were with me last night! For we heard the veeries most beautifully in the very spot where I first heard them, in the same sort of green twilight, with almost the same magical effect. (When the first experience of anything beautiful has been exactly right, I don't suppose any repetition can quite equal it.) When we arrived at the spot, there was a great deal of other song in the woods—flycatchers, chickadees, water thrushes, ovenbirds, and even discordant cries of night herons flying over the creek. Finally the sound for which I'd been straining my ears—the short "Whew" that says veeries are about. And at last the songs began, the first so far off in the woods, or so faint, that I had to hold my breath to hear at all. But oh—unmistakably!—a veery. Soon others began, some quite close to us. As perhaps you found, they seem never to sing in chorus, but responsively, one voice quickly answering another. And all that unearthly quality—"of a spirit not to be discovered" as Mr. Halle[24] said—was there. But one of the spirits revealed itself, for suddenly a slim little bird materialized on the branch of a dogwood, almost over our heads. Oh, how I wanted it to sing, then and there! But that was not to be. In a minute or so it flew off into a tangle of honeysuckle along the path. Then there began to be suspicious movements in the low growth at the very edge of the path. I was just beginning cautious investigations when three people came over the foot bridge. So we tried to look as if we'd never heard of a veery, for you can hardly imagine the rating a person must have with me before I'll reveal even a *possible* site of a bird's

[24] Louis J. Halle, author of *Spring in Washington*, first published in 1947.

nest. "Have you heard anything?" they asked. "Oh, yes—there have been water thrushes—and ovenbirds." Being very cautious, you see. They looked disappointed. And after all, they each wore binoculars, so I relented a bit. "And the veeries have been singing." You should have seen their faces brighten. Obviously that was what they'd come for, so I was doubly glad when the spirits began calling again. As soon as we came home, I looked up Mr. Halle's description of the song—it could hardly be improved on.

I was going to write more but think I'll mail this now, as my greeting for today. Maybe there will be word from you tomorrow. And guess what? I love you.

Rachel

JUNE 5, MID-AFTERNOON

Darling [Dorothy],

I haven't resorted to the typewriter for a long time, have I? But time is far from dim today, so I know you won't mind.

First—in answer to *your* answer to my veery letter—I thought the whole episode pretty starry, beginning with the fact that, as I learned the other day, while I was in Rock Creek Park listening to veeries and wishing for you, you were walking along your road listening to wood thrushes and wishing for me! And then, of course, to think that you did have your lovely and satisfying veery experience before you received the account of mine. Oh, darling, I'm so glad that now you have really heard them and understand how I feel about them. I agree that Mr. Halle's description is superb. The bit about the "overtones—as if the bird carried its own echo within itself" is especially telling. I thought the other night I should copy that bit for you. I'm sending it to you in a few days.

Tell Stan that I have the *Collier's* article "Bread from the Sea" though I must confess I've only glanced at it. There is a large scientific literature on marine plankton and its utilization—I wish I could spend an afternoon at the Woods Hole MBL[25] Library with him and help him find it. I'm sending him a few reprints from my own collection—he can return them to me this summer sometime. I feel sure someone at the Oceanographic could be helpful if they knew his interest.

Yes, I've been told there is "another" *La Mer*, but haven't heard it so far as I know, and don't know the composer. Darling, you have mentioned Debussy's *La Mer* several times, and I haven't responded—deliberately. Now I'm beginning to laugh at myself, so I guess I will tell you. Of course I know and love it—that wasn't the reason. The summer *The Sea* was published, RCA asked me if I would write the commentary for their new recording of *La Mer* by Toscanini, and I did. I wouldn't have had the temerity to attempt it if I hadn't known that, in this particular instance, what they principally wanted was something about the sea, rather than a competent analysis of the music. Anyway, by the time I knew you well enough to be talking about such things, I also knew that you are

[25] Marine Biological Laboratory at Woods Hole, Massachusetts.

so far beyond me in your understanding of music that I guess I just got very self-conscious about having you know anything about it. And now you do. I decided today that you'd probably discover it yourself sometime, and then wouldn't I be thoroughly scolded! Perhaps I will anyway. I looked at it today and one word stood out—evocation. I believe it is a word I have used a good deal without thinking much about it, but now you have made me very conscious of it. Oh, also on the subject of *La Mer*—I remembered this morning there had been something in last Sunday's *Times* about a new recording that sounded interesting, so I looked it up and am sending it for you.

If there was a recent "deluge" of Freeman mail, darling, it was a very delightful one, every piece of it bringing its own particular bit of happiness. However, if I'm not mistaken, you had mail every day this week except Wednesday, and several pieces the week before. The only trouble with that, of course, is that on the rare days when the postman fails to deliver what is expected and longed for, there is such a sunken feeling!

I have found copies of two early books of Tomlinson's—*Gallions Reach* and *Tidemarks*; someday we can at least dip into them together. Darling, I don't think your copy of *The Face of the Earth*[26] will be here for some time; it had to be ordered from England and the "book post" always seems slow. So it will have to be an un-birthday present. And for your birthday—something made me decide today to send to you at once an advance on your remembrance from me, so when the first package comes you may open it. You will know why then, I think. The other you should keep for the proper day. And by the way, as soon as you know what you will be doing that day, and when, I wish you'd tell me. I might be thinking of calling you, you know.

[26] Written by H. M. Tomlinson, first published in 1950.

We made a change in Jeffie's medicine several days ago, and it seems to have brought about some real improvement. So the last few days have been a little less anxious ones.

Do let me know how Martha got along the next time you write. I hope the ordeal is well over now and she has forgotten it.[27]

[27] An operation to remove a small growth on an eyelid.

Yesterday Marie sent me an astonishing clipping from *Publisher's Weekly*, saying *The Edge of the Sea* is scheduled for September 13th. Guess I'd better get back to work!

All my love, dearest—
Rachel

JUNE 16

[28] The first page or pages of this letter not preserved.

[Dear Dorothy,][28]

I think sometimes in regard to the book that if only there were someway, without anyone being hurt by it, that I could be free of all responsibility and worry for even one month (of work on the book) it would make all the difference in the world. But that couldn't be, and it's the feeling that there is no way out that gets me down. Or I suppose there is a way—to have what it takes to rise above all these things and just go ahead, but that's where my weakness comes in.

Darling—am I distressing you? I do hope not. Because I hope you know what it means to have you to write all that to (and I didn't intend to write it—oh dear!). Anyway, just think back to all I've tried to tell you about what you are to me, and know how much you are helping me, by your sweet understanding!

One thing I've resolved—after the writing commitments are met (and you see I'm assuming now they will be) there is going to be a long, healing interval of no writing, in which I shall get straightened out in various ways. And in which, I hope, we can do some happy things together.

And darling, I hope you have some idea how very happy you have made me by what you have written in your recent letters—about yourself. To know that you really do see some improvement in your condition is the happiest news I could imagine having. It is what I have hoped for ever since I came to realize what you have been enduring. I must leave it to your understanding to know what it does for me to have you associate me with that improvement. Darling— there has been such joy in having you—and if "having you" has had that effect, or in any way contributed to it, the joy is immeasurably increased. And to think Stan made the connection, too! From a purely medical standpoint, darling, it is plausible—happy emotions are a great medicine and I suspect they work their magic through mysterious chemical reactions that could well be all-important in a condition such as yours. But why analyze it? If you are happier, and have less discomfort and disability than a year ago, that makes me supremely happy.

I have a few other things to say that I think I shall write separately—this is all on a rather emotional level, isn't it? Be sure to tell me just when you are leaving (the 21st is all I know) and when you are leaving Southport to return. As I suggested in my recent note, you may have "only" about two letters during your time there. (Don't you think, we should write once a month?? Can you remember that once we discussed that!)

About Stan's book—it came yesterday and I really think the damage is so slight—mostly to the jacket—that the desirability of having it early makes it possible to disregard that. I do think he will get a lot of ideas from studying the color photographs, and would probably like to do that before he returns to Southport. So I think I shall anticipate his birthday, and send it about the last week of June.

I'm glad you liked my inscription in *Spring in Washington*. I knew you would read it correctly—but that no one else could!

Now, my dearest, no more until you are at Southport, where I so wish I could be that week!

My dearest love—always—
Rachel

Darling [Dorothy],

This time I shall really try to be brief; as you know, there is new incentive for concentrating on the work I ought to be doing. And probably I shall try to write less often, too. I MUST get certain chapters out of the way before I can allow myself to go to Maine, and also I MUST get them in shape for Mr. Shawn[29] to see them soon.

When we are together I will tell you more about him and my feeling about having the *New Yorker* do this. It is a feeling I acquired out of my experience with *The Sea*—my experience with him editorially, and my contact with *New Yorker* readers. It all adds up to the fact that I'd rather have the new book appear in the *New Yorker* than anywhere else, although I realize that probably takes a little explaining to anyone outside the publishing world. (I know I was quite amazed when Marie sent them a chapter of *The Sea*.) But as I told you the other night, the enormous boost to my spirits came not so much from the prospect of a *New Yorker* sale, as from what Mr. Shawn said. Darling, I thought you knew I have been simply obsessed by the conviction that this was very far below what readers of *The Sea* were going to expect. As Bob Hines[30] said when I told him the news, and my psychological reaction, it is a good thing to have a little self-doubt, but real gloom about what you are doing can be very crippling—and that's what I have been suffering. Well, I hope I can hold the mood of the present.

The proofs of the sand chapter came yesterday and on the whole I am pleased. These have to go back; I shall try to get also a plain run of galleys to keep—then you can read that chapter in type.

I am going to mail Stan's book in a day or so; then he will have it to look over at home before he goes to Southport next. He said not to mail the slides back, but I think I'd better, for as you know the time of my arrival is so uncertain and he may want them soon. I'd love to see some of them projected, but it has been fun to look at them through the viewer. I can hardly wait to get there and help him find some of the many colors of starfish that live on my shore in the region of good low tides. Perhaps we should do something about an aquarium. And you, darling, turned out to be quite a photographer—I'm much impressed with your skill, only I think you'd better pick a better subject in the future!

I thought two of the Beston quotes very beautiful, the other mystifying. Remember to tell me more about *your* impressions of Northern Lights[31]—and remember to tell me more about your book! You are slippery as an eel on that subject, but I shall succeed in pinning you down someday. You see, I really want you to try, and I have a very definite belief in what you could do.

In connection with my Rutledge[32] quotes to you, I meant to remind you that we met him in the course of my long southern trip in '52, and have visited Hampton Plantation on each of our later trips. He is of the historic Rutledge family that included a signer of the Declaration of Independence and a framer

[29] William Shawn, editor of the *New Yorker* magazine, who was considering first serial rights to *The Edge of the Sea*.

[30] Staff artist for the U.S. Fish and Wildlife Service and illustrator of *The Edge of the Sea*.

[31] Chapter 7 of Henry Beston's *The St. Lawrence* (1942) contains a legend entitled "The Fiddler of the Northern Lights."

[32] Quotations about love, beauty, and the sea from Archibald Rutledge RC sent to DF for her June 15 birthday.

of the Constitution, and the plantation itself goes back to those days. He is about 70 and now very frail, but it is always a wonderful experience to talk to him.

Darling, I hate even to suggest this and raise your hopes when it might not come about at all, but recent developments have raised the possibility that I might need to see Houghton Mifflin. Once we are at Southport, I can't leave Mamma overnight to go, and it would not be feasible to break our trip to let me do it then—once we start, we shall have to go right on through as fast as I can drive it. So—if it turns out that I really need to, I might come up next week. I suppose I'd fly up some morning, and spend much of the rest of the day with H.M. Then I'd try to stay over that night with you, but would have to come back the next day. But it is very tentative, and if I can avoid the break I will, for it will only delay my coming to Southport.

The Park Book Shop will mail your *Sea Beach*[33] direct to you, presumably tomorrow.

It was sweet to talk with you Friday night, darling. I didn't try very hard to resist my immediate impulse to share the good news with you, for I so wanted you to know. And I especially wanted you to have that news to offset the gloom that I was afraid had pervaded the letter you would have in Saturday's mail. I was horribly tired then and correspondingly low in spirits, but I did have enough sense to get several good nights' sleep. That, and the *New Yorker* news, have me feeling immeasurably better.

I do hope this week at Southport will be a happy one. Will you be driving back alone Friday? Oh, I wish I could join you!

My dearest love, darling, and perhaps I won't write again till Wednesday—then I'd send that letter to West Bridgewater to greet you when you return.

I love you.
Rachel

SATURDAY NIGHT, JUNE 26

Darling [Dorothy],

Two letters from you today, and I suppose you had a shower of notes from me—at least I hope the "special" reached you, along with my regular letter and its postscript, and perhaps Stan's book. (And by the way, I'll mail his Kodachromes to him, by first class mail, the first of the week.)

Before I forget this, dear, I was so glad to have your report on the road. I certainly don't want to spoil my white side-wall tires! And of course more seriously, to get the car out of line, as I did the Chevrolet. So I telephoned Mr. Plummer[34] tonight, and he will put two or three loads of gravel on the worst places before I come—then we can see if it needs more. He will do that for about $6.00 a load, and I'd rather just do it myself, if no one else is interested, than leave it undone. It is a wonder that Mr. Mahard[35] has endured it this long.

I loved your Goldilocks story, dearest, as I hope you knew I would. I only

[33] *The Sea Beach at Ebb Tide* by Augusta Foote Arnold, first published in 1903.

[34] Elbridge Plummer, a Southport handyman.

[35] One of RC's nearby Southport neighbors.

wish this bear could have come in and found you. I often think about the dream house as you call it, there all alone—I really do love it quite dearly, you see—and it has given me a very warm and lovely feeling to think of your visits to it, and your presence in it, darling. Perhaps as though *it* would be glad to see you come in. And there is more to the feeling about you and the house—as though all the happiness and all the fun that you and I had there in May have become part of it, for always. Oh, I'm so glad for that time, too!

As for our departure, it begins to seem more real. I've gone so far as to make lists of things to take or send, and aside from the makings of the book, it doesn't look too staggering. As you know, I'd felt I must get another major section of the book ready before I left—but in the heat and with other adverse conditions here I'm progressing so slowly that I've about decided to abandon that goal and just count on working that much more intensively when I get to Southport. However, because of the holiday week-end, during which I don't want to be on the road, that still means leaving on the 6th.

You darling—it is so like you to have all these thoughts of loving concern about the drive. I do think the night driving will be best, though of course it has features I won't like. But I do promise you to rest and sleep as much as possible before starting—I know I must. And we'll take lots of coffee and probably I'll use Dexedrene or some such aids to wakefulness. I just don't think Jeffie (Have I told you his favorite delicacies? Loin lamb chops, broiled, and nicely seasoned. And Tavern bleu cheese crackers.) could take the heat of daytime driving, especially in his case, well ventilated though it is. Of course if there should be some drastic change of weather, we could just take off by day instead.

It was 99° here today (no—100°) and felt even worse till a late afternoon storm (66 m.p.h. winds!) cooled us off. I was caught in that coming home from the afternoon with Marie, so the car has been broken in, in that respect at least. We had a very satisfying visit, and it brought me a sense of the realities of the writing world that I lose when I am too long away from her. There were more details of Mr. Shawn's reaction (his opening remark was "She's done it again.") all of which were good to hear. Paul Brooks is delighted with the *New Yorker* prospect—I rather thought he would be. (Absence of pictures makes the difference—now no reader will think he has it all in the magazine.) And Marie says the *Reader's Digest* is pressing her for a look at it—either for condensation in the magazine or for their quarterly book club volume—which last is very profitable, she tells me. (And since the *Publisher's Weekly* announcement of Sept. 13, for the publication date, she has been deluged with letters from foreign publishers, wanting to see galleys! Poor Marie.) So—all looks rosy if the author just produces! All this is a tremendous stimulus, as you understand so well; also, as you understand—there are still days and days of agonizing effort. And even in the week (heavens—is that all it is?) since the *New Yorker* news came along, there have been days when the "wind" died down again. I found your metaphor very apt, darling—it really seemed to express exactly what I've been going through.

Oh, I meant to tell you I now have a set of galleys on the sand chapter. First I thought I'd send them to you, but decided against it. I'll be seeing you soon, darling (what a lovely thought) and I'd rather you read it when I am not too far away. You see I remember past reactions—and if the mountains and the seas begin to rise I want to be able to put my arms around you and bring you back to reality. Oh my darling!

I am being lazy, writing this in bed—and if you look back over it you will make no more apologetic remarks about your letters. You don't know why those two were so sweet and wonderful, dear? Basically, because of their depth of understanding, my darling—and in my recent state of ragged nerves, there is nothing more healing than to be understood and loved—all of which came to me in those letters.

Oh dear, the phrase "in those letters" reminds me of what I've felt I should say in a letter, since somehow it didn't get said at Southport, though I meant to. I suppose it didn't because it belongs in the category of things that are hard to talk about because of what they imply. I haven't quite decided whether I shall carry my complete collection of letters with me or leave the bulk of them here, but what chiefly matters is that I have (many weeks ago) put with them a note of instructions—if anything happens to me, they are to be destroyed, unread. I think perhaps I did tell you that, for I know at one time you told me that you had told Stan to return mine to me. Darling, I don't believe that is enough. I believe you, too, should put written instructions with the letters—perhaps to return them to me, or to destroy them. I don't care which, so the instructions are firm and leave no uncertainty about your intention. This is something we must discuss further, darling, and I'd wait for that but perhaps you are going to leave them there and will want to do something of this sort before you see me. Ever since I became acutely aware of the public's prying curiosity about an author's life, I have shuddered every time I see announcement of the publication of some poor wretch's letters! And my shudders aren't wholly with reference to our letters, darling, though heaven knows you are the only one I've written to in volume since *The Sea*—it's just the principle of exposing something that is wholly private and personal and should be sacred. Well, dearest, we must talk about it more, but meanwhile—put something in writing!

To answer a question: either the yellow-billed or black-billed cuckoo could be at Southport. The former would be near the northern limit of its range there; the latter is a northern bird. I used to know bird songs, and call notes rather well, but have become very rusty. I'm very anxious to sort out these thrush songs with you. Last year after we got there I seldom if ever heard a wood thrush, but we had hermit, all around us. And the hermits sit up in the uppermost branches of the spruces to sing. The wood thrushes, in most localities, are lower down, even when singing. We'll get out with binoculars and settle it. I hope the mosquitoes are gone!

Darling, you know I want to hear all about Martha. I loved all you wrote.

When can I meet her? You know, ages ago, you asked what she would call me, and I don't think I ever answered. Children always call me Rachel. Would that bother you? But probably the problem won't become acute this summer!

Roger is much impressed with the Oldsmobile. When I first told him about it (on the phone) he turned to his mother and reported, "He's got me new car." (The third person pronoun is always "he's.") Then he said, "Rachel bring my car." I WON'T take another sheet of paper!

My dearest love, darling—
Rachel

When do you take off for Southport again? Friday afternoon?

SUNDAY, JUNE 27

My dearest darling [Dorothy],

Can you believe it—if all goes as we hope it will, it is now a matter of *days*, not weeks, until I'll see you. You could really count the hours from the time you receive this.

If you received the note I sent to Southport along with the Berrill[36] article, you know that I'm not expecting to get away until Wednesday night. Since I talked to you I've written the Swiss Chalet at North Windham (Conn.) and had a reply—they will be glad to have all three of us[37] at any hour—"just ring the night bell" if they are not up. I'll wire him the day we are to leave and he will reserve a cottage from that evening.

Today I'm in the midst of going over files and reference notes—most of the books are packed. The files and manuscript I'll carry in the car. Of course there are copies elsewhere of everything that's really done. Tuesday afternoon the man who cuts our grass and does occasional odd jobs for us will come and wrap cartons for mailing and put the heavy things (such as microscope) in the car. That morning (Tues.) I'll have my new curls shampooed, so I won't be immediately at the mercy of Boothbay beauty shops! Darling—you know how references to "Alice" delight me and usually I'm not so slow about recognizing them. I don't know why I'd forgotten the frog and the fish and their curls. Which one are you?

Presumably I have all the mail that's coming my way—at least that's what you *said* in the letter that came Saturday—the one written Thursday. I'm so happy you have veeries where you can hear them easily every spring. I, too, think we shall find them at Southport. I had wondered about the Labrador Meadows—on the basis of a story Mr. Pinkham[38] told me about "one of the summer ladies."

I have laid in a supply of Jeffie's medicines. Oh, how I hope the long drive doesn't upset him badly. We had at one time planned to take him for "practice drives" during the spring, but of course his various upsets have prevented that. Just now he is limping badly again, apparently having strained something about

[36] N. J. (Norman John) Berrill, zoologist and author of several books, including two in 1955: *The Origin of Vertebrates* and *Man's Emerging Mind*.

[37] RC, her mother, and Jeffie.

[38] Charlie Pinkham, owner of the West Southport general store.

the poor little left leg; but otherwise he seems all right. Just before that happened he'd actually been able to *run*. I know you will love him darling, and I know you do understand better than anyone else could that your introduction must be gradual—or at least that he must take the initiative. His nervousness has to do always with the fear of something touching him or falling on him—even a sheet of paper falling on him would startle him horribly for he'd think, at least, it would hurt his little back. Yet he will come and stroke against me, or roll over on his back; as long as he's deciding what to do it's all right.

I still don't pick him up, though sometimes I think he wants me to.

Darling, I feel just as you do about summer seeming so short—in relation to Us, I mean. I know now that my idea we had three weeks this time was based on my being there in June, and your staying when you came for the Fourth. At any rate, my dearest, please don't worry about whether I shall be anything but honest with you about my time. Among the truly wonderful and satisfying things about Us is the depth of mutual understanding. I *know*, for instance, that you know I'd love nothing more than hours and hours of you every day. So I shall have no fear of your misinterpreting my deepest wishes when I have to curtail those hours. Oh, why couldn't it (the book) have been done! I was so sure it would be. But dearest, we do *have* to have many hours alone together, somehow—there is so much we need to talk about!

Of course we shall plan to be together on the 12th. I had been thinking of that, too. "Together" in some special way, I mean—for I hope to see you every day.

It is almost certain to be Thursday that I'll call you, dear, and I'll make it before one or after three. If the day is decently cool, we might get on our way that afternoon, and so go to bed at Southport before dawn comes! I'll be prepared with a road map when I call you—but darling, I don't think you really should come to meet us when you will be making preparations to get off the following day—and we'll be together Friday, you know. I'd dearly love it, of course, but if it would take hours out of your evening, please don't.

Now I suppose I should stop. If I think of anything that *must* be said I'll mail you a note tomorrow. Otherwise, our next communication will be by phone. Except in our thoughts, of course! You will be with me all the way—with every mile bringing you nearer. And I will be careful, darling, I promise.

I love you so very dearly, always.

Rachel

AUGUST 21

Darling [Dorothy],

I think I'll have to go to Boothbay this afternoon after the Brookses[39] leave. Can I do anything for you? I'll come over and see—around 3:30. A nice errand would be to take you with me—but we shall see about that and other plans.

[39] Paul Brooks and his wife, Susie.

Tell Stan that the more I think about last night's slides, the more impressed I am with how beautifully they illustrate many of the points I want to make in my December talk. And I couldn't possibly have gotten them from anyone else.

Here are the Brookses!

Know what?

R.

WEDNESDAY, SEPTEMBER 18

ALSO UNDER DRIER

Darling [Dorothy],

This—for you—must be tiny for I'll soon be ready to go, and want to mail it in Boothbay.

Dear, perhaps someday we can laugh together about that maddening, frustrating parting, but this morning I didn't think it was funny! Probably I shouldn't have allowed it to happen, but I did, and anyway I knew you understood all the reasons for it, and how exactly it was just what *would* happen, right down to the goodies ring[40] incident! And because of all that, it was especially sweet to have your call, darling. I hope you know how much it did for me to hear you, even if I couldn't say what I wanted to. I think probably you did. Anyway, thank you so much for calling.

As I told you, I went back to bed and read most of the morning, largely to take my mind off missing you!—and also to carry out your instructions to rest, darling. And after tomorrow I'll rest more. Don't worry about me, dear. And please do try to take decent care of yourself. You know why. And what! I do, allways. (Can you figure out that spelling? It was unintentional, but you are responsible.)

Rachel

[40] "Goodies ring" refers to being given food by a mother to take on a trip. RC and DF appropriated the phrase from a recorded parody of *Little Red Riding Hood*.

SEPTEMBER 18

Darling [Dorothy],

I would have written the enclosure earlier and mailed it to West Bridgewater, but the mails, as you know, are now too uncertain.

I want you to have it *after* you reach home, so please don't read it now. There is nothing in it that you shouldn't read here—it is only that I want you to have mail from me on your arrival, and this is the only way.

You know I'll be thinking of you, sharing every mile of the trip. I love you so.

R.

My darling,

By the time you read this, if you have kept it as I shall ask you to do, you will be at home and the passing of the hours will already be bringing closer those happy days we plan to have in October. That is one way to look at it. Another is that during all these coming weeks when the miles separate us, there are, for both of us, ways in which we can turn them to constructive account. And to the extent that we do, I think we shall enrich and add to the joys of whatever periods of actual togetherness we can achieve this winter. You know the things I mean. For you, darling, a beginning on that writing project that has been in your heart so long—long before you ever heard of me, I know. I do hope so fervently that your knowing me has not, in some horridly insidious way, weakened your will to do it. It is very hard for me to tell you how much it would mean to me to have you achieve what you have in mind. I know better than most that writing is hard and full of anguish and disappointments, but I know also that it brings deep satisfactions and rewards that have nothing to do with best-sellerdom. And I know that the rewards outweigh all the misery, and so I want you to experience them, my dearest. But I do so hope that when the hours of doubt and frustration and despair come, you will remember that they are part of the life of almost every writer, and will not take them as proof of your own inability to achieve your goal in the end. Live through the dark hours somehow, and then go on!

And also for you, darling, the care of your physical self that has been too long neglected—too much sacrificed for others, including me! Please, please, dear—uninteresting and dreary and even unpleasant as it all is—do it for me and remember how very much it means to me, now and for the future.

And darling, for my part I promise you that I shall make a real effort to straighten out my difficulties, in order to get the present book done, and for the long-range view as well. And I want you to know that you have helped me to see more clearly what I have more or less known all along—that the real difficulty is in me, and that I am the only one who can change things. Thank you darling, for all the hours of listening with so much patience and sympathy and love. As I told you, I'm sorry to have devoted so much time to such things, but they are part of my life and if there are to be no reservations between us, I suppose some such talks are inevitable. Anyway, now you have a much truer picture than you had a year ago. I think you must love the real person with a love that is rather different from what you felt for the semi-mythical being of September, '53. But darling, I would rather have the kind of love you feel for me now. This, I know, is real and lasting.

As for this summer, my regrets are all for its seeming shortness and the impossibility of doing together all the things we wanted to do. But how many happy hours and days we did have—and of them all of course, the ones that are most dear to my memory are the ones when we were alone together, no matter what we were doing.

Now, dearest, I must say goodnight. I hope you are not too terribly tired. And I hope that in spite of the ache that I know is in your heart—for it is in mine—there is also a deep happiness that will carry over into the every-day life that now seems uninteresting to you.

Darling, I couldn't possibly tell you, ever, what it has meant to me to have you this summer—or to be able to look forward to other times of happiness to-gether—or how deeply I love you. I can only hope you know these things.

I love you
Rachel

WEDNESDAY NIGHT, SEPTEMBER 22

Darling [Dorothy],

If you could hear the surf tonight you'd think another hurricane was not far off—and the wind itself gave that impression during the day. Another of my poor trees—one of those on the slope back of the house—rocked and swayed so that it visibly lifted the earth around its roots, and we could even hear the roots snapping underground. But it hasn't gone—yet. The tree at the corner of the sun deck—the one split by "Hurricane E"—was sagging so ominously that at 5:30 I called Mr. Plummer and he came to the rescue, doing a very neat job of bringing it down without damage either to the house or to the little red pine nearby. Another summer like this would ruin us!

(It's 9:30 and there is such a tumult on the shore that I think Marjie and I will have to go down as soon as Roger is more securely asleep.) (Oh, last night we did—with him in tow—and there was a tiny bit of phosphorescence. But he looked *up* and of his own accord began singing "Twinkle, twinkle little star."

Today, there was another letter from Henry Beston, which I must save for you to read. Two books from him arrived also—*The St. Lawrence* and his book of fairy tales.

We took Mamma to the clinic today for a treatment and have to return to-morrow. I think her knee has been bothering her more than she admits and I don't want to risk another acute attack. On the way home we drove around the island and went down to the Tower Landing at Newagon. Roger asked, "This is Wagon water?" Was that where you and Stan took him? Incidentally, he was busy this evening with pencil and paper and said he was writing to Uncle Stan. If I can find it I'll enclose it. He enjoys going to the post office, also to the kitty store to see Mr. Pink One.[41]

[41] Many cats con-gregated around the entrance to Pinkham's gen-eral store on Southport.

Everyone enjoyed your letter, darling, and you must know how good it was to be assured that your trip home had been accomplished safely and with-out particular strain. And how wonderful that Stan got home that night! I hope you really have been relaxed and reasonable about the horrid task of unpack-ing, sorting, and putting away. The last weeks here were not easy ones—now, af-ter your *vacation*, take a rest!

I have been thinking about the slides. When you come in October would you mind bringing back the lot we earmarked for my December use? I really should spend some hours going over them and deciding how I'm to put my story together. I can do this while you are here with the viewer—don't bother about the projector.

We do want to hear all your hurricane news when you come. Was the mess on the windows, etc., very terrible? Imagine still having no street lights!

Have you any idea how much we miss you? Nothing is quite the same since you left. All summer I thought I was aware how very much it meant to have you and Stan—but now I *really* know!

It seems like a dream that summer has ended—even by the almanac, today. Will October 8 bring our Indian Summer? Our love to you all—

Rachel

My darling [Dorothy],

I must add a few words more—those two sheets were really quite empty. It was sweet to have your special note yesterday (but then I've written you since then, somehow it seemed long ago) and another today, which really didn't surprise me.

Everything about your morning program sounds fine, darling—Stick to it and there are bound to be good results. Already we seem very star-dusty; the letters we wrote Tuesday both discuss your looseleaf notebook—which, darling, is the real beginning and foundation of your project! Dearest, I do believe in it—and you—so deeply. So must you.

THURSDAY, 1:45 P.M.

And that was all last night, darling. Were you awake at five this morning? I was, and looked out of the kitchen door, into the same sky where once we saw the dawn come. But this time there was no dawn—in the dark sky were all that remains of our harvest moon, and several incredibly bright stars. Had you been here, I know I would have suggested that we dress and go out to enjoy that beauty.

Now, again, there seems no time to say to you any of the things I'm thinking, but perhaps there is no particular need. Breakfast, bed-making, the trip to the clinic, marketing, and lunch have again eaten up half a day, and I want to mail this and your mother's little birthday remembrance before three. But you know, darling, that my thoughts of you are all full of tenderness and love, and of gratefulness for having you. I am trying, as you know, not to write often or at length—and I know you understand the reason.

Darling, I think I did a very poor job of telling you the things that trouble me. Perhaps if I had written them I could have been more coherent and less disorganized, but that, somehow, makes little things take on too much importance. Anyway, darling, it helped, and thank you for your sweet understanding. I love you so much.

Rachel

Natural history notes: In Wednesday's big wind, about 12 to 15 gulls were apparently "trapped" in the air above our shore, circling around screaming and seemingly unable to get down. Their feathers were being blown back and one was almost turned over as it tried to come down. Eventually they disappeared.

Moose have been on the island all week. This morning one was at the lobster pound.

THURSDAY, SEPTEMBER 30, LATE AFTERNOON

Dearest Dorothy and Dorothy's dear ones,

This afternoon we are enveloped in one of Southport's heaviest fogs— London might almost be glad to claim it. I can scarcely see the water from my study window, and everything is dripping and sodden. When we go to the post office shortly, we hope maybe we'll see a moose—or at least a deer. Marjie found very fresh deer tracks on the road behind the property this afternoon. And there were new moose tracks yesterday. So we still hope—though just what we shall do if we meet the beast I don't know.

Yesterday and the two days preceding were autumn at their best, all gold and blue and something special in the air. We had magnificent surf at Pemaquid on Tuesday, though the trip there was something of an ordeal because of the road work. I'm sure it has never been as cold here as your Boston reading in the 30's—as far as I know high 40's have been the coldest.

Roger has been having the time of his life, but I suppose I must wait till you come to tell you his adventures—it will soon be dinner time. But every trip to Boothbay Harbor is a series of delighted encounters with old friends: the kitty store, the poss ofus, the deam chubble that lives in a sand pile by the road, the dirty bridge, and John Nagle. The last two may need explaining. The dirty bridge (the drawbridge) puzzled us for days—why dirty? Then finally the other morning I heard his mother reading from the little book you gave him about the child's fingers—something about "a sturdy bridge they make." I said, "What do they make?" and the answer came back as expected. The *John J. Nagle* is a filthy old fishing trawler that is in dry dock in the Harbor. Roger fell in love with "him" on sight. Every day is lost until we have gone to see J. Nagle. Yesterday he took his bus along so he could show it to J.N. Then we actually took him down alongside of it, and I wish you could have seen the look of ecstasy. Marjie had photographed all these things so he can have them to enjoy this winter.

Stan, he was really delighted with your letter. I don't know how many times he has had it read to him—and several times we have heard him reading it to himself, with interpolation of some of his pet phrases like "peshious little darning," and much about trucks dancing, chickens, etc. And there is talk every day about Uncle Stan and Aunt Dorsey.

I gave you Marjie's plans for flying home Monday, with a brief stop-over in Boston. (By the way, we have had confirmation of the 4:30 flight.) I should have told you not to try to get word to us as to whether either of you would be in town and free to visit with them—if you are, just go to the airport. But as I did say in that note, please don't make a special effort, for she will get along all right. Of course they would both be delighted. M said a little while ago: "I sure would like to see them both again."

We have all loved your wonderful letters; for the two of us who will be here it is wonderful to think that the real people will be substituted for them so soon. I'll probably write only once more before then.

We do hope the weather was good on your mother's birthday and that you were able to make the trip to Marblehead. Tell us about it.

I hope I told you that Jeffie loved his birthday cards—at least he sniffed them with great appreciation. They were so cute.

Our dear love to all,
Rachel

SUNDAY NIGHT, OCTOBER 17

My dearest Dorothy,

I have just accumulated an impressive pile of eleven pieces of mail, representing that many items of business that I know I ought to attend to before leaving. Now, please, may I write to you while you paste 11 stars on my chart?

Somehow I forgot to mention last night that I drove over to the Head yesterday on my way home from Boothbay—all seemed as we had left it except that our screen door and porch screens have now been taken off, so I suppose the closing of the house is official. Your tide looked very high, but you didn't have the rough surf I found when I got home. Ours was quite thrilling again today, and there is a new sound when one is close to the high tide—so many small boulders have been moved in and piled against the sloping rock that there is an audible grinding. And also a lighter sound caused by the thousands of periwinkle shells being washed up the slope by a breaking wave, then rolling down again. This evening just after sunset there were again the long streamers of ducks in the sky, but the procession didn't continue as long as it did Wednesday night.

Here in the study I'm surrounded by piles of cartons and more discouraging piles of stuff still running loose—and suddenly I remembered writing to you last year under just such circumstances. Remember? And, as you often say, I didn't know you very well then!

On the whole, however, the packing seems pretty well along and even the organizing of kitchen shelves, etc., so when the boxes depart to the post office and all possible items are taken to the car tomorrow, the worst should be over. Tomorrow's schedule also calls for having the car attended to (oil change and grease job), calling on Father Manette,[42] finding a couple of gifts at the Smiling Cow,[43] and, I now imagine, starting another series of treatments at the clinic, for

[42] A clergyman living in the Boothbay Harbor area whom RC's mother occasionally visited.

[43] A Boothbay Harbor gift shop.

the knee is giving trouble tonight, and difficult as it is to get them in, I'd rather make the effort than risk another acute attack.

Oh, I undertook a little landscaping job today on sudden impulse. I decided there was a perfect spot for a small spruce among the big rocks to the right of the steps; by piling up a few small rocks I could create a deep depression, fill it with soil, and have a place a tree should really thrive in. It proved a bit more effort than I expected, but I'm pleased with the result. And it is wonderful to see the "hurricane tree" erect and firmly secured.

Sitting in the study last night, I could actually feel the vibration from the big waves breaking on the shore. I don't remember ever being conscious of it before.

Dear, I forgot to tell you that we will have the essentials of Jeffie's steps[44] with us. That is necessary because of the other night's stop, so don't be rearranging and contriving. And I'm sure I did tell you we will have food for him.

I have been looking over the 3-A book about possible stopping places for Thursday night. (Much as I'd love to stay over a second night with you, darling, I really feel we must get home sometime Friday, and it is too far for one day.) There are two plans possible. One is to leave early Thursday and get to Perryville, Md., that night, where we enjoy the Canvasback Inn. The other is to leave you early in the afternoon, and try one of several motor courts that sound all right, in the vicinity of Meriden, Conn. With an early start Friday, we'd be home by dinner time. That is what I'll be tempted to do (and you know why) but perhaps we'd better make the final decision Wednesday. I am sorry not to leave Tuesday and make our plans fit with Stan's—or rather I would be sorry if I didn't feel perfectly sure he would be going with us just for the sake of helping me with the driving, for I know he can go more quickly and easily by train. And this way, thanks to the new motor court at West Bridgewater, the trip will be very easy for me anyway. Do you know how wonderful it will be to see you again? And some of the "curse" is taken off leaving here just because of where I'm going that day!

Now, to confirm instructions: I'm to call you from the new Howard Johnson midway along Rt. 128, then meet you in a First National parking lot in or near Stoughton, where there is a traffic light and a Shell Station. I still think I should meet you nearer home, but will leave that to you.

Goodbye till Wednesday, darling, and our love to all.

And to you—know what?
Rachel

[44] RC had devised steps for her injured cat to use when climbing up onto and down off of furniture.

My dear one [Dorothy],

There are not many copies of this first edition[45] in existence, and I should be sad if you didn't own one. We both know the part the book has played in our lives, but in sending you this particular volume I want to tell you this.

Years ago on a night when rain and wind beat against the windows of my college dormitory room, a line from "Locksley Hall" burned itself into my mind—

"For the mighty wind arises, roaring seaward, and I go."[46]

I can still remember my intense emotional response as that line spoke to something within me seeming to tell me that my own path led to the sea—which then I had never seen—and that my own destiny was somehow linked with the sea.

And so, as you know, it has been. When finally I became its biographer, the sea brought me recognition and what the world calls success.

It brought me to Southport.

It gave me You.

So now the sea means something to me that it never meant before. And even the title of the book has a new and personal significance—the sea around Us.

Keep this for me, dear, and understand all it means. My deep love—

Rachel

My dearest [Dorothy],

Estelle[47] is here, roaring around with the vacuum overhead. We are both going downtown early this afternoon to have our hair done and the car washed and serviced so perhaps this is a good time to start your week-end letter. (I still find it hard to relax completely while The Treasure is here, but perhaps that will come in time. Even so, it is a wonderful help to be relieved of doing the things she does, and if I can't concentrate completely while she is here, I can and do get little desk chores done.)

Speaking of desk chores: I feel so virtuous this morning there is scarcely any living with me. Can you imagine why? Yesterday may have been a holiday for some people, but not for me. I worked on the accumulation of correspondence until, for the first time in years—I suppose since The Sea was published—my desk tray for incoming mail is EMPTY. Of course this was accomplished with the excellent help of Mrs. Rivera.[48] And to be completely honest I must admit that some were so hoary with age that I just shut my eyes and dropped them in the wastebasket. But most were answered, and they are all typed, signed, sealed, stamped and ready for the mailbox this morning. There were somewhat more than thirty, many requiring fairly lengthy answers. To do that many in a day left

45 RC had enclosed a first edition of *The Sea Around Us* with this letter, and had also sent DF a first edition of *Under the Sea-Wind*.

46 The last line from the poem by Alfred, Lord Tennyson.

47 A housekeeper.

48 RC's typist.

me feeling rather drained of energy, but oh, so relieved. Now perhaps I can keep up by setting aside one evening a week to deal with correspondence. The trouble is I have just been doing the easy ones and letting all that required much time and thought pile up.

Recently I wrote to Paul Brooks and told him that I am really determined to finish the manuscript by the end of January. He replied with his usual considerate kindness that they could manage all right with such a schedule, though anything later would make it difficult for them. I don't know definitely what month they have in mind for the advent, but probably September. We can celebrate at Southport. And that will be too late—thank goodness—for the Smiling Cow to have an autographing party.

[49] Bob Hines.

There was a wonderfully interesting letter from Bob[49] a few days ago. He was then still in Alaska but about to start home and will be in Washington sometime next week. I sent his letter on to Marie, but after I get it back will send it to you, for I think all of you would enjoy reading of his adventures. Stan will wish he had been there with his camera.

All of this week has been one beautiful fall day after another—cool but not really cold with those intense blue skies that so impressed me when I first came to Washington from grey Pittsburgh. Most of the nights have been cold, leaving frost on the ground in the early mornings. Has it been clear enough there for you to enjoy the moon this week? You know, I'm sure, it is the first one we have missed seeing together since June. Always, now, when I look at the full moon I am imagining what it is like at Southport, coming up behind the spruces, shining on the water, and finding all the little snowflakes of mica in the rocks. Do you remember, one of those last nights when you and Stan were there, those brilliant flashes on the water, and how we couldn't be sure at first whether they were caused by phosphorescence or the moonlight? (Do you remember! Silly question!) But does it all seem very long ago to you? It does to me—not that I don't remember it all very clearly, but it just seems so long ago.

No, I don't know the book *Exploring Nature*—but it should be worth looking into.

And that makes me think of Martha (what a pity you missed talking to her Saturday night) and of the fact that I wanted to ask whether you ever did anything about getting her a "Chessie"[50] from that shop in Connecticut? If not, do you mind if I appropriate the project and get it for her Christmas present from me? Now if you really want to do it yourself please say so!

[50] A stuffed toy cat.

Roger still adores his Chessie so that when they went out to Wheeling a few days ago for a little visit he worried about taking her along—he was afraid Chrissie, the baby there, might have designs on her. He was quite excited about the train trip. We made up a package containing about six or eight small ones, to be opened at intervals for his entertainment, and Marjie reported the idea was a great success. His conversations are really funny and he is developing quite an imagination and a taste for little games of "pretending." For example, he presumably was telephoning Virginia[51] the other day and he said, "Dinny, this is Marjie—*Marjie*, your sister." Another time he took his phone and said, "Is that Roger? This is Mommy." Then he pushed the phone over to Marjie and said, "Here, talk to Roger." The time he had stitches in his scalp naturally made quite an impression, and gives occasion for imaginary calls to the doctor. The other morning poor Marjie had one of her upsets, and Roger reported to us, "She sick at her stumkum. Docker Healy have to come and sew it up."

[51] Virginia King, RC's niece and Marjie Williams's sister.

Well—enough on Roger, but you say you like to hear of his doings and I know you do. Just wait till Martha starts having real conversations—you can tell me all about them.

The combination of African violets and a Pussy Willow[52] sounds bad to me—just made for Trouble. For many years my own indoor gardening has been strictly conditioned by the fact there were Cats. Why don't you get Stan to install a shelf half-way up the kitchen window? Or would he (P*W) climb the curtains?

[52] The Freemans' new kitten.

Dear Jeffie is doing very well. Much as he loved Maine, I think he is happy to be back in his first home. In many ways he seems less troubled by his back— often he startles me by getting up on something without benefit of steps. On the other hand he seems afraid of the stairs. He spends most of his time upstairs, but sometimes I carry him down in his basket. He can then go up himself. But the other day he was playing with a bit of paper and apparently batted it down the stairs and followed it. The poor little fellow is so patient about his handicap that my heart aches for him when I think of all the fun he ought to have, and is denied.

SATURDAY MORNING

I have not felt I had time to attend the Audubon lectures for several years, but now I have decided I'd better go to the next one (which is all that stands between us and my own appearance) just to refresh my mind about procedures and facilities. It is next Tuesday and I think I shall go to the afternoon presentation, probably trying to get in a little Christmas shopping before it.

Tell Stan I have not yet had a chance to talk to the firm where I got my microscope but shall try soon to find out whether it can be used, with or without some sort of adapter, for micro-photography. And I have recently had a good idea. Audubon lecturers are not paid any princely sums but I believe (as usual I can't find the correspondence) I am to get $125. This particular lecture, however, is going to lean very heavily on the slides of Mr. Stanley Freeman. So I have now solved a problem that was bothering me. I shall devote that fee to some piece of equipment that will aid in exploring the world of minute things photographically. In that way both Stan and I can enjoy it, next summer.

Now I must get to work. As extra activities, I agreed to do a joint review of Burton's[53] *Margins of the Sea* and Hans Pettersson's *Ocean Floor* for the *Herald Tribune*. The latter book just arrived this morning so I shall soon need to get at it. The former I have read, with some disappointment, and all the while being dis-

[53] Maurice Burton.

tracted by the fact that the author can't make his verbs agree with their subjects, and that often one wanders in bewilderment through a whole sentence without ever meeting a verb! Why don't editors edit these illiterate scientists?

Another small job: *Life* sent me yesterday advance sheets of a feature on Albert Schweitzer and wanted comment, which I think I ought to give. You know he is in the news now because he just went to Norway to accept last year's Nobel Prize. We must talk about him sometime. I think he is an extremely significant figure—his Reverence-for-Life philosophy is of course somewhat like my own.

Oh—one more thing I wanted to ask you. Did the Mary Poppins volumes you read give any information about the author? Recently I borrowed Marjie's volume of two of the books combined. On the jacket was a very interesting biography of Miss Travers. I hadn't realized she is "among the more notable of the young Irish poets" and had an early career on the stage. Or that Mortimer Browning composed a *Mary Poppins Suite for Orchestra*!

Oh—please do send me from time to time your suggestions for records. You know I'm counting on you for that. And *if La Mer* is packaged for mailing (it seems to me I left it as it came to me) you might send it; otherwise don't bother and I'll get it sometime.

Now I must stop. Our love to all of you. And you know, don't you—

I love you
Rachel

SATURDAY MORNING, DECEMBER 11

Darling [Dorothy]—

You said not to write this week—and I promised to make it short if I did. So I will. I'll hope to write more on Tuesday, but even that probably won't be a "real" letter, for I ought to be working even harder on the book than I have on the lecture.[54]

[54] RC's lecture, accompanied by Stanley's slides, was to be given to the Audubon Society of the District of Columbia on December 13.

It seems I just can't do anything quickly and easily, and I've suffered and burned the post-midnight oil over this, despite the fact that most of it is being taken out of the manuscript. But selection and arrangement and timing—oh, you know! Mrs. Rivera will type it for me for my little notebook today. I won't read it, but if it is all down where I can go over it repeatedly, I'll stick to the time better and will get in the right facts, approximately as written. It will run about an hour and 15 minutes, I believe. (About what is expected in these talks.)

My little white hat was acquired at Garfinkle's on Wednesday. The shape is quite different and its veil is not star-dusty, but I think it's very nice. *Maybe* you'll see it in New York!

I had to plan to have my hair done today (so will have to sit up in a chair tonight and tomorrow night!). But my girl doesn't work Mondays, and besides

I'd rather rest that morning than have to make an extra trip downtown. So that takes up this afternoon.

The lectures are at 5:15 and 8:15, with a dinner between! I don't expect to eat much, for various reasons.

Of course I don't need to tell you that in my thoughts you and Stan will be there. And somewhat more tangibly, too, for of course Mr. and Mrs. Freeman have to be introduced to my Audubon friends. (Requests for tickets are still pouring in, I hear!)

Really, now that the preparations are about completed, I'm not worried and expect to come as near enjoyment as is possible for me at such a time. (But I agree with Hemingway that writers should *write*—not speak!)

Here is the review I mentioned, in which *The Sea* is mentioned in connection with the sky book. I've been wondering why I have started deluging you with such things. I think maybe I'm trying to get you in trim for next fall, when presumably you may have to see that name in print a good deal. Maybe you can come to feel my detachment about it.

Now darling—we'll talk Tuesday night. Maybe we'll try a 4-way conversation for a few minutes—I expect Mamma will want to put in a word. (Oh, of course she's going—and all the rest of the family.) But it makes it a little hard to hear when the extension is in use too. And I know she will write you.

This must be all for now. My dearest love, always

Rachel

Please return the clipping sometime.

Another package just came! I did not open it, as instructed.

TUESDAY MORNING, DECEMBER 14

My darling [Dorothy],

That was a sweet, sweet note—just right for the occasion and the hour, and it brought you very close. I wanted to wait until I was ready for bed before I read it, and I did. When I said on the phone, "I thought you'd be asleep by now"—I didn't mean you, dear—I hoped you were in bed but I knew you'd be awake living it all with me at least until you thought I was home and abed. And you were with me all through it, darling. And really it was a happy and pleasant occasion—not an ordeal in any way. And the slides truly looked beautiful—I'm not just trying to make Stan happy. I wish you both could have seen them—you couldn't have been other than satisfied and delighted with their appearance on the big screen.

Darling, I'm worried about you—when did you get this laryngitis—and are you really staying in and taking care of yourself? *Please* do, for me.

I had a wild desire to call *you* early this morning—then for various reasons controlled it. I know I'll be tempted to call you as planned tonight. We shall see whether I do! (Probably I won't, darling. But you know what.)

So far I haven't been able to relax much—didn't go to sleep till after 1:30, was awake at 7:15 and got up for coffee, then around 8 decided I might just as well get up to stay. Now, after breakfast, I've gone back to bed to talk to you.

Oh, darling—I do so hope these changed Christmas plans,[55] whatever they are, aren't a disappointment to you. I am guessing it means you have to go away in order to have Martha for Christmas—or else have your observance a different day. Whatever it is, I want to hear your dear voice on the real Christmas day, so be sure to tell me how I can.

Dearest, I'm sure you know my heart is full of things I'd like to say to you, and especially in response to your last long letter, but I won't try. We have New York before us when we can talk. And that will be much better.

Twenty-one days, now, darling!

I want to mail your package this morning and have a quick session with Christmas greetings, so I won't linger with you now, much as I want to. Did you say the package I mailed last Wednesday didn't come till yesterday? Heavens— that's no special handling!

Darling, I'll write again briefly after your letter comes. Short ones whenever we can is the rule now, isn't it?

On January 4 we won't have to remember poems. But until then, dear, do.

I love you
Rachel

[55] Plans were changed due to the Freemans' daughter-in-law's pregnancy.

FOR CHRISTMAS EVE[56]

[56] DF had asked RC for two Christmas Eve messages, this one to read on December 21, the eve of her Christmas celebration with her son. The second message begins on p. 67.

My dearest [Dorothy],

Now it is Christmas Eve and we are alone together, for I am there in your heart as truly as if I were actually present. You have been looking forward to this little interval of peace and quiet; you see, I know that without being told. And of course that is one of the most precious and wonderful things that has come into being during the past year—that each of us can know, with unquestioning certainty, the sort of thoughts and feelings that are filling the mind and heart of the other.

Darling, I know we both look forward to years where the miles between us will be fewer and we can spend more time together. But what a wonderful year 1954 was for us—looking back, there were so many joys, so many happy experiences, so many wonderful milestones that marked the growth of our love and understanding, that it would take a long, long manuscript to describe them all. I doubt that either of us, last Christmas, really understood the gift of happiness that 1954 was to bring. And so, I am sure, 1955 holds the promise of unsuspected joys.

What can I say to you tonight that has not been said before? Or that is not already in your heart? What new words are there to describe this beautiful experience we are sharing?

We both know that no new words are necessary—that the three simple words that were first said a trifle shyly in a pre-Christmas letter in 1953 still say all that need be said. But for tonight, my dear one, I would like you to think of those words as written on the Christmas sky in letters formed of stars, shining with the reflected gleam of that invisible light of which we know.

I love you,
Rachel

AUGUSTA, MAINE, DECEMBER 23, 2:30 P.M.

RAILROAD STATION

My Dear Ones,[57]

Of all places! I have an hour to wait for the train to carry me back to Stan in Boston and how better could I spend it than getting a message off to you? Our Christmas is all over, and if it had to be this way, we all feel it has worked out successfully. Of course, we are tired but now we can rest. I feel that Stanley had the difficult part for he had the responsibility of the travelling, plus the care of Martha and the act of being both Mommy and Daddy. He felt after driving with her from Suncook to W.B.[58] in one of the worst snowstorms of years that he could manage the trip back to Orono easily. But we didn't want him to have to for it is an eight-hour trip and of course it is not like summer driving for some roads are not clear of ice. We compromised by my coming to Augusta. We left W.B. at 8 A.M.; stopped in Portland for lunch which was really fun for me for Martha really is so cute (incidentally, her choice of friends to take in to lunch was "Widdow"—and if you don't know who "Widdow" is you know him better as Chessie—you see, when Martha arrived at W.B., before her wraps were removed she made friends with "Putty-Widdow" (whom she loved). When she opened Chessie, before he was out of the box she said "Putty-Widdow"—so "Widdow" he has become. We hope you won't mind).

We were in Augusta at 2 P.M. This is much better all around for I'll be home tonight and can rest and relax for the whole week-end. Besides, I think the little family in Orono will enjoy being reunited without anyone else to consider—they won't even have to bother getting me to the train to-morrow. It's really been quite an experience for them all.

Martha travels beautifully. You know, Stanley has arranged the back seat with a board which she can play on, sleep on, move around on, with all her friends and books. Besides he has a little seat with wheel, gear shift, etc., on front. She used that very little, preferring to be on back. It was so sweet to watch her playing, talking to herself unmindful of us.

There is so much I could tell about us, but what is more important is to tell you that all your shower of gifts was so exciting and sweet and loving. We de-

[57] This is the first preserved letter from DF. It is addressed to the Carson family. Occasionally, RC and DF sent in the same envelope a family or sharing letter and a separate more personal message, often containing the salutation "Darling."

[58] Suncook, New Hampshire, home of Stanley, Jr.'s, in-laws, to West Bridgewater, Massachusetts.

cided we could enjoy them more if we opened them on "our" Christmas Eve while Martha was asleep. We had already let Martha have "Widdow"—and when Stanley came out after covering her he said, "Well, 'Widdow' has the place of honor tonight—the other 'friends' around but 'Widdow' in her arms."

I haven't the space to tell you about each gift now—but you may be sure each of us was made very happy from Vira[59] all the way through to Pussy Willow. But I want to tell Mamma that her choice of "Peace in the Heart" was a happy one for me. The little book of Mr. Rutledge's I read this summer made me know I wanted to read more of him. And the first page of this filled a need at the moment. I have the book with me and shall read it on my 5-hour train ride. Also I want Mamma to know that her letter about the lecture came on my Christmas. I was so glad I could read it to Stanley. I know she stole time from a crowded Christmas program to write it & I do appreciate it. Getting toward train time so I'll just send a deep thanks to you all—Marjie and Roger, too, for all the gifts and the Christmas cards from you all.

My dearest love,
Dorothy

[59] DF's mother.

My dearest, dearest Darling [Rachel],

It seems so odd that I'm in Augusta, of all places, on December 23 with my Christmas joys behind me. Augusta, darling, that has so much meaning for us.

I did so want to get a message off from here to you for you must know how very close you are to me here.

I've written the other note first and now I feel hurried for there is so much I want to say to you.

Your mail to me, dear, has been so sweet to have! There was a lovely one in the mail on Tuesday after Martha arrived and then on my Christmas came yours with my good-night message for Dec. 24. (Just as you hoped.) Oh, darling, I feel so guilty about that, for after the precious message that I read on Dec. 21, I don't need anything more—it could so easily have done for both Christmas eves.

In your Dec. 18th letter—you must remember for New York, to tell me your thoughts about the Ocean Point slide of "Us." New York, dear—less than two weeks away—and nothing of importance for me between now and then. You still have Christmas to occupy your mind and time. I can simply lose myself in happy, happy thoughts.

Darling, I brought all your Christmas Eve notes with me to read them over again. How very sweet, dear. And I wonder when you read my Christmas Eve note to you if you will find the Stardust very thick. Neither of us knew what the other had in mind—the theme was the same—ending with the invisible light. Similar in thought, but darling, yours, as usual, was written with so much more grace and effectiveness. But, of course, it should be.

Darling, Guess what was the name of the diner where I've just had dinner? No, you probably won't believe it.

Hermit Thrush! What was it I wrote only a few moments ago?—so many *things* bring you to mind!

The train is late, but I know Stan is waiting. Good-night, darling.

I love you,

D.

FOR CHRISTMAS EVE

My precious darling [Dorothy],

This is to say goodnight to you on Christmas Eve. This is to bring me even closer to you than I have been all day, or all of every day. This is to share an intimate and precious moment, for I know that even as I am there with you, in those moments before you turn out the light, and after—so you are here with me as I read your sweet messages and dip into your "golden hours" and perhaps even open your package.

Darling, many thoughts have been crowding into my mind and I want to tell you some of them, at least. I have been remembering that my very first message to you was a Christmas greeting. Christmas, 1952. I knew then that the letter to which it replied was something special, that stood out from the flood of other mail, but I don't pretend I had any idea of its tremendous importance in my life. I didn't know then that you would claim my heart—that I would freely give you a lifetime's love and devotion. I had at least some idea of that when Christmas came again, in 1953. Now I know, and you know. And as I have given, I have received—the most precious of all gifts. Thank you, darling, with all my heart.

And then I have been thinking of the wonderful year behind us—but less of the tangible joys we have shared than of the intangible things—the steps by which our love and understanding have acquired that depth and firm foundation that will last for all time. We passed through a phase when we asked "why" and tried to find reasons and explanations for this wonderful experience. I am glad to remember we decided long ago that there was something beyond the sum of all the "reasons" we could put forth—a mystery beyond all the explainable mysteries. The writings of Einstein seem a most unlikely place to find anything that relates to Us—yet I discovered a few lines recently that I want to quote for you. Of course he was speaking of the ultimate mysteries of the physical universe, rather than of the spirit, but I think his words have meaning in both realms.

The most beautiful and most profound emotion we can experience is the sensation of the mystical. . . . To know that what is impenetrable to us really exists, manifesting itself as the highest wisdom and the most radiant beauty which our dull faculties can comprehend only in their most primitive forms—this knowledge, this feeling is at the center of true religiousness.[60]

[60] From *Living Philosophies* (1931).

And then, darling, there was the parable, expressed in your own inimitable way, of the fairy emeralds held in our hands in the darkness of the night, and of the crude flashlight that destroyed them.

And so I think the year has taught us to be content that some of our mystery is beyond comprehension, even as it sheds its radiant beauty on our lives.

Darling, when we talked today (Sunday) you asked if I had read the little prayer on the card that enclosed your Christmas Eve letter. So I did, assuming that much was permissible. (The letter is still safely sealed, of course.) It is sweet, dearest, and so are you. And God has blessed me far beyond anything I deserved or dreamed of, by giving me you. And he has a constantly renewed petition to take care of you for me, darling.

Perhaps your Christmas won't be "merry" in a literal sense, but may it be filled with a deep happiness and joy, my dearest. And in a few hours I'll hear your voice. Now goodnight—go to sleep remembering how I love you.

Rachel

DECEMBER 24

Darling [Rachel],

This is the morning of Christmas Eve. I am in bed, quiet, alone, resting after the strains, both physical and emotional, of the past week. Stan has gone, Mother is not yet up. To-night people are "dropping" in—they will stay late, I know.

And because I am alone—really alone with no effort to contrive to be—I chose this time to read your Christmas Eve note.

You of the understanding heart, will forgive me if it is not exactly the time you had in mind—but the circumstances are what you would wish, I know—just as I wish. Darling, by reading it now I have had peace and quiet and time to re-read it at least ten times so that it is already deep in my heart and to-night I won't need to read it before I turn out the light (although I'm sure I will). I can almost say it by heart now.

I am deeply happy I have read it. I am not sorry now or even guilty that I pleaded for two messages for, darling, I have now two of the most precious letters you have ever written me—and most beautifully written.

No need to tell you that the tears were on my cheeks when I finished reading. Darling, although I don't need to be told, nevertheless, it is a wonderful experience for me to have you express your love for me in words I can read and go back to again and again.

As I said in my note to you yesterday about "my" Christmas Eve message from you—the theme is the same but the quality of expression is incomparable.

Again you will find more Stardust to-night as I have this morning—there is no need for me to even point it out.

The quotation from Einstein, darling, is pure poetry. I am so glad you used it for it is an expression of what I have been trying to say—the unexplainable mystery. I wonder if I have ever told you that the one thing in common that I have found in the writings of the men you have led me to this past year is that element of the awe and wonderment of the mysteries of life. Each one has expressed it in some way. Of course, you know all that—but for me it has been a beautiful discovery—that great men, too, find mysteries they cannot and even do not want to explain.

Darling, this all means more to me than you can ever comprehend—perhaps I shouldn't say that. Your good-night is so sweet and so precious and so all inclusive of the deep love and mystery between us. Love is such an expandable thing—and every day since I have known you it has been growing so much it hurts. And what a lovely hurt!

LATER

Now, it is almost noon. Darling, to-day there is "peace in my heart." It began yesterday on my ride to Augusta when Stanley and I talked over many of the things that had caused turmoil in my mind in the past ten days. I left him feeling very happy and content, knowing that everything is quite right with him. The unhappiness which you must have sensed in my letters has passed. I'm glad we had our Christmas as we did for now Christmas Day itself can truly be happy for me. I shall want to tell you all about it. When we reached home last night we called them and had long satisfying talks with both Madeleine[61] and Stanley— heard the reactions of our precious darling to her home-coming. She told her mommy "Gam-mamma gone train."

So I went to bed with that peace that continued overnight to which, this morning, your tender good-night was like a benediction.

I hope you don't mind that I read it so early on Christmas Eve. It was the loveliest time for me to have had it, and to-night when you are reading my message to you I shall be very close to you for the lovely words I have of yours—and have had all day.

Darling, to-morrow is really Christmas. For the rest of our lives I know we shall count the Christmases we've had together for it all started at Christmas time.

Now my dearest, I loved what you wrote of three words formed of stars in our Christmas sky. I shall think of them that way to-night—and all nights— they are mine for you to see also.

A blessed Christmas for you, my dearest one.

I love you so very much.

Dorothy

[61] Stanley, Jr.'s, wife.

Darling [Rachel],

I love your sweet notepaper with the butterflies and yellow roses. How do you like mine? Stan gave it to me little realizing, probably, how much the promise of spring means to me. We'll find violets in our Maytime this year!

I had talked to myself all morning to prepare myself for the fact that your letter couldn't possibly be in the mail to-day. But It was! How lovely. I read it then and now at sunset time I've read it over and over. Oh, darling, why is it these written words mean so much to us?

Almost always I read the For You part first. For *some* reason I read the family part first to-day. Of course, I found the reason when I read my letter—you had suggested it. It's things like that, dear, that leave me breathless with wonder.

I am so happy about the flowers for, as I wrote Marjie, if they couldn't be freesias, the little white sweetheart roses would have been my second choice for they would be like you, darling—dainty and fresh and pure and modest.

I, too, thought the little hermit thrush was rather nicely done. When I found the collection of birds in the Audubon rooms (I was looking for a print of a hermit thrush) I was thrilled for I knew my search was ended until I discovered there wasn't a hermit thrush. You can imagine my delight when I was told I could order one. Then, of course, I wasn't happy until I had it for with the poem it seemed so right for me to give you this Christmas.

I'm sure Mamma will enjoy her pewter pitcher and I think it was sweet for you to give her one. I love mine—and now with the candleholder and my pewter plate I have a lovely and unusual, I think, arrangement for my buffet. I used all white candles again this year.

Pussy Willow wants Jeffie to know that after the decorations were arranged he was returned from his exile—he just was beyond control while the boxes of decorations, greens, etc., were strewn around. He has had a rare time with the little tree. After our Christmas it went out on the porch. The floor is strewn with broken ornaments, tinsel, ribbons. This afternoon he thought he would help me by taking the balls off the tree—I picked up ten whole ones not counting the broken ones. How he got so many off I can't understand.

He loves to get in large paper bags. To-day he had one on the floor in the pantry. He had chewed a small hole in the side of it. When I went looking for him he was inside with only his head out of the hole he had chewed. Too cute!

By the time you read this you will know that my first typed letter was to you—as you suggested I might do. Darling, I'm not quite as bad as that. We just had fun while I was doing it going at top speed and letting the mistakes fall where they would. Another thing we had a laugh about was the way the Tryolaris bubbled when I tried to gargle the first time. I felt like a human bubble pipe!

New York—darling—a week from this moment I shall be with you if all goes well—and it must! Yes, I think we can be casual if we meet at the desk—just a chilly glance I'll give you and say, "Glad you made it."

But just you wait!! I'll pay you back. I shall be eager for my letter tomorrow. I have to go to hair-dresser's (first time for a number of weeks—fortunately I could do it myself—I really haven't been out of the house but once since my throat got bad except to Augusta and to Norwood Sunday). I meant to go to see Marione Shaw this week but I'm not. So I won't be here when the mail comes—a good reason to hurry home.

Darling, I'll mail this after I go to Brockton and consequently it will be my New Year's greeting to you.

My darling, 1955 is going to be another milestone in your life. My greatest wish for you will be that it can hold only joy for you—all kinds of joy—the joy of finishing the new book, the joy of seeing it in its finished form, the joy of a warm and hearty reception by the waiting world—and selfishly (on my part) the joy of having me this time to share all the joys—for somehow I believe (shamelessly, of course) that the fact that I can be in your life at this time will add to your pleasure in your success. (My, what a thing to say!)

And, of course I don't need to tell you what 1955 is going to mean to me—just because of you!

So, darling, my sincerest good wishes for this wonderful new year, with, as always, deep, deep love—beyond expression, really, my dearest one.

I love you,
Dorothy

1. So I guess
the Edge of the Sea!
was nothing
it your reaction
meant there were

JANUARY 6

Darling [Rachel],

Did you notice a rosy glow about this room?[1] For some reason it seems to have disappeared. I wonder why! I can't get out of it soon enough. The bureau is empty. The bathroom is empty. I feel empty—and not my stomach for I just dropped in at a rather nice little place on 58th St. near 5th Ave. and had a luscious grapefruit and more coffee.

Darling, the whole world is different since you turned that corner. Thank you, so much for staying last night. I realize now what a desolate night I would have had alone.

I couldn't get Stan when I first tried. Now I've talked with him. He tried to drive in this morning. The roads were glare ice so he gave up and only drove as far as Ashmont. That is all right only I feel so sorry that he made the attempt for he could have taken the train. He was very late to work. I think predictions are for warming so roads should be all right by night.

He spent most of *my* call telling me about Willow. He let him out when he got home at 11 last night. When Stan was ready for bed he called. No Willow. Stan redressed and went out. No Willow. Stan read. When the clock struck twelve Willow returned!!

Do you suppose he might be needing an operation?

He got in the bathtub while Stan shaved this morning.

I walked over to Schwartz's. It's just around the corner from here on 5th Ave. That store drives me almost mad. I wish you could see the dolls—they are becoming more and more real every year—the most beautiful faces.

They did not have and haven't had for some time the book I wanted but the girl knows it—in fact owns it. The name is a "Child's Grace," pictures by Constance Bannister—published by Dutton. She thinks it is not out of print though so I shall try in Boston.

Spent some time examining kitten and cat books—just for fun. If I should do anything with that idea I think I'll do a bit of research on cat books first!

Well, darling, I'll finish packing now and move on.

[1] From January 4 to January 6, RC and DF had stayed at the Barbizon Plaza Hotel near Central Park in New York City.

Now you'll be getting mail from me to-morrow. And I might just write a bit on the train to mail in Boston which would mean Sat. for you. Then if I write to-morrow you will have received your quota.

Oh my darling, how wonderful to have had these hours—how many?—approximately 44 I think.

Thus far I have no regrets. How wonderful also.

Bye for the moment, darling,

You do know what, don't you? I L Y.

Dorothy

JANUARY 6

Darling [Dorothy],

Now it is 12:35 and I suppose you are on your way to the train, or perhaps already at the station. I have just come from the diner and we are in Maryland somewhere, having crossed the Susquehanna while I was at lunch. Also, during that interval, we ran into rain, which I hope you may escape for your drive home this afternoon. I had a series of cat naps between New York and Philadelphia, and now feel quite wide awake.

(What an odd handwriting! The combination of train jiggles and rough surfaced paper seems to be especially unfortunate.)

(Sorry—I would pick a sheet I'd already started to make notes on).

Darling, it was a lovely interlude and I am so happy we could have it. Now with these memories the weeks ahead will go much more smoothly, I know. And when I see you again the major writing problems will all be solved and all but the tag ends of this undertaking completed, I do hope. How different I'll feel!

I have been thinking, darling, how wonderful it is when two people mean so much to each other that they will set aside everything else for several days just so that they can be together. And how wonderful that it was possible—that, out of all the possibilities, there were no circumstances that made either of us feel she shouldn't or couldn't make the trip. Thank you dear, for coming. And thank Stan for letting me borrow you.

Of course I've thought of many small and not very important things I meant to say, and one longer discussion I rather wish we'd had—the latter has nothing to do with us, darling, and is chronic rather than acute so it can come another time. But so it would always be unless we could be together every day, I know, and this time there is no feeling of any important omission. It was all very happy and lovely and satisfying.

Just now I've been thinking of two little hearts in furry bodies that are going to be made glad this afternoon. What purrings and loving there will be! This is the first time Willow has had to do without you, isn't it?

Really I think I should stop; this writing is getting worse and worse. I'll mail this in the station but will mail another tiny note tomorrow or Saturday just to report on the completion of the journey.

My deep love, darling—
Rachel

JANUARY 6

Darling [Rachel],

It's only 12:30 and I am safely "set" on the Yankee Clipper which is going to carry me farther away from you! You'll understand why I'm using pencil.

I just saw something which made me so wish we might have seen it together. Just at the Vanderbilt Ave. entrance to Grand Central as I came through the door an oil painting—illuminated. At first I thought it was a Shelton[2] for it had that same luminous quality that I have felt he achieved so well. Darling, the subject was—and I can almost believe it—the setting for our fairy pool. It was exactly the view that I had as I stood above looking down on you and Stan as you explored it—the high rock wall rising above the level carpet of sea moss—two or three small tide pools and of course, the dominant sea rolling in, in a glory of light.

Tears, of course, for memories and for wishing we might have viewed it together. It would have been so stardusty!

NEW LONDON

We've just passed a buoy boat with all the floating buoys on its deck. How Roger would love to be here.

Darling, for the first hour I read The Lecture—you know, I only read parts of it in New York. How thrilled Stan is going to be. I'm so anxious to run off the slides with it.

Since then I've dozed—between waking and sleeping—rather a blissful state with all the lovely thoughts I'm having to accompany it. It was all so sweet.

I didn't fully realize—altho we did speak of it—just how much it added to the joy of it not to have to account to anyone else for all of those 44 hours. I think we should plan perhaps to make it an annual event for the time that we live so far apart.

PROVIDENCE

The time has sped. By the time I get my hair combed and some lipstick on we'll be in Boston. The landscape has been so drab & now the fog is settling down so I'm glad I came on this train.

Darling, you won't carry out that threat not to send me any more manuscript, will you? You'd be depriving me of an experience that brings me great joy. I think you have shown me that I mustn't let the quality of your writing influence my thinking about something I might attempt.

[2] Alphonse Shelton, a Wiscasset, Maine, artist whose paintings of the sea and Southport area RC and DF admired.

I promise you, dear, I'll try to take a very detached attitude toward it—enjoy it and bask in it and love it.

So, please when and if you find some you'd like to share don't hold it back.

Now it's time to say good-bye again. I am and have been very happy since 12:30 P.M. on January 4. You know these 4 hours alone and quiet have been sweet—to daydream about and with you.

Within the hour I shall be chattering, you may be sure.

Even as I cling to you at parting, I cling to the pencil—I hate to leave you—even this way.

My dear, dear love,
Dorothy

JANUARY 7

Darling [Rachel],

Now I've written the other, I wanted to make the introduction to the fact that we shall be looking for you to spend time with us while you are working on the book with H.M.[3] and, dearest, I do want to emphasize what I said about becoming one of the family at such times. Maybe a year ago, I might have thought of you as company, but honestly, darling, I won't. Didn't I tell you I thought of you as my little girl? So when you come it will be exactly as when Stanley comes home.

And I meant to say before we parted that if occasion arises *before* February or whenever you had contemplated coming, you are to simply say you have to come. You know how much joy it will bring me.

Of course, darling, all my thoughts have been with you since we parted. I drifted off to sleep with you and you were with me in a dream just before the alarm went off—not a pleasant dream—the car had been stolen from where it was parked in Damariscotta and I didn't know the new license number—so I was quite worn out when I woke—but the alarm snatched you away from me. Were you awfully tired, dear? I'll confess I was, but nothing that some sleep won't remedy. Actually I think physically, I feel quite a bit better. I think perhaps, I was getting neurotic over my cold—probably because I was over anxious to be completely well for my time with you. Anyway I think the change was good to break the spell.

Oh, darling, I do so hope nothing develops with you—no cold nor grippe. I shall feel badly if it does.

Darling, again let me tell you how sweet every moment of our being together was for me. Another lovely memory to be added to so many others. Of course, I believe the setting for our type of happiness is at its best in the natural world but if we can't always have that we can create our own "quiet bower" in a man-made environment, can't we? It wasn't too bad, was it, dear?

How queer, almost, to see the moon above the skyscrapers? Well, what really matters I suppose is that we see it together!

[3] Houghton Mifflin Company.

Darling, I have only the happiest thoughts about every moment. *Every* one was right—so right. I hope you find it the same—and will continue to.

I shall write so you will have my next letter by a week from to-day—which will be Jan. 14 (& Time moves on!). Until then you know that I love you very much,

Dorothy

SATURDAY MORNING, JANUARY 8

Darling [Dorothy],

Well, here we are again—Christmas season over, New York behind us—back at the old weekly letters!! With a difference this time, though, for now mine are going to be VERY short until the ordeal is over. I've said it before, but this time I mean it, and I know you approve and understand, for after all, you have suggested *no* letters. But that would be too hard on me.

I do so hope the roads were all right Thursday night and there were no difficulties about getting home. My train was a little late getting in, but Washington's rain was over though the skies were still grey. I was home shortly after 2:30.

Willow's escapade made me laugh—I think he was just protesting your absence. Now *my* child thought up an even more effective protest—he simply went on strike and didn't go to his toilet the whole time I was gone! But within five minutes after I'd entered the house, everything was attended to. Know any good cat psychiatrists? You will share my happiness in this, I know. I've told you the darling's back seemed so much stronger. For weeks I've been tempted to try picking him up, but just didn't dare. But this morning I did, at his request, and with no ill effects.

Marjie has had a very bad throat and we hear that many others are having it too; even our doctor has laryngitis. So far Roger hasn't developed it, thank goodness. And I'm not going near them, so don't worry about that. And I didn't get anything in New York. How are you, darling? Please just take it easy for a while, till all the after effects are worn off—of your cold, I mean, not New York!

I don't think I told you adequately how impressed with your typing I am, dear. The little quotation you typed for me was practically perfect, and the bit of manuscript you showed me was as good as lots of scripts turned in to publishers, believe me. (It took me years to learn, and accept the fact that publishers think nothing of words x'ed out, irregular margins, and such. In fact, I believe they consider it more professional that way, in reason, of course.) However, your typed letters are going to look much better than mine, I'm sure.

Such an extraordinary bit of fan mail was waiting for me that I must share it with you. I would like it back with your next letter, however. Whatever will "my husband" think of it—all these terms of endearment, and on a postal, too! And even my children mightn't like it—especially my son Geoffrey. Needless to say, I never so much as heard of this person before, so references to my goodness and kindness are baffling. I have a theory that most of it was copied out of an Indonesian text on How to Learn English in Ten Easy Lessons. Don't miss the little details on the address side of the card.[4]

[4] The fan mail from Jacatra, Indonesia, was addressed "To Her Excellency: Miss Rachel Louisa Carson" and sent regards to her husband and children. "Geoffrey" is Jeffie, RC's joke on the fan's reference to her children.

Now, darling, I must go. It was so, so lovely to have those hours with you, and the happy glow of remembering it all will help in the weeks ahead.

Rachel

I forgot to say that the notebook containing my lecture and the slides that belong to me can stay with you until I come. And before that time, I'll carefully go over all other slides I have here to be sure I haven't kept anything of Stan's.

Will you be getting a tide calendar from Fisherman's Wharf? (It's done by Neptune Press, Boston Ltd.) I have an extra one if you want it. The very low tides of May are the 22nd, 23rd, & 24th; – 1.9, – 2.0, – 1.8, very early morning but after sunrise / June lows of – 1.8 are 20th & 21st.

SATURDAY, JANUARY 8

My darling [Dorothy],

Now just a word with you before I go to work. Two notes from you—one yesterday and one today—have been lovely to have, and I shall hope for a bit Monday to say that your drive home wasn't too bad. Ice always worries me!

So you had a glimpse of our tide pool fairyland as you entered the station. New York was amazingly full of stardust wasn't it? I wish I'd been with you to see it. And we must see those Shelton paintings next summer—*this* summer, I mean.

Darling, it was all very satisfying, wasn't it? I found it so, and hope you did, too. I have looked forward to it so long. If we'd had to make a long postponement there would have been a terrible ache of disappointment. Now there are more memories, and such lovely ones.

Darling, about the manuscript—I truly believe it would be better for you not to read any more for a while. But *please* don't think I fail to understand, or am impatient with you because of the way it affects you. I understand only too well from my own experience of wishing very much I hadn't read something. For example, I'm afraid to read any more Tomlinson till this book is finished. With you, I know, it is not only the fear of seeming to imitate, but the fact that you haven't as yet convinced yourself you can write in a way that will satisfy you. I sincerely believe, darling, that you shouldn't read any more, of me or anyone else that might so affect you, until you have a good, solid start. And *keep going*. You will fall into the style and treatment that is right only after long work—maybe on page 25, maybe page 100 or 200—but not on page 1. So don't keep looking back—plunge ahead. And darling—I think perhaps I misunderstood your references to the Harper Prize book and Eugenie Clark as "excuses" for giving up. If I seemed cross with you about it, please forgive me. I wasn't really—not in my heart, I couldn't be. I was just trying to jolt you out of what I thought was a mood of defeat.

Now darling, I really must stop. I do hope it won't be hard on you to have only short notes for a few weeks—shorter than this, I mean. You'll still know all that's in my heart, won't you? And that I love you very, very dearly and tenderly? Because I do.

Rachel

Darling [Dorothy],

This is very wicked, I suppose, but I just felt like having a word with you before I return to the typewriter. I have been struggling for days with an unwieldy first chapter—trying to make it wieldy, perhaps—till I'm all worn out with it. I even spent one whole day quite unexpectedly creating a sort of prelude, in an effort to take the curse off all the heavy facts that must go into Ch. I. Whether that will stay in the book I don't know. What I need is to feel terribly fresh and full of vigor some morning and just sit down and rewrite the chapter *fast*, not stopping till it's done. That's what I did with the "Island" chapter of *The Sea*, I remember. Well—I'm probably being ridiculously optimistic, but I hope to have a complete, tho still somewhat rough draft of the book by the end of the month and then go to New York to see Marie. If I can make it by the 25th I can take in the Book Awards ceremony and also the Zoological Society's annual party, which would be fun. Meanwhile I've written Paul B. that I hope to be ready to see him in February. So you see I do mean it.

Friday I am going to squander on having my new permanent, taking the car to be reglazed, and clearing up various things at the library. Probably your week-end letter will get written at the hairdresser's, which may mean it won't be very satisfactory! But I'm hoping so much yours may come tomorrow, otherwise I won't get it till *Friday night*! Horrors!

Darling, I've thought of so many things I wish we'd talked about in New York. I think I was in a mental state—induced by the near-completion of the book—that must have made me an unsatisfactory companion, though of course you'll deny it! But it will be otherwise the next time, I hope. Also, the next time, I'll make a list!

This is not in any way a reply to your dear letter, or an installment of the next. I just wanted to talk to you, and so I did. And you know why—and what!

My love dearest, always,
Rachel

1955 | 81

Are you feeling rested? I do hope you are.

Will you, after all, send the note to the *Register* about the lecture? I had good intentions but this is such a bad period for me that I'm afraid I'll delay it. Anyway, I think you would do a better job on it. Anything you say is all right, as long as you don't solicit future bookings!

WEDNESDAY EVENING, JANUARY 12

Darling [Rachel],

I'm terribly torn—shall I pour out my soul as I usually do, or make this very short? If you'll promise you won't try to answer it, I'll probably go on at length. You see, I know what a temptation it is for me to want to answer at length everything you say. And knowing you, I can believe you are tantalized in the same way, and I would spare you—or would I? I have a feeling you are not going to be spared now.

So we'll see—and my next letter will depend on your restraint after this one. Oh, darling, I don't need to tell you that it's only for your own good that I hesitate. You do know how much your letters mean to me. But for now I can stand it, hoping that for the rest of our lives it might never have to be this way again.

Darling, I was terribly worried that you were ill after you returned home. You see your Saturday letter didn't get here until Tuesday so from Monday noon on I began building up visions of a disabled you until your letter brought relief on Tuesday. Of course, I was berating myself for going to N.Y. at all with whatever I had—but, oh, darling I was so much better than I had been and I wanted to be with you so badly. So I was glad to know that you were all right.

Darling, I listed all the activities between Friday afternoon and Tuesday in the other letter to prove that I really do feel so much better. I know that New York did me worlds of good—I never could have even thought of such a program before I went.

Of course, as I told you I was quite tired the day after my return but I'm not going to tell you about the slump I went into—purely from being tired, I think. I wouldn't mention it now (I was going to tell you the next time I saw you) except that I snapped out of it entirely—as I hope I've proved to you.

And physically, I haven't had so much—can I call it—pep—for a long while—more, an interest in doing something, I guess. So, darling, if you came through New York without being exhausted or catching a bug, I'm awfully happy we had it. It was lovely and I shall live on its memories until we are together again.

Another child's definition of love akin to the "sending more postal cards": "when you see a lot of each other and then get used to each other."

Darling, you said in your letter "how wonderful when two people will set aside everything else"—Darling, darling, all the sacrifice was on your part—

you were the one to set aside such important work—you were the one who was going to have to work harder because of the interlude—and because it was you, darling, can you understand how honored I felt because you wanted to and did—honored and humbled, darling? You were so sweet to want to.

I'm sorry that there was anything left unexplored in our conversations, and, of course, now you have me awfully curious—what is it that is not acute—but chronic? Won't you tell me? Well, of course not now for that would mean writing.

Do you know what my reading has proved to be other than a few magazines? I went back to *The Wind in the Willows* (and even that could have a "bad influence on me" if I would let it). You know I wonder if children really enjoy it. How old were the girls when they read it? I know that when I read *Alice* I was too anxious to get on with the story, as I told you, to stop for the poetry. And so in the *Willows* I find passages with no action at all which I feel pretty sure I would have skipped at that age. But, oh, how delightful now! Darling, when I read chapter 7—"The Piper at the Gates of Dawn"—I was all quivery with stardust. Read it, darling, especially from where Rat and Mole get out the boat—page 129 in my book—so many, many lovely thoughts—and on page 134—"suddenly the Mole felt a great Awe"—and on and on, darling. Read it and think about Us. I think you'll find the same thoughts I did.

Now about your special note in yesterday's letter. Darling, if you have manuscript that you could share with me, please, please don't deprive me of that joy. You know that anything I am doing is so far remote from a finished product that Time will take care of any present effects your writing might have on me. It's only for a short time now that you can share it with me in the form it is in. Soon it will belong to the world. Surely you can't realize how much it means to me. Is this the price I've got to pay because I've promised to *try* to write?—To not have your manuscript?

Don't you see it will make me not want to try? And I am so close to not wanting to. It would be so much simpler not to. (Oh, dear, I hope that isn't going to make you unhappy.)

Just send me some manuscript if you have some, and don't worry about the effects on me!

One thing I wanted to say, dear. I hope so much, darling, I can be near you when the reviews come out. I suppose that would be near the publication date so when you know that couldn't we plan to be together? You would want me, wouldn't you?

Darling, now please don't worry about your short notes. Of course, I'll "still know all that's in your heart, and that you love me very, very dearly and tenderly."—Oh, my darling.

Oh, dearest, I do so hope this isn't going to disturb you in any way—to make you feel the need of writing more than a note.

Remember I said at the beginning we'd see—and if you answer back at any length I'll know I must not write much or in any vein except mere daily routine.

Oh, darling, I love you so. I haven't spoken to you since Friday—and this is Wednesday.

Now darling, good-night.

I'll think of you as I always do when I go to sleep. I love you very much.

Dorothy

FRIDAY EVENING, JANUARY 14

Darling [Dorothy],

Now you are putting me on the spot! If I really answer your letter I get a tiny note in response! Now I'll be waiting to learn the penalty for the extra one you got today—or I *hope* you did.

All right, I'll be brief, but partly because I want to take this to the box this evening in an effort to reach you Monday. Also, of course, because we have agreed to this and for a few weeks more it is for the best. But don't fuss with me about the extra one. I think you must have known I really needed those moments with you.

Now I wish I hadn't said that about the phone call, for I know you'll be on edge expecting it, and maybe I won't call. I shouldn't, I know.

Darling, when we are together please tell me all about the "slump" after New York. If I'd taken any proper care of you while we were there it probably wouldn't have happened. Now don't push your recovery too hard—I don't believe you know how to rest!

You remember I said I had no new problems and I think that is true. I know I just didn't feel much like talking about any of the old ones while we were in New York—then coming home on the train I rather wished I had. But it was just an aspect of a situation you know—probably the "most chronic" of my worries. And it will keep perfectly well.

About manuscript, darling! You know I'm only trying to do what seems best for you. Now I feel as though *you* are *my* little girl—and a problem child at that, refusing to eat her spinach because mamma is withholding the candy!! Well darling, let's settle it this way. At the moment there is really nothing I'd want to send you anyway. And I'll be perfectly honest and say that at this trying stage I would rather not give thought to selecting sections, fiddling with them, and getting them off to you. I fully expect to see you within a month. At that time I'll have a complete draft of sorts. We can then discuss whether you are to dip into it. I promise you, darling. I won't hold out if you really feel strongly about it. Did it ever occur to you, my dearest, that you don't really have to make any great decision *now*, this winter, about writing a *book*? The actual doing of that is such a long, long process. You can decide much later whether this is actually to take book form. But meanwhile, you can go on getting your thoughts and feelings on paper. And I think that's what you are doing, despite all the backing away from it.

I'll look up the chapter of *Wind in the Willows*—remember it vaguely. Dearest, I think I will take this to the box now. Don't be surprised if a tiny one follows in a few days.

I love you dearly—

Rachel

SUNDAY NIGHT, JANUARY 16

Darling [Dorothy],

I suppose after this you won't write to me for a month! But really I am not trying to break the pattern of weekly letters, and don't want you to either. The irregular one last week was just because I was feeling strain and really needed to talk with you. Tonight's is just a postscript to your weekly letter, though perhaps an unnecessary one. After this I'll probably fall back into the pattern.

I am behind my schedule but despite that feel rather optimistic. At last I can sort of get the feel of it as a whole book, and it seems to me (darling—this is one of those "shameless" things one would say to so few) the kind of book I myself would like if someone else had written it. That was what I was able to feel about the other two before they left my hands, and I think one should have that reaction.

Quite surprisingly, with this filling my mind—for I really have been concentrating intensively since I saw you—I have also been getting rather excited about the book I'm to do for Harper[5]—seeing it as potentially an important book, perhaps more important than anything else I've done. Can I tell you about that in February?

Darling, I think I really needed to add this to my Friday letter to be *sure* you understand what was in my mind about the manuscript, and that I am not going to be stubborn about it if you really feel you are being deprived of an experience that means much to you. I hope my teasing response Friday didn't hurt you. And that you can understand my failure to send any more for a few weeks had nothing to do with our conversation—it is just not a good time for me. And darling, there will be *months* before it "belongs to the world." We can talk it all over in February, and I'll have it with me. Some of it, such as the introduction, I really want to read *with* you. All right?

Now don't scold me for writing all this—you must understand I have to get away from work at intervals. And don't make your letters tiny!

I love you dear—so very much.

Rachel

[5] Harper and Brothers had asked RC to write a book for their World Perspectives series. She was considering a book tentatively titled "Remembrance of Earth" about the origins of life.

Darling [Dorothy]—

I held this to see if there would be a note today—and there was! So I'll just add a few lines.

In spite of my recent confusing behavior, dearest, I really believe the weekly schedule is best. It cuts down that morning of "waiting for the mailman" to one, and I never quite settle down to work while I'm looking or listening for him. So as far as the expected letter is concerned I think one a week is best, but that doesn't mean darling, that I wouldn't welcome with joy a little unheralded one now and then, if you feel like writing it. I've already exercised that privilege myself, and as you understood, that was because I needed to talk to you. But it is unfortunately true that expecting a letter every day or so doesn't help calm concentration, so this time I'll be hard on myself and say no when I'd rather say yes.

About the call, darling, I'm afraid that was a silly idea that ought not to be acted on—an early morning one I mean. It would seem so crazy to anyone else. So for the present I think I won't call—or if someday I just *have* to I'll try a more conventional hour, person-to-person.

I love you darling, very, very much.

Rachel

Dearest [Dorothy],

Today was a milestone of sorts. I sent Marie all the manuscript that is approximately ready, and it made such an impressively large package that I could really see that "shimmer on the horizon" that means The End. If you ever bought a ream of typing paper you know it comes in a box of substantial size— and my brainchild nearly filled one of those. (Not nearly that many sheets, of course—they seem to sort of fluff up after they are typed on.) Anyway, it began to seem, at last, that something has been achieved. The sad truth is that I have a very great deal still to do on two chapters, and finishing touches on all others— but still I feel good.

Other achievements of the day—we both went to have our hair done (I *can't stand* a new permanent till it's washed), took the Oldsmobile to get its new wheel discs, saw Bob at Interior and discussed drawings. Also, quite unexpectedly, took poor Roger to the doctor as we went downtown. He and Marjie had gone to the store—he was marching along with hands in his pockets, stumbled, and fell flat on his face on the sidewalk. Damages were a badly chewed lower lip, two teeth loosened, and a bloody nose. Doctor says it will all heal nicely and teeth will probably firm up again, though nerves might die. By this evening he was able to take a little liquid food—it hurt too much before. He was very brave and patient about it though.

I'm glad Stan had a satisfactory reply from Dr. Stine. You know the Exacta is the camera I've been talking about, and that Jack Culbeath recommends. (No, there is no R in it—but I can see why a New Englander might not be sure!) I think I'll have to get one before summer—but not, of course, until Stan and I have discussed other possibilities.

Well, didn't Mr. Pinkham give up journalism in a hurry! I'm glad you sent in your contribution, but sorry *you* had to do it, chiefly because I'm afraid you wouldn't say enough about the pictures.[6]

By the way, Russell Mason, of the Mass. Audubon Society wrote to ask about a lecture (or rather a series of lectures) next season. Guess you know the answer to that!

Dear, you mentioned the possibility of going to Orono some week-end, and that reminded me I had intended to say that after thinking it over I really imagine my visit to Boston in February had better be during the week, (whatever week) so that I can be sure of all the time I need in the H.M. offices. So don't let that enter your thinking about Orono. Maybe the *next* time I come can be built around a week-end. Also, I'll have to avoid two family birthdays—Roger's on the 18th and Mamma's on the 28th. But as I said, I'll know better what to try for after seeing Paul next week.

Jeffie had a lonesome afternoon and was *so* glad to see us—had a grand play, ate a lamb chop, and is now sound asleep in his basket on the bed beside me. He still squeezes all of his nearly-ten pounds into the little old basket, only occasionally using the big one. We are so happy that all is well with Willow. I'm so anxious to see him. This is all for now, dear. I hope it reaches you Monday.

Our love to all,
Rachel

My dearest darling [Dorothy],

I'm so glad you asked me about our moon—I hadn't seen it since it began rising after I went to bed. So I set the alarm for 6:30 this morning and propped your letter against the clock so I'd remember instantly *why* I set it early, and not just go to sleep. But Jeffie decided to call me about 10 minutes earlier, and I went to the window in the bathroom—our only upstairs window facing east. (By the way—from what window do you see it. I can't think which way your house faces.) The moon was just a little above the horizon. And the Star! How blazingly bright and how enormous! Thank you, darling. It occurs to me how much more attention I've been paying to the moon since I've known You. For instance, I don't think I *ever* saw the moon in New York till we saw it above the skyscrapers!

For your information about the telephone difficulties—first we got 2065-M (horrors, what a jolt when the wrong voice answered), then my operator told yours we got the wrong number—in a minute a Special Operator answered, heard the story, did some research, and reported there really is a 2069-M and to try again—my operator got yours again—yours said, "But that is a *party* line."—

[6] Charlie Pinkham, proprietor of the West Southport general store, had been a correspondent to the *Boothbay Register*. DF had sent him a report of RC's December Audubon lecture in which RC had used Stanley's slides.

mine said, "Yes, we know it is and we are calling M"—then success at last. It sounded to me as though there was just a very stupid operator (There was more conversation than I've quoted—she misunderstood the number several times—repeating it with one or more numbers missing) in the Brockton office. The rest of the story about my difficulties of the morning I want to keep till I see you. Really it was awfully funny.

Your letter did come Thursday, darling, and made me very happy. As you know by now, it (the call) did me worlds of good, and for my own sake I'd be self-ishly glad I made it; now I can be glad for your sake, too. Of course I knew you *couldn't help* expecting it and being "on edge"—I know I would. But I want you to tell me more when we are together, as you say you will—how "it made a dif-ference" in your frame of mind and your attitude. Did you really need the sound of my voice? As much as I needed to hear yours?

Oh, darling, there is so much I want to say but I'm going to try to keep this short as I promised. Think I'll turn in as soon as I finish this because I am tired and probably will only waste time trying to work. But Saturday and Sunday I must accomplish a lot. Dearest, I would love to be able to share parts of it with you as I go along—for instance, the day I got the idea about the chapter to pre-cede the original Ch. I, and began to work on it, I suddenly wanted so much to tell Someone about it, and of course the Someone was You! Well, we'll read it in February. I know I shall be working very hard on it (the whole manuscript) right up to, and through, the galley stage for I do want it to be as good as I can pos-sibly make it—and it needs a lot of work yet. (Guess you can tell I'm sleepy and tired—none of my pronouns have antecedents, I find on re-reading!)

Darling—I should learn not to talk about important things when I write in a hurry as I did last week! And I am *not* starting one of those exchanges of re-grets now—I know it isn't necessary—but just let me recall to you Tomlinson's phrase about words casting shadows. They *were* shadows, darling, not the real meaning and I just hope your hurt-prevention insurance was working when you read my inept remarks about not sending manuscript and about your de-cision regarding your own book. I am sure you understand what was in my heart, even though badly said. But darling, I do feel we need a long discussion of my relation to your writing—I hope you know what I mean. It is the one sub-ject on which I have a great fear of hurting you by saying the wrong thing—or by not saying something I ought to say. I don't *want* to feel that way—so let's talk about it when we are together. I am sure both my feeling and any possible rea-son for it can be removed by talking it over freely. Darling, I do so want you to throw yourself into it, your writing—happily, without all the doubts and hesi-tations you seem to me to have. I believe in you, darling—if you had equal faith in yourself all would be well!

Now I must stop (says she, going right on!). About your letters, dearest—I am weak as water! How about a Monday letter another week at least? Besides the Thursday or Friday one, I mean. I do love them so. And you. You will have this early in the week and perhaps I'll write a little account of New York on the train coming home, Thursday. You should have that Saturday if I mail it at the station. Darling, is it hard to think of my being in the world and of sharing me? I smiled at that, but it was a smile of complete understanding. You see, I had already thought of that myself.

I love you dearly
Rachel

FRIDAY, JANUARY 28

My darling [Dorothy],

I don't know whether you will want to share the card[7] or not, but this is just for you, even though it will be very short and probably not say the things I want to say. Your recent notes and letters, and the calls, have brought you very close, dear, and that has been sweet and has helped me. And I am so glad you have said what you have about your thoughts and feelings at this time, and when we are together I want you to tell me *all* you are thinking. But even this much makes it possible for me to talk (when we are together) about it, and I think that will help us both. Without that sharing of thoughts, darling, the next year could be very hard for *both* of us. Had you thought of that? Probably you had. But the things we both fear won't happen if we talk about it now, I'm sure. Darling, I *do* understand how you feel, but I want to help you to feel a little differently. It can be a happy time for you and I want it to be all happiness. And you can help to make it especially happy for me.

As I said this morning, we have a great deal to say to each other, don't we? And the time, at best, will be short and I'm sorry for that. However, I think we'll both be happier if I get the business out of the way first, darling. Then you may be sure I'll stay as long as my conscience will let me. But you do understand the problems, don't you, darling?

It was sweet to have your goodnight note. I believe it was nearly one o'clock when I read it. You must know that in all the whirl of New York, you were never far from me.

There is much to tell you about the book and related things, but probably I'll keep that till I see you.

Darling, on second thought, probably I won't mail anything more till Monday. I've promised Mrs. Irey (the New York typist) a big section of mss. on Monday, and that probably means getting it off by special delivery Sunday.

I love you, darling, and you are very precious to me. And very necessary. You know that, don't you?

You are, And I do
Rachel

[7] In the preserved notecard RC had written of happily anticipating her February West Bridgewater visit.

My darling [Dorothy],

In part this is an experiment to see whether an *air mail* letter that is picked up Saturday evening may reach you Monday.

But mostly it is just to say I love you, and to have a few minutes with you before dinner.

Last night before I went to sleep I reread (for the ninth time!) a number of your recent letters, darling. And if there is any one thing I especially want to say as a result of that reading it is this: I think it is so truly wonderful that we feel we can say to each other exactly what we are thinking and feeling. I do, darling. It makes all the difference in the world. When I said (for example), "Is it hard to share me?" I wanted the kind of answer you gave, so please don't ever regret having written it. Perhaps after sending off yesterday's letter, in which I said that we must talk about all that, and that I wanted to make you feel differently, I have feared you will think I am unhappy about it. Don't think that, darling—I'm not. On the contrary I'm deeply happy that you care enough to find the sharing hard. But I do want to go even more deeply into the sharing of our thoughts about all that might lie ahead, for I think it will help us both. But dearest, don't, in the meantime, feel I am worried or unhappy about anything relating to us.

Darling, I am afraid I am often very unperceptive. I had no idea that my letter with its "shameless confession" that now I feel better about the book was going to bring you such happiness. In retrospect, I can understand that it would, for I do know your heart ached for me in my great dissatisfaction. But I'm afraid I tossed that bit your way quite unthinkingly! I loved what you said about the difference it makes when one can *see* the end, even if there is a considerable distance to cover. Of course that is the real reason I now feel so much lighter in spirit, even though I haven't reached The End! I know where it lies, and that it can be attained, even though there is tough going ahead. Now, my darling, you will hear again toward the end of the week. And I'm living for a letter soon—maybe Monday!

I love your dearly, and for always,

Rachel

MONDAY MORNING, EARLY, JANUARY 31

Darling, my dearest [Rachel],

Last night I spent with you from one to two o'clock. Reasons enough for lack of sleep: a rather stimulating day, the disconcerting news from Norwood,[8] plus 9 cups of coffee which is a record for me—if not for you.

While I struggled for sleep I finally arrived at our Maytime, and particularly did my mind wander through your home as I first knew it. Oh, darling, live over those days to-gether sometime. Such happiness as those days brought to me. I remember the morning I got up before you did, to stand at the window

8 Norwood, Massachusetts, where DF's aunt was ill.

for a long while looking down on your own special world. Darling, the tears came that morning—the whole situation was so lovely—so far lovelier than anything my wildest imagination could conjure up. Do you remember?

After a while with no suggestion of sleep I thought of the February letters. So to them I went. Do you know it took me a whole hour to read all you wrote me in that month? So how many valuable hours did you consume in the construction of them!?

What wouldn't the world give to have them? For, my darling, they are the most beautiful expressions of love I have ever read. So tender and loving and beautifully said. They began with the hyacinth letter[9]—the Revelation.

If I could save only one letter from my mighty collection that would be the one. It is so precious. Of course, I practically can say it by heart for I must have read it literally a thousand times. You shall read it over when you come up for I want you to remember it all. I couldn't help thinking as I read "Just suppose I hadn't asked 'Why' so many times—you might never have written it" and how awful if you had felt as you did and I hadn't known it. And then the letters that followed as the result of that one.

There were smiles for me as I remembered all we experienced in that month. But what amazed me was the depth to which our love had gone in that time for after all we had been together exactly the 6½ hours at Southport in the summer previous plus the 13 hours here in December. What magic letters can work!

And in one letter there was an exclamation from you about such depths—as though we had already been to the bottom! Oh, darling, how little we knew then.

How much we have discovered in this past year. I can remember thinking in the midst of those exchanges "How long can this last?"

Darling, I'm sure now that with me it will last as long as I shall live—the year has not dulled my love and devotion to you by one little neutron—in fact my love is as infinite as that beautiful morning star which is my first ritual of each day—to look out at it and speak to you, to reach you in your subconscious for I always hope you are asleep. This morning I thought what a lovely experience it would be if we could watch that star rise together. Did you ever set yourself to watch for the rising of a star? I did once—I think I told you—on Mt. Holyoke—only that was in the evening.

My darling, reading your letters last night was so warming I could almost feel your arms about me—and afterwards I went back to bed and dropped into a lovely sleep.

Oh, darling, can I ever make you know how much you mean to me? That was the burden of those letters—how much and why we need each other.

And you must know that I continue to need you and the year has taught me that you do belong to me.

[9] RC's letter of February 6, 1954. Over the years, this letter gained in significance for RC and DF and was always referred to as "the hyacinth letter."

Now, darling, the world calls. It has been so lovely to talk to you this morning to revive the year's memories.

The letters have been so precious always—but never more so than last night.

My darling, do you know how very very much I love and adore you?— I do.

Dorothy

[EARLY FEBRUARY]

My darling [Dorothy],

A year ago I tried to tell you, in terms of a white hyacinth, one of the reasons I love you and need you.

May these white blossoms[10] repeat for me all that I said then, and bring you my dearest love.

Rachel

[10] RC had asked Stanley to deliver white hyacinths to DF with this note.

THURSDAY MORNING, FEBRUARY 3

Darling [Dorothy,]

Two small paragraphs only, before I go back to my barnacles.

I don't know why I hesitated, dear, when you asked about reading the paragraphs describing the two high tide pools. They belong with the slides and I wish you would. (The slide of the "blue pool" is, I think, my favorite of all Stan took.) Any possible objections that might apply in another situation don't apply here. In the very unlikely event that anyone says "I'd like a copy of that"—then the answer would be no. Only *you* may have that, darling. But please read it if you want to, and I'm sorry I didn't say that first. I'd like very much to have you do it.

Item 2: In retrospect I thought you were wondering how much time *I* wanted or needed with the Brookses. My business on the manuscript will of course be confined to the office. Actually, I have various little plots in the back of my mind, but my first objective will be accomplished if you and Stan have time to visit with the Brookses and you all have a feeling of being friends when they leave. So for that reason don't cut their time down too much. But do keep everything easy—they are very casual people and will like it that way.

Oh-h! I'll have to add a paragraph #3. While writing this a phone call came: the U. N. asks whether I will go to Rome for them in April to cover an international conference on "living resources of the sea." I'm sure the answer has to be no, but a request like that still seems quite exciting.

Now darling—goodbye. I'm living for the 13th.

All my love—
Rachel

Darling [Dorothy],

Just another brief "report." Late this afternoon I sent Paul the manuscript—all, that is, except the problem chapter that may turn out to be only an appendix. That I'm going to take to him in rough form, as agreed. I am wondering at what point I'll know I'm *really* done. Probably when I return the corrected page proofs! But though the actuality keeps skipping along out of reach, I've been basking in the light pouring in through that open door for weeks. (Don't you think I'm entitled to mix metaphors at this point?) Dear, please don't worry about me. The weariness of achievement is a very different thing from that of frustration and despair. I am quite all right, really. Yes, I think this pressure at the end is inevitable—for me, at least, and I believe for most writers.

I smiled when I read your thoughts inspired by Mr. Faulkner—not because of what you said, but because of the stardust! There had been a few paragraphs in the *Washington Post* yesterday that just "set my teeth on edge"—not only because of that column, but as a foretaste of what is ahead. Somehow I think I'll hate all the publicity angles even more than I did before. So that was one thing I had listed for our conversation!

How will there *ever* be time enough?

Darling, I do want to say this. There are always uncertainties in our plans, and you have a situation in the family now that could easily call for changes of one sort or another. Please promise me that if, for example, your aunt should be ill enough that you ought, especially for your mother's sake, to be spending a good deal of time there, you will let me know. A short postponement would no doubt be possible, or in any event I'm certain to have to return to work with the production people and you are coming here for Spring in Washington. It comes to us early, you know. (The more I think about Rome, the less I think it makes sense—but we'll see!)

You will probably hear Saturday. Or if not, on Sunday in Brockton!!

All love dear,
Rachel

Darling [Dorothy],

I see I forgot "the liquor problem." You said not to write about it. I know, but I planned to so you can decide in advance.

To be truthful, I know the Brookses do like "something stronger"—but I have been known to give them sherry and as you see, he still plans to publish my book! I think your own customs should prevail, darling. If you seldom or never serve strong drinks, there is certainly no need to now. However, if you don't object, how about offering a choice of sherry or — ? But don't bother with cocktails. Paul seems to be a great Scotch or Rye man and I think Susie takes the same. So some such plus soda (which I hate) could be a simpler and most acceptable alternate.

Darling, do I need to tell you—perhaps I do—that I'd be happy and proud to have you entertain anyone I know. And *do* get over this notion that people who write or publish books are some separate and exalted order of beings. If for no other reason, get over it because it isn't fair to them. (What did I write once about pedestals?) And I can say because I really *know* that Paul has a very modest opinion of himself and his job. And Susie is just "like an old shoe." Both of them love the out of doors and camping and canoe trips. Now please just enjoy them.

Darling, can it *really* be so soon? Somehow it seems impossible.

You know what!

R.

SATURDAY MORNING, FEBRUARY 19

Darling [Dorothy],

I wrote the other first[11] which means there really is little time for this if you are to be assured of Monday mail.

Your notes came Wednesday and Thursday, and the longer letter yesterday—a bright sunny day as you hoped, and Roger's birthday activities to fill it. For various reasons, darling, I won't reply at length, though I can't simply "acquiesce" as you ask. I know that you wrote on a gloomy day, after several days of sadness following our disappointment. So especially for that reason I'd rather not reply now, for later I think you will feel otherwise. You say you thought long about it—but not long enough, darling. You haven't thought out all the implications of a policy that says, in effect, "No happiness that can't be guaranteed weeks in advance." By force of circumstances, I've learned I have to snatch what happiness the hour or the day offers—I can't be sure of anything a *day* in advance! Darling, I know May is most uncertain,[12] and so is anything we might plan. I know you thought I was feeling I couldn't do it and you were trying to make it easier for me. But I am not willing to give up, and I hope as you think about it all you can come around to feeling that, while knowing we can't count definitely on that or anything, we shall seize whatever opportunities come and be grateful for *"even an hour!"* Remember the phrase? Darling, your note has come while I've been writing this, and it echoes another thought of mine—that we have drifted into a terribly negative, unhappy mood about various things, and we really must pull ourselves out of it. I miss the joy we used to have. It isn't your fault, darling, any more than mine. But let's both decide to go back to the happy things and let problems take care of themselves for a while.

My feelings about the curtailed visit[13] are of course somewhat like yours, darling, especially as to the deep disappointment for all we had to give up. Yet I

[11] The "other" letter, a long, chatty, public letter that accompanied this private letter, is omitted.

[12] RC and DF were hoping to make a trip to Southport in May.

[13] RC had arrived in West Bridgewater on February 13 and departed on February 15 when a telephone call home had aroused concern about her mother and Jeffie.

knew all along, as you know, that I might have to come home Tuesday. Of course the particular turn events took, as to human complications, bad weather, etc., made it especially trying. But never for a moment did I regret having gone. And I'm truly thankful for the hours we did have.

Dearest, if there is an emergency and we have to postpone your visit, of course I'll tell you. But I'm looking forward to that as a very happy, wonderful time—with much of it all to ourselves, darling. Now dearest, let's escape from all the unhappiness and just find joy in all we have. I love you dearly—

Rachel

MONDAY MORNING, FEBRUARY 20

My own darling [Dorothy]—

Of course I opened the sealed note at once—it was better that way than wondering, for it would be impossible to "shut my mind" to it. Perhaps I am less upset by it than you thought I'd be—but only because the subject of your distress is so easily disposed of. But of course I grieve that you have been made so unhappy. What in the world *is* the matter with us, darling? I want *you* to be happy, you want *me* to be happy—and here we seem to be under some wicked fairy's spell so everything we do or say has the wrong effect! Remember how you used to write me fairy tales, darling?

Well, dearest, I'll be brief, but you are torturing yourself with thoughts of "whatever did I do or say" to make me say I'd "keep out" of the handling of your manuscript. Darling—I thought you'd know what I meant, or I would have been more specific so let me explain now, briefly. We'll talk it out next month.

Over the years of my own experience in writing I have acquired a point of view about the marketing of literary property that is different from the way I'd have felt ten years ago and different, I know, from yours. I have realized it is a cold matter of business—however charged with emotion the author's feelings may be (and should be) about his production. But the marketing end is professional, calling for knowledge of what various editors want, and so on—and this is especially true of magazines. Of course, a new author going at it blindly may happen to do the right thing, as I did with the *Atlantic*[14]—but from there on I floundered badly till I got professional help. I am not suggesting that you get an agent until you know what and how much you are going to do, darling. But I'll confess—if you hadn't realized it—that almost as soon as I became aware you were serious about writing, I began to wish I could help you—by suggesting markets or by bringing about helpful contacts—to break into print and regain a little of that self-confidence you need so badly. Then, belatedly, I began to feel my zeal was misguided, because it may be important for you to know that whatever happens, you have brought about entirely "on your own." Darling, I *do* understand that feeling. You are so afraid "they" will say you were published, not

[14] RC's first magazine article, "Undersea," had appeared in the *Atlantic Monthly* in September 1937.

because of your own merit, but because of influence—because you knew me. Whether you are right or wrong is beside the point—if you have that feeling it will destroy your own satisfaction and joy. So I feel it is important for *you* to know I had nothing to do with it. That was all there was to it, darling. And that isn't so terrible, is it? I'm just trying to be sensible and protect you (and Us) from future hurt. And I am certainly not hurt about it now. I can remember back far enough to realize I might have felt the same way. Now, of course, I think no more of having someone sell a manuscript than I'd think of calling in a real estate agent to handle a piece of property. It's just business, but I feel that you, *quite understandably*, are not ready for any such detached point of view. Darling, you didn't ever say or imply you wanted me to "keep out." You did say last week that you knew if you ever had a line published, people would say it was because you knew me. And that just reminded me of what I had told myself months ago.

Perhaps, when we can talk at length, we can acquire a more matter-of-fact point of view about the whole thing. I do hope so. But meanwhile, darling, please just believe me that I am not hurt and didn't mean to hurt you.

Now I am trying to remember whether the letter you are reading today is apt to be disturbing. I do hope not. I think that for a variety of reasons, our spirits are at a very low ebb and so our recent disappointment was especially hard to take. I know that, for myself, there is a very great physical weariness deep inside—remember what I told you that very first night on Dogfish Head—about writing *The Sea*? I realize it is the same now, for I have begun (too soon) to let down a little, and then I feel it. Also, the wonderful sense of freedom I expected to experience is somehow being spoiled by the fact that other, less tangible bonds (Meaning family problems, of which you know.) seem now more restricting than ever. And you poor darling, having been elected to hear all my troubles—well if the bower isn't a place of peace now it isn't your fault! I'll feel better soon, darling, and shake off all this depression. I am looking forward, truly, to much joy and happiness while you are here. I think we should try to forget troubles then as much as possible. Darling, you do bring me deep happiness and peace—nothing is changed. Now, let's remember nothing matters except that we love each other dearly. Let's just be happy, dearest.

I do love you always.

Rachel

Darling—now don't worry because I said I'm very weary. Of course I am—the long strain is bound to be felt, but it's nothing serious. And I've planned definitely not to work on the new book this summer—I shall be a new person at Southport.

Now cheer up, my dearest—and not just on the surface but deep inside. You want to help me—I know you do. Just now that will help me more than anything else. And I'll try to do the same for you. Yes, I think we should laugh at ourselves for making problems and tormenting ourselves, instead of just being full of joy because we have each other. I am, dear, and I know you are, too. So let's forget everything but—you know what!

I love you,

R.

Darling [Dorothy],

Just a word to say that your Sunday letter was a wonderful help, and something I needed very much.

It is odd how the goal seems to recede as I approach it. I am just suddenly so weary—physically, mentally, emotionally—that at times The End seems unattainable. This is not to worry you, darling—only to explain, and to tell you how healing and comforting was your sweet letter today. I never want you to be unhappy and it helps to know you are less so. And now dearest, March 28[15] is a lovely star on our horizon. I know it will bring much happiness.

My dearest love,

Rachel

[15] Date of DF's planned arrival for a six-day visit with RC in her Silver Spring, Maryland, home.

Darling [Dorothy],

I shall send you a note today after all—I didn't go to have my hair done yesterday so am there now, and will use the time under the drier for you. Your letter written Wednesday came today along with the card (of course you couldn't resist it—just made for us!). If I've been deluged with mail this week, so have you, darling. In fact I'm now very confused as to what I've written you when—just something every day, I think. In that little note yesterday, I believe I said I was just beginning to feel that the revision of the coral chapter was going right, and I must devote myself to it. Well, from that moment until now has been a blank as far as work is concerned. I won't take time for details, but Marjie had some sort of "spell" of feeling very ill, and the situation seemed to demand me for the rest of the day and evening. It is, unfortunately not the sort of situation that can be remedied by a "tonic" as my mother always thinks, but I am sure demands some sort of complete rehabilitation that again involves me. There are serious physical complications, of course, but the psychological ones are perhaps almost more important. Well, I think the crisis is past for the moment; if not perhaps I can install a nurse or something, but "sensible" solutions are always more easily prescribed than applied to other human beings.

Now I've written this much I almost wish I hadn't, for you will be able to imagine, even if I say no more, what the whole situation does to me at this particular time. By writing of it at all, I seem to be failing to keep our resolve to "cheer up" and write of happy things. And yet somehow, darling, I need to tell you that the period since I saw you (and it seems an eternity) has been almost as black as any I have known. I think I wrote you a year ago that my great problem was how to be a writer and at the same time a member of my family—now you know what I meant. It is that conflict that just tears me to pieces. Now, so near the end, I wonder why I can't have peace for even ten days, but I have thought of no practical solution. You know I can't go away now.

Darling—there is no need for you to write of this in any detail—it just helps to tell you that the going is pretty rough—and at the same time I feel like a heel to tell you, for I know it will distress you. Try not to let it, darling—stay "cheered up" and write me happy letters with thoughts of a happier future. Believe me, dearest, that will help, and at the moment there is no other way you could.

Looking back over this, I see I should be more definite. M. is back to more or less "normal" today, and it is not likely I'll have to go over again to help. And maybe nothing more will happen till I'm over my own crisis. Now don't be upset darling—that won't help!

There were various things in your recent letters I wanted to comment on, but I'll just mail this and let them wait.

Darling, I couldn't do without you—don't ever forget that.

I have asked the family in for a little buffet supper Monday night—nothing elaborate and Vera[16] will come early and help.

Now I'm dry. I love you dearly darling as you must know I do.

Rachel

[16] RC's sister-in-law, married to her brother Robert Carson.

M O N D A Y   N I G H T ,   F E B R U A R Y   2 8

My darling [Dorothy],

I'll start a note before I turn out the light, but will probably not finish it until after mail time tomorrow.

Dearest, we should laugh at all this and I hope you can—we could if we were together, I know. (Remember how we laughed under the October moon?) The bad fairy is still about, and she told me to call you today, knowing perfectly well—the fairy did, I mean—that you weren't at home and news of the call would only upset you more, whereas what I was trying to do was to counteract the effect of my upsetting letter!! Oh dear—how I wished I *hadn't* called when I found you weren't there! But now it's all right, isn't it, darling?

Of course, I know you *want* me to tell you anything that disturbs me, dearest, and of course I feel free to do so. But there is just no sense writing when I am in the depths of one of my darker moods, when by the time you read the letter I shall in all probability have snapped out of it. And so it was this time. A productive and undisturbed day yesterday made a different person of me. You say you are the victim of strong emotions—and I know I am one who swings from despair to hope or even elation very quickly, at least at certain times, and I think those times relate to critical stages of whatever writing is under way. And of course this is a particularly critical stage—the Last Chance, as it were—so my nerves are a bit ragged. But darling—it's all right now, really.

There is a real spring thunderstorm in progress now, just a little after midnight, and for several days there has been a definite feeling of spring in the air. It is really wonderful to feel I can have time to enjoy some of it this year—for several springs now, I have felt so trapped.

Darling, glance over *Spring in Washington* before you come and tell me whether there is anything Mr. Halle describes you particularly want to see. The two paths along the old canal certainly, and there should be many early migrants then. It was sweet to have your note of Friday, dear. Yes, the Sunday letter that I said "helped" me was, in part, about your reaction to "The Rocky Shores."[17] That was not the only reason it did me good, but definitely it was one of them, darling. One of my own disappointments about the abruptly terminated visit was the fact that there was no time for that subject, when of course I wanted very much to know how you feel about it. So thank you dearest, for writing it, and of course I could ask for no more than the things you have said. Let's talk some about it when you are here. (I want you to read a few sentences of Elizabeth Bowen's about a writer's critical faculty as applied to his own or to another person's writing. I have always considered myself a poor judge of another's work, and what she said was illuminating. Incidentally, I don't know her *House in Paris*. The only novel I know is *The Heat of the Day*, which I have, along with her *Collected Impressions*.)

Dearest, we shall have to go over some of our letters and translate, I see. For instance, *I* am now mystified by what you say of applying my remarks to the publishing world generally, instead of to yourself. But I am quite content to wait, and we can explain all happily, I know.

Oh darling, it will be so *wonderful* to have you. Please stay as long as you feel you possibly can. Goodnight dear.

TUESDAY A.M.

(March 1st—this month I'll see you!)

No letter this morning, they seem often to be taking two days now, so I'll expect it tomorrow. Having talked to you last night, I guess I can wait that long!

Darling, I'm certain we can visit the cave pool together, and more than once. I'm not even sure it requires a spring tide—it may be exposed on every low, but certainly several days out of every two weeks. I think you didn't go because we had nothing very special in mind when Stan and I wandered up there—you know the tide had been rising for some time and I didn't think of going to that pool. But darling—maybe you can be glad you didn't if you think of this—knowing you hadn't seen it, I tried to describe it *for you*, so it would become real in your mind.[18] Perhaps without that objective, the result would have been very different.

[17] A chapter of *The Edge of the Sea*.

[18] The cave is described in the opening pages of "The Marginal World" and in the final pages of "The Rocky Shores" in *The Edge of the Sea*.

Dear, I'd love to hear now of your lecture plans. Will you tell me when you come?

And I do want to talk, and at length, about your writing, darling. I realize more and more that the whole subject of creativeness is a terribly complex psychological problem—I realize it from my own experience, I mean. I wish someone much wiser than I could consider your problem and advise you. There is no question in my mind, darling, that you could write. The question is whether the effort would be good or bad for *you*. You say you have "shut the door" on the problem for the present, and that is good. You can take a fresher look at it a few weeks hence if you have forgotten it temporarily.

I am skipping around over your letters—just picking out a few things. Darling, *of course* I didn't misunderstand your turning to other reading "to break the spell." You didn't need to explain, I approve heartily. (And there I tagged along with you through the Bowen novel!)

Now I must go to work. The storm brought a nice, steady rain—good for staying in and making progress on the manuscript polishing!

Please darling, no more regrets, please, and no more foolish thoughts about being a "hindrance," and all that. If you really knew how indispensable is "the part you play" your heart would be so full of gladness there would be no room for negative thoughts.

My dear, dear love, darling.
Rachel

Darling—*perhaps* I won't write again till end of week. All right?

TUESDAY A.M., MARCH 8

Darling [Dorothy],

Your Sunday letter is here, and I realize I should mail a note (?) today so that you will have it before you start for Orono.

You know now that my goal has been moved on a week. It seems the other was only in my mind, for Paul swears March 15 has been his date all along. I told you I think, that Friday and much of Saturday had been lost out of consideration for the inflamed eye, but I put in a tremendous day Sunday and got to the Post Office just in time (8 P.M.) with five newly composed pages for the opening of Ch. II. These were going to Marie so she could turn the whole mess over to Mr. Shawn yesterday or today. She is going to Florida on the 25th, for a week, and hopes to have a reaction from him before that. So do I! This is the time, as they say, to keep our fingers crossed.

I am now working on the appendix and really hope to send everything but picture captions to Paul by Saturday or Monday. Poor Bob is still feeling wretched and I imagine his part will fall a little behind.

The morning mail brought a letter with a Boothbay Harbor postmark—Mrs. Burgoon requests a talk for the Monday Club and Garden Club—I was a little uncertain whether they are one or two but at any rate I judge the meeting would be combined. Was this the request you hinted at on the phone? I will put off a decision on this for a while, for I want to discuss it with you and Stan. It has to be cooperative, if at all!

After my Sunday chore was completed, we all went to Virginia's for dessert—a birthday cake and ice cream. Mamma had gone to M's[19] in the afternoon to see "Zoo Parades" cat program and have supper. I had persuaded her I was getting along beautifully and had lots of time to prepare my own dinner. So I thought early in the afternoon but as it happened I had barely time to tuck away a cheese sandwich while putting the mss. in its envelope and snatching my hat and coat. Those frantic rushes to Post Office or mailbox are so much a part of the end of any literary labor for me that I rather enjoy them. I *don't* enjoy the eye trouble, but it, too, is a sign of the approaching End. I remember it was much worse with *Under the Sea-Wind*. So don't worry darling, it will clear up.

But about Sunday—I started to say I wasn't the only one who found the day tough. When I took everybody home from Virginia's, Roger got his cap and coat off, gave a big sigh, and said, "This has been a very hard day." I almost believe he's had enough birthday celebrations for a while.

Oh—he now has his sail—a green and white striped one—installed over his bed-boat, and is simply delighted with it. He already sails here and there to pay imaginary visits to friends. I am so pleased with the quality of his imagination.

Now, darling, when you hear from me again you will be back from Orono and I shall be almost Free! Oh, I do so hope for good weather. Please let me hear as soon as you are home.

All my love—
Rachel

No, I hadn't heard of Mr. Bent's[20] death, but I know he had been very frail for a long time. What you said about his being little known locally was an odd coincidence, for only yesterday I had read this: "The man of significant achievement may be scarcely known in the particular locality in which he lives." It was in a leaflet the "Who's Who" publishers send to their so-called "biographers," to explain what classes of people are included, and why. In Mr. Bent's case, his work is certainly an enduring monument to him.

The moral of the Louise Rich[21] story is (for me) "never write about Silver Spring!" Let's hope Boothbay Harbor (in the person of the Smiling Cow) never gets such an idea! (If it recognizes itself in "The Rocky Shores.")

You know what
R.

[19] Marjie's.

[20] Arthur Cleveland Bent, author of *Life Histories of North American Shore Birds*, first published as pamphlets in 1927 and 1929 and as books in 1962.

[21] Louise Dickinson Rich, author of, among other books, *Innocence Under the Elms* (1955).

Darling [Dorothy],

The Post Office failed us at the wrong moment. Your Wednesday airmail didn't come yesterday, but today, and I left home before mail time and returned only a short while ago. However, perhaps a "special" will be delivered to you Sunday, or Saturday evening. And probably you have inferred the reply from the letter you should have today or tomorrow, in which I told you I had declined the medical association's bid. So far as I know or can imagine, dear, I shan't need any of the slides—mine or Stan's—before summer, if then. So don't hesitate to accept this or any other invitation—and use any of the lower slides if they fit and you want to.

A letter from Paul today brought a wholly satisfactory reaction—the manuscript had duly arrived on the Ides, he had read the new parts, and feels (she reports shamelessly!) that it has passages superior to anything in *The Sea*. On second thought, I guess that isn't shameless at all—after all, he only compared Carson with Carson, not with anyone else! But you know I relaxed a little when I read that, and now perhaps I can overcome my inertia and do the rest of the job! For I'm sorry to say that severe inertia set in the moment the manuscript proper was mailed, but now I think I can handle the rest. Still no word from the *New Yorker*, and I'm getting restive.

Now darling, this must go to the mailbox. Soon I am going to count up the hours. I must tell you that when I read your opening words: "Unforeseen developments." my heart stopped until I went on and discovered that you were NOT telling me you'd have to postpone your visit!

My love, dear, always—as you know.

Rachel

My darling [Dorothy],

Because I have said I'm "busy" and that the week ahead will be "hectic," I'm concerned lest you begin to worry and think it is too soon for you to come. So I want to tell you, dearest, that you couldn't possibly come too soon! I *need* you more than you know or can imagine, I'm sure. The very thought of your not being here next week is intolerable. This is not an easy time, and only you, darling, can bring me the sense of peace that has been lacking for so long. I think that, even if we had never had this lovely plan of your coming, I should have had to ask if you would, for I do need you, darling. You are not to understand from all this that there is any fresh crop of troubles that we need devote precious time to—it is just that the whole situation of which you know gets me down at times and this is one of the times! Of course I'm feeling pretty drained of nervous and physical energy with the worst of the manuscript work behind me. But just escaping from it all *with you* will be heaven, darling, and will be wonderfully restoring. Somehow the letters of the past week or so have brought you especially close—have you felt that, too?

I love you darling—
Rachel

Darling [Dorothy],

I suppose this might be your last letter until—you know what?

First of all, will you thank Stan for his good letter of information about the cameras, and tell him I have decided, since there is so much choice of equipment and so much money involved, I should not rush the purchase but take time to check—perhaps getting more confused in the process, but at least I'll feel I tried to get the right thing. And really, of course, I don't need it just now.

Then about Sunday—as I told you I'm perfectly sure I'll be at the gate or even a bit nearer if I can, though of course I won't know your car so can't actually meet you as you step off. But as an alternative, let's take your suggestion of the Travellers' Aid booth—to sit near it, I mean, because of the possibility of telephoning. I believe that is along the waiting room wall that parallels the station concourse, whereas the information booth I mentioned is sort of out in the middle near one end of the waiting room. And in case you had to call—and if you got no answer here—Marjie's phone is Juniper 5-0028. I don't know what possible series of catastrophes could make all this necessary, however, I shall probably eliminate parking worries by driving only part way, even though it is Sunday, so I shall be alone and Mamma will be here to answer the phone.

The weather this week has been freakish—78 yesterday, dropping to freezing at night, with rain and high winds (tornado warnings in afternoon!). So for that and other reasons I'm glad we chose next week. Other reasons are mainly that if it were this week our time would be half gone already!

Yes, I did suggest Edwin Teale, and am so glad to hear he did the script. He probably doesn't know how it happened, and I probably won't tell him.

Marie says she will phone Mr. Shawn if she has heard nothing by tomorrow, because she is leaving for Florida Friday. However, she may get to stay only for a long week-end (it's her mother's 70th birthday) because of office complications.

Oh—your package came Monday, and it seems very nice to have your things hanging in my closet!

Now I must stop, dear. Our love to Stan and your mother, and kiss Willow for me. I know he'll miss you.

My dearest love,
Rachel

Darling, my dearest [Rachel],

Even the angels in heaven are playing the Hallelujah Chorus! Could they be you and I?

Oh darling, I am so happy for you—and that makes me happy for myself. Isn't it wonderful that the good news came before my visit, to make that momentous event even more happy—if that could be?

You must have sensed that I couldn't express myself adequately last night. What I wanted to do was hold you in my arms to be able to tell you just what your happiness means to me. Can you possibly know?

Your voice came over so clearly that you seemed to be quite near—so near, dear, it made me ache to be with you. And there was a sparkle in it, too, dear.

I suppose you know how wonderful it is for me that you want to and do share such things with me.

Well, darling, with the blessing of the *New Yorker*—you, having "enchanted" it (I love that), surely the publishers won't have to work too hard on promotion, will they? Lucky they to have *you* for an author.

Darling, it is only 5:45 A.M. but I've been awake for a long while. I wonder why. There's to-morrow to get through and then it will be Sunday morning, but there's still 48 hours between.

Somehow I think you are as eager as I am for this next experience for you and me, that eagerness which is beyond expression. This *is* ALL until I see you.

I love you,

D.

My darling [Dorothy],

This will be only a tiny note, with no time to say all that is in my heart, or even try to. I will just ask you to try to know and understand all that I might say.

Some of the subjects we made such a tiny beginning on I hope we can return to next month. Darling, I do want you to feel a part of all that happens about the new book—and that is for *my* sake even more than yours, as I think I can make you understand. It is something I have counted on ever since I began to feel close to you. Anything else would be very, very hard for me to bear. Please try to realize that.

And darling—we did not return yesterday morning to the subject of my paragraphs on the nights on the shore, so I want to repeat here that my decision to eliminate them—which I should probably have done anyway—is a firm one with no regrets involved. We shall really have to take a detached attitude about things like that, darling. If it were two people who were less close there would be no objection to their writing about the same thing (provided, of course, they didn't use each other's words!) but with us it just wouldn't do. About your own piece (sorry—I know you don't like that word. But all editors use it & I have acquired the habit.) darling, work till you are reasonably satisfied (you never will be, completely) and then start it on its rounds. And don't think all is lost when rejections come. They do to everyone. Beyond that word, I'm going to keep out of it, darling, not because I'm not deeply interested, but because I think you prefer it that way. I understand, and am not hurt.

Darling, the few hours we had for ourselves were very sweet and precious and I am thankful that at least we had them.

Now I must go. I hope you will find a letter when you come home, for I don't want you to have to wait till Wednesday.

My dear love, darling,
Rachel

APRIL 4

Oh, my darling [Dorothy],

Do you know all I'd like to say—all that's in my heart? I hope you do, for I want to mail this when I go out, and I'm almost dry.

Everything in the letter was so sweet, and found echoes in my own thoughts and feelings, darling. Those were precious days and have left only the happiest memories. I think we dealt constructively with all the problems, dearest, and I have no regrets or fears about any of them. Even the prospective handling of the writing problem seems to me, in retrospect, most constructive.

Now that I understand one of your worries was the fear of being "imitative" I think the tentative choice of subject for your first attempt is ideal. In subject matter and flavor it's a world apart from anything I have done or could do. Once you have handled that you will have established your own handling of the whole theme and will, I'm sure, lose your fear of subjects that might come close to "our" world. More of this when I'm not so rushed, darling, but I want you to know I'm happy about it, and I think you know now that I *never* had any feeling of not wanting to be close to all your efforts and hopes. So far, our weather since you left has come close to my ideal "Spring in Washington" but now this complication of Robert's illness[22] has arisen. I'm so thankful we didn't choose this week.

[22] Robert Carson, RC's brother, had required gall-bladder surgery.

Darling, I'm ready to go home so I won't write more now.

Yes, I am living over all the memories—so lovely.

I love you—as you know
Rachel

Darling [Dorothy],

Doing the captions could hardly be an easy job and I didn't expect that, but neither was I prepared for it to be such an exhausting one. I'm "all in"! I've struggled for two days and am scarcely more than ⅓ done—if I can pick up a little speed I might finish *Friday*! Good heavens! It's all the fussy little details that wear me out, I suppose, and then it's just not easy to write a good caption. I don't know whether these are good or not; I suspect many are too long. Or maybe I'm worn out from the frustration of wanting to write you and being unable to. Last night and tonight I dashed off incoherent little notes as I was about to go to the Post Office, but they don't count. So for my own satisfaction, dear—I want to write a short letter, at least, before I sleep.

Darling, I thought you were going to write only a note on Easter and then your long, lovely, wonderful letter surprised me this morning. I read it through twice when it came, and then returned to it so happily after my late journey to the Post Office (Silver Spring, not our Woodmoor office, for late mails) when I could come upstairs and get into my robe, and then settle back against the pillows and relax. (That's where I am now—with Jeffie curled up in his basket beside me.)

There is so much I want to say and of course so little time. One of the most important, darling, is how deeply happy I am for you about Stan's new work,[23] and his feelings about it. How wonderful it is turning out this way. I'm so glad, darling, and I'm sure he really will make something big of his opportunity. And I wanted to ask if he would mind your having told me that he is to develop a new field of work for his company—if it's all right I'd like to say something to him in the way of congratulations. Perhaps this is too early—I'll wait till you think it's a good time.

And then, darling, about the dedication[24]—though probably I should write what I want to say in another letter. Well, I can repeat part of it. Dearest, as so often happens, I didn't say clearly what I meant—I gave my words a negative twist when they should have been stated positively. What I should have said was that, in my thinking, what really matters about a dedication is the underlying *reason* as understood between the author and the people concerned that there is (or should be) more than appears on the surface—more than the public will ever know. Unless there is that underlying meaning, there should be no dedication at all—or so I feel. In this instance, of course, it is the depth of meaning—the "rightness" of it—that makes me so happy about it. That was what was uppermost in my mind when I said a dedication was something between the author and the person—or persons—to whom he dedicates a book—I mean the *meaning* darling, not the statement of the identity of the person. I did go on to say that there were all degrees of explicitness (as to identity) from initials to the full name, and I was trying to get your reaction. (Remember, I felt I should have

[23] Stanley had become director of a newly created department within the Chas. M. Fox Company of Boston, a distributor of dairy feeds.

[24] For *The Edge of the Sea*, which reads, "To Dorothy and Stanley Freeman who have gone down with me into the low-tide world and have felt its beauty and its mystery."

your permission to do this at all! So I also wanted to know how completely you wished to be identified.) My dearest, you have been honest about your reactions (bless your dear heart) and I'm being honest in return. Believe me, darling, there is not the slightest shadow of the thought in my mind that I *don't want* the world to know to whom I refer. If there is any leaning on my part toward "Dorothy and Stan" it is simply because that is the way I think of you and so it is more comfortable and intimate. But I am by no means certain I want to be "comfortable and intimate" in print—perhaps in the long run I should be happier with a degree of formality, or perhaps dignity is the word. And darling, I think it is lovely, and really lots of fun, to think of all the people who know you, but don't know that you know me—to think of their discovering it that way. Without the last name they wouldn't be sure. So let's have it that way. Truly, dear. I know I wouldn't regret that—and the other I might regret, too late.

If I've had hesitation about the whole thing, darling, it concerned my doubt that the book is good enough. I thought of waiting for another—but who knows what else will be written, or how that will turn out. So I guess you have to take *The Edge of the Sea!*

Darling—there was nothing unsatisfying about your reaction to my announcement. You were a bit stunned at first—so I knew you had never thought of such a thing, and I was happy it was such a complete surprise. For my part, I'd often wondered *how* I'd tell you—then when the time came I couldn't remember anything I'd planned so I guess I just—told you. I can't even remember how I approached it, now. But I meant then to suggest that I had considered the Problems you mention in your letter—and I think our feelings on that run parallel. And for many reasons, I think the solution I found is a happy one—I am pleased to have it this way. (Shall I dedicate "Remembrance of Earth" to "my Beloved"? Remember, darling, you are the only one who knows the title or the real idea of that book. I haven't talked of it and don't want to.) I liked your story of the TV play and especially the two sentences. They give a positive note to an action that had seemed to me agonizingly destructive and negative. Well—let's talk of it in that light sometime. When you think of it, that *is* a wonderful way to keep something forever yours, secure from "the world."

Darling—time is slipping away. I was tired and sleepy when I began and almost bogged down after a few paragraphs. But now I feel refreshed—I wanted to say these things to you. I'll add a few lines in the morning. Now I shall go to sleep—perhaps I shall hear a veery. Goodnight, darling. I love you.

And now good morning! I think quite possibly I'll call you Friday morning if circumstances here make that a good time—I know it's your "Hazel[25] Day" but after the hint I dropped maybe you'll be looking for a call soon. I love you dearly—

Rachel

[25] DF's house cleaner.

I didn't mean to "spill over" to another page but here I am!

Darling, I got Anne Lindbergh's book[26] but so far have only glanced at it. It's very short and could probably be read in an hour—which I shall do next week. Then I'll be so glad to lend it to you, if you haven't read it meanwhile.

I phoned Mr. Greenbaum[27] and he is rushing through another tax return that will reach me tomorrow. He assures me it will be all right if checked in at Internal Revenue Monday—especially since the Government owes me money!

Darling, your letters are very precious and bring you so close. And you know I love that—and I love you.

Rachel

26 Anne Morrow
   Lindbergh's
   Gift from the Sea
   (1955).

27 RC's tax attorney.

28 To Southport for
   a weekend.

TUESDAY EVENING, APRIL 19

Darling [Dorothy]—

Now there is so little time left for you! But from your note today (two when I came home, dear!) I believe I'll hear your voice Friday morning and that will be wonderful. You will be Going Away,[28] you know, and I'll be lonely without you! So it will help to hear your voice before you go, dearest.

You know I loved, and understood, your little story about Saturday night, darling. Perhaps I could almost match it myself. At any rate, I know the feeling, and the sweetness of it.

About the "gray beginnings" of the dedication, darling—I'm not sure. I really don't know when the idea first occurred to me, except that it was very early—but you know we did get pretty far in those first months. It was certainly before last summer, and probably before May. But it's just one of those things that seemed so natural—so "right"—(the word keeps recurring) that I can scarcely remember when, during the time you've been part of my life, I didn't have this idea. Not very satisfying, perhaps, but I doubt if I can do better.

Darling, I loved every bit of that letter of "thoughts" that you wondered about. Yes, I think you are right about the similarity of background and general way of life. Perhaps that helped, but it's only a small fragment of the explanation, I think. Probably I have in mind various *other* people who have similar backgrounds, but with whom no semblance of this feeling ever developed! But of course you're right, dear, it does ease the way. Suppose you'd been an Aleut and I a Hottentot—I have an imagination, too.

The minutes are running away! I have the feeling of so many things I want to say—to tell you—and that I fill my letters with all the *other* things. But perhaps you, too, read between the lines.

Now I shall take this to the box. I'll try to have something longer in Monday's mail, darling. I love you so.

Rachel

Dearest [Dorothy],

I want to get this in the mail tonight if I can; is it possible that only a week ago tonight I was also rushing to beat the mail collection, failed, and went to the Post Office instead? Probably that is what I'll do tonight, but I have errands.

Springtime in Maine with the first forsythia showing and frogs peeping—and hermits beginning their song—all seem not only far away but off in some distant past, for the contrast here is so great.[29] Thank goodness the heat didn't continue and yesterday and today have been quite delightful, but everything looks more like summer than spring.

There is a great deal of news. The *New Yorker* is using Bob's pictures. Just which ones or how many we don't know, but at least enough to give him a very substantial check, to create a precedent that will set publishing circles to buzzing, and so to be very good for the book. *New Yorker* publication has been set for the first three weeks of August, which Marie feels is an excellent time. Realizing that I shall be very busy with galleys until the end of this month, I have asked her to suggest to Mr. Shawn that he try to work with me the first two weeks of June. So the next six weeks or so look rather crowded! I am going to try to clean up everything I can in the interval before galleys start coming in—empty my correspondence box, for instance!

Now we hope that H.M. will decide to publish in October, since the *New Yorker's* decision gives them a chance to follow rather closely. The manuscript has actually gone to the printer, Paul told Marie, and he has agreed—with a curious show of reluctance—to send galleys to *Reader's Digest* and Book-of-the-Month. I am getting an extra set of galleys to keep, so even if some of the sheets have gone back before the end of the month, I'll hope to have a chance to show you *The Edge of the Sea* in print when I come up for the Conference[30] on the 26th.

Robert isn't going back to work next week after all—the doctor says not for two weeks more. He is getting along all right, but is not to have any undue exertion that soon.

Now I'm beginning to think I won't have any chance to work on the Jail Project[31] until I return to Southport—but you know I'm counting on your being there, too, and shall make you help me! Okay? I must admit I read the lady's letter rather hastily before sending it to you, but I got a bit confused toward the latter half. All I know is that the 13th has been chosen. I meant to suggest that Stan let them know what kind of projector they should get, since obviously they will have to rent one anyway. We might just as well ask for the best—there is no point doing it at all if the slides are not to show to best advantage.

Oh, I think the funny brown seaweed is Scytosiphon: you will find it in Yonge,[32] p. 66, and I also found it in other books. Several of the weeds on your shore have never appeared on mine, at least in summer; it would be nice to know whether it is a seasonal difference or one of location. I'm so glad we had a

[29] RC had gone to Boston for a meeting at Houghton Mifflin. Then, as they had hoped in February, RC and DF had been able to visit Southport from May 3 to May 5.

[30] A sales conference at Houghton Mifflin.

[31] RC had been asked to give a benefit lecture in Wiscasset, Maine, by the Lincoln County Cultural and Historical Association and was planning to use Stanley's seashore slides.

[32] C. M. Yonge, *The Sea Shore* (1949).

low tide at a good time of day for leisurely exploration, for really I've never had a chance to see as much early in the year.

Now I suppose I must go; I haven't done anything about that jacket material and it must be mailed tomorrow.

All my love, dear—
Rachel

Dearest [Dorothy],

Today should have some special mark on the calendar, I suppose, for the first galleys arrived—the first two chapters. I imagine there will be another batch the first of the week. As far as the type is concerned, I think it is easily read and makes a nice looking page—I think it is the same Stan saw on the sample layout pages. I am finding rather a lot I want to do, especially in the second chapter, which has never pleased me very well, but actually I don't think it involves much resetting. Miss Phillips, the copy editor, seems to have used great restraint and so far I don't object to anything she has done or suggested.

If the rest of the proof comes in as rapidly as I think it will, I suppose I'll have most of it read before the conference. If we have time for veeries *and* a bit of reading, shall I save the coral chapter to read with you? I think you read an early version, but it has been largely redone.

Next week looks pretty hectic—several dental engagements and I'm also trying to get in lunch or dinner with at least three people on the list, so with work on the galleys that means a full program.

Thursday night I heard veeries calling in the park, and one tentative spiral of song. I think it is a bit early. Also thought I heard an olive-back, but it always got mixed up with a woodthrush song and I wasn't sure.

You said you went over your dates for the summer, making them more definite. I'll be eager to see the result—I hope any changes mean more time at Southport, rather than less. It is going to take some doing on my part to be ready to go by mid-June, but that's my goal.

Friday, I really did a job on my desk, with the result that practically all of the correspondence is cleaned up, or will be when Mrs. Rivera delivers the typed letters tomorrow. That's a relief, as you can imagine, and I was so glad I got it done before the galleys began coming.

Robert did go back to work last week after all—there was some sort of crisis that made him feel he must—but he seems to be making out fairly well.

Roger went along to listen for veeries—his first bird walk, I guess, and I'd like to have had a movie. He was told we'd have to be quiet, so he tiptoed along the path with elaborate caution, talking in a loud whisper. He seemed to find the whole experience very exciting.

As plans are now, dear, I'll fly to Boston late Tuesday and have that night and Wednesday with you. Thursday is for H.M.—then home that evening. Perhaps I can make a tentative decision about the plane before this letter goes, but remember it might have to be changed. But you know I'll plan for every possible minute with you.

All my love, dear,
Rachel

SATURDAY AFTERNOON, MAY 28

Dearest [Dorothy],

I have just followed your advice and made a list—no doubt incomplete—of things to be done before June 15th. As one result, I have turned to the typewriter to do your letter—I feel the need for speed in all things henceforth!

You will know that I have been thinking a great deal of you and Southport, wondering what you are doing each moment, how Willow stood the trip and how he likes his summer home, about the thrushes and the tides and everything else I'd love to be enjoying with you. Perhaps I'll hear Tuesday or Wednesday.

As you know, it was a quick and pleasant trip home—it's really magical, isn't it—in my own home just a little over three hours after we left Boston airport. I read *New Yorker* proofs, but got diverted from duty by that article on tornadoes in the current *New Yorker*; then we had dinner en route, so the time passed quickly. I had to sit over a wing so couldn't see much, but at ten thousand feet on a cloudy day I suspect there wasn't much to see.

It was such a happy time with you, dear, and so lovely to be able to enjoy the beautiful setting of the garden for some of our reading and talking. And one of the loveliest of my birthday gifts was the intangible one of hearing veeries so beautifully with you! (That wasn't achieved on my actual birthday; we had a picnic supper in the park in veery territory and heard much calling but no song.) And the tangible gift from you and Stan was quite the most impressive one I received. I hope you know how delighted I am with it, and if I needed any reminders, it would bring you to mind all of every summer day, no matter from what quarter the wind blows.

Now there is much activity on the *New Yorker* front, all quite in character—two long phone calls in as many days. One from Mr. Shawn's assistant, the other from Mr. Vanderbilt, the "Profile" editor. It is following such a familiar pattern: in the preliminary stages, especially in indirect dealings, they can seem so exasperating and indifferent to things that matter to others; then when we move on into direct conversations, they are so kind, considerate, and eager to work out difficulties that all earlier annoyances simply dissolve. It has been agreed that I'll mark all changes I want made on these proofs and send them up next week. Then if either they or I feel that we need a personal conference at this stage I'll go up for a day during the week of the 6th. Mr. Vanderbilt feels we can iron out all editorial problems by phone in July. The omission of "Coral" was a concession to space problems, regretted on their part, I take it; but will be a cause of rejoicing by H.M., and I'm really glad, too. (After all, they paid me the full price, says she in mercenary vein!)

And of course I still have to finish H.M. galleys; hope to do both this weekend, but that will take some post-midnight oil.

Tell Stan a phone call yesterday announced my camera has come. I'll probably get it Tuesday.

Tell him also that Miss Burrage's letter of May 1 (I've heard nothing since) said: "There is a permanent 8' × 10' screen in the high school auditorium, and a 16 mm. projector for films, and a film strip projector for slides. I am sure we could rent anything else if these facilities were not what you wanted." I don't know a thing about film strip projectors, but I should doubt one of them would be powerful enough in a gymnasium that will accommodate 1,000 people. And is the screen large enough? My feeling is that we want this presentation to be as "right" as we can make it, and since we are doing it without charge I think we should feel no hesitation to ask them to provide first-class projection equipment. But I wish Stan would take charge of that department. Maybe when he comes in June will be time enough.

There is a letter from "Jean Vann" (Eugenie van de Water) of Station WCSH in Portland, saying she has heard about the lecture from Miss Burrage and wants to know whether "Stan" and I will appear on her program. (I wasn't clear whether she knows you or whether the first name was just the habitual chumminess of such people.) I'm afraid the answer is no, for this half of the team, anyway.

Roger has acquired a little "nawn mower" so he will be prepared to take care of his estate when they move. He had a wonderful time at our "pinkink" last night, especially because there was a "snide" nearby. (He really does better on some words!)

Now I suppose I must conclude and try to get a bit closer to the point of checking something off my list.

My love to all, and very much to you, dear.

Rachel

Mr. Webster seems to be another Mr. Plummer. His labor charge for the planting of 5 laurel bushes was $4!

Darling [Dorothy],

Even this note just for you is going to be typewritten, for after all I know you want me to surmount this mountain of things-to-be-done just as badly as I want to.

When I read your sweet birthday note,[33] dear, I felt that all your hopes had come true, for I had only a sense of happiness and satisfaction and peace about the hours together. And I really believe you did, too, darling. I do understand so much better than I did, and now it doesn't bother me in the least to realize that there is further understanding to be achieved in the years ahead. I do think

[33] This note, possibly one RC received from DF on May 27, RC's birthday, is not preserved.

our clarification of the word has been a great help. I do so hope, my dearest, that in your afterthoughts you didn't return to any feeling of being disturbed or upset because of anything I said to you in explaining my own early reaction. If so, please remember that I didn't then, or ever, want to hurt you; it just seemed better that you understand how it did appear to me. And I needn't say, but shall once more, that there is no longer any vestige of being hurt on my part; everything is, and I think will continue to be, "all right." I am so glad we could have this time now, darling. We had gone a long way to clear up the problem in our letters, but we couldn't go all the way.

It was all so sweet, darling—every bit of every hour. It seems to have made me want you all the more, if that is possible and apparently it is—because I do! Are you living it all over, too?

Darling, I am so glad you read me as much as you did of what you have written. Of course I wanted to hear it all but I am grateful for even that much of a sample. I wish you could understand that the deflation you felt on that earlier re-reading is just one of the less pleasant experiences every writer has—or at least this one definitely does. And such deflation is not a sign that you should reach for the wastebasket! To judge one's own writing is very hard, but one does learn to have some ability to do so. The self-discipline of a writer includes the patience and perseverance to write and rewrite until the result comes at least fairly close to his ideal. I doubt that one should ever feel complete satisfaction and probably no good writer does. I am sure you are, at this stage, expecting your early attempts to come closer to your idea than you should. Go on and get it down, darling. (When you can! I know there are weeks and weeks ahead when you can't.) Then you can revise and rewrite. But truly, darling, in what you read me, I felt the creation of a special world and its atmosphere that is, in essence, what I have long felt you could do. I think your material has character and charm and meaning and I feel confident you CAN do something with it if you will. You will find many thoughts worth treasuring in this Willa Cather preface I mentioned; I'll bring it to Southport.

And that reminds me, darling—I wish you would keep the copy of *Gift from the Sea*. I'll get another. I think it is something one would like to return to from time to time, and for reasons you will understand I'd like to be the one to give it to you.

As usual, I keep thinking of things I want to tell you or say to you, but I'll *try* not to write again until something you'll have the end of the week. That list looks pretty long and difficult.

Darling, I'm very happy and very much at peace. And I love you dearly— I always will.

Rachel

Dearest [Rachel],

The days filled themselves up—I wanted to mail a letter to you yesterday but it didn't get written. Now, I've gotten up before the rest so that I'll have a little written to mail as we go home.

Willow is asleep in my lap. I could fill my letter with him—as I guess I did the Fri. evening one. Well, as long as I'm on him I'll finish. He has responded to the place even more wonderfully than we hoped. Stan took him for a long walk Fri. eve with the leash as it was dark. He didn't mind the leash at all, just walking along, exploring all the places and things he wanted to with no straining or pulling. Then Sat. morning early I took him out again and we "did" the Head, including both coves, the rocks, the Head itself, all the juniper and bayberry and the big oak.

From then on he's been on his own, always returning to the house before we began to get concerned about him. He's made a good impression on the Amblers[34] and as they like cats, I'm sure he'll find a second home up there this summer. Tammy, Aunt Pink's[35] little dog, has been impressed, too. As with the dogs at home Willow has taken the initiative. It was really funny to watch Willow approach Tammy while Tammy stood frozen to the spot—Willow just went close and sat down. Tammy held herself motionless—finally moving away cautiously without moving her head, just one foot at a time.

Then late yesterday Willow walked through our path all the way and back to Deep Cove with us. I wish you could have seen his joy—tearing by us, pounding like a little pony, plume waving, darting into the underbrush, climbing trees, smelling the juniper, playing with a lady's slipper (they are blooming all through the woods now.) I worried that he would get too tired so we tried to carry him occasionally but he would have none of it.

Stan had him on the beach at high tide yesterday and said that he had a wonderful time playing with the edge of the water. Now to-day he has to ride home but I think he won't mind that too much. We think we won't put him in the case.

All the rest of our visit has been such a happy one. Saturday we worked quite hard, especially Stan, but with a satisfying sense of accomplishment at day's end.

Yesterday was our expedition to see Martha which worked out beautifully. The weather had us worried for a while as there was much cloudiness here and wind but as the day wore on it became warm with plenty of sun. The meeting place was a delightful park in Belfast with plenty of green grass, the most beautiful larches I have ever seen amidst other shade trees, the broad lawns sloping down to the sea. The beach itself was pebbly but at least a place for our Martha and her cousin, Iris (who had come to visit with Mad's[36] mother), to explore, to

[34] Longtime Freeman family friends and summer neighbors at Dogfish Head.

[35] DF's aunt Bertha Rock ("Pink").

[36] Martha's mother, Madeleine.

find shells and seaweed; to throw skimmers into the gentle waves, and of course, to get feet wet.

I guess grandma tried too hard to educate Martha. I took some shells from here for her & we talked about them when she found the seaweed. I told her it was knotted wrack. She wanted to take it home to show mommy. Later when I asked her what she was going to tell mommy it was she said, "knotted shells." Poor darling!

Before lunch the girls had a wonderful time in the swings. Grandma took Martha a new seersucker dress which she wore home to show mommy.

Of course, it was all fun for Martha so she was very happy. She is really awfully cute looking now, not beautiful, but bright looking with a small face with big brown eyes and an adorable little smile. She sang songs to herself—as she swung. However, she is at the stage where she'll do what she wants to herself but if you ask her to sing "Old King Cole" she says "I don't want to." Stanley says she says the whole of "The Night Before Christmas" but only at her own instigation. She was very affectionate with us and called us by name. She calls her father "Stan" or "Daddy Stan."

I cooked lobsters Sat. & opened. Instead of making sandwiches, I took all the ingredients for salad, sandwiches, etc., and made them as we ate. It was fun.

Had a chance to talk with Stanley about house, school, plans, etc. Everything seems to be nicely under control & if the baby arrives before summer school (July 5) he thinks he can manage very well while Mad is in hospital— good neighbors, and a girl they have been having to take care of Martha, whom Martha loves and who loves Martha.

All in all it was a most satisfactory day. Spring is just now here. I never saw apple trees more lovely—such profusion of bloom—everywhere in this area. Every tree is completely covered with pink glory. The lilacs are at their best, too. And along the road back of Lannings' is more rhodra than was there last year. I was afraid when they cut the roadside last year they might have destroyed it.

But by far the high point of this visit, dear, is the discovery of veeries, singing in the woods between Huskins' and Sheridans'. How I wish you might be here to hear them with me. It is laughable that last year you were calling people in New York, the Bestons, the Audubon Society to find out about veeries in Maine! And here they are. Oh, I do hope they'll still be singing when you arrive. If not, you'll just have to plan to be up here for a few days, at least, at this time next year.

We did a bit of tide-pooling Sat. & Stan tried for a few pictures but all pure experiment.

Last night we went up to hear the veeries again. This time we went deep enough into the woods to be close to them and to discover what I wondered about—whether there was water about. It is a bit swampy there—probably in a normal season (this one is very dry here) there would really be water.

The hermits & white throats were singing, too. We drove over to your place to listen for bird songs there, but nothing very close. Your beach seemed to have more sand than we remembered so we went down the steps to explore. We think there definitely is a lot more and of a finer character. But the fascinating part was the quantities of empty periwinkle shells—not scattered all over the beach—but lying in windrows—as though marking the edge of waves. Such quantities!

Well, darling, this is only some of it. The sea has been so glorious—full of motion—high winds most of the time making much white water, splashing over our rocks. Last evening there was a fascinating disturbance I wish you might have watched with us—in the west, heavy thunderheads piled up. Suddenly, in front of them a huge swift moving black cloud, extending the length of the Bay as far as we could see. It moved so rapidly that in ten minutes it had disappeared in the Boothbay direction, but while it passed a hurricane wind, black water, white caps, white rocks—& lightning flashes behind it. Do you wonder I am weather conscious? Now it's time to clean house for the bride and groom who come next week-end.

Dear love to all,

Dorothy

Oh, my Darling [Rachel],

How can I find the right words to give you this—my perfect birthday gift to you.[37] In the field of the intangibles, darling, I can think of nothing else I could offer you that might bring you more delight. Do you know what I'm going to tell you? To-night, my Beloved, I heard veeries singing on Southport—in West Southport—on the Dogfish Head road—but best of all—and can you believe this?—at the juncture of the road where we turn to go sharply around the corner to the Dream House.[38] As I said at the beginning "Oh, my Darling."

It was like this. As we were coming home from Boothbay about eight o'clock I said we must listen for thrushes. As we turned to the left near the Pink Houses Stan slowed down & after we passed Huskins' house I was startled to hear what seemed to be the veeries' call. Stan stopped. And it was repeated. And then, darling, before I could hardly believe it the little magical bells (at least that's as I think of them) began to tinkle. Not once, but on and on—all through that area to the right between Huskins' and Sheridans'.

At last, the perfect setting—no drone of traffic—only the wind in the trees.

Can you imagine how I felt, darling. The end of our quest within a quarter of a mile of the Dream House? You must know the warm glow that spread over me, but you must also know the dull ache, too, because you aren't here to share it.

Oh, how I pray they'll stay until you come.

I just can't tell you how I felt. Then, later, as always in the usual places

[37] DF began this private letter on May 27, RC's birthday, completed it the following Monday, May 30, and enclosed it with the preceding letter.

[38] A term for RC's cottage.

from Deep Cove down, Hermits and White Throats filling the evening with lovely sounds. And again I heard the "Wee" that I had begun to think I had mistaken for the Chewink. But now I'm convinced it was the Hermit.

MONDAY, 7 A.M.

Oh, darling,

I've been away from you so long! And yet every minute I've been conscious of you—how I've wanted you to share it all.

How sweet to find your clothes mixed in with mine, dear—that brought you near. I've wanted you so when I looked at the moon, when the tide was high; when the water made wild sounds in the night; when we went tide-pooling; when the anemones were exposed for a few seconds as the water rushed away from the cave; but most of all, darling, when I went back to the veeries—

Saturday alone, and I went into the woods a bit and lay down on the moss near a blooming apple tree, so filled with flowers that the air was drenched with fragrance. The wind was high that evening so there was a strong rote mingled with the veeries' songs.

Darling, can you at all imagine my emotions? Oh, my dear, every sound, every twig, every lovely odor, every soft bit of moss, every bit of beauty, darling, means you are here.

There was a crowd on the porch yesterday at high tide—children, grownups—laughter and I was so lonely in the midst of it.

Do you know why? Darling, I am so happy that before I came back to the "Versaille" room,[39] I could remember the laughter we shared in it. The unhappiness has been dispelled—it never came into my mind until this moment, honestly, dear. Isn't that wonderful that as I've been walking around here with you I've thought only happy thoughts? I hope you, too, are happy.

Thank heavens for those hours in West Bridgewater.[40]

This has been written in installments this morning. Now it is time to go.

We are leaving around 10 o'clock on a foggy, drizzly day so the parting isn't as hard as it might be.

Darling, my hope is that when next I'm here you, too, will be here. Then my happiness will be complete.

I love you so—you know, don't you?

Bye, dearest,
Dorothy

WEDNESDAY, JUNE 1

Dearest [Dorothy],

It was so good to hear your voices last night and to know you were safely home—you know I couldn't help worrying about that holiday driving. And then to have more details by mail this morning. Of course the discovery of veeries just where they should be—at the turn of the road from your house to

[39] DF may be referring to her garden in West Bridgewater or perhaps to a place in the woods.

[40] RC had visited the Freemans on May 24 and 25 prior to attending a sales conference at Houghton Mifflin on May 26.

mine—is so wonderful and so right in every way that it is the thing I must mention first. I feel sure they will be singing for many weeks to come. I know I have heard them at Woods Hole late in July. But who would ever have dreamed of finding them so close? I had thought of the swampy interior of Southport, or of the ponds on the way to Boothbay. But you know that area between Sheridans' and Deep Cove, on Sheridans' side, was very wet and full of frogs when we were there a month ago, and probably there is much wet land all around. Now I can't wait to hear them with you.

It is perfectly wonderful about Willow. I never supposed he would become so perfectly adjusted to new surroundings in so short a time. What a lovely summer he will have!

And it was good, too, that your week-end could be made perfect by having a picnic with Martha. "Knotted wrack" indeed! I think her compromise of "knotted shells" was very good. Last year Roger was just reaching the "pinky-winkie" stage.

This morning I had a reassuring chat with Mr. Vanderbilt—after seeing the marked-up proofs he assures me he thinks we can handle all difficulties by mail and phone. We were mutually complimentary about the other's patience and understanding so apparently all will go smoothly, and thank heaven I won't have to take time for New York. I have the Coral Chapter ready to mail to H.M. this afternoon, and will dispose of the first two chapters tomorrow, I hope. I need to, because Friday my eyes will be taking a holiday.

Of course I wish I could see your garden now, but having seen it last week I can visualize the lovely new developments.

I'll send Stan one of the Exakta books in a day or so. I have several of the regular Kodachrome films and two of the new Ektachrome. My question last night was where we could have the latter processed in a hurry, but I assume there would be a color lab in Portland. The old Kodachrome goes to Eastman as before, I understand.

Now I must hurry, dear. Do you know why? I have a real incentive to put checks on that list.

All my love
Rachel

I am sending the tornado piece from the *New Yorker* under separate cover. Don't return—it's yours. The Wilderness Society is sending you a replacement of the magazine, which they say they sent some time ago. If you get both, just pass on the extra one.

Darling [Dorothy],

Knowing you as I do now, I can guess that you are reading this very early in the morning, or maybe even in a wakeful interval in the night. Whenever it is, you know I wish I were there to tell you, on this day of yours,[41] how much I love you. I think you know, but I like to tell you and I think you like to hear it!

In a little while, dear, I shall be talking to you—then in only a little interval I shall see you! That overshadows all other reasons, happy as they are, for longing to get to Southport. In looking ahead to this summer, I think in a way, it should be even happier than last. There was a certain tentativeness then—we wondered how and how often we could be together, we resented the world's intrusions, we were struggling to establish a pattern. Now I feel much more settled and secure about it. Do you, dear? I know it will be a summer marked by interruptions and outside demands on both of us, but we know that and I think are prepared for it. But oh, I know there will be many beautiful and happy hours, dearest, sharing the loveliness of that spot, enjoying its beauty with you as I could with no one else. Darling, isn't that one of the wonderful things we have found in each other? Somehow the sharing of beautiful and lovely things is so much more satisfying with *you* than it has ever been for me with anyone else. My life has been so much richer for having you, dearest. And can it be that two years ago I'd never seen you?

I shall love going over some of those early letters with you, darling, and I agree they should be kept—the record of the unfolding of a lovely flower.

Darling, I wish I could be with you on your birthday, but at least the day will be filled with preparations to speed to you. May the year ahead be filled with deep happiness for you: with moonlight on the shore and the distant sound of rote, bunchberries in the spruce woods, sun shining through drifts of apple blossoms, the song of veeries at twilight and hermits at dawn; with laughter over breakfast coffee and sherry by the fire; explorations of fairy pools; freesias and white hyacinths—oh, you know the list—all this and more. And darling, may the year deepen the growing understanding between us—and may I, who love you so dearly, bring you only happiness.

Goodbye for now, darling, for only a few hours and days.

I love you
Rachel

[41] DF's birthday was June 15.

Darling [Dorothy],

The note that went to you today contained nothing just for you, and I was sorry. I meant to write that this morning but was somehow very weary (largely, I guess because I'd just gotten "the curse") so stayed abed until almost noon. Then, on the way to town, I found your dear letter at the Post Office. Now I'm in the funny little beauty shop where I believe you used to go (once I met you across the street from it. Remember?). I didn't want to wait for Mrs. Hanson's Saturday date—partly because I'm cherishing a hope you may be here!

As you know, dear, all the loveliness of Southport is so bound up with thoughts of you and memories of all we have shared that now everything I see or hear makes me long all the more to have you with me. Once again after you left the hermit thrush was giving his "wee" call—but until Sunday morning I had never before heard it near the house. And the olive backs are still singing, though less often, I think. Another week or two will probably still all the thrush voices.

I think, darling, that I have not yet really learned all of Mrs. Lindbergh's wisdom—that is, in the sense of gladly accepting growth and change in things that are dear to me. For I do find myself longing for the fresh, lovely, less complicated relation we once knew. That, I suppose, is immaturity. But I do. Must there really be what you call "worldliness" tinging our attitude toward each other, darling? I wonder. Somehow, for me, part of the wonder of it all, was the special, untouchable quality of everything relating to my thoughts and feelings for you—an immunity to the worldly corrosion that now and then invaded all other human relationships. But perhaps that is just illusion. Don't let this sadden you, darling—they are just random reflections. Nothing in the recent past or ever—has lessened that need for you or the wanting you that I have so often expressed. And I am sure I have selfishly thought too much of my need, and too little of yours, taking more than I gave.

And darling, lest you doubt it now, Friday afternoon did make me very, very happy and restored the peace of mind that had been lacking all week. You will know what I mean, I'm sure, when I say it was easier to see you go after the sweetness of those hours, and the understanding we reached then. Do you feel that, too?

Dearest, I am going to keep everything uncommitted from Friday night on, hoping so much Stan may decide to come. If you do, you are still going to stay on a few days, aren't you? (I do so hope Stan may decide to get an Exakta, for a really fine instrument will get results another can't, and he has such skill and such a fine sense of composition he deserves it.) Now, my darling, I'm dry and must close. More soon!

You know I love you dearly.

Rachel

WEDNESDAY, SEPTEMBER 21

UNDER DRIER

Dearest [Dorothy],

By now you are home, I hope. This is just a tiny note to say—guess what? *I miss you!* It would have been a lovely day to watch surf somewhere together for it has been blowing hard all day, though here in town one doesn't notice it. I hope it wasn't bad on the road, for I think it is tiring to fight a wind for hours of driving. Mr. Plummer came early this afternoon and we looked over the new lot and also planned for the new rock retaining wall and so on. So that will be done before you come back, I think.

While he was there, the *Esso Rochester* went up the bay, moving fast and without its tug. The season's last tanker, for us, I suppose.

Willow did look so sweet coming up to the car with you, and we had a final glimpse of him just before we turned off the Dogfish Head road, riding along on the back of the seat. I'll be so eager to hear his reaction to home. I'm sure he would remember.

I hope it warms up a little for the Bestons' visit but I believe the forecast isn't encouraging. I did most of the marketing for tomorrow before coming in here, for it will be 5:30 or so when I escape.

This must be all for now, dear. I'll write a longer letter soon, and will send Stan the correspondence with the man about the trace elements in soil, etc.

It was wonderful to have these recent days in the woods and doing things together.

All love,
Rachel

MONDAY, SEPTEMBER 26

Dearest [Dorothy],

This is another shining autumn day, and I wish you were here to enjoy it with me. Yesterday began the same way, then clouded over and was very windy, but I spent some time outdoors in the afternoon nevertheless, doing some trimming and transplanting of wild things. Then again we had a night of exquisite moonlight. I am so sorry that the full moon will have come and gone before you return! Can you tell me why in the world some of the blueberry is in flower at this time? Is that usual? And of course the foliage of much of it, and the huckleberry, is scarlet now, and today I want to photograph a spot on that rocky slope above the drive, where the bright red blueberry is pushing through the carpet of grey lichen. Dear, I don't think the foliage will have dimmed when you come. Of course last year was spoiled by the hurricanes, but the year before, I remember, the colors flared up brighter than ever in those last days we were here. It made me so glad we had stayed, instead of leaving the end of September as we once planned!

I seem to be taking your advice—at least, I sleep later and later in the morning, so that any time from 9:30 to 10 is now a normal rising time. Of course I waken earlier, but just turn over and go to sleep again. And in spite of the accumulation of letters in the study, I'm not doing much about them, or about that magazine piece. But perhaps I shall be fresher for it later on if I just enjoy my surroundings now.

The books have not come and I have not had confirmation of the publication date—perhaps there will be some word today. Bob, too, received a proof sheet, and is bubbling over with happiness about the whole thing. By the way—in giving you his address, I think I made a mistake in the apartment number. It is #575, Colonial Village, 1913 Key Blvd., Arlington. He is going to design the bookplate, and perhaps will have some sketches here today or tomorrow.

I think Mrs. Bennett[42] is coming today for a cup of tea and to bring the cedars, which I could not ward off, though I made a feeble effort to. Oh well, they can be chewed up by deer, or something of the sort, if I don't like them.

I am sure you were all distressed, as we were, by the news of Mr. Eisenhower's illness. I imagine that settles the question of a second term—but who can come along on either side to replace him?

Now I must go to the Post Office, dear, so this will be all for now. I suppose Willow is securely in possession of his estate once more, and keeping the neighborhood dogs in check. Do let us know about him, and how you all are.

Very much love,
Rachel

SATURDAY, OCTOBER 1

GUESS WHERE?

Dearest [Dorothy],

It was so good to talk last night. And fun to have the reason I did for calling you! If I'd had the planning of it myself, I don't think I could have done much better. You know we've thought all along it would be wonderful if we could be together at publication time. And now we can. Paul's party[43] may turn out to be fairly large, I don't know, but at any rate the tone will be friendly and informal and I know that among the people there you and Stan will find a number you will enjoy. His idea is less to have people because of who they are than because they are friends of theirs or mine who will be happy about the book. In other words, a real celebration. (In still other words, to say "Thank God, she did finish it at last!")

I think, dear, that because it is such a habit and also because we have much to discuss, I should stay with Marie that night. But if Stan doesn't absolutely have to leave at crack-of-dawn, I am now inviting myself to join you at your hotel for breakfast on the 26th. With luck, the *Times* and *Tribune* will carry the first reviews that morning. So we *can* share The Day to that extent, at least, and I hope that makes you as happy as it does me. The other affair, as I told you, is still pretty indefinite as to what and when. I've asked Paul to tell me the second possible date. While H.M. will no doubt keep me pretty firmly in their clutches for

[42] Christine Bennett, neighbor of the Freemans at Dogfish Head.

[43] Paul Brooks's party in New York for the October 26 publication of *The Edge of the Sea*.

that visit, I can have at least a tiny bit of time with you! Your letter came this noon. I'll write you more over the week-end. I think Stan is a dear to be willing to go to N.Y. for I know it's a busy time.

All my love,

R.

OCTOBER 26[44]

For the Author of The Edge of the Sea

Dearest Rachel,

This little Shell[45] is to be for you, a symbol of all that you have given us from the sea. We thought we knew the sea, but through you we discovered how slight was our knowledge. It was you who really unlocked its "beauty and mystery" for us. For all that we are everlastingly grateful, as you well know.

But now we have an added debt to you.

For the great honor you have done us in the dedication of your unusual and, for us, most meaningful book, *The Edge of the Sea*, we want you to know we are not only proud but deeply humble. Our thanks to you is beyond expression and comes from the depths of our hearts.

May we always be worthy of this tribute to our friendship.

With enduring affection,

Dorothy and Stanley

Beloved [Rachel],

What can I say on this day when I am so proud and so humble? My heart is full of so much that you know. I told you I wished I might have a gift for you for to-day that was just for Us! You said that my gift to you is the intangibles. And so, darling, it will be that way.

In your precious letter written after I left you (I found this in *The Open Heart*[46] about a collection of letters: "They reflect the affectionate, high-spirited, often passionate individualism of men and women *reaching across the silence of space for the sympathy of that other heart.*" (I love that last phrase.) You said "I wish I could tell you in some way all that you meant to me, and the sense of peace, I feel when I am with you." Darling, if I could give no other gift, you have told me the one I would most wish to give you. And because I want you to remember it now because it belongs with that idea, I'm going to quote again the little poem that seemed made for us as long ago as the first time you came here for an over-night visit. Do you remember? Its title is

Peace[47]

Peace flows into me
As the tide to the pool by the shore;

It is mine forevermore,
It will not ebb like the sea.

[44] This letter from DF and Stanley and the following one from DF had been written to mark the October 26, 1955, publication date of *The Edge of the Sea*.

[45] A diamond pin in the shape of a seashell.

[46] By Edward Weeks, published in 1955.

[47] By Sara Teasdale.

I am the pool of blue
That worships the vivid sky;
My hopes were heaven-high,
They are all fulfilled in you.

I am the pool of gold
When sunset burns and dies—
You are my deepening skies;
Give me your stars to hold.

Darling, I think that says everything, for I know you can read into it all that I do. Dearest, for all the moments that I have destroyed that Peace you find with me, I beg your forgiveness. And I know, because you understand me, I have it.

The list of other intangibles I would give you is long—happiness and health and laughter and beauty and music and friendships and now success for *The Edge of the Sea*.

For it, and for its dedication and for the experiences I have shared with you in your toil over it, for its poetry and for all that it evokes in me I give you my deepest gratitude. Darling, you never had a book dedicated to you (and such a book!) did you? So you can't quite know all that it means to me to see my name on the page of an important piece of writing—To Dorothy—with all that I know it means.

Last night I read in *The Open Heart* what Mr. Weeks had to say about a particular dedication of a book, which made me realize vividly how much meaning is read into a dedication by people like him, who know authors well.

And I know you must have been fully conscious of that when you made your decision. That, darling, is why I am so proud and so humble—that you were willing for the whole world to know. Can you understand how I feel?

Beloved, may *The Edge of the Sea* bring you joy as deep and enduring as the very sea itself—allways![48]

Oh, my darling, I love you,
Dorothy

OCTOBER 25

EN ROUTE TO NEW YORK

My darling [Dorothy],

Now I have read the letter[49] that only you could have written. I waited until we could be alone together on the train, and it has been sweet to have you traveling with me. I had wanted to write you a little message for tomorrow, also, to hand to you at the party tonight, and although writing on a speeding train is not what I would have chosen, I think I'm glad I have waited until I had read your precious note. Darling, if one can assume anything so unthinkable as to suppose I did not know why I had dedicated the book to you, your letter would make it all clear. It is because there is no one else like you in my life—now or

[48] After RC's misspelling of "always" in a summer 1954 letter, DF and RC came to use "allways" or "all ways" for its added dimensions of meaning.

[49] RC had received the preceding note from DF in time to read it during her trip to New York City on the day prior to the publication of *The Edge of the Sea*.

ever. As only you could, you summed up in the pages of your note all the sweetness and joy and deep happiness of the past two years and made me feel it all again in its fresh and delicate beauty. The one thing I wish today above all else is that as the years pass we may never come to take for granted this beautiful sympathy and understanding that exist between us, but may always feel their shining wonder as we do today.

For me—and I think for you too—it is set apart from all other experience. No one but you, darling, has ever expressed such lovely thoughts so beautifully as you have in your letters and in some of the precious moments we have had together in the woods or by the shore or under the night sky. And who but you would care so deeply as to wish to know what I am doing each hour of every day? When I read that in a recent letter—though it is not a new thought between us—it somehow touched me very deeply and made me wonder if I could ever express to you the warmth and joy that come with knowing you do care that much. And I am sure you must know there is a returning flood of love as deep and lasting.

If I could have been granted only one wish for the day of publication of *The Edge of the Sea* it would be to have you share it with me. And now the wish is being granted. All I would change would be to have more of the day with you, but whatever there is will be precious.

Darling, I have told you that the dedication has been planned for many months—certainly for well over a year. Since it first entered my mind I have considered no other. There could be no other that would be a true expression of my feelings. I am glad that it makes you happy, dearest. But for me, too, there is deep happiness that I have been given friends so dear and precious to me that I could feel as I do about the dedication—so completely satisfied with its rightness.

Now, darling, I must close. In a few hours I am to see you. I hope and believe it will be a happy party. I know our little private celebration tomorrow will be happy.

Goodnight, dearest, I shall be thinking of you as you read this. You know I love you deeply and tenderly—and all ways!

Rachel

OCTOBER 27, AFTER LUNCH, 12:50 DST

Darling [Dorothy],

For some reason my train didn't leave until 10:45—though scheduled for 10:30—and meanwhile I had plenty of leisure to reserve a chair, have a cup of coffee in the station restaurant, and buy a book (*The House on Nauset Marsh*).[50] Once on the train I skimmed through the *Saturday Review* and *New Yorker* (such depressing stuff! They should have more Carson—and how about a Freeman for a change?) read some of the Crile book,[51] and took the *Nauset Marsh* to the diner where I had an all-but-inedible lunch. Now here we are! If you are on time

[50] By Wyman Richardson, published in 1955.

[51] *Cancer and Common Sense* (1955) by George Crile, Jr.

I suppose you will reach Boston about two, with several hours to spend before you can join Stan, but perhaps you will spend those more happily there than alone in New York.

And now, darling, October 26th has come and gone and has become one of our memories. That is the especially happy part for me, that it is in *your* memory as well as mine. And that all but about 4 hours of the day itself were spent with you. And one of the sweetest touches, dear, was that I heard the very first review from your lips. How long ago you said to me: "If only we could be together when the first reviews are published," and we were. When I went into the Doubleday Book Shop in Penn Station and asked for the Richardson book, the clerk led me to a table, took the book from a shelf and laid it down right beside a pile of—guess what? Then I asked to see Sinnott's *Biology of the Spirit*; it was produced and laid on the other side of *The Edge of the Sea*! (No—I did *not* tell him!) About *The House on Nauset Marsh*, my first impressions are disappointing. If you ever want to read it you can have mine but I doubt it is really something you'd want to own.

Darling, don't dwell too much on what I said about my reaction to having returned to Silver Spring. Of course the whole situation there is not exactly a happy or favorable one, but I'll get adjusted to it again. So don't be disturbed, dear one. I think probably the best I can do is to make what improvement I can in the present surroundings rather than try to make a radical change this winter. But I can think of that for the future.

Wasn't it lovely that we gained that hour this morning by your misreading the clock? How short our morning would have been if you hadn't! The time together was so sweet, darling—every minute of it.

Now we are about 20 minutes out of Washington. I imagine the day there will be mild if not actually warm—the sky is so clear and bright. I wonder what Mister Jeffie will do when he hears me come in—the dear little black thing. You, I suppose, will have your nose well "sharpened" tonight.

Darling, it is wonderful to know I'm to see you again so soon. I'll let you know about the plane soon.

Do tell Stan again that I think he was a dear to take the time to come. Love to all—and a very special share for you.

Rachel

SATURDAY AFTERNOON, OCTOBER 29

AT HAIRDRESSER'S

Darling [Dorothy],

Now I can begin my week-end letter to you. My hair has "gone by" very rapidly and I decided I might as well come down today, and so make the timing with next week's appointment about right. Miss Woods isn't ready for me, so I have a little extra time with you, besides that under the drier.

Your precious train letters came yesterday, as I thought they might and were far more satisfying than mine, I'm afraid, would be to you. I was more weary and tense than I realized and could not seem to settle my mind on any-thing—reading or writing. And now I know you know why! The wonderful thing for me, darling, is to have you understand so completely. This sharing, not only of events, but of what is in my own thoughts and feelings, is exactly what I have longed for almost from the time you walked into my life. (I am speaking now especially of all that relates to *The Edge of the Sea*.) But such understanding is a rare flower, difficult of cultivation, and I didn't know whether we could pro-duce it. Now I feel that we have, and I am deeply happy. I, too, think it helped very much to have you actually present at the party, and with me on The Day, able to note and interpret all the little signs I didn't realize I was giving you. But don't fear, darling, that I will consciously withhold what I am feeling, for the thing that makes me especially happy is to have someone with whom I *can* share those inmost thoughts.

My present state of tension is something quite different from the previous experiences, and I suppose only a writer who has achieved what the world calls a great success with an earlier book can have quite these feelings. The odd thing about *The Sea* was that, in writing it, I expected very little. I was just grateful I had a publisher for a book written as I wanted to write it. Even after various signs pointed to something a bit out of the ordinary, I was still completely un-prepared for each development—each review, each sales report, each Sunday's "List" was so far beyond expectation that I think I was always quite relaxed, just happily accepting what came. Now, to borrow something Virginia Woolf said about Joyce, I have myself made it impossible that anything of the sort can hap-pen to me again. I know that, even if this book achieves acceptance, acclaim, and sales that by any reasonable standards amount to "success"—still, by com-parison with *The Sea*, it will fail. What I want for *The Edge of the Sea* is for it to be judged on its own merits, but that is most unlikely to happen. So of course I am tense, waiting for each review, each "straw-in-the-wind."

However, you will know from what I'll write in a sharing letter that for the most part the early reviews have lowered my blood pressure considerably. I was particularly happy with Lewis Gannett's, who was able to see the forest despite the multitude of trees; with Paul Flowers, who placed it, not *under The Sea* but side by side with it as one of a trilogy; and with Virginia Kirkus, whose chief em-phasis is on the quality of the writing. I am making many little notes of things to tell you when I am with you—Stan will like to hear them, too.

LATER—MIDNIGHT, IN FACT, AND ABED

I know I am going to be much tempted to call you tomorrow; by the time you receive this you will know whether I yielded to temptation. For one thing, darling, I am so concerned to know that you are all right—that you didn't catch my cold.

Even before your letter came, I was planning to try to tell you how wonderful it is for me to feel now that we really can share all that will happen. There have been times when, looking ahead, I have been afraid that the sharing I had so longed for was an unattainable dream—that once more there would be a barrier erected. Now I know that hasn't happened and I am so relieved and happy.

I will call the airlines tomorrow and, subject to schedules, see no reason why I can't arrive in Boston[52] early Monday afternoon. So we could have about 24 hours together, darling. But oh, how short that is—gone almost as soon as it begins. November 8 until—when? We must try to contrive some little oasis before Christmas.

I want to mail this tomorrow morning when I go out for papers—I want to pick up the *Baltimore Sun* and *Washington Star* to see if they have reviews. So now I must close. Unpacking and putting away is a weary business and I am tired. Goodnight my dearest. How sweet it was to be with you in New York.

I love you.

Rachel

There is much more I want to say, but for the sake of early mailing think I'll take this along. Yes I do.

R.

TUESDAY AFTERNOON, NOVEMBER 1

Dearest [Dorothy],

This morning Paul sent me a few clippings and I am sending on two of them, though I've already quoted from each to you. The Kirkus one has apparently been mimeographed from her "Bulletin" to booksellers. I know you will like to read Gannett in its entirety. Just hold them until I come.

There was also a phone call from Paul—something called Books Abridged wants to do it in their February volume. Little money involved, but H.M. thinks it good promotion. Best of all, Paul said Julian McKee reports from New York that the book "couldn't be going better." And while it is much too early for any great number of re-orders, Paul said some store, (I forgot where) that the trade regards as a good weathervane, has just sent in a re-order for 500 copies. He also said that instead of being interviewed by the Museum Librarian for their own program, which is carried by a "tiny station, and Brad Washburn[53] was worried about it"—I am to be interviewed by Marjorie Mills. You remember she wrote up the jail! However, we'll still just do a tape recording at the Museum, before the reception.

Did I tell you the N.B.C. "Monitor" program has scheduled a review for Nov. 13, and I am to talk about the book myself for two minutes, this to be done here day after tomorrow by tape recording in a local studio. I must get my remarks down on paper this very day!

Here is something I especially wanted to tell you and Stan. Perhaps you

[52] For a Boston Museum of Science reception honoring RC.

[53] Henry Bradford Washburn, Jr., Director, Boston Museum of Science.

have heard me speak of Else Ström, a Swedish newspaper-woman here, who has family connections with Tiden, my Swedish publisher. In fact, it was through Else that *The Sea* (and later *Sea-Wind*) went to Tiden. I lunch with her now and then, or occasionally go to dinner. She shares a house in Arlington with a woman who is in the photographic section of the State Department. Both attended my Audubon lecture, and were enthusiastic about the pictures. And of course Else has heard me speak of you otherwise. Well, I had a long telephone visit with her yesterday—first we've been in touch since spring. After saying many nice things about the book and its hoped-for success, she said, in her very Swedish accent: "There is no one in the world who deserves good luck more than you, or for whom I wish it more, but I keep thinking what wonderful luck you had to find the Freemans in Maine!" I had not told her about the dedication, she had found it for herself and was delighted by its "rightness."

Now a note in different vein: Marie's associate, Elsie McKeogh, died Saturday. I haven't heard directly from Marie, but it was in Sunday's *Times*. Under the circumstances, it is possible to feel only relief, for her and for Marie. But the weeks ahead will be sad and difficult ones for Marie. I do hope she can find someone to take on part of the work.

Last night (Halloween) Marjie had dinner with her friends, the Brockmans, and in the evening she and Sallie dressed up Roger and the little Brockman boys, about 2 and 4, and took them out a little in the neighborhood. M. said Roger would peer into his paper bag after each donation and shout, "We got marshmallows"—or whatever it was, or if he couldn't recognize it he'd say, "We got something inersten' to me."

Thanks for the report on Boston book stores. Brentano's here had no window display last week, but a good pile of books just inside. I am most interested in the lack of *The Sea* at Lauriat's. It fits in with a remark made to me last night by the manager of the Airport Bookshop (he wanted me to appear at some Book Fair). He said he didn't think Oxford had been on the job—that in his experience each new book by any author revives sales of earlier books. I was going to see if Marie wanted to speak to Oxford, but now I know she must be so busy I want to keep my affairs in the background.

Oh, I hope your flowers haven't all "gone by" when I come. After all, it's only a few more days. And I'm so anxious to see Willow.

Now this must be all for now, dearest. I'll send a note by the end of the week. And will see you Monday[54]—how sweet.

> Our love to all
> and you know what
> *Rachel*

[54] RC stayed with the Freemans on November 7 and attended the Museum of Science reception with them on November 8.

Darling [Dorothy],

Your wonderful, long letter is here, as I hoped it might be, and I have devoured every word twice,—but from the beginning, not starting on page 3 as you suggested!

I wish I hadn't sent that little note yesterday, for now I suppose you will worry. I am much better today, dear—up and dressed and have even been out in the yard for it is a beautiful, sunny day. The throat is better, the "tight" feeling gone from my chest, and a day in bed did much to erase the weariness. But I shall continue to take the capsules as precaution for "they" say the bug prevalent here has a way of returning to bite its victims again.

Darling—*did* I ask for a letter every day? I didn't mean to, although of course I'd love it. But I know we shouldn't make that our routine, for many reasons. *So*, I'll send something Thursday, to reach you Saturday, and that will be all from me this week! And a week from now our hours together will be running out—oh dear. But I will try to come to you in December, darling, and perhaps you will come here in January.

Your letter today was so sweet, dear, I loved all of it. And I am so very happy to feel that we *are* sharing these experiences just in the way I had hoped we might. You know, I'm sure, that what I feared was that in some way—through seeing me publicly cast in the role of "famous author"—that horrid barrier might rise again, and then, in trying to tear it down, I'd have to withhold things instead of just pouring them all out with no restraint. Now, darling, I know that the barrier is forever destroyed, and I hope you know how happy that makes me.

But darling, in my earlier efforts to protect you from a great let-down if the book didn't do well, I see that I overdid it and made you suffer all the preliminary jitters I was experiencing. I was *so* afraid the reviews would upset you—afraid, too, you would expect too much in volume of sales. Well, darling—maybe you are enjoying these early good reports all the more because I infected you with my pessimism. I know I am! Isn't it fun? Yesterday while playing invalid I skimmed through the pages of Virginia Woolf's diary (the book published about a year ago) and was amused and enlightened to discover similar jitters with the publication of each of her books—"what would they say?" (and in particular, what would a certain reviewer say?—would he do the book at all?—would he be patronizing or evasive?—and then the vast relief when "he" said the hoped-for things)—would it sell well?—would people like it as well as some other book of hers? And so it is—we always think our problems are peculiar to us, and then finally discover how many others have gone through exactly the same thing. And much as I suffer during the writing itself, I begin to think it is easy for me compared with the agonies she relates!

No, darling, I hadn't seen the "Poet's Column" but now I have read all three with delight. It is almost uncanny how often there is something, precisely timed, that seems planned especially for Us. This is one example. The hermit thrush chorus on July 12 was another. (I do hope you kept the poem about moonlight and "heart light"[55]—I want it [a copy of it] for my collection.)

Yes, I'm sure that with my precious You to help, my hair will be all right, and I certainly don't want to clutter up Monday or Tuesday with having it done. It is in good enough shape today, from last Saturday's doing, so I can be optimistic. I am of two minds whether to wear the New York dress or look for something else. I'll need something a little more "covered" looking for some occasions, anyway. If the weather is good tomorrow or Thursday, I may have a look. In any event, I'll be wearing a hat.

Now dear, there is an assortment of news I'll write in a sharing letter. But please tuck away in your heart and never lose it, the thought that this whole experience is warm and glowing and happy for me in a way it couldn't possibly be if you weren't part of it.

I love you.
Rachel

S A T U R D A Y , N O V E M B E R 19

Dearest [Dorothy],

We do seem to have kept each other well supplied with mail this week, and yet there is so much unsaid and untold! I'm so glad your cold did not materialize into anything disabling, and that Stan's tough week at the office is behind him—I hope that also means he is over the peak of the autumnal mountain of work and can now relax a little. As for myself, I did spend yesterday in bed except for going down for meals. Cora—mother of a maid we used to have—spent the day with Marjie and was quite a godsend, attending to meals, tidying up the house, and entertaining Roger. He liked her so well he invited her to come every day. M. seems to be much better today and is able to cope with things herself. Thank goodness, because Cora couldn't come today and there is a heavy, wet snow, so I'm glad not to go out. But I do feel better, dear. There is still a little nagging soreness in my throat, but the aching all over has subsided and I feel much more like my ordinary self.

Now—what have I left untold? The dinner Monday evening was an interesting experience, for as you know I have attended nothing held by the Institute[56] since the May ceremonies when I became a member. There are, of course, many more men than women in the group, and this was reflected in the dinner attendance—probably between 30 and 40 men and 5 women (Malvina Hoffman, sculptor; Marianne Moore and Phyllis McGinley, poets; Isabel Bishop, painter; and myself.) There was a brief cocktail hour in the library (of the Knickerbocker Club) before dinner, where my chief conversation was with Louis Untermeyer,[57] until Will Beebe[58] and I spied each other. Soon the poet Auden fell into conversation with us—he is very, very British, a bachelor, studied zoology at some time, an Oxford man, and is fond of cats, of which he now has one or two, I forget which, but it or they have the usual feline fondness for

[55] "Heartlight" by Georgie Starbuck Galbraith reads: "With magic the silver-fingered moon / Transmutes the commonplaces of noon— / The shabby street and the tattered elm— / Into beauty's exotic realm. / The heart, too, loving and waxing full, / Can work this enchanting miracle, / And a world bathed in heartlight lies / Lovely and strange as paradise."

[56] Institute of Arts and Letters.

[57] American poet, author, and editor of, among other works, *A Treasury of Great Poems, English and American* (1955).

[58] Dr. William Beebe had placed two chapters from *Under the Sea-Wind* in his 1942 anthology, *The Book of Naturalists*, and he and RC had become friends.

lying all over his manuscripts. At dinner I sat between Will Beebe and an architect by the name of Smith, who turned out to have a very intelligent interest in geology and paleontology. I told him about *Conversation with the Earth* and he wrote the title in a notebook so he could look it up. The after dinner business was a discussion of candidates for the Gold Medals in sculpture and music, and I realized then that most of the guests represented one or the other of these fields. Deems Taylor[59] and Virgil Thomson[60] both spoke about the candidates in music (Copland, Sessions, and Varese). There was a long and rather confusing (to one who knew nothing about it) discussion of the six candidates in sculpture; then finally Marc Connelly, the president, introduced Ogden Nash, who concluded the proceedings on a light note.

Tuesday I made no attempt to get out early. Marie went to the office and I stayed behind and made numerous phone calls, then met her and Maria Lieper[61] for lunch. Then Marie and I went, on sudden impulse, to the Bronx Zoo, Marie having first called Christopher Coates to tell him we were coming. So all the official red carpet had been rolled out; Mr. Coates was waiting to greet us and take us to speak to Fairfield Osborn[62] and other dignitaries, then asked what we wanted most to see. We had only a little more than an hour. Not knowing what this involved, I mentioned the duck-billed platypus. And the nursery where Mrs. Martini presides. The platypuses (what is the plural?) had been established in winter quarters down in the lower regions, but all the doors were unlocked and we were conducted down winding stairs and along passageways, as in a medieval dungeon, to the basement room where these strange creatures spend the winter months. They are so very shy that they are poor exhibit animals at any time, but we had an excellent view of the female, who has stronger nerves than her mate. Then Mr. Coates took us to one of the cat houses, where Mrs. Martini, who had been alerted, was waiting to give us an introduction to assorted lions and tigers she has raised from infancy, and also to take us into the nursery. It was a fascinating experience, and she urges me to come back when they have baby tigers, when she will allow me to hold one. The potto I mentioned is a very primitive primate, something like a lemur, with big round eyes and pads on all its toes which allow it to cling tightly to trees (or cage bars) for apparently its sense of security depends on knowing it won't fall. Mrs. Martini detached it carefully and lovingly, one toe at a time, and got it wrapped around her wrist; then she managed to transfer it to mine, where it cuddled up quite confidingly, and nibbled my fingers. There was a little Asiatic deer wandering around in the nursery, never more than six inches from Mrs. Martini, and with no eyes for anyone else.

We had an appointment with Dick Pough[63] for late in the afternoon, but he was still at the zoo, where he had been attending a meeting, so he brought us home in a cab and came up to the apartment for a chat before he went to the Audubon Dinner. (It was in the midst of that that I called you.) After he left I tried to take a nap, feeling rather all in, but couldn't really sleep. Paul arrived from

[59] Author of, among other works, *Music Lovers' Encyclopedia* (1939).

[60] American composer of operas (e.g., *The Mother of Us All*, 1947); film scores (e.g., *The Louisiana Story*, 1948); and ballets (e.g., *The Harvest According*, 1952).

[61] An editor at Simon and Schuster.

[62] Conservationist and author of several books, including *The Limits of the Earth* (1953).

[63] Richard Hooper Pough, Curator of Conservation, American Museum of Natural History, and author of, among others, *Audubon Land Bird Guide* (1949) and *Audubon Water Bird Guide* (1951).

the airport about 7:30, and Marie had planned for dinner at home, so that was much easier than going out. And as you know, Paul took me—or what was left of me, I was really feeling miserable—to the train about 11:30.

I had told Marie about the Boston talk with Paul on Monday evening; then she and Paul and I talked it all over and wound up with the decision that she would lay the cards on the table to Cass Canfield, the Harper editor, some day this week. But I wasn't happy about it and told her Wednesday evening (by phone) to do nothing until I had an opportunity to think it over at leisure. Paul's first proposal of a deal between H.M. and Harper did not seem to make sense, as we discussed it, and all that is left is for me to ask to be relieved of my contract obligation. That I don't like, and I know Marie doesn't. So at the moment I am inclined to write for the Harper series, as briefly and simply as may be, exactly the book they asked for, and save my major theme for a later book.[64] The ramifications are too complicated to write, but I think this is what it will come to, and perhaps it will be for the best this way. I do not think I will be comfortable with any other solution.

By the time you read this, you will no doubt know that *The Edge* rose from 15th to 4th place on the *Tribune* list (Paul says this is "probably a record for a standing high jump") and is making its first appearance on the *Times* list, in 8th place. Paul reports that in Boston the fastest selling H.M. books are *The Edge* and their new novel, *Cash McCall*,[65] with *The Edge* on top. In New York, he says, these two are both selling so fast that they hardly know which is on top.

Developments in the *Reader's Digest* field: The *Digest* has arranged for a 6-page extract to appear in the February issue of the magazine, and has contracted separately with Bob for four drawings. H.M. considers this a good "ad" for the book—not enough to make people feel they have sampled the whole. It does not necessarily preclude the much more lucrative use in the Digest Book Club, but at the moment there is no real hope of that. A good run on the best-seller list might, however, change that situation. And we can still accept the Books Abridged offer, for next summer, if we wish.

I think, dear, I'll send you (In separate envelope.) a batch of recent reviews; just asking you to return them within a few days, for I don't want to get too far behind with my scrapbook. But by the time I see you, too much else will have accumulated. Marie had a typewritten copy of Jack Berrill's review, which I will also send. It is one of the loveliest yet. However, Paul sent a printer's proof of it from the *Saturday Review*, and I see it has been somewhat condensed. But it is still very, very good. We don't know in what issue it will appear.

I think I told you of Mr. Fleischmann's death.[66] We had known he was in a hospital in Charleston, but did not realize how serious his condition was. They took him home a few days before his death, so I suppose they had been told there was nothing more to be done, and Charles wrote they were so thankful he was able to know he was at home before the end came. Charles says that when

[64] Harper and Brothers had asked RC to write a book on evolution for its World Perspectives series. RC's reference to her major theme concerned the contemplated book on the continents.

[65] By Cameron Hawley.

[66] A Carson family friend from South Carolina.

his mother is able he will bring her to New York for a while, and that they will break their trip in Washington for an overnight visit with us.

It was hard to realize that all those flowers could be in bloom at Southport in November. I knew there was a whole new crop of snapdragons coming on when we left, but supposed they would be nipped by frost long before now. I'm glad the new plants look all right. Had the storm window been put on? I have had no bill, or other word, from Mr. Delano, although Mr. Sherman[67] sent his bill for taking care of the water. So the little "squirnie" is right on the job, ready for a hand-out! I wonder just where he curls up to be secure from the winter winds and snow.

Goodbye for now, dear. I know I'm going to be tempted to call you tomorrow. We shall see. Our love to all.

Rachel

For some of the oddities of my typing, you can blame Jeffie, who "helped" considerably.

Now darling [Dorothy]—

This time is just for Us. I have written all the major news in a long family letter, and now I can talk to you. There has been only one day since my return from New York with no letter from you (Thurs.) but today there were two, those mailed Thursday and Friday. After your letter yesterday I longed so to hear your voice that I almost made up my mind to phone you last night. But you had spoken of a week filled with engagements, and I thought probably you would be out or would have guests, and at best it could hardly be a satisfactory call. I think very likely I shall try you tomorrow morning, darling, hoping to reach you before you become involved in the day's activities, if any. Why? Just to hear your voice, dear, and to compensate for Tuesday's very unsatisfactory call. Yes, darling, you *do* know me well enough to understand I'd be disturbed when Tuesday's events began to hem me in so I couldn't get away to phone you. I had originally timed the call for what I thought would be the end of my New York stay, knowing very well the difficulty of "escaping" for a private conversation at any other time. Then the change of plans upset everything. But I couldn't bear not to call and at least let you know what was going on.

I am so concerned about Stan—and for you because of the worry I know it must cause you—and I do wish there were some way he could shift some of this nerve-racking detail to an assistant. With at least a possibility that next year he might not have his present secretary. I do wish he could find someone—or persuade the company to give him someone—to be responsible for this annual tag headache.

I am taking your recent letters item by item. I loved the fact that Mr. Tomlinson proved to be the custodian of the missing letter![68] Now I must ask him if he has mine—your *first* word to me, darling, on the bunchberry card. It makes me sick every time I realize I don't know where it is. You know I put it *somewhere*

[67] Maurice Sherman, Boothbay Harbor area building contractor.

[68] DF had discovered a misplaced letter in her copy of an H. M. Tomlinson book.

to take with me to Maine that first summer (before I had ever seen you) and I've never seen it since. Mr. T. doesn't have it, of course, but when I go through all my papers, as I want to do before I start another book, I do hope I shall find it. Darling—*of course* I wrote that note only because I wanted to (I think I was so afraid you might just slip out of my life!) just as I went to the Head that night because I wanted to—and kissed you goodbye because I wanted to!

That was sweet about Martha and the caterpillar and Rachel. What fun it must have been to see the changes in her and Richard.[69]

[69] DF's grandson, Martha's brother, born in June.

Yes, I did wear the new brown dress at the dinner. Marie liked it very much. *And* a new hat which I'm eager for you to see, but it's too special to wear traveling. It's tiny—sort of a golden brown with a little veil and a slender, curving feather. Perfect, I think, for that dress, and I could also wear it with one of my suits if I wanted to be very dressed up.

As you know by now, I didn't see Elizabeth Bowen at all, but I had expected only to see her briefly at the bookshop. Mr. Bader was quite upset when I phoned to say I couldn't come. Evidently he had been telling people I'd be there and had promised autographs.

I like your coffee hour idea, dear, though I want you to do whatever will seem best to you. But I was realizing that a luncheon would take the whole afternoon. And you know how I begrudge Our time, darling. I do hope I can come, my dearest, and am planning for it, but please don't let yourself count on it absolutely, so that the disappointment would be too bitter if I just couldn't. But I will, darling, if everything is all right here.

Heavens, it seems so LONG already since you put me on the train at 128. And it is simply incredible that only a calendar month ago today we were arriving home from Maine, and that since then I've made two trips to New York and one to Boston—with all their associated events and ramifications.

Now to today's letters: Darling, I smiled about your concern at not mentioning the *Tribune* List in your Tuesday night letter. I suppose I might have noticed, and even been disappointed, but for two reasons. As you know, there is always a state of confusion as to what letter the other is answering, as I didn't remember you knew at that time. Also, things happen so fast that the big news of yesterday is swallowed up by the news of tomorrow, so that particular event no longer seemed so important by the time I heard from you. Its importance is purely historic, as the First Occurrence! Didn't I expect it? Well, yes—and especially in the light of post-publication happenings. But my dearest—don't you understand how easily it might not? The fall season is murderously competitive. The day I went to New York I counted the *Times* list of books published on that single day—41!! So to rate the *Tribune* list a book has to be among the top 20 out of at least 1500 books published in the fall; for the *Times* list the top 16. So how could anybody count on it? I knew I'd feel sick if it didn't—not because I myself have any illusions about it—but because of what everyone (not *you*, darling, you do understand) so unreasonably expects and takes for granted. Robert, for example, wonders why it isn't in first place! Of course, I suppose I wouldn't like it if everybody was astonished, would I?

Darling, I don't think I shall try to write you all my thoughts about this problem of the next book—or books. Doubtless it will still be a problem when I see you, and we can talk it over. In brief, Paul's "solution" does not look so good on further examination. As Marie says, I am not a baseball player, to be bought and sold. So the issue is really one between Harper and me, in which H.M. has no part other than interested spectator. Harper might release me, but I'm afraid I wouldn't be comfortable. So I think I shall do the evolution book they asked for, as simply as possible. But I'm grateful for the discussion with Paul, for it saved me from wasting a major theme on a book in what seems to be a rather obscure series. The big book will take years to mature. Meanwhile, the essay on the origin and evolution of life will clarify my thoughts in a field that is basic to the other.

Darling—these letters will take half your day to read! Why don't I stop? I will; only I am sure I haven't as yet said any of the tender things that have filled my heart ever since I had to tear myself away and leave you—and for many, many months before that. With all your intuition, your sensitiveness, your deep understanding, I doubt if you can ever fully realize the place you occupy in my life—the warm glow of happiness that every message from you brings, and every thought of you—and the deep sense of peace and contentment you have given me. Try to realize it dear. I want you to know all that, and how much I love you.

Rachel

SUNDAY NIGHT, NOVEMBER 20

Darling [Dorothy],

[70] Clippings of reviews of *The Edge of the Sea*.

I can't send these[70] without tucking in a note, in spite of the volume that went to you yesterday, and our conversation this morning. (Did you really expect me to call, dearest? You didn't really explain what you meant by saying "Even to the minute!" But I chose eleven because I thought *if* you thought I might call, that would probably be the time you'd expect it.)

Now I'm amusing myself by comparing the mail situation with Thanksgiving week last year—do you remember? I think I knew you had written, for I know I confidently expected a letter Wednesday, and then it didn't come, and I felt horrible, knowing I then had to wait till Friday. So perhaps the letter you will mail Tuesday will follow the same pattern. But I guess I can stand it, darling, though that would be almost a week! Imagine such a thing!

So far we have made no Thanksgiving plans. I suppose we'll have Marjie and Roger here, but doubt we'll do more. I hope you will just have a quiet day too—it sounds as though poor Stan needs it. I'm so sorry about all his troubles and worries.

Such a lovely surprise in the mail—another letter—the one written in pencil and mailed when you went to the store Friday afternoon. You see, my Saturday mail contained one mailed Thurs. in W.B. and one postmarked Friday in Boston—so I thought that was the Friday letter you meant. So now I *can* live through till Friday if I must, darling!

How glad I am I didn't hear the wretched "Monitor" thing![71]

Your "celebrity" phone call brought me a happy smile, darling. Really, I think that is all very sweet, and it *does* give you an insight into "how it feels."

(No more of that paper upstairs!)

Darling, this is a good point at which to say that I *truly*—even now—don't expect *The Edge* ever to reach the #1 spot, and (what is more important) I won't be disappointed. And I'll be happy that it is Mrs. Lindbergh's book and not something sensational or trashy that holds that position. I simply don't see how I could go much higher than #4. There is an element of regionalism in my book, whatever else it may be or say. And the stores represented by those lists are scattered over the entire country. Not more than a fourth are truly eastern. So my *Tribune* count (18 stores out of 36) meant *The Edge* is definitely a best-seller outside of its area, but I just don't see how it could ever be so reported by all 36! I am very happy with the present situation, darling.

I talked to Marie yesterday and my decision is made to go ahead with the evolution book for the series. I shall be happier that way, and perhaps in the end will feel the big book is the better for it. I'm writing Paul today.

Now this must be all, darling. Just maybe you won't hear again till the end of the week. I must get all these books out, catch up on correspondence, and *start* Christmas shopping.

I love you, darling. Do you know?

Rachel

You came to me in a dream last night—a very sweet one.

[71] A radio interview with RC that had not been presented in the context she had expected.

WEDNESDAY, NOVEMBER 23

My own darling [Dorothy],

In this week when I thought I might go letterless until Friday, I've had four in three days! And such sweet ones, dearest, especially your Thanksgiving note, which came in the same mail (today) with your long, satisfying typewritten one. Darling, you do find such beautiful things to say for these special days, as well as for all the many days that are "special" only between Us. You must know the item that heads your list of blessings is also number one on mine, and that all your thoughts about it are enclosed in my heart.

Even on our *first* Thanksgiving, darling, there was a sweet message from you. Do you remember? I do—it was enclosed with a greeting, and it gave a special glow to the day.

I think you would approve of the way I've spent most of the past week—just lying around reading a good part of each day, sometimes not getting dressed until afternoon. I do feel a lot better, though I'll have to admit that some soreness persists way down in the larynx, where it seems unlikely a gargle can reach it. If it isn't better by Friday I'll probably see the doctor. I'm sure you are tired of hearing me say that, but the fact is he hasn't particularly encouraged me to come, and I think they just don't know what to do for this affliction, which so many seem to have. But I do want to get rid of it, darling, and you know one important reason.

I smiled at your preparations for that Sunday call that hadn't been arranged for, and I loved our late afternoon visit as you described it. Yes darling, we would have had much to discuss. But when wouldn't we?

In reading underway and planned, I feel I have already entered upon what Edwin Teale calls the "delightful stage of research" for the evolution book. It *is* a luxury just to read, and not try to write. So you see, darling, already *The Edge* is becoming a little dim in my mind, with my thoughts more on the future than the past.

Did you notice that I had replied to your comment about first place on the list before that comment reached me? So now you know how I feel. I've had the experience of a long run as first, and it was good, but I don't covet it this time. There will be no disappointment. By the way, I almost think I may write to Mrs. L. after all.

Your Saturday party sounds lovely, darling. I can't think of any food that would taste better on a snowy winter evening and I know they would all enjoy the pictures. Now this will be all for now, darling. I do hope Stan's tooth is better for the present, at least till his dentist recovers. I'll try to mail a note tomorrow, but I want you to be sure to have something the end of the week.

I love you darling.
Rachel

NOVEMBER 24

Beloved [Rachel],

It is the morning of Thanksgiving Day. I have already told you what I consider my major blessing but it can well be repeated. Darling, I am so thankful for *you*. Do you know?

Now, for a little while I want to try to answer two letters—my own part that came in your long wonderful letter on Monday, and the lovely one that came with the clippings. I am typing some of my comments about them (the clippings)—this is what I would talk about if we were alone together.

Stan said after reading the reviews last night, "Aren't you afraid to write to someone who can write like that? I am and you'd better tell her so." And then I began to analyze the situation. Perhaps I should be afraid—or stand in awe.

And then your own feeling about all this came to me. "I think of her as someone else." And darling, I'm beginning to wonder if perhaps I'm acquiring the same attitude. Do you mind? What you mean to me and what I hope I mean to you is so far removed from all the fame and publicity that She does seem quite apart from Us.

And yet, darling, I would not have you think that your great gift is not a part of my You. You know that, too, don't you? It is all so complex. I think, probably, what I'm trying to say is the thing you tell me you strove for so long—no abysses, no barriers, no pedestals—just a warm glowing understanding.

Yesterday's note had a plaintive little query—"How could you live until Friday if no letter came on Wednesday"—I smiled as I read it for I knew what quantities of mail were on their way to you. So you remember the mail of a year ago? I do, too, and of two years ago. And, darling, it was *three* years ago I was beginning to think of my first letter to you. Three years, darling. Of course, that first nine months was rather sparse as far as mail went, but the seed was planted. Do you know, the fact that I wrote last week—that you *wanted* to write that goodbye note in September—is quite a new thought with me. You may think that odd—but somehow, darling, it has never dawned on me—at least for me to really grasp it—that you could have been interested in me then to the extent that you were "so afraid you might just slip out of my life." I know you have told me before, but you see, I had to discover it for myself. I suppose I was so concerned with my feeling about you at that time I never for a moment gave any consideration to the idea that the feeling might be reciprocated. Indeed, that would have been in the realm of pure fantasy.

So, darling, can you understand what this means to me now—two and more years later? Of course, I have known and believed for a long time that I do hold a unique place in your life, but to know that you were objective about it from the beginning throws the whole lovely affair into a new rosy light.

I hope you find that bunchberry card sometime for I am curious about its message that caused you to answer.

The letters did *not* take half a day to read—but what if they had—can you imagine any way I could have been happier for a half day?

And I'm so glad you took time for your declaration of love on the last page—darling, I know, of course, all that you wrote but it is so very sweet to hear it and to read it!

Thank you, dear, for writing as fully as you have about the "next book" problem. Although the conclusion is not the one that I felt you were hoping for when you left me, I'm sure it is the right one for you will be fulfilling your obligation to Harper, but at the same time not wasting what you told me "might be your most important book" in an obscure series. And besides I know you want Paul for your editor for that effort.

So I'm sure all the conversations and consultations have served their purpose even perhaps to bringing you to start on the new book with a happier out-

72 Positioned on
Seguin Island,
located to the
southwest of
Southport Island,
is a warning bea-
con for ships.

look—looking beyond it to the next—and the work on it proving to be the basis for the "big book," you say. How wonderful to have such a distant horizon—the air has to be very clear to see so far—like finding Seguin[72] on a crystal morning.

The other big thing, darling, is about your attitude toward the best-seller list. I believe you, dear, that you are not going to be disappointed if *The Edge* doesn't make the #1 spot. And I am not going to be a prophet to say that it will. You know far better than I the vagaries of that situation. Perhaps if the Lindbergh book had been on longer the competition would not be so keen. I saw an example in Jordan's. Two women came along to the counter where *The Edge* was piled beside the *Gift*. "Oh, here's Anne Lindbergh's book—I've been meaning to get it" and the second one said "Yes, I think I'll get it too" and the sale was made without a glance at *The Edge*—no reflection on *The Edge*, I'm sure, for they were not choosing between them—just buying the one they'd been hearing about all summer.

But, darling, who knows? Of course, I wish for Robert's sake it would rise to the top!!

And I, too, am glad that it is the type of book it is that is its rival.

Anyway I made a sale for you at lunch at Schrafft's the other day. For half the period four women had eaten in stoney silence—I didn't seem to find the right opening. After one had left, the ice seemed to melt, and we were off. And believe it or not, I was *not* the first one to say I go to Maine for the summer! My companion goes to Goose Rocks which is the setting for *My Love Affair with the State of Maine* or something like it. She was eloquent about the book. What better lead could I have to say "and do you know Rachel Carson's book, *The Sea Around Us*?" And she did, so I simply said "She has a new one out, you know" and modestly said nothing more. Can you believe it? When she left she said "What is the name of the new Carson book? I must get it."

Darling, I loved Jack Berrill's review, for several reasons. Of course, the fact that he *knew* how it was written—the studies, etc.—helped make it an intimate-feeling review. I loved "does not actually take the reader by the hand" and then gives the feeling that she does. And she does.

And his explanation of the closely knit relation of text and pictures is the best yet.

Let's read it together when you come for I'd like to comment on it sentence by sentence but Time is beginning to "rear its ugly head" and I must cease.

Went to dressmaker's yesterday where I saw an exquisite piece of material, embroidered all over, which I wondered might resemble your brown dress.

Looked for tripod for Stan in Boston but became so confused as to models, prices, etc., that I decided to tell him what his gift was to be from me and let him get it himself. But that makes me unhappy, as I always like to have a real surprise for him and my mind is a blank in the field of surprises.

Do you know if there is a model number of your tripod?

Now dear, this should be all. I hope you can read all through it that I love you very much. And I am so happy that on this Thanks-giving Day the burden of the book that has been on your shoulders all the other Thanks-givings I have known you has been so happily lifted.

Allways I love you,
Dorothy

SUNDAY MORNING, NOVEMBER 27

Darling [Dorothy],

Even as I begin this "postscript"[73] I realize the futility of attempting even to suggest all my thoughts. What I long for, of course, is the opportunity not only to report events but to discuss them with you as they come along, wandering down all the by-paths of thought they suggest. But darling, there is a warm happiness even in *imagining* our doing so, and in knowing that we can have that sort of companionship whenever we are together. And meanwhile, all the sharing of recent weeks has been lovely for me, dearest.

It has just occurred to me that the timing of *The Edge* in relation to you and me is good. What if it had been published during the first year of our friendship—or even last year? I don't think I would have dared to send you these reviews. But now, even when you reported your little conversation with Stan about whether you should be "afraid" to write to me, it didn't bother me, for I feel that you have really overcome all those earlier feelings about vast "gulfs" and unattainable "mountain peaks," and so I am just serenely confident none of this can come between us. And darling, I'm not sure you can ever know what that means to me.

Bless your dear heart—I *knew* some of those clippings would make you weep! As for myself, darling, I don't know that I have shed any tears, but that is only because I am protected by that feeling of unreality. If I believed what they say to be really true, I don't know just how I would react. But dear—truly—I am too conscious of the many flaws in my work to accept some of these high estimates without strong reservations. They are something to try to be worthy of in the future and perhaps that is the only way I can regard them.

I loved what you said about the clear atmosphere in which I could see beyond the next book to the one beyond, and the reference to seeing Seguin. And speaking of Seguin, I know you're going to enjoy Mr. Bok's[74] letter, which I shall try to enclose. (I enjoyed his introductory near-apology for a second letter, and his remark about "prowling" for "lions.")

As to the future writing program, dear, perhaps it will not surprise you that I have not discussed it at home. There was no point, for I knew the reaction would have stemmed from resentment of Paul, and now that my decision is what it is, there is even less need. Except for Paul and Marie, you and Stan are the only ones I have discussed it with. I'm sure my decision is the right one, even if it is the long way around. In the long run, I don't think the major book will suffer. But more on all this when I see you!

[73] On the previous day, RC had sent DF a letter for sharing with her household.

[74] Publication of *The Edge of the Sea* had prompted Curtis Bok, author and soon to be associate justice of the Supreme Court of Pennsylvania, to write to RC.

As before, the correspondence is beginning to raise problems, and I think I am now more conscious of them, especially where they raise (indirectly) the question of the extent to which I should retire into my shell like a periwinkle at low tide! Some are easy, of course, clearly calling for a negative answer, others are not so simple. I know I have said something to you about my feeling of acquiring certain obligations as a result of recognition, and when it is a question of people really wanting whatever it is they feel I have to give, then I am troubled about taking the easy course of declining, and wonder whether I should not make an effort to be (temporarily and occasionally) that Other Woman who is different from the one you and I know best! A specific example is an invitation to come to Vassar in April as the Helen Kenyon lecturer, to give one public lecture and then, for two or three days to have less formal contacts with the students. I was unable to reply with an automatic "No," but instead have asked more details as to the type of lecture appropriate. It occurred to me that just possibly a section of the Harper book might serve as the basis of the lecture, so that I would not be diverting too much time from the book if I felt I wanted to accept. Well, we shall see. Probably it will have to be settled before I see you, if they reply promptly to the letter I'm mailing today.

And then, in lighter vein, there is the problem of "lion hunters" (definitely not Mr. Bok!). But while I feel I can identify them, it is not easy for me to deal with them, being perhaps too sensitive about hurting people's feelings.

There is an amazing proposal from the head of the firm of attorneys who handle my tax affairs. It has to do with a round-the-world voyage in which Rachel Carson assumes the role of a modern Charles Darwin all to be duly sponsored by wealthy backers among his friends. I shall save this to tell you and Stan about. At the moment, I can see only the funny side of it, although I suppose some of Beebe's expeditions have had just such an origin. (Don't worry, darling, I'm not going!)

Now, my dear one, the world is beginning to demand my time and I suppose I must end this happy hour with you. After breakfast, I came back to bed to write. Jeffie is overflowing his basket on the bed beside me, after coaxing in vain for me to get up and play with him.

I have several letters I must get in the afternoon mail along with the batch from Mrs. Rivera. Some I find too difficult to dictate, needing to ponder too long—and these I have to do myself.

My throat feels some better already, darling, but now we know it is nothing to worry about.

Dearest, please don't push yourself too hard in your effort to do Everything in the Next Two Weeks! You mustn't get sick, you know. And *don't* try to write much or often—really dear!

I love you dearly

Rachel

Dearest [Dorothy],

Have decided to get a note on its way today, so you'll be sure to have it before the week-end. Some of the mail (not yours, as yet) seems to be getting slower.

Your Sunday letter (that wasn't going to be written) came yesterday for a nice surprise. I enjoyed your going to see *Pipe Dream* in all innocence, not knowing you were to be right at home in a tide pool! Evidently when you wrote me you hadn't seen the enclosed,[75] and maybe you missed it. Don't bother to return it.

[75] Enclosure not preserved.

Paul phoned this morning and while we were talking his secretary handed him an advance copy of next Sunday's *Times. The Edge* has advanced from #5 to #4! Paul jubilantly surveyed the rest of the list and declared no other book had gone so far in so short a time. He remarked that the only ones ahead were the old timers who should be moving along anyway. He hooted at my conviction that #4 was about the summit for *The Edge*—but I'm still to be convinced. Anyway, everyone at H.M. Co. is very, very happy. Books are slipping away from them at the rate of more than a thousand a day. By the way, Paul sent a very lovely letter (to him) from John Enders, whose research led to the polio vaccine, and who was a Nobel Prize winner last year. I'll have it copied before returning it. I think I'll send Paul the Bok letters sometime.

Dear, if this fits into your own schedule, I think I'll make two return reservations—one for the Federal Wednesday night, the other by plane about midday Thursday. Then circumstances can dictate which to use. I know you are going to feel that a return Wednesday is too soon—and it is—but from experience I know that repeated brief absences are less upsetting here than one prolonged one. And I think you'd rather see me several times during the winter—even briefly—than only once.

In spite of all the letters I did last week-end with Mrs. Rivera, and a great pile I did personally yesterday—the difficult ones—my desk is still horribly cluttered. And I must start the chore of Christmas greetings. So probably you won't find me in your mailbox again until early next week.

Our love to all, and a special share to you.

Rachel

Darling [Dorothy],

Your Sunday letter was a joy, as always, but especially so because I had told myself there would be nothing in Tuesday's mail. But truly darling, I am getting worried about your Christmas chores. I am going to keep my extra messages on greeting cards to a minimum, but I think you probably find it hard to do that, and I don't see how you are going to finish—unless you write shorter *and* fewer letters to me. I can stand it, darling, with December 12th on the horizon.

I have actually bought or ordered a number of Christmas gifts, and may try to do a little more today, though there is such a cold and blustery wind that going out isn't inviting. But I also want to go to the library—for already I find my mental processes falling into the now familiar pattern—my brain cells sorting over and storing away facts as a squirrel with its nuts, and scenting an interesting lead and eagerly following it—if you can follow the badly scrambled metaphors! And I am enjoying it darling, as you sense, and that helps. There is far more new and significant work in the field of evolution and heredity than I had realized. So *I* am learning a great deal, and that also helps. And I'm able to feel it is important to do this Harper book—that there really is something that needs to be said.

Darling, I don't really know how long you had counted on my staying, and I hope I am not disappointing you badly. You know we have to act on the principle that something is better than nothing. I have discovered that the recent absences of 2 or 3 nights were not too upsetting here, and that leaves me free to plan to go again, whereas the prospect of my prolonged absence is very likely to precipitate a harrowing crisis. Please understand, darling. You know how greatly I want to be with you.

I'm glad you thought my inscription in the Littles'[76] book all right, darling. I had a hard time with it. Later, in autographing a book for my correspondent, Mr. Schultz, I used a few lines from the T. S. Eliot poem in *The Book of the Sea*[77]—"The sea is the land's edge also—" etc., and then rather wished I had used that for the Littles'.

Around Jan. 17th, when I am to be a guest at the dinner of the New York Zool. Soc., I'll be in New York for a couple of days. Soon after that, I hope you are coming to visit me, darling. Probably I could then plan for a February visit to Boston.

As you must know, from my recent letter and in other ways, I do long to be near you, darling. And soon I will be for at least a few golden hours.

> I love you dear
> *Rachel*

FRIDAY NIGHT, DECEMBER 2

Darling [Dorothy],

Tomorrow looks like a full day, so I shall write just a note before I turn out the light, so I can mail it tomorrow. Somehow, I feel you especially like to receive mail before and after the week-end. I know I do.

Where did you ever find the lovely card you used for your message of Wednesday morning—the Emerson lines on friendship?

Darling, I think some of my recent letters can serve to remind us of topics we want to explore more fully—you know I never remember to make an adequate list. But I will remember to bring some of your letters, for of course there are many conversational spring-boards in them.

[76] Walter and Flora Little. Walter Little was president of the Bridgewater Grain Company, Stanley Freeman's former employer.

[77] A. C. Spectorsky's *The Book of the Sea* (1954) contains a passage from T. S. Eliot's "The Dry Salvages" (*Four Quartets*, 1943) and from *Under the Sea-Wind*.

I don't think I mentioned receiving a call from "Omnibus"[78]—again wanting me to do script for them, but this time it is no last-minute rush to get narration for a program already scheduled, and that makes it more inviting. In fact, I'm inclined to look very favorably on the opportunity to get acquainted with them, for I think it might give me a chance (in future programs) to present some thoughts that seem important to me to their large audience. And I don't have to appear in it, or even speak my own "piece," and that is good. The subject the man has in mind now (though very willing to think up something else if I'll just do it!) is "Clouds," "a poetic and sensitive interpretation—a new look." I said at once, "You should have Mr. Guy Murchie for that," to which he replied "I know you're good at thinking up someone else to do these things, but we want *you*." He has since talked to Marie and their terms seem generous. I shall probably go and look at some of their film in January, if not before, and see what I think. Really, I should see television now and then—I don't know what these programs are like.

The Edge is #4 in the *Tribune* again, Paul reports, exulting as I creep up on Mr. Peale,[79] whom he seems particularly anxious for me to replace. (20 stores reporting Carson; 21 Peale.)

Darling—what does it do to you when you read of "projects ahead"? Nothing unhappy, I hope. You must tell me when we are together.

I am really laughing at myself for even supposing I could take any appreciable "time off" before beginning the new book. I am taking to this research like an old alcoholic to his bottle. Really, it is so stimulating, and I find my mind in a ferment of ideas. It is such a different kind of book from *The Edge* that the very change is refreshing. And in the years I have been sailing the ocean or exploring its edge, I have quite lost track of the exciting research in pure biology. Well—undoubtedly you will hear much of this soon! I really hope to have this far along before Southport, though doubtless we'll be laughing at that statement then. But I'm trying to think of it as a very long (maybe 2 part) magazine article, rather than book length. Just today I began playing with the idea of going to Atlanta for the A.A.A.S. meetings ("incidentally"—you know—but there is no You in Atlanta!) after Christmas, if I could discover that I would have an opportunity for even a brief chat with some of the men whose work is basic to this book. Some of them are ordinarily in California, and all are so scattered that the meetings might be the one chance to see them.

Oh—it is 1:15 and maybe time to go to sleep. But I did have a nap this afternoon, darling, so don't worry. You should have this just one week before you see me! Dear, I think if weather is all right for flying, we really can have a Monday-til-Thursday visit.

More clippings today—nice ones, too. Will bring them.

I love you dear.
Rachel

[78] A C.B.S. television program sponsored by *Omnibus* magazine.

[79] Norman Vincent Peale, whose *Inspiring Messages for Daily Living* was on the *New York Tribune*'s best-seller list.

Your Thursday morning mail came this morning, dear, and I'm returning the note you sent. *Yes, why don't you?* I did have a memo to myself about something along that line to discuss with you. And I shall.

Lunch with Dr. Hard[80] was pleasant, but I'm weary. It was a warm and terribly humid day—everything glistening with moisture though the sun was shining, and I think that sort of weather drains one's energy.

I have my reservations made, dear. It won't be long now, will it? Only this past week has seemed very long.

Now I'll mail this, darling. You do know what?

I do.

R.

[80] Dr. Frederick Hard, president of Scripps College, Claremont, California.

DECEMBER 15, 2:30 P.M.

10,000 FEET ABOVE YOU

Darling [Dorothy],

We are flying in brilliant sunshine above a sea of clouds, with never a hint that there is an earth somewhere below this upper world. It has been a serene and uneventful flight, and we are expected to make our landing about 3:30. I'll drop this in the Airport Post Office, and should get through Washington before the rush-hour traffic. I'll wait until I get home to send your wire.

Now here is a puzzle for you to clear up, though perhaps it was created by my imagination. When you gave me this writing paper, I *thought* you said, "And here's one for you"—and it was then I handed you (or showed you) the tiny note which I tucked under the electric-blanket "controller" on your desk. And a few minutes later I said "Where is my note?" and *thought* you said you'd put it in the envelope—which I then tucked in my bag. Anyway, when I took out the envelope to look for it, once we had climbed into the sky, there was no note, darling! But there were *two* little correspondence sheets in their envelopes, one for Mrs. Guymont, the other—? Oh, I can read the invisible ink, darling—is that what it was? Or *was* there an actual note, and did *I* somehow leave it behind, or did *you* pick up a blank by mistake to put in my envelope, or what??? Well, whatever the answer, don't be disturbed, dearest, for I have so many sweet memories that you are right here with me in a very true sense, so the disappointment is not as sharp as you might fear. But if you find it, send it to me please.

Either that cloud sea is adrift at a higher level now or we have come down to a lower altitude—it is just below us—so dazzling a white in the sunlight that the eye cannot linger on their shapes. Clouds—I suppose I may be preoccupied with them for the next few weeks and will no doubt discover for myself new thoughts and meanings. It's something like starting out on a journey into a country only *dimly* (yes, that is the word, but I stopped short before writing it!)—only dimly known. Well, that's what they said they wanted—"a new look at clouds—to make people feel they are seeing them for the first time."

Goodness—there is land below us. When I look down very intently, peering into spaces between clouds I can see light streaks (roads) and variously shaped patches through the murky gray air and the effect is almost exactly like just barely making out objects lying on the floor of the bay (our bay) when the water is its usual turbid green.

I loved the episode of the book during our unexpected time-dividend at the airport this morning. And darling, I shall love telling you what I am reading. Don't you know that it will keep me from feeling "alone" during the writing of this book if you will go along with me, all the way? I don't mean, of course, to wade through *all* my bibliography—just the key things so we can talk about it, for after all you do have other things to do. (Like doing a little writing yourself!) Darling, it was all a delight—these days with you. They added many precious memories. My thanks and love to all of you. And my special love to you.

Rachel

WEDNESDAY, FEBRUARY 1

Darling [Dorothy]—

Now I have several letters to answer, for my recent notes haven't been very satisfying. But I am planning this to reach you on Friday, when the Amherst occasion[1] will be behind you, and you will—I hope—have had your evening with Stanley and perhaps be looking forward to his return for another night, at least.

What a hard time you have had since that tiny oasis here, my dear one![2] I am so distressed by your worries. But please don't *ever* feel you should withhold them, for it would distress me even more to find that you had, and, darling, it makes me feel so close to you when I know you will tell me of your worries. It is such a relief to know that Stan's crisis is behind him. But now I know you won't be quite easy in your mind until those stomach X-rays are repeated and definitely interpreted. But what a blessing these clinic visits can be. For if he should have an ulcer, it is so much better to know it early, and regulate his life accord-

[1] On February 1 Stanley received an alumni award from the University of Massachusetts, his alma mater, for his agricultural work.

[2] The Freemans had visited RC from January 22 to 24 coinciding with a Washington, D.C., business trip for Stanley.

ingly. Maybe that, and the stress of office crises, have been working in one of those vicious circles to cause much of his trouble. Well I do hope it will all be understood, and under control, soon, darling. But do tell me, dear. Goodness knows, I have poured out my troubles to you enough that you shouldn't hesitate!

I doubt that you would want to go to New York quite so soon as next week, but let me know if you do. Otherwise, I doubt I shall stay over at all. I think I'll take the overnight train Monday and then return Tuesday evening. I may or may not attend the Book Awards ceremony. *If* you wanted to come, I would stay over Tuesday night, but if I'm going on with the program[3] there will be other February opportunities. And if I go next week, it will mean I *am* going on with it.

[3] The "Omnibus" television program on clouds, for which RC was producing a script.

Darling, you are such a comfort. I think you know what it means to be able to speak one's inmost thoughts. And apparently you read my thoughts even before they are spoken! It's a curious thing, but I know now that idea about *The Edge* had been wandering about in my mind for sometime without being definitely identified until we talked. I think once (a long time ago) talking of *The Sea*, I tried to describe the thing that happens when one has finally established such unity with one's subject matter that the subject itself takes over and the writer becomes merely the instrument through which the real act of creation is accomplished. And when this mysterious something happens, one always knows it. I suppose it happened sometimes in writing *Under the Sea-Wind* (in fact, looking back, I can remember when it did and even locate the passages, but I was not then analytical about such things) but I first recognized it while writing *The Sea*. That was what *didn't* happen with *The Edge*, or at least it happened so seldom and in such a limited way that I didn't write the book I might have written. And I know that, in order to have this happen, the writer must for a time lose himself utterly in his work. In those four years I could never do that. That is the problem I must solve if I am ever again to be the writer I could be.

There is a bitter little corollary to the thought I expressed last week, but I won't write it. Oh well, I will, or you'll wonder. It is the awareness that all that followed the publication of *The Sea*—the acclaim, the excitement on the part of critics and the public at discovering a "promising" new writer—was simply blotted out for me by the private tragedy[4] that engulfed me at precisely that time. I know it will never happen again, and if ever I am bitter, it is about that.

[4] Marjie, unmarried, had become pregnant with Roger.

Now darling—you know my inmost thoughts on this, but it does no good for either you or me to brood over them. There is a new opportunity before me, and perhaps the Harper book will be what I want it to be.

Meanwhile, of course I am eager to hear your thoughts on possible solutions of the difficulty. I feel I'm going to see you in New York *this month*, or if not, in West Bridgewater early in March.

I think I won't send the various letters & clippings I spoke of this time, but I will as soon as I've replied to the letters, one of which balances the Hawkes review so nicely that I want you to have them together. Actually the review isn't bad, on second reading, except in one or two spots. And I think you'll get a laugh out of this latest Bok letter, so I'll send it, too, next time. Darling, I do hope I didn't upset you when I asked you to assure me that you weren't really "jealous." And I hope I didn't make you feel you mustn't say joking or teasing things about him—I like to laugh about it, too, it was just that one little word you used that stuck in my mind and I wanted to banish it. I'm sure you said it lightly, but I just wanted you to tell me so.

Now, darling—this is like ending a phone call—but I suppose I must stop. What has happened to the schedule? And who cares? At the moment, at least, I think we both have a real need to write whenever something "occurs to" us, as the Judge says. I do hope there can be post-Amherst word from you this week—only I don't see how there could be. But by Monday, *please* for you know I'm going to New York. Dearest, I do hope your mind is easier by now. And remember how much I love you—all ways.

Rachel

THURSDAY AFTERNOON, FEBRUARY 2

Dearest [Dorothy],

This will be a hasty note, but I want to tell you something that I think will please you. Apparently I am going to do the *Woman's Home Companion* "piece"[5] after all! You know the whole thing collapsed last fall because they would not meet what Marie considered a reasonable price. So everybody said "Sorry" and dropped it. Last night Marie phoned to say the *Companion* had called to ask if I would write the article—at my price. I said yes, provided they could wait until the "Omnibus" job was done. I'm glad, for I always had a little feeling of regret about it—it seemed something worth doing.

Your letter mailed Tuesday came today and made me very happy. Now I'm so eager for further word, after Amherst, but I know I can hardly expect that until Monday.

More enclosures for you to read and return someday—no hurry about it.

My dearest love, as always—
Rachel

Can you guess (from enclosed letter) what the non-fiction winner is?[6] I still can't! I don't think it's anything on the Best-Seller list, and of course it doesn't have to be. And I'm sure it's nothing I've read.

FRIDAY NIGHT, FEBRUARY 3

Darling [Dorothy],

Yesterday when I read the first sentence of the letter you wrote Monday afternoon after reading my thoughts on Mr. Bok and Us (remember what you said?) I knew I had to send you at once the valentine I'd been saving so carefully

[5] "Help Your Child to Wonder" was published in the *Woman's Home Companion* magazine in July of 1956 and in book form as *The Sense of Wonder* in 1965.

[6] Enclosed letter not preserved. The 1955 National Book Award winner for nonfiction was Herbert Kubly's *An American in Italy. The Edge of the Sea* had been a nominee for this award.

for you. Here it is; now look at it and then we can both laugh! Darling, your letter made me feel as if you had done just what you said you wanted to do, and now I've dismissed that word from my mind and feel better. And I think there is a lot to laugh about, and I want to. In fact, I was beginning to have a little fun about comparisons even before you were here—remember I said I'd have to discuss a writing schedule with him? (And I think I should—there was ANOTHER LETTER today!) Well I won't answer this one for at least a week, so there! And besides he's gone to Florida. (Do you think I should have sent him one to read his first night away from home? You see I have an imagination, too!) Oh darling it is funny, isn't it? And I still say what in the world is he getting out of it? Maybe he is the kind who pursues something with great zest for a while and then drops it. If so, he'll probably get bored any day. After all I'm sure we are very, very different. (He says today he is "an extroverted male with many introversions." Should I reply that I'm am introverted female with few or no extroversions?)

Yes his comment about metaphors bothered me, too. I'm sure he means similes. At the moment I can't think whether Tomlinson refrains from them, but I agree with you that he makes expert use of metaphor. I confess I can't always follow the dartings of his thoughts (Mr. Bok's) as about "sardonic" today, and once or twice I got confused in his philosophizing about war. Now that he has told me who got the award, I know why I couldn't guess—this book seems never to have come to my attention! He is a little hard on Mrs. Lindbergh—maybe that's the "extroverted male" viewpoint. But I did have to laugh at the way he described the voting!

Now it's time to change the subject! Darling, it was wonderful of you to write Wednesday—how did you ever squeeze that in! But it did make me so happy to have it. And I'm so glad you could go to see Alice[7]—I know it was wonderful for her and would give her a real lift.

I have spent most of today reading and thinking along the lines of the Harper book, so that I may at least appear to have some ideas when I see the Canfields[8] tomorrow. Now that the *Companion* piece has come up again, I feel a bit like a juggler with several balls in the air at once, but that article always did seem to me worth doing. And at the rate "Omnibus" is holding off almost final settlement of terms, maybe I won't be doing "Clouds" after all!

My "problem" was underscored yesterday when poor Marjie had another attack of whatever she has, and I spent so much of the day there that nothing usable was left of it. Now she can't start her clinic tests until Thursday (if I go to New York) for even if I just sent her over in a taxi we'd have to keep Roger. They found albumen in her urine the other day, so that is a worry until they do some blood chemistry to see just what it means. And she is to have X-rays of stomach, gall bladder, and colon. When these crises develop there seems to be nothing for it but for me to go—by the time we know about it Roger is needing his breakfast and she needs something—even if only a cup of tea—so she won't have an in-

[7] Alice Mullen, the Carson family friend from Amherst, Massachusetts.

[8] Cass Canfield, Harper and Brothers editor, and his wife, Katharine.

sulin reaction. Well, I do hope they'll discover something that can be cured. Meanwhile, what is needed is a near-twin of me who can do everything I do except write, and let me do that! When I feel, as I do now, the pressure of all the things that seem worth doing in the years that are left, it seems so silly to be spending my time being a nurse and housemaid.

Darling, I'll perhaps mail something in New York Tuesday. I won't call you—it looks like a very hectic day. But I'll probably write you at length on the way home.

Know how much I love you? I hope you do.

Rachel

Reading over this letter, it seem so lacking in expression of all the tender thoughts that are, and have been, in my mind. Please read the invisible writing!

SATURDAY AFTERNOON, FEBRUARY 4

Dearest [Dorothy],

It was really wonderful to have word from you from Amherst, and best of all to know, before the week-end hiatus, that you are safely back in West Bridgewater despite the snow! It seemed to me you made really wonderful time both ways—I think your return route was more or less the road we followed to Amherst when we stopped with Alice on the way home in 1953. Of course I am eager for all the details, and especially to read the citation, but I'm so happy for Stan and for you, too. How wonderful that you could be there, and what an appropriate and graceful way they took to acknowledge your part in Stan's achievements. Will you have prints of the pictures they took? I'd love to see them.

I do hope Stanley made the planned-for trip so that he could enjoy all this with you, too. It was such nice timing and I hope weather didn't interfere. We have had rain all day today, freezing on trees, bushes, and sidewalks, but so far not too bad on streets. However, I didn't take the car this morning but called a cab, not being sure what might develop before I got home. I went down early and had my hair done, then met Mr. Canfield at the Mayflower. (Mrs. Canfield didn't come after all, having discovered that she seemed to be "expected" for lunch at the Achesons', whom they are visiting.) But that probably gave us a better opportunity to talk of books and the writing of books, and a very pleasant conversation it proved to be. He is an older man than other editors I've dealt with, and knows so many writers. For instance, he knows Mr. Tomlinson well, and said he wished I would write to him—he thought it would please him. I think I left him feeling quite happy about my contribution to their series; I was surprised myself to find that in telling him about it, I seemed to have a pretty good idea what I was going to do!

It was really wonderful of you, dear, to take time to visit poor Alice, who must really have had a wretched time since Christmas with her affliction, and I know your visit will provide her with happy thoughts for a long time to come. And if I could possibly have had doubts on that score, a delightful card came this morning—"We had a wonderful and rewarding visit yesterday with your darling friend Dorothy. I can't tell you how dear I think she is.—I'll write a long letter about our visit. Thank you for letting me know her." I know she would be really delighted to have you and Stan stay with her if you could, and actually I think you and she have a lot of interests in common—music, for example, about which she knows a lot. And books—she has always been a great reader. And gardens; really there would be quite a list.

I talked to Marie last night and she still had no satisfactory word from "Omnibus"—nothing negative really, but just that they are "working on" the business details. That puts me in the unpleasant spot of committing my time to something that may or may not prove satisfactory. I have told Marie I didn't want to go up again until they had signed an acceptable contract; but if I am to go over the film with Dr. Schaefer[9] I have to be there this Tuesday. So at this point I don't know what is going to happen, but we feel they are not very businesslike, for in theory all this was ironed out in December.

Are you tired of reading Bok letters? If not, here is another; I think you'll be interested in what he tells about the Book Award, and the way he tells it. No wonder I couldn't guess! Probably there are references in his letter that you won't understand without mine, but I've been writing in longhand without a carbon. Now I'm going to *not* write for a week or ten days, so just return this sometime during the coming week for my attention!

This week-end I'm going to try to clean up other letters (between you and Judge Bok my other correspondents get scant attention) and read a lot of meteorology references I've picked up during the last few days. I don't think it's time lost even if I shouldn't do clouds.

This will be all for now, dear. Our love to all.

Rachel

Your mother's good letter, and yours to Mamma, came several days ago. Thank you both.

WEDNESDAY, FEBRUARY 8

Darling [Dorothy]—

To my great happiness, both your letters were waiting for me when I got home last night about 12:15, and I saved them until I could get into bed. One of them I read twice before finally turning out the light. It was sweet to have them, dear.

And of course I loved our talk yesterday morning—it all worked out so nicely at both ends, thanks to our system of telepathy—you ready to receive the call at the time I was freest to make it!

Darling, I do hope your mind is easier about Stan by the time you read

[9] Dr. Vincent Schaefer, chemist, meteorologist, discoverer of cloud seeding, and director of research for the Munitalp Foundation.

this. Of course I've known for about two months that an unnamed something was worrying you—which worried me as much as if you'd told me. And I do so hope that worry is removed, and the stomach X-rays favorable.

I know you will understand if I write only notes like this until next Tuesday, when the major job for "Omnibus" must be done. I confess I'm pretty weary, and the situation here is no more conducive to work than usual—some worries about Marjie today, and tomorrow morning will be consumed by the clinic visit.

Now it seems a very long time to wait to discuss all these things you are putting away in the "Rachel file." If you have a magic solution maybe I should know it now—but please forgive me for doubting (as I do) that there *is* any magic way out. (That wasn't your word, I know.) And what is this "serious" side to the "Bok story"? So many riddles! But write to me, darling, even if I cheat you a bit now.

I love you dearly,
R.

SATURDAY AFTERNOON, FEBRUARY 18

Dearest [Dorothy],

Now I have a little time to write—got home about two o'clock after being down to have my hair done, had a late lunch, and am now relaxing in bed, although I could do better without the typewriter. But it does keep the words coming faster. We are going to have dinner with a certain four-year-old gentleman tonight, and will take his packages then (a Stieff hand-puppet black cat; book of Bible stories from his Grandma, Winnie the Pooh, and wooden beads and other makings of flower pots full of flowers.) Marjie reports they survived the party, though the host was in tears at the end.

Our trip to New York was a great success. It was a little train that starts in Cumberland only an hour or two away, and had only one coach. The trip to Washington takes about 25 minutes, at least 15 of which are spent maneuvering around the yards so they can back into the station. But that was fine, because it gave us a good view of simply dozens of trains. We hadn't been on our way ten minutes until Roger announced, "I'm so hungry—s'pose we go into the dining car." He seemed rather shocked to learn there wasn't any, but otherwise he approved highly of the entire trip. We had our "bite to eat" in the station restaurant, rode a car, a torpedo boat, and a horse in the waiting room, then came home by streetcar, bus, and taxi! Meanwhile, "Mommie" had a chance to bake the birthday cake, which had animal crackers standing up all around the edge.

As you might guess, I have still heard nothing from "Omnibus," neither by phone, letter, nor carrier pigeon. Of course if they ever communicate, I'd love to say I'm not available at whatever time they suggest, but on the other hand I want to get the thing over and forget I ever heard of it. (I do hope I'm not spoiling "Omnibus" programs for you!)

You may remember Judge Bok's enthusiasm for a new novel called *H.M.S. Ulysses*.[10] I have since bought and read it. It really is a wonderful story, in my mind far superior to *The Caine Mutiny* and *Cruel Sea*, with which it has been compared.[11] It is hard to put down and yet, as Mr. Bok said, it is such a terrible story that one almost has to stop now and then for relief from tension.

I am curious about *An American in Italy*—I looked at it today in Ballantyne's. It was published by my old friends Simon and Schuster, but if they have ever seen fit to advertise it (even since it received the award) their effort escaped me. One of Ballantyne's buyers, with whom I talked, said she had tried to read it, but couldn't get interested.

I am afraid Jacquelyn Berrill[12] has been "scooped" as they say, on her Schweitzer book. I saw a new one today (also written for young people) called *The Story of Albert Schweitzer*. I thought hers was to appear in January, but I have seen no notice of it.

My present prediction (you know how good they are, but maybe I can do better on other people—besides, come to think of it, I said *The Edge* would never be No. 1) anyway—I think this silly *Bridey Murphy*[13] thing is going to scoot right up and crowd Mrs. Lindbergh, if it doesn't actually displace her. The *Tribune* says this week there are 120,000 copies in print, and the book is only four weeks old! *The Edge*, by the way, is No. 6 this week—up one. Gunther[14] is down to No. 9.

Now I suppose I have to stop and get the birthday packages ready. We are due there in about half an hour. There is still much I want to say, as usual. And this is all about myself. But you say that's what you like to read.

I shall be so eager to know about your Garden Club program. I can understand that your task now is to select and eliminate, for on such a subject there is so much to say.

More soon, dear. Meanwhile, very much love.

Rachel

Discovered too late that I'd been writing on my backing sheet. Excuse patch work, please.

SATURDAY AFTERNOON, FEBRUARY 25

Darling [Dorothy],

There hadn't been even a shadow of a plan to call you last night, but I'm sure you understood why I *had* to. That was a horrid thing to hear—without any of the details that would have reassured me—on the way home.[15] So I was deeply thankful to be able to go to bed knowing you were safely at home.

Snow was falling for some miles either side of Philadelphia, as it had here Friday morning, but there was only light rain in Washington last night. Today the wind has been tremendous, but it rushes through the sky with the hollow roaring sound that, to me, means March and spring. And now there is such a

[10] Authored by Alistair MacLean.

[11] Herman Wouk's *The Caine Mutiny* and Nicholas Monsarrat's *Cruel Sea* were both published in 1951.

[12] Jacquelyn Berrill, wife of Jack Berrill, authored the children's books *Wonder of the Seashore* (1951) and *Strange Nurseries: Another Wonder Book* (1954).

[13] *The Search for Bridey Murphy* by Morey Bernstein.

[14] John Gunther, author of *Inside Africa*.

[15] RC and DF had met in New York City on February 23 to see *Carousel*. After they departed on separate trains on February 24, reports of snow and a Boston train wreck had concerned RC.

tumultuous drumbeat of rain on the roof that it got Jeffie out of his basket-on-the-bed where he had been napping, and sent him downstairs to seek security under the platform rocker in the little bedroom.

Dear, I do hope the trip to New York was even half as rewarding and satisfying for you as for me. It was wonderful of you to come. I did need very much to talk with you, and it did me a great deal of good. I am thankful you realize that, as with most human situations, there is no cure-all that can suddenly take care of all aspects of the problem. I'm sure it will have to be worked at, a little at a time. But, dearest, you have helped me see some things much more clearly, and you have strengthened my determination to change some of the things I can change. I do hope even that much is a satisfaction to you, as it should be.

All of our time together was so sweet, dear. I hope (and believe) it was for you, too. And now we both have the freesias to remind us—though we need no reminders.

No doubt the "Omnibus" people are behaving quite normally—*for them*! Apparently all is sweetness and light! Just frantic, last-minute jugglings of programs, so that of course they are always occupied in desperate urgency, with *next* Sunday's program. In theory, according to yesterday's information, I should be working with them beginning March 5, or later that week. But don't rearrange your life to be near a television set March 11, for probably there will still be one or two changes of date!

Dear, I had to laugh when I looked over the accumulated mail last night. You know I said to you that there was no cause for concern about the pace of the correspondence with Judge Bok, for I had written a letter he would get Monday, and Tuesday's mail had brought *no reply*. But that, it turns out, was the fault of the Post Office, for I found a letter written and mailed in Philadelphia on Monday! Quite a long one, too, continuing his philosophical thoughts on war, and amplifying his views on *An American in Italy*. He also comments on my picture in the *Tribune*—I remind him a little (if he may say so) of England's Queen Mother. Well, I suppose there could be less flattering comparisons, though she too, is a little overweight! I'll either save the letter to show you, or send it after I have replied, which I shall *not* do today, and perhaps not for another week.

This morning there was an urgent invitation in the mail to contribute— as a "guest author" who doubtless had other, more lasting publishing commitments—to a series Dodd Mead is planning—"1001 Questions" about this and that, mine obviously, about the sea. Edwin Teale is doing insects, Rutherford Platt trees, etc. All made to sound very easy and profitable. Well, we shall see. Too many distractions from the big jobs, I fear. And I think I'm going to feel the same way about any time-consuming relative to the Maineland film.

A letter from Mr. Delano this morning. I gather they have had much more snow than usual; he thinks my plants should survive well under their blanket.

Now I shall try to put "Omnibus" out of my mind for the next week. I hope I can get the tax data in shape tonight and tomorrow, and then I shall try to do

¹⁶ *Woman's Home
Companion*.

a first draft of the *WHC*[16] article this week. If I could do that, I ought to make
the end-of-March deadline comfortably.

Paul writes that sales have passed the 70,000 mark. Not bad, BUT on tomorrow's *Tribune* I have slipped to #9. AND, that wretched *Bridey Murphy* thing
has displaced Mrs. Lindbergh! That is really a blow. One doesn't mind having
something really good move ahead, but I'm sorry that the book that broke her
first-place record couldn't have been a better one.

Incidentally, in Penn Station yesterday I went into the Doubleday Book
Shop to find some train reading (got a 25¢ reprint of Cameron Hawley's *Executive Suite*, which I raced through before Washington). A girl who was ludi-
crously drunk came in and somehow conveyed the idea that she wanted a
book—any book—as a gift for someone. She said—"Give me something I
couldn't understand!" The clerk, somewhat nonplused, finally selected *Bridey
Murphy*, for some reason. After she had staggered out, another clerk said, "Why
didn't you give her *Roget's Thesaurus?*"

Well, darling, this must be all. *Maybe* my letters will be brief for a while.
But please, if you don't know it, let me tell you that my heart is full of gratitude
for all you have done, and all you mean to me.

All my love,
Rachel

TUESDAY, FEBRUARY 28, BEDTIME

My darling [Dorothy],

At such a time I long so to go to you—or at the very least to call you—as
I'm sure you understand. One is impossible, the other might not be satisfactory
and there is always the deterring thought that others must think we are crazy!
All this, too, I know you understand.

On first reading your letter surprised me; then as I re-read and thought
about it, I began to see it as a natural result of New York. For every solution we
considered then came up against a stone wall—*me*!

Tonight, in the midst of birthday company, I've been thinking of an analogy that might help us. Suppose you and I were writing a play. We've managed
to get our principal character involved in a dreadfully complex situation and we
have to work out a solution. We think of one thing after another but reject all
these ideas for the same reason—the actions they involve wouldn't be "in character" for the person we have created. So our play wouldn't be credible, for the
audience would say—"But she just wouldn't do that."

Well, I needn't go on, but I think it illuminates the difficulty we've experienced, not as playwrights, but as one precious friend trying to help another.
No solution can last, or bring relief, if it calls for actions that are "out of character." That isn't to say, darling, that I think all your suggestions were, but I
think it is the difficulty we've sensed in regard to some ideas.

Darling, there is a great deal to be said and thought, and at the moment I'm not very clear about it. I rather wish I could find time to write at length on it before we talk again, for I think more clearly on paper than in spoken words. Perhaps I can—but the price of seeing you soon (end of March, I mean—NOT "soon") is devotion to the jobs on hand.

But for tonight, my darling, a few thoughts. *Please* don't reproach yourself. *Of course* the situation is one that you resent, in my behalf. Loving me as you do, and having been subjected for so long to my cries of anguish, I don't see how you could do other than urge strong measures. I'm sure *I* would, if the situation were reversed. And I'd probably be quite impatient with you if you didn't agree! So I do understand, darling, and if possible I love you all the more for the way you have tried so hard to find a way out for me.

Even now I think there is probably some middle ground, if we could only discover it—something between just running away from the problem or letting it engulf and destroy what I think, at least, I am or could be.

Darling, there are things in the years (I'm still referring to the current situation, but that antedates Us by several years) before I knew you that I don't even want to talk about—there is nothing to be gained, and it is too painful. But there was a time when I longed so desperately just to run away from it all, and then in time I learned that you can't do that. But dear, my attitude is one that has developed over a period of years. And I think that yours, too, must evolve—and is evolving—and that takes time. And so, darling, I have understood some of the reasons for views (of yours) that didn't agree with my own.

But heavens, I seem to be suggesting that all this time I've been a model of saintly resignation, when the truth is that I've been complaining and crying out for help. It's just that I have long known the thing you now realize clearly—that there are many attractive and quite sensible solutions that I can't accept—just because they call for something I couldn't do, or would be so troubled about doing, that my "last state would be worse than the first."

Sleepiness overcame me then, and now (Wednesday morning) your Monday letter is here, darling.

I mustn't write much more now, but I just want to stress one thing. You must get over this sense of having "failed" me, darling. You *haven't*—you have helped and comforted me enormously. I hope you can realize—and I think maybe you are beginning to—that the help you have given is not to be measured by the fact that I have or have not adopted your suggestions. It is something much less tangible than that—and something that, in the end, counts for much more!

So darling—don't talk any more of "not forgiving" yourself, or of "failure." Please!

I am thankful if there was anything comforting in the letter you received Monday—I was afraid it was very general and impersonal!

[17] A neighbor.

This will reach you Friday, I suppose, and perhaps I won't write more in this vein until the end of the week. We are going to Eleanor's[17] this afternoon, you know, and I want to spend tomorrow and Friday on the *Companion*.

Darling, one more thing! I said to you in New York that I couldn't discuss the basic problem with Marie, because she would come up with purely practical solutions that I—in my weakness or whatever it is—couldn't accept. I don't believe you could have thought I was putting you in that class, but I want to be sure. (As evidence, I *do* discuss it endlessly with you.) And, dear, in all you have said, I have been aware, perhaps more than you yourself, that you *were* recognizing the limitations that my own character imposes. You might have wished I would "become hard boiled" but you did understand the difficulty—you dear, precious darling. And now this thought—if you had taken the opposite view of passive acceptance, that too would have kept me from opening my heart to you. The only other friend who knows the true nature of the family situation is Elizabeth Dickson.[18] Dear as she is, she simply isn't intellectually capable of understanding what all this does to me as a writer, and that is a complete barrier to discussing it with her. I know she deplores the financial drain, and the monopoly of so much of my life, but the really destructive part she couldn't understand. And you do, darling. As I said last night, I think there must be a middle ground and that is what we must find. And you can help enormously darling—and not by keeping silent, either!

[18] A nurse and friend of RC's from her earliest days in the Washington, D.C., area.

So, in the month ahead, think when there are quiet moments, but not with a sense of terrible urgency, dear. There is time. And make notes. And then we'll talk—and March 27 is the date I'll try to be ready.

I love you darling—so very dearly.

Rachel

Re-reading, this—I feel like throwing it away! Again a whole letter about *me*! Darling, I'm really ashamed of it. And it isn't the way I feel, believe me. Everything that touches you does concern me so deeply. In extenuation, I can truly say, as to this letter, that I felt you were disturbed and I wanted to set your mind at rest. But dearest, I do know you have other concerns and problems, and they concern me, too, as affecting you. Even if I haven't said so in this one-topic letter!

You know what?

THURSDAY, MARCH 8, MAIL TIME

Dearest [Dorothy],

This is only a report that I'm home and have spent most of the day sleeping or dozing, and so feel almost human again.

(Roger has just told me I look like "a penguin wearing a beautiful flower.")
I believe "Clouds" is scheduled for 5:30, but better be at your TV set at 5 and be sure!

How lucky we didn't time your New York trip for this occasion—that would have been real frustration!

I meant to ask what time you listened to "our" concerto.[19] It was played between 9 and 9:30—and very beautifully!

I am unexpectedly having to read proof on the Books Abridged version of *The Edge*—that has occupied my waking hours today—getting started, I mean.

Darling—I'll write a real letter tomorrow. All my love.

Rachel

[19] Mendelssohn Violin Concerto in E minor, referred to in RC's letter of December 8, 1956.

MONDAY, MARCH 12

Dearest [Dorothy],

It was sweet of you to call last night; I hope you know how much it meant to me. I'll try to tell you when I see you.

My chief reaction to this television experience is that I'm glad it's over, and that I seriously doubt it would be worthwhile to get involved in such a project again. But you never know till you try something, do you? It has just occurred to me that Mr. Cook didn't mention Dr. Schaefer or his Foundation, though I understood both were to be credited; also, he didn't explain the speeding-up of the pictures, though we specifically discussed the need of doing so last week!

I think you will be interested in details about the "Philadelphia weekend."[20] I've just replied to the recent letter, so will send both with the following additional comments. I think it was in one of the letters you still have that he made another very lovely remark about *Under the Sea-Wind*, and in replying I suddenly had the thought that if he didn't have the original edition I'd like to send him one from my hoard. So I asked him and received his reply of March 2. My next communication was a note from New York to confirm the March 11 date for "Clouds," since he said he wanted to see it. In that I asked him where to send the book; he only occasionally writes from Radnor, and I had the idea that perhaps they spend only a rare week-end there, but I have no Philadelphia address except the Court. To this, he replies on March 8. In replying, I think I have handled the question of Mrs. Bok all right—at least I hope so. I told him I'd enjoy coming, but there was some uncertainty with me about the date, and perhaps when his wife returned he'd find she already had plans for that "nice looking week-end"—so could we confirm it later? Then I explained something of my schedule and how it might crowd April 14, and said if that didn't work maybe I could come later in April or early in May. (Even if I were sure of the date, I didn't want to accept definitely until I'm invited by her. What do you think Emily Post would say to my handling of the situation?) Also, I've decided that when or if I go, it will be a Saturday to Sunday affair; not the long week-end he suggests. In case we all hate each other violently, it will be good to have it short, and I'd much rather they regretted its shortness than its long duration! I do like his

[20] RC had been invited to spend a weekend at the Boks' home near Philadelphia.

sense of humor. I loved that "I said to me" about *The Sea*—and don't you love what he says about that book (says she shamelessly!)? Did you ever look him up in *Current Biography*?

I've had some very odd correspondence lately. One woman addresses me as "Dear Mermaid Carson" and signs herself "Affectionately (how can I help it?) yours"—but actually a very nice letter. A man wonders if I, or someone I know, would like to buy his statue of "Lady Purete." At first I thought he was the sculptor, but I guess not. Then someone from your state tells me a long tale about Saint Somebody who, in crossing the ocean, lost his crucifix overboard; on landing on some Indian Ocean shore, he met a crab advancing toward him out of the waves, bearing the crucifix aloft. Can I tell him what kind of crab it probably was? And may he quote me in an article he wants to write for a Catholic magazine? (I replied I was afraid I could make no useful comment!) And today a man sends his copy of *The Sea* (without return postage, of course) and says would I please inscribe it with a few lines on the meaning or purpose of life. (This from the Home Study Department of the U. of Chicago.) Do all the nuts read Carson—or what??

Publication of *Man Under the Sea* has been postponed until May 9, one of the Harper editors tells me so I've asked Mr. Brown for a postponement on the review.[21] That will help.

IF I can get along with the *Companion* article, I'd still like to plan for Boston the last week of March and then go south the following week. But everything depends on progress the rest of this week. I have one of those horrid Audubon Board Meetings tonight; then no more interruptions, I trust.

Forsythia is in bloom and frogs are singing, so spring is on the way!

I do hope all is well there, dear. My love to all.

Rachel

[21] Francis Brown of the *New York Times* had asked RC to write a review of James Dugan's *Man Under the Sea*.

THURSDAY, MARCH 15

Darling [Dorothy],

If you don't go to Orono, you should have this Saturday; if you do, perhaps it will greet you on your return. It was so wonderful to talk with you yesterday, and as we agreed then, I didn't try to put anything in the mail yesterday for a Friday send-off.

I'm struggling hard with the article for the *Woman's Home "Bepanion"* as Roger calls it. I asked him what he would think if he saw his picture in a magazine, and he gave a very knowing laugh and said, "Oh, you can't put pictures in magazines!" Last night I bought him a silly record at the grocery store (of all places!)—something about Siamese cats, and the song mentioned their "domicile." This morning he said to M.—"Domicile—that means their home"—but none of us had defined the word for him! To return to the article, there is no dearth of material, it's just a question of finding an appropriate form for it, and so far I'm floundering. But the solution will come, I trust.

I see Sir Laurence Olivier is quite disenchanted with what TV did to his film. Poor man—I have a certain sympathy. You try it once and that's enough. Did I say to you that I was shocked that Mr. Cook didn't mention Dr. Schaefer—without whom I would never have attempted the job? But *I* was presented as the expert, which was really embarrassing.

The plan that you might come here that last week of March seems better and better, the more I think of it. I do have to see people at Harvard sometime, but if I go to Boston now I'll miss seeing Stan, and maybe I could go later while he's being a gentleman of leisure and we could all have some fun. Boston will be more pleasant later in the year, anyway, and maybe this time we could show you a normal Washington spring, instead of the frigid blasts that greeted you last year. And the combination of Bernstein and Our Symphony [22] seems too wonderful to miss. I've reserved tickets, in hopes. (Please tell me if you don't share my preference in seats. For the symphony concerts, I like the balcony, so I can see what's going on. I've reserved seats, in the front row of the balcony, but can change if you prefer orchestra.) So you see it's all taking definite form in my mind, dear. I'm sure I can be ready for you to come *here* that week, but my trip to Boston would entail some preparation to see Dr. Wald,[23] etc. And as you know, I may want to go south the first week of April, so this is the perfect solution!

A letter from Alice this morning, with rather distressing overtones. Kitty[24] has just had another "spell," so violent that Alice was actually frightened. I don't quite know whether K. is out of her mind or just thinks it useful to pretend she is. K. had gone to the young rector, who is evidently not as bright as he might be. He came to see A. and told her that if money was the difficulty, she should be the one to make peace and go away—that anything she might have done for K. in the past is of no importance now—it is the future that matters. And he is said to have told K. that the fact A. was her sister didn't matter—she owed her nothing! Poor Alice is searching desperately for work—says she must establish some income before she can do anything.

Remember what I said once about other people's troubles? Yes. I know you do.

Dear, I loved what you wrote about the "Clouds" script. (Would you like a copy of it sometime?) Our neighbor Mr. Delaney came over to give me his reactions, and said he would have known I wrote it even if my name hadn't been mentioned. You will laugh at this, but several times while working on the script I paused at that sentence containing the words "awareness" and "dim." It seemed to be trying to tell me something, and the something was connected with *you*, only I couldn't quite get it. Now I know! My trademarks. Wasn't that silly of me?

Thank you for telling me about Stan's fresh honors from Amherst. Tell him we are very proud of him. I do think it lovely that all this well-deserved recognition is coming his way just now—it will give him some pleasant things to think about while in the hospital.[25] Yes, by all means keep *Ulysses* for hospital

[22] Tchaikovsky's Sixth Symphony, listed in an advertisement for the concert enclosed in RC's letter.

[23] Dr. George Wald, biologist and Harvard professor.

[24] Alice Mullen's sister.

[25] For tests to try to determine the source of internal bleeding.

reading—it certainly is diverting, even if grim. I have been meaning to ask whether Stan sees the magazine *Modern Photography*. The last issue is devoted to 35 mm stuff, and has a long list of possible markets. I can't think of any reason why he couldn't sell some of his beautiful stuff if he wanted to. And it has this advantage—if he sold even one, he could consider any expenditures for equipment or films (within reason on the latter) as business deductions for income tax purposes. Mr. Greenbaum told me that, quite definitely.

I have been meaning to ask you what about my white hyacinth bulbs. When can they be planted—spring or fall? I have just let them sit, without watering, since the blooms faded. Is that right?

Now I suppose I must return to my job. There is much unanswered in your letters, I know, but I'm hoping to answer them in person. Guess what? Last night, after days of rain, I had a first glimpse of a fresh new moon!

> All my love —
> *Rachel*

On Sunday. Roger could hardly wait to tell me a "joke" he learned in Sunday School. (Not, I take it, as part of the official curriculum.) This is the way it goes: "You know what?" "No, what?" "That's what!" And so on, through endless repetitions, each with gales of laughter!

APPROACHING NEW YORK, MARCH 30

Darling [Rachel],

I'll try to get this written in New York so writing won't be too jiggly. The miles are dividing us. Queer, how different one's feelings depending on the direction in which one is heading! I felt like weeping as you slid out of my sight but perhaps in 25 more days, you'll be in my sight again.

I began by knitting but I fear there will be no sweater on Martha's birthday at my rate of progress. But it's not important as I have other things in mind for her anyway.

Then I went on to Mr. van der Post.[26] Darling, probably you wouldn't remember but in the Preface and lst chapter there were passages so significant in relation to our conversation last night that it seemed like pure stardust. I may copy some of them to send back to you for now is the time for you to know what I mean rather than a few weeks later.

I can see that I am going to enjoy him—one reason is that there is some of you in his writing—"awareness," for instance—oh, I don't mean just the words alone—a quality, too.

Then to prove I did nap, I missed Wilmington altogether and was amazed to awake at Philadelphia.

There was the usual scramble for the diner at the regular lunch hour so I waited till 3 o'clock and it was quite perfect. And for some reason the food was

[26] Laurens van der Post's *Venture to the Interior*, published in 1951.

of better quality—I actually enjoyed my lunch—I only wished you were facing me instead of only being there invisibly—there was a vacant seat across from me but it wasn't vacant.

You know how my thoughts were living over all the hours together. We have added so much to your storehouse of memories this winter. This visit will take up an unusual amount of space in that storehouse, darling.

Sometimes I have feelings of regret that new experiences tend to displace some of the treasures of the past—but I mustn't, for there are years ahead and we can have such lovely times going back over some of the cherished memories that can't help but fade with Time. Like "This is the letter I wasn't to write (you said)"—what a queer delicious tingle that sent all over me!

I'll have to admit I'm enjoying the luxury of my accommodations. You'll laugh at one touch that I like especially—the "wall-to-wall" carpeting. I doubt if I could travel really happily on long overnight trips unless I could have the best but I hope you understand how I feel about this—for me, just to be able *to go to you* is a luxury—and I hesitate to add what really is an unnecessary expense when it is an indulgence just for me.

You were so sweet when you were about to make your suggestion at the station—the little quirk around your dear lips—I almost melted for you made me think of a little child pleading for candy. But, darling, I think it was better the way I decided.

Did I thank you for everything, darling? Sometimes I fear I am so concerned with being with you and then leaving you that I forget to be polite. Of course, you know how much I appreciate all you do for me—not only the spectacular things like the concert but also arranging my pillows for my morning coffee.

I really haven't many "regrets" this time. This one, though. I thought you handled the dishes situation so well—very clever of you—but I feel as though I might have helped there. Do you realize I didn't wash one dish? Next time, dear, why couldn't I wash while you pick up, get the dessert or the coffee, etc.? I'll try to remember.

On our way as you can judge and on time, too. Blue sky—partly cloudy which I hope will prove to be the case at 128—no sleet or drizzle!

You made me very happy when you told me that knowing Mr. Bernstein and Our Symphony came from knowing me. You have brought so much that is new and beautiful into my life, darling, I'm glad if I have made a tiny contribution to yours. And how wonderful to share—I'm sure you found a difference in the quality of your joy in hearing Our Concerto and Our Symphony (she said shamelessly).

Now, darling, I'll bring this to a conclusion. I've copied more from *Venture to the Interior*—and there is more I might have. Some chuckles! Delightful as far as I've gone.

I suddenly had the bright idea that I might telephone home from the train to find out if Stan was all set to meet me. But it was a frustrating experience—the circuit was busy (the "mobile one") for the whole half hour I was trying—no chance even to get the operator for if you hear conversation, busy or a ringing you have to hang up—and I never got a clear line. Heard one man trying to get California so I gave up! As it was getting so late that Stan might have left & I feared mother would get upset, if connection was poor, as it could be, if she didn't know where I was.

So I settled for a fresh fruit orangeade. I ate quite heartily between 3 & 4 so I didn't want more food.

We'll be in Providence soon and then it will be time for me to clean up.

Hasn't been a bad ride at all—in fact, it would have been quite perfect if you'd been along.

Think there's a mailbox at 128—if so I'll drop this there. Pen ran dry—Awful writing. Train is flying!

Darling—it's almost as hard to stop talking this way as it is to wave good-bye.

Thank you again for everything.

I do hope you will feel well for the rest of your writing endeavor.

> Good-night Beloved,
> I love you
> *Dorothy*

Love to all!

Dearest [Dorothy],

Just a little note to wind up this latest period of happy being-together. It was so wonderful that you could come, and having you here helped me so much to relax and feel better. Really dear, I can return to the article now with a very different attitude, and I feel better physically, too. I hope you at least feel none the worse for the visit, but you had the hard part, with two long days on the train. I know neither of us will ever forget that concert—nothing of that sort that I ever heard gave me so much delight. And in the time I have known you, you have already opened my ears to so much I was not aware of in music that I owe a very large share of the other night's enjoyment to you.

I've spent a relaxed afternoon reading and resting—didn't have to take Florence[27] home after all, for her daughter telephoned that she would come for

[27] A housekeeper.

her. It has turned quite cold and windy in spite of the sun. I do wish your winter would have disappeared before your return, but I suppose that's impossible. But maybe there will be a real warming up soon.

I shall hope for a little note from you Monday, dear. This is just to carry my love to you as speedily as may be, and I'll probably write again over the weekend. I hope Stan's trip was a good one and that he had no travel difficulties. And tell Willow I'll send a catnip greeting soon.

Our love to all—
Rachel

SUNDAY EVENING, APRIL 8

Dearest [Dorothy],

I shall take this out to the box tonight for a very early morning pick-up, and perhaps if the Post Office department exerts itself you might get it Tuesday. Probably not until Wednesday, I suppose.

The act of getting off the manuscript was accomplished about 4 o'clock. I had taken all but a few concluding pages to Mrs. Rivera last night—I had to finish it in the small hours. Then I got her material early this afternoon and copied the end myself, since she was not to be available for work today. It turns out to be quite long, and I just hope it doesn't have to be cut too much, for that will pose some difficult choices. I'll send you a copy soon, dear. Even though it is too late to profit by any suggestions, of course I'd like your reaction. Mrs. Rivera's was quite encouraging, for I take her to be fairly typical of the readers of the magazine. She doesn't always comment on what she types but this time she did. Now, as I told you today, I shall be waiting to hear whether Mr. Moskin[28] feels the need of a personal conference either on illustrations or on cutting the text. Even if I don't have to see him, I'll go to New York no later than next week to see the *Life*[29] editor.

By coincidence—or is there a better word?—the day I was trying to decide what answer to give Life I had a delightful letter from Dr. Schaefer in answer to my attempt to thank him for all his help on the "Omnibus" job. He said (she reports shamelessly) that it had been "a real privilege" to work with me and to watch my developing interest in the atmosphere, and he hopes it represented the beginning of an even more active interest, winding up by saying, "We need persons like yourself to tell about such things." So I felt from that that he would be pleased to know I am about to invade his field again. I imagine *Life* would want some of his pictures. Wish they would use his beautiful cloud pictures in color!

I think I mentioned the new purple snail incident. One night last week I answered the phone to discover that someone was calling from Key Biscayne, near Miami. Immediately the thought, "purple snails," flashed into my mind. (I think I did tell you about the earlier call.) Sure enough, it was a kindly reader who was determined that I should see some of the snails that had come in on her

[28] J. Robert Moskin, *Woman's Home Companion* managing editor.

[29] RC was considering writing an article on the jet stream.

beach that morning, floats and all. "I'd love to but how can I?" I said. The answer was that her son was flying to Washington that night, returning to classes at the University of Virginia, and he would bring them in a container of seawater and leave them at the ticket office at the airport. He was arriving about 4 A.M. and going right on to Charlottesville. Well, it was horribly inconvenient for me to go over that morning, for I had counted on an unbroken day of work on the *Companion* piece. Nevertheless, purple snails with bubble rafts aren't offered every day, and I couldn't say no. So after a lengthy and pleasant chat with Mrs. O'Neill (who told me that every day she says, "If only I could walk this beach with Rachel Carson!") I made some tentative plans to show the trophies to Bob after collecting them, worked extra late in compensation, and finally went to bed. Next morning at seven I phoned the airport just to be sure the young man had remembered to leave the snails. Lucky I did—no planes had been able to land in Washington since 2 A.M. on account of fog. The flight I inquired about had been put down in Richmond, I was told. So that settled the snail problem, I thought, for surely the boy would go to Charlottesville without coming up to Washington. I'm afraid I was sneakingly glad, and I got a good early start on my work. But about noon the phone rang—young Mr. O'Neill had been taken to Pittsburgh, had just gotten back to Washington, and would leave the snails at the airport. But by that time I was certain the poor creatures would be dead, if indeed they had been alive on starting out, which I doubt. So I was able to arrange with the curator of mollusks at the Museum to send over for them and attend to proper pickling of the specimens—for which help I offered him a share. So I'll go down in a day or two and collect mine.

I was horrified to hear you were having more snow and probably lots more. The snapshots Olga[30] showed us of her place looked just like excavations for a base camp at the North Pole. What do you suppose will happen to all your bulbs and other things that have already started to grow?

So *David and the Seagulls*[31] isn't up to advance billing on the photographs, at least! Judging by the Museum exhibit and all publicity, I expected something quite superior. It is hard to know what makes a child's book go over—or any book for, that matter. I hope you meant your suggestion seriously. By coincidence (that word, again) a day or two before your letter came Marjie had remarked that she thought you ought to write books for children. See how many people you keep disappointing! Why don't you do one on the sly and surprise them??

An advance copy of an intriguing looking book was sent me yesterday by Harper—some such title as *The World of Night* by Lorus and Marjorie Milne, a husband and wife who have collaborated on several books with a biological basis. I was glad enough it hadn't come until my article was finished, or I might have been afraid I'd been influenced by it. A few days ago I realized that this piece had certainly brought out my own preoccupation with night—something I myself hadn't realized. But so many of my incidents and illustrations had to do

[30] Olga Owens Huckins, a writer for the *Boston Post*, owner of a home near Cape Cod, and friend of RC.

[31] A 1956 book by Marion Downer, photos by Yoila Niclas.

with nocturnal activities that it was really funny, and I had to write in some other unplanned things to restore some sort of balance. But now I do expect to enjoy the Milne book.

I don't think I'll try to do anything about *Life* this week—just relax by such restful occupations as spring-cleaning a closet or two, trying to catch up on correspondence, maybe buying a television, and reviewing that confounded book for the *Times*!

We are so happy that Willow is home and appears to be making a good recovery this time. I always remember the time one of our Persians had to be in the hospital about ten days for a serious operation. That was years ago and we had taken her to Baltimore to our old vet there, for she was so sick no one here thought she could survive, and he was very skillful. I remember that she talked all the way home from Baltimore, in a hoarse little voice that showed there had been little conversation at the hospital. Then all night she kept coming and rousing me, to tell me something else she had forgotten.

My notes and letters since you left have been so sketchy I don't know what I've said, and probably I'll realize after this goes that there are unanswered things in your letters. But I'll get around to them.

I do want to hear all about Stan's latest honor at Amherst. Tell him I hope he knows he's lucky he didn't have to pay for it by making The Speech of the occasion—at least I assume he didn't. I feel like Tommy Tucker, having to sing for my supper—only I won't sing. But to return to Stan, I do hope, too, that the extraction wasn't a difficult one and that now he is relieved.

There was a great deal about letter writing in the *Times* today—did you see? Among other things, how people are really writing mostly about themselves, or to express themselves. Which this letter seems to prove.

Our love to all, dear. Tell Willow to be good and I'll soon send him more catnip.

Rachel

Later

There is lots more I want to say, darling, but if I take this to the box tonight I suppose there's just a chance you'll get it Tuesday. And it's now ten o'clock, so I think I won't write much more. Anything I mail tomorrow you should have Wednesday—so I'll have a little visit with you later for mailing tomorrow.

It was *so* good to hear your voice this morning—but how fast that half hour went, leaving so much unsaid! I wanted terribly to call you Friday, for I was so eager to have a good report on you and Willow, but I resisted the impulse, and I'm glad I waited. Then too, I wanted to be able to say "the piece" was done. Darling, I do hope you'll like it. Mamma and Marjie read it tonight for the first time and both wept—maybe *you* should have some Kleenex on hand—though I didn't intend it to be sad! I'll mail a copy tomorrow. Left the "Cloud" script with Mrs. R. to be copied, so you shall have that soon, too.

[32] DF had sent RC some quotations concerning the creative process from *Venture to the Interior*.

Darling—I can't quite comprehend in what way you would think the van der Post quotations[32] would bother me, however I interpreted them; I think he stated the heart of the matter very perceptively. I loved his phrase "a contract with life." So please—you dear, precious, funny darling—stop worrying and know that by sending along his words you gave me a real lift. (And I *know* you were joking about the cattle boats, and so was I!)

Darling, sometime maybe I'll annotate the *Companion* piece just for you with an account of all that happened yesterday—The Last Day of Work on it! But somehow I could laugh inwardly and it seemed I could work quite well between episodes, so maybe I *am* learning to live with it!

[33] An operation for Stanley's ulcers.

I wish I could tell you how relieved I felt when your letter came Saturday, and I knew you had received reassurance from Dr. Dick. I had felt you feared maybe an operation[33] was in prospect so I couldn't help being anxious. And now it's all right! More tomorrow, darling.

And now—all my love—
Rachel

MONDAY A.M., APRIL 9

Darling [Dorothy],

Now I'm regretting that I sent the long typewritten letter by air—skies are sunny and unclouded here, but with a report of up to 13 inches of snow in the Boston area I suppose your airport is closed again. So maybe the letter will be held up for days. I used to think they just automatically changed to train mail if flights were cancelled, but in the last big snow one Boston letter (H.M.—not yours) took a week because it was airmail!

I can hardly bear to think of your being under all that snow again. And just after your tantalizing glimpse of spring!

The morning mail *did* bring the promised 3 pieces, dear, which was very sweet. Today I'm just feeling relaxed for part of the day, at least; I must do millions of letters with Mrs. R. tonight, but that isn't like "a piece."

Yes, I think it did finally "tell" me how it wanted to be, darling. It's an odd thing and very difficult to explain. I do think if you could realize how very different my early drafts are from the final version—really crude and in places amateurish—you wouldn't be so discouraged by the first drafts *you* produce. ("And whose fault is it that I don't see the early drafts?" you say. Well I know, but I have a terrible block against letting anyone see them—even hate to myself— so please just take my word for it.) Darling, when you read the piece you will find *us* in it—in one of two spots at least. (When I see you, remind me to tell you about a ridiculous dream about ~~a ridiculous dream last night, about~~ (Sorry—I was interrupted here and repeated without looking) the letters "U S." Really fantastic.) Also dreamed I met Judge Bok on the shore in front of the "Dream House"—he didn't look at all like his picture but was so "low-voiced" I could scarcely hear him. That dream resulted from a sense of guilt that I hadn't answered his letter of a week ago, and I'm a little afraid he may think I am in some sort of state about the Kubly business. So I *must* write today.

Darling, I have only a general impression of the message on that Easter card I sent you. I know I was happy to find it, for it said what I wanted to say. I had found nothing I wanted for you before that (the day you left me) and had decided to send nothing if I couldn't find the right one. If you still have it, maybe you would copy it for me. Yours to me was so sweet dear—and so true. Yes, peace is what one needs, perhaps above all else, and perhaps it is attainable if one thinks of things in the right way.

One problem I know I must solve is that of finding someone who can come in at least while I am away, for I know it is not safe to leave Mamma alone. For example, there was another fall—miraculously, no harm done, but had I not been within calling distance, so that I could help her up, I hate to think how it might have been. And then the vagueness and forgetfulness, involving things that might cause tragic mishaps, especially with regard to the gas range—when I face these realities I know I should never again leave her alone. For various reasons, no one in the family seems to be the answer, so I must work out something else.

Darling—won't it be wonderful to be at Southport again? Hearing veeries and hermits and olive backs, living under the skies where we belong!

One bit of Stardust I forgot to mention. I have always been horribly tempted by those train telephones, but have never tried them. So during that Friday afternoon I thought, "Maybe she will telephone Stan to find out whether he will be able to meet her."

Heavens, darling—do you suppose my scales do underestimate? But very oddly, the day after I read the startling 133, it was down to 130, and I know my diet isn't *that* good! Besides, I do slip now and then.

Darling—do you remember the little note you had inserted in Stan's letter? I don't remember which day it came, but I had been hoping so for word from you (probably hadn't had any since the day before!) that when a quick inspection of the mail failed to disclose your writing I had a little sinking sensation of disappointment. I thought, "If only there would be a note from her enclosed in Stan's letter—but of course there won't be." But of course there was! And as I have already tried to tell you, it changed the whole day and made it a very good one.

I suppose I must stop, dear one. Have decided to enclose this along with the manuscript.

> I love you, dear
> *Rachel*

Oh, my Darling [Rachel],

Thank you for letting me share what I knew would be lovely—but not *how* lovely. "She's done it again." Oh, dearest, your signature is all through it and yet the public is going to find a new you—the you that I've known from the start, the you of the Starry eyes, the elfin you, whimsical, fanciful you who appealed so much to me.

Somehow, I wonder whether I'm going to like sharing that you with the world. But the deed is done, and I guess I'm glad the world is going to have this glimpse of you. I loved it all as you must have known I would. I wonder if I would have noticed the predominance of the nocturnal note if you hadn't called my attention to it in a previous letter. But it is all so lovely, dear—and I'm sure it is not out of proportion—in fact I think I like that emphasis very much. Would it be because so much of our joys have been of the night? And there is a harking back for me, for long ago—and I think I could lay my hand on the letter—you wrote that you thought you were a "nocturnal creature."

Of course, you knew that to find Our-night-on-the-Head[34] would be a surprise for me, and such a delightful one. If I wept, it was when I read that—oh, there were other spots, too—I know exactly where Mamma's and Marjie's eyes were moist. And of course you and Roger on the stormy beach was reminiscent of my morning with Martha when the surf made her laugh.

Stan was home early—here when I returned from town. I started to read the piece aloud to him upstairs—and guess who wanted also to hear. A little furry boy jumped into my lap much as to say "I want to hear—I know what she's talking about."

LATER

Darling, it is moving on toward midnight—a scandalous hour for us. I had meant to finish this by answering your letter enclosed with the Piece. But we went out for dinner, made a call, and when we came back Stan and I began talking about Writing—and it developed into the longest sustained conversation we've had in the evening for a long while.

So now I think I'll send this by him in the morning for I know you'll be anxious for word from me as to my reaction. Then I'll try to write to-morrow before the mailman comes.

I think, or, I hope I have conveyed to you the thought that I feel very much a part of your Piece, darling. I feel close to it and to you through it, darling.

Good-night and I love you,

Dorothy

[34] In the *Woman's Home Companion* article (published July 1956), RC had described an evening RC and DF had spent on Dogfish Head in Southport. The description appears on page 54 of *The Sense of Wonder* (1965).

Dearest [Dorothy],

Will write a few paragraphs before dinner for the evening mail, aimed to reach you Saturday. Your Tuesday night note came today and was so good to have except that I wish you would take your housecleaning a bit less seriously — this is no time to get yourself all worn out!

I talked to Marie yesterday about my New York appointments, and think now I shall go up late Monday afternoon, see everyone Tuesday, and return that evening. The reactions to The Piece, from New York, are all I could ask. Marie who does not usually make extravagant comments, wrote it was *lovely* (italics hers) and this afternoon I had a phone call from Mr. Moskin who said he called just so he could tell me personally that he thought it was "just great" — that they were all thrilled and happy to have it and wanted to carry every word if space permitted, as he thought it would. (Phew — is she ever shameless!) I am to see him Tuesday morning and talk about pictures — he says they have some they have shot for it which he thinks I'll like very much. Then I am to have lunch with Mr. Whipple and someone else of *Life* Tuesday, and am also to see Mr. Greenbaum that day.

Mrs. Rivera has been sick all week so the letters are still hanging over me — may be able to do them tonight. But other items have been checked off the list: I actually cleaned out three closets AND think I've settled on an RCA television. If I give the word I'll have it tomorrow or Saturday.

(Please notice the pale appearance of my typing at the top of the page. I wondered what was the matter, then remembered that Jeffie had begged so hard for the typewriter last night that I set it on the floor for him and I guess he changed the adjustments to suit his own purposes. This morning as soon as I got up he ran, purring, to the typewriter to invite me to make the keys go for him. Maybe he wants to answer Willow's nice letter. Well, he will try to remember to tuck in another sprig of the magic herb.)

Another letter from Judge Bok this morning, full of laughs. I don't know whether to send you recent correspondence or bring it. He discourses at length on the reasons (or at least, *his* reasons) for answering a letter at once, and they are all reasons you and I understand all too well. But he doesn't wish his correspondents to feel they must do the same. Well, maybe I'll just bring the letters. Even if I restrain myself on my replies, there will probably be one or two more before I see you.

Did I tell you Roger was quite sick for a couple of days? High fever, and the doctor thought maybe he was developing measles. But today he is back to normal with no further symptoms so I guess he wasn't. I remembered to send Martha a birthday card yesterday. It is the 13th, isn't it?

I'm going down Saturday to have my hair done and maybe do a little shopping. And I hope to get a letter in the mail that should reach you Monday.

Maybe over the week-end I'll indulge in a spree of looking at new houses. I think I should know what the possibilities are in that direction before I decide what to do. In some ways, I wonder if my original plan,[35] or a realistic modification of it, may be the answer, with a view to the future. Either way it will be an upheaval that I rather dread, but in many ways this is the best time it could happen.

Love to all, dear. And please treat yourselves to some real rest over the week-end.

All my love

Rachel

[35] RC was considering moving Marjie and Roger into her own household, either by purchasing and renovating the house in which RC and her mother lived or purchasing another house.

SATURDAY, APRIL 14

Dearest [Dorothy],

So many things to say and not much time to say them! I'm under the drier now and have to hurry home to—guess what? A television set! It's an RCA console type 21 inch. It was delivered shortly before I left and already I can see what a hit it's going to make with Mamma. You can imagine I don't know a thing about tuning or adjusting the things, so I wasn't pleased with the picture I was getting and said "Let's turn it off till Robert comes and can show us how to handle it." But she said "Oh no, I'd like to watch it anyway—I'm so afraid something's going to happen to that white horse!" So we left it on. I'm relieved to find I don't hear it upstairs. I called a little while ago and she reported—sounding as happy as a cat with a saucer of cream—that Robert had it working beautifully and they were watching "The Lone Ranger." So I guess she and Roger can be happy for hours at a time with it. M. & R. will come for supper tonight to see it. R. is *so* pleased that at last poor Rachel has a television.

Dear, of course you can have a copy of the *WHC* piece a little later. The trouble was that Mrs. R. did not have her big typewriter that week-end and had to use a borrowed portable that wasn't very good and couldn't make as many copies as I wanted. So I wanted to have your copy again until I see whether Marie is going to need it. But you shall have one soon.

Of course I love all you've written about it, dear. I'm so glad you liked it— and you must, if you want Stanley and Madeleine to be influenced by it. I'm greatly relieved that I can feel it does contain most of the ideas I wanted to convey.

I *have* heard from Dr. Wald but he will be out of town and probably unavailable for some time. Alternatively, I'd like to see Dr. Bigelow, and will feel also that I might profit (for the *Life* article) by seeing Charles Brooks at the Blue Hill Observatory and perhaps someone at MIT. That I can judge better after I see the *Life* editors Tuesday. None of these have been set up and they could be either April 24 or the following week, as far as I'm concerned. I think I'd better try to call you from New York Tues. afternoon and we'll decide. Now, *don't fret* if you have plans to be out that day; I'll call from home (later) if necessary. I have lunch with the *Life* people and unless something happens that I don't anticipate, should be taking the 3:30 or 4:30 train home, and would probably call you from the station. Time up and all the rest I want to say must wait for tomorrow. My dear love—R

APRIL 13[36]

About the house problem

As you see, this is being written in sections, and this particular one will be all on the above subject. Maybe I shouldn't write about it tonight (have gone to bed early to relax by talking with you) for suddenly the whole business makes me very weary—a sort of "oh! what's—the—use" or "what's—it—for—any-way" feeling. But I can at least report developments and some of my thoughts.

Mr. Simpson[37] sent some men today to appraise the house. I haven't heard what they reported to him, but his own guess the other night was around $18,000. I've made some attempts to learn who would be a reliable person to call in for an estimate on remodeling, but so far with only confusing results.

One reason my thoughts have reverted to the scheme I unfolded to you in New York is this: for many reasons I don't feel confident that the present solution of Marjie's living problem is a very durable one. When we were house-hunting for her, I felt we should look for something all on one floor, but she said she would be nervous at night, sleeping on the ground floor with windows open. But when I spend any length of time over there, as I did a few days ago when Roger was sick, I can see that the stairs are exceedingly hard on her. Trips to the second floor and trips to the basement, and lots of them; and it's hard on a heart like hers.

And then from the money standpoint, all the expense of keeping up the yard and property where there is no man, and not even an able-bodied woman, to do a thing. Storm windows to be taken off, leaves raked, grass cut, etc., all mean Earl[38] and money! And I can't help feeling that with the semi-consolidation I had in mind there could be a good deal of saving on help, inside and out. And remembering that I already have $14,000 invested in that place, and am now considering maybe 20 to 22 here (with renovation) I can't help wondering if I couldn't get what I want for the combined figure.

SATURDAY

At that point I went off to sleep—I was really tired. Now I'm at the hair-dresser's but will continue this discussion a bit before turning to other things. A point mentioned by you in this morning's mail was the very thing I was coming to next—a room for a housekeeper or even someone to come in at irregular times to stay overnight. I know I'd be foolish to *buy* anything without providing for that situation. So I *shouldn't* give up that little bedroom. But that changes the character of the whole project I visualized so radically that I don't like any of it.

[36] RC enclosed with the Saturday, April 14, letter two separate sheets both dated April 13.

[37] A neighbor and attorney acting as a broker between RC and her landlord, Mrs. Gover, concerning RC's potential purchase of her rented house.

[38] A handyman.

I think I am developing a sort of complex about sunlight, darling. If there is one thing I long for in considering the ideal house it's *light*. I want lots of it, and if possible windows open to views of sunrise and sunset and moonlight. A living room that is both small and dark and has no view to anything just aggravates that complex unbearably. So I don't think I should doom myself to it—and neither, I'm sure, do you, darling. So I think it comes down to this: about the time I'd get this house bought and remodeled, some development in relation to either Mamma or Marjie might well make the whole situation impossible. So I should try to anticipate the future as far as that can be done.

The disadvantages of not owning the place you live in have oppressed me a good deal in recent years and I don't like to go into another rented house. You think of things you'd like to do outside or in, but you don't because you always have that tentative feeling. Besides, I guess the rent we are now paying is ridiculously low, from what Mr. Simpson told us of others, and to get what I'd find acceptable would probably involve a big jump in rent.

So——guess I'll start looking at houses, dear. Maybe spring is going to be a pretty busy time after all!

APRIL 13

Darling—something in today's (the Wed. night) letter made me think of Roger, and I laughed. Do you remember the day last summer that you and I went off while he was there—I think it was the day we went to the Sheltons. Roger was upset at my going and his grandmother told him he should be glad Rachel had gone out to have a good time with Aunt Dorsey. So later he said to Marjie, "I'm not *very* glad she went." And still later, "I'm a *little* bit glad, but not very glad." Do you know what I'm comparing? Your "I wonder whether I'll like sharing that you," followed by "I *guess* I'm glad—." You funny darling! I wish I could be there and make you laugh and *know* you're glad!

Do you know, darling, I suppose it *will* reveal a different me. And for a long time I've thought—and I wouldn't say this to anyone else—that that was exactly what Marie hoped would result from this. You see, for a long time after *The Sea* there was a great deal of pressure from the *Companion*, *Ladies Home Journal* and others, for me to allow someone to do a piece about me. This, of course, I wouldn't agree to, and M. always approved of my refusals. But when the *Companion* asked for this article I think she saw the possibility that I might indirectly tell a good deal about myself and to some extent satisfy that demand. And so I think her suggestion to the *Companion* that I might tell some of it in terms of Roger was an astute way of insuring this!

[Love, *Rachel*]

Darling [Rachel],

This is an experiment. I have just lived through an hour of suspension in time that I would like to try to express. Perhaps you will understand—perhaps you won't—why I am writing it to you. I feel the need to put it on paper— somehow if I say it to you, I may come more nearly to saying what I want to say than if I make a simple record for myself. I am shut away in the back bedroom in the corner that belongs in my heart only to you—you know where and why. It is dusk outside—the rain began sometime ago. I became conscious of it be- cause of the sound the automobile made driving through it even before I knew it was falling. Blue-jays have been screaming; the sparrows chirping as they will do in the rain, but in the tree outside the window has been a voice—the owner invisible, plaintive and poignant like a canary full of sadness, if you can imagine that. I don't know the song, but it, and the now heavily falling rain, fit my mood.

The mood is compounded of many things. I came upstairs for a nap. Stan was having one in his room. I told mother if there was something she wanted to watch on TV to feel free to do so, but she said rather forlornly there wasn't. That belongs to my mood for there is my guilt feeling—we left her alone last evening and yesterday was her wedding anniversary—her 59th! In my callous way I have felt since my father died that anniversaries wouldn't mean much to her. But suddenly last night as we were talking about that fact on the way to Littles'[39] I realized with a wild rush of feeling—suppose it were I? Wouldn't the date of the day I was married still mean the same to me—perhaps more, even—if Stan wasn't here to share it? (You know how anniversary conscious I am—not just weddings!)

And so I am guilty for last night, and for now, having shut myself away from her this dreary afternoon.

I was also feeling guilty on another score. This morning I spoke crossly to Stan. He was hurt, I knew. For once I didn't let it stand, and asked his forgive- ness in his arms. But the deed was done.

When I came upstairs I meant to finish *Venture to the Interior*. I tuned in on the Philharmonic, then under way, on something I did not recognize (and never did learn what it was—but I must find out some way).[40] I was shut in from all the world and lost myself in the book—the music being only background. Darling, somehow this book seems to hold some meaning for me—I was prepared for adventure but not for the philosophic overtones—the implications of human destiny—a mysterious study of personality. The last few chapters have moved me beyond reason—I don't know why—my mood, I suppose.

Suddenly, at one of the most dramatic moments in the book before its cli- max—the music overpowered me so that I had to stop reading. Floods of tears just streamed from my eyes. The music had been subdued and at times a rich human voice had become part of it. At the time it reached me it was carrying an

[39] Walter and Flora Little; he was for- mer president of the Bridgewater Grain Company, where Stanley had once worked.

[40] A note, in RC's handwriting, on this letter identi- fies the music as Symphony No. 3 in D Minor by Mahler.

exquisite melody in the high strings with dark shadings in the lower strings. It seemed to complement the book completely. Then I began to think of Stan asleep in the other room and suddenly underneath the lovely melody was a pattern of discord in the brasses, incongruous and intruding—almost a warning to me it seemed. And then I knew that somehow I've got to tell Stan how wonderful has been my life with him, how good he has been to me, how rich our life together has been. He's made me so happy—given me so much. I feel I have in no way repaid him for his years of devotion. Of course, I know I am thinking deep inside me, "What if I should lose him?" And so to-night I'm going to try to put into words all this that I feel. It will be good to do for there is never enough expression, in words of one's gratitude, is there?

I listened to the music to its conclusion. I don't know who wrote it, but it could have been our Mr. Bernstein for there was in it the melody and lyrical quality of the old school, but a touch of the disharmonies and discords the moderns seem to like—and which he understands.

Afterwards I finished the book. Those last chapters are so profound and so moving—the exquisite descriptions of the natural world on top of the plateau with the counterpoint of the drums of the wild African dance—and under and over it all his musings on life—its heights and depths.

Darling, do you understand why I needed to write it?

It is almost dark now—the rain is almost like that African drum—my face is hot and my blood is throbbing—the tears are dry but where they have been my face burns.

Now I'm going to get up. I hear Stan stirring. I'm going back to my world. It seems to me that I've been away a long time. I've just heard Willow scratching on the window seat in the dining room below me—his elbow beating against the wood.

I know most of what has affected me this afternoon is the book—I have marked so many passages for Us for there is no one else who could share this with me but you.

Perhaps back to reality—or is it illusion?—I shall not be so moved & when I read it to you I may wonder why all this.

But as I said at the beginning I have been suspended in Time—and outside my private world.

[Love,
Dorothy]

This is for the Strong Box. It is not about Us. It is about me, but sent because I have felt you close to me all the time.

Dearest [Dorothy],

It was wonderful to find a nice fat letter awaiting me last night. This will only briefly supplement my train letter, for I have to go downtown to get my car—too late to pick it up last night, as I expected. And I may shop a little. I believe Thoreau said: "Beware of any venture that requires new clothes," but somehow my wardrobe appears to need supplementing before the Bok weekend. Specifically, I'd like to find a very simple but just-right dinner dress that I could take there and also wear for the AAUW dinner.[41] Now I see I've anticipated my story. A letter came this morning that makes everything all right. They are most understanding; it's quite all right for me not to give the address and they've already made other arrangements for that and all they require of me is a brief response—any length I choose. So all is well on that front, and in view of Mr. Greenbaum's opinion I feel much richer this morning. Really, though, it just about strikes a balance. I awoke still feeling as allergic to *Life* as when I went to bed. That wasn't changed by a Special that arrived from Marie. The editor had called her after I left. They *are* doing a feature on the weather, but he doesn't think that would necessarily interfere. So they would like a piece from me on the jet streams IF I could say they do this and do that—a whole list of specifications. Well I can't and I won't and they can go to you-know-where and ask the Proprietor there to write it for them! Well, one does live and learn and I'm a lot wiser than when I went to New York. So now you know some of what goes on behind the scenes of *Life*, and so do I, and I can't imagine that I'd ever write for them.

Judge Bok is most eager to see the "tide-pool pictures" and I'm happy that things are working out so that I can bring Stan's rather than having them mailed. Of course a very few of his lovely scenes would be wonderful, too. I'm afraid I seemed to exclude them in what I said on the phone. I always feel hesitant to have many of those beauties in my possession even briefly, and of course I do think the chief reason for taking slides is to show them the world they don't know, but just the same I can't imagine any Maine enthusiast who wouldn't be thrilled by seeing some of the landscapes. So if it's all right, put in a few of those. I'm taking my own projector—he says his is 16mm, and I imagine he really means a movie projector. He says "the dogwood will have to hurry—only leaf buds so far"—and he guesses I'll just have to tell *them* about ours.

Tell Stan to behave himself and get a lot of rest over the week-end, to get in practice for resting in the hospital.[42] And give our love to him, and to your mother, and to Willow.

And you know what.

Rachel

[41] A dinner held in Washington, D.C., on June 22 to present RC with the 1956 Achievement Award of the American Association of University Women.

[42] For an operation on April 25 to address Stanley's internal bleeding.

My darling [Dorothy],

Can you understand what it meant to me to have you take me into your heart as you did in that letter? I think perhaps you can if you will think about it and that should erase any possible lingering regret that you did write and did send the letter. To be chosen as the one to whom another feels she can communicate something so intimate, so sacred, so intangible that it is most difficult to express, is a very wonderful experience, dearest, and makes me both deeply glad and humble. It was the first thing that came to my mind when I opened my eyes this morning.

Please don't insist that the letter go into the Strong Box, darling—at least not immediately. It is very precious and wonderful—containing, or implying so much that is uniquely You—so many of the qualities that make me love you so dearly. Of course your deep sensitivity is one of them. It is not always a comfortable quality to possess, I know, but perhaps its rewards—the awareness of so much that is unnoticed and unappreciated by all but a few—are compensation.

I know I was deeply impressed by *Venture to the Interior*, but I must read it again—in fragments with you, and also in its entirety. And I think I can understand a little about the music, though I have heard very little of Mahler and probably would recognize nothing of his. But Alice felt so deeply about his symphonies and I heard much about them from her—enough to suggest to me that they have an extraordinary quality that could affect you just as you describe.

Last night on the train I told you I had such a strong sense of coming home to you. And how much of you I found! Darling!

Looking back over what I've written, I don't seem to be saying all that I want to say, nor to be able to find words to do so. Perhaps for now it is enough to say that everything in your letter—your insight into the deeper meanings of the book, your response to the music, and your transfer of those emotions to your own personal situation—all make me love you even more deeply and tenderly than ever, if possible. And I am so glad I am to be with you so soon.

Now I must go, darling. My dearest love—

                                                                          Rachel

TUESDAY, MAY 1

Dear Stan and Dear Dorothy,

Letters from both of you today brought you close and helped close what already seems a very long gap of time since I saw you—imagine, it is all of a week this afternoon since the three of us visited in the hospital![43] But how much has happened since, and how happily it has all turned out. I'm so delighted, Stan, as all of us are, with the good reports we've had from Dorothy in letters and by phone. By the time you read this you'll be almost ready to go home. But

[43] RC had combined a visit to Harvard with a stay at the Freemans' home at the time of Stanley's operation, April 24–26.

don't you dream of going until the doctor pushes you out—better an unnecessary day or two than one too few!

I'm sure Dorothy has relayed my first, glowing account of the happy Philadelphia week-end. Of course there are many details to fill in, which I'll try to do in a letter soon. But the important thing is that I was simply charmed with my hostess, my host, and their daughter, that the visit was even more wonderful than I had dreamed it could be, and there was nothing about it I would have changed if I could! I do hope my pictures turn out, so that I can give you a glimpse of the people and their home. Oh course I'd love to have taken many more, but I didn't want to spend too much time on that for the hours were too few as it was.

Temperatures Saturday and Sunday were high in the 80's but not uncomfortable, and it was lovely to be able to sit out without a wrap. The shrubs and the garden were coming on with a rush, but still far behind schedule. They had cut a large dogwood branch and brought [it] into the house in time to have it in bloom, so that the promise of flowering dogwood was at least symbolically fulfilled. Sunday morning I heard the first wrens and catbirds of the season, and now this morning—the first of May—I heard a wood thrush when I opened my eyes. Earl came to cut the grass for the first time today, lilacs are in bloom, and at last winter seems well behind us. But it was much cooler yesterday and today, and poor Jeffie seems to have caught a cold—his eyes are running and he seems a bit listless. I am dosing him as best I can, and it is wonderful to know Dr. Dennewitz is here if we need him.

I haven't worked out a schedule for Pittsburgh[44] as yet. Probably I'll take a train the morning of the 10th, stay over that night with my classmate, and return the next day, though that is really holding my time there to a minimum, and I suppose I ought to see my relatives even very briefly. I'll let you know my plans soon. Tomorrow seems to be taken up but I think the rest of the week is pretty clear. I want to talk to Mr. Simpson tonight if I can—did I tell you he said the appraisals (by two different firms) were fairly close—one $19,000 to 19,500; the other somewhat less. He had written Mrs. Gover but hadn't heard. She will probably be jolted by his report. He said if I bought it he was going to tell her he wouldn't charge her a full commission, just to help things along. I want to ask him what he thinks I might offer her (I mean, how much less than I would actually pay) for I never know just how to play that game. In this happy situation he is working for me even more than for her, so I feel free to discuss such angles with him.

Now this must go to the Post Office. If the hospital has two deliveries, maybe you'll get this tomorrow.

Stan, I did tell Dorothy but must repeat now, that the Boks and their guests were delighted with the slides. Your sunsets, the autumn and storm scenes of the Head, the tidepools and the fairy cave brought the most ohs and ahs, I think, but they loved them all. It was so good of you to lend them again.

[44] RC was planning a trip to her undergraduate alma mater, Chatham College, to receive an alumnae award.

Tell me if you want me to mail them—or shall we just hope I can bring them fairly soon?

Both of you take care of yourselves! As always, a lot of love goes to you both from us all.

Rachel

WEDNESDAY NOON, MAY 2

My darling [Dorothy],

Two more notes from you this morning, one written Sunday night, the other Monday afternoon, but both bear an 8:00 P.M. Monday postmark. Perhaps all hospital mail goes out then. I hope you and Stan may have my letter today, but yours to West Bridgewater will probably be for Thursday night reading!

No word yet from either of the visitors from New York, so perhaps Dr. Vishniac[45] didn't come. That would suit me just as well. It's a rainy day, and even if he came to the house I'd have to go out and rent a projector. Dr. Anshen[46] will be here, I'm sure, and our dinner is set for 7:30. I just have to hear which hotel.

Jeffie seems better today, for which I'm so thankful. He worried me last night—it was so much the way Muffie's pneumonia started—and I planned to take him to Dr. D. this morning. But his eyes have stopped discharging and he is much more active and ate a good breakfast, so I just talked to the doctor and will follow his directions and see how the baby is tomorrow. I really think he's definitely better.

Darling, I'll write a long letter soon giving all possible details on the Boks—about their house, their grounds, what we had to eat(!), what we did when, and all that. That will be for all of you. But for you now, if I'm not interrupted by a call, I'll try to add to my report of Sunday night. You say this morning that you are glad I've wanted to share the development of this friendship. But you must know, darling, that once again, as in so many other instances, you are the *only* one with whom I would have shared, not only the letters, but my feelings about them, and that for me there has been a warm and happy glow in having you to share it. It has been a lovely experience, and I think can now go on to an even happier phase. I'm sure you know that for some time I have wondered how Nellie Lee (the name somehow suits her perfectly) regarded her husband's correspondence, or whether she even knew about it. Now I know there was never anything furtive about it (she would say, "When you wrote to Curtis about" so-and-so; or he would remark to her—"You remember Rachel wrote about—") and all is so obviously right between them that all my doubts and questionings are erased. And so I don't have to wonder whether it is all right to continue the friendship.

The saddening thing is that he does look so much older than he should at 58, and so worn that one knows his illness took years from his life. His hair is almost white and his face has lines that his age couldn't have put there. It must be

45 Dr. Wolf Vishniac, microbiologist and professor at Yale, had proposed making a film of *The Edge of the Sea*.

46 Dr. Ruth Nanda Anshen, editor of the Harper and Brothers World Perspective series.

a real heartbreak for her to see him start for Italy in June (the 27th, I think) but one has only to see the light in his eyes when he speaks of it to know how much it means to him, and I think she is wonderful to understand that.

They told me many things—past and present—about the girls and all I heard and saw of their family life is quite lovely. The parents, as you know, are Quakers, but Nellie Lee said both girls had felt strongly attracted to the Episcopal Church and have been baptized in it, though not yet confirmed. Enid went off to church Sunday morning. The father and mother, between her illness and his, have gotten somewhat "out of the habit" of going to church, Nellie Lee said, but she goes with Enid as often as she can. They have a silent grace at meals—very nice, I thought.

Curtis speaks very matter-of-factly of "my older children," and Enid mentioned "my brother Ben" (or Derek) in the same vein, so whatever the situation was, it seems to have been resolved in a very civilized fashion. There are several grandchildren—four, I think.

Of course the lovely thing—so hard to define or describe—was that sense of being so comfortable and at ease with each other. It was definitely present from the beginning, but so strongly all day Sunday—a warm glow of mutual understanding and even affection.

Yes, darling, I did know you were very much with me all the time, and as I suggested yesterday, my regret at leaving them was softened by my eagerness to get home and tell you about it! Now for the future, what? A summer with little communication, that's *sure*! Then maybe a visit in the fall, but it's a big maybe. Goodness, darling, am I glad *you're* not going to sail to Italy! And that your coming to Maine isn't just a maybe!

Speaking of that, as soon as you decide which week of June you'll spend there, do let me know. I don't know what I can do about it, but it's pretty sad to think that if you're going to have only four weeks there, one of them would be while I'm far away. Oh dear! And if it's the week including the 22nd I'd have to lose a big chunk of time with you even if I were already established at Southport, which seems unlikely. Oh dear again!

Darling, I don't think I'll do the *Life* article—certainly not now. And the Blue Hill visit was to some extent just taking advantage of an opportunity to get Dr. Brooks's point of view. He is not a jet stream authority. But I still feel so negative about them that I'm not inclined to reverse my decision.

Now I suppose I must halt this conversation with you, dear. Your little "postscript" yesterday was duly noted. I know I'll want to call you again this week some night. Then after that Stan will be home and, though I know you'll be busy caring for him, I do so hope you can get some rest and take it easy. I'm really concerned about you, darling. We are to go to Robert's for dinner either Thursday or Friday and that will probably determine which night I'll call.

Darling, I do understand and share that odd feeling about the weeks ahead—no definite date as a rallying point for our thoughts and hopes. But we do know that the summer must have many lovely hours in store for us. I wish you could plan to be with us that last week of June, before all the summer people are there—if Stan goes to Conn. could we hope for it? I do love you.

Rachel

MONDAY, MAY 14

Dearest [Dorothy,]

No letter went off yesterday or early today, as I had planned, and this must be short if it is to make the evening mail. Our sudden hot weather (93° yesterday and about the same today) has taken everybody's energy, but just the same I've found it necessary to be pretty active.

Here is a bit of news I wish I'd known yesterday so I could have told you on the phone. My *Herald Tribune* "Books" was late, so I didn't know that *The Edge* has returned to the list—No. 12 on a list of 19. Probably I wouldn't even have looked but there was a note from Paul today, rejoicing. So maybe there will be a vacation spurt.

We found a real dream house last night—brand new and open but the agent wasn't on hand to tell us the price. (However, I put on my own price tag—$35,000.) Today I learned the tag is $33,500, though it promptly dropped to $30,000 with hints of going lower, when I said that was not for me. Though it still isn't, after seeing it I'm convinced I should do a lot more looking before buying this. Another in the same beautiful area (4 or 5 miles toward Baltimore, from here) was only $23,500 and while it had been decorated in wretched taste it is basically a very nice house—both 3-bedroom ramblers on sloping lots so that a ground level recreation room (beautifully finished in each case) looks out on a back yard with lovely trees—even a trickle of a stream on that one, with over a half acre of ground. With the large lot there would be opportunity to do the thing I have talked about from the beginning—make a place for Marjie. I'm sure it seemed impractical as I described it, darling, but I always keep coming back to it and really I believe it's the only thing that makes sense—at least to buy something that has that future possibility. I feel more and more that the time is coming, regardless of what anyone may want, when Marjie will have to become part of the household in one way or another. Her feet are now giving her a great deal of trouble, suggesting that the circulatory troubles of advanced diabetes are setting in. And you know I've felt that the stairs, and indeed the whole set up there, are just too much for her, and she said as much to me today. I am sure that the sooner I get her away from it the better, in terms of the years of life left to her. Of course, as you might suppose, the idea of leaving here is most unattractive to Mamma, and I can see that the idea of any changes (even so much as a coat of paint) is also unattractive. But I've been talking to her about the situation as I see it in relation to Marjie, and I think she might become reconciled to a change for that reason. I might even decide to build what I need, and I imagine Mrs.

Gover would leave me undisturbed here for some time if that should be my wish. As you see, dear, nothing is as yet very clear to me, but at least I think I'm beginning to see some things I mustn't get involved in.

Oh dear—a long phone call from Bob has eaten up most of the interval to mail time.

We do hope the convalescence will go more and more smoothly, and that the weather will prove ideal for long, healing days in the garden.

Love to all—
Rachel

Oh darling—no time now to say what I wanted to. Yesterday I was afraid I may have seemed to be complaining about the length or quality of your letters, dear, and *of course I wasn't.* I haven't wanted you to write nearly as much as you have under these trying circumstances. What I was referring to was the few things you seem to be putting off for summer conversation. Oh dear—this must go to the box! But I love you—do you know?

R.

TUESDAY, JUNE 12
───────────────────────────────────

My own darling [Dorothy],

For your birthday, this is to tell you—as if you didn't know—how dearly and tenderly I love you. You have come to occupy a place in my life that no one else could fill, and it is strange now to contemplate all the empty years when you weren't there. But perhaps we shouldn't regret those years—perhaps instead we should just give ourselves over to wonder and gratitude that a friendship so satisfying and so full of joy and beauty could come to each of us in the middle years—when, perhaps, we needed it most!

Darling, I loved the little clipping pasted on your letter today. It says so perfectly what each of us would say.

I hope you will read this before we talk Friday—and now I think it will be the 8:30 morning hour. And I know I'm going to be tempted horribly to call you at Southport tonight! Always wanting to share every bit of everything, you see! Darling, do you know how wonderful it is to have you? I hope you do.

I love you.
Rachel

P.S. The enclosure[47] darling, won't wait for your birthday, for it applies to your trip to Maine so directly that I must send it now. You know, I've *said* this to you many times, so it was quite stardusty to find it on a card.

[47] A birthday card to DF from RC.

Oh dear, so many other things I wanted to say, but mail time is impending! I'll write to Southport, dear, aiming for Tuesday.

You know I *will* be with you all the time. And I, too, am relieved to know you'll have neighbors there.

A sweet note from Nellie Lee Bok today—they hope Curtis can come home to continue convalescence there on the 15th—and they are planning to go to Maine in early August—no European trip! She says there is extensive heart damage, which he seems not to realize, but if he can adjust he should have "years of reasonable activity." Now I must go, darling. It is so hard never to have time to say what I want to say.

But I do anyway!
R.

JUNE 15

Darling [Dorothy],

I wish the enclosed[48] had come in time that it might have been sent as a special little birthday greeting to you. But actually, I didn't expect to have them until next week, so this was a surprise.

The same mail brought your sweet letter written under Our Spruce. Perhaps I can answer it (briefly—don't fret) this evening—just now Roger and I are waiting for our patients. It's really wonderful—we haven't had to come in rain yet, so he can play on the lawn.

I forgot to tell you I received an advance copy of the *WHC* piece some days ago—just sheets torn from the magazine—and I guess the July number will be on newsstands next week—around the 20th to 22nd. That makes a big week for me, doesn't it! With a wonderful one to follow, if all goes well.

Now home—lunch—packing—errands! Will mail this, even though I suppose there is no chance you'll get it tomorrow.

All love to my dear on her birthday, and always—

Rachel

JUNE 23

THE DAY AFTER

Dearest [Dorothy],

Once-upon-a-time, you wrote me a letter from this hotel.[49] Remembering that, I was moved to bring home a bit of hotel stationery last night, on which to send you my account of the affair.[50] This will be only a note, for this is Mrs. Johnson's[51] last day and I want to put every minute to good use. But I do want to mail something this evening.

It was all very lovely, dear—especially the warmth of the informal reception afterward, when nearly every woman present must have come to greet me. You see, the identity of the award winner was a secret even from this group, except for a few individuals. Apparently there is keen interest in it, and from what they had to say (she reports shamelessly) I gathered they were pleased with the selection of the committee.

The dress was comfortable and seemed right, though there were more short dresses than long. However, with so much attention focused on me, I felt

48 A second birthday card from RC.

49 The Sheraton-Park Hotel in Washington, D.C.

50 The American Association of University Women dinner at which RC had received a $2,500 award for outstanding scholarship.

51 The nurse attending to RC's mother, who was convalescing after hospitalization for knee problems.

the long dress more appropriate. The blue is much the color of the border of your card, and if I can find an extra deep seam I'll snip off a bit before I put the dress away. The shell pin was delicate and lovely with it, and picked up the sparkle of my rhinestone necklace. I wore the blue-and-rhinestone earrings, but not the bracelet. My corsage was two small white orchids with deep pink throats, no net, a bit of pale pink narrow ribbon. I was glad I had it, for there were no special flowers for me—just a little pink carnation corsage, at each place at the speakers' table. My own little talk went off all right and—here she goes being shameless again—there were some very satisfying comments about it. I think the thing mentioned most often was what I said about the loneliness of a writer's work—that or the indicated subject of the new book.[52]

And while I was talking, you, I hope, were settling down at Southport. I do hope the trip was comfortable. It is horribly hot and sticky here. Relief had been promised for tomorrow, but now they say more of the same. If only we can get a break Tuesday night it will be heavenly.

LATER

Our dear Mrs. Johnson is gone now, but with promises on both sides to keep in touch. She says she would come to stay with Mamma while I have to be away any time she wasn't on a case. I have also sounded her out as to whether she might even consider coming to us in the capacity of housekeeper, and I think she might. She would be very competent, I'm sure. She did a major defrosting & refrigerator-cleaning-job today, so now it will be simple on departure. She cleaned and reorganized the compartment under the sink(!), washed up the kitchen floor, got meals, washed dishes, went to the Post Office with me to carry packages in and out, carried the microscope and other heavy things to the car, etc., etc.! Do you wonder I call her a Treasure?

As to packages, dear, three cartons containing blankets were mailed, Special Handling. I should think they'd arrive Tuesday or certainly Wednesday. If you will just set them in the house we'll be sure of being able to keep warm. (She writes on a 90-degree day!)

The other things are all going by Express and can take their time. They will be delivered to the house, you know. This year I'm sending a small trunk, so the car won't be so jammed and Mamma will be more comfortable.

And will you, when in the house, unlock the Study screen? You might then just set something against it so it won't blow open. That will give me another way to get in. It's so nice you have your phone this year, for I can call you from along the road.

(This pen is driving me mad!)

Fan mail on the *Companion* piece is beginning to come in. A lovely note from Anne Ford, who likes it best of anything I've written. And a mysterious envelope with no name or address, containing a little Japanese card in its own en-

[52] The contemplated book on evolution.

velope. The inner envelope is inscribed: "For you who wrote 'Teach Your Child To Wonder!'" And on the card is written

> God must be glad
> One loves His world so much.

That's all!

This morning one of the nice men in the Post Office spoke of it (the piece) to me.

Oh, I must tell you Roger's compliment when I returned last night—they had stayed here with Mamma. Of course, I had changed back into "traveling clothes" before leaving the hotel—a little white linen suit he hadn't seen before. On it I wore the orchid corsage, and I was wearing my little blue feather hat. He cast an appraising eye over me and said, "My, you have a nice design, Rachel."

I think we are taking a Pink Cottage[53] for the last 2 weeks of August then the Steeveses'[54] for 2 weeks of September. That, plus some time with us will give M. & R. a nice long stay. Did I tell you he said recently, "I can't wait to see good old Maine and the wonderful Bay!"

Well, dear, pray for cooler weather here. If we get it, I *think* we'll start Wednesday, but whether we can go through in two days depends on how well Mamma's knee stands the travel. I'll wire you when we start, and communicate in some way during the trip.

So maybe this is the last *letter,* tho I'll try to send a note the first of the week. I love to think of you *there.* And I love you, as you know.

Allways—
Rachel

WEDNESDAY A.M., AUGUST 8

Dear Stan and Dorothy—

This morning I achieved the difficult feat of getting up without disturbing anyone but Jeffie, so maybe I can write a letter before breakfast.

Knowing you can't be at Southport as soon as you want to be,[55] I'm always of two minds now about talking of the place or telling you anything special that happens—should I share it with you, or is it mean to talk about things you want so badly to see or do yourselves? That, in general, is my predicament, but this time I *have* to tell you about something strange and wonderful.

We are now having the spring tides of the new moon, you know, and they have traced their advance well over my beach the past several nights. Roger's raft has to be secured by a line to the old stump, so Marjie and I have an added excuse to go down at high tide. There had been lots of swell and surf and noise all day, so it was most exciting down there toward midnight—all my rocks crowned with foam, and long white crests running from my beach to Mahard's. To get the full wildness, we turned off our flashlights—and then the real ex-

[53] A cottage on the Dogfish Head road, rented by RC for Marjie and Roger.

[54] A neighbor's cottage near RC's, also rented by her for Marjie and Roger.

[55] In July the Freemans had returned to West Bridgewater where Stanley had undergone transfusions and tests for internal bleeding. RC had stayed with DF on August 1–3 and had visited Stanley in the hospital.

citement began. Of course, you can guess—the surf was full of diamonds and emeralds, and was throwing them on the wet sand by the dozen. Dorothy, dear—it was the night we were there all over, but with everything intensified: a wilder accompaniment of noise and movement, and a great deal more phosphorescence. The individual sparks were so large—we'd see them glowing in the sand, or sometimes, caught in the in-and-out play of water, just riding back and forth. And several times I was able to scoop one up in my hand in shells and gravel, and think surely it was big enough to see—but no such luck.

Now here is where my story becomes different. Once, glancing up, I said to Marjie jokingly, "Look—one of them has taken to the air!" A firefly was going by, his lamp blinking. We thought nothing special of it, but in a few minutes one of us said, "There's that firefly again." The next time he really got a reaction from us, for he was flying so low over the water that his light cast a long surface reflection, like a little headlight. Then the truth dawned on me. He "thought" the flashes in the water were other fireflies, signaling to him in the age-old manner of fireflies! Sure enough, he was soon in trouble and we saw his light flashing urgently as he was rolled around in the wet sand—no question this time which was insect and which the unidentified little sea will-o-the-wisps!

You can guess the rest: I waded in and rescued him (the will-o-the-wisps had already had me in icy water to my knees so a new wetting didn't matter) and put him in Roger's bucket to dry his wings. When we came up we brought him as far as the porch—out of reach of temptation, we hoped.

It was one of those experiences that gives an odd and hard-to-describe feeling, with so many overtones beyond the facts themselves. I have never seen any account scientifically, of fireflies responding to other phosphorescence. I suppose I should write it up briefly for some journal if it actually isn't known. Imagine putting that in scientific language! And I've already thought of a child's story based on it—but maybe that will never get written.

Then everyone got up, and the day began!

The tide was very low this morning (1.8′) but I didn't go out. I could see surf on Bull Ledge as I was writing.

Now I'm at the Witch's,[56] about to have my hair fixed so I'll have to wear a hat all the time!

Dorothy, I'm going to call you—or try to, Thursday night. I hope I'll hear of lots of improvement.

I know it must be hard to be patient—but just remember those doctors have all the skill needed to get you back home as soon as possible. Our love to you both—

Rachel

[56] Nickname for an unsatisfactory hairdresser.

Dear Dorothy and Stan,

We have spent the morning at the clinic and in BBHbr, had lunch, and now I want to get at least a note in the afternoon mail.

The enclosed clipping[57] has just been sent to me by Dick Pough, whom you met at the "21" party last fall. Please return it after you have had your share of laughs out of it.

The morning mail also brought a letter from Curtis Bok; being in Maine and actually having had a trial sail on his boat seem to have transported him to the seventh Heaven of delight. They are starting their coastwise cruise Saturday and will do it by leisurely stages, stopping at Friendship and New Harbor, and arriving here Monday sometime. They will probably stay over Tuesday and leave Wednesday. He suggests supper aboard Monday, which would be fun; then I can have them here Tuesday and show them shore creatures by microscope at least. I don't know whether he should actually do any tide-pooling. But the timing could hardly be better for me, so I am delighted.

As I told you, Dorothy, I expect the Teales[58] Wednesday or Thursday of this week. Marjie and family move to the Pink Cottage Saturday. Moppet has really been a very nice little visitor. We haven't dared let the two cats together, but they sniff noses and then spit through a crack of the door and might eventually get acquainted. Roger understands about the closed doors, so it works all right. Incidentally, he dictated the enclosed letter while we were waiting at the clinic this morning.[59]

Mamma thinks the combination of microwave and ultrasonic is doing wonders for her knee. They use the former about 30 minutes; then follow immediately with a brief ultrasonic dose. Dr. Gregory says the two complement each other, being very different wave lengths, and he thinks the combination more effective than either separately. Stan, maybe you should try it for your shoulder. I'm trying to persuade Marjie to give it a try while we are making the daily trips anyway.

I know the time must seem very long to both of you, but how good to be that far away from the wretched attack[60] that began the hospital stay. We know that will never happen again, for you would detect early symptoms if it ever should begin. You know we are thinking of you both very many times each day. Must go now.

Our love to you both,
Rachel

[57] Enclosure not preserved.

[58] Edwin Way and Nellie Teale.

[59] Roger's letter to Stan reads: "Dear Uncle Stan—I love you. I went down to a dock today. Now we're waiting in the car for Grandma. Now we went to see the building ship. We went in wading on the beach. *We* are Rachel and Roger. We got some "debiled [devil's]" apron. Love + + + + Roger."

[60] The onset of internal bleeding on the night of July 27 had prompted Stanley's hospitalization.

Darling [Dorothy],

You will forgive the typewriter, I know. I want to mail this with Stan's let-ter, and the time is short so it is the only way. Your dear note, written Sunday morning, came on the noon mail—wasn't that wonderful? Now I shall try to tell you more coherently about the earrings. When you admired them so, I decided immediately that I wanted you to have a pair just like them. But I knew that if I told Mrs. Babcock that I wanted to give them to a friend, she would not allow me to pay her for them. So I wrote her that a friend had admired them so much and wished to have a pair—so would she make them for you but send them in my care, since you would be here at irregular times. I don't know whether she saw through my stratagem, but at any rate, when she sent them she said firmly that the question of payment must never come up—that it would be her great plea-sure to send anything of the sort that any friend of mine fancied. So now I shall tell her who the friend was, and I know she will be especially happy that they are yours.

Darling, you must have known even as you read the "firefly letter" that I deliberated before writing it, and wrote it with full knowledge that it would bring sadness as well as joy. But as I weighed the two, it seemed the joy would be the greater, so I took the chance. I suppose I was remembering, too, the times you have been here when I could not come—and one time in particular when I thought I might not come at all that summer—yet I wanted to hear all you told me of what you saw and felt. And I believed it would be the same with you, just as you say it is.

Darling, it does seem to me that you can have real hope of coming a little later. And with most people gone, the place would be far better for Stan to have real rest and healing quiet than during the confusion of summer. I think you should begin to believe a little, now. After all, peace and rest are almost the most important elements of the treatment for his condition, so you would not be tak-ing a chance and risking interference with his recovery, once he is able for the trip. And you know, darling, if it was best for you to put him on a train and fol-low by car, I'd be simply delighted to meet him and bring him the rest of the way—from Brunswick or Wiscasset.

Must go to the Post Office, now, dear one. I love you.

Rachel

Darling [Dorothy],

This will be only a tiny goodnight, for the hours have flown with closing the Steeveses' cottage, packing, mailing, trips to Wiscasset and Boothbay, last errands and preparations for the travellers, and now in an hour we must go.

If it were possible, dear one, I'd love you more than ever before for what

61 Marjie and
Roger, returning
to Silver Spring
from Southport
by train, had
DF's company for
their stopover
in Boston.

you are doing today.[61] It is a tremendous load off our minds, as you have rightly understood. And I don't know anyone else, darling, who would voluntarily and happily do what you are doing today to give us this peace of mind. Bless your dear heart!

I have been re-reading *Venture to the Interior* and, of course, finding rich rewards on almost every page. This one I want to speak of now—the dedication to his wife, "to defeat the latest of many separations." And I thought how all our writing of letters, and our telephone calls (both of which we are constantly re-solving to curtail) are really efforts to "defeat the separation" that is so hard for both of us.

Darling, you know I am going all the way home with you tonight and lov-ing you dearly. And I'm counting days until you return.

All my love.
Rachel

S U N D A Y   N I G H T ,   S E P T E M B E R   2 3

Dearest [Dorothy],

Today's predicted rain held off until after dark and now is making pleas-ant sounds on the roof as I write, perched on my bed and making use of my writ-ing case. Tomorrow morning I'm going to have my hair done(!) so I'll write a bit now for mailing then.

Last night I crawled off to bed early feeling as though maybe a cold were coming on—but it isn't. I probably slept it off for I didn't get up till late. Then I thought I'd go back to bed and read, but instead an odd restlessness kept me on the go all day, which was good, for I do have some results. I explored all the woodland from Mahard's new lot back to the one where the woman is going to build, and began to wish very much I *could* buy those lots. Of course it doesn't compare with the woods near you, but is quite lovely with its mossy cliffs and its unexpected open patches where only the reindeer lichen covers the rock. The trees are good—several splendid white pines among them. Well, I'm tempted, and if the other project weren't looming I probably would. More of that later.

I brought back several loads of moss and fern and lichen to plant on the slope behind the house—a tiny area, really, but I find it can absorb several wood-carriers full of materials and still leave lots of room for more. Well, maybe I'll finish it before we leave.

Then I went at kitchen shelves, and you should see how many stale crack-ers and potato chips I got rid of!

Yesterday at the store I got several pieces of "change" from Mr. Pinkham. One, that the Dogfish Head Road is going to be widened. Maybe that is the meaning of the markers we've noticed. I don't know when it's to be done. He swears they are not going to bother our little lane through the woods—I told him I hoped it would always stay as it is. The other item was a strong hint that some of Mrs. Gaynor's companions (in the Steeveses' cottage, you know) are not exactly desirable. Added to the hint you received, it doesn't make me feel happy about the possibility Mrs. G. might turn up as a permanent neighbor. So I wish I could buy *that*! Soon I'll want the whole island!

Without prearrangement, Mr. Delano dropped in to see us last Wednesday, so I told him what is in my mind. At first I thought there was no hope of his doing anything in time for next summer, but as we talked I felt he was trying to find a way to get it in. I'm to see him soon to get down to more specific details and see if I can afford what I want. As I expected, all costs have risen—he says this house would cost ⅓ to ½ more now than when he built it.

Now my "week off" is shaping up about like others. Tomorrow, hairdresser's and maybe Mr. Delano. Tuesday, a meeting in Wiscasset of a group interested in forming a local branch of the Nature Conservancy. I feel I should go. Wednesday, Dr. and Mrs. Vincent Schaefer and a couple of friends are coming—he phoned Saturday from Schenectady. They will probably stay over, and so maybe I'll have to do a tide with them Thursday. That gets me through the week to Friday—and you know whom I hope to see that day!

MONDAY A.M.

Still raining! Jeffie insisted on coming in at 7:30, so I got up and made a fire and then came back—so here we are! He's having a jolly time romping over my bed and looking out of the windows.

Oh, I do hope there will be dry, sparkling weather while you're here!

In a way, of course, it seems long since you left, yet it's hard to believe Stan is already starting his second week of work. I do hope all is going well, and he isn't getting too tired.

Now I guess I must start the day's program, dear.

My love, always.
Rachel

New birds today: Brown creeper, 2 yellowlegs on shore.

Maybe I'll find a note from you on way home today. Know what?

FRIDAY, OCTOBER 5, 10 P.M.

Darling [Dorothy],

Now we can talk a little—sitting in front of the fire as we did some evenings not long ago.

It was sweet to have your call so that my thoughts of you could again find definite focus, knowing you were home. I *almost* called you back, for as soon as I put down the phone and went into the living room, the spectacle I shall describe in another letter began to pass across the sky. And as always I wanted to share it with you instantly, some way. You can imagine the memories it called up, for always before this has been something we have shared.

I was so glad I had returned for mail this evening, and so had your under-the-drier letter before you called. (It was postmarked at noon on the 3rd.) The other, which somehow arrived first, was a bit disturbing as the *only* message from you, but I felt there must be another on the way—and there was. Darling, I'm so sorry Wednesday[62] had to be one of those days filled with irritations and frustrations. But I *know*, as you must be aware from some of our conversations and you should know, too, that I am far from being the "angel" of patience and forbearance that you picture. But when my own irritation flares up, it is always about 50% anger at myself that I should let it, or that I should be so annoyed and upset.

All right, dear, I will copy the passages you want from Curtis's letters. But as to the one I think you especially have in mind in this connection, remember I read it to you in amusement because I thought it so inaccurate an impression!

Now don't worry so much about me, dear. I admit the nights are hard—the hardest part, really—for I do love my sleep and can hardly bear to get up. The last couple of nights there have had to be extra risings to give the Demerol, so never more than 2 hours unbroken.[63] I think I'll make up with daytime naps, but I don't for there is so much I want to do—some quite pleasant.

And at that point I had to give in and take a nap, which was my undoing, for now it's after 10 *Saturday* night, and I have a feeling I won't get everything said this time, either. And I do want to write a short letter for you and Stan.

Dearest, dearly as I'd love to have you, you are not to think of coming again. Your place now is there to do what you can for Stan, and if he should have any sort of setback I'd never forgive myself. I am thinking seriously of trying to get Mrs. Johnson to come for at least a few days before we leave and of course to return with us. I think that's the answer if she can and will. I can see that after a couple of weeks of this I'm going to be more tired than I ought to be for that trip. And the trip itself will be unusually taxing—each stop so hard—and Mrs. J. would be a wonderful help.

Darling—your trip letter was here, amazingly, at noon today and now I feel I've had such a wealth of mail from you. It's been very sweet, dear. I am not letting myself think of The Long Night,[64] either.

If I do build my little house[65] I feel sure I'd need to come back to see Mr. Delano—unless he can do nothing on it in time for next year.

And, if Mary Poppins Johnson comes to take care of us (her name *is* Mary, you know) I'll just plain come to visit you.

Now and then I realize that this present mishap has decided certain things once and for all. Mamma can never again be left alone while I go away, for example. Indeed, I don't think she can ever be left alone even for half a day. And never again can I bring her here alone. All summer I've been haunted by a feel-

[62] DF's first day home after a Southport visit from September 28 to October 2 to close the Freeman cottage.

[63] RC had to wake up frequently to tend to her mother's knee problem.

[64] The night of Stanley's internal bleeding attack.

[65] RC may have been contemplating having a small outbuilding constructed on her Southport property.

ing—"What if something serious happens? We're 700 miles from home." So there *has* to be a Mary Poppins.

The parallels with Edwin's mother keep suggesting themselves. Those falls, after which she "lost her sense of equilibrium," he said, so that she always had to have help to walk. I don't think this is a matter of equilibrium, exactly, but a terrible unsteadiness that has the same result.

But somehow, dear, I feel the present crisis will work out. And surely I can get help when I get home, and then I can sleep. Marie called as soon as she got my letter and offered to come for the last few days, but I assured her I'd be all right. And I will, dear. Now I must go and leave so very much unsaid. But you understand why.

I love you dear,
Rachel

Oh—I forgot this. Of course it was all right to tell Stan about Curtis and his Board.[66] I wouldn't want it to go beyond you two at present, for you know I am merely Curtis's candidate; the others can also present names and I may not be chosen. But to have him want me, and for the reasons he gave, is quite enough for us to be happy about. I'm glad you did tell him, dear.

[66] Board of the American Foundation.

SUNDAY

Darling, I *want* to keep talking to you but I mustn't. I must try to pack books tonight.

I love you,
R.

OCTOBER 7

Dear Dorothy and Stan,

I hope this may reach you on your anniversary, but whenever it comes I know you will accept it as a little observance of that occasion. You know this is the first year since I have really known you that I have had to *write* in order to wish you happiness on the day, and many years of continuing happiness together. Having shared Your Day to some extent for the past two years, it has become a sort of Anniversary for me, too, with deep meanings that I know you understand without my putting them into words.

There are certain events that I've come to associate with the week—if not the actual day—of your anniversary, and now I must tell you what happened Friday evening. It had been one of those bright, clear days with a piercing wind from the northwest, and at sunset there was not a cloud in the sky. There had been a thought in my mind all day, and shortly after sunset I went into the living room and began to scan the horizon. Almost instantly I saw a faint line like a wisp of smoke above the Kennebec—then more and more until I knew that one of those great migrations of waterfowl was moving toward Merrymeeting Bay.

All, as far as I saw, were far away in the western sky, but with the glasses their formations and even the individual birds stood out clearly. And the flights continued until dusk made the drifting ribbons invisible. One more detail: I had also had in mind that on that evening I should see the new moon—the moon of the month in which I must leave here for another season. But when I looked into that clear, after-sunset sky I couldn't see it. Behind the spruces on the far shore of the Bay the sky was a pale orange, fading above into yellow and then a cold, gray-blue. Then the ducks appeared, and as I was searching the sky with my glasses, suddenly I saw the moon just above the horizon, a thin sickle, but so enormous that at first I could hardly believe it actually was the moon! Its color was so close to that of the sky that without the glasses I couldn't see it. Last night it was clear in the evening sky, and soon, I suppose, I can begin to watch for its reflection in the Bay.

This was quite a different sort of day—heavy rain in the night that slackened and turned to fog by the end of the morning. I went out with the camera and tried some tricky shots. If the slides look like what I saw in the viewer they will be good. And the light meter encouraged me to try!

The day of the high wind I explored the shore and adjacent woods from Daniel's place north for a short distance. If only that could be kept always just as it is! If ever I wish for money—lots of it—it is when I see something like that. How many acres would you guess are in the land from Daniel's road north to where the Head cottages begin, and between the Dogfish Head Road and the Bay? Just for fun, tell me what you think, and let's pretend we could somehow create a sanctuary there, where people like us could go, as my friend said of the Bok Tower and grounds, "and walk about, and get what they need." Well, if no one ever thinks of it, it certainly won't happen; if someone does think hard enough, it just might. Of course I am just thinking aloud, and quite confidentially, to two dear kindred spirits. But it's fun to dream of such things, isn't it?

We get along after a fashion. At the moment I just can't imagine steps, or getting in and out of the car, so the problem of the trip home seems far from solution. All the complications of sending Mamma by train or plane seem worse than the car trip. Another ten days may make quite a difference, of course. I'm using hot packs on the knee now, for it is quite painful, but does not seem stiff. Mamma seldom makes any complaint, but I get it out of her by questioning that her back pains her constantly, and she has to take the Demerol pills about as often as she can. I really think I shall see if Mrs. Johnson can come, for I know what a help she could be. Marjie wanted to try to leave Roger with someone and come, but I declined that—there are too many complications and besides I need someone much more rugged physically. By the way, Roger is simply delighted with school. I talked to them last night, and when I asked him how he liked it he said emphatically, "*Very* much!" So that hurdle is taken successfully.

Now my dears, I must stop. I'm going to try to call you Tuesday night for a further word. And you know that with the devotion and loving thoughts that always go to you, there is a special portion from us both for this particular day.

Always your
Rachel

Darling [Rachel],

This is for your anniversary. You may have forgotten that *The Edge of the Sea* will be officially, at least, one year old on October 26.

You must know that was an important day in my life, too. To have you publicly proclaim our friendship was a lovely thing for you to do.

But we both know that it needed no public proclamation to make it the most beautiful thing in the world for me.

Its essence is in this little quotation[67] which I believe I have already sent you at some time. But it bears repeating and when I found it in this form I knew it was meant for us.

Darling, I fear I have failed at times to live up to the thought in this paragraph. But I know you have forgiven me. For that I thank you. On your part I know you have sifted the heedless things I've said and with the breath of kindness blown the rest away. For all that wonderful understanding, darling, I love you more, if possible.

I wish I could be with you on the Anniversary.

All my love,
Dorothy

Dearest [Dorothy],

Here is a little oasis in the midst of a busy day, so— propped up on my bed with the typewriter on my lap—I'll talk to you a few minutes before Our Treasure has the dinner ready. Then I'm going off to an Audubon Board meeting.

The car has been whining and groaning on starting out for the past several weeks, and so I finally got it down to the dealer this morning to have the hydromatic adjusted. Now it floats again, as on air, and they have also adjusted brakes, which were not quite what they should be, and fixed some unsuspected "leak" about the power steering, so now my transportation seems assured for a while.

I had been called yesterday by an agency about a possible Mary Poppins, so I arranged to see her at their office today. She turns out to be a *Hazel*— wouldn't it be funny if I took her?—and while it is dreadfully hard to tell, I believe she may be worth a try. She is middle-aged, has good references, including one place she worked four years with all care of house and children, and her husband has been janitor of a Lutheran church about a mile from here for the

[67] The quotation, entitled "Friendship," by Dinah Mulock, reads: "Oh the comfort, the inexpressible comfort of feeling safe with a person, having neither to weigh thoughts nor measure words, but pouring them all right out, just as they are— chaff and grain together—certain that a faithful hand will take and sift them, keep what is worth keeping, and with the breath of kindness blow the rest away."

past 12 years. I could get her for a 5½-day week for $35—quite a bargain compared with our Treasure. She will have her husband bring her out Sunday for further discussion, but at the moment I am fairly hopeful.

Mary[68] did not exactly endear herself to me last night. I suggested she take the evening off, since we were having Elizabeth Dickson for dinner, and Marjie and Roger for a while, and I thought we'd enjoy the evening more without her in the offing. The only stipulation I made was that she return not later than 11, since I wanted to drive Elizabeth home. She returned blithely at 12:15—simply had no idea I'd said what I did!

My program for today also included the seeing of the new Walt Disney film, *Secrets of Life*. I told myself I really needed to see it, in view of all that is transpiring re the Vishniac Edge-of-the-Sea project. Now that I have, I do want you and Stan to see it. I scarcely know whether I was more impressed with the wonders of Nature, or the wonders of modern photography! In any event, it is a wonderful picture, and I do really hope you will see it.

One October day, on the porch at Southport, I read you a letter from Curtis Bok asking me if I would accept membership on the Board of the American Foundation. He has now written to say that the Board has met and elected me to membership, in which fact he expresses due, or should I say "undue," pleasure? He goes on to discuss a problem soon to come up relating to chimes for the Tower, and then says he is anxious for me to see the place, and that the Foundation will send me down at any time I can go. He and Nellie Lee, and perhaps the girls, are going late in January, and he suggests it would be nice if I could just get on their train in Washington and go with them. Yes, it would be wonderful, if I could be free to do that, *and other things*, and who knows, perhaps I can. As you know, I was very deeply touched when he asked me about membership on the Board, but I don't think the full import of the thing got through to me. Now I believe it has, and I feel overwhelmed.

Darling, someday soon, if not before you [read] this, you will receive an invitation to the affair on November 27th.[69] You will know without my saying so that nothing would make me happier than to have you and Stan there. It is for the book of which you are "godparents" and I suppose it is the most important single thing that has happened for that book alone. Nevertheless, I realize there are many reasons why you cannot be there, and in asking to have you invited, it is with no real hope that you can come in your physical selves—I know you will be there in spirit. But I did want you to be included among those invited, if only so that you will have this memento to file away. A letter from the Committee chairman (There is also basic information about the Council of Women—Inc.! which I'll send you after I've digested it.) today says that Mrs. Kimbrough has had to make a lecture engagement for the 27th, so they have adopted the custom of some other organizations, asking the previous year's recipient to make the award. BUT, since Mrs. Lindbergh did not herself receive the award, they have asked her publisher to make the presentation. This I must say, is a slight disappointment, for I am not 100% sure that Mrs. Lindbergh would have refused to do this. I think they were a little offended that she did not come. Perhaps this is the moment for me to write to her—I don't mean to influence this situation, but as a link between us affording the opportunity.

There have been several letters recently that I think you will enjoy. Darling—I must stop if I'm to mail this on the way to the Board meeting. Wonderful messages from you today—thank you, my dear. And I'm *so* happy about your slides. NOW maybe you'll go on next year!

All my love
Rachel

SUNDAY NIGHT, NOVEMBER 18

Darling Dorothy,

I've just made a discovery—the Philharmonic concerts are rebroadcast at 10 P.M. Sundays. When they disappeared from the normal Sunday afternoon spot last year I thought they'd been dropped completely. Maybe they were then—but here it is now, and I almost like this hour better. I have the radio beside my bed right now, tuned in softly on the Haydn symphony. Oh—it's ending now—and you know what's next? Did you perhaps listen today? *Our* violin concerto!—Need I tell you, darling, in what a very special way you have been with me during *that* half hour, and need I list the memories that came with the music: of listening to it with you at Southport—and once with you and Willow—and another time I heard it only in my heart, but told you about it, and then it became Ours. Remember? And now this reminds me of what I've been thinking recently—that our store of memories is already so large that many of the separate items get lost, or nearly so. Every now and then I uncover the memory of some shared experience or precious moment, with such surprise, realizing I hadn't thought of it for years—or at least months! Not that I'm complaining about having so many memories stored away, you understand! But it is wonderful, darling, and in such a short time, really. Three years ago about this time, you sent me your first Thanksgiving greeting! And I remember how I loved it, and I know what you wrote!

Darling—an intermission announcement at today's concert, in case you didn't listen, concerned the fact that a long-playing record has been made of the *Symphony of the Birds*, which they performed in October. Didn't you hear it or tell me something about it?

More about Leonard Bernstein in today's *Times*—I'll send it. And would you sometime return the clipping I mailed today?

I have probably got you thoroughly confused and even upset by all my chatter about somehow trying to get together this month. I know I shouldn't think of it, really, under the circumstances, but I do want to so much! But I'm afraid it's unfair to involve you in one of these very uncertain schemes, with only a very short visit possible at best. Well, let's talk about it Thanksgiving, and if we feel we mustn't, please forgive me for raising the hope, dear one.

All my letters recently seem so fragmentary and unsatisfactory. I don't know where the hours go. And I seem to have said too many times that I'm tired. Please don't worry about that, dear. Of course I am, but under the circumstances I don't know how it could be otherwise.

Your Friday note came today, dear—this is now *Monday* and I'm under the drier. And did I say your Thursday under-drier letter came Saturday as you (and I) hoped.

Now I must go, dear one. I haven't heard your Thanksgiving plans. If you won't be home that morning don't worry—I'll then try Thursday evening.

All my love,

R.

S ATURDAY, D ECEMBER 1

Dear Dorothy and Stan:

It is good to think that you will be together again before this letter reaches you, and probably I shall have spoken to you both tomorrow. I do hope the weather is being kind to you today, for the return from the hospital.[70] You may be sure we are thinking of you and hoping all goes well. What a happy cat Mr. Willow will be! Even after only 36 hours' absence, I received quite a welcome from Jeffie.

Stan, it was wonderful of you to write out all those directions for the exercises. They came this morning, and I have told Marjie; she was really touched, and I hope they will prove to be something she can and will do. I think she is suffering less pain, but is quite limited in the movement possible in that arm.

I know you want to hear more details of the New York affair. As I told you, Dorothy, it was a smaller and less formal party than I had visualized, but that made it much more pleasant. I am no good at guessing numbers, but I'd say there were from 100 to 150 people there. The very happy part was that I knew so many of them; one thinks of New York as rather an impersonal place, so it was really wonderful to be able to greet so many friends and acquaintances. Last year the award was presented at a fancy party at the Waldorf, the award itself consisting merely of a scroll with some appropriate words inscribed. The Committee Chairman told me they decided it was foolish to let the Waldorf get all the money; that they'd rather have a simpler affair and provide a money award for the author. Very sensible, I thought!

As I commented to Marie, my past, present, and future publishers made up a substantial fraction of the gathering: three from Oxford, two from Simon and Schuster, three from Houghton Mifflin, and three from Harper. And of course many other publishing houses were represented, as well as book review-

[70] Stanley underwent further diagnostic tests for internal bleeding in the hospital on November 24–30.

ers, people from *Publisher's Weekly*, etc. I know I told you Will Beebe came, and also Mr. and Mrs. Tee Van from the Zoological Society. And Edwin Teale, and my tax lawyers, and others I can't think of at the moment. The Carnegie Foundation Building in which it was held is a structure of modern but very pleasant architecture and furnishings, near the East River and the United Nations. It is available only to tax-free organizations of various kinds. Along one wall of the room there was arranged an exhibit of the books that had received some support for the award. Beside the central display of *The Edge of the Sea* were the two runners-up: *Nectar in the Sieve*,[71] which I seem to remember you read, and *Greenwillow*.[72] The chairman told me, however, that *The Edge* was so far ahead of any others in votes that they were not even citing these for honorable mention. Then in panels at each side were the other books, each of which had received some votes. I noticed that Pearl Buck was among them, but at the moment I can't think of any others. I arrived about five, at which time only a few were there. After about half an hour of milling around among the gradually increasing crowd, the award was presented by the gentleman from Pantheon Press, and I responded and then had Edwin put my $500-check in his vest pocket for safekeeping! By about 6:45 there seemed to be no new arrivals, and most people had gone, so Marie's dinner party left en masse, for a very pleasant evening. Margaret Cooper Gay is quite delightful, and her husband, Francis Smulders, is a smiling, easy-going Dutchman—they live in the midst of 35 acres of Connecticut countryside which has, besides wonderful woodland, a lovely stream with a 30-foot waterfall. They brought pictures of it, and I took pictures of Muffie and Jeffie to show her. Besides the Smulders, Marie's guests included Edwin, Paul Brooks and Jack Leggett from H.M., her friend Phil Gustafson, and the little Frenchman whose name I can't spell, but who is going to cross the Pacific in a fiberglass boat.

Back to the Award Party for a moment: all the women of the National Council that I met were middle-aged or elderly, all most pleasant and gracious, and quite dedicated to their program, I would suppose; although how much they actually accomplish is anybody's guess. I presume most of their meetings are exclusively feminine affairs, and I was amused to overhear a comment: "My, isn't it exciting to have so many men here!" Another stage-whispered comment Marie heard soon after our arrival was: "Doesn't she have a nice figure!" Guess I'll forget my diet, which hasn't reduced me a pound anyway.

The business meetings of the next day were all interesting, and promise enough activity to keep me busy for years if all work out. Walter Oakley of Oxford and Al Leventhal of Simon and Schuster came to Marie's office to discuss the juvenile adaptation of *The Sea*:[73] Oxford is expressing no objection and S&S only eagerness and willingness to let me have veto power over text and illustrations, so all is set to move forward. S&S would like to publish in time for Christmas, 1958. Because all new illustrations have to be made, and color takes time, no earlier date is possible. This means, however, going ahead very rapidly on

[71] Authored by Markandaya Kamala and first published in America in 1954.

[72] Authored by B. J. (Beatrice Joy) Chute, published in 1956.

[73] *The Sea Around Us* was published in a junior edition by Simon and Schuster's Golden Press in 1958.

text, and the adaptation would have to be made and in form approved by me well before Maine, 1957. (You see, that's the way I date things!) Then my work in checking illustrations would come in the fall and early winter.

On the Vishniac movie, there are now at least four possibilities as to backers, quite different in character and therefore presenting various pro's and con's. This item is, of course, most confidential, but I had written Laurance Rockefeller in the hope he might be interested. He replied he did not think he could undertake it directly but had discussed it with Fairfield Osborn as a possible project of the Conservation Foundation, in which Mr. Rockefeller would presumably take some part. Mr. Osborn had expressed interest, and I hoped to talk to him while in New York. I couldn't, so wrote him on Thursday. I had just returned from mailing the letter when a phone call came from New York: Mr. Osborn calling to discuss this project with me! You know what *we* would call that! He will be out of town until Wednesday, at which time Marie is to see him. In many ways, this sounds like the best bet.

There is also, as I told you very briefly, a proposal from Simon and Schuster via Maria Lieper that I undertake to edit a *World of Nature* series that would be, at least roughly, a counterpart of the *World of Mathematics* they have recently published, with 100,000 sets already in print at $20 per set! (They are sending me a set of the mathematics books, so I get this out of it, anyway!) This would presumably be of more modest proportions. If I could find enough people of good literary judgement to help me with the library drudgery, it might be financially worthwhile. Maria talked at length with Marie (how confusing!) on Thursday, and I'm waiting to get details by mail.

Then William Shawn of the *New Yorker* wanted to talk about some idea of his by phone Wednesday, but I didn't have time to connect with him. Oh dear, why can't I be twins and then I could be rich enough to buy all the Tenggren[74] property!

Of course you understand that all these things are still so nebulous that I am not mentioning them to anyone not immediately connected with them.

Now I must go out and do the Saturday marketing. I'm looking forward to direct word by phone tomorrow.

My dear love,
Rachel

[74] Owners of much of the undeveloped woodland around and near the Freeman and Carson cottages on Southport.

WEDNESDAY, DECEMBER 5

Darling [Dorothy],

Enclosed is the map you need—I hope in sufficient detail. It was as simple as picking up the phone and asking for it. I could have done the whole job for you that way, if only I had thought quickly. My 3-A membership really pays— today I had trouble with my 7-month-old battery and had to summon Emergency Road Service. (Battery now replaced.)

Your Monday night letter came today—airmail pays, too, at least in this direction, and especially in December.

I am returning Dr. Roberts's letter, which I enjoyed—I gather you viewed *Mr. Sun* with mixed feelings. I meant to see it, but somehow didn't. What I read of it made me glad I hadn't and all I heard in New York confirmed this feeling. Bell Telephone was one of the sponsors Dr. Vishniac had in mind, and this rather gave us all cold chills! If even Walt Disney is learning (as in *Secrets of Life*) that one need not stoop so very low to reach the average person, why can't the others?

Darling, I did so long to talk to you last night—to call you, to be with you somehow! You were the one person in the world who could have shared and understood my mood—and I needed you. I haven't time to explain now, but I shall try before we talk again. (soon? Monday?) I was thinking about the *World of Nature* project (or *The World of Life*, it may be) and while thinking I put myself under the spell, first, of Mendelssohn's Violin Concerto, and then of Beethoven's. Have you ever become almost intoxicated by music? I'm sure you must have— and I did, and it was a wonderful and creative experience in which the whole conception of how I would handle this project came into being. Mingled with it all, of course, was my great dream, and I was almost overwhelmed by the thought that at last—*really*—I was seeing a way it *might* be accomplished.

Oh, so much to talk to you about, dear. Suddenly I can see all the separate parts falling into place—almost as if the dream was "meant" to come true.

Dear, I shall talk to you soon. This must be all for now. But you know I love you dearly.

R.

SATURDAY MORNING, DECEMBER 8

9 A.M. AND HAVING COFFEE ABED!

Darling [Dorothy],

What fun and how lovely it would be if only you were right here this minute! There is so much I want to say to you, and by writing it I'm afraid I shall be making *you* want to steal time to reply. Don't, dear—but if I can write some of my thoughts today you will have them before we talk again. It is a bad season to have so much happen in my world—so many plans, ideas, and dreams whirling in my mind, but these things do not respect even Christmas!

There are two things I want to try to convey to you even briefly today: one, to share with you before it fades out even for me, something of that recent evening when something creative happened and I was able to know what this one project could be, and what it might mean. The other is to try to give you my perspective on the whole thing that is happening, for quite suddenly and amazingly there are enormous potential changes on my horizon. It is important to me to have you understand how I feel about it all, darling. At your 500-mile distance, and having heard only fragments, it could easily look different to you and so I must talk about it.

Perhaps the larger picture first. You know without my rehearsing them the various financial responsibilities, now and stretching far into the future—the known and the potentially greater ones through disability—that have weighed rather heavily on me. And I haven't dared let myself think much beyond my existing resources in planning how I'd cope with it all. The books of the future weren't written—maybe (my darker thoughts) never would be. So how care for the ever increasing expenses of caring for Mamma, keeping Marjie and Roger clothed, fed, and housed, paying their medical bills, even planning for Roger's education?

And along with all this, most illogically, a dream began to take form—a dream in which you, darling, had a larger part than you could ever have realized. Certainly in its earliest stages neither you nor I realized what was going on. It had to do, of course, with the Lost Woods[75]—and with a growing resolve that, if I could possibly bring it about, directly or indirectly, they should *not* be lost. At first, of course, it was only an impersonal hope—maybe I could get others to do something about it. I think it was still largely impersonal even this fall, when we made our "Lemon Squeezer Expedition"[76] and when I wrote you and Stan of plans—but they were plans to interest others. Now I see a way to do it, at least substantially, myself! Oh darling!

Do you remember (as if you wouldn't?) the day in May, 1954, when we sat in the warm sun and you read me "A Lost Woods"? Or the day all the thrushes came and sang to us? Or the picnic lunch by the shore? Or the exploration last October? They all played their part, dear. And other hours, too.

And now, like the scattered parts of a puzzle suddenly falling into place, everything seems possible! When I stop to pinch myself I can scarcely believe it. It is like an answer to prayer—and yet I confess I have not prayed for it, unless my life, not words, were the prayer. But for a good many years I have believed that in order to achieve one must dream greatly—one must not be afraid to think large thoughts. And now, suddenly, as though it was "meant to be," the way seems to be opening up.

In the writing of these pages, dear, there has been a happy interlude for the reading of two letters from you. (The clippings, etc., came, too.) And I see that you have grasped the enormity of the change that has come over my thinking. I shall probably save some of the details of the projects for another letter. This one is for the "overtones."

The junior edition of *The Sea*[77] is, of course, largely a by-product. There will be work for me, but it will be for the most part routine checking, not creative. So, with no special effort required, here is something that has the possibility, at least, of caring for M. and R. for some years to come. You see, Oxford has not balked at the 75% to me. This means a guarantee of $15,000. This much is

[75] RC and DF had attached this name to the Tenggren property in reference to the essay "A Lost Woods" in H. M. Tomlinson's *Out of Soundings* (1931).

[76] A large crevice in a cliff at sea's edge on the Southport shore between the Freeman and Carson cottages.

[77] In 1958 Golden Press would publish an adaptation of *The Sea Around Us* for young readers.

sure, and to Marjie, spread over several years, the taxes will be small. Beyond this, the almost certain sale would carry the income well over $50,000, with possibilities considerably higher. Fantastic, but true! So it is not unreasonable to hope this project alone would see Roger well along.

Royalty rates on the so-called *World of Nature* project are still subject to negotiation. *If* it sells as well as the *Mathematics*,[78] the income, after commissions, fees to assistants, etc., should run from $70 to $100,000 on a minimum royalty, perhaps to $150,000 on best of possible rates!! Again: fantastic, but possible.

This, of course, is a project involving Herculean and heart-breaking labors, but considering the goal, who cares?

In other words, the other project, with its prospect of caring for my long-term dependents, makes it possible for me to dedicate this one to A Dream!

To The World—at least until the Dream can be revealed—it may appear that I am commercializing my art in devoting myself to a money-making anthology instead of to works of my own creation. But *I* know the reason, and *you* do, so it doesn't matter.

Besides, after that experience recently, the anthology project has revealed itself as possessing enormous creative possibilities, the end result probably more valuable than anything I could write myself.

I suppose I mustn't take time for all that today: there are other "practical" letters that must find their way into the mail, too. So I shall try to be brief.

When the project was proposed, as an anthology of natural history, I said to myself, and to Marie: "But there are so many nature anthologies—this must have something to distinguish it, besides just being *bigger*!"

One evening earlier this week (you will know when—I don't) I played the Mendelssohn Violin Concerto before dinner—heaven knows, there were interruptions: coffee for Robert, a crisis about repairing the doorbell, getting dinner—but it did lay the foundations of a mood that reached its peak later in the evening when I heard the rest of this record and went on to the Beethoven (do you have it?). How shall I describe it to you? I know you would understand, for I can compare it to your experience on hearing the Mahler Symphony last spring. The nature of the emotions was different but their intensity was probably the same. That Mendelssohn Concerto has meant so many different things to me! First, as I listened to it in the winter of 1955—with closed eyes, trying to nurse them into a state where I could complete the editorial touches to make *The Edge of the Sea* ready for publication—a mood of resignation and peace. The book was done; it would live with or without me. Then we heard it together at Southport that summer, and the morning you left me, in our last moments alone, I kept hearing that most hauntingly beautiful of its themes in the ears of my mind!

Then Tuesday or Wednesday night—whenever it was—I was really quite overwhelmed by emotion. I think that Mendelssohn filled me chiefly with the beauty and wonder of The Dream, and with awe that perhaps it was going to be

[78] James Newman's *The World of Mathematics* (1956), part of the Simon and Schuster series to which RC's contemplated nature anthology would belong.

possible to achieve it, or at least make a beginning on it, through my own efforts. Later, listening to Beethoven, the mood became, I suppose, more creative, and rather suddenly I understood what the anthology should be—the story it should tell—the deep significance it might have. I suppose I can never explain it in words, but I think you understand without words. It was a mood of tremendous exaltation, I wept. I paced the floor. And I wanted to have *you* beside me so badly it tore me to pieces! There now, darling—that is for us alone, for I am still shy about revealing such moods to the World. But only when I have felt myself so deeply moved, so possessed by something outside myself, can I feel that inner confidence that what I am doing is right.

The revelation? Well, briefly: the anthology should not be confined to "nature" as generally understood. Rather, it should present the whole story of Life on our earth, the geologic setting, the beginnings of life, its amazing ramifications and adaptations, its relations to its physical and biological environment. On a canvas of such noble scope, what a picture one might paint! I am sure this is the right approach—the opportunity to make a true contribution to popular thinking. I have told Marie and she is delighted. The idea will be presented to S&S later. *They* are in the mood to hail anything with delight!

As to practical procedures. Obviously, I have to have capable help, of various kinds. I am not the sort of person who can delegate basic decisions to others, but the library work is exhausting, as well I know, and I think I should have two people here in Washington to take much of the physical burden. (Bless your heart, darling—of course you will help, in hundreds of intangible ways, and maybe in some more tangible as well.)

I shall send soon, if not in this letter, a *New Yorker* column about James Newman, editor of *The World of Mathematics*. He lives in Washington. I said I'd like to talk to him about procedures. Instantly, as if Aladdin had rubbed his lamp, Mr. Newman telephoned and invited me to dinner at his house in Chevy Chase, Friday evening, December 14.

As to the conversion of all this to The Dream: there are two things to do very soon. One is to discuss general procedures with the Nature Conservancy. I have a tentative appointment with the secretary—or maybe he is more an administrative officer—here next week. Second, I must write a very long letter to Curtis Bok. He can advise me expertly on two counts—his legal knowledge, and his experience re his father's foundation. (Another piece in the Meant-to-Be Jig-Saw Puzzle—that Curtis came into my life at this moment!) I suppose some sort of Foundation must be established, to own and control the property, so that all income from my project, conveyed to this Foundation, might be tax-exempt. Otherwise, there would be only a small fraction left.

Darling, I have dreams about what might be done with this place that include you and Stan in important ways. But that is for the future.

Meanwhile, I go into a positive cold sweat at the thought of how, when, and through whom, to approach the Tenggrens. Suppose they prove intractable!

But there! I am idealist enough to believe it is Meant To Be. Perhaps before we all meet at Southport again the outlines will be clear.

On a different level, my dearest, isn't it all crazy and fantastic! Here am I, your "darling"—once your "little girl"—shy, retiring, not well known to most of our summer neighbors—solemnly juggling sums that run well into six figures! You know how I love you, darling, anyway—and allways.

Rachel

FOR CHRISTMAS, 1956

My darling [Dorothy],

Even that first Christmas we did this—Christmas of 1953—when really we had known each other for only a few hours, beginning a custom of Christmas Eve letters that it is hard to imagine we shall ever break. And now for me there is that shining little interlude after all the preparations for the Day are completed—tree trimmed, piles of gifts in place, stockings filled, and the household put to bed—when I can be alone with you for a half hour. And it always seems you *are* here, dear one. There is so much happiness in those quiet moments, so much peace, so much warmth and tenderness and love.

And *you* began the custom, darling, just as you have brought so many other lovely hours into my life.

I have said this many times, yet almost daily it comes over me with the freshness of new discovery—"Whatever would I do without her?" For you, dear, are the one in all the world who can share most fully, and understand most deeply, all that is closest to my heart.

For your blessed love and understanding, dear one, my deepest thanks. That is always your most precious gift to me, at Christmas and all the year.

And now the shining star on the horizon for both of us is The Dream we share, toward which we may work together. I hope fervently I have not built up unfounded hopes. But somehow I do not think so. In one form or another, I believe something will result from this that will live on into the future, the symbol of what we both so dearly love. And because it is something we can share, it is doubly precious to me.

Darling—may peace and happiness and love fill your heart this Christmas season. And may the New Year bring health to all you love—and to you!—and may it be a year of joyous affirmation in which your dearest hopes and dreams will come true.

My deepest love, for always.

Rachel

My Beloved [Rachel],

My answer to The Letter can never tell you all that has been in my heart, all that has been whirling through my mind since you shared with me your Great Dream. In the first place, to think that you wanted to and did share with me so much that is so intimate, so much a part of you, so holy, even, made me know (as though I never had) the place I hold in your life. The glory of that knowledge overwhelms me by its immensity and its sweetness.

In the second place is the lovely thought that music has taken on such meaning in our relationship. When the note[79] which served as a prelude to The Letter[80] came, asking if I had ever been intoxicated by music I knew we had found a plane on which we could share our feelings without the use of words. What this means to me can hardly be expressed except by music. I think I have told you of my longing for someone to share and to respond as I do to the language of music. In all my life until I met you there have been only two who might have filled that need. One is a man whom I scarcely know but during an evening when I talked with him I intuitively knew he had the quality I was searching. The other was Winnie Clarke. The sad part of that was that I only found it out about the time she went out of my life, by a chance remark she made about the Prelude to *Lohengrin*.

And then Dear Heart, you came into my life. Now added to all else you have given to me to enrich my life is this bond I have longed for intensely. And it can be for "as long as we both shall live." Can you imagine how I reacted when you wrote, "While thinking, I put myself under the spell of the Mendelssohn Violin Concerto and then Beethoven's—and it was a wonderful and *creative* experience"? As I think I told you, I, too, put myself under their spell that afternoon, pondering all you had written of the dream of the Lost Woods, knowing, I believe, as fully as anyone could of another's mood how it had been with you. To think that music has played such a part in this drama!

With this kind of preparation I was emotionally ready for all the wonders of the Letter itself.

You began by saying it was important to you to have me understand how you feel. Out of all the world I am the chosen one! Darling!

As you went on, another thought humbled me: the realization that you had confided in me so completely during our friendship that I understood, with no need for you to explain, the staggering financial burdens of your future. And consequently, I could understand how much it meant to you to have found a solution to them and thereby to have found freedom to proceed with your Dream, the Dream that grew out of our Maytime—an hour in the woods with a book and a singing thrush. Can you imagine what it is going to mean to me as the Dream unfolds? Even if the Dream were about some place I knew only casually

[79] RC's December 5, 1956, note.

[80] RC's December 8, 1956, letter.

it would be exciting to know I was there when the first spark was struck. But the fact that the Dream means saving a part of my Beloved Spot

> God gave all men all earth to love,
> But since our hearts are small
> Ordained for each one spot should prove
> Beloved over all.[81]

[the theme of my book, you know]

is like music rising and stirring my heart to its depths! That this is happening to me is still in the realm of magic. Of course, ever since your first Christmas message I've been living in that realm. Sometimes you haven't approved of that idea of mine. But I like to soar. We are all earthbound too much. (Surely both you and I have been this year.)

I think even you are beginning to know there is a quality to it outside reality.

And now we come to the part that sets this Letter apart from all others— that gives it a touch of sublimity. You write, "It is like an answer to prayer—and yet I confess I have not prayed for it, unless my life, not words, were the prayer."

Darling, that sentence should have been written in words that could glow—for here is the light that illuminates your whole being. Always, dear, I have thought of you as different—as not like all others. And here is the unconscious answer in your own words. Your life *is* a living prayer! I have marvelled at your complete selflessness—no wishes or desires for yourself—always thinking and doing for others.

And now this Dream—I know its accomplishment will have its satisfaction for you, but beyond that, the joys and rewards are going to be shared by so many others that even in this you are losing yourself.

Do you wonder I worship you? Now, dear one, as you are finishing my 1956 Christmas letter to you please know that my greatest wish for you this Christmastide is that your prayer—Your Life—may receive rich blessing in the fulfillment of your Great Dream.

For it and for countless other gifts from you my undying thanks and devotion.

On this Christmas Eve and as on every other evening

> I love you.
> *Dorothy*

[81] From the poem "Sussex" written by Rudyard Kipling in 1902.

UNDER THE DRIER

Darling [Dorothy]—

I'll start this now and finish later for mailing tomorrow. Every evening now I seem to be so lazy and so sleepy that letters are beyond me, so I didn't even try to talk to you last night. Then this morning there was more furnace trouble, and a man was still working on it when I left.

Ida[82] is still a joy to have, and it seems to me I'd have had an intimation of clay feet by now, if they existed. She's been with us nearly a month, you know. And she keeps the house in excellent order, with no direction really necessary. Best of all—and if only *this* lasts!—she doesn't seem to be resented and there has been no friction.

I'm going to have a talk with her maybe this afternoon about the possibility of her taking an occasional "night duty." I know she isn't eager for it, but may be willing to accommodate me. I just don't want to have anything to do with Mary[83] again, and Ida would be so much better.

Darling, I see L.B.[84] is conducting next Thursday, Friday and Saturday. I assume there are also other January dates, but this was in the *New Yorker*'s listings for next week.

By the time I talk with you Tuesday, I should know what I can or must do, and then we shall see.

I tried to make some crude measurements of the Dream Woods on my Geological Survey map of the area last night, and now agree that I was way off.

The shoreline does look more like half a mile—maybe even less—and the maximum depth from shore to road about $\frac{1}{5}$th mile. By further crude computations, I came up with an estimate of roughly 50 acres. Of course I have no idea where this gets me, as to possible price, except that it should be less than I'd thought!

I guess I must soon write out The Dream for my lawyers and see what they think. Curtis says the actual establishment of a foundation is very simple. Three people, as directors, file papers and that's it. But he wants my tax lawyers to advise me on where to incorporate (which state) how to keep it tax-free, and which should come first—my contract or the incorporation. One thing I think I know is that I can't hold back any of the proceeds of the contract—The Dream must get all or none. So if it should turn out that I could swing it alone, I'd rather keep full control, accepting no contributions that would give others a voice in what to do. Of course I guess if the contributor does not stipulate any restrictions that is all right.

The choice of a third director is causing me to think hard. I think definitely it must be a man, one thoroughly in sympathy with our vision for the place, and a good businessman. Edwin meets the first two qualifications but I'm not entirely sure of #3. He will be in Washington the week of the 20th. I think

82 Ida Sprow, a new housekeeper.

83 Mary Johnson.

84 Leonard Bernstein, as he was commonly abbreviated by RC and DF.

I'll tell him of my plans, perhaps without saying anything about a directorship, and judge from his reactions. Any other ideas, dear? Of course I want it to be someone I know quite well. (Though you and I could always out-vote him!)

Among other thoughts I want to write about at length later is the feeling we should have some sort of consultants (who would advise but not vote) among the local people. Mr. Pinkham, of course, among purely local residents; one of the Bestons, to go farther afield. And others. But I do think a sense of local pride and participation is very important. ("Sharing is important," in the words of a wise young lady.)

S*ATURDAY P.M.*

I came home to find your letter—certainly *not* "unsatisfying" as you thought! (A bit of stardust there: we were both so tired after Christmas, and unable to write the letters we had in our minds. But *I* hadn't had a houseful of people, and I did have Ida before and after, so you must have been ten times as tired.)

Last night the Delaneys and her parents from Philadelphia came in and I showed them Maine slides. And tonight I'm going to the Algires,[85] who are entertaining a group for supper.

[85] Dorothy Algire, a friend and biologist, had assisted RC with research.

Marie telephoned and I've made tentative plans to go to New York the latter part of the coming week to talk to Maria Lieper about the anthology. I think this must be done soon in order that the project may begin to move. When I call you New Year's Day I should know whether I have to squeeze in any other business, and we can see whether that seems the right time for you to come, dear. Otherwise, I could probably make it during one of the following two weeks. I shall want to take the chance to see Edwin during the week of the 21st, and if I *do* go with the Boks that would be the week-end of January 25–27.

Ida promised to discuss the problem with her husband last night and reported today that they did not feel she should be away overnight. The husband drives a truck in some sort of interstate transport and often is away, and they did not wish to leave the boy alone. However, she suggested a niece, who may be worth a try on a one-night absence, and said she herself would stay through supper if, for example, Marjie were coming. So we shall experiment a bit.

Of course, I want to hear all about your Christmas, but maybe now you can save that to *tell* me! Can you believe it? And do you suppose we'd ever stop talking?

Stanley will certainly have a busy time. Will his degree[86] be conferred at the midyear commencement? (I suppose there is one.) What a nightmare about the copies of his thesis!

[86] Stanley, Jr., had received his D.Ed. from Columbia University.

Now I must go, dear, and try to organize my thinking on paper for Marie—about the anthology, I mean. I hope you'll get this Monday.

All love to you, as you know
Rachel

My darling—my dear [Dorothy],

Now how can I "answer your answer" in such a way as to make you know all that I am feeling? I told you the letter brought tears to my eyes, and perhaps from that you know much of what is in my heart.

Darling, the sharing of my Great Dream with you was so natural as to be inevitable. And if it was wonderful for you, it was equally wonderful for me to have you a part of it—don't you know that, dear one? Had you never come into my life there would be no one to know it all. Oh, of course, I'd have communicated the idea (if there had ever *been* a Dream) to others, just as I'm doing now, but there would be many parts of it withheld—locked in my own heart. So, dearest, try to realize what a warm and joyous experience it is for me to have someone to whom I can express it all—someone who understands all that it means—and who cares about it as intensely as I do.

Yes, darling, I do think it is lovely—and most appropriate—that music should have been a part of it. And I'm touched and grateful if, even in that field, my responses should be satisfying to you—a field in which you have gone so much farther, and know so much more, than I. I can only claim an intuitive sort of response, but perhaps that is enough.

As for your third point, what can I say, darling, except that, as so often before, I feel completely unworthy of your conception of me. Of course what *I* meant was that all my life has been directed—even in "oblique" ways—to the sort of thing that is symbolized by the Dream, and that possibly that sort of devotion to a course was a wordless prayer. But you have given it a beautiful and "sublime" interpretation. Bless your darling heart!

Sometimes I take time to think, as I know you do, of the amazing contrast between my present mood, and that of the summer. And the whole transformation brought about, as by the waving of a wand, within 24 hours in November!

Despite those occasional moments of shock and alarm, I can't help feeling, darling, that it is all "meant" to work out. And there is some of that feeling that I've tried to describe in relation to the impact of *The Sea*—that it is something that will happen through me, rather than something I shall do.

On the purely personal plane, darling, I can't think of anything happier for us in the years ahead than to work together to make this Dream a reality—something that means so much to us both, something that will last and be part of our immortality. So I feel that the time-worn phrase, Happy New Year, has special meaning for us both this year, for in 1957 the outlines of the Dream should become clear.

This is not properly part of the "answer," dear, but I want to comment even though briefly on your suggestions about the anthology. Very stardusty: I have had all those thoughts myself. You are absolutely right: a "World of Nature"—as the word "nature" is generally understood—would be far easier to do. It would take less out of me, and because you love me, you *ought* to prefer it, and I understand and love you for it.

But on the other side, two thoughts: almost the moment this project was proposed to me, I had a slightly negative reaction, which I expressed to Marie— "But there have been so many 'nature' anthologies"; if this one is to attract attention—to stand out—to have the stupendous sale they are talking about, it must in some way be *different*. I think that first, instinctive reaction was right. But just how it should be "different" did not become apparent to me until that night of "intoxication," when Messrs. Mendelssohn and Beethoven told me. And having had that vision, darling, I'd be wretched if I didn't try to live up to it as best I may. It is new, it is exciting, it is a tremendous challenge, and so is something I can believe in. Actually, dear, the theme I have in mind is so flexible, and gives me so much "room to turn around in" that in one way it would be somewhat easier. Strange as this may sound, "Nature," in its conventional definition, might prove somewhat restrictive in a work of this size. The theme of "Life" provides for so much diversity, and allows me to pick and choose. And somehow I can feel such a work *could* command 100,000 buyers or more; of the other, I'd be very dubious. Of course, in the *World of Life* there would be ample place for the wonder and beauty of nature.

Darling, the afternoon has melted away and I must go. I have a feeling I shall be with you soon.

I love you
Rachel

MONDAY, JANUARY 7, 2 P.M.

Darling [Dorothy],

Probably I'll send this "Special" for I would like you to have it tomorrow, and I know you couldn't otherwise. The reasons for speeding it are two: I know you want a bulletin on my progress, and I must dispel the vague notion that I might come to you this week. The doctor has been here this morning and says by the look of things I'll have *It* at least a couple of days more. He still thinks I have intestinal flu—it's apparently true to form except for persisting so long. After it is well over, he'd like to have some X-rays just to see if there is any special reason for its lasting so far beyond the usual period—an inflamed diverticulum or some such thing.

Now I'll set you a good example of candor—I'll tell you I have been so miserable that I shudder to think it might have developed a day later and caught me in New York. When I called you yesterday I really did think I was beginning to feel better. Then the pains began again and seemed to get progressively worse. Temperature rose some, too, but broke in the night, and today I am making somewhat fewer trips to the bathroom. Doctor gave me a new medicine for pain and already I feel better—more comfortable, I mean. I'm on a very limited diet, but can't say I care. Ida is going to stay to get our evening meal—bless her heart!—so I won't have to go downstairs. It's moving around that seems to start up the pain.

There now, dear, I've told you everything there is to tell, and there's nothing to worry about. It's just the kind of thing that has to wear off itself, the doctor says, and there isn't much he can do except make me as free from pain as possible. Antibiotics would only make it worse because they irritate the intestine.

Yesterday, during one of my expeditions out of bed, I set up the record player beside the bed, and the record albums, and started playing some of the Beethoven symphonies, with the analyses. I love what L.B. has to say about Beethoven (Did you get that? And what Beethoven symphonies do you have? I have #1, 3, 5, 6, 7 and 9)—in his analysis of the *Eroica*, and as I recall his comments on the Fifth in the record I sent you.

For me, the best part of yesterday's Philharmonic concert was knowing you were sharing it with me—the miracle that we—500 miles apart—were hearing in the same split-seconds of time notes sounded midway between us! Otherwise, I must confess the program was not one I would have selected. To my unsophisticated ears, the Bartok number was little more than jumble of noises! But it would have been fun to *see*, as well as hear, L.B. in the concerto. The applause sounded tremendous and in the background of Mr. Fasset's concluding remarks did you hear the shouts of "Bravo"? Also, did you notice that at least half the audience seemed to have dreadful coughs? It was too bad we missed the *Romeo and Juliet Overture*—it must have been the concluding number.

Well, darling, it was a lovely dream that we might have been there together. The difficulties we've had this time make all the more wonderful the almost effortless achievement last March, bringing you and me together with L.B. and Our Symphony!

Of course it was a disappointment to have to postpone discussion of The Dream—but that wasn't the only disappointment, dear! However, I have this bit of progress to report. About a week ago, in writing Mr. Greenbaum about taxes, I mentioned that I'd probably want to discuss the Foundation with him soon, and gave him a very sketchy resumé of what it is about. He is always a most comforting and reassuring soul, and seems to resolve problems by magic. He suggested, in a letter today, that we could very well go right ahead and set up a tax-exempt conservation foundation, stating its purposes broadly enough that they could cover other projects in which we might later become interested, in addition to Our Woods, or alternatively in case that didn't work out. He seemed to feel it was a simple matter.

In my present thinking, I feel that perhaps there is no need to wait until papers are signed with Simon and Schuster (let me call them S&S hereafter) before I approach the Tenggrens in a preliminary way. If it later proved there was no deal and no money I don't see that any harm would have been done by their knowing what I wanted to do. I am going to try to draft a possible letter soon, hoping I may be able to go over it with you next week! Meanwhile, be thinking and making notes yourself, won't you?

Here is one of my thoughts: maybe the best approach is that I have long wished to bring about the preservation of *some* tract of Maine coastal woodland in its natural state—and that theirs is one that appeals to me—leaving the thought that I have alternative possibilities in mind. If I reveal how fully my heart is lost to *that one*, I'm afraid I have no bargaining power left.

And I suppose I'd better state it as a personal project, which at the moment it is in terms of financing. Granted I might later solicit contributions, if I told them that they'd think there would be endless funds available for the purchase. After all, if they are wealthy enough to own it, why mightn't I be wealthy enough to buy it?

Darling, I know I sounded gloomy about everything yesterday and no wonder you suggested that my mood probably extended to the Dream, too. I think now my illness had been coming on all week—I felt miserable New Year's evening when Bob and family were here, and then seemed so tired and faintly nauseated the rest of the week. So I *did* feel depressed and worried even about the Dream. I'd had a long telephone conversation with Mr. Newman[1] Wednesday, and of course was left with the feeling it will be a long and difficult job.

[1] James Newman, author of *The World of Mathematics* (1956).

But those moods come and there is no use taking them too seriously. Already the curve is starting upward again. In fact, I have dimly sensed for some weeks that such an anthology could be important for *me*. I'm still groping and can't say clearly what I mean but I can see at least sketchily the outlines of perhaps the rest of my "life's work" in writing, and this seems to be a step in it. All part of a vast theme that others keep trying to state effectively, but can't. Maybe I can't either, but I keep feeling I can *almost* see how, and perhaps if I try long enough, I can. And in a sense this anthology would be a part of it and a personal preparation for the other.

And if, at the same time, the doing of it could secure Our Dream—how could I hesitate? I know it is impractical. Of course my present investments don't secure me against all contingencies. Curtis said, too, "Please be sure of your own security first." But really, there is no such thing as absolute security. If I live beyond the anthology—as I expect to!—there will be more writing and more income. Meanwhile, I can live comfortably, even if not in elegance, and there is enough for any reasonably rainy day. And in the Dream, I am taking care of a spiritual security, by "laying up treasures" in an earthly heaven. So you see, I still believe in it, darling.

Now this must be all. Really I think I am improving—much less pain now. So maybe, next week!

All my love,
Rachel

Darling [Dorothy],

At last I hope I can write a few lines for mailing to you tonight—your first from me in I can't think how long. Your dear letter written after my call Tuesday night was here today. It has been wonderfully comforting to have your letters dear—do you know? But for all that, the fact I couldn't write to you has given me such a curious sense of isolation. *You* must have felt that much more.

Marjie came home at noon today—very thankful to be home but pale and weak.[2] The doctor insisted on an ambulance (of course she was the only one with any other idea!) and said the men must carry her upstairs. I was waiting for her at the house with Mrs. Shaw, the nurse. Moppet had crawled into M.'s bed when Mrs. Shaw came in and was waiting there. (Mrs. S. loves animals but Moppet just doesn't know her yet.) The two animals seem very, very happy.

Doctor says Marjie must stay upstairs at least until Sunday, then perhaps come down briefly. I was discouraged to learn yesterday that, even after all the B-12 and other injections, her hemoglobin is 62—if I'm not mistaken, that's a point or two lower than when she went in!

Roger is lively as 17 crickets, so it has been next to impossible to hold him down today. In fact I'm the only one who can, so he has his innings while I'm out.

I think it must have been after I talked to you that his doctor came to check him. The chest is clearer but still has rattles. Dr. Mullwater says it is an "influenza-type infection" and that a low-grade fever may persist "for weeks"!!! For the present he wants him kept in bed or at least as quiet as possible. Says if it (the low fever) continues after chest is clear he might let him be taken out a little but not to go out to play or school.

Darling, there was no reason not to mention your siege with Stanley. To begin with, it is most unlikely Roger would get whooping cough after the modern shots, he has no recognizable symptoms, and I can't believe the doctor wouldn't recognize it. He says this is not a serious condition just a persistent thing that requires patience and care. I gather he has lots of other cases like it.

I think my life will be much simpler now with no little creatures up there looking to me for care, and no hospital visits. Marjie seems to like Mrs. Shaw and

[2] Marjie had been hospitalized on January 15 with pneumonia.

I hope she will work out all right. At present, I think Marjie needs a competent nurse. Later, if only there were a twin sister to Ida, that would be ideal.

I loved the picture of you with your teddy bear, darling. And you didn't have to tell me which one you were! There is a bit of stardust in the fact that among the things I had packed for New York were several childhood pictures of me! If I can find them now I may enclose them.

Darling, of course I know you understand as well as anyone could who isn't on the scene just what my days are now. But the possibility of working or even writing a letter, no matter how urgent—has been at least as remote as a personal trip to the moon. So if my reply sounded abrupt please forgive me. I have eaten a fair number of meals without sitting down—bolting a sandwich while doing something else. From the moment I get out of bed the Emergency has claimed me, until I fall into bed again. Last night I got into the tub for the first time in days and days.

But I'm all right, dearest—really I am. Probably at such times one draws on reserve sources of strength unsuspected before. It must be so. But don't worry.

Yes, I've thought before this how good a long southern sojourn would be for *all* of us. In fact, before Marjie's illness took such a serious turn, I was playing with the idea of shipping her and Roger to St. Simons for several weeks. Now I doubt if she will reach a point, for some months, at which she could safely go away alone.

Now to clarify my last-resort plans for Florida. *If* I'm able to leave at all, I'll take the Silver Star about 2 o'clock Thursday, arriving at West Lake Wales at seven-something Friday morning. The Boks are staying at the Mountain Lake Club at Lake Wales, about 5 miles away. They will have the train met, and I suppose we'll all have breakfast together at the Club. They had planned to leave on the Silver Meteor Saturday, at 12:18 and I now have space on it. So we'll have all afternoon and evening to visit on the train, and I'll be home Sunday morning.

I have consulted Nellie Lee about suitable dress for the club—she says they "dress" for dinner only on Saturday night, and suggested that the black and white silk I had worn at their house would be perfect for Friday dinner. I think I'll take my white linen suit and some summery dress, and travel in suit and brown cloth coat.

Oh dear, there are whole volumes of things I want to "catch up on" with you! There has never been such a time for us before, has there?

Of course I loved Martha's comment on your letter. I'm hearing quite a few gems from Roger, but no doubt I'll forget them before I can pass them on.

Well, remember the happier days, and remember how much I love you. Because I do.

Rachel

Darling [Dorothy],

The beautiful freesias are here. Somehow, even as I began to open the box, *I knew*. You precious darling!

I don't suppose we can ever again be completely surprised by Stardust, but you can hardly have imagined the amount existing here. I had been planning to plot with Stan that he would take you, for me, a bunch of freesias the latter part of next week, to keep you company in case I went to Florida—or just to whisper messages to you if I didn't! (Now I'll have to sneak up on you sometime later.) And yesterday I was ordering a pot of pink hyacinths for Marjie, and "happened" to ask Mr. Mason if he had any freesias. He *said* none had come in as yet. Was he already in cahoots with you? What was in my mind was that just maybe I'd pamper myself by having some freesias in my bedroom, allowing their fragrance to bring happy memories.

And now I have them, darling, from you! It was such a sweet thing to do, and so like you. Thank you dear one.

Marjie looks a little better today. Roger same as ever—his doctor wants him taken in for lab tests the first of the week.

Your good letter of Wednesday night was here this morning, dear. Yes I know you'd have come if you could, dear. I do understand.

And I love you
Rachel

SATURDAY EVENING, MARCH 23

Darling [Dorothy],

It was wonderful to have that visit with you Thursday night—it actually seemed to take away a lot of my weariness,[3] and I woke the next morning with a happy thought of the long letter that was coming. And it was a delight, dear— why do you always say such harsh things of your letters?

Now today your note written after we talked. You are dear and precious to want to do this, darling, but for many reasons I think it should wait, probably to be combined with the trip to Maine. You see, dear, I could not send a 5-year-old alone. I know people do, but I couldn't. So even if we came by day, at coach rates, it would be quite an outlay—2 round trips for me plus one at half fare for him— or around a hundred. If I were not planning the later trip probably I wouldn't let that stop me, but I am. I had thought about that, dear, that if I could time it conveniently for you, I might leave Roger with you for a few days after we'd had our glimpse of Maine—hoping, of course, you can share that with us.

I feel, too, that since Roger isn't used to your climate, and has to be watched with special care just now, a later period would be wiser and allow you to have him outdoors more without anxiety.

Sometime next week I suppose we must repeat that test and then consult

[3] Marjie had died on January 30. RC had adopted Roger. DF had visited them from January 31 to February 6 and had offered to have Roger visit West Bridgewater. DF's diary indicates that RC and DF had exchanged letters between January 25 and March 23. None are preserved.

with the doctor. If we can get the operation[4] out of the way in April I'll be re-lieved. And if we were counting on his going to you now, and then about next Thurs. or Fri. the doctor said "No" that would be upsetting.

Of course I know why you want to do it, darling, and I love you for it. But maybe I'll need the relief even more later—and it's a luxury I can't avail myself of very often. If only you lived as near as Philadelphia even! But from a 500-mile distance, darling, I know most of your help must come in the form of moral support! But just knowing of your love and concern is a great help—believe me, dear!

Will mail this now. More soon.

I love you dearly
Rachel

[4] Corrective eye surgery for Roger was being con-templated, but was determined to be unnec-essary.

WEDNESDAY NIGHT, MARCH 27

Dearest [Dorothy],

And still I haven't been able to write you, although I want to so much. Per-haps later tonight, but I'm going to shopping center and want to drop this in box for the 9 o'clock collection.

And I find myself wanting terribly to call you but for various reasons I mustn't. But you do seem so far away. I hope you are all right, but I can't help worrying a little.

I suppose you know about Mr. Bernstein's Bach program—this Sunday, for us. And you know, don't you, that "Omnibus" will be no more after this year? L.B's views on himself, TV, and music are quoted in the new *TV Guide*. I always wonder how faithfully his interviewers portray him—these things don't agree with my own conception of him from seeing him in person and on TV.

More soon, dear. I hope.

All love, as ever
Rachel

THURSDAY, MARCH 28

Dearest [Dorothy],

Now I shall try to spend a little time with you so that you may have some word before the week-end. The days have been full and really should have been even busier, but I have not been feeling quite myself all week and am oppressed by all I've had to leave undone.

I could easily feel discouraged on the slow progress of the building proj-ect,[5] but guess I must steel myself to endure such. The redrawn plans weren't presented until yesterday; today a man came to interview me about the mort-gage—says he can get it through in a week. But I can easily imagine frustrations and disappointments about getting to Maine. However, I suppose I can't achieve the high goal of getting settled in my own home without sacrifice of some sort.

[5] RC had decided before Marjie's death on the con-struction of a house in Silver Spring.

⁶ An addition to
RC's Southport
cottage had been
planned.

Mr. Delano, as I think I told you, is almost ready to begin.[6] His report after inspecting the site was that the "split-level" device wasn't really necessary—in fact he visualized some trouble about the steps down in relation to ceiling height unless he also dropped the level of the new dining area, which I wouldn't want. However, I have written him again about all this, with the further point that I want the screened porch enlarged (it had to be cut to take part of it into the house, leaving it *too* small, so now I want to extend it a distance of 8 ft. or so behind the addition). This will change the roof and may alter the situation about dropping the level.

I think, with you, that bunks are not practical because they are horrid to make up. Besides, I can visualize fancy high-dives out of the upper bunk. So I think one single bed goes in Roger's room, with perhaps a fold-away cot tucked in a closet for a possible little-boy visitor.

On the big house, I'm beginning to get a picture of sorts of what I want living room, dining room and den to look like—trying to treat them as a unit in a way, for on entering from the hall one will see all three. So I think variations of a basic color scheme, founded on greens and "earthy" tones with something bright for accent, will do what I want. I haven't decided whether to use stone or brick for the fireplace, but think that entire wall (from corner to door into den) of living room will be stone (or brick) up to a height a little above fireplace opening, then paneled above. There will be no mantel, and no projection of the structure into the room. The den fireplace is a corner one and would probably be handled same way, or might carry stone or brick all the way up.

Picture windows in l.r., d.r, and den will give lots of light. Also, I want dining room to have lots of glass in wall separating it from porch—ideally, sliding glass doors (all glass) but these cost extra. French doors wouldn't.

Think I'll try to sketch plan roughly, though proportions will be all off.

Den will have picture window in front, French door & window on back wall. Wall without windows to have long work table and cabinets (something like picture, which please return). (Sorry—*not* enclosed—I need it now.) Desk one side of picture window, *Fisher*[7] on other. Love-seat-width bed-sofa in front of back window. Can you see it?

Big bathroom will have one of these new vanity affairs instead of ordinary basin, to contain towels, soap, etc.

Shower in master bedroom's bath has sliding glass doors.

There, that's enough for now!

You have a busy week coming up, I remember. And thoughts of traveling later in the month. How about that nice plan for a drive southward? If it doesn't work this spring, why not in the fall, to visit the new house?

But remember I'm hoping, even if you can't *both* come this spring, that you will come in May for a preview.

I don't think I commented on the clipping about Mr. Wing[8]—I was really very sorry although I scarcely knew him. His wife and I used to chat at store and P.O., and I'm glad that one day I introduced Roger as a devoted admirer of her husband, via his records, and told her Roger had said Mr. Wing sounded like "such a kind man." She seemed so pleased, and said she would tell him.

For the enclosed poem, part of which might well be printed on an introductory page of my *next book*, I am indebted to Dr. Gesell (*The Child from Five to Ten*).[9] On the negative side, my reading of this book is punctuated by private exclamations of horror at what little beasts children appear to be, with little relief in sight within the dreary wastes of time encompassed by this book—just progression from one phase to another even worse!

Well, dear, this must be all for now. You seem a million miles away, so don't be surprised if I put in a call soon to discover whether you really are.

I love you—

Rachel

P.S. All the foregoing was written, darling, before the arrival of your precious telegram. The date[10] had been in my mind, you may be sure—even if I don't keep a diary!—and as I had more to say to you anyway this postscript can serve a double purpose.

Now I think I may try to call you tonight, instead of the Sunday call I'd had in mind. I've wanted to *every* night for days, and it's getting hard to wait. And this is, after all, An Anniversary! How very long ago and far away it seems—part of another era, a lost time that will never quite have its counterpart. For I grow more conscious with each passing week that my life will never again be the same, and that when it might otherwise be possible to do the things I had thought to do, the sands will have run too low. But no more in that depressing vein—I was only recalling that while I may have thought myself "encumbered" during our lovely 1956 Spring-time, I didn't know "from nothin"! How I wish we could look at the Bernstein-Bach Program together!

I know I have said in almost every letter recently how far away you seem—probably I shouldn't dwell on it but it *is* the feeling that fills my heart so forgive me if I keep expressing it. Somehow I feel terribly alone with my problems, as I suppose I must inevitably be. And sometimes I even have a panicky feeling that I *can't* go through with it, but then I see again that there is no gate in the wall; there is no alternative. And then I'm haunted by the thought "What would become of Roger if something happens to me?"—and for that, as yet, I've found no answer and it frightens me.

Of course you would know that, while it is good to have the happy diversion of the house the underlying problems remain and I can't shut them from my mind except for certain intervals. The fact that I'm not feeling especially well doesn't help, of course. I suppose this is only weariness and reaction—nothing very definite but unpleasant and a nuisance.

[9] By Arnold Gesell, published in 1946.

[10] RC and DF had been together a year earlier in Silver Spring and on March 28 had seen Leonard Bernstein conduct Tchaikovsky's Sixth Symphony.

Darling [Dorothy],

I hope you mean it when you say you aren't looking for mail and I hope you don't expect it to amount to anything when it comes! There seems to be less and less time to sit down and put my mind on anything more pleasant than income tax (which has driven me frantic today). On the other hand, there have been letters from you practically every day—most of them long ones—and I feel very far behind in my responses. The trouble is that if one doesn't answer soon, one never does, for the response is swept away in the tide of new happenings and new thoughts. You said, dear, you didn't want me to answer your sealed letter last week. Perhaps you really don't. But I want to answer parts of it at least, darling, for as you should know, some of it touched me deeply. However, I can't say what I'd want to say when I'm hurried or tired, so it must wait, perhaps even until we can talk.

Your June baby sitting had slipped my mind until you mentioned it recently, and now I gather you might go on the 30th and just stay on. So of course the thought came to me that Roger and I might make our Southport visit then—during your first week, I mean, for I think one child would be sufficient distraction under those particular circumstances! I imagine Mr. Delano could postpone interior finishing until that time, even if he could otherwise have reached that point earlier—I don't know how fast he plans to work, but he does know I want it finished in June.

So, darling, could you plan to come here by early or mid-May? I hope there will be at least a hole in the ground to show you by then! I'm getting a little discouraged. Rain yesterday prevented work on clearing the site, but this was accomplished today and it was fun to be able to stand in the various rooms! But precise locating of the house is still to be done and I seriously doubt there will be any excavating this week.

Much of this area was once occupied by the Quaint Acres Nursery, which still exists on smaller scale on Colesville Road. I think this accounts for the wealth of climbing roses, of which I have great tangles. Lots of them, in the house site, had to go, but they also grow luxuriantly in the lower corner and here and there elsewhere. Today I noticed a nice little apple tree—crab apple, perhaps—showing pale pink buds, in the future backyard. And there are several lovely hawthorns, a legacy from the nursery, I imagine. There are several large maples, including a handsome one in the front; a big sycamore, some willows, poplars, and lovely pines of all sizes. (Also a large tulip tree.)

If I used the term "landscape architect" it's no wonder you are alarmed. If it was on the phone, I may have said "landscape gardener" for certainly I have no one so fancy in mind—just someone who will do the work I ask him to do. My development of the place will probably be considered unconventional, but at least the mistakes will be my own, not hired ones! Yes—a whole corner left as a wild tangle, wet underfoot for birds and frogs. And few, if any, formal beds or borders. Of course it will take time and money, and I may be unable even to begin this year.

I think I'll send you one of the preliminary blueprints of the floor plan, even though it was done from a rather rough sketch and doesn't show all the final changes. But it's almost impossible to trace a blueprint, and this will give you the main features. The relocation of the stairs was a vast improvement, I feel. The stairway will have the same panelling and finish as recreation room into which it leads, with door at head of stairs, and stairs enclosed on both sides to reduce noises from below. Also, there will be acoustical tile ceilings in the downstairs bedroom & rec. room.

A night of wild wind—that brought tornadoes to the Carolinas and even as close as Norfolk—brought thoughts of Carol and Edna. Really, some of the gusts seemed almost as bad. I've been wondering what you had today.

Of course I loved all you wrote of your Saturday experience, and also your reaction to L.B. on Bach. But now it's very late and I'm sleepy.

> All my love, dear
> *Rachel*

WEDNESDAY

I'm mailing blueprint in separate large envelope—first class, but I'm afraid to put this in it. Spent morning on lot and finally got house located subject to surveyor's corrections tomorrow. Such heart-rending decisions! It's such a long house that even on this big lot there are problems. So I had to weigh one tree against another, etc., but I believe we finally came up with the best answer.

I've taken a couple of snapshots of the other house that is somewhat like this one—it is within 3 weeks of completion—and will send them soon to give you an idea of style of house.

Again in haste, but always with love,

> *Rachel*

THURSDAY, APRIL 11

AT BEAUTY SHOP

Darling [Dorothy]—

Now guess who has been cleaning out desk drawers? And you shall inherit the kittens, and maybe even a fish or two. I eliminated a large wastebasket full of trash from my desk last night, and felt virtuous, even as you say you do after such accomplishments. But I guess I'll feel I've earned wings and a harp by the time I've gone over the whole house!

Your note this morning brought not only snowflakes but a certain amount of stardust—you speak of the endless "lists" of things to be done and ask how I manage. I'd been reflecting on the same problem just yesterday and arrived at a certain philosophy about it. I guess I can just make myself shut my eyes to the millions of little things (and some not so little!) that I leave undone, but this is the only way I've been able to accomplish certain Big Things—and when I list the major projects that have been gotten under way since January I do feel a bit complacent! But I know the tangles of neglected things would drive a more orderly person mad.

Now I'm under the drier (can't neglect that completely!) so will be able to mail you a week-end greeting after all.

Before coming here, I had a satisfactory talk with the architect who is going to keep a supervisory eye on things for me. He is the Bank's recommendation and I like him very much. Tomorrow the surveyors will confirm the house location and Monday the iron monster moves in.

Mr. Mahard telephoned one evening this week—they had been in Washington several days. He says they may go to Southport on the 19th—even as you!

I enjoyed Mr. Pinkham's dissertation[11] on the Fire Dept. very much—he really is wonderful, isn't he? And I read the ads with interest—will probably drop a note to the typist. Perhaps you are also noticing whether any housekeeper offers her services—please let me know if you see such. Maybe *I* should advertise, but of course I wouldn't want to engage anyone I'd never seen.

So our Wild Winds brought you snow! Such queer weather. I really should keep a diary as you do and it's odd that, as a writer, I don't seem able to stick to such a project. I wish I would, now I've become a landowner. (But I didn't for my Maine land—oh dear!) This is a silly note, but if it takes you my love by Saturday that is really its purpose.

I do. R.

[11] In an article in the *Boothbay Register*.

SATURDAY AFTERNOON, APRIL 20

Darling [Dorothy],

This will be waiting for you on your return, I hope. If your temperatures are even within 10 or 15 degrees of ours, you must be having a spring-like day for Martha's party and your trip to Southport. I do hope so.

All else I might have written is overshadowed by the tragic news that came to us by telephone from Amherst last night. Dear Alice[12] died in her sleep Thursday night. I really know few details—I was too shocked by the news to ask many questions of the friend who called—a stranger to me. I do know that Alice was alone—you remember Kitty went to France in February—but I'm not clear how it happened that someone went in and found her yesterday. She was in her bed and probably just slept away.

[12] Alice Mullen.

A heartbreaking touch was the arrival, today, of an Easter greeting post-marked in Northampton at 7:30 Thursday evening, evidently mailed on the way home from work, a few hours before her death.

Kitty is expected to arrive Sunday, and the friend said something about services Tuesday. However, all of Alice's friends here know it was her wish to be laid beside her husband in Fort Lincoln Cemetery here. Whether Kitty will re-spect this no one can tell. Sorry—this was left unguarded for a few minutes.[13] I have sent her a wire at Amherst asking if there is anything I can do at this end, and another friend has made a similar offer, so at least she will be reminded.

If she does decide against bringing Alice here, I would of course wish to go, but really don't see how I can. Apart from the usual difficulties, there is the Philadelphia matter I must attend to, Roger's polio shot, and critical decisions about grade and foundation levels at the house-in-construction.

Added to my real grief over losing Alice is my regret that I have been so neglectful of writing for so long—I'm sure she understood but I could have helped so much more than I did. Now I'm so thankful that I called her one eve-ning last week and we talked half an hour or more. I told her of my building projects and she was so pleased. She said she'd been sick with a cold for about two weeks, but had kept going to work and claimed she was better though "very tired." In answer to my question, said she hadn't had her blood pressure checked recently. You know it was very high, and some heart trouble was dis-covered last summer. I felt then she was rather disturbed about her condition, but she was so afraid Kitty wouldn't go to France she wanted to make light of it.

Darling, I think you can imagine much of what I have been feeling. As we ourselves have said, not often in one's whole lifetime does one find a real kindred spirit. In their different ways, both Alice and Marjie were that to me, and in an interval of less than three months they have both gone. Now, more than ever before, darling, I'm going to be haunted by fears about You! My heart has been very heavy since the news came and the night had many sleepless hours, thinking of things we had shared and now can never share again. Alice used to write such sweet letters of appreciative reminiscence—wondering if she had ever said enough about what we had meant to her. Have I, dear one, to you? I suppose one doesn't, really—coming almost to accept or take for granted, and then suddenly it is too late.

In my efforts today to reach people here who should know, there have been, for the most part, reminders of passing time and change—people no longer in phone book, phones disconnected, etc.

Dearest, I shall call you very soon. Had I felt definitely I'd be going to Amherst, I'd probably have tried to reach you in Maine, but I'd have hated to break into what I hope is a happy trip with such news.

All my love, always,
Rachel

[13] The bottom of this page of RC's letter contains markings by Roger: his name roughly printed, surrounded by a very irregular circle.

Darling [Dorothy],

By now you are, I imagine, well on your way home—perhaps at your New Hampshire stop. I do so hope it was a happy week-end in every way. With 89° temperatures here, I hope you had 70° at least.

Perhaps I shall talk with you before you read this. How I have wished to be with you, dear—here, there, *anywhere*—just to be together. For I have needed you, darling, terribly. I wanted to write you Saturday night, but when I could I was too weary. Then again Sunday, but that, you know, is the Worst Day of the Week! Perhaps it was as well, for my Easter meditations would have been inappropriate ones, concerned with Death rather than Life.

By this time I am able to feel happier for Alice herself—her problems were so dreadful and seemingly insoluble; now, by a master stroke, all are solved. And I am sure if she could have chosen, her end was what she would have wished. A disabling illness, in Kitty's care or in a hospital, would have been so hard for her to bear.

What I really want to say, darling, is that this loss has focused my thoughts so clearly on You and all that you mean to me. Of course, the place you fill in my life is unique. That I have known from the beginning. In spite of the differences in kind and degree, there was with Alice, too, a wonderful sharing of thoughts and interests and feelings. Losing her has made me know, in a small way, what losing you would mean. And really, darling, life would be so empty I don't think I could go on. Perhaps the two deaths in so short a time have been too much— I have been dreadfully depressed since the news came—and somehow quite unrelated problems have seemed even less endurable than usual.

I don't think I'm expressing at all what I want to say. And perhaps I could *say* it better than write it. But what I feel most clearly is that we must never again for a moment forget what a precious possession we have in our love and under-standing, and in that constant and sometimes almost puzzling longing to share with each other every thought and experience. There has never been anyone else, darling, with whom I have known that to a degree even approaching the way I feel it with you. And there never could be another, I know. If ever I have seemed to forget the wonder and fragile beauty of it, darling, know that I won't forget again.

Before this cloud came over our Easter, I had been thinking so much of the beautiful Easter morning letter you wrote me—can it be three years ago?— the one in which you introduced me to "A Lost Woods." And I planned to spend an early morning hour with you in the same way—then when the time came I was too heavy hearted.

I must see you soon, dear one. When I can pin down Roger's doctor to some definite decision about whether to have the operation, and when, perhaps we can plan.

Meanwhile, activity flourishes on the building project—the basement walls well along, and the first lot of some 2,000(!) bricks on hand. I chose a rather light rose or pink shade, preferring it to the usual reddish colors. I'm to have a conference with the architect tomorrow—I want his reactions on fireplace design and a possible change in roof line over *study* end—maybe a gable after all.

I have decided to have what is indicated as porch and carport be all porch, and maybe extend something from back corner of porch toward rear of lot as a gesture toward car shelter. Or maybe just let car sit on drive.

Door from study to porch can now be shifted away from fireplace. I want it for light and ventilation—a picture window doesn't let in much air! The general throughway will be via dining room to porch. Window in side wall of study will be high enough for desk (or something of such height) to sit under it. View will be near horizon—a little grove of pine trees, so not distracting, just restful. Without window on that side, I couldn't keep moon under proper observation!

Now, my dearest, I must go. I do plan to talk soon—I trust the cables are behaving now.

My dearest love, always
Rachel

TUESDAY AFTERNOON, APRIL 23

Darling [Rachel],

To-day has been a promise of Spring. The temperature has climbed to 70°, which is a record. The sun shone this morning but now the clouds are thickening with a threat of rain. I worked hard all morning, physically, and ended the effort by raking the front lawn, just because I wanted to be out. Clusters of snow drops are showing their snow, ready to burst into bloom.

By quitting time I was terribly tired. So for the past hour I've been lying on the bed in "My" room, reading and finishing Ellen Glasgow's autobiography.[14] When I finally closed it, I lay for a while thinking of so many things it had evoked within me. Foremost of course is the thought of you. And that is why I'm writing to you now when a thousand other things are shrieking to be done. But I feel the need of talking to you—we've had so little time recently to be together This Way—do you know what I mean?—to talk about things outside and beyond us. In a way my mood is much like it was the day I wrote you after hearing the Mahler 3rd. This time no music is involved, but there is a quality to my feelings that takes me back to that afternoon. Actually, I have nothing important to say—it is only that if you had been lying on the other bed, as I was reading, from time to time I would have said "Listen to this" and read you a bit that we could then have talked about.

Isn't this silly, dear—suddenly as I write I find myself crying. I'm far from unhappy. I'm remembering all the lovely moments we've had together with mu-

[14] *The Woman Within* (1954).

sic and books and bird songs and sunsets and lost woods and ocean and surf. All that seems far away now. I'm sure we'll have them together again.

But back to the book, for it was that which made me rise up to write to you. It has struck me as odd that I should have discovered it at this particular time in *your* life, dear, for it is the inner life of a writer. Not that it parallels your case in anyway, dear, but she had her tragedies. Besides, there are many situations, many episodes that bring to mind something we have talked about. For instance, and because the time may never come to share the whole book I'm going to copy a paragraph and you will understand why.

"Collectors and colleges are asking for my original manuscripts; but they are a generation too late. When I left home after the tragic death of my sister, I left all my manuscripts in my own handwriting, and a number of letters I valued put away on the high top shelf of a deep old closet in the upstairs hall. In my absence, Emily, the eldest of us all (and divided by an uncomprehending generation from myself) came to live with father. I returned 5 years later to find that my housekeeping sister had burned every manuscript and every letter, and that the shelves had been scrupulously scrubbed and cleared of all literary associations . . ."

And there is more on keeping "papers." I do think we would find many passages to interest us if we could read it together. The night after I had talked with you when I realized you were at a low low I read this: "One human being could bear so much, and no more. Was I never to have a breathing space while I lived? Was my whole life to be smothered in tragedy?" Do you wonder you were near as I read it? Tragic as it was there were lovely experiences and happiness. England was a joy to her. "Caroline (her best friend) and I were gazing on Fountains Abbey under scattered flowers of sunshine and low drifting clouds. 'All this beauty!' we repeated, together, and fell into each other's arms in sheer ecstasy."

I could go on but this should give you an idea of why you were with me.

But with it all, I'm sorry to say the picture she drew of herself and her life did not arouse my sympathy—it all left me a little cold except for a few high spots. I wonder why I can't quite describe it.

In the midst of all this I had a morbid thought that set my mind a-whirl with the problems it might present. Darling, don't laugh. I pictured you and Roger flying to me. The horrid thought which pricks at me every time you fly "Oh, if anything should happen to her!" came as usual. But added to that now is the possibility that something might happen to *both* of you at once. Heavens, what a mind! But, dearest, when you revise your will won't you take that horrible idea into consideration? You see, I wondered who then would be ready to grasp Roger's share of your fortune—knowing what I do and knowing your Dream for a Lost Wood project, I tried to think out how you could provide that, after your family needs would be taken care of, the rest could go for some form of a Dream project!

Darling, I suppose you are laughing at me. Of course, it's my mood, but somehow I would hope you could protect your Dream—I don't mean South-port specifically—just the idea of some preserved wilderness.

And I am the one who had vowed *not* to worry about other people!!

But I think the preface of all this sets the spirit of this little visit with you. This is a queer sort of letter. I think you will understand it.

I am so relieved that the manilla letter arrived intact. Queer, isn't it, where it had been? Perhaps, though, it was all for the best for I've learned a lesson. The mails can't be trusted, and I shall try to be extra cautious from now on. Perhaps we can work up a little code of understanding when we are together that will enable us to say some of the things we might want to say. One thing I do know is that I'm going to get at those letters right away & I think, dear, you should just burn the lot of mine immediately. If you move you won't have time to go over them, & why carry them on to a new place? Really, dear, why not relieve your mind on that score—one less thing to worry about!

This isn't the letter I had planned to write next to you—it was to have been about Orono—but here it is. I trust you will understand.

WEDNESDAY, 8 A.M.

The rains came. The wind blew. And I had a delicious sense of being near you before I drifted off to sleep.

There will be a different letter later in the week.

I love you allways,
Dorothy

SATURDAY, MAY 18

Oh darling [Dorothy],

It was so wonderful to feel last night that you might be with me soon. I do need you so. And I don't mean just about the house—there is so much else that I can't write and don't even try to write. Of course I long to show you the house and talk over plans for it. It is such a big thing in my life that it has grieved me not to have you part of it. But there are so many other reasons why I need you and want you! Oh please do say you'll come! And stay just as long as you can!

As to my major problem—darling, I haven't even tried to discuss it with you in letters. That's so futile. Please understand, and understand also that my own feelings about it ebb and flow like the tides, with my own changes of physical and emotional well being. Sometimes I think I *can't* go on; at other times it seems possible. But always I know I must. Life is such a queer business—great visions, great opportunities opened up, and then a door slammed. I don't understand it; I never will.

I do know, darling, that if the situations were reversed, I'd be distressed even as I know you are. So I do understand the little you have said, and all that is unsaid, better than probably you realize.

From the tone of this letter, you may know this has been A Hard Day. Saturdays always are, but this has been worse than some.

I think I shall try for nursery school—or day camp or whatever they call it—during the month of June, then look forward to some all-day arrangement in the fall. Public kindergarten is only 3 hours a day, 4 days a week—and I can't earn a living, and live myself, in 12 hours a week!

Dearest, this must soon go to the mailbox.

I'm living for May 26th. *Please* come.

> I love you dearly.
> *Rachel*

WEDNESDAY, MAY 22

Darling [Dorothy],

This will almost certainly be my last letter before you leave. I still can scarcely believe you're coming!

Stardust about veeries in our letters that crossed! And after reading yours yesterday I found time to slip down to the magic spot, alone, last evening. Veeries were calling in the distance—a good sign. One usually has to walk up the path, which I didn't do, to hear the song. But the olive-backs were giving a concert that transported me right to Maine. And a barred owl was whooping somewhere across the creek. There is no traffic there now, for a bridge is under repair, so it's wilder than usual.

My only birthday plan, dearest, is to be with you. Marjie was the one who remembered, baked cakes, and planned celebrations. Virginia remembers, and will probably ask us in for dessert, but would be quite willing to have that observance another day. Robert never remembers, so that takes care of that. If it's a nice evening, we might take supper to the park, near the veery woods. Otherwise we'll eat quickly here, and go.

About the train, darling. I have your letter saying you and Dot Pease had both decided on the later train. Meanwhile, you will have one from me giving reasons why I hope it will be the earlier one. Probably I'll have some later word from you, and whenever you say in that you're arriving, I'll meet you. Of course if I don't show up in reasonable time, go to the telephone but I'll expect to be at the gate. Now don't protest, darling—*I want to.*

I think bathroom tile and fixtures are decided on—another major item checked off.

Probably the panelling vs. plastering crises will be upon us when you are here—all tied in with fireplace material and design. And all involving the basic decorating scheme for living room—dining room—study, so that's an excellent point at which to get a new viewpoint.

Tonight I'll try to finish marking plans for electric outlets.

We've had cloudy, chilly weather all week, but mostly without rain. Now it's supposed to get warmer.

I hope you can know, darling, what a tremendous lift it is giving me to look forward to having you. You mustn't think of it in terms of taking time from what I'm doing. You can help enormously with some important decisions, and just to have you beside me will rest and refresh me more than anything else in the world. Less than 109 hours, darling!![15]

My dearest love,
Rachel

[15] DF visited RC from May 26 to May 30.

JULY 14

FOR THE FIRST NIGHT IN YOUR NEW HOME

Dear Heart [Rachel],

> Peace and rest at length have come,
> All the day's long toil is past,
> And each heart is whispering,
> "Home, Home at last."

There is so much I would say to you at this moment if I were with you. First, of course, is the wish that you will find "peace and rest" as the little verse says, in this new home which has been your dream for so long. When did we first think about it?—not recently—it must have been in that first sweet year of our growing love and understanding, when we found the kindred spirit who could listen to our troubles with sympathy.

Oh, Darling, I do hope this Dream House, which is now a reality, is going to mean a new happy life for you with many of your problems solved by its possession. Probably, to-night there are still many cares associated with it, but for the future I trust your life will flow more smoothly because you have it.

I am enclosing some excerpts I have found that may find application, at least, in part, to you and your new home.

> This above all:
> "A world of care without,
> A world of strife shut out,
> A world of love shut in."

If I were shut in with you, darling, you know there would be a world of love,

Good-night
Dorothy

SATURDAY MORNING, NOVEMBER 2[16]

My darling [Dorothy],

Once more this will be brief, for I want it to get on its way so it will reach you Monday. It was wonderful to *talk* last night; as you know I would, I'd been wondering minute by minute what was going on, and was so disturbed at the thought of your having such a very sick man at home, so far from the kind of

[16] The lack of October letters is likely explained in part by the Freemans' October 14–17 visit with RC in Silver Spring.

help he was likely to need. So the call made me feel better at least in that respect, and I know you feel, too, that it is far better to have him in the hospital.[17]

[17] Internal bleeding and chest pain had continued to plague Stanley. He had returned to the hospital on October 31.

And how I have lived it with you, darling! My experience alone with Marjie that awful morning of her return to the hospital, when within only three hours she changed from a reasonably convalescent patient to one in desperate condition—and with only me to look to for help for what seemed an eternity—makes me know all too well how you must have felt on those nightmarish days. That morning is something I'll never forget, as I know these experiences have burned themselves into your heart.

And what a horrid experience in the ambulance! And then yesterday's storm! I didn't realize until I heard the weatherman on TV last night what a widespread storm it was, and how much worse in your area. We had only a rather heavy rain with some wind, but nothing violent.

Darling, in case of especially bad weather, won't you stay in Boston overnight? If you could always carry an overnight bag so you could, and perhaps have some frozen things in the refrigerator so you mother would be all right, I'm sure Stan's and my minds would both be easier about you. And it is wonderful you wouldn't need to have concern about Willow if you did stay.

Mamma is deeply distressed at the news and, as you would know she would do, is praying for Stan and has already asked the prayers of Robert and Vera, the Delaneys, and Father Manette. Not to mention Roger, whose supreme faith in his own prayers certainly ought to make them heard!

Now I suppose I must stop, darling. I'm not going in today, and want to give this to Robert, who, I think, plans to come in this morning. I'll try to keep notes, at least, on their way to you each day. And you know I want yours to be brief, for I want you to spare yourself all you can. Give our dear love to Stan. And you know, dear, how much I send to you.

Rachel

MONDAY, NOVEMBER 4

My darling [Dorothy],

Before you read this I shall have talked to you, I hope. At least I shall have some further word of Stan tonight when I call.

Two letters from you this morning. And of course I should feel much reassured had I not talked to you last night. But I do remember that there were ups and downs the other time, and I can only trust the darkness of yesterday has been followed by a brighter day.

Several times last night I was aroused by something, and each time you and Stan came instantly to mind. Surely, darling, with all the resources they can bring to bear, they can save him for you—and once that is done, what matter about the future? To have each other, in any circumstances, is all you need. And I am sure that, for people of your resources and intelligence, there are many ways to provide the necessities of life besides working for the Chas. M. Cox Company! Once relieved of the strains of his job, Stan would no doubt be quite able for other things that would bring in some income. And surely his company would do something fairly substantial in the way of retirement income for him even now.

Darling—you do know that we are living each moment with you, and are hoping and praying that Stan will soon respond to treatment and pass this crisis?

As you will know before you read this, I called Anne Ford this morning and asked her personal attention to flowers for Stan and for you. This seemed far better than trusting to a telegraphed order. Anne is really a sweet person and I think was genuinely pleased to be entrusted with this mission. I gathered from her really lovely letter about Marjie that she is Catholic; this is confirmed this morning when she said, quite spontaneously that she would "say a prayer" for Stan; "in fact," she said, "there is a little chapel near the florists, and I'll stop in and light a candle for him." Their ways and beliefs are of course not mine, but I do respect their sincerity and cannot help believing all this counts for something.

Darling—I have copied the firefly letter and am now returning it to you. I shall have to see how the *Holiday* article[18] develops before I decide whether to include this bit in it. As you know, I have a partial manuscript—which is intended as a chapter in "Remembrance of Earth"—and by rights I suppose this bit belongs there. All will depend on how the *Holiday* material shapes up.

A letter from Marie today reports a visit from Paul; she told him of the *Holiday* article, and he said he'd like to get this whole *Holiday* series for a book. (This amuses me, for she was very luke-warm about the whole thing!) Paul also assured her they would be advertising *The Edge* for Christmas.

There is also a request from the Peoples Book Club (distributed through Sears Roebuck) for a mail order volume of the three Carson books to date. Paul, I gather, is eager for it; now we await Oxford's reaction.

Darling—don't explain and apologize for your thoughts about "Remembrance of Earth." Apparently I have never made it clear that I consider my contributions to scientific fact far less important than my attempts to awaken an emotional response to the world of nature. So the "wonder" book, and "Remembrance of Earth" I should consider more important than any mere reporting of scientific fact. The trouble is, there is not enough material at hand for "Remembrance." But I should begin on it, I know. After all, who can say what is one's "last" Book?

Darling, isn't it strange? You had your earthly "hell" a year ago last summer; I had mine last winter. Now yours is beginning again. But I do trust that, while it may well be "the end of an era" it is also the beginning of a more peaceful "Indian Summer" of life for you both; in which curtailments and readjustments may have come sooner than you expected, but which will nonetheless bring you happy years of life together on a different plane.

[18] "Our Ever-Changing Shore" appeared in the July 1958 edition of *Holiday* magazine.

Now I must close, dear one. I'm still in trouble as to my vocal cords, but don't feel too bad otherwise. I have cancelled all clinic appointments, to be on safe side. Ida is here and I'm taking it easy. So don't worry.

I'll be talking to you, of course, but want to have something in the mail.

I love you dearly, as you know,

Rachel

I was startled, too, by address on envelope, although I did know the "firefly letter" was written while Stan was in hospital.

TUESDAY, NOVEMBER 5

Darling [Dorothy],

I can't tell you how much relief the call brought last night. You had sounded so sad and worried Sunday night that I never dreamed the news could be so good only 24 hours later. Surely the worst is all over now.

I'm staying in bed today. There's a tiny temperature (just under 100) but enough to make me feel a little groggy so I decided to take things easy while Ida is here. I'm having a good time going over old field notes, sorting out facts and ideas for *Holiday*.

Darling, I loved all you wrote about my next books. It was sweet—and fun to be talking about such things again. Really, this is the first time in a year or more it has seemed likely I'd ever write any more, isn't it? By the scientific book do you mean the Harper project? That, if ever done, will be largely philosophic, as I see it now. And when I say I don't think the scientific aspect of my writing is most important, of course I should qualify and explain. I mean, I don't think straight scientific exposition is my "contribution" to the world. It is, I agree, what you call lyricism. But if that lyricism has an unusual quality it is, I think, because it springs from scientific fact and so rings true. I loved what you wrote of the *Monitor* excerpt from *The Edge*, dear. It seemed unfamiliar to me, too!

"Jessie" is spending the day on the bed beside me. (Well, that was good—it probably gave Stan an extra laugh.)

Oh, darling—would your "Rachel" file also yield that piece on Cape Cod?[19] If so, would you also entrust that to me sometime within the next couple of weeks? But *don't* search!!! I have it somewhere, but at this point goodness knows where.

No mail from you today, darling, though I know from what you said there are at least 2 on way. Oh well, tomorrow will be A Big Day! My dearest love to you, darling. And now I can think of you so much more happily.

Rachel

[19] "Shallow Waters," an April 1953 article by RC published in the *Cape Cod Compass*.

Darling [Dorothy],

Two letters from you in today's mail!

Dear one—I'm sorry I caused you any distress about the flowers. I see now that, in the actual mood of Monday, it was all right. But remember, darling, that when we talked Sunday night, things looked almost as black as they could. I couldn't imagine you wanting to wear, or have, anything that looked gay and partified. I discussed this with Anne, and she suggested that the florist near them had had, only a few days earlier, sprays of "those tiny orchids that look like violets." This sounded exactly right, but alas, they didn't have them that day, as I know now from her letter. But I told her to use her judgement on both, feeling it was good—and it's all right. But you see why I said "Pooh" that night!

I'm glad the chrysanthemums were yellow. I always feel that sunshine color is best for one who is ill.

Of course I wanted you to have something all your own, darling! It's been dreadful for you, as I know only too well.

And I know the weeks ahead will be hard, too, for these things are not solved overnight.

But what a strange future we all have to face! It seems to me all I have ever said or believed has lost much of its meaning in the light of recent events.[20] Probably you have not had time to think beyond the personal problem with all its worries and uncertainties. I have to some extent—and I feel ill with a distress that has nothing to do with my cold!

As Tomlinson suggests over and over—there must be a Truth that has eluded man's understanding. If only he could grasp it—and its intimations are everywhere about—surely all this could be avoided!

It seems to me that what Tomlinson—and I—and others have to say should have been said a generation ago. Is it too late?

Darling—I'm sure much that has happened has been lost for you in the immediacy of your distress. But it is all deeply disturbing.

Now—let's get back to the everyday world.

I have agreed to be the "guest of honor" at a tea given by Dr. and Mrs. Warner (of Roger's school) on Sunday, the 17th, celebrating the beginning of Book Week. This, of course, just because I want to promote happy relations there for Roger's sake. Also, I do like Mrs. Warner very much.

Roger has a "best girl friend" and a "best boy friend" but at times complains bitterly about going—especially for the full-day session. I just hope and pray he soon gets to really like it. It is really funny but the French seems to appeal to him more than anything else. He goes around muttering "Bon jour, madame" and other sentiments, to himself. A new child came in Monday and the French lesson (once a week) was yesterday. Roger commented in surprise— "She didn't speak a word of French!" He and another little boy have been made

[20] The Soviet Union had just launched the first artificial satellites, Sputnik I on October 4, and Sputnik II on November 3.

responsible for seeing that she is taken care of—finds her way to station wagon, etc.—which I thought was good strategy, removing from Roger the stigma of being the "newest" child.

Mrs. Warner told me that the young woman who drives Roger's station wagon is a student at the Adventist College and available for occasional baby sitting—especially on Sundays—so that may be good to know.

Another clipping from the *Monitor*—my, I do have a friend there, don't I?

Darling—I'm trying to remember *my* first orchid. Of course it had to do with becoming an author, but I'm sure *Sea-Wind* didn't produce any. I think it was the party at the National Press Club launching *The Sea*. Thereafter, of course, they came thick and fast but my preference has always been for the smaller ones. Perhaps H.M. knew that. And I love the delicacy of the Cypripediums (sp?)—several of those, with baby's breath, formed the loveliest corsage I ever saw, in Columbus. Anyway, darling, I'm touched and happy to have provided your "first"! They do last amazingly, in spite of looking so fragile.

Dear, I think I am feeling some better, and if the weather is good I ought to be out this week-end.

I've wanted to tell you how lovely the moonlight is here. I ate dinner by it last night, in the dining room, for I've been trying to keep my cough away from the others. And my bedroom has been filled with moonlight. And for the last two nights Jeffie, or some other kindly spirit, has wakened me just in time to see the nearly full moon about to set, right outside my bedroom window. Southport, almost.

Darling, *of course* I didn't get my cold from you—so long ago! I think it most likely I got it during my two days at Clinic! But I was also at hairdresser's, where a coughing, sneezing woman preceded me, and in various stores. But I do feel better—haven't checked temperature, but for first time since Sunday feel I have none.

Now I *must* stop, for I want this to go with Ida.

I love you dearly, darling. You know, don't you?

Rachel

NOVEMBER 12

Darling [Dorothy],

Just a tiny note to go with Ida. I do want you to know I'm feeling considerably better. The doctor was here this morning and said my lungs are "clear as a bell." I can stop medicine but continue salt water irrigation of nose and nose drops, for there is still a far from normal state there, and it probably keeps up the cough indirectly.

I had him over chiefly to check on Mamma. When I sat at the table with her last night (first time in about a week) I noticed she was quite short of breath. However he says her heart is as usual, but her pressure is up—190. So he has increased her medicine. I know she has been worried about me—sure I was getting pneumonia—so now she knows I'm not maybe she'll improve.

Two letters today—Sunday's and the one enclosing Cape Cod piece. (You hardly knew me then, did you, dear?) And that reminds me I wanted to ask: did you remember, when you read the second *Monitor* clipping, that I wrote the description of the sea cave for *you*—so you could see it through my eyes, for at that time Stan and I weren't sure you could ever make the trip to it. Remember? And that reminds me to say that I recently had a second letter from the college girl in Wisconsin—whose first, over a year ago, was so unusual that I showed it to you, with my reply. Apparently she didn't then know *The Edge*; now she had discovered it and sat up until 3 o'clock to finish it. One of the things she mentioned was the description of that cave. She has never seen the ocean but feels she knows it through me, she says. Maybe you'd enjoy reading her letter after I answer it.

By the time you have this perhaps the X-rays will have been taken and some of your questions answered. I'll be so eager to hear, of course. I do hope the hospital session may be behind you by this time next week, although of course it is better to be sure all is well before Stan leaves.

Oh darling—how good it would be if we were where we could talk every day on the phone, and often have a lazy afternoon to just sit around and talk—about the things that worry us and even more about the things we love!

So sorry about your mother's arm—sounds like a wretched experience. Now it's nearly time for Ida to go.

All my love, as always.

Rachel

I can go out Thursday if weather is good. How about coming to do my hair for Sunday?

NOVEMBER 13

Hello darling [Dorothy],

Just a note, but somehow no day seems complete without a word with you.

Such activity today: the floor is re-laid (with new tiles), service man came and installed missing part in oven; plumber is here replacing cracked toilet in basement, and washing machine is promised for Friday! This morning I ordered a couple of pieces of unpainted furniture for Roger's "study"—so in a couple of weeks we may be in business.

Last night I read a lot in Tomlinson—wishing all the while that you were here and we could read it sentence by sentence and talk about it. I seem to get some new meaning or significance each time I read him. You do have *The Face of the Earth*, don't you? Then read his concluding pages, beginning on 242. Especially, of course, his last paragraph, and his last sentence!![21] Then there was much in "On the Chesil Bank" that I'd love to enjoy with you!

[21] The last paragraph of the essay "The Little Things" reads in part: "Still, though irrational, he [a thrush] was also disturbing. . . . But it does seem hard that our earth may be a far better place than we have yet discovered, and that peace and content may be only round the corner, yet that somehow our song of praise is prevented; or does not go well with Hesperus, unlike that of a silly bird."

Still floundering around to find the mold in which to cast the *Holiday* piece. It's still a hundred different bits in my mind, lacking the idea that will bring them together. I'm still better. And of course anxious for news of you and all that concerns you.[22]

[22] Stanley returned home from his three-week hospital stay on November 20.

I love you.
Rachel

NOVEMBER 25
_____

Darling [Dorothy],

I looked for a Thanksgiving Card for you but of course could find none that said the right thing. How could they? For you are so special, and the reasons for my thankfulness so related to you, so intangible, so indescribable, that no card could express them. Even you don't half know or accept them, darling. But all the love and tenderness and companionship—yes, and understanding!— you have given me have brought such a warm glow into my life that I could not help giving thanks, even were there nothing else.

I think I told you recently that I remembered your greeting and its message for Thanksgiving, 1953—and how I tucked it under my pillow and took it out to read first thing the next morning. Need I say—but I do anyway—I love you.

Rachel

MONDAY, DECEMBER 2
_____

Dearest [Dorothy],

Here is the Cape Cod piece, returned to your efficient files. As my study gradually settles down I find things, among them the manuscript of this.

Two letters from you this morning, *all* they contained so good to know. I'm afraid your mail from me was unsatisfying—and perhaps will be until THE PIECE is done. Can't say progress has been substantial but at least I have a better feeling, in that I think I know what I want to say. You know all the bits and pieces were there waiting for the central, unifying idea. If I'm satisfied with this now, it's at least partly due to an evening of Beethoven last night, when, in the study, I played his 6th, 7th and 9th symphonies and the violin concerto. Some little bit of his marvelous creativeness seems to seep through into my brain cells when I listen to him—or perhaps I should say into my emotions. Will you listen to the very first few bars of the 9th and see if the chills run up your spine as they do mine? To me it is the perfect expression, in music, of my first morning at Ocean Point, when there was nothing but fog and rocks and sea, and the time might well have been Paleozoic. I don't know whether I can say that in my "piece" but I shall try.

With one "hand," last night, I was thinking of *Holiday*, and with the other of the Harper book and what I shall say to Nanda[23] Wednesday. Somehow these

[23] Dr. Ruth Nanda Anshen.

two, plus the wonder book, seem opportunities to say, in different ways, some of the things I want to say before I lay down my pen.

Of course I'll send an autograph for your submariner friend (picture enclosed). And of course I couldn't help enjoying his tribute. Something rather similar in a letter from Vincent Schaefer this morning. He has just returned from a wonderful trip to the African coast of the Indian Ocean—many interesting things and perhaps you'd enjoy his letter after I've replied. Anyway he said the head of the British Petroleum Exploration Co. told him *The Sea* is required reading for all their engineers.

I hoped I was watching the Bernsteins with you yesterday, was I? Quite different from his other programs, of course, but fun. And I hope you saw the "Science" program with Eric Sevareid—what a contrast to puppets vs. cosmic rays!

Now I must stop, dear one. It was *so* good to talk to you both Wednesday night. Will try to say more soon, but you understand. I love you.

Rachel

P.S. Has your Yosemite book come? I had a statement from publisher Saturday, showing a refund due me, which seemed to mean they had sent paperbound edition instead of cloth, as ordered. Sorry!

My headaches have about disappeared, dear. However, I still have that tight little cough and a no-account feeling—both of which I'm very tired of.

Know what? *R.*

WEDNESDAY, DECEMBER 11

Darling [Dorothy],

This is a queer, nightmarish interlude—and not the least of the nightmare is feeling so out of touch with you. But perhaps it is better that way, for if I were writing at length my letters would hardly give you a lift!

Although the doctor claims to be satisfied I must say I'm not, and there is a tight little knot of anxiety inside me all the time. Mamma is very weak, and has to be pushed to do the amount of walking about the doctor considers advisable. Left to herself, she just sits in her chair and sleeps. I rouse her up to look at certain programs, or for meals, then off she goes again.

Mary[24] was surprisingly helpful and I have asked her to return this weekend. She keeps Roger entertained, and it will mean unbroken sleep for me those nights.

According to the paper, you must have had a deluge Monday or Tuesday. I hope it was rain instead of snow, but I'm afraid it wasn't good for Stan's return to work, whichever.

When I called Roger this morning it was raining a little. When he left an hour later the ground was white, and until noon it looked as though we were in

[24] Mary Johnson was again in RC's employ.

for a repeat performance. But it has stopped now, and the snowplow has been through, so we are not cut off from the world. However, at 1:45 in walked Roger! I'm afraid that school is just too cautious! Of course I have my fingers crossed for the morning.

Of course I am really desperate about *Holiday*. I find a little time to work—then interruption! I think "Tonight perhaps I can work all night." But when I get the household settled—or even before—I'm in such a state of exhaustion I can't. And as each day passes I get more tense about it. And the approach of Christmas leaves me numb. If it were not for Roger I'd just pretend not to notice until it's over. I'm finding it's even harder than I thought—in unexpected ways, like the bright, thoughtless messages people write on their cards. Now I must go, dear one. My thoughts of you help me through the days and nights.

All my love,
Rachel

THURSDAY, DECEMBER 12

Darling [Dorothy],

Last chance to get a note to you before the week-end—and of course with holiday delays even this may not make it.

A lovely flood of mail from you today, written Sunday, Monday and Tuesday. It brought you very close, dear, and helped more than you know. *And* your three packages—that was certainly quick.

I think you do know my regret that there will be nothing tangible for you at Christmas time, from me. I care greatly about that—for others I don't seem to. I haven't even *bought* a single card and shall probably send only a handful in the end.

It is almost unbelievable how closely I have been confined most of the time since our return—whatever shopping I might have meant to do would have been impossible. In the past ten days I have been in to the Woodmon shopping center *once*, otherwise right here!

Darling, I'm afraid that was a forlorn note I sent yesterday and I'm sorry. It was the way I *felt*, goodness knows, but there was no use passing it on to you.

Maybe someday I'll have less to worry about and feel well again myself!

Meanwhile, the effort to work on the article is just agony, combined with annoyance at myself that I can't rise above worries, aches and pains and just get it done. Everyday I think I'll stay up all that night and work, and then my physical self won't do it!

Bitter cold last night and today. But school didn't close, at least. Talk of more snow for tomorrow!

Darling—you do know in your heart, surely, that even being able to think of you is my greatest help and comfort. I went to sleep last night remembering some lovely things we have shared.

Yes—two months gone. Imagine! What months they were. Don't give up spring time hopes, darling. I'm living for that.

Mary will come again this week-end, as perhaps I told you. I can't remember and am sure I keep repeating.

Goodbye for now, darling I love you so dearly.

Rachel

TUESDAY MORNING, DECEMBER 31

My darling [Dorothy],

I will try to write something else to go with this, but now I want just to talk to *you*. And how I wish I really could—talk all night till the dawn came! Or the moon set—did you see it yesterday morning, still above the horizon at seven, and looking so enormous? —And just now the mail came, and I know you were to be up at 6:45 Monday, so I guess my question is answered! And there is much stardust in the opening paragraph of your letter: The Sunday that didn't bring the chance for the letter you wanted to write—and your wish for a real "bedtime chat."

Darling, there is so much to say I hardly know how to begin or indeed what to say for I feel badly confused. And, of course, rather hopeless and desperate. It is just another chapter in my same old story of frustration—but somehow each new guise the frustration assumes seems a little worse and more insoluble than the one before.

LATER

But first as to facts: From the preliminary report, at least, on fluoroscope and X-rays, there is no organic trouble in the digestive tract. (Roger's, of course, not mine!) So, unless there is something most obscure and difficult to detect, there is no physical trouble except in the tonsils. Dr. McDonald is more and more inclined to think this is chiefly emotional, and believes the shock resulting from Marjie's death is only now coming to the surface—says it is quite possible it could have been there but hidden all this time. And of course there have been occasional remarks that made me wonder just what was going on inside, these going back for some months. And from many little signs, I felt that Christmas— in anticipation as well as when it came—brought back a flood of memory to him even as it did to us. So I think there is a logical basis for it all—but what to do?

I went over this morning for a talk with Mrs. Warner, who is most understanding and eager to help, but I don't think either of us found an obvious solution. However, I think it will help for each of us to know the other's side. And in all seriousness, I did ask her to recommend a psychiatrist, as a last resort if the situation continues to deteriorate.

As a no doubt logical part of the picture, the poor child's demands on me have increased to the point where—even though understanding or trying to— I think I'll explode! He will scarcely let me out of his sight. And what this meant in terms of the *Holiday* article, I leave it to your good imagination to picture. For no matter how I explained the situation—yes, and no matter how hard-boiled I got about it—nothing helped very much—he was at my door every little while to see "how much work" I had done. And I actually believe he convinced himself he was "helping" by staying away even for a few minutes at a time. When it was finally done he seemed more relieved than I was able to feel; as I told you I was too exhausted and numb to feel at all.

And he seems to be getting so neurotic—several times a day he comes to me about some new ache or pain—or he has chills and can't breathe—or he's had a nightmare, etc., etc.

Darling, I do feel so sorry for him, and so inadequate to cope with the situation. I suppose if I gave myself to him every minute of the day it would help—but I can't help fighting to preserve something of myself. And even while hating myself for it, I can't keep thinking, "Why did this have to happen to me?"

And I can't help feeling black resentment against those who could help so much if they weren't so engrossed in their own lives and pleasures. If someone would give Roger an occasional happy outing, what it would mean to us both! Or if someone would say, even once in a month or two, "I'll take over for the evening—go out and do something you want to do." In the past year I've been out two evenings. Those were to meetings, and with a hired baby sitter.

Darling, you are the only one who understands and cares enough to *do* something when you are within range. I feel I never have half-expressed my gratitude for the joy you gave Roger many times last summer, and the chances you gave me to draw a relaxed breath, and do some work. Please know, dear, how I love you for it. Well, that's enough—too much—complaining, dear. It's what I'd probably pour out, weeping on your shoulder, and then we'd try to forget and be happy together. How I wish we could.

Darling, about the *when* of our being together: If Stan should be really very much better, I'm still hoping so you can come in the spring. Don't say now you can't, though I know things look black. But let's still hope. I do think it was better though, not to be setting up definite plans in this interval, and then having the heartbreak of seeing them wrecked.

WEDNESDAY A.M.

Now I want to finish this and perhaps get it out for the mailman. There is so much else I want to say—things that have been in my mind for days or even weeks, it seems, about you, about Stan's problems—and, I suppose, more about *me*. That last seems to be all I do write about.

Darling, your letters have all been so sweet and have brought you very close. And in spite of all our telling ourselves and each other that we shouldn't write so often, I realize that I still feel just the same—my heart leaps when I see the mailman, but if a certain handwriting is missing I feel suddenly empty, and so I know what hope caused the leaping heart! I suppose I always will feel that way, darling—I really hope so for it's one of the real joys the days bring.

Darling, I'm glad you could "put your hand in mine" and send the little verse and say what you did about religion. It's too bad we have been so inarticulate about it—and I suppose, self-conscious. Let's try to talk more about it when the blessed time comes that we are together. Maybe we could find out that way what we do believe—of course part of my trouble is finding anything definite I can really feel is true. But I am sure, there is a great and mysterious force that we don't, and perhaps never can understand. Maybe the Truth that Tomlinson felt was being uttered by the thrush, but which men have never grasped, and so struggle on under their compulsions, and are unhappy.

One of the things I've had in the back of my mind to comment on was a TV interview with Frank Lloyd Wright, of which I happened to hear a little weeks ago. Something he said (while it didn't really surprise me) stuck in my mind with a sense of shock. It was to the effect that long ago he had had to choose between "honest arrogance" and "hypocritical humility"—and had chosen honest arrogance. It somehow crystallized my belief that a large share of what's wrong with the world is man's towering arrogance—in a universe that surely ought to impose humility, and reverence. Well—I didn't start out to give a lecture! Oh darling, how good it would be if we could *talk* about such things.

And there was a lot I wanted to say about Stan. I shall try now only to suggest it. In so many ways, I feel I can almost put myself in his place and know what he is suffering—mentally, I mean. For few people can understand what this sort of thing does to one's capacity to carry on the usual work. By "this sort of thing" I am comparing, for Stan, a serious physical illness and the worries and uncertainties that would inevitably accompany it; and for me a vague and, I'm sure, relatively slight physical disability, plus the mental and emotional stress of the condition of others close to me, and the uncertain future. But either one, in such an insidious way, undermines one's ability to undertake and carry through one's normal work. And the more we become conscious others don't understand, the more difficult it becomes. The searing agony of the *Holiday* piece is of course fresh in my mind, and, as I know you realized, the feeling that others couldn't understand why, in spite of everything, I couldn't just sit down and *do* it, only strengthened the forces that blocked me. And so often, during it all, I thought of Stan, when you wrote of his immediate physical reaction to some controversy that arose at work, or of his fear "people would think he's lazy." So often, before the thing was somehow done (and at this point I don't know whether it's good or awful) I would open my eyes in the morning, remember everyone waiting and not understanding, and I'd want only to go to the bathroom and be sick! I didn't, but I felt like it. And there is another point we have in common, dear one: in our different ways, we both have You. I know you have understood all these things, as they relate to Stan or to me. And truly, I don't think anyone else does. Marie, for example, with her brisk competence and her "slide-rule solutions" only drives me to retreat further within myself, which is unfortunate. There *is* no simple solution—people are people, not puppets to be pushed around even though one has power to do it. And I am myself, and what I do has to be true to that self—not someone else.

Because Stan has *you* with him every day, to care for him when he is lowest physically, and to understand him, he is luckier than I. But his physical problem is, of course, far more serious, don't think for a minute I'm minimizing that.

All this is just a round-about way of trying to say I understand!

Now, darling, this must be all of this rambling letter. Of course the mailman came long ago, so I'll mail this when I take Ida to her bus.

All my love, dear one.
Rachel

Part Three: **Silent Spring**

ng is moving well,
r mind the ~~tired~~
rom you. Just to
ing is all I ask

y love, dear,

Doroth

J A N U A R Y 5

[Dear Rachel,][1]

   . . . Roger and I could find plenty to do, and I would be sure he made no demands on you, you know, I can give him loving care, too.

   Darling, you say you are desperate. Please come. And I want you selfishly, too. We could be so happy together in spite of our worries. Don't you think we could?

M O N D A Y M O R N I N G

   Sunday is not the day, I find, to complete a letter to you. Rather than hurry it at a late hour I decided to hold it till to-day. I'm glad you could write about the little prayer I sent you. I have been struggling to express to you something of what I feel, as you could tell in that other letter. For those who talk about prayer, in its formal sense and who are sincere, I think the idea must give a real sense of being helpful. It must be satisfying to say "I wish there was something I can do to help—at least I shall remember you in my prayers—or I'll light a candle," or all the other forms it takes.

   And I'm sure we are remembered in their prayers, and it's a comfort to those who have remembered to feel that they are helping.

   I'm not being cynical, dear. I only wish I could get the same comfort. I fear I have denied formal religion too much, for when the time has come when I feel the need for saying "God help me, God give me strength, God help him, God help her," the thought always comes "You've been too independent too long to have the affrontery to expect God to listen now." Darling, do you understand what I'm trying to say? And yet when I do read some expression of faith that might help, I want to snatch at it. Perhaps just words do have a way of helping.

   As for my belief, I know I have a reverence for the overall Mind—well, I might as well use the word God—which my more formally religious friends don't even know.

   For example, dear—Thursday night at sunset time, I was driving out from Boston. Snow was heavy on the evergreens, but on the leafless twigs it had been turned to glass. A lovely rosy glow enveloped the whole landscape but the touch that made it unusual and breath-taking was that every twig of glass was turned to amethyst—do you wonder tears formed in my eyes? And it was then

[1] The first several and last pages of this letter not preserved.

that all these thoughts flooded over me and I went into my cathedral. And I said a prayer for you, and I lighted a million candles!

Perhaps this should be my stopping place, but I have more random notes from your letters, and as I have yet an hour before the mailman is due, I'll continue.

Darling, I did see that moonset last Mon. morning, just as you thought I might. The reason I remembered especially is because I could see it out of my own window just before I got up & I wondered—usually I only see it from Stan's room. Wasn't it huge?

You spoke of the possibility that Christmas was reviving memories within Roger. One might wonder if children as young as he could remember a year ago. I have proof from Martha's memory & she's a year younger than Roger.

A year ago I used my Irish Belleek nut cups on the table. Now they are on my "treasure" shelves in the dining room. Martha climbed up in a chair to look. She said, "There are those dear little dishes that are so thin you have to be so careful."

While Martha is here—a few more comments from her. Mad wrote that when they had finally opened their last package of their third Christmas at home Martha sighed & said, "Well, I never thought Christmas could be so pleasant." Her reaction to the ballerina doll they gave her. "There's nothing like a beautiful doll for a girl." . . .

[Love, *Dorothy*]

FEBRUARY 1

[2] The first pages of this letter not preserved.

[3] Promised for the Harper and Brothers World Perspective series. RC had dropped her December 1956 idea of a profitable nature anthology. The high price of the Southport land she had wished to purchase had ended this dream.

[Dear Dorothy,][2]

About the book:[3] I'll see if I can make any sense about it briefly. The theme remains what I have felt for several years it would be: Life and the relations of Life to the physical environment. (The older ideas of dealing just with theories of the origin of life or with the course of evolution were discarded long ago.) But I have been mentally blocked for a long time, first because I didn't know just what it was I wanted to say about Life, and also for a reason more difficult to explain. Of course everyone knows by this time that the whole world of science has been revolutionized by events of the past decade or so. I suppose my thinking began to be affected soon after atomic science was firmly established. Some of the thoughts that came were so unattractive to me that I rejected them completely, for the old ideas die hard, especially when they are emotionally as well as intellectually dear to one. It was pleasant to believe, for example, that much of Nature was forever beyond the tampering reach of man—he might level the forests and dam the streams, but the clouds and the rain and the wind were God's—the God of your ice-crystal cathedral in that beautiful passage of a recent letter of yours.

It was comforting to suppose that the stream of life would flow on through time in whatever course that God had appointed for it—without interference by one of the drops of the stream—man. And to suppose that, however the physical environment might mold Life, that Life could never assume the power to change drastically—or even destroy—the physical world.

These beliefs have almost been part of me for as long as I have thought about such things. To have them even vaguely threatened was so shocking that, as I have said, I shut my mind—refused to acknowledge what I couldn't help seeing. But that does no good, and I have now opened my eyes and my mind. I may not like what I see, but it does no good to ignore it, and it's worse than useless to go on repeating the old "eternal verities" that are no more eternal than the hills of the poets. So it seems time someone wrote of Life in the light of the truth as it now appears to us. And I think that may be the book I am to write. Oh—a brief one, darling—suggesting the new ideas not treating them exhaustively. Probably no one could; certainly I couldn't.

I still feel there is a case to be made for my old belief that as man approaches the "new heaven and the new earth"—or the space-age universe, if you will, he must do so with humility rather than arrogance. (I was pleased to notice that word in the little editorial on snow I sent you. I think I wrote you of Frank Lloyd Wright's use of it.)

And along with humility I think there is still a place for wonder. (By the way, I hope you didn't think I was serious, some weeks back, in asserting a claim to the word "wonder.")

Well, darling, that's not an outline of the book, but at least indicates the approach.

Of course, in pre-*Sputnik* days, it was easy to dismiss so much as science-fiction fantasies. Now the most farfetched schemes seem entirely possible of achievement. And man seems actually likely to take into his hands—ill-prepared as he is psychologically—many of the functions of "God."

Glad you are reading Conrad. I don't remember ever studying him formally, but of course I've read a good deal of him. Does your book include selections from *Mirror of the Sea*—which I love. See Bennett Cerf's biographical note on Galsworthy for an incidental bit on Conrad.

Rain on the roof now—maybe snow tomorrow. Had an interruption a couple of pages back to hear the announcement of the launching (?) of an American satellite. Still a maybe as I write.

Perhaps I'll put this out in the morning for the mailman who comes early Saturday. If it snows I probably wouldn't go in later.

So I'll say goodnight, my dear one, in case there's no time to say more tomorrow. Now to sleep—perhaps to dream—Guess what?

I love you
Rachel

Darling [Dorothy],

The documents that would prove it are wrapped and tied and sealed, so I shall not look them up, but I'm sure that by the time you receive this there will be an Anniversary for Us—the anniversary of a certain very precious exchange of letters.[4] A white hyacinth is the symbol that represents that exchange, and all it means for both of us.

Much has happened since then, dear one, but I am sure that if we could read together the letter you most often refer to, I could tell you that all I said then is true today—perhaps it has even more meaning. Almost from the very beginning you have assumed such an indispensable role in my life. Even in those weeks after I had met you but before I really began to know you, I felt through some intuition that you could fill an empty place in my life. And you have, darling—far beyond my imagining!

As you know, I keep no diary, but have usually had a day to day calendar on which I made notations. Recently I got out the one for 1953—really to look at the photographs. But what memories were stirred to life by several notations. "Sunday, Sept. 6—Freemans." And "Thursday, Sept. 10—saw Dorothy at Dogfish Head." And then for Wednesday, Dec. 30, just "Dorothy." Probably meaningless to anyone else, but how much these notes mean to me.

You have said more than once that I am more mature than you, but I doubt it, dear. Certainly not if my dependence on almost daily word from you is any gauge. The happy thought of you is still part of returning consciousness each morning. And try as I will, I can't still the hope that the mail will bring some word, nor master the black disappointment if it doesn't. Childish, I know, but I can't help it. For I love you even more—

Rachel

Darling [Dorothy],

I'm going to start this now but probably won't mail until tomorrow. It's bitterly cold with a high wind so I think I won't brave the elements to go to mailbox. Besides, I have a notion I'm going to call you tomorrow morning. I'd made up my mind to do that if there was no word from you today—now I want to even though there were pages and pages!

You see, the Post Office slipped badly this week, and your wonderful, long letter mailed Wednesday never reached me until today. With it was Thursday's note. I can hardly hope to tell you how I felt when I saw them for until they came I couldn't help feeling worried and desolate. Silly, I know, but *you* will understand!

[4] RC and DF's correspondence in February 1954, including the "hyacinth letter."

I might as well start over for none of the foregoing amounts to anything—except to prove I managed to spend a few minutes with you yesterday. Such a lovely and satisfying conversation this morning! I am so glad I called, for it all worked out very well. And you will know not to be looking for any mail from me for a few days—this won't get on its way until Monday.

I do hope you found Bernstein on one of your channels, for we enjoyed it so much. (Checked up on "Last Word" on other set from time to time but heard nothing of my query.) I didn't tell you, but last week I rented a tape recorder, with the idea this would be a quick and easy way of assembling a lot of my poison-spray material[5]—then Mrs. Rivera could transcribe it. Well I haven't put it to its primary use as yet, but have found one can have lots of fun with it. Roger is simply charmed with the sound of his own voice! Well, this apparent digression is to explain that a brilliant idea dawned after Mr. B. had been talking 5 or 10 minutes, so I hastened to set up the recorder and now have the rest of it so I can hear it again—and again! I used to wonder why people wanted tape recorders—now I know!

Of course I loved his exposition of musical creation—as I know you would, if you heard it. In better days, how much "writing" I did just lying on my back with my eyes closed!

Dear one, you *did* make a wonderfully satisfying response to my little attempt to give you the background thinking for my book,[6] even though you seemed uncertain this morning what you had said. It was lovely and encouraging, darling, and added definitely to my wish to do the book.

Sometime when you wish to practice typing, perhaps you would copy for me the two or three paragraphs of my letter that describe the book. It *did* help to talk about it to you, dear, and no doubt I should have made a carbon.

You refer to my autobiography, which needless to say will never be written. But if it were, it would contain this: "I first stated the theme of my book on life in a letter to Dorothy." For I had never expressed it before, darling, to anyone. . . .

[Love, *Rachel*][7]

Darling [Dorothy],

You can thank Jeffie for this. He demanded the freedom of the house at 6 o'clock. After the necessary arrangements I decided I would take back a cup of coffee—thought a while in bed with coffee—and got so wide awake I decided to write to you until time to get up.

The moonlight was so beautiful last night that it hurt that you were not with me, as you might have been. And we seem, after all, to be having a run of good weather. But because of my cold I know it was best to wait. And we can hope for other full moons at Southport!

[5] The first indication in this correspondence that RC, prompted by a letter from Olga Owens Huckins describing bird deaths from pesticide spraying, had embarked on the project that would become *Silent Spring*.

[6] RC refers to her February 1, 1958, letter about the book planned for Harper and Brothers on life and its relation to the physical environment.

[7] The last page or pages of this letter not preserved.

Your long letter mailed Monday did come yesterday, dear. That, and our talk Monday night, brought you very close.

I am so happy about your changed outlook and the reasons for it, darling. Of course I had worried greatly about your back, too, wondering just what was in store for you—so I, too, feel relief. To be able to change the situation through your own efforts is wonderful, and hard as I know it is, I hope and believe you will stick to it, with the prospective rewards so great.

You describe your changed outlook and this new sense of "exaltation or well being" very clearly, dear—so I think I can understand it. And isn't the sharing of thoughts, feeling, and emotions the very essence of friendship? So don't say "does it make any difference?" It does, dear, all the difference in the world.

And I, on my part, am coming to have a new feeling about my ability to carry on my work—a routine is being established that does give me hours of un-interrupted time, and it's a good feeling. I *want* to get into the study and begin the minute breakfast is over.

Yesterday was quite a morning—given over to editorial conferences. I had 4 telephone conversations with New York and one with Boston. Fortunately all but one were at the other fellow's expense! Paul is just back from England and wanted to discuss book.[8] Mr. Diamond called to discuss it. Then a long dis-cussion of Junior *Sea* with Mr. Le Corbeiller. Most importantly, Mr. Shawn called—quite his usual, wonderful self and we talked on and on. The startling news is that he would like to think of doing it as a long, 2-part piece![9] Of course this will greatly increase its impact, so I'm glad of that. Also, they will of course pay more, and since I'd be doing as much for the book anyway, that's good! He also mentioned in quite general terms an idea he wants to discuss for the fu-ture—about nothing less than the Universe!! I countered by telling him a little of the Harper book and suggested we might get the two ideas together. He wants to hear more, and of course we shall need to discuss the other material as it develops (well all right—*you* give me a label for it!) so I shall try to manage a few hours in New York early in May.

Then I wanted to report all this to Marie, so that made my 5th long-distance discussion!

I had to spend a long time correcting the map-maker, Lowenstein's, chart of ocean currents, but at least got this with long letter, into mail! Quite a day.

Le Corbeiller has a deadline of April 20 to get all color work to printer. It seems to me there is still quite a bit to do, so let's keep our fingers crossed.

[8] Houghton Mifflin was in the process of contracting with RC for *Silent Spring*. The contract was signed in May 1958.

[9] William Shawn had proposed publishing a 20,000–30,000-word *New Yorker* article by RC based on her insecticide material.

Now, Roger off to school, I'll stop and be ready to work after my breakfast. Ida has just come in.

Of course you know I want you to come Sunday if you can! And you can decide that at the last minute.

My dearest love
Rachel

How sad about your poor Marione Shaw! One wonders *why* such things have to be.

Darling [Dorothy],

The ridiculous card I mailed you yesterday is not, of course, your real Easter greeting. But I couldn't resist it, for it summed up the way I've been feeling—and perhaps looking and sounding—and stood for the chief reason we haven't been together this week. This, instead, is to carry your real Easter message, although probably it must only suggest it and you will have to know all I'd say if I had a morning to write.

When I think of the Easter season in relation to ourselves, do you know what I always remember at once? The beautiful letter you wrote me on Easter morning of 1954—it must have been, the first spring I knew you. You said it was your sunrise service. It told of the awakening beauty of your garden, and of the song of birds, and it told of your discovery of "A Lost Woods." You copied a long quotation from it. That was my introduction to this particular essay, too, you know. Later you gave me the book, during our Maytime, and one day we sat in our lost woods and read it together.

And there was much more of that sort of thing—the discovery and sharing of beauty, a newness and freshness in the world—that prevailed in our letters all that spring. I remember without even getting them out to read. It was a quality that belongs to Easter, and to spring. And it also belongs to that sudden discovery that came to each of us, that here, at last, was a kindred spirit. I know you have often felt that magical freshness and wonder could not last and perhaps has not lasted. But I don't think so, darling. It is there, all the time, perhaps temporarily obscured by other things, but awaiting only the touch of a spiritual spring to bring it new life. For it is, I know, the very essence of Us.

Do you know that too, darling?

Spring is beginning to come at last—though not, I fear, in Massachusetts. You must have been having dark skies and rain instead of the sunshine that has at last come to us. The morning paper says the magnolia buds are opening and herring are running in the Potomac. My swamp maples have put forth their red buds and the willow branches are bright with color. Last night in the nearly full moonlight Roger and I walked down the street to hear the chorus of the frogs at close range—really it was so loud we could scarcely make our own voices heard! How I hope they continue for 3 more weeks! When the real springtime will come, regardless of the weather.

My deep love,
Rachel

Darling [Rachel],

I fear you are going to be cheated out of a real letter after all. Last night we got word that Walter Probert, Stan's step-sister, Dorothy's, husband died suddenly yesterday afternoon.

I want to do some cooking to take over this afternoon. To-morrow I had a date in A.M. for hair-do which I need to keep as Thurs. is the day I show slides for Helen's Guild—that's a luncheon. And the funeral is to-morrow afternoon. So, darling, the week is well eaten into up to Friday.

Not that I won't get some messages off to you, but not the usual length.

Have just hung out a wash and it is so cold. I wandered around the garden—it is cold, and soggy and looks discouraged. A year ago I discover in my diary we had crocus, scilla, snow drops, arabis all in bloom. Apparently have lost all of ours—I imagine the long drouth of last summer was their death knell.

Dear, I wonder if you have Tomlinson's *The Snows of Helicon*— 1933. It's a queer thing and written in quite an obscure vein. Very meaty sentences will be tucked away in a paragraph which sometimes I might lose if I didn't reread. But it is as always delightful for me, and the theme is for Us—the saving of Beauty in a material world. There is one vivid, meaningful passage which you must read before you write your Life book; in fact, I think you'll want to read it all, but it is so different in content that you'll be surprised. I have it from the library so if you can't get it—I can. Also have *A Swinger of Birches* by Sidney Cox—a portrait of Robert Frost—records a Damon-Pythias friendship over four decades!

Darling, now it isn't two whole weeks until I see you! How wonderful. With my week-end trip to Orono, the time will be helped to pass quickly—now, you see, this week is going to be crowded for me—and before I know it, it will be Sunday, April 20! I hope, and I rather believe that your days, too, will be crowded & the waiting time will not seem long to you.

Stan was really shaken by Walter's death and I was a little bit worried for a while. I suppose he was being subjective about it. He said, "It sets such a whirlwind of thoughts in my mind." But I think he's all right. The funeral may be hard for him. He's felt closer to Dot than to any of the others of the step-family.

My back, altho' not what one could call cured, is so much better it's amazing! How wonderful I went to the Clinic instead of trying to live with it.

I do hope your cold begins to show improvement. Now I must cook— Darling, my dreams are all of being with you soon.

How I love you!
Dorothy

UNDER DRIER

Darling [Dorothy],

As mail has been going, I need to get this on its way if you are to have it Monday! Apparently the note I mailed last Saturday didn't reach you until Tuesday. As for yours, the card from the Station was here Monday—the letter written Sunday came Tuesday—the train letter Wednesday—and now one today.

It has been a full week, of course. When I learned of Glenn's[10] death, I called Irston Barnes[11] and asked if I might recall the dinner invitation, but had him come in the evening for our talk. Edwin came about 4 o'clock Wednesday and stayed until 10 or so—a delightful visit. Then yesterday we went to Glenn's services at the Cathedral. Vera went with us to help. Fortunately, I am not to see Mr. Canfield until Monday, when I'll meet him for lunch.

Funny how the parts of a jig-saw puzzle suddenly fall into place. If the bluebell reached you in fair shape, you must have known it is a *Scilla*—even I said that when Irston brought it. Now I have found it in a garden book by Norman Taylor which Paul has just sent me. It is *Scilla nonscripta*. Flowering date is given as April. Says it is sometimes incorrectly listed as *Scilla nutans*. Called also Wood Hyacinth. He gives as a "related plant" the Spanish Bluebell, *S. hispanica* (or, incorrectly, *S. campanulata*) which is the *Scilla* you marked for me in the Wayside catalogue. So now we know!

I meant to bring your letter with me but, in hurried leaving, forgot.

Pachipandia at Quaint Acres is $25.00 per 100. Myrtle there is $45, but $30 most places.

Suggestions for the wet patch: native Vibernums, deciduous holly or "Christmas berry", or red osier dogwood.

Thank you for the *Saturday Evening Post* news. It sounds like the series about which Marie had an announcement some time ago. A catch to that was that articles must be part of a book already under contract for publication. That gives possibilities for the Harper book, but if Mr. Shawn wants it I'd rather give it to him. However, I shall be most interested in the articles. Sounds like a new departure for the *Post*, which, as you've probably guessed, I don't usually care for.

The azaleas are bursting into glorious bloom. My only complaint is lack of variety. Dogwoods everywhere are glorious now.

Two long and interesting letters on the spraying problem—one from the Mayo man—Dr. Hargraves.[12]

That reminds me: you didn't like my phrase "the poison book"—now I don't enjoy your "Tommy."[13] Let's compromise on both.

But I did enjoy your comments on the book. Stardustily, Edwin and Nellie Teale have just been reading it!

[10] Glenn Algire, cancer scientist and husband of Dorothy Algire.

[11] An economist, writer, and officer of the Audubon Naturalist Society of the Central Atlantic States.

[12] Malcolm M. Hargraves, M.D., of the Mayo Clinic.

[13] "The poison book" refers to the work in progress that became *Silent Spring*; "Tommy" perhaps was a DF nickname for Tomlinson.

All of your post-visit letters[14] have been good to have, dear one. This is not a reply to any—just a report in a snatched moment.

I'll tell you now, because apparently we can relax. I learned Monday Roger had been exposed to scarlet fever at school. He has been stuffed with penicillin all week and incubation period is now past. I kept him home Tues. and Wed. to avoid further exposure if someone else got it. But penicillin apparently does the trick now.

More soon—dear—but now I'm about to go.

All love,
Rachel

THURSDAY MORNING, JUNE 12

Oh, My Darling [Rachel],

What can I say? I'm quite speechless and breathless and overcome with the loveliest perfume. You just can't believe in what excellent condition your tribute[15] arrived. I put them in the refrigerator for an hour and now they are pouring out their fragrance on my desk as I write.

Of course, to say I'm thrilled (as you said I would be) is putting it mildly. I hope I didn't temper your joy by guessing what it might be. When you intimated whatever it was needed to come through in a hurry, and then that we'd both be thrilled I began to puzzle. Suddenly I was sure it couldn't be anything else.

And, dear, I quite understand how much it means to you to be able to send me for my birthday a flower which has had meaning for us which *you produced yourself*. And such a product. I never dreamed they could be of such astounding quality—really huge blossoms & such fragrance. Oh, darling, how truly delightful it all is. Just the type of episode that spells out the bond between us.

And now I'm full of questions. I wonder if they'd grow in our climate. I want to try so I must find out where you sent for bulbs. Do you think they will live over for another year. Are there other colors? Are they all blooming? I just can't believe that those tiny blades I saw in April have resulted in this loveliness.

What a lovely fragrance when I opened the box. Stan was backing out of driveway but I made him come back so he knew it, too. There was no time to write this for him to take, hence the note on envelope.

Don't take time to answer my questions now—We'll talk about it when we are *together*. Darling, how thrilled you must be to send me a birthday remembrance that you *alone* could have sent! The kind of thing I always long to do!

Mr. Kent brought the special handling box at same time, but I see Roger's name so I shall save it until Sunday.

Darling, you are so precious!

I love you, dear, need I say, for this and all the other myriad of lovely memories you've given me.

Dorothy

Rachel Carson at work.

Dorothy labeled this "Rachel Carson by the Edge of The Sea, summer 1954."

Dorothy, Southport, October 1954.

Dorothy labeled this "Rachel Carson July, 1955, on her wildwood lot, West Southport, Maine."

Dorothy labeled this "Summer 1955, Rachel on platform under The Spruce, a favorite spot."

Rachel and Dorothy.

Rachel, Roger, Marjie, and Dorothy, waiting for moonrise over Ebenecook Harbor.

Martha Freeman and Roger Christie, summer 1956.

Stanley, Dorothy, and Rachel with squirrel, summer 1955.

Rachel and her mother, Maria Carson.

The Freeman Southport cottage, 1950s; Dorothy and her moth
Vira Murdoch, on porch.

Rachel and Dorothy: a Southport picnic.

Rachel's Southport cottage, 1955.

Jeffie.

Rachel and Stanley in New York,
December 1963.

Dorothy at Rachel's Southport cottage, autumn 1975.

ON TRAIN

Darling [Dorothy],

Here we are—on noon train from N.Y., due Washington at 3:50. I've decided this should be waiting for you on your return home Sunday—I assume your plans haven't changed.

It has been a very good trip, with all major things accomplished and really a lot covered in the short time—*New Yorker*—Joan Doves—Fairfield Osborn—lawyers.

The visit with Mr. Shawn was really a delight and most satisfying. We talked for 2½ hours! He is completely fascinated with the theme[16] and obviously happy and excited at the prospect of presenting it in the *New Yorker*. Best of all, I can (indeed, he *wants* me to) present it strictly from my point of view, pulling no punches. He says, "After all there are some things one doesn't have to be objective and unbiased about—one doesn't condone murder!" Besides the importance of the theme ("We don't usually think of the *New Yorker* as changing the world, but this is one time it might") he feels the material is just plain fascinating, and now thinks he'd like to have 50,000 words!! (This would mean 3 installments, I think—that alone will emphasize its importance in their eyes.) Since I had meant to keep the book down to about this length, it will mean the two will be about the same.

I'll probably save until I see you some of the "side issues" of our conversation—about E. B. White's awareness of this problem many years ago and his almost prophetic vision regarding it—he says Mr. White will be utterly horrified when he gets all the *facts* I present—about the profile of Dr. Newton Harvey,[17] which did result from my suggestion some years ago—about my proposed Harper book, which seemed to impress him so greatly that I guess that, too, could well find space in his pages. Now I've suggested Vincent Schaefer as a profile subject, and also given him a little horror story on radioactivity which I got from Edwin Teale. It concerns Dick Pough—I planned to send you the letter after I've answered it. Mr. Shawn wrote it down at once, is going to call Dick Pough, and I imagine it will appear in "Talk of the Town."

From there I went to the New Weston and got established, and about six Joan Doves came over with our Scandinavian agent in tow—he just happened to be in her office. He stayed for "a drink"—then left and we had dinner and talked until eleven.

This morning I went to breakfast at the Osborns' at 8:15. We had about an hour to talk, then shared a cab as far as my hotel. From there I went immediately to Mr. Greenbaum—I have asked him to keep on the will, which has been a thorny problem, and still is, with tremendous decisions to be made.

[16] RC was by now deeply involved in her pesticide research and continuing to consider an article on the subject for the *New Yorker*.

[17] Edmund Newton Harvey, physiologist, and author of, among other books, *Living Light* (1940).

[18] A Harper and
Brothers editor.

And that took me up to train time! It was really a good trip. The only thing I couldn't carry out was seeing Elizabeth Lawrence,[18] who left for a western trip yesterday, but that was chiefly a courtesy call so it didn't matter.

Now—enough about me. By this time your week in Maine is over. I do hope Stan came home minus any traces of his cold, and that you are refreshed by your time there. Your account of that first week-end sounded very full of people, but probably that changed Monday.

[19] Izetta Pinkham,
wife of the West
Southport gen-
eral store owner.

I laughed at Mrs. Pinkham's[19] question. Did you say "Yes, *almost* every day"?

Darling, about your birthday, you know I'll want to call you but now that I've gotten organized enough to look at the calendar I realize it is Sunday. As you know, I can be more sure of peace and quiet to talk when Ida is there. Besides, you may go out. So how about Monday morning, about 10 o'clock?

How I'd love to hear that early June chorus of birds! And see the flowers. Maybe, sometime.

I don't think you'll want to read any more of this—and my arm is getting a cramp from trying to be legible.

How nice you have *The Return of the Native* before you! I confess I remember only two parts—the wonderful opening passage, and the scene about the glow worms.

All my love, dear.

Rachel

SATURDAY AFTERNOON, JUNE 28

Darling [Dorothy],

I'm on the porch on the new chaise (did I tell you?—aluminum frame, plastic cushion covers in a figured pattern, shades of tan and a touch of dull orange—very pretty and *very* comfortable). We've had two days of lovely weather, after two of horrid heat—and I spent both of them downtown!

Darling—as always now I feel hurried and I suppose I won't express myself very well or adequately. But please know I understand your feelings and your mood at least better than I must have seemed to when we talked Tuesday morning. I know now I must have failed you horribly when you asked, "How do you feel about all this?"—and I was so obtuse I didn't know just what you meant! But now I've thought about it, darling—asking myself how I'd feel if the situation were reversed—and I know I'd be sad, too. So I *do* understand, dear one—maybe even better than you do, for you are trying to convince yourself and me that it isn't the lack of letters. But, in large measure it *is*, darling! If I could somehow keep putting on paper the sort of thing I used to write—and which I still feel and think about—I know you wouldn't feel so desolate.

And of course I know you are not happy about my project. Perhaps I can help you to feel differently when we are together, dear. No doubt I make a mistake in that I tell you all the wrong things—but I never learn, I just pour out whatever is in my mind at the time! I know you dread the unpleasantness that will inevitably be associated with its publication. That I can understand, darling. But it is something I have taken into account; it will not surprise me! You do know, I think, how deeply I believe in the importance of what I am doing. Knowing what I do, there would be no future peace for me if I kept silent. I wish I could feel that you *want* me to do it. I wish you could feel, as I do, that it is, in the deepest sense, a privilege as well as a duty to have the opportunity to speak out—to many thousands of people—on something so important. You say you know this is important to me. But I can't, at this point, feel sure you are also convinced of its importance to (as examples) your children and even more to your grandchildren. Do you really know that, dear? And if you do—can you possibly wish I were not doing this—no matter what the cost?

My "disease" is, no doubt, aggravated by the nature of my subject, and also by the fierce drive to get it done—but we can't lay it all to that dear, for I was miserable much of the time in Maine last year, even when doing practically nothing.

And, of course, to immerse oneself almost completely in a project is ideal—something I haven't been able to do since *The Sea*. Remember some of the things Bernstein has said along that line—we have discussed them and I know you have understood and responded to his thought.

But it isn't forever, darling! And this time there seems to be no choice. It can't drag on as *The Edge* did. The old problem—why am I not twins?

Darling, I've probably not helped by this—all that will help will be to *see* you. Which brings me to this. *If* you are going to Maine the week I go, and for only a couple of days, I gather, *why* can't you make it the 9th instead of the 8th?? If you go the 8th you'll waste a day (says she, shamelessly!). You know I won't arrive until the end of the afternoon on the 9th. Oh, it would be so wonderful to know I was going to *you*. It would be empty, otherwise. And so I'd hope your stay was all ahead of you, instead of a day already gone.

As to route—when you and Stan went back last October, you used the Mass. turnpike. Where did you enter it, and do you think this better than Conn. parkway?

Now I must take this to box and then get to work.

> All my love, dearest—
> *Rachel*

Was glad to hear you decided against the house-party—hope you are having a lovely time right now.

Darling [Dorothy],

We're having our morning coffee together—do you know? This can't reach you until Saturday, I suppose, and it *may* be my last before we leave.

Your letter of Sunday was sweet to have, dear. I know you have meant what you said when you've been telling me not to write and that you didn't want me to—but I also think (shamelessly) that you couldn't help missing the letters. I know *I've* missed them!—for even writing to you keeps you closer.

The call Sunday was not so much because your letter made me sad (though of course it did) but because I was afraid my reply, written so hastily, was all wrong. But now we are to be together in a place we love *one week from today*, so nothing else matters.

I have been glad we weren't on the road yesterday or the day before—even with air conditioning the stops are hard in such heat. The car seems to be back to normal and looks new in its waxy coat.

Ida will come Monday prepared to spend the night and get us off on an early start Tuesday, then stay to close the house. *Why* didn't I think of that last year? I've arranged that I will call Mary Shoemaker[20] from a place I usually stop for coffee, this side of the Delaware River Bridge. That will give them plenty of time to reach our meeting place, off Exit 9 from N. J. Turnpike.

I've had to call a halt on library work—just couldn't get ready otherwise. My "getting ready" seems peculiar this year—taking very few books except for my working collection, and many things I used to think necessary don't seem to be. Actually, I guess we'll be there about as long as last year, but it seems a very short time to look forward to.

Darling, I thought I might try to call you Wednesday between 12 and 1, if possible, to tell you about when we ought to arrive. I don't know whether you'd find it possible to be there to greet us—you know it would be sweet if you could—but I certainly don't want you to waste precious time waiting and not knowing when we'd arrive. One thing you must promise, darling. You are *not* to do anything in the house. The water is in and other essentials taken care of by Mr. Delano. We'll stop at Pinkhams' for supper and breakfast things, and with Mary to help on beds all should be simple. What fun to be really thinking of being there—and to know you will be there makes all the difference.

Now I must go, darling.

All my love,
Rachel

[20] A young friend of DF who was traveling to Southport with RC.

Darling [Dorothy],

This is to greet you at Southport and to remind you that I am following in hours so few you can easily count them, whenever this reaches you.

I wanted to send a note to reach you at home Monday but couldn't, so this instead.

The trunk and several smaller items went off by Express today and I shall mail a couple of laundry cases Monday, so our car load should be tolerable.

Aside from the heat—something one can't get aside from!—there has been the usual run of perversity on the part of most mechanical objects I'm associated with—car air conditioning refused to come on yesterday (a fuse had blown out—but why?—so guess I'll have to go down Monday and ask); then one of the big fans overheated and stuck—Robert fixed it today; dishwasher finally was repaired Thursday after nearly 2 weeks; cabinet front is still to be replaced so heat of dishwasher pours into kitchen unhindered—etc., etc.! Then Moppet has seemed not well, but I think it's hair balls plus heat; Roger is getting 2 molars at once—etc.—etc.!

And the heat has me feeling like a dishrag; but I still believe we'll get off Tuesday.

SUNDAY

I still do so believe, but there are more complications. However, if you haven't already heard otherwise before you leave, you'll know we are on the way.

Virginia became quite sick yesterday, and there is still some uncertainty as to just what the trouble is. I won't go into details, now, but unless she is improving and her trouble better understood I'll probably need to postpone departure.

And Elizabeth,[21] on way to hospital early yesterday morning, fell and shattered her left elbow. She is in hospital, of course, arm in traction and most uncomfortable. I must take time tomorrow to go down to see her before we go.

[21] Elizabeth Dickson.

MONDAY A.M., COFFEE TIME

All that was not the reason for writing, but as usual I pour it out.

Showers last night cooled us off 20 degrees or so, but I'm afraid today is to be hot and sticky.

Car is partly packed—Ted put in microscope for me. Ida will help with what remains tonight.

Darling, what I really want to say is that I hope you are not sad about our recent letters, and particularly about anything I have said. In my thinking since Thursday when your long letter came I have come to realize that I can and should limit the job now—as to length and time spent—so I can soon be free to move on into happier projects. And there will be occasional "days off" at Southport, I promise you. Also, of course, "hours off" when you can come to be with me!

Darling—since I didn't get this off Sunday you won't have it until Wednesday's mail—just a few hours before you have me!

I would hope we'd arrive between 4 and 5. Perhaps we'd better just say you'll come when you can, and that I won't telephone, even when we do arrive.

Now I can say "day-after-tomorrow"—!!

All my love, dear
Rachel

WEDNESDAY NOON, JULY 9

Dear One [Dorothy],

Had all gone well, we could have been looking forward to a moment of great happiness in only a few hours. I'm sure you know that my decision was an agonizing one because it involved destruction of that lovely prospect. However, when I made it, I still believed we could leave early this morning and perhaps reach Southport by noon Thursday—and so salvage something. Now that I'm to miss you, I don't seem to care when we go. And that's as well, for tomorrow is definitely out and all I can say is "next week."

It was frustrating to have such a poor connection last night. I don't know how much of the story you got, so will repeat. (Don't feel "guilty"—all work materials are packed or shipped, so today is gloriously empty.)

Monday was a hectic day, full of the things that can be done only on the last day. To add to its complications, the smell of gasoline (of which I'd been vaguely aware before) was very noticeable as I drove about on my errands. I was also conscious of considerable light-headedness, but attributed this to heat and strain. By the time I got home in mid-afternoon with laundry, ice, etc., I decided I must have car checked, so called and arranged to take it down. While I stood beside him the man looked in all the wrong places and none of the right ones (I know now) and declared there was no leak and all was well.

I filled tank Monday. As we started out Tuesday I was aware that gasoline smell was stronger than ever. Soon I noticed that tank was ¾ full—and before long ½! We made it to an Esso station about 5 miles this side of Catonsville with an empty tank! On adding some gas, the attendant found the fuel pump simply spraying it out! They told me of an Oldsmobile place about 7 miles farther in. Of course I was by that time thoroughly alarmed about fire or explosion, and thinking frantically what to do with my passengers. The single motor court on that road would have none of us because of the cats, although I explained all circumstances and promised to keep them in carriers! Then I thought of the Rices, and left them there while I went on with car.

When examined, the trouble proved all the more infuriating because it was something the dealer here had done—a gasket improperly installed. Probably it has been leaking a little for some time, then got suddenly worse.

When car was ready it was nearly 11:30. I knew this would put us in New York at a terrible time. Also, I was feeling pretty woozy and doubted it was safe for me to continue long at the wheel. (Both Mamma & Roger were apparently unaffected.) And I was concerned about the cats, although for no specific reason, so it must have been pure intuition.

When we got home both cats were obviously glad, but I thought they were all right. A half hour or so later, Jeffie staggered across the bed to me, panting heavily, his tongue a horrible blue. So was the roof and lining of his mouth. After a rather unsatisfactory talk with a local vet, I put in a call to Sarasota, in desperation, and was so relieved when Dr. Dennewitz answered. He was shocked by the whole thing—said he was so thankful I hadn't gone on, and that we were very fortunate I hadn't been suddenly overcome at the wheel.

Jeffie improved somewhat with the treatment suggested—color of tongue was much better within an hour. However, he is still far from recovered and seems to have difficulty swallowing today. Doctor thinks he will be all right, but that several days of rest and care will be needed.

And little Moppet is far from her lively self, though showing no specific symptoms, but just lies and sleeps most of the time.

I am all right now, dear—the dizziness, etc., have worn off. But we were all very fortunate that there was not a tragedy of some sort.

Of course I can't pretend that I don't dread the trip horribly now. Yesterday I realized more than ever just how vulnerable we are when anything goes wrong. If we'd had another able-bodied adult with us it wouldn't have seemed quite so bad.

But at least I'm deeply thankful the trouble developed when it did, instead of on one of the Turnpikes, hundreds of miles from home.

Darling—do you know how terribly I hated to call you? I knew all too well what I was going to do to you—you had told me, you know, that you planned this trip especially to be there when I came! Knowing all that, I ached for you even more than I ached within myself!

But now that all possibility of seeing you this time has vanished, I shall be truly glad to rest here a few days and perhaps get my back and my "innards" in better shape for the trip.

Poor Elizabeth—it actually made me feel faint to see her swollen and blackened arm in traction Monday. Now she is to have an operation probably tomorrow to see what can be done for her shattered elbow.

Darling—I'll try to call you Sunday about eleven and I do love you—do you know?

Rachel

AFTER SUNSET

Darling [Dorothy],

Five years ago you sat on your porch at sunset and wrote me a goodbye note.

Tonight I watched the sun just before it set, from our beach, where the water colors were those you read of today from *Under the Sea-Wind*—but instead of skimmers I had gulls. Later I watched the actual sunset from the porch, all the while planning to write this note.

It must be brief, for you may come and I want to give this to you. But I can't let you go, and see the summer end, without telling you how much better I feel after our talk this afternoon—particularly the last few minutes on the island.

As you must have known, I have been heavy-hearted for some time, and I think you have too. Most of the time you seemed so far away—and I was groping for you as through a fog. Today it seemed as though I found you again in that conversation, when you told me that you do understand and accept the things I felt had come between us. Somehow I feel now that you really do, and the weight has lifted.

I hope that you, too, are more at peace, although I'm afraid I did little to bring that about.

And although this summer has held fewer of those moments of beauty and loveliness that seem to belong especially to us, there have been some, and we shall cherish them through the months ahead.

That interval we must take as it comes, I suppose. Now I look toward mid-October, if no little surprise visit to Maine is possible before.

But the important thing now—the certainty I want you to take home with you in your heart—is that, as ever and always, I love you and I need you.

Rachel

FRIDAY, AUGUST 29

Darling [Dorothy],

Of course we have been thinking about you a great deal as we listen to news of hurricane watches, alerts, warnings, etc., for the southern Massachusetts coast, and do hope you will have nothing worse than heavy rains. Yesterday afternoon we brought a supply of wood to the porch, checked candle supply, and laid in a little hurricane food just in case the power should go. But from all we can hear this morning we, at least, aren't likely to be in the path.

Wednesday night I lay on the chaise a long time looking at the nearly-full moon as it rose above the spruces. I wondered whether anyone at home could believe I was wearing a wool robe, tweed coat, had a folded blanket around my shoulders and another over my lap—and needed them all! Several times while I lay there towhees spoke to each other from the evergreens beside my drive. It was all beautiful, and guess who was in my thoughts?

I'll mail this for the afternoon mail, but suppose you won't get it until Tuesday, because of the holiday! So I'd better be definite about our Thursday meeting.[22] It would be a miracle, dear, if we got there before one or two o'clock. You know my household, and though I shall have Mary[23] to help about breakfast, beds, etc., she is not easily hurried. So I wouldn't expect that we'd get away a minute before 9, and it might easily be an hour or more later. I won't wait until the last minute to call you, but start 10 or 15 minutes before I think we'll close up and leave. If I don't get you I will leave the message at Pinkhams' but would also try somewhere along the road. Failing all else, why don't you plan to be there at one, with reading or writing materials, since you say you won't mind waiting. But if we should be quite late leaving we'd probably need some refreshment stop en route there, and you know that takes lots of time because of the slow and difficult process of getting Mamma in and out.

The bit from the Record announcement is lovely—almost in the Tomlinson vein, isn't it? I'm returning it at once, for I don't want to mislay it for you. I never get anything about the records now, and as I told you the last two records that I expected to receive never came, so I think I must have been inadvertently lost. As soon as I get home I must write them about it.

The Spocks[24] proved quite delightful. Mrs. Spock is a spry and spirited old lady of 83 or 84, with a wonderful sense of humor. They came by boat (it was a perfect day) and after lunch I brought them here for a couple of hours. Our mothers visited on the porch while we exchanged information in the study. Miss Spock and Miss Richards are approximately my age, I suppose. Poor Miss Richards, who has the misfortune to be allergic to many chemicals, looks terribly frail. The Spock place, as I understand it, overlooks the passage between MacMahan and Georgetown, so we can't see it from here. They bought the place early in her married life, so her memories don't go back as far as your mother's, but do include the boat trip from Boston—in fact, she was on it the night it was "shipwrecked" in the fog, somewhere out from the mouth of the Kennebec, I think. You probably know all about it. She says she has the account of it that was published in the Bath paper.

The rainy day we went to Bestons' we missed a caller who came all the way around from Sagadahoc Bay—my bookstore friend, Mrs. Rose, from Silver Spring. You know I told you she has been summering there since she was a child—her grandparents from Boston established it. (Their summer home, I mean.)

Yesterday we called on Father Manette. I sensed that Mary did want to go, and she seemed to enjoy it. In fact it was a great help to have her, for when Roger got restless she took him over to see the fishing boats, where they heard much talk between Coast Guard and fishermen about the hurricane.

[22] Near West Bridgewater.

[23] Probably Mary Shoemaker.

[24] RC had corresponded with Marjorie Spock and Mary Richards because they had been plaintiffs in a lawsuit in the spring of 1957 to prevent the spraying of DDT on Long Island, New York.

Heavens, dear, I must stop. This is so much more fun than other letters I might be writing.

So glad you are feeling better and that you are getting some of the rest you need so badly. I couldn't see that you had any here! I hope Stan's trip didn't wear him out and that your mother is all over her upset. And good for Willow that he's beginning to fill out again. Ours get fatter and fatter all summer. I'm sorry for them having to go home, where dogs prevent my taking them out. Someday I shall have to install a fence around a small part of the yard so I can.

Juncoes, sparrows, and bluejays are busy at the seed outside the window as I write.

See you soon, dearest—how wonderful! (It helps take the curse off leaving!)

All love,
Rachel

SATURDAY A.M., AUGUST 30

Darling [Dorothy],

After our experience with Saturday mail, I don't know when you'll get this—but by Wednesday at least, I hope, it's just a note to say I love you and have wished for you to share these last nights of moonlight. Last night I moved my bed so I could lie beside the front window and look out every time I opened my eyes. I even saw it dropping toward the horizon as day was coming. All that loveliness makes it especially hard to go, and yet, in completely different ways, the routine of school and Ida ahead looks like a haven to be longed for.

Yes darling, I do feel so much better about Us. That awful weight is lifted. And I scarcely know how it happened but suddenly there was a change and everything seemed to be all right. Was it that way with you? I keep groping for a simile in someone's writing—possibly Thoreau—about the sudden coming of the thaw in spring: one day all was a frozen winter landscape—then, suddenly and as if by magic, there was sunshine and release—and spring!

When we are together in October, darling, I think I must make one more attempt to have you understand something in me that you still do not understand. I know you have tried, but the solution you have reached is not the true one. I know this because of one sentence you uttered that day in the car on Pratt's Island. This is not reproach, darling. But it concerns something that is so basic to my whole present life that until you do really understand it I cannot fully open my heart to you. Will you let me tell you—and will you be willing to substitute my knowledge of myself for what you now think?

In any event, darling—don't ever again say or think that you are "just another." It would be easier for us both, I suppose, if I did not so desperately need to pour out my heart to you—but I do, and nothing changes that.

Wendell is here (as of 10 A.M.) and he and Mary seem to have a big weekend planned. Unfortunately, they are going places where I feel Roger would not be safe in the somewhat preoccupied care of a pair of lovers—Ocean Point and Pemaquid. But I shall spend much of the week-end packing up, and not expect any time to myself.

Already I'm planning for those all-too-short days in October. Do squeeze out every possible hour for us, darling. If you and Stan can come to us first, we can have our general visit and "settling down" out of the way—then when he goes to his meeting we will be ready to enjoy every minute. You know, with the Hide-a-bed in the study and even an extra bed downstairs we have plenty of room. Now, until Thurs., darling, a goodbye—and so much love.

Rachel

Horrors! I didn't investigate the envelopes when I bought this paper!! Hope you will overlook Ye Olde Gift Shoppe touch. Horrid, aren't they?

LABOR DAY, SEPTEMBER 2, 8 A.M.

Darling [Dorothy],

Not a creature is stirring—except the mouse-catchers, so I'll have a moment with you as I have my coffee at the study window.

You may not even have this before I see you but I wanted to tell you about the birds at Pratt's Island yesterday. It was sunny but foggy—the sort of day when you can't see far offshore. I took the family while Mary & Wendell were away, & Roger and I walked through the woods to the place you and I sat that last day. The tide was high so the little island containing the bird bath was smaller and completely cut off. It had become the resting place for a large party of birds—about a dozen terns, a few semipalmated plover, and *eleven* turnstones! Some were sound asleep, heads tucked in their back feathers. One bird I wasn't sure of proved (according to plate in Forbush)[25] to be an immature turnstone. The island next farther out was devoted to gulls; the long ledge in the distance to cormorants. These, in the fog, looked immense. It would have been easy to take them for people. One spread its wings and remained motionless in that pose for an incredible time.

I'm also happy about solving the mystery of the little vine. (Perhaps as you felt about the flycatcher.) The Bennetts called yesterday & Christine said she thought it was a cranberry. Later, in looking for that, I came upon the snowberry. Under a lens, the little brown bristles leave no doubt. I want to take home a bit to try to establish there. This is my last word from here, dear. With it, all love.

Rachel

[25] Edward Howe Forbush's *Useful Birds and Their Protection*, first commissioned by the Massachusetts Legislature in 1905.

Darling [Dorothy],

All you wrote yesterday was not only sweet, but found answering echoes in my heart. And if you thought I looked "lovely and precious" and all the rest, it is only what I thought of you. I regretted later that I hadn't told you how sweet your hat was—so soft of line and color, and so right (with the suit and the lovely pin) for your blue, blue eyes. But most of all, of course, how sweet you were!

Of course, dear one, I wish I hadn't written that letter from Maine, but it must not for one moment make you feel other than your earlier conviction that "all's right" with our world.

We long ago recognized that we do not, and probably cannot understand each other *completely*. So when I said you didn't understand, I was speaking of one specific thing (concerned with my motives for doing certain things I have done) and I did not mean to imply a general lack of understanding.

As I think you know, I am a creature of moods; what I wrote then came of a mood of rather black despair and a crying need for you to understand. When I am silent, darling, it is out of fear I'll say the wrong thing and deepen misunderstanding—as I've been known to do! But I will try again—although doubtless it is hopelessly unfair to expect anyone to comprehend my changing moods.

But what is important, darling, is that you have filled—and I'm sure always will—a unique place in my life.

It is lovely that, for both of us, there are echoes of the Beginnings.

As always, I love you.

R.

MONDAY MORNING, OCTOBER 20, 7:30

Darling [Dorothy],

I've just settled back in bed with a cup of coffee—and you. And you can picture it as you read, which of course is one of the many happy things about having you "visit" me.[26]

I am so glad, darling, that you can feel better about my situation. There is every reason to. So many problems have been solved, and with better results than I ever dared hope. Except for the occasional bad days, I am reasonably content. I think the house itself contributes to serenity—I do love it, and everything I can find time to do, inside or out, gives me real satisfaction. And Roger's happy adjustment to school this year is such a help—he was actually bitterly disappointed yesterday about being sick because "I don't want to miss any more school!" And I can see already that as he grows up many things will become easier. And darling, even though I seemed unable to be satisfying about it in conversation, I'm actually excited and happy about the book. For all its unpleasant features, it is something with so many complexities scientifically that it is mentally stimulating, as are the contacts with many of the people I talk or write to.

[26] The Freemans had visited RC in Silver Spring from October 13 to 16, coinciding with a business trip for Stanley.

Of course I fret for more and more opportunity to throw myself into it to the exclusion of most diversions, but all in all my feeling about it is good.

Darling—I am always touched and humbled when you really open your heart to me as you did as we sat by the stream. I wish I could help more positively, but I am so happy that my role as listener was in any way helpful. Please, please, dear one, don't regret having poured out some of your inmost thoughts. It was a precious interval for me; far from detracting from the loveliness of the day, it added to it, as something to cherish—like a certain dawn in Maine.

LATER

Dr. McDonald has been here—Roger has flu (not Asian!) but he believes R. will be over it in a couple of days. He is being a good little patient, and with Ida here all is serene. I do love you, darling, *terribly*!

Rachel

MONDAY AFTERNOON, NOVEMBER 24

Dearest [Dorothy],

Only a brief report for Ida to mail. I don't think we are doing too well, but it is hard to judge. The doctor hasn't been here yet today but we have conferred by phone. Mamma's temperature is up somewhat and heart seems more irregular. She is very weak, but completely rational—actually looked at a little television. In the most part, though, she just sleeps. I'm having a hospital bed sent in; it should make handling her easier on everyone. Vera will be here again tonight but I think I must look up a nurse or two.

Guess you won't hear again until the end of the week, darling, on account of the holiday.

Your long Saturday letter was in the mail today—so good to have, but of course I won't attempt to answer now.

All love to you,
Rachel

SUNDAY EVENING, NOVEMBER 30

Dear One [Rachel],

The days roll by. Every time the telephone rings my heart stands still. Perhaps, after all Mamma is improving. And yet from what you told me Friday morning that scarcely seems possible. And so I picture all you are enduring in these long days. If it seems long to me since Friday I can't imagine what it is like for you, dearest. I wish I could talk to you. Stan has just suggested I call you, but I know I mustn't. I couldn't help and I fear I might be interrupting some precious moment.

Darling, this was the day of the first Bernstein concert. Of course, I doubt that you watched and yet if Mamma had rallied to any extent perhaps you did. I should not write about it at all except that it had such an emotional impact in relation to you and Mamma that I can't bear not to mention it. I shall not write the details now. I should like to tell you about it in person and I will do that when we are together. I longed for you and Mamma to be listening and yet I knew it would be agony for you, but bliss for Mamma. If you did see it I'm sure you will know what I mean. You were beside me every moment of that hour, darling, and my heart was full of longing, I wanted your mother to be sharing it knowing her feelings for him.

The program was Beethoven's 9th with the Philharmonic and the Westminster choir and 4 marvelous soloists. When it was over I felt that Television has at last come into its own, and surely all the people who saw the vision of producing such a program should receive grateful thanks from all of us up-to-now disillusioned viewers. Your Robert Saudek and Alistair Cooke were listed.

Even most of the commercial was dignified—two touches they could have omitted but I'll forgive them those bits.

As for L.B.—he was his usual self—simplicity, feeling, passion, depth. When I think of the work that must have gone into training that huge orchestra, chorus and soloists, he seems like a superman—well, he is, that's all. It doesn't seem possible that any following program can quite equal this.

There were wonderful close-ups of him, in strong lights and shadows that gave him the appearance of being sculptured. I think that there will be such a demand for a repeat performance, that if you didn't see it this time there will be a second chance.

I think I shall jot down now all the things I want to tell you so that I shall not forget—the things that would have been so fraught with emotion for you if you were watching.

In a lighter vein I think you will be happy to know that he has had his forelock shorn so that he was free from having to keep that in place—a big help.

This has been a cold day here—scarcely risen above 20—with strong winds forcing the cold in around the cracks.

Stan remains comfortable—but does so by sticking to his very restricted diet and using the extra drugs. If ever again he can have a bit of fruit I think perhaps I'll be happier than he—it seems so awful not to have any relief from the monotony of starch and protein. But he doesn't complain—he says it's all in the head—and goes on enjoying custard and cream of wheat.

Then your call came, dear.[27] Darling, I feel so useless—and so helpless. From what you said I feel you must have adequate help now, but somehow I think you must be very lonely in the midst of these sad days. I long so to be near you. Your dear picture is on my bureau and now the wistful look I have loved from the first has an added quality of sadness.

Of course, I can't free my mind from the idea that I must go to you. But I seem to feel that you may need me more when you will be trying to find your way back into the everyday world than you do now. Darling, I have talked to Stan to-night. He remembers how wonderful you were more than once when he has been sick. If he continues to be as well as he is now I could go to you, darling,

[27] RC had telephoned to report her mother's deteriorating condition.

even if for a very short time. This is what I want to ask you. If you do feel the need of me, will you please ask me? I promise you in all good faith that I would be honest and if I felt I shouldn't leave Stan, I would tell you so.

There is another thought that I have harbored, too—that we would so love to have you and Roger come to us if that idea seemed at all workable and feasible.

Whatever you want or need is what we want. I'm sure you are numb now and to think beyond the present is impossible. But know that I am as near you as I possibly can be, with my arms stretched out to you, darling. Will you ask me to come when you need me most? We all send our dearest love. Thank you for the call to-night, dear.

Good-night, my darling,
I love you so.
Dorothy

Why I even dare to suggest that you ask me to come, is that after I talked with you to-night I suddenly visualized what it would be like if I were the one who was going through your tragedy—and how terribly I would want you. So I hope you want me—and I don't want you to hesitate to ask because of my situation here.

MONDAY AFTERNOON, DECEMBER 1

Dear Heart [Rachel],

What can I say to you now that Mamma has gone?[28] Even as I write the word, Mamma, I wonder if I ever explained to you why it seemed more natural for me to call her that than anything else. You see, dear, your pronunciation of Mamma is quite different from the sound we New Englanders give to it. From the first, I loved hearing you say it, and began myself to use your way in speaking of your mother. Mamma, as you say it, means only *your* mother to us—it distinguishes her from all other mothers.

I have thought of so many things I want to say to you, but I have decided to write of only one—something I'm sure no one else could or will write. I told you in my letter last night that the Bernstein program yesterday held a great emotional content related to Mamma and to Us. As long as I cannot be near you in these next sad days, I want to tell you of that experience for, from henceforth Beethoven's Ninth will always mean Mamma to me.

Knowing her intense interest and devotion to Mr. Bernstein, it seems almost prearranged that this marvelous first performance of his should have had, for me, the quality of a final tribute to her. Darling, this may sound odd to say, but at one point in the music the thought swept over me, "If Mamma is hearing this she can truly die happy." Perhaps, dear, even then, she was hearing sublimer music.

I so wish I could remember Mr. Bernstein's exact words—they are always

[28] RC's mother, Maria Carson, had died on the morning of December 1 at age eighty-nine.

so right—as he gave his conception of the meaning of this masterpiece. I shall try to give you the thought briefly.

The symphony is a vision of life—the inexorable order of the universe—the struggle, the fatefulness, the beauty, the energy, the mystery, the despair and the joy. The first two movements evoke the struggle—the heights and the depths. Then the third movement brings exaltation—the vision of heaven (now I long so for his exact words) when, after the fire and struggle of life one has a glimpse of eternal glory. Then follows the great relief, as when one realizes a terrible pain has ceased. Then it was that my heart nearly burst for you and Mamma. I even noted the exact time when he said those words. Darling, if you have the Ninth, play that Third Movement when you can be alone for I know you, too, will find exaltation and relief in it.

Before he played the great joyous fourth movement he quietly appealed to each one to do nothing for the next twenty minutes but to listen to the glorious climax—to let oneself be lost in the music and in Time. And it was in those minutes, dearest, that my mind dwelt on Mamma—on all that I know of her life, of the wonderful person she has been, of her great love for all living things—"the darlings"—of her spiritual qualities and of her belief in eternal life, and above all of the happy fact that she had given a priceless contribution to the world—and to me—You.

So you see I was very close to her in what proved to be her last hours through the medium of our mutual friend, Leonard Bernstein. There are a thousand things I could say now but we will talk about them when we are together.

I shall miss her, darling. Do you know when I think I shall miss her most?—When we shall sit down to a meal together and she will not be there to say Grace. From the first I have loved those blessings. The world needs more of them.

The fourth movement of the symphony is based on Schiller's "Ode to Joy." Darling, now you are sad but let me quote some of the English translation for Mamma knew the Joy that comes from loving "the brothers of the world's all-loving Father."

> Joy, thou source of light immortal,
> Daughter of Elysium,
> Touched with fire, to the portal
> of thy radiant shrine we come.
> Thy pure magic frees all others
> Held in Custom's rigid rings;
> Men throughout the world are brothers
> In the haven of thy wings.
> Millions, myriads, rise and gather!
> Share this universal kiss!
> Brothers, in a heaven of bliss
> Smiles the world's all-loving Father.

Do the millions, His creation,
Know him and His works of love?
Seek him! In the heights above
Is His starry habitation!

From your sadness, darling, comes a lesson for me—that having known your patience and kindness toward your mother, I must strive to be more like you towards mine.

Know that I am near you in spirit and that my love flows toward you with the strength and depth of the sea around us.

I love you truly,
Dorothy

Darling [Dorothy],

This is not the letter I want to write, and shall write soon, but after devoting the afternoon to other correspondence I find I can't pass up the last chance to have a place in your mailbox Saturday.

Your wonderful letters yesterday comforted me as much as anything but your actual presence could have done. And another sweet note today. They have all been most precious to me.

After a grey day the skies have cleared somewhat, but now I see a fog stealing up from our stream and woods. There was much fog yesterday, plus rain that was sometimes heavy.

During that last agonizing night, I sat most of the time by the bed with my hand slipped under the border of the oxygen tent, holding Mamma's. Of course I didn't feel she knew, and occasionally I slipped away into the dark living room, to look out of the picture window at the trees and the sky. Sometime between 5:30 and 6:00 I did so. Orion stood in all his glory just above the horizon of our woods, and several other stars blazed more highly than I can remember ever seeing them. Then I went back into the room and at 6:05 she slipped away, her hand in mine. I told Roger about the stars just before Grandma left us, and he said, "Maybe they were the lights of the angels, coming to take her to heaven."

Darling, I shall call you Sunday, as near our usual eleven A.M. hour as possible.

All my love,
Rachel

My darling [Dorothy],

There is so much I want to say to you—that can be said to no one else! Most of it I shall save until we are together. I hope it will not be too hard for you, but I know it will help me to pour out to you some of the recent agony, with your arms around me.

This, however, I want to say now. We have talked, especially when you were here in October, about regrets. Now it is too late for me, but it is not for you. Although I have told myself for a long time that surely there were not many months or years left, I seem not really to have believed it. If only I could really have understood that time was running out—that there were just so many months, or weeks, or days, in which to be kind and tender and understanding! This may sound dreadful to say, but if only I could have realized, through a comparable loss by someone close to me, I would have been different in those last weeks. This, darling, is the opportunity you now have.

What I have learned is that one never regrets the kind words, the acts of understanding and consideration, the putting aside of one's own wishes or needs for the sake of another. These are indeed the treasures we may store up for our earthly heaven. It is the other sort of thing that rises, when it is too late, to haunt us.

These are hard days, and hard nights disturbed by dreams of death— even those long gone live again in my dreams to die again. I don't know whether it is good or bad for me that I must put on a cheerful face for Roger's sake.

Darling, I am sure we can be happy much of the time you are here. But you will forgive me, I know, if I pour out some of the agony to you, who alone can really comfort me.

All my love, dearest—
Rachel

CHRISTMAS

My darling [Dorothy],

As you know, this is the saddest Christmas I have ever known, yet I can't let the season pass completely without at least a token observance of the lovely custom you began on our first Christmas. This will not reach you for reading on Christmas Eve, I know, but perhaps there will be a quiet moment alone some-time soon.

The only thing I really want to tell you is something that seems impossible to convey—how much you mean to me, how dear to me you are. I doubt you can ever fully know, my darling. Indeed, though I've thought I knew all these years, I have gained so much deeper an understanding of it these recent weeks that my earlier comprehension seems "dim" indeed. What I'd have done with-out your sustaining love, my dearest, I have no idea. Even though nearly 500 miles separate us, except for such an occasional lovely interval as the recent one,[29] yet you are always near me, and my heart is warmed by the knowledge of your love, and of the fact that you really care.

I tried to express something of this Sunday on the phone, when I said "How wonderful to have someone who cares enough to come all the way from Boston to be with me." That is a symbol of it, of course, but it goes far deeper. It is the constant, day by day, hour by hour caring that counts—my knowledge that whatever happens matters to you.

[29] DF had visited RC from December 14 to 17.

The "others," of course, so soon forget and drift back into their own concerns.

For all this, darling, there is no way to thank you except perhaps to say that I hope I can always be to you, whenever you especially need my love and understanding, what you have been to me.

The thought of summer with you at Southport is a lovely one.

And for you, darling, I do so hope 1959 will bring a happy and satisfying start on a new life, with Stan restored to better health and all your hopes realized.

Now, darling, do you know how much it means when I say "I love you"?

Rachel

SATURDAY, JANUARY 10

My darling [Dorothy],

I feel so helpless! If only I could put my arms around you and let you pour out all the agonizing doubts and fears that must beset you, I'm sure it would help us both. In whatever help it is, know that I am living all this with you.[1] It seems to me that for an endless time (though actually for only a few weeks) my preoccupation has been with the incomprehensible mysteries of life and death, and now my personal grief seems to have merged with and flowed into your own fiery trial, torn between hope and despair.

If one is to be honest, there is no disguising the stark facts you must face, whether Stan leaves the hospital or not, and I doubt it is kindness to you to say "all will be well." But darling, as I did say before, it is quite possible that after this difficult period, the new medicines may bring about a condition by which you may have Stan with you for years to come. Provided his pain can be controlled, I'm sure both of you could find happiness in that. After all, life can be adjusted so that there are few tasks requiring physical strength, and for these hired help can be found.

And now your Thursday note is here, with its enclosed poem. It is always so good to find something from you in the mail, but darling, I don't want you to feel any compulsion, in these difficult days, to write. I know you *want* to, and that is enough.

[1] A heart attack had sent Stanley to the hospital shortly after his January 1 retirement.

[2] A handyman.

Mary is here but Elliott[2] failed to come—I don't know why. Roger's new bed is supposed to come today and I have planned for Elliott to take this one down, so that is a complication. However, until Roger's new bookcase headboard is ready, things can stay as they are.

Darling, there is so much we might *talk* about, and even a 30-minute telephone conversation is no substitute. How I wish I could come to you! You know, I hope. Now I think I shall try for a nap in preparation for the evening. I'll mail this on my way.

5 P.M.

And I had a nap, and now it is time to start Roger's supper (I made life simple with a TV turkey dinner, which he loves) and get dressed. It is bitterly cold and windy so I am wondering what to wear to be comfortable. The windows are making quite a difference in the house—wish I had done this last year.

Darling, we shall talk before you read this. I do so hope you can have had some reassurance.

My dearest love, always—
Rachel

MONDAY, JANUARY 12

My darling [Dorothy],

This is a bright, sunny day, and at last the wind is still. I meant to ask you last night whether you had seen the young moon, but the question slipped my mind. And according to the paper there was a good chance of a display of northern lights, following the sunspots. I looked several times during the evening, but our neighbors across the street had their blinding outside lights on, so I could easily have missed an auroral display, if there was one.

[3] By Lois Crisler, published in 1958 and about the experiences of Lois and Herb "Cris" Crisler in raising Alaskan wolf pups. RC and Lois became friends and correspondents.

Darling, I have thought ever since I knew the book that you and Stan should have a copy of *Arctic Wild*.[3] Now I think I shall send mine to Stan in the hospital, but it is yours and his to keep—I'll get another. I'll do it that way because anything else would take time. I gather Stan can read some, or perhaps as his convalescence lengthens out you will spend some of your hospital visiting time reading to him. Poor dear—the hours must drag for him, and if I've understood you correctly, they don't use sedatives much.

Elizabeth Lawrence writes of the Crislers: "Lois and Cris are exactly the people you would expect and hope them to be. She is more beautiful than the photographs indicate—her eyes perhaps are a difficult color. Not large or small, but with a kind of magnificence about her. Cris is rather small and very compact—simple and direct and friendly.—Lois's new book, *Gift of the Wilder-*

[4] Unpublished.

ness,[4] is the story of her meeting with Cris and the world he opened up to her in the Olympic Mountains, Alaska, Florida, Colorado." I must answer her wonderful letter soon—Lois Crisler's, I mean.

I do like the Harper people very much. As I may have said, Mr. Canfield—though by no means ancient—fits my ideal picture of the old-fashioned editor or publisher, a man of immense integrity, with good taste and good judgement, highly intelligent, courteous, urbane. As everyone says, he *is* Harper's, and when he says something one does not have to wonder whether a higher-up will reverse him. So I find myself drawn to them strongly, and am more or less inclined to commit the "Help Your Child to Wonder"[5] derivative to them, at least in my private thinking, though Marie may consider it better to appear to make no decision yet. Then there is the sea anthology they've suggested, besides Dr. Anshen's book. There is no pressure from him on any of these. Did I tell you Marie will be down this week-end, provided neither of us develops a contagious malady in the meantime?

I may devote tomorrow to library work. Wednesday morning I see Dr. Alfaro about my aching face, and then have my hair done as an antidote.

Virginia saw Dr. Healy Saturday about her back, which had improved scarcely at all in the week since her fall. He thinks it is a sacroiliac sprain, but will report on X-rays today.

Robert and Vera have been busy house hunting—were excited yesterday at the thought they had found It at last. Decision is to be final in a day or so. It would be miles out toward Frederick—probably 25 miles from Washington, which seems an awful drive to be committed to but I suppose no more than Stan had. It is almost new and they are pleased with many features of it.

Now darling, I have chattered on about many things of little relative importance, but if the skies are not too dark when you receive it, you may like that kind of letter for a change.

It was lovely to have you open your heart last night and tell me something so poignantly beautiful. Your need for just such a talk with Stan had been so much in my mind since our previous conversation, and I hoped I had not dissuaded you by what I said that night. How wonderful that it came about as it did, at Stan's own initiative. As you say, it will last for all time—for whatever time you have him with you, and for beyond. I may not have been very satisfying in my response last night, darling. It opened up such recent anguish in my own heart that I could not trust myself to say much, but I hoped you understood.

Perhaps you will have this before we talk again, but perhaps not as the mails go now. I hope so, for I mailed nothing yesterday.

Darling, how earnestly I do hope that from now on the convalescence may be uninterrupted by more setbacks and that you may both look forward to quiet and peace by your own fireside soon.

All love, dear one, as ever and forever—

Rachel

[5] RC's July 1956 *Woman's Home Companion* piece that was later published as *The Sense of Wonder* (1965).

My dearest one [Dorothy]:

There is nothing that really needs to be said, I'm sure. I should be sad if I thought you really needed to be told again that the message of the "Hyacinth Letter" is as true as when it was written; or if I thought you really needed the tangible reminder that the flowers themselves will provide. But this year I especially wanted to send them—a year that has held such anguish for both of us, a year when we have needed each other as never before. In all my sorrow, dear one, the knowledge of your love and devotion has sustained me as nothing else could. And I like to think this has been true for you, too.

So put the flowers where you can see them often, dear one, and let them tell you how much I love you, and how your love provides "food for my soul"—as it has ever since those first magical days when I came to know you.

I do trust the florists have carried out their mission acceptably. I stressed that there could be no substitution—that if no white hyacinths were available they must wait until they were. So I don't know when you will receive them.

Darling, you know that I could not even think of life without your love and all you mean to me.

Rachel

Darling [Dorothy]—

I may have an errand near the Post Office this morning and will write this note to mail then. Probably I'll write more tomorrow while having my permanent but I do want to say now how my heart aches for you in the hard decisions and plans you are having to make. I felt yesterday that you have thought I would be critical (at least silently so) of the nursing home.[6] You do know now that I don't feel that way, don't you?

There is no comparison to be made with any situation I ever faced, darling. Mamma never had a really prolonged illness. And most important, there was never the need to consider the strain on anyone but myself. That, I know, is what makes your problem so acute, and really, darling, the decision you seem about to make seems the only sensible and right one. I just do so hope the place will prove so satisfactory in every way that you won't have a moment's worry on that score.

I wish you'd tell me more about your plans for the actual trip, darling. I do think you must have *very* competent help with you—can't you take a nurse?

You may remember that the year Mamma fell and I was wondering how I'd get her home, Curtis Bok wanted to provide a "Cabulance." All I know of that is that it's more like a limousine than an ambulance and costs somewhat less. Or have you thought of renting some kind of car that would allow your mother almost to lie down?

6 DF's mother had had a stroke which prompted a decision to place her in a nursing home.

Well—I'll write more tomorrow, dear, It's hard to believe you may be in Maine so soon—and "me too"!

Yesterday when I returned from taking Roger to Bill's house a whole family of killdeers was on the lawn—father and mother and 2 of the cutest babies! One adult put on a "broken wing act" on seeing Capt. Hook coming to meet me.

Dearest love—you know
Rachel

FRIDAY NIGHT, OCTOBER 2[7]

Darling [Dorothy],

I'm weary but must say a few words before I go to bed, for Saturday is a "rat race" and I can't count on time for writing. This will probably be my last gardening week-end, and I'm hoping we can dispose of the rest of the bulbs.

It was a sweet surprise to hear your voice, dear. I wondered later why I didn't take the extra minute required to shift to my bedroom, for though news was on I didn't feel *quite* as free as I like to, especially toward the end, when news was off! I know you understood!

I hope your day (today) hasn't been too tiring, and that you have found Stan no worse for his trip to Augusta. No wonder you are anxious for his retirement, darling—I just do hope it works out without disappointment.

All this sudden crossing of our paths with Olga and Mrs. Rich[8] is really odd—something like the ecological networks I love to trace! Of course I'm returning both halves of the start of your new correspondence (do you have a spare file drawer?) for you will certainly want yours. I don't see how she could be other than delighted to accept your invitation! Are you going to tell her about your book? If so, darling, I sincerely hope she will be able to find those right words of encouragement that I have somehow never achieved.

Was it in answer to your suggestion of suspending letter writing that I wrote the hyacinth letter? It seemed to me that followed one of your often repeated "Whys"—but you have the letter so you ought to know! Well, darling, I didn't propose anything so drastic as *no* letters, and my suggestion still stands. I have believed for quite a long time that you felt you might get down to something if you could salvage part of that letter-writing time. And I'd like to do something to help! (Only you must promise not to turn nouns into verbs or I won't do without a single letter!)

Heavens, darling, you startle me. I thought your diary was quite terse and objective. What can you have written in it (for posterity to read) about Us that can have brought up these regrets? Please get busy with ink eradicator! And *please* try to eradicate those memories from the pages of your heart, dear one. I think all such unhappiness is far better forgotten. I forget easily, until you remind me and then I have to forget again! Please, darling, for your sake and mine, remember only the happy things!

[7] DF wrote several long descriptive letters from Southport in September and early October 1959, which are preserved. This is the first RC letter preserved following her May 18, 1959, letter.

[8] RC perhaps refers to Olga Owens Huckins and Louise Dickinson Rich who both lived in Massachusetts.

Do you know the book of photographs called *The Big Book of Cats and Kittens*? It is not new—though I believe this is an enlarged edition. I couldn't resist it when I saw it in Brentano's. Often I don't like books of cat pictures but every one of these is so precious, or so laughable. I was thinking you might like to consider it sometime for the Littles, or for Stan (and you).

Speaking of books—it was a coincidence that just after returning the proofs of the book about the Kalahari Desert,[9] I should see an ad for a new book by Laurens van der Post—*The Lost World of the Kalahari*! I got it at once, but have taken little time for reading it. I doubt it is up to *Venture to the Interior*—and perhaps does not portray the place as satisfyingly as Mrs. Thomas does.

My intention is to send the book for Martha and Richard as an *un*-Christmas present. Since I practically ignored Christmas last year. I'm sure I sent them nothing, and, like you, think I will generally keep things on a simplified basis. I now have my supply so will get a few into the mail when I can get them wrapped!

Now to bed, darling. Probably I'll add to this before mailing. But remember how I love you!

Rachel

Now Saturday, end of afternoon, and I'm dog-tired. But I have an errand in Four Corners so will mail this. Tuesday, I fear, may not be a mail day.

But today was, and it brought your sweet note. Brief as it was, darling, it brought a glow to the day. That is the sort that goes under my pillow, to bring you to me in the quiet hours.

I love you dearly, and I need you! You know that, don't you?

There are good developments on the book—some wonderful letters, and very influential people getting aroused through hearing of my project. I feel, darling, that this may well outweigh in importance everything else I have done. I hope that can make you glad I'm doing it—as I am.

My dear love
Rachel

OCTOBER 3

Hello, darling [Dorothy]—

I love you so very, very much. There is so much in your recent letters that has revived lovely memories—things I want to talk about, but have not yet found time for. You do understand, I hope! When I am forced to brief and cryptic notes, it's not because I want it that way. And I love every word from you, whether your letter be one page or "a volume."

When I see you, may I read the "hyacinth letter"? Do you remember that, after receiving it, you telephoned me? And I remember that, with characteristic obtuseness, I had assumed you already knew everything I said in it, and was somewhat surprised that it moved you so deeply!

Your "very precious" enclosure,[10] now returned, puzzled me, too, as to its dating, but now I think I know. I'll tell you when I see you.

Probably I'll take my courage in both hands next week and ask Ida about staying while I go to Boston. As I told you the other night, I have held off somewhat in the hope of seeing Prof. Williams. Perhaps I'll write again and try to get something out of him.

Now I think I'll take this to box, darling, and hope to find moments to share with you tomorrow.

I love you
Rachel

[10] Enclosure not preserved.

SUNDAY NOON, OCTOBER 4

ON PORCH

Darling [Dorothy],

I think this is the last of my "apple stationery," but not, of course, the last of the apples.[11] Your long letter yesterday, mostly written under the spruce, brought me a great deal of happiness, because it brought you very close. Of course I loved your sudden, almost un-understood impulse to go tide pooling, and most of all the heart-stopping sight of the flight of wild fowl just above the spruces. Don't ever dream I wondered at your tears. I've had the same response too often—perhaps always when alone. (I suppose there is a certain inhibition in the presence of anyone else—or almost anyone!) The experience I relate in *Under the Sea-Wind* about the young mullet pouring through that tide race to the sea is one that comes to mind. Of course I guess I didn't tell it as a personal experience, but it was—I stood knee-deep in that racing water and at times could scarcely see those darting, silver bits of life for my tears. So I do know. Of course you knew I would.

I am so happy for you to have this interval, short as it is, alone with all the wonder and loveliness. There can't be the same feeling in the season of "invasions."

According to Paul Reimers,[12] a flight of geese went over here Friday evening. Unfortunately, I'd been very tired and had flopped on my bed after dinner and had a nap—so I missed them. That sight always seems so stirring to everyone. (Wait till you see the bit from the *Times Book Review* I'm sending you.)

And the other—a reminder it is never too late to become a writer! Am glad to know Alice has now taken up the cause—I'll leave it to her and perhaps she will succeed where I couldn't. At any rate, I am saving some of your lovely accounts of these fall days—if you could reassemble all such from your correspondents perhaps you'd have a book in spite of yourself.

Your recent reports on Stan had been so encouraging until this last. I do hope the change you noticed was only transient.

[11] RC and DF had begun to use the term "apple" to refer to a private letter from one to the other enclosed in an envelope along with another letter to be shared with family.

[12] A Silver Spring neighbor of RC.

Heavens, how time melts away! When do you now plan to leave, darling? I know not till after the 12th, but I'm vague about the projected schedule. I remember last June you wished I might have a magic carpet to transport a vast company (including, I remember, Dr. Alfaro and Ida); now I wish the same for you, so that the entire migration might be accomplished at one time. Poor dear—my heart aches for you! . . . [13]

[Love, *Rachel*]

OCTOBER 13, 10 A.M.

My Darling [Rachel],

This is a rare occasion. I am absolutely *alone* on the Head. The Dexters[14] have gone for the day; Stan is off to B. Bay for a haircut, which gives me this hour alone, and how better to spend it than with you! Oh, dearest, so much I should like to share with you of these last days, but I shall have to limit myself to what can be contained within this hour for there is the refrigerator yet to be done, dinner to get, a trip to see my mother,[15] attempt to line up men to lift her into car on the 20th. But actually the worst is over as far as work goes. Oh, I could still clean putty & paint off panes of reset glass. I had planned to wash couch covers, pillow tops, etc., but weather didn't cooperate so they will wait until spring.

I did get a letter off to Lois last night. If I can remember I shall enclose hers—do you know about the grant of $1,000—the source I mean?

But first to answer yours of yesterday.

Thank you for writing as much about the work as you did. It helps to bring you closer when I know some of the way your hours are filled. When I go home from here leaving all the loveliness you and I share, and about which I know I understand when I write, I am fearful I shall feel very far away from you. West Bridgewater really means very little to you for you scarcely know it. Darling, your work sounds so enthralling and I marvel at your ability to absorb information in so many fields—absorb it, to digest it and give it back to the "Young," shall we say. A crazy metaphor but somewhat like the Mother Gull with her cheese sandwich! Please laugh, dear. And I can well believe that all you are discovering in medicine, chemistry, physiology, biology, and piecing together may be exactly like one big Detective Story. No wonder you are excited. You didn't mention being exhausted in this letter but I'm sure you must have days of weariness to the point of aching.

Please be kind to yourself—if you know how. Mrs. Davis II,[16] I'm sure, is a treasure.

Yes, I thought of dear Mamma in the investigation of the Quiz programs.[17] I remember how aghast and almost insulted she was when I questioned the complete authenticity of the workings of it. Hank's name has been in the paper but thus far I haven't seen Elfrieda's. Poor Charles V.D.—even if he was all above board himself the publicity and spotlight can't help him.

I do hope my under-drier note reached you. If not perhaps you haven't received my thanks for our lovely anniversary card (yes, 35th). It was such a beautiful one, wasn't it? When I showed the collection to mother, before knowing it was yours, she picked it out from the bunch to hold up to call my attention to what a lovely one it was. I loved the blank spaces that surrounded your answer on my questionnaire about the Book!! More telling than words.

New plantings sound interesting—surely will look like an Estate by next spring.

I shall write for details of Atlantic Contest—ahem! And of course, Maria Dermont is an inspiration—think I'd enjoy her book, wouldn't you?

Arrangements for mother all set except to get 2 men lined up to-day, definitely. Have some leads.

Now to Life here in the past few days. I've got a long list, but most of it I shall touch lightly.

We got the wood under kitchen shelf down to a minimum so decided to give it thorough cleaning before bringing in more wood. Way in back, on the floor was a large, soft, fluffy nest (with no inhabitants) made of pink drapery materials shredded to a fuss. That mystery is solved.

The day Martha & I walked in the woods in the rain a hermit thrush sat on a tree flicking his tail at us. At Engelbrekt's Mon. I was called to identify a bird—it was a catbird eating berries on a shrub close to house, but he was so fat no one believed it could be. But—more important while I was looking, a hermit thrush stood for quite a while on a summer bench on the lawn.

At Bennetts' there is the most fantastic display of fungii I ever saw. Stan has tried for pictures which I hope can show better than I can tell. Not only quality but *quantity*.

We had planned to take pictures of children at tree, at stump, etc., but rain spoiled all that. We did take some flashlights in doors of family group as mementoes of 35th. One we all hope comes out well, for Willow who was sitting on a green pillow on my lap gave a great yawn just as it was snapped. We had disturbed his nap. Yesterday he crawled into Stan's suitcase as might be expected.

I have had proof that he knows me just to look at me and not just my voice. The other day I was out on the Head. He did not go with me. As I started back he was in the path almost over to Flat Rock beach. I just stood still. When he saw me he made his almost inaudible cry & came walking toward me. I'm sure he would have run from a stranger.

The foliage has been so slow & remembering that glorious year when you & I took pictures at Campbell's Pond, quite disappointing. There is practically no color there yet. The River Road is gorgeous now, but actually the roads on Southport are about as lovely as one can find. Yesterday A.M. for our Coffee Break we went up near Wings' (sold, incidentally) & just sat in the sun looking back the slope at the flaming maples. One has the greatest variety of color I ever saw on one tree. Willow liked the sight, too.

Conants have now bought the Wellses' property which joins theirs going toward B. Bay—30 acres along the shore down Love's Cove! and an old house. Winslows delighted because they look directly at it.

Sat. was an *Argo* Foliage trip. Eliot[18] invited us as his guests, and although she had told Eliot she wouldn't go, I prevailed on Mrs. Winslow to go. It was the ideal day—so clear and warm enough to be completely comfortable. Crossed the Sheepscot via the Cuckolds & then up the Kennebec, close to the new destroyers at Bath & down Sasanoa. We sat in front row in bow! It was simply lovely and I think now perhaps going *up* the Kennebec is more appealing than down. It is quite amazing how the passage is closed in at certain points. We must do it next year. Hell's Gate was in full action—deep, deep whirlpools—at times boat stood almost still.

Mahards joined us so we heard some of their trip. She was the most animated I have ever heard her—very enthusiastic about trip & full of anecdotes.

That night & the next day Stan didn't seem so well—didn't say much—rested & retired within himself so I was discouraged again. But yesterday he snapped out of it & did as much work about closing up as he ever did—oh, not so strenuously.

Dale & Norman Gaudette came at 3:30 & carried everything up to car, brought in wood, etc.! Stan packed car & we were all relieved when that was done. So actually the hard part is over. Food is coming out about even, which I like.[19]

Now I think I'll clean that refrig. & save the best (I think it is) till last—maybe this evening, for I've used more than my hour.

EVENING

Everything well under control at 7:30. Now for another hour with you and then to bed. We have had two days of small craft warning winds—over 30 miles an hour, they say. Naturally we could feel it indoors but we kept warm. But I wore a kerchief to bed—too much motion around my head. And what a blessing electric blankets are. I can remember other Falls when, no matter how much clothing I wore to bed, I could not keep warm.

There is a spot on the short cut I wish you might have seen these past weeks. Everywhere the lovely lavender asters have been profuse—the Head had a bountiful supply mingled with the goldenrod. I'm sure you remember the shrub with the white berries—snowberries some people call them—we found them on Barter's Island. The spot to which I refer was a mass of the lavender asters combined with the snowberry—wild, but no landscape architect could have contrived anything lovelier.

Mr. Maurice Sherman came over one late afternoon to talk remodeling again. He crawled under the house to determine condition of underpinnings & as far as he could get and see things are in a fairly good state. Now we have another plan which will give us "quite a house"—it involves a room upstairs over

[18] Eliot Winslow, owner and captain of the *Argo*, a cruise boat sailing from Boothbay Harbor on day tours of the area's island.

[19] DF probably refers to the amount of food left in the cottage for meals compared to the number of days remaining before departure.

the new part to the living room. We shall see, but it's all fun anyway. In that way we could have a study downstairs—a place to write or "paint"—where we wouldn't have to pick up. Wish it could be done this winter but I don't want to rush into it, until I get the property all in my name.[20]

Sat. eve when I was feeling a little low because of Stan I spent almost an hour on the Head in the moonlight. It never did touch the Bay, just the edges of the shore—the water was rough. But it was lovely & all I needed was you.

Did I tell you that when the children were here, we all stood on the porch in the darkness, calling attention to "no lights on Mac's," shutters on the houses, only the sound of water. Richie said "I wove [love] this peace and quiet."

And so do I—I think I know now that the reason I long to stay here, that my heart is here, is because I'm so close to elemental things. Here the outdoors is my home. In W.B. my home is a house.

Yesterday I walked in the woods alone. After the heavy rain all was wet, and sodden. The reindeer moss never looked more like snow. But the sun was filtered through the spruces and gave no warmth. The only life I saw was a red squirrel, and a chick-a-dee upside down on the tip of a pine branch gleaning something desirable, I suppose.

And so I was glad to get out to Deep Cove to the warmth of the road, gay with maple colors.

And I was aware that I have had more than my share this year and perhaps I would not be happy to watch the loveliness fade and drabness take over. I really knew the woods could hold me little longer.

And I suppose home will look good.

Now, darling, I'm off to bed. Somehow I feel as though I'm leaving you behind—all this I love belongs to Us and without it I shall miss you even more.

Good-night, dear one. Remember the next week will not give me many moments for writing—I'm sure you understand. The rest[21] is my farewell-from-Southport gift to you.

I love you,
Dorothy

SATURDAY NIGHT, OCTOBER 17, 10:30

Darling [Dorothy],

Now at last the moment of luxury I've been waiting for and looking forward to ever since your long letter—the last-from-Maine-came yesterday. (Now I also have the card and the first-from-W.B.) The meeting and my talk[22] are over and I'm tucked in bed, weary but wanting a few moments with you before I give way to sleep. For I *am* tired! Of course I ended by putting a good deal of time into organizing copies for my talk, and have been burning the candle quite late all week! Tomorrow I'll relax.

Darling, all of your letter was a joy, but your account of the morning (and evening) flights of geese quite took my breath. You really made me feel I was

[20] DF had begun investigating whether cousins shared title to the Freemans' Southport cottage.

[21] An enclosure, not preserved, describing flights of geese. RC's October 17, 1959, letter makes clear the subject of the enclosure.

[22] To the Audubon Society of the District of Columbia.

there. (Did you make a carbon for yourself? If not, I'll certainly have to return this for your Book—much as I'll want to keep it.)

Somewhere in my own little notebooks there is a record of those morning waterfowl flights as I observed them several years ago—Fall of '56, it must have been. But my observations were from the house and more "remote" than yours, out in the open with the birds overhead. But the sight made a strong impression, nonetheless. It was the year Mamma had fallen in the kitchen, and in the remaining weeks our nights were pretty broken. Often when I had been up with her early in the morning, I'd just settle down at the picture window instead of going back to bed. What impressed me so was the reverse pattern of flights in gulls and waterfowl. The gulls toward the open sea at sunset, but upstream in the morning—the ducks and geese just the reverse. Of course I imagine that the evening flights of waterfowl are always new migrants from the north, and that those seen heading down the bay in the morning are resuming the southward journey.

Sometime, somehow, I hope I can take you to Lake Mattamuskeet in North Carolina. That experience was something I'll never forget—the countless thousands of Canada geese wintering there. During the evening and—I seem to remember—even far into the night, the throbbing chorus of their voices rose from the lake where they were resting. But the greatest thrill came when we went out just before sunrise to watch the flocks rising up and heading out into the neighboring fields where they forage by day. They would pass literally just over our heads—so low the sunshine made their dark heads and necks look like brown velvet. And all the while the air filled with their music.

Now I'd give a lot just to have one small V of them pass over here!

My eyes are getting too heavy—I'll tell you about the speech and comment more on your letter tomorrow.

SUNDAY

Another day, and I turn to the typewriter for speed. There is so much to say, and if I mail this today it will perhaps be waiting when you return Tuesday from your difficult pilgrimage.

About yesterday: I felt rather as though I were a professor lecturing to an extraordinarily attentive and diligent class. I was surprised to discover they were all equipped with pencil and paper, and from the moment I began, throughout the 30 or 40 minutes I talked, they all scribbled away for dear life, taking notes. (Or so I assumed—could they have been writing letters home???) By the way, I loved your simile of the Mother Gull—in fact, I laughed aloud when I read it, and irreverently thought of it yesterday. Perhaps a subtitle of *Man Against the Earth*[23] might be "What the Mother Gull Brought Up."

Quite a delegation from Florida was present—Russ Mason, formerly Executive Sec. of Mass. Audubon, Mr. and Mrs. John Storer, who have now retired to Florida (he is author of *The Web of Life*, and quite well known in conservation

[23] This was RC's working title for the book that became *Silent Spring*.

circles) and one or two others who proved interesting for one reason or another. Charles Mohr of the Phila. Academy of Natural Sciences was there, and later my companion at dinner. Well, I can't begin to name everyone. After the meeting at the Brookings Institution in downtown Washington, we all went out to the home of one of our members, to be entertained at what I thought was to be a buffet supper. Instead, we all were seated at tables in her really palatial home—some 35 or 40 of us, I guess—and were served a delicious turkey dinner—roast turkey with dressing and gravy, sweet potatoes, peas, tiny onions, cranberry, celery and carrot sticks, ice cream, cookies, after dinner coffee and mints. Before this there was a "cocktail hour" in the library with an open fire, but so far as I observed, an excellent sherry was the only alcoholic drink offered. (Guess what I had?) Her grounds are truly park-like, and I shall want to go back sometime when there is plenty of daylight to observe them. There are huge magnolias as high as the house, lovely hedges of Chinese holly, and an exquisite border of some diminutive holly—the kind with spiny leaves—around the patio. Mrs. Lee asked me to come upstairs to autograph her copy of *The Sea*, and a copy of the young people's edition for her cook, who was brought forth, all atwitter, to meet an honest-to-goodness author. Ellen, the cook, is quite an exceptional person, according to Mrs. Lee—who I think lives all alone in that magnificence. She says Ellen (a young colored woman) goes out on bird walks with her around the place, and is exceptionally good at spotting birds before anyone else sees them.

Roger visited Virginia and Lee[24] while I was thus engaged, and said he had a "gorgeous time." I had just bought him a Monopoly game, and they all three played, afternoon and evening. Roger had prayed that I would make a good speech, so you know I had help.

[24] Lee King, husband of RC's niece, Virginia.

Oh—one very surprising and rather amusing angle—the President of the Michigan Audubon Society, as it turned out, was sort of Dr. Jeckle and Mr. Hyde. All unknown to anyone there, he proved to be an employee of the Dow Chemical Co. Of course, as soon as I had finished, he rose to his feet to challenge me. However, I think that I was able to take care of him, with some very able help from Mr. Barnes.

You thought you detected an exhilaration in my voice the other night, which you attributed—and rightly, I'm sure—to my happiness in the progress of The Book. The other day someone asked Leonard Bernstein about his inexhaustible energy and he said "I have no more energy than anyone who loves what he is doing." Well, I'm afraid mine has to be recharged at times, but anyway I do seem just now to be riding the crest of a wave of enthusiasm and creativity, and although I'm going to bed late and often rising in very dim light to get in an hour of thinking and organizing before the household stirs, my weariness seems easily banished. For example, I was terribly tired last night, but after 8 hours abed I was completely refreshed.

[25] Enclosure not preserved.

[26] Beverly Knecht, a young correspondent of RC, who was blind.

Dear, please don't read the enclosed clipping[25] until some moment when you can give it your full attention. I was so deeply impressed by it that I bought extra copies of the paper for you and Lois, and I want to read it to Beverly[26] on tape. It is not only his thought but his exquisite way of expressing it. I have often realized that this must be an extraordinary man, and someday I hope to meet him—though quite possibly that might spoil my impression. Didn't I send you something he wrote about *The Wind in the Willows*? And at other times he has referred to *Alice in Wonderland* and other things I love, in a way that shows me that he not only has a very keen analytic mind that contributes to his ability as a commentator on public affairs, but a wonderful sensitivity.

I also have numerous clippings on Bernstein to send you soon. Don't return them.

I loved your story about solving the mystery of the pink drapery material. This should go in Your Book. And also that precious remark of Richie—the Wover of Peace and Quiet. He is a very remarkable little boy. Won't it be interesting to watch his personality unfold?

Now I must stop, dear. Roger and I will put this in the mail this afternoon. I'd like it to be there to welcome you home. Of course I do so hope all went well, and that you can feel at least reasonably happy about the new surroundings for your mother.

> All my love—and more before long,
> *Rachel*

THURSDAY A.M., OCTOBER 22

Dearest [Dorothy],

Just a word now, but will enclose some Nature Notes.

Last night I went over your letters since we returned, and am going to return to you soon all the accounts of nature-in-Maine. I *hate* to let them go—but I have good reasons for doing so. Will you *please* make a project, soon, of typing up all those portions of the letters? I think you'll be surprised to discover you already have the nucleus of "Something." Had a wild idea of having this typing done—feeling you'd be the more aware of the quality of all this if you unexpectedly saw it all typed—but Mrs. D.[27] is just too rushed.

[27] Jeanne Davis.

By the way, you asked me once if I'd "mind" if you wrote the Teales and sometime went to see them. Darling, how could you suppose I would? On the contrary it would please me very much.

Somehow it seems good to have you home again. Partly, I guess, because I've been dreading this transition for you, and am so relieved it has been accomplished.

It was wonderful to have you call Tuesday night. Thank you again.

Till Sunday—and my dearest love.

> *Rachel*

I'm on the porch—again, for there has been a long interruption and it's the end of a hot afternoon—and have just heard a great fluttering and flapping—a starling having a good bath. We have a fair *variety* of birds but few in number. However, I seem to remember it was so last year until later in the fall.

There has been no recurrence of the pain that caused last week-end to be a "lost" one. Mostly, I feel fairly good but I do realize that after several days of concentrated work on the book I'm suddenly no good at all for several more. Some people assume only physical work is tiring—I guess because they use their minds little! Friday night (when I missed the geese) my exhaustion invaded every cell of my body, I think, and really kept me from sleeping well all night.

I spent Thursday at the N.I.H.[28] library and got some wonderful material—some of it just published. In something so live as this subject, I just can't shut off the research—ever.

Must get us something to eat, I guess—though I seem to loathe the thought of food, especially when I have to prepare it! Will save space for a good-night word.

Was the moon still in your sky at 7:30 tonight? I went out then to change the sprinkler and saw it just above the line of trees in the west. Thought of it over the Bay—then tried to think whether at that moment you could still see it. Somehow it seemed to make our separation official, for it was a different moon—one we hadn't seen together.

Now I must go.

Love—always you know—
Rachel

Nature Notes

Yesterday morning—Wednesday October 21, I discovered there had been a perfect eruption of white throats into the area. During the night the wind had shifted around to ENE and maybe that had something to do with it. Anyway, as I looked out of the study window toward the group of pines, I saw that the grass was fairly bubbling with white throats—scores and scores of them all moving about purposefully, intent on gleaning seeds from the lawn. So when I had sent Roger on his way I took the bird glasses and went out for the half hour until Ida came—just on my own place. There were a good many chickadees, titmice, and downies—hardly enough to suggest any such wave of migration as the white throats, but many more than we've been having. But I had one very special reward for going out. A movement in the big pine by the corner of the porch caught my eye—a golden crowned kinglet! First I've seen in years. It must have been a female, for the crown was very golden; Peterson says the male's is orange.

There were a few sparrows I wasn't sure of—grasshopper, perhaps.

Their breasts were the softest, warmest buff imaginable, but I didn't see their backs well enough to be sure.

After an early morning filled with sunshine the day turned gray and rather bleak, with a sharp wind. In late afternoon, from the study, I could see countless birds pitching down from the sky into my wild corner. While trying to spot some of them from the window, for identification, again I saw the kinglet, her crown visible across the length of the lawn, for she was in a pine down by Apple Grove Road.

Then I saw the scores of feeding white throats again, this time in the front lawn. I wondered if they had been sleeping all day and were getting ready to continue south. This morning I haven't seen them. And I thought about White Throat Village, no doubt closed for the winter now, and couldn't help wondering if I might have entertained some of yesterday's guests before.

Ann Morgan's *Field Book of Animals in Winter* says meadow mice remain active even in winter—have burrows under snow with tunnels to sources of food. I do wonder what became of Templeton?[29] Maybe when we said goodbye he knew there'd be no more corn muffins, and moved elsewhere.

[29] RC and DF had named a mouse after the character in E. B. White's *Charlotte's Web* (1952).

THURSDAY, NOVEMBER 19

Dearest [Dorothy],

So much I'd like to write, but I won't attempt to cover much today. Perhaps over the week-end. Of course I was tremendously interested in all you wrote of the Audubon Society meeting. I had known about it, and in fact had reasons for interest in it on the basis of my conversations here with Allan Morgan,[30] and later correspondence with him. He is the new Russ Mason, you know—though I doubt he is quite a Russ Mason. I think I shall write him now and ask for a copy of Dr. Sears's paper. Yes, I imagine—or at least I surely hope—I know most of the facts that would be presented, but it is interesting to see the emphasis and interpretations given.

[30] Executive Secretary of the Massachusetts Audubon Society. Dr. Paul B. Sears was Professor of Conservation, Yale School of Forestry.

Yesterday I attended the big Cranberry Meeting,[31] which was most interesting. Flemming[32] certainly went away up in my estimation; he handled the whole thing with such quiet dignity and courtesy, but they didn't ever put anything over on him! At the conclusion of a speaker's statement, he would gently pick up the very thing I'd been hoping he would demolish. I think he's going to stand firm. I was delighted by the support he was given from various independent organizations that had asked to be heard. And I was impressed by the fact that the tone of industry spokesmen was on the whole mild and conciliatory. I had been told privately that industry heads had been shocked when they really began to look into the situation, and their attitude yesterday bore that out. A Congressman from Oregon—whom I had expected to be full of pleas for the industry, took quite a different line. He said that, sad as this might be for the industry, it has served to point up the whole enormous problem of contamina-

[31] Congressional hearing on the United States Food and Drug Administration's ban on the sale of cranberries sprayed with aminotriazol.

[32] Arthur S. Flemming, Secretary of Health, Education and Welfare.

tion of food by pesticides and other chemicals, and called for better laws and more rigid enforcement. I was so impressed that I called his office later for a copy of the statement. You will laugh, as I did, at the response. When it became necessary to give my name for the mailing of the document, there was a sudden brief silence, then—"You frighten me—could you have written *The Sea Around Us*?" I assured her that, though I had, I was quite harmless! As you may have heard, the industry's prize exhibit was a doctor from Tufts who says he uses the chemical clinically in treatment of the thyroid and it could not be harmful. Oh dear—his testimony can be shot so full of holes as to be absolutely worthless, and the disheartening thing is that he must know this full well, if he is the great specialist they say he is. For those who might not see the holes, however, it was good that Consumer's Union had sent a man who gave the opinion of a leading cancer specialist of the U. of Chicago—exactly the opposite of the man from Tufts. And my files are full of things that refute the Tufts man!

I believe Roger Peterson[33] showed his flamingo pictures here—either that or he's going to this winter. Of course we are his "home" group. But I never have time or opportunity to go now so I'm not sure. Of course I would love to have seen the slides, too. Perhaps I should ask Mr. Morgan for a list of the photographers represented, so that when I ever get around to collecting the actual pictures for the book I can investigate them. Up to now, as you know, we have been concerned only in equivalent samples as a basis of cost estimates.

If I'm to send this with Ida, as I planned, I must stop now. It seems to me the weeks now are about 2 or 3 days long—no more, ever. I wish I could find some way to salvage the week-ends for work, but I never accomplish much then.

All love, dear, to the others and to *you*.

Rachel

[33] Roger Tory Peterson, author and illustrator of several field guides to birds.

MONDAY NIGHT [DECEMBER 7?]

Dear [Dorothy],

Yesterday's talk was such a treat—perhaps all the more because nowadays it is rare. It was all so satisfying and good. I've had a big day and am weary—not trying to work tonight. Was up until one last night preparing to get the most out of my interviews—then up early so I could be dressed and breakfasted too before Ida came, for I needed time in the library with Mrs. D. before my 10 o'clock appointment. That was *wonderful*! I had expected what I wanted to ask Dr. Weinbach would take no more than half an hour; instead I was with him more than 2 hours! He is the kind whose eyes shine with the wonder and excitement of what he is doing, and—he gave me a 2-hour seminar lecture on biological oxidations! The entire subject of energy-production through phosphorylation is something developed long after my Hopkins days—since this really basic process is disrupted by some of these chemicals, I have to bring to life for my readers what goes on inside the cell and even inside the mitochondria! (We used to see them, knew their function was "unknown," but I can't remember we even wondered. Now they're known to be the basis of practically everything!) Well, I decided after all that to skip lunch, so Mrs. D. got me a package of cheese crackers and a chocolate bar while I ran through all the volumes she had assembled and marked passages for her to copy. Then an hour with Dr. Hueper,[34] mostly picking up loose ends and clarifying, but very good! I must say I'll be glad to have a day at home, working in solitude except for Ida's ministrations, tomorrow. Dr. H. says he thinks the time now is right for the book for people are beginning to want the facts—sooner would have been premature, he thinks.

I can't remember the dates of the family's visit, though I do know your Christmas is the 19th. I do hope it can be a happy time for you, dear. You'll have fun with the children, I know.

Thought you might like Miss Worrell's 50-year reminiscences now. No hurry about returning any of this, of course.

All for now, dear. Very much love—

Rachel

Dearest [Dorothy],

The enclosed clipping[35] is a spare that was sent me, so you needn't return it. Thought you might have fun being surprised when you turn to the second page—just as I did!

Among assorted things I've been meaning to tell you is this—in the course of other reading I happened to discover that our familiar Usnea moss is the source of an antibiotic, which also has a powerful physiology effect on biological oxidations. I didn't have time to pursue the subject, but of course wondered what the commercial process is, and to what extent it's used. But I was quite fascinated.

I'll be so interested to hear what you learn about the doings of the storm at Southport. Of course our papers dealt in generalities except for Boston.

I'm glad you could go to your Round Robin[36] gathering in spite of your back. Be careful how you sneeze hereafter! I do hope you are feeling much better now.

Cass Canfield just sent me a book that looks fascinating—*No Room in the Ark* by Alan Moorehead. It's about the animals of Africa, and it's beautifully illustrated.

Oh, I promised to write for you what Carl Sandburg said to Beverly. Here it is: "Dear Beverly Knecht—Your sentences inform me that you dwell in the wide airs of the sky, the earth, the heart, and the mind. I salute you and send loving greetings. Yrs, Carl Sandburg." Isn't that lovely? She says his letters are obviously self-typed on a battered typewriter, also that he tends to use abbreviations, such as "Yrs."

How wonderful you had the kinglets so close. Is Stan taking any bird pictures this winter? I'm buying seed in 100th lots now—I can have it delivered

[34] Wilhelm C. Hueper, M.D., of the National Cancer Institute.

[35] Enclosure not preserved.

[36] Nickname for the correspondence maintained for fifty-nine years by DF and thirteen women college classmates.

from the store in Georgetown; at a great reduction at that quantity. And how they make it disappear. Do you know, I don't think we ever have the hairy woodpecker, except in the woods.

A letter from Lois, I'll send you this and earlier one soon. She tells of Cris working to enclose the garden for Wildie.[37] She built fires to thaw the ground for post holes!

[37] A wolf-dog born to one of the Crislers' Alaskan wolves.

Love to all—
Rachel

FOR CHRISTMAS

Sweet memories and friendly thoughts are like stardust scattered on a Christmas tree.

Darling [Rachel],

Another Christmas—our seventh that we have known each other.

What can I say to you that I have not already said? But it all bears repeating. Three words—I love you. And so many ways and for so many reasons. I hope you like to have me repeat.

I chose this card for the words "You alone." You alone have been nearest and dearest to me in this past difficult year. It is hard for me to approach Christmas without the sad memories of a year ago—yours and mine. But I try to "shut my mind" to them, to remember only "the happiness we've known." Darling, so much of what happiness I've been able to achieve this year with, or without you, has stemmed from my increasing awareness and delight in the natural world. To the wider opening of that door I am deeply in your debt. Seven years ago I was blind to much I now see—I see because of you.

Perhaps here is the right place to quote you a little poem I came across in my old faithful, *Star-Points*.[38]

[38] A poetry collection edited by Mrs. Waldo Richards and published in 1921. The poem quoted is by Maxwell Struthers Burt.

As We Go On

As we go on, grow older, grow more wise,
Grow friendlier with every friendly thing,
The honorable trees, grave dusk, the swing
Of upland meadows upward to the skies,
And even the old new fraudulent surprise
Of that quaint smiling paradox the spring,
How greatly beauty once again can bring
In smaller ways tears to our tenderer eyes.

We do not wait on mountains or on seas,
For there's a little lake between the hills,
That rustles with the sedges and the bees;
And great adventure found in daffodils
Stirs April gardens, when the world again
Is quick with mice and moles, crickets and men.

If only for the last line alone, I knew I had to send this to you. But there is meaning for us beyond.

What would these difficult months have been for Stan and for me without the unfolding interests we are sharing in all forms of Nature. Thank you, dear, for being our guide.

And for something very tangible I thank you, too—the many telephone calls when you let me pour out my troubles. I doubt if I can ever in words express what it meant to me to be able to talk so often, so easily and so freely to the one person in the world whom I felt understood.

It has always seemed some kind of a miracle that after over fifty years of living someone I had never known could come to hold such a unique place in my life. The first amazement is still in my heart.

Darling, when we talked last Sunday of Templeton's request to Hurry Back, I recalled that exquisite moment on December 30, 1953, when you used the same words. Remember? You had supposedly been put to rest. You called "Hurry back"—sweetest music to my ears!

Oh, My Darling—

Your lovely white lamps light my page as I write. The one over my bed is often used in the wee hours of a dark night. Each time as I turn the switch my heart says "Rachel."

And so you may know that whenever you read this, my heart has said "Rachel."

Darling—may the year ahead be kind to you in every way. I long so to have your path more smooth.

If only I could help someway!

And now Good-night, my dearest one, a blessed Christmas.

> With deep, deep love,
> *Dorothy*

TUESDAY A.M., DECEMBER 29

UNDER DRIER

Dearest [Dorothy],

Just a quick note to say Happy New Year! I daren't send it airmail, for the fog rules that out, but perhaps you'll have it Thursday, anyway. The vacation days are melting away—as all days do now—and in no time Roger will be back in school. Yesterday I spent several hours in the library with Mrs. Davis—first I've had her for about 10 days, for she suddenly became swamped in family Christmas activities. However, she's coming here tomorrow, so we can clear up some of the back log of letters, at least. Did I tell you Jeannette[39] sent me a big box of evergreens, club mosses, cones, etc.—plenty for decorations throughout the house? Also a box of such cunning, cute Christmas cookies. And from the Fleischmanns a perfectly beautiful scarf that reminds me of the favorite one I lost—the one I wore when I made my December trip to Boston. Remember it? Light background—flowers in very soft colors. I learned Saturday morning

[39] A college-age woman from Wisconsin with whom RC corresponded.

why it took me half an hour to get my call through Christmas night. The paper reported a record number of long-distance calls that day!

Did you see that "my" Dr. Hueper received the A.A.A.S. award in Chicago (this year's meeting place) for distinguished contributions to the study of cancer? Overdue recognition, but I'm so glad it happened. The chemical companies won't be happy. As perhaps I've told you, I'm giving a full chapter to the subject of cancer—something I hadn't expected to do. Did you realize how much that little Christmas Eve call from Mr. Shawn meant to me? I'm confident now about all of it.

Must be dry now and I want to go as soon as they'll release me. May 1960 bring all of you health, peace of mind, and deep happiness.

My dear love,
Rachel

Saturday, January 9

Dear Heart [Rachel],

The letter that has just come shall take precedent over the many that are still on file in your drawer for I must talk to you at once. Oh, Darling—one more burden for you! I wish you might have followed my thought processes as I read your startling news. When you wrote it wouldn't be playing the game if you held back and didn't tell me and "to be honest, I'd much rather not" and that you "had developed a new ailment," dearest, I was so afraid—and I might as well name the fear—that you were going to say cancer that the words duodenal ulcer came almost as a relief. But, of course, you know I'm shocked. And terribly, terribly sorry that you will have a new limitation to contend with. And do you know how I long to fly to you just to see you for a little while and to hold you in my arms?

Darling, of course, I shall do a certain amount of worrying—it wouldn't be like me not to, would it? But at least this is something I've had firsthand experience with and can understand. (And know that one can live with it even happily, if one is faithful to restrictions.)

First let me say that if it had to be, it is good it is the kind that gives pain, and consequently warning. And because of the discomfort, it was discovered before it got to the disastrous stage which we both know. And knowing of it, you will do all that you should to control it, I'm sure. Oh, darling, if you had had to be rushed to the hospital!

It's wonderful that you have the reassurance of Virginia's recovery to help you on your way. I suppose your diet will be quite limited for a while—mostly milk. But let me say that, really, Stan and I are living on an ulcer diet—of course quite liberal now—and enjoying it. I, of course, eat fresh fruit but very little else that he can't eat and I really enjoy it. I know you will miss salads, tomatoes and such, probably more than I do. I never bother with salads anymore—lettuce or celery occasionally. But as you say, it will be a nuisance—the diet I'm thinking of particularly for I suppose you will still want Roger to have things you can't.

I'm glad you could find the early morning warm water an agreeable substitute for your coffee. I felt sorry for you when you told of that for I know how you enjoyed it. Well, dear, *now* will you let me bring you your *warm water* in bed? I'll fluff up your pillows, help you on with your bed jacket and put my arms around you with a warm kiss on your neck.

And even before you mentioned sherry my mind had leaped to it for I always felt you derived a certain amount of comfort from it. But I know you will be faithful to your diet. Probably after a while you may be allowed an occasional sip although I feel that sherry is not so important to you that you are going to mind its absence too badly.

I wonder if you are having to take sedatives. Of course, Stan did because of the bleeding but perhaps it won't be necessary for you. I do hope not for I know you need to get on with the book and to be under sedation makes it so difficult to want to do anything but sleep.

What is Maalox—a cereal food or perhaps medicine to serve the same purpose as Stan's Creamalin?

And about the Book in relation to the ulcer. Darling, that is why I wish you could have followed my mind as I read your letter. Perhaps you cannot believe me, but this is the absolute truth—until you said "I hate to tell you because I'm sure you'll feel the book is to blame," the Book had not entered my thought as a cause. Cross my heart! And I still do not think of it as a major factor. The marvel to me is that you did not develop an ulcer years ago. When I think of *all* the causes that could be contributions—all I have known about, and all that came before I knew you—! An ulcer doesn't just happen overnight, does it? And it is due to emotional strain and worry, isn't it? Who has had more of those in eight or nine years than you? I'm sure I don't need to list them. And, of course, you, I think, are the type—the person who, on the surface, keeps calm, shows no emotion, and goes along apparently unruffled with all the tensions bottled up inside. There have been times when, if I had been you, I would have screamed.

As for the Book, I have felt that you have been happy working on it, and especially this Fall you seemed to be deriving such satisfactions from your work that I could not blame it except for, as you say, the pressure to complete it. If you have been unhappy about it I feel *I* have been the cause of that unhappiness and now I have more regrets than ever that I did not encourage you from the start. I have asked you to forgive me before and I do again. Of course, you know that I have come to believe in it as completely as you do—or do you know? My only worry now is what will happen after it is published—not how it will be accepted—I'm sure it will be a best-seller—but how the spotlight of publicity will be turned on you, and how can you escape. Will you be dragged to hearings, etc.? I hope in some way you can perhaps disappear for a while at the time of publication—remember where there is a "quiet bower"!

Actually, darling, now with this latest development in your physical health, I do so wish you could give your body and your soul a real "vacation"— a vacation in which you can be free in spirit to do all the sweet lovely things you and I know can bring healing. It would take a lot of planning, I know, but once your work is done and before publication couldn't you make some plans?

I suppose when you thought I would say the Book was the cause of the ulcer you also thought I would say you should stop work on it. Not at all. I think if you can feel well enough to work on it you should get on with it as quickly as possible within limits of not pressing yourself beyond reason. What does Dr. Healy say?

While I'm on the subject of the Book I can't help once more mentioning "poetic prose." Forgive me, dearest. I fear you haven't understood at all what I have meant. I am smiling—you say "Let's let the poetry wait for the next book." Oh, darling, if I were with you I would take you in my arms and tickle you to make you laugh, for listen to this—in the same breath (or sentence) you say "I just want it to be simple and clean and strong and sharp as a sword—for it has work to do"! Perhaps you don't think of that as poetry, but I do! You precious dear!

I never said that "poetry was the criterion—the thing I was going to look for, with consequent disappointment if it is not there." I *know* it *will* be there. My wonder has been all along, how?—no doubt as to its presence. And now in a sentence to me about the book you have answered my "how?" You didn't let the poetry wait for the next book. You see, it *will* be there!

How I would love to curl up beside you on the sofa in the study with a fire to gaze into and just talk on and on. Oh, darling.

Now back to the ulcer—oh, dear I am so terribly sorry for you. As to telling Stan, I did not read him your letter for I had already produced the clippings as its contents. (Don't return any more of that collection—I didn't mean for you to return anything except the one funny little poem from the *Register*—maybe you used them as a vehicle for the important letter. O. K.) However, I do not feel it will do Stan any harm to know of your difficulty, in fact, I'm sure he would be most sympathetic and understanding. It would be another bond between you. I suppose he will have advice for you but you would understand that.

But if you'd rather he didn't know that is all right, too. I thought if he did know it would give you more freedom in writing to us since you do feel restricted in some ways now-a-days.

I will wait until I hear from you. I wouldn't want you to have to write all the details again as in this letter but you could say it briefly in writing. Then after we had talked again I could give him the details that you have already written me.

Someway I want to read to him what you wrote about the A.M.A. and aminotriazole. I think I can easily do that & also your comment on the black jelly bean episode. Of course, I never dreamed you would be watching at that hour but I'm so glad you were. Darling, I am not the "average viewer"—I don't watch the "Dave Garroway Show" because I "like him." In fact I know he is only a puppet, and any views he may express are put in his mouth. The reason I watch "Today" is because in spite of many silly, stupid, irritating, disgusting moments, I find there is scarcely a morning when I do not learn something, see some famous personality, hear a worthwhile interview, and in many ways have my outlook on national and world affairs broadened. We do not sit glued to the TV for 2 hours. We listen to the news and then go about our business, keeping TV turned on so we can hear what is going on so we won't miss something worthwhile. Just seeing "your" Cass Canfield is an example!

At the moment we are quite disgusted with the little 2 minute "ad-libbing" that goes on so frequently.

So please don't feel you can't say something criticizing that program to me.

MONDAY NOON

A sparkling day bringing in many birds. I was out at 7:15 to feed them— 8°. It felt good. Stan says he has no pain. Has been down for meals, but staying in bed. He says he expects to be O.K. to go to Clinic on Wed.

I've had a profitable morning. Washed up all Christmas linens—quite a batch besides a wash in machine & also ironing. I find it is easy to take the things to be ironed out before too dry & iron. Saves sprinkling & works out well.

Now I'm off to Bridgewater. Will mail this on way & then I'm going to try to call you.

What a terribly long letter![1] You will be weary after reading it.

It carries so much love.

Dorothy

Our first goldfinch just appeared while I was dressing. Bridgewater friends have had them & I've been envious.

[1] DF's letter had been written in installments over three days. The long Sunday portion containing domestic news is not included.

² In a previous let-
ter, DF had com-
mented upon
RC's failure to
date her letters.

Darling [Dorothy],

Your letter came yesterday and was perfectly wonderful. I read it through, not once but twice practically without stopping—and again at bedtime. It made me feel so warm and relaxed and surrounded by love.

No darling. I need *more*, not fewer letters like that! Oh, not as to length—it wouldn't be fair to ask or expect that, but the same kind of letter.

Thank you dear, for all you said about the book. You made me very happy. And I laughed with you (and at myself) about the poetry. Well, I guess there will be *some*!

I won't try to answer your letter in detail but am marking some parts for later comment.

That letter you got last Friday had been mailed (by me) *in* the *Post Office* before noon on Tuesday!! No excuse for that delay.

Till Sunday, dear one—or maybe you won't have this till later.

> I love you
> *Rachel*

THURSDAY, JANUARY 21

Dearest [Dorothy]

I no longer know dates so can't date my letters! Anyway, it's a better day with more progress. In fact, I was allowed to sit up in a chair to eat my lunch. I confess I was glad enough to crawl back, but am sure I'll gain strength faster as I can get up even for short periods. And guess what—the ulcer has been behaving so beautifully that Dr. H. says I can try a little stewed chicken tonight! That really makes it a red-letter day.

My 3 black nurses (Jeffie on night shift) are still with me but whether J. will have to take over all 3 shifts Saturday remains to be seen. Perhaps one of the others can come part of the day, at least.

Your letter written Tuesday is here. I'm sure you would feel concerned about Aunt Pink—it doesn't sound good but I do trust it doesn't prove serious.

Your night of sleet there was one of wild wind here—literally screaming around the house all night. Sometime I'll tell you more about that night for me—that and the following were the low points of my illness—but somehow it seemed too a night to annihilate distance, for not only were you much in my thoughts but you seemed very close. And also I found my thoughts traveling to Lois—thinking of her isolation. . . .

> [Love, *Rachel*]³

³ The final page or
pages of this let-
ter not preserved.

My darling [Dorothy],

It surely seems some Voice must have spoken to me this morning, telling me to call you. I am so glad I did, and even that I chose that particular time to call, for at least I can feel it comforted you a little to talk. Darling, please don't ever feel you should withhold such news from me even if I'm sick. I want to know, always.

Oh, you poor precious, I am so, so sorry. My heart aches for you—knowing, as I do so well, what it means to you. And you know I understand all those undercurrents, without need to have them stated or described.

Of course I know you have every possible reason to believe the present situation can be handled well and satisfactorily and that is a great comfort. I'm so glad you went immediately.[4]

[4] To the hospital on January 13 due to Stanley's chest pains.

When we were talking this morning I was longing to put my arms around you and feel your head on my shoulder. If only I could go to you. But I know you understand my own health doesn't allow me to think of even a day there.

Darling, I'm going to call you Wednesday evening. I'll try about 9:30—later if no answer. I realize you might stay over in Boston some night (please always go prepared to in case of snow) so if I can't get you I'll assume that is the reason.

[5] Perhaps Mary Johnson.

I'm going to cross my fingers and entrust this letter to Mary[5] for mailing on her way home tonight. You know you and poor Stan are constantly in my thoughts. Do give him our love.

And to you, darling, my dearest, truest love—

Rachel

WEDNESDAY, JANUARY 27

My darling [Dorothy],

You could not have wished for—or dreamed of—anything lovelier than the great box of freesias that arrived early this morning! They are a wonderful golden yellow—much like the color of those I raised—and each stalk is laden with perfect bells, and with so many buds I know I shall have them for many days. And all as dewy fresh as though they had just come from someone's springtime garden. I'm so glad they waited for these to come in! Darling, it was sweet and dear of you to do this. It brings you very close.

If only I could talk to you every night now while you are so alone. Even while we're talking I feel so helpless and aware that I can't *really* do anything for you and I long to so desperately. I do wish there was someone there who could give you understanding and comfort.

As I write (in the study) a white throat has just sung, very tentatively but sweetly. I'm much tempted to wrap up and go out for five minutes' worth of sunshine. Think I will after lunch.

Do you suppose Stan could have had a touch of flu, which then brought on trouble with the ulcer? One kind prevalent around here seems to be marked by pain and diarrhea, with no "cold" symptoms.

Tell me if you ever did get the letter I wrote Sunday, and asked Mary to mail that evening. I wouldn't put it past her to forget all about it.

Darling, I'll be calling you Friday or Saturday evening, depending somewhat on what I hear from you in the meantime. I love you dearly and tenderly and I'm *so* sorry.

Rachel

MONDAY A.M., FEBRUARY 8

Darling [Rachel],

Stan is off to Brockton so I'll just send a little message to tell you how sweet it was to talk with you last evening. How I wish I might have been close to you to celebrate.[6] How would we have celebrated? Not with sherry I'm sure.

I think if you could have rested in my arms, for you were so weary, it would have been the loveliest celebration I could imagine. What do you think?

I do hope you can really rest considerably before you get back into the routine of concentrated work again.

And when *that* work is over please think of a long, long vacation.

I find it good, after these last few months, to have nothing I have to do. Of course, I know I wasted time, but even that is good!

A letter later in the week, dear. This is to tell you what you know so well.

I love you
Dorothy

[6] The anniversary of the February 6, 1954, "hyacinth letter."

WEDNESDAY, FEBRUARY 10

Dear One [Dorothy]—

I've just re-read (again!) your Letter About the Hyacinth Letter. What a sweet and precious message for me to cherish. And how many wonderful memories it revived. They have been sweet to remember as I lie here and day after monotonous day flows by. The "companionship of your letters" (that was a good phrase) has never meant more to me than now.

The Anniversary was seemingly unobserved by me this year, but you know why, and you know it was observed in my heart, don't you darling? I am so glad I wrote that original letter. It was one of those things done so naturally and so effortlessly—you seemed to have questions in your mind, and I knew all the answers, so I wanted to give them to you. It was just that simple to me. And I remember how surprised I was when you called me the night after you received it, seeming rather overwhelmed. I think I kept saying, "But you really knew all that already, didn't you?"

No, darling, I don't suppose I did understand what it meant to you. *Perhaps* I don't now, but with the Gulf bridged and the Pedestal destroyed, I think I can look back and see more clearly how you may have regarded the Author, as distinct from the person who loved you. (Sometimes I wonder whether the Author even exists anymore—it rather seems Fate has been otherwise minded these recent years. Very puzzling, to one who thought there were important things to be done.)

Yes, you did tell me why you needed me and what I meant to you, very beautifully. I think the phrase "kindred spirit" antedates that, however—I associate that with a letter you wrote me at Myrtle Beach after I had "happened" to give you my address there. But after the hyacinth letter you wrote of the sharing of those "things of the inner being" and there, I think, you touched on the very heart of our relationship—the element that brings that surging wish to share something—an apt phrase, a lovely description, music, a special bird, a cloud, a sunset, a whimsical thought—not once but many times a day. To share with the Other, in a way no one else could share.

Darling, there was much more I wanted to say—just to go on talking, remembering things, in this way being with you—but the afternoon wears on and if Mary gets here on time Ida will soon leave. I want to send this with her. Considering the weather, you probably won't get it till Saturday, anyway.

I'll talk more soon. Meanwhile, dear, know that as I lie here I am always so conscious of your love, and of your thoughts flowing to me and surrounding me—always. And by that I am sustained as by nothing else.

My dearest love
Rachel

MARCH 24

Darling [Rachel],

[7] RC was anticipating surgery to remove breast cysts.

When you read this you will be installed in a hospital bed.[7] If you feel like reading I think this letter, just arrived, from Alice might carry you away in your thoughts from your surroundings.

We, too, rowed to Green Island, didn't we? I'm sure you will find in it much the same thoughts as I did. I wish we could read it aloud—together. I imagine you know it, the poem, anyway, but things shared, as we both know are so much lovelier.

Apart from the sea mood I like especially "thought unbraids itself and the mind becomes single"—I'm sure that would have great meaning for you after the work you have been engaged in.

And the last verse, darling!

"And thrift is waste." How wonderful if we could be unthrifty with Time.

If this doesn't get lost in your hospital routine, I would like to have the letter returned sometime. Or just save it and bring it to Southport where we can once again visit a Ragged Island.

I hope that your mind can be at peace, that your home cares are solved sufficiently so that you can perhaps, in a way, enjoy this little island in time which is to be yours for a few days. Be sure I'll be on that island in thought.

> So, so much love
> *Dorothy*

FRIDAY, MARCH 25

Dear Heart [Rachel],

Perhaps you'll be reading this before the operation. I rather hope so considering the title of the tide-pool poem. Is this the one you meant? I do hope Peace[8] will flow into you, darling, whether this arrives before or after.

This is the day that you and Lois are having together. Can you think of anything that would be lovelier, as a pre-operative absorption? Of all people—Lois! How wonderful, wonderful, wonderful.

There was the loveliest lilt in your voice last night, dear—the first real lilt I've heard for many a moon! Of course, I know some of it came from the relief that the visit was to be Friday instead of Saturday.

Well, I've been projecting myself into your Study this morning—did you know there was an eavesdropper? I've been imagining the conversation between two writers—especially the two whose viewpoints on Life and Nature are so similar.

I am so happy for you. Your new robe sounds adorable. I only wish I could be there to put my arms around you in it, as I have in the old one.

Darling, I have all the confidence in the world that all is going to be right with you.

Hurry to get well.

> I need you—and love you,
> *Dorothy*

MONDAY MORNING, APRIL 4, 9:30

My Dear One [Rachel],

About now the time is approaching[9] and my thoughts are with you as they have been constantly for so long. Each time I woke in the night my mind leaped to you. It was the kind of a night I like to share with you—rain beating against the windows with wild wind voicing the storm.

But I have shared other nights with you. I remember at this moment one when we were younger and far happier. We had climbed down over the slanting rocks, clinging to that arm of juniper, to your beach which moonlight had made white. The old log was silver. We sat for a long time watching the moonlight touching every cresting wave—I can see it now. Can you? I don't remember what we talked about. It was noisy for there was a wind and there was much tumbling and rumbling of the sea. I doubt if we talked.

But there was no need for talk. We knew.

[8] The enclosed poem, "Peace" by Sara Teasdale, reads: "Peace flows into me / As the tide to the pool by the shore; / It is mine forevermore, / It will not ebb like the sea. / I am the pool of blue / That worships the vivid sky; / My hopes were heaven-high, / They are all fulfilled in you. / I am the pool of gold / When sunset burns and dies — / You are my deepening skies; / Give me your stars to hold."

[9] RC's operation planned for the prior week had been postponed. On April 4 the surgery revealed a malignancy and she underwent a masectomy.

That is only one of many memories.

Yesterday Clifton Fadiman had a list of 200 Great Books in "This Week." Yes, *The Sea Around Us* was there.

Oh, my dear, I do hope everything goes well at this moment. For you, I feel confident that our miracle drugs have destroyed all nervousness—that you are waiting quite calmly. And it helps me to know that it can be so.

Before you read this I shall know how you are.

Remember how dear you are to us and if we *can* help in *any* way we are yours to command.

My dear, dear love
Dorothy

APRIL 5

My Dear One [Rachel],

If only I could sit beside you now to talk. I'm sure there is much we could say to each other but so difficult to write. Of course, you will know that I spent hours in the night thinking of you and what we would talk about if I could go to you. At times I even thought I should try to go. And began planning which would be the best way to travel. But there are two ways to look at the proposition. I shamelessly believe it would make you happy. But, as I came to learn, while Stan was in the hospital, perhaps the presence of a loved one could be too much of an emotional strain when one needs all one's energy to get well.

Dear, both Stan and I think you are a remarkable person. If we hadn't known it before, that telephone conversation last night proved it. Just the very idea that you wanted to call—and I know the motive was to reassure me (and it most certainly did) was so courageous. You sounded far stronger than you have many a time in a regular conversation. And all the details, you remembered to speak of—mail, flowers, poems, glucose, transfusion, the people who were with you, the hour of the operation, when you came back from recovery room, the telegram to Lois, and much else. How could you, darling? Because you are a miracle.

So, dear, you surely accomplished what you wanted to—to let me know that you had come through the ordeal well. Of course, it was also reassuring to know that you are on Elizabeth's[10] floor. And I was glad you were to have a night nurse to know you'd be kept as comfortable as possible.

I have written to Lois this morning and went quite into detail about our conversation last night for I think it should reassure her, exactly as it did me.

I can think of nothing else to-day but you. And I don't want to think of anything else. If there is such a thing as thought transference your "line" will give off a busy signal constantly for there is not a moment when I am not sending you waves of thought to strengthen you and hasten your recovery.

Of the operation itself I have decided to shut it out of my mind as much as

[10] Elizabeth Dickson.

I can. When we can talk *together* maybe you will want to tell me what it means to you.

In this era I'm sure that the future can be entirely hopeful.

For the moment, I want you to get well and to get home just as fast as you can.

I wish you could have been here this rainy morning to see what we had for breakfast!—in fact, before breakfast. As I looked out of my upstairs window to the feeder at our back steps the ground was full of motion. All among the purple crocuses and the emerging heads of hyacinths was a convention of goldfinches busily feeding. They are in such a mottled state of plumage now that in spite of the dark day it looked exactly as though they were flecked with sunlight—the gold and purple promised Easter.

They ate while we did, too. And they were joined by male grosbeaks—whose yellow also brightened the morning and by red polls who need real sun, though, to produce the ruby flashes.

I told you we thought we saw a pheasant. Well, I just happened to look out the back window at the right moment (queer how that so often happens) & there under our bridal wreath bush was the same creature. Rush for Mr. Bausch & Lomb! Well, we are sure it is a hen pheasant but its plumage was so fluffed out it looked almost too large. We had put grain out back after we first saw it. We have decided she's broody from her actions. She finally wandered off into our tangle of blackberry vines, etc., & we hope perhaps she's looking for a location for a nest. Now wouldn't that be wonderful?

Stan goes to dentist this P.M. and will mail this then.

Darling, if ever you thought you knew what you mean to me, multiply that to infinity and you may have some idea!

> I love you so,
> *Dorothy*

SATURDAY EVENING, APRIL 30

My Dearest [Rachel],

Was it all a dream that I have had two nights and days with you? It doesn't seem possible that I could ever be so happy, considering the awful thing you have been through. But, darling, you are so wonderful in all ways, it left room for some happiness in spite of the overwhelming sadness I feel—to see you thin and your eyes expressing the suffering you've been through was hard to bear. And although you were brave, and courageous and even casual, I knew you were terribly uncomfortable while I was there.

I do hope my visit didn't tire you too much—we were lazy, yes, but you drove the car twice and that afternoon at the files was strenuous. And there was one other time when you forgot to favor your hurt side!

That night on the train I lived it all over. I suppose I did sleep some but there was much time of consciousness when I was with you again. As I told you, I read the chapter before I went to bed so it was very vivid in my mind, which couldn't let it go. I thought about it so much.

I want to read all that I brought home over again. Do you want me to tell you my thoughts on what you have written, or had you rather I didn't make any comments? You might prefer it that way. (Please don't interpret that sentence in a negative way.) Stan is deep in it now & I'm sure you'd be exceedingly pleased with his reactions. I think he will write you about them so I won't.

I have tried to give him some idea of all you showed me Thurs. afternoon—of the prodigiousness of your work—but no one could believe it without seeing it. I hope sometime that Stan can.

Darling, I do hope that you weren't suffering so much that you couldn't enjoy those lazy hours in my room, talking and catching up on so much that has been unsaid.

I was glad you told me of your unhappy problem of Beverly.[11] It is such a sad situation. I'm sure I sensed what proportions it could grow to when I heard one tape recording last summer.

Such a difficult quandary for you. You are tactful, dear. Can't you figure out some way to suggest she reduce the length of her tapes—the time you must put on the book after this interruption should be an approach.

It was fun to talk about the title. I hope perhaps your mind found some avenues of thought to pursue. I wish I could have stayed longer to explore that with you.

I wish I could have stayed longer period! But I do think we covered a lot of ground and I came away satisfied. Were you?

I do so wish you would write to E. B. White. Surely he'd be wonderfully sympathetic with your subject and with his ability to turn a phrase neatly he might come up with something. I don't mean for you to ask him outright for a title, but can't you find some excuse for a little correspondence with him about the book.

And above all I do hope you can get up to N.Y. for the award program.

Had a note from Lois to-day written Thurs. "It is beyond dreams that you can go down ("up"?) (I wrote her about "down Maine") to see Rachel!" "And your letter, telling me how she is—that I already long for." "May this trip be a lovely one. Rachel wrote that a lace of green, and delicate pink apple blossoms look in at the window of that room where the morning light on pale ceiling and walls is so lovely. You will sleep there, no doubt, in that room." I wrote her a brief note yesterday but promised to write at length soon. I'm sure she will be delighted when I tell her how happy we were. I trust it will be all right with you if I tell her about my guided tour behind the scenes of the book and that you let me have 2 chapters to bring home.

When we talked last night I detected a touch of discouragement in your voice. Darling, I know only too well how discouraged one can be when striving

[11] Because of her blindness, Beverly Knecht used audio tape to compose letters to RC.

to get well fast. And I'm sure in your case every aspect must be multiplied. My salvation came from comparing one Sunday with the previous Sunday & knowing then there had been improvement in the week. I hope you too can find cause for reassurance as you look back.

With such a major operation I should expect the doctor would want to see you for several weeks. Just think Stan was in the hospital almost a month after his operation & the surgeon came in every day to have a look.

And incidentally, I took a good look at his scar to-day. It does *not* go above the diaphragm. He says the little needles used for the heart apparatus were inserted in his chest—3 in about these locations[12]—they were inserted before the operation while he was still conscious & could see it work (the heart machine).

This has been one of our loveliest days thus far. I worked in the garden—Tommy mowed the lawn—Stan helped with the oak leaves. It is fun to be gone a few days to discover what's gone on. My bleeding heart shows sizable buds now & the bluebells are practically blooming. We wandered around the lot discovering patches of violets, daffodils, etc., which we had tucked away and forgotten under the trees.

A flowering crab which Stan took from our big tree two years ago has a multitude of buds. A hemlock we brought from Maine, after several years of struggle has become vigorous & healthy. Violets are everywhere—purple & now the white ones—of course, for the neat gardener a pest—but a mound of them at the base of the birch is lovely to me. Wish I could give you some of the lilies of the valley that are now showing through.

We both rested on the chaise, practicing with our new glasses. The trees are full of grosbeaks & their sounds are exactly like a frog chorus.

MAY DAY *MORNING*

Those words have a subtle connotation for me left over from my childhood—memories of happinesses of several varieties—my first May basket, full of violets; May parties of costumed children, May poles, (all typical of Somerville) and later May breakfasts followed by May walks.

So I rose before Stan & took my hot orange juice into the garden—guess who accompanied me!

For our May breakfast we had Stan's trophy from his fishing trip—he'd frozen it—one perch (and it was delicious) divided among three (Willow had the skin) supplemented with bacon and, for me, hot cross buns.

Now I've been working in the garden—oh, what a state it's in, but I'll have to shut my mind & eyes to the bad features & enjoy what's left. So much work I could do—or someone could. Our peach tree is in bloom & quince about to burst into loveliness.

There, I mustn't turn into a Beverly with too many details. I want to write to Lois and get both of these letters to the P. O. before three & it is now 11 o'clock with dinner to get in the interim.

[12] The letter contains a sketch of a chest with incision points marked.

I keep thinking of so many things to write about my visit. One—did it occur to you how nicely we got on without sherry?

And, darling, there were many things I might have said to you that could help to convey to you the depth of my understanding of all you have been through. I hope that in spite of all I didn't say you do know how I feel.

I hope you read it in my eyes when I looked silently and deeply into yours. I hope words really were unnecessary.

I still have to pinch myself to believe I've been with you.

After the nightmare of the past months for both of us it was balm to my spirit to have a sweet dream that proved to be a reality.

Oh, my darling. All my love flows to you constantly.

I love you,
Dorothy

Dearest [Dorothy],

I shall talk with you tonight and tell you then about yesterday and today, but since we are going to the P.O. I want to put in a word for you.

There has been a strange stillness in my heart since you both left,[13] and I knew that for a while at least you would not be returning—something that came of knowing the phone would not ring to bring me your voice, and that I would not hear the crunch of your tires on the drive!

Much fog today—and yesterday heavy fog closed in around the island before we left. Terns are screaming and diving over the bay—there must be fish.

Roger had a gay but rather adventurous afternoon yesterday—I'm afraid Larry may not be the ideal baby sitter from the parental point of view! (He was home for the week-end.)

I do hope for somewhat better news when I talk to you tonight, but of course I realize any change will be slow. You know I am thinking of you constantly.

All my love,
Rachel

[13] RC was writing from Southport after DF and Stanley had returned to West Bridgewater.

THE LAST NIGHT—BEDTIME, SEPTEMBER 8

Dear [Dorothy],

How better spend a few moments before turning in than in talking to you?

Going back and forth to the car on last errands, the sights and sounds of this last night were the nearly full moon in a clear sky—a cricket chirping—the tolling of the buoy carrying through the still air—the rote. Later I carried Jeffie out on the deck; he twisted around in my arms to look straight up at the sky, purring.

Knowing I shall see you tomorrow takes some of the hurt out of leaving—but how I do hate to go! I have never had a summer with so little time to enjoy the place but I have never loved it more. And as I sit here in the study for the last time this year, of course I find myself wondering what new changes will have entered our lives before another summer. For you, I know, some sorrow and anxiety are inevitable, but I do really feel that your worries about Stan are going to gradually lessen. He does seem so much better than in June. I hope and believe there are good years ahead for you.

And darling, I look forward to next summer as a carefree and happy one, with time to share the joys of the place we both love. And in the meantime, some thaws in the long Winter! I could say all this to you tomorrow (and probably will) but I, too, know there is something in the written word. It will be hard to say goodbye, darling.

I love you dearly,
Rachel

[*MID-SEPTEMBER*]

Darling [Dorothy],

Just an extra word or two before I mail this. I have not really told you since our return how it warmed my heart to be with you again in your home, even for so short a time. It closed that long gap of years since I have been there. And I, too, loved the few moments we had all to ourselves.

And darling, I can't even begin to tell you how my heart aches for you. Of course, seeing your mother made it all the more real to me, but I am so glad I did, for many reasons. And I can imagine your sleepless nights. I know what mine were during the comparatively short time Mamma lay here in the oxygen tent. For you, the indefinitely prolonged misery is so much worse. Oh, darling, I am so sorry.

Now I shall put this out for the mailman. With it goes so very much love.

Rachel

FRIDAY, [*SEPTEMBER*]

Darling [Dorothy],

Now a few more minutes before I'm dry. It was *so* good to talk to you Tuesday—and we did keep it fairly short, didn't we?

Darling, my heart does ache for you. I can imagine all too vividly what this situation must be doing to you, and what your thoughts and feelings must be. And there seems to be nothing I can do or say to help. I do imagine it is true that while your mother is quite clear in her mind in most ways, nevertheless her faculties are probably dulled enough that she is far less aware what her condition is than you are. And if she sleeps a great deal that is all the more true. At least I suppose you can feel reasonably assured she is not in pain. But oh, darling, I know it just tears your heart, whether you are with her or lying awake on your bed.

About your own physical state, darling. I do hope that the next time you feel any concern whatever you would at once invest the necessary time for a visit to the Clinic. There is no tonic so fine as being told by a doctor you trust that there is nothing seriously wrong. In your situation it is inevitable that you would worry about things you might not notice at other times. But instead of merely telling yourself that, I think you need the boost you'd get from *professional* reassurance.

Now I'm almost dry, so I'll bring this to a close. You are very close to me in all my thoughts, darling. But how I'd love to be with you again—even for an afternoon, as on Sept. 9![14]

All my love, dearest,
Rachel

[14] The date of RC's recent short visit to West Bridgewater on her way home from Southport.

SATURDAY, OCTOBER 8

Darling [Dorothy],

Just a tiny note to reach you Monday, I hope. Perhaps you will put it away for a quiet moment in the evening after everyone is gone. I do hope it will be possible to have the services[15] Monday for I think it is easier not to have this interval prolonged. I know so well how hard these days will be for you, but when it is all over I hope the present sadness will be replaced soon by deep thankfulness that release has come for your dear mother. I know you do feel that to some degree even now, as all of us must who had any idea of her ordeal.

[15] DF's mother, Vira Murdoch, had died on October 7.

I am especially glad now, darling, that I did see her in September. I had such a feeling there could be no later time. And certainly she knew I was there and I think was pleased that I had come.

Last night I thought of our mothers' last summer at Southport, and realized for the first time that that summer of '58 *was* the last for both of them in that place. Poor dears—their end-of-summer farewells were always saddened by the thought it might be the last.

It was lovely to know, darling, that you were using that dress. I will talk to you soon, dear one. Meanwhile, you are constantly in my mind.

Dearest love—
Rachel

WEDNESDAY, OCTOBER 12

My dearest one [Dorothy],

This life is so different from anything I've known before in all the years since we met. Just no time for letters—no time to read—no time for anything, it seems, unless it is somehow related to the great projects that are uncompleted. I suppose as I grow older and become more aware that life is not only uncertain but short at best, the sense of urgency grows to press on with the things I need to say—things that may be less important than I think, but to me at least it is necessary that they be said. But I do think back with a bit of nostalgia, darling, to the times when this urgency seemed less. I like to *remember* at least, days when I spent a whole morning (or more!) writing a leisurely letter to you. As I addressed your letter this morning I wondered with a smile how many times I've written that address—and how many times my heart has leaped (as it still does) to the sight of the familiar handwriting in return.

And right now I do long for even a day with you, when you could say the things you want to say, and I could tell you some of the little things that never get written, and that I'd rather talk about, anyway.

A mockingbird is pouring out *his* heart to the whole world just now, as I sit in the study, writing. One day recently I recorded some minutes of song coming down the chimney.

Darling, I continue to be so relieved that this long ordeal is over. All those weeks I was so aware that each visit to your mother must just tear your heart. And how I know the feeling of dreading to waken each morning to that leaden weight. There will be sadness now, I know, but of such a different kind. Now, for the first time since Stan's retirement, you should begin to have some of the enjoyment of leisure that you deserve. You must feel so much better about him than you did even at the beginning of the summer. Now begin to take care of yourself, too, darling. Because I love you—remember.

Rachel

MONDAY NOON, [OCTOBER]

Darling [Rachel],

I've been at my desk all morning trying to clear it of so much that has accumulated since mother went. But with all the writing the thought of you has dominated my thinking with sadness, as it has ever since yesterday.

So before I go out to the mailbox I feel the need of sending you my love.

Here it is, dear,
Dorothy

MONDAY MORNING, [OCTOBER]

Darling [Dorothy],

Although in my mind yesterday I composed long letters to you, experience has taught me that there is really nothing I can say that will change your feelings when your mood is as it was yesterday. I can only hope time will bring a change.

Just one or two things I must say before we drop the subject into that limbo of things that should never have happened between us. Although it is true, to my great regret, that I have hurt you many times, I have never done so deliberately. When I decided to choose my own time and place to tell you about Mrs. Kennedy,[16] the reason lay in the scars of old wounds—I was trying to avoid more heartbreak for both of us. When I came home that day, full of things I longed to share with you, I almost went to the phone to call you. Then I remembered certain things, and I was afraid, and the phone stood silent.

That is the tragedy of these awful misunderstandings between us. They are a black shadow on the present, and they reach out into the future as well. Two of the things you said yesterday are examples of words that are hard to forget. You implied, at least, that you would never trust me again. And you spoke with regret of the time you had spent "feeling sorry" for me because of my cold, and my ulcer, etc. That is going to make me try very hard not to invite sympathy again, darling.

To me it all seems so tragically unnecessary. But when one incident makes you speak with such bitterness as you did yesterday, I can't help wondering if the fragile beauty of all the lovely things over the years is as precious to you as to me—as precious to you as I thought it was.

I called you yesterday so lightheartedly, ready to start a day's work but feeling a need I once tried to describe to you. I put up the phone feeling sick, and 100 years old. Does it have to be this way, darling? When I said I was sorry, couldn't you have let that settle it, couldn't you love me enough not to let this happen?

Because I do love you—

Rachel

Dearest [Dorothy], And of course this is just to say how happy I am now that the horrid weight has been lifted from my heart. I hope you are as happy. I had wanted to call—or hoped you would—ever since Sunday, and last night decided I couldn't sleep again until I had. It was wonderful I reached you when you could talk about what we both needed to talk about.

Your Monday note was in the mailbox this morning. It must have been delivered to someone else who then just placed it there. And your sea poem[17] came today, yes, the mood is right. And perhaps it says poetically what I tried to say in prose.

Anyway darling, all is well now and once again there is peace.

And again—and always—my love.

Rachel

TUESDAY, NOVEMBER 22, AFTER OUR CALL

My Darling [Rachel],

As I walked to the car, there in a clear sky was the young moon and two bright stars.

It was so lovely and belonged so to us that somehow it seemed a sign that all will be well with you.

---

[16] Upon Jacqueline Kennedy's invitation, Rachel had met with the Women's Committee for the New Frontier.

[17] Poem not preserved.

I'm glad I called. It is good that you could share your anxiety with some-one—for I'm sure it is an anxious time for you.[18]

If only I were within an easy driving distance—how many times I have longed for that!

How I would love to sit beside you before the fire and feel your head on my shoulder.

Last night our sunset was one of those gorgeous coral affairs with clear turquoise on the horizon. I was ironing but I dropped what I was doing & hur-ried out to the porch to sit quietly letting myself bask in its beauty as it turned to ashes of roses and then to gray. And you were there!

I longed for you so. And now I long for you even more!

I shall mail this on the way home so you should have it Friday.

I'll be thinking of you with Bernstein on Thurs., dear.

All my love,
Dorothy

[18] There had been evidence of a spread of RC's cancer.

FRIDAY, NOVEMBER 25

Darling [Dorothy],

For me it was so wonderful that you called Tuesday, but for you, I'm afraid, it was not. My definite plan had been to write you all this news *after* I had the report and decisions had been made. That, I thought would be Tuesday or Wednesday, so that you would have the letter after your holiday, at the end of the week. Then when your letter came Tuesday, telling of plans for family and other activities extending through the week-end, I resolved I must not write until the end of the week, for truly, darling (although my later actions may seem to belie my words) I did not want your week-end or the holiday clouded by any unhappy thoughts. Tuesday was a difficult day, for I kept expecting Dr. Sanderson to call, and he didn't. That was much worse than almost any certainty, so by the end of the afternoon things seemed pretty bleak. And I confess, darling, I wanted you—and by force of circumstances and my own determination, felt cut off from you. So it was almost uncanny when the phone rang—and it was you!! Just at first I still felt I must keep back what was in my mind. And then it all spilled out, and though I felt I should not have done it, I felt so much better.

The Thanksgiving call was designed (as you must have realized) to give you the comparative peace of mind I felt from having facts instead of guesses. But it must have seemed to Stan a horrid thing to do—to choose Thanksgiving to call and give you news of a fresh problem! I hope it *did* ease your mind some, darling. I knew that otherwise you would have to wait till Saturday or probably Monday to learn what the X-rays showed.

Well, as you will know from the other letter, I start treatment Monday. The time this represents now when it is all so precious is of course horribly frus-trating. But naturally there is no choice.

Of course I wish it were possible to determine the nature of this thing, which may be quite innocuous, but this way we shall never know. But they don't wish to cut into it, which is understandable. Well, I shall believe the X-ray therapy will take care of this, and I shall try to cross no more bridges at this time. Of course it is true that I thought a door had been closed last spring, and now it has opened a little or so it seems.

Today your note came, as you hoped it would—the one you wrote Tuesday after we had spoken and you had seen the moon and two stars. (I know the stars you mean.) It was sweet to have, dear, and brought you close again.

In quite different vein, isn't this *New Yorker* carton perfect?[19] I laughed aloud when I found it tonight.

I'm trying to finish the chapter on herbicides over the week-end—trying rather desperately so I can discuss it with Paul. I've gotten some wonderful material for it—partly through Justice Douglas,[20] you know, partly thru Dr. Egler[21] of Connecticut, and now a wonderful, thoughtful letter of comment on this problem from Dr. Olaus Murie.[22] And I have included my own observations, driving the Back Narrows road to the Y Camp! But the ecological folly is so apparent in this war on vegetation.

Now I must let sleep take over, so I can get up fairly early and work—I hope. I'm indulging in 1 Miltown at bedtime for a while—it gives me a good rest. I wish you were here, dear one.

All my love to you,

Rachel

FRIDAY MORNING, NOVEMBER 25

My Darling [Rachel],

I was so glad you called yesterday. Of course, I couldn't help being glad I knew, and was prepared for the news you had for us, for when I realized how shocked Stan was I imagined how I might have reacted.

It was good to know you were more at ease in your mind, but I don't have to have a great imagination to know that this is a terribly difficult situation for you. Darling, if I didn't know that every available hour for work on the book is important to you I should want to go to you. But don't entertain the thought for a moment—time out for New York (which I hope you will feel up to doing) will use up valuable time.

Please know that my mind and heart are with you constantly.

Richie is standing beside me asking "Why are you sending her notes?—like you always do!" How does he know?

I told him "because I love her."

I do, my dearest,

Dorothy

[19] The cartoon by Barney Tobey shows a woman in a phone booth saying into the receiver: "Oh, nothing special, Agnes. I was just passing one of those booths and thought I'd call."

[20] United States Supreme Court Justice William O. Douglas.

[21] Dr. Frank Egler, ecologist and owner of Aton Forest, Norfolk, Connecticut.

[22] Dr. Olaus Murie and his brother Aldolph explored the western United States. Olaus Murie authored *A Field Guide to Animal Tracks* (1954) and Aldolph Murie authored *A Naturalist in Alaska* (1961), illustrated by Olaus.

Darling [Rachel],

Just a note. This is the afternoon we go to the 75*th* birthday Open House. The children left at 10 A.M.—we spent two hours straightening house & now need a nap.

This, our first Thanks-giving with our grandchildren, was completely satisfactory. The children were happy all the time—there was no dissension. They played hard. They love our stairway, and spent hours on it—using the drapes as curtains for their puppet shows. Of course, they also love grandma's passé finery to adorn themselves.

The pilgrimage to Plymouth was the high spot—Martha said "This is the best time of my life." Will give you details sometime.

Richard was wearing Roger's coat in which he looked like someone from "Brookes Bro." Very stylish. Martha loved the Bird Records & each night she wanted one side played before bed—I hadn't thought of using them that way.

But with it all, darling, you were always in my heart. We talked of you a lot as we always do.

I was so happy that you called us on Thanks-giving. Stan and I haven't had much time alone to talk but when we did get away for a moment alone he always spoke of you at once. We are terribly concerned for you, dear, for we know these treatments will interrupt the flow of the work you had planned. We do hope there will be no discomfort but fear there may be. Darling, you know I love you, don't you? So much,

In allways,
Dorothy

Darling [Rachel],

Just a wee note to put out for the mailman. You are so constantly in my mind it is hard to think of anything else. I almost called you—or at least, I had thought of calling you last night but company came at 8 and didn't leave until 10:15, which I thought was too late.

I am hoping and praying that chills and fever are gone, that they were not related to the treatment.

I'm sure until you know it is a great worry for you.

Yesterday afternoon I went to the Nursing Home for the first time since I gathered mother's belongings.

I was so welcomed that I vowed I would go often. Dear Mrs. Ward seemed so touched. What a pitiful case hers is.

Darling, did you see the white, white moonlight last night? If it hadn't been so cold here I think we would have gone for a walk.

Do I need to tell you that my heart longed for you?

Dearest—if there is anything Stan and I can do to help you—*anything*—you wouldn't hesitate to propose it, would you? Remember we want to help.

Does loving you *help*?
I do—*so* much,
Dorothy

SUNDAY NOON, DECEMBER 4

Darling [Rachel],

Have been writing Christmas messages all morning. I succumbed to the "group" letter idea again this year—so many we write to only once a year, and I felt this past year, again, needed more explanation than I wanted to write on each card. The letter will be ready on Tues. so I've been addressing the "far away" ones with a personal note on the cards. And I find it really fun when I'm not pressed for time for I've been re-reading last year's letters—which I had almost forgotten & some are truly lovely. Have already had such a fine letter from the couple in Victoria, B.C., that I felt I wanted to write a letter to them. They live near the sea and had a wonderful experience watching a killer whale "put on a terrific display for us."

But, darling, with all this writing I cannot lose myself completely for you dominate my thought. I would not have it otherwise although I wish the thoughts could be happier ones.

Last night again I wanted to call you. Suddenly I felt terribly tired (for no real reason except that I sewed all the time I listened to the opera broadcast & didn't rest) & at 7:30 I took a bath and got in bed. And dropped off to sleep. And didn't get up until after 8 o'clock this morning. Now that I've talked with you, I'm glad I chose a good time, you said.

Darling, I think no one can appreciate how truly miserable you have been, and are, than I. It sounds so much like my June episode. Those enervating night sweats (the only good feature—when they began, the chills were gone) the results of the high temperature, the "visions," the don't care, desperate feeling (I remember Stan raising the curtain so I could look at the sunset, and I was so miserable I couldn't open my eyes to look—and I almost didn't care.)

All this is bad enough. To have the worry of your new "mystery" with the necessity of making some kind of decision as to how to proceed must be cause for desperation on your part.

I'm so glad you've had someone there. I remember how desperate I was last February when I grew so sick alone with Stan in the hospital. When I realized I couldn't make the effort to go down to feed Willow I knew I had to have help. That's when Mildred came. When I hung up after talking to you Wed.

night I had that same feeling for you so I was decidedly relieved when your letter said you had called for Vera.

Think I'll send Stan to P.O. with this while I get dinner. It's only a message to have some familiar handwriting in the mail, but it carries dear and tender love as always,

Dorothy

DECEMBER 14

ABOARD PLANE

Darling [Dorothy],

It is something of a triumph that I can write "aboard plane."[23] There were times I thought I'd never make it. You *know* nothing would ever go smoothly, and now I can relax. I'll tell you some of the tribulations of the past couple of days if you'll promise to laugh instead of cry!

Of course, Ida couldn't make it Monday but Tues. about 7 she phoned she was starting and had word buses were running. Somewhat more than an hour later she called again: power had failed on streetcar line, and after sitting a while she had walked somewhere to get a bus, but would be too late for her connection in Silver Spring. I told her to try to get a cab, and if she did tell the driver to wait and take me in. I'd moved on my hair appointment to noon, but knew it would be difficult to get a cab to come out. She arrived about 10:15 and I went in; did a little shopping, had a bite of lunch, and had my hair done.

When I left there I spent one hour on the street in bitter, windy cold before I could get a cab. When I finally did I talked to the driver about the problem of getting to the airport this morning. He said the company was not taking any "time calls" but that if I could tell him the hour he would come for me. We settled on 9:30 and I told enough of the situation that he knew I *had* to get there. Well, I'll finish that story before I introduce other complications. Nine-thirty this morning came, but no cab. With each passing second I got more jittery. I tried to call the cab co. but got a perpetual Busy signal. About 9:35 the phone rang. It was the cab driver. "What time is it you have to be at the airport?" He'd had a trip downtown, couldn't come for me, but would send someone else! I told him his company wasn't answering the phone, but he said he'd radio in to the stand at Four Corners. Knowing no cabs have been on stand for days, I hadn't a grain of faith he could keep his promise. Besides, a cab should have had me in it *right then*. I tried every cab company in Silver Spring—Busy. (I think they just take the phone off the hook.) In desperation I called the police and asked if they could somehow get me a cab. A very nice man said he would certainly try. About a minute after that I saw a cab coming down Berwick—sent by my faithless one. It was then 9:50. However, my habit of always allowing lots of extra time for airport trips paid off, and I was there with 5 minutes to spare to get my ticket by 11.

[23] RC had decided to fly to Cleveland to consult Dr. George "Barney" Crile, Jr., an authority on breast cancer.

Plane was due to leave at 11:30. Actually it was long after 12—didn't notice exact time. We've now had lunch and, at 1:15 are flying over a Christmas card landscape, most of the mountains now behind us. I don't know just what our route is, but imagine we have only about another half hour. Perhaps we are near Pittsburgh—a big river is looping across the landscape and there are towns.

Well, the other major complication is that we have frozen water pipes in the downstairs bath. This was announced by Roger and Ida when I got home yesterday. A plumber came early this morning (I had telephone advice last night) but there is little to do but wait watchfully for the thaw, which will tell the story of whether the pipes have burst. If so, it means tearing out the bathroom wall. Ida is to shut off the main water valve when she leaves today. (Roger is spending night with Newtons.)[24] Or if she sees signs of a leak meanwhile she shuts off. Well, at least I'm glad it happened while I still had time to get the situation under some sort of control before leaving.

Roger's school was to have closed for the holidays Friday noon after the Christmas pageant. All schools in the area have been closed since Monday, and yesterday Mrs. Brooker decided just not to reopen! So a good long vacation it is. As Doris Newton said last night, "All eternity seems to stretch out before us."

I wonder about you and the snow and cold, darling. I hope you didn't lose your phone. If you didn't, I'll probably talk to you before you read this.

Now I'll stop and have this ready to mail in Cleveland. I know your thoughts are with me, darling. I can feel them!

All my love,
Rachel

[24] Silver Spring neighbors.

THURSDAY, DECEMBER 15

Darling [Rachel],

Waiting at the Clinic. Stan had his 3 mo. check-up and Dr. Dick suggested I might as well see him. In a way, I'd almost rather not because I'm in good condition in his department. But I think he wants to be sure all stays well.

If we get out in time I think we shall deliver our Christmas packages to Needham & Norwood on the way home & that will be done. More bad weather is predicted. I do hope it's rain. Boston streets, even the main ones, are a mess! Went to Littles' last night. You know he had something last spring which I'm sure was a "shock" altho no one called it that. He gets around with a walker beautifully and as they had an elevator installed he is quite free to move about. I think he's going to be at least 88 in March—maybe 89.

Well, darling, yesterday and to-day were to be eventful days for you. Of course, I've been thinking steadily of you, wondering if you did go. And if you did hoping that you are happy with the outcome.

This is the month in which I always relive that first December—1953— all the little messages flying back and forth. Even then you were too busy—

I remember, trying to get your paper done—and yet you found time to write to me. There was a verse "A little bird sang in December—it's nearer to spring than it was in September." And it is, darling. Of course, I know with you perhaps you wish spring were a bit farther away for you'll be terribly pushed to get the book done with this long interval of non-work.

LATER

All is well with me. How I wish you could write the same.

Christmas mail, I suppose, will slow up the "regular"—but even if it is slow reaching you, be sure I'm thinking of you all the time.

Love,
Dorothy

FRIDAY MORNING, DECEMBER 16

My Dearest [Rachel],

I long to write volumes to you but what can I say? First, to tell you of my gratitude that you called me last night. I knew you would, of course, when you had something to report but I hardly thought it would be so soon.

If one can be glad over sadness I suppose I am glad that you are in such competent, understanding, and well informed "hands." I don't doubt that what you have learned is a terribly serious situation.[25] Neither do I doubt but that you are facing it with calmness and patience. The waiting period will be so difficult.

If only I could help. Dear One, last Christmas you sent me some lines which now I want to return to you. I have a feeling that they are original with you.

Do you remember them?

How shall I wish you strength?

A tree says "strength" so silently.
How shall I wish you joy?
A bird sings joy and needs no words.
How shall I wish you peace,
When snow breathes peace so perfectly?
Yet these are the things I wish for you.
At Christmas time, and in the year to come.

Darling, no telling when this will reach you but remember it is written soon after we talked.

It would be so easy to think only of the dark side of all this. Instead, as you wish and ask, I shall try very hard to believe with strong faith that good will conquer and that the future will be well with you.

If loving could make it so, then it would be.

All my love,
Dorothy

[25] RC had learned that her malignant breast tumor had metastasized. Dr. Crile had recommended radiation treatment in Silver Spring.

Darling [Dorothy],

This is a mere token letter—but then Christmas itself is a token and a symbol, isn't it? But I do not want to break that precious custom we began on our first Christmas which now seems rather long ago. For this is the time of year to remember and to say that the gift of love is the best gift of all. Christmas without the knowledge and the sweet reminders of your love in your many dear messages would be bleak indeed and you know that in return mine flows out to you in an ever running stream.

It is sweet to remember, dear, the happy sharing of lovely things in the years we have had. Though perhaps there has been much less opportunity for doing happy things together recently. I think we have learned to cherish every such moment, and even this past difficult year added to our store of memories. And there will be others.

Perhaps you won't have this until you return from your Christmas journey. But no matter—it is only the reassurance of what you already know—that I love you deeply and tenderly and for always.

Rachel

B. BAY HARBOR, DECEMBER 23

MID-TOWN MOTEL

Darling [Rachel],

It was foreordained that we should make our call on Southport to-day. Blue skies, sun, and bare, dry roads made our decision before we crossed the state line at New Hampshire.

Thus far it was a good decision for other than wind and cold all else is perfect—and neither wind nor cold make it disagreeable.

We telephoned ahead for our motel so went directly to the Head, reaching there at 3:15.

We were able to drive all the way & were only stopped at the parking space at the end of the road by a snow pile left by the plough. All else is bare.

The grove looks exactly as in summer. Some snow patches in the woods, but otherwise less snow than at home! The wind was blowing strongly from the southwest so we didn't want to linger on the porch. Sun was less than an hour high & from our porch was hidden behind Aunt Pink's house. Imagine.

There was ice on our living room floor where snow had beaten under the door so while Stan chopped and swept that out I went out to the Head (temp. about 20°) to have a glimpse of Seguin which, due to some atmospheric effect, looked as though it were detached from the sea and floating in space—and so much larger than in summer. I did not linger.

Our beach is filled with huge logs & heavy with seaweed. The storm & high tide of Wed. had strewn debris far higher than ever and at the lighthouse beach seaweed had been thrown into the Gardners' driveway all across the street. I should like to have looked on that in the process.

All seemed secure around our place. Foam in the cove was thicker than whipped cream & was being blown like milkweed through the air. No gulls.

I took time to saw a foot high balsam to take to Orono—just for old times sake.

I suggested I walk from Deep Cove over the hill to your place but Stan said "Oh, we can drive around." I never would have dared attempt the little lane by Mrs. Kenrick's but he did—it was mostly ice and ruts but as it was all down-hill we made it. I wouldn't let him try your hill so he drove down to Steeveses' to turn around while I walked through your woods to the high ground overlook-ing Steeveses' (snow only in patches) & by "our" path to your road. There was snow in the path and some creature had preceded me. I like to think it might have been a red fox but probably it was a Gardner dog. My main object was to check on your porch. From the steps behind your house I could see the sun shining through the screens through your French doors. The effect was so warm looking and inviting that it could have been a summer's day. I wanted you inside to welcome me!

You will be happy to know the porch is complete even to an excellent coat of paint. There are spaces between the boards so the light shines through, which I should think would be a great improvement.

I could not linger there—the wind was too strong, and I did not go down to the beach. But I did note that about 20 minutes before sunset time the sun was exactly over the chasms on Georgetown where the surf dashes in so excit-ingly in a storm—the place you want to explore sometime. Quite a contrast from early July!

But I did go up the snow-covered Dorothy Freeman Highway to the open lot where the one and two ft. high spruces standing in snow looked like a min-iature forest where fairies might gather by moonlight—only they'd need over-shoes and something warmer than gauze for clothing—probably mole-skin jackets. There I picked the checkerberries. And all the other greenery is from your Estate!

As I started back down the hill through "our" path again, the quarter moon hung in the southern sky causing me to draw in my breath sharply—and you know why! Stan was waiting at the foot. While I caught my breath we drank coffee from a thermos from home.

Although the road was icy we made our way safely out to the lighthouse beach to watch a red sun set in cloudless sky while rough seas pounded into the wall. Seguin was still floating in air—a queer effect. (Three ducks were swim-ming in the cove and flew off to sea.)

When the sun had disappeared we climbed the hill to the store where from the steps we watched another sunset—even more beautiful for the bare-ness of the trees has opened up wider vistas and more of the Bay is in sight.

[26] Charlie Pinkham, West Southport general store proprietor.

[27] Charlie Pinkham's wife, Izetta.

[28] Ethelyn Giles, Boothbay Harbor area realtor and the Pinkhams' daughter.

Charlie[26] was in the store & quite thrilled, I think, to see us. Then we went up to see Zetty[27] & I do believe we made her very happy. Both of them seem to be holding their own. Christmas for them is to be at Ethelyn's.[28]

On to the P.O. gaily decorated with lights, magnified snowflakes on the picture window, and chimes playing on the door as you enter. The "Postmaster" greeted us gaily but with tales of woes—including a break-down of her washing machine, two flooded floors as a consequence and other troubles of which I shall spare you. There was other conversation which you and I could grow hilarious over—I shall try to remember when I see you altho' I doubt if I can impart the true flavor!

After a rest we dined in one of the two available "Restaurants"—Etta's Diner. The atmosphere is not similar to the Ritz but the food is worthy of any Duncan Hines' recommendation. More of that when I see you—the customers were natives, I judged from their accents and conversations!!

A long evening opening cards which arrived before we left, an hour of Christmas on TV & now we are ready for bed.

Darling, I have just reread your Christmas "token." I was so glad I read it in my quiet bower last night—for I had it then and now I can have it again and again. Darling, I can well imagine that when you open my special Christmas Eve message that Stardust will spill out of the envelope all over you as it did me last night.

Was it some hidden longing to be alone together in our woods that made us each choose such similar scenes? Your miniature is so sweet. And if your message was, as you say, only a token, it proves again that you have the magic gift of expressing in a few words the very ideas that I ramble on into page after page—the Gift of Love, and all you said so beautifully and so typically you.

Darling, I love you. The wind, the sea, the woods, our favorite spots, even the moon compounded to bring you very close this afternoon. You walked with me in the woods. And I thought of what you would have said if you were there.

And now Good-night, my dearest one. I shall hold you in my heart as I drift off to sleep.

I love you,
Dorothy

DECEMBER 24, 8:30 A.M.

Off for Orono via shore route. Beautiful day. Wish you were here!

CHRISTMAS

My Dearest [Rachel],

Eight Christmases—eight sweet Christmases of knowing you! If only there had been more—the one when you were five and I was fourteen—wouldn't that have been fun? I might have read *The Wind in the Willows* to you!

Queer what a difference the decades can make. Or the one when you were the earnest young student trying to decide between biology and writing. Or most of all the one when the girl was writing what the world knows as *The Sea Around Us*. Oh, I wish I had known you always! Thank goodness I wrote that Christmas card in 1952. At least I shared some of the experience of *The Edge of the Sea*. Do you remember the lovely moment when you told me of your intention about the Dedication?

This morning I relived with my diary the Christmases since I have known you. I've tried to explain to you the glow and excitement that stirred within me all during that first December. I found my agitation was even recorded. Those feelings I still remember so well. What a wonderful time in my life. Never, all during those Christmas holidays, did that undercurrent of YOU leave me.

There were a few Christmases not tinged with anxiety and sadness, but so few. The minor key began to dominate. Darling, for me to have had you during all these years of trouble has been my strength. I hope in some small way you may have felt the same way about me.

Last evening as we had a delicious fire just for ourselves, "shut in from all the world about," we felt there would be no better time to enjoy our gifts. First we opened an accumulation of sweet, funny, lovely cards—many with good letters. When I came to your gift I would have known from the wrapping, so typical of you, dear, that it was from you even without your name and sweet explanation.

(A telephone conversation with you.) Oh, My Darling! After we opened our gifts (and I have told you now that they are both sweet and precious to us) I settled into the wing chair before the fire to communicate with you and Bernstein and Beethoven. You were beside me, your hand in mine. You had written of being moved to tears. Perhaps, dear, we can use this symphony symbolically. Our beginnings were like this—gay, thrilling, happy. Suddenly—after the gaiety of the first movement, that long drawn out minor chord introduces the sad slow movement (the past four years, darling). But the sadness ends while the music rushes and skips along in a joyous dance to a happy ending. It shall be that way for us—the sadness will end and we'll be happy again.

Darling, I keep trying to tell you how much you mean to me—how knowing you has added zest to a life which needed a new outlook—finding in you the kindred spirit to share the lovely things of life—this Seventh Symphony, for example. Here in verse is the perfect expression of how completely you have filled my life. If I haven't sent you this before, I don't know why I haven't. If I have, it bears repeating at Christmas time:

My life is a bowl which is mine to brim
With loveliness old and new,
So I fill its clay from stem to rim
With you, Dear Heart, with you!

My life is a pool so small it can hold
But a star and a patch of blue;
But the blue and the little lamp of gold,
Are you, Dear Heart, are you!

My life is a homing bird that flies,
Through the starry dusk and dew,
Home to the heaven of your true eyes
Home, Dear Heart, to you.[29]

How better can I tell you?

[29] "My Life Is a Bowl" by Mary Ripley from DF's well-used *Star-Points* anthology.

Darling, the card took my eye for the winter wonderland of the forest. I wish you and I could walk this Christmas time in just such a setting. Somehow the solitude, the beauty, the nearness to all the little creatures, the music of the spheres are the accompaniment of what I long for Us to share.

So, darling, when you read this try to think of us together, sharing, as we have so many times, in so many ways all the Beauties which have come to mean so much to us in these years since that first Christmas.

Always I send you love—I wish there was a new way to express it. But after all, to say "I love you" is to say it best. I do.

Dorothy

WEDNESDAY, DECEMBER 28

Dearest [Dorothy],

I was so grateful to you for calling at once to set my mind at rest about your safe return.

Roger's first edition of his newspaper proclaims: "Scoop! Roger Christie Gets Telescope! Sees Moon and Venus! His Grandad Gave it to Him!" Now if I were running a newspaper, my lead story would be: "Rachel Carson Gets Capehart . . . Hears Beethoven and Bach . . . She Gave it to Herself." For that is the big news of the day. A Silver Spring firm (or rather a Washington firm with a SS branch) had just gotten the exclusive agency for the Capehart, and advertised the other day, offering substantial discounts to celebrate the occasion. I went in today, fell in love with its tone the minute I heard it—and ordered it! It is the first one I've heard, not excluding the Fisher, that I've admired without any reservations. I'm getting for $289 one designed to sell at about $100 more. It is a lovely piece of furniture as well. Delivery is promised for tomorrow. So I guess you know I'm thrilled.

Treatments continue without hitch and with no further reactions. I should have reached the half-way mark today, but now they hedge a little and say the 10 is "approximate." Well, maybe it will be only 9!

Your Boothbay Harbor letter came yesterday and was such a treat. I loved every word of it, and the evergreens testifying to your thoughtfulness. And Roger was thrilled with the card. More soon, but I want to give this to Ida.

So very much love—

Rachel

Darling [Rachel],

How is the Capehart? That was a lovely surprise—of course. I hope you realize I couldn't hear the music too well—just that there was music in the background.

I felt you might have been disappointed because I didn't recognize it.

I am so happy for you—I think you will get hours of enjoyment—and it may also be a pleasant way to work!

I can imagine how thrilled you are. Won't it be wonderful when we can share it?

As I told you I shall let you decide the time. After talking with Stanley to learn that he is planning to spend the week of Jan. 22 with us while he visits schools around Boston, I suppose I must be home that week. Other than that time, I could go to you any time.

I do want terribly to see you for as you said in the Apple, "There is so much to say—things that can only be said." You say you "cannot be sure from my letters just how much you have let this recent cloud disturb you."

Of course, you can't be sure, dear. I will tell you this, and I'm sure you will understand that on that Tuesday afternoon before Thanks-giving I was awfully upset—upset for all I felt the new "opening of a door you had considered shut" would do to your peace of mind—how it would affect your work on the book, as well as your outlook for the future. I think there were many days when I could think of nothing else—and I'll confess the thoughts were negative. Suddenly I realized such thoughts were bad—for you, and for me. After that I tried hard to concentrate on positive thoughts, on a happy future—of summer and the lovely things we are going to share. Then came your news of your contact with Dr. Crile. If you remember the letter I wrote you then, I tried to express in words the great sense of relief that flooded over me that morning. And, darling, since then I can truthfully say that it is so much easier to think happy thoughts, even to the point of real faith that this shadow will be conquered.

Through all our letters and long conversations you yourself have conveyed to me in words and in attitude only hope. Darling, if you have felt despair (and I can believe you must have) it has not come through to me in any way.

It will be so comforting to talk together.

This is the last day of 1960—a tragic year for both of us. Let me repeat the words of your Christmas message.

"The promise of a year where everything goes well with you and those you hold most dear."

What finer, better wish could I make?

Be assured, darling, my love is boundless as the Sea. Forgive me for all the mistakes I have made in this past year which may have caused you not to believe me.

> For I love you beyond expression.
> *Dorothy*

1 9 6 1

TUESDAY, JANUARY 3

UNDER DRIER (NO GLASSES!)

Dearest [Dorothy],

I have only a few minutes, since I'm about to have a manicure. Dr. Caulk is inclined to agree with me that there is already a suggestion of shrinkage. He confirms my thought that once we are sure it is going down, he can go ahead with local radiation. (He would eventually use that anyway. It is important now to learn whether it is endocrine-dependent.) So I think, dear, if you can come next week that is the best bet—unless we waited several weeks more. (I'd rather have you *soon*.) So maybe Sunday or Monday?? As I said on the phone, we'll be very sensible and if weather is threatening, or anyone has a sniffle, or anything else is wrong, we'll just postpone.

Dr. Caulk will want to see me one day next week, but I'm afraid that would be true of any week. I'll ask him if the appointment can be Monday, if you are coming that day. Anyway, he is very prompt and his examination takes only a few minutes.

I do *hope* your New Year's Day rain didn't turn to snow! And how lucky your Maine trip wasn't that week—at least I heard some northern N.E. places had 17 inches.

The mail hadn't come when I left, so I hope for a letter from you when I get home. I think you said one was on the way.

I will write more when I can see better! This is just to confirm that I hope you can come next week, and that it would be Heaven to have you anytime.

All love from a not-so D.D.[1]

---

[1] Distinguished Democrat. RC had written for the Democratic platform and been invited to an inaugural reception for distinguished Democratic women.

Dearest, I had to rush home to release Ida, without time to get an envelope and mail the enclosed note. Now I'll mail it this evening, when I have to go out on another errand.

As I hoped, your letter was here and I loved having it. Since you say you can come anytime except that one week, I'll assume we can hope that this time a week from now we'll be together! You say the day, darling, according to when you want to travel, but I'd hope for either Sunday or Monday. I have done so little writing for weeks, and there is none of that long lost "momentum" of the summer to interrupt, so this is really an ideal time, and I hope you will stay as long as you feel you can be away from home.

The Capehart continues to be a delight, and I am finding unexpected pleasure in the FM radio. Before you come I want to get one stereo record just for the sake of comparison. Perhaps they *can* sound better than my regular LP's, but I'll have to be shown.

Of course there is much more I want to say, but what a joy to hope I can say, not write, it soon!

I'll call you the end of the week, darling, for further plans. Tell Stan I think he is dear to be willing to share you.

All my love,
Rachel

Dearest [Dorothy]—

Just a line to keep in touch until I call you, which I'll do Friday night. All goes well here—weather cold but sunny, and most of the snow gone. Now I hope that is the last for many weeks. I was so thankful to hear you decided to forego the New Year's Day trip in the cold rain—which might so easily have begun to freeze. A *fireplace* and Beethoven sounded much better! (Beethoven's 5th in my background now.)

Only one more treatment in this series. The ulcer has been painful, but today is yielding to diet and increased medicine. Dr. Caulk says it is not unusual for radiation to cause an ulcer flare up, and advised consulting Dr. Healy. I did, but knowing the routine by this time, was already doing everything necessary. Darling, we wouldn't let a little thing like a misbehaving ulcer interfere with our visit! A cold, yes—but not that. Besides, once the radiation stops, it should clear up promptly.

I continue to feel the swelling is going down. Really, this is very, very good. As I understood Dr. Crile's estimate, the chances it would do so on withdrawal of hormone stimulation were 50-50. Of course it *will* when treated directly, but the knowledge it is hormone-dependent (when confirmed) gives us additional weapons for the future. Had we continued the direct radiation in the beginning we'd never have known.

Next week does look like the ideal time for you to come, so I do hope weather and all other factors cooperate. No treatments, I'm reasonably sure.

Today's mail brought an invitation that will cause me to go carousing with other D.D.'s on the afternoon of the 18th—a "Reception for the Distinguished Ladies Attending the Inauguration." At the National Gallery of Art. It should be something for an old lady's memories, (when I reach that stage) so I shall hope to attend. Yesterday I read in the paper (not knowing I was a D.L.) that those attending would properly wear afternoon dress and either a new hat or a special hair-do (How about a wig—if my hair lady can't mold mine into something special??) We can laugh and have fun planning for this—but really I think it will be an experience. And Roger will be *so* proud. He is already bursting with pride over a letter his "mother" has from the President-Elect. (Just a gracious note of thanks—purely routine, of course.)

There is also an invitation to the Inaugural Ball, but this I shall pass up.

Jeanne was here today—the first since just before Christmas, and we got caught up on letters. There is some work to be done at Public Health downtown that she can attend to while you're here, But I do want to manage a brief get-together if I can, just because I'd like you to know each other.

There is bad news from Lorraine. Larry[2] is having serious trouble again, and soon has to choose between amputation of his foot and a drastic operation with months of convalescence and no assurance of benefit. She says "only he can decide."

I'll send this airmail, dear—partly to speed it to you, but also for the more prosaic reason that I've used my last 4¢ stamp!

There is a growing pile of things to share with you. How can there be hours enough?

Love to Stan, Willow, and—You!

Rachel

[2] Caretakers of RC's Southport cottage.

JANUARY 9

My darling [Dorothy],

Can you possibly know how happy I am that you are here?

Recently I re-discovered the little poem[3] enclosed. Perhaps it should be our theme in the days ahead—not that it is new to us, especially the last line. But I like it for us, so very much.

And I love you always, all ways.

Rachel

[3] From "Auguries of Innocence."

To see the world in a grain of sand,
And a heaven in a wild flower;
Hold infinity in the palm of your hand,
And eternity in an hour.

William Blake

My darling [Dorothy],

If I could I would travel with you, but let me be near you as you travel in the only way I can—in the memory of hours listening to the Capehart, of hours before the fire, of reading shared, of thoughts and feelings so freely exchanged. It has all been sweet—"a magical thing and sweet to remember"—but perhaps best of all was that chance to share each other's thoughts and in their light to exorcise any lurking dark spirits. I want you to think only happy thoughts of me from now on, darling, and now that we have faced this problem together I hope and believe you can.

Have fun reading on the train. I shall be with you in *my* thoughts all the way.

Remember how truly and tenderly I love you.

Rachel

JANUARY 13, 1:30 P.M.

Darling [Rachel],

I'll have to take advantage of the station stops to write briefly. Train travel is not conducive to good handwriting.

The car my porter chose, he told me, was "the best"! I'm sure he'd never ridden on it. After we got going, it began to jerk and shake unmercifully. At first I thought the roadbed must be rough—I really never knew anything like it. There were some jocular remarks about the situation as the conductor went through. But it wasn't funny to me for I didn't see how I could endure it for 8½ hours. Desperately, I went exploring. I discovered that the second car back rode as comfortably as the one in which I had gone down to Wash. So before we got to Baltimore I transferred my bags, & have been as comfortable as possible ever since. I've had some milk & a miserable sandwich put up by the Penn. R.R. I won't even describe it—at least, not now.

NEW YORK—ON TIME

Always when I leave you, I travel with a dream-like quality—half waking, half sleeping. Today the feeling has been heightened by *The Immense Journey*.[4] There is a sense of being suspended in time. And when I return the book I'll send you some pages to read to help you understand what I mean.

Darling, I approached this visit with a feeling of sadness. But there was such a charming, magical quality to it, that in spite of the underlying sadness that we can't deny I have come away with a certain sense of peace which you had hoped (in a letter) I might do.

I hope you are as content as I am that we found the way to bring to the surface the thoughts that were lying so far below. Only between two who love each other as we do could there be the possibility of saying what I did to you. Now it has been said, I'm sure all will be easier from now on. I know the problems you

[4] By Loren Eiseley, first published in 1957.

face. It seems there couldn't be more difficult ones. But you are so wonderful about them all, that in a way it has helped me. You see, I rebel so terribly that this serious situation has confronted you—you, my darling, the talented, gifted, giving, precious one—whose path has never been smooth since I've known you. Even when all is well, as I now believe it will be, I shall still rebel at the time you have had to sacrifice to it, as well as the worry and anxiety it has brought you. It would have been so wonderful if you might have gone on to the completion of the book with the uninterrupted momentum you had achieved.

To have learned of your fine relationship with Dr. Crile, and the knowledge that you will be watched over not only by fine competency and skill but also by interested friendship, helps me to rise above the more depressing thoughts.

I have read your train "apple" over hourly. As always you have caught the spirit of our being together beautifully and simply.

I leave you, inspired, darling. Yes, the beauty we shared will be a living memory for weeks to come. I feel that Capehart will bring you unending joy as well as much peace.

I need not tell you how happy I am that you played Santa Claus to yourself.

From Roger's comment this morning we gathered that Santa Claus fills stockings, *at least*. "Yes, Virginia, there is a Santa Claus."

NEW HAVEN

8 minutes here so I'll finish this. So many thoughts, deep in my heart. If you and I were sitting before the fire I think I could voice them. One thing I've been pondering is your contemplated California trip.[5] Oh, I do so hope you can go. And I want to reiterate my offer for Stan and me to housekeep for you. Darling, it would be so much easier for you, so much more freedom to move about if you didn't take Roger. He has a long lifetime for such treats. If you have talked it over I suppose he would be disappointed but who isn't? After our (Roger & I) pleasant little session before the fire last night I have the feeling he would accept us happily, which might temper his disappointment.

And, darling, you know we have wanted to help you some way. It would be no hardship for us. It will be a delightful time of year—it would give us a chance to see your place at one of its loveliest times. And we would see you, dear, before and after!

Think seriously about it. All you'd have to do if we go down would be to walk out—no arrangements to make—or at least not nearly the number you'd have to make otherwise.

The sun is casting long shadows. In three hours I should be receiving Willow's welcome.

I have reread your note. You *have* travelled with me, dear, in many ways. Now I'm going to the Diner for a cup of tea and toast to break the next 3 hours. It will be a far cry from the setting of yesterday's tea and toast!

[5] To speak at Scripps College, Claremont, California.

And how far a cry, little I knew. I will spare you the details now.

One hour to go, and in spite of the poor writing it means, I'll finish this while jiggling along. You'll understand.

The return journey is always so hard. None of the anticipatory glow that I shall be seeing you in a matter of hours—only long weeks without you stretching ahead.

But isn't it wonderful that I made the journey at this particular time? Of course, I felt so distressed for your indisposition & I know that you kept up because I was there—but I want to believe that perhaps you felt as well as you have for a long time. And of course, the weather was ideal at both ends—and in the middle, too. Just to have those few moments to walk out with you *and* Jeffie was an unexpected delight—in January, too!

If all is well at home, it will be a good ending for a perfect 3 days *and* 4 nights!

I shall not soon forget the hours before the fire with The Capehart. (That personifying touch—I never speak of my record player as The Zenith.)

And, darling, we *laughed* together. Do you realize it?

Like cutting off your voice this morning, it takes fortitude to end this letter. But we are getting closer to the Mass. line and the writing is miserable.

I have enjoyed *The Immense Journey* so much—but the reading of it lacked the ability to turn to you & say "Listen, to this" or even to express a thought that it aroused in me to you. That would have made it so much lovelier. Well, at least we had some hours of that kind of loveliness.

Now, my darling, I'll say good-night. Not as I said it last night but at least with a vivid memory of that moment.

> I love you deeply
> and highly and widely,
> *Dorothy*

TUESDAY NIGHT, JANUARY 17

Dearest [Dorothy],

I'm sitting where we spent many happy hours, on the study sofa, the Capehart playing softly. But no fire on the hearth, no loved presence beside me. By talking to you, though, I can bring you near.

I am so glad to be able to send you the enclosure,[6] not only because I know you'll be happy to "meet" the Criles, but because I hope Jane's message may do for you something like what it did for me. Her revelation,[7] so calmly and matter-of-factly made, somehow made my spirits soar like a shot of psychological adrenalin. I think even her picture will tell you she is so vibrantly and joyously alive. Now to know she, too, has encountered this shadow and in spirit at least has triumphantly overcome it is a wonderful example. And it will make you know the sympathy and understanding that underlie their desire to help me.

[6] Enclosure not preserved.

[7] Dr. Crile's wife, Jane, had breast cancer.

Now darling, I want to try to help you understand something, and the talks we had should make it easier. You know that I can see many reasons for a hopeful attitude, but you also know that I have faced all the possibilities. Out of that has come, I think, a deepened awareness of the preciousness of whatever time is left, be it long or short, and a desire to live more affirmatively, making the most of opportunities when they are offered, not putting them off for another day. So when the California invitation was renewed, it seemed to me this was the time to accept. But from the very beginning the intention of taking Roger was part of the decision—and not because I didn't know what else to do, but because it was an opportunity to do something lovely with him—to give him the memory of a wonderful experience we had shared. If it must be that his world has to be shattered again before he reaches manhood, at least I want while there is time to share as many "wonders" as possible with him. And if we could carry out this great adventure of going to Lois that might be the summit of the whole experience. At any rate, darling, my desire to go to California is composed about equally of two parts—the fact I have something I want to say at Scripps, and this wish to create something Roger can keep always. You do understand now, don't you?

WEDNESDAY, UNDER DRIER

But I won't have long to write because of my manicure. This is the day of the reception, you know. Grey and rather threatening skies, but I trust they don't mean rain or snow. (There was talk last night of Thursday snow.)

Well what a tea party you had on the train! I couldn't imagine what the story was going to be. You wonder what I would have done and I scarcely know. Perhaps when it became too offensive I'd have summoned the waiter and asked him to move my tea to another table, without explanation, probably—certainly none to the man, but the action would speak for itself. But how disgusting! No, I can't laugh about the incident. Perhaps I could offer some thoughts on it, but I won't now, because time has sped on and I'm now at home, soon to get dressed and fare forth as a Distinguished Lady.

The day is cold and rather windy but the early threat of precipitation seems to have disappeared from the skies.

A couple of items to chuckle over: Yesterday's mail brought a letter from an unknown woman writing on very "distinguished" stationery, printed with the "distinguished" name, Mrs. Grasvenor Atterbury. "You won't believe this," she began, "but I really want to know what you feed your dog, cat, monkey, bird or whatever—not commercial feeds but something very special between you and your pet." She is compiling an animal Cook Book—purpose to aid an Animal Shelter on Long Island. Shall I tell her loin lamb chops and blue cheese crackers?

The other item was inspired by your report of Roger's term for my intestinal difficulty. He has always had a horror of having diarrhea himself—why I don't really know. Anyway the term had impressed itself on his mind at an early age. He was also impressed by all the hurricanes and their names, even when he was only 4 or 5. Reminiscing one day several years ago he said "you remember that one they called Hurricane Diarrhea?" Not bad, is it? (I think he meant Dianne.)

Well, my H.D. is intermittently better and worse—clears up for a day or two and then returns. Fortunately this is one of the better days.

Your Sunday-Monday letter is here but I won't attempt to comment now—time to dress and go. I want to mail this on the way.

Of course I'd like the Criles' card soon.

Your grosbeaks and Mr. Pheasant sound so special!

Tell Stan his "salmon wiggle" sounds good even to me! I looked up the recipe. I assume "cooked salmon" means canned?

All my love—and such happy thoughts of last week—

Rachel

My dearest [Dorothy],

Everything in the enclosed letter is information I really wanted you to have—so don't be disturbed about my taking time to write it. However, the result of segregating all of that sort of thing is a letter so different in tone from my usual outpourings to you that I had to laugh when I re-read it! I hope you will, too. But I also want to say, on this tiny card, that, in retrospect, neither does my long letter mailed yesterday seem to have conveyed half of what was in my heart to say to you, despite its length. Perhaps the typewriter got in the way—producing quantity but perhaps not quite conveying my feelings. As always, though, I count on you to understand. There have been such beautiful things in your recent letters—more than ever, I mean. The part about the fire yesterday—yes, darling. I know what you mean and feel as you do, but we must have time and opportunities to enjoy this now! And in the letter before that—one of the loveliest things you ever said to me—that because you have come to love me, you have realized anew the depth of your love for your family. There are few things that could make me happier than that. And so I could go on and on, picking out the thoughts that have brought me so much happiness, and that make me love you—though it hardly seems possible!—always more and more.

R.

TUESDAY, JANUARY 31, LATE AFTERNOON

Darling [Rachel],

I like this time of day to talk to you. There is still a cold light in the sky but the street lights are on, the birds have taken their last seed, the silhouette of the bare branches against the sky is fast fading. Inside, I've just turned on my dear lamp over my bed, all is cozy, the house is quiet, Stan is writing, way off in the study, and Willow is taking a last breath of fresh air. This is the bed where years ago you lay for a rest—a rest I thought you needed, so left you alone—and as I started downstairs that sweet little voice made my heart leap—"Hurry back." That was all I needed. I did.

Now in this setting where you always are, I have read again the Hyacinth Letter. How very, very precious it is. I shall always remember the warmth that flowed through me as I read the words, so exquisitely expressed, which told me that you needed "the particular combination of qualities that is you," and why you couldn't stop writing even for the "bread" of the book. No wonder you didn't need to read the card that accompanied the pot of "white hyacinths" yesterday. As I said recently I wish so much I had taken this letter for us to read together during my visit. It is so full of lovely, expressive phrases—"the lovely companionship of your letters has become a necessity to me," "what sort of nourishment a writer's spirit must have," "someone who is deeply devoted to me as a person, and who also has the capacity and the depth of understanding to share, vicariously, the sometimes crushing burden, of creative effort, recognizing the heartache, the great weariness of mind and body, the occasional black despair—someone who cherishes me and what I am trying to create." "And then, my dear one, you came into my life!"

Dearest, can you *now*, did you *ever* understand what all that meant to me? Remember that then you were the Famous Author, on a pedestal, with that gulf between us. In that letter the gulf was bridged even altho' it took a long time to destroy the pedestal. Its destruction came when I grew to know you as a person who had worldly cares and burdens and heartaches as I had. It is paradoxical that I could bring you down off the pedestal and yet continue to worship you as I do, isn't it?

There are five long pages of this letter. I used to read them every night for months, I do believe.

You go on to say—"there is another side to all this—but I can't see that *I* can possibly be giving you anything comparable in return." "I, unlike you, simply accept the fact that evidently I have filled some need in your life. What it is doesn't matter. Perhaps you don't even know."

But I did know and I think that I answered that question. If you could go back I think you'd find that my answer was that I felt in you I had found a kindred spirit—someone who loved and enjoyed the things of the inner being—which I so much needed, for at that time I had no one with whom I could share my deep feelings for music, night, moonlight, sunsets, The Sea (remember) and all the other intangibles which are food for that inner self.

Now 7 years have spun themselves out. And during them you have not only been that kindred spirit in a thousand ways, but you have enriched my life beyond measure. I wonder if you realize in what ways. I could list so many—but I shan't try to think of them all.

Probably the fact that knowing you caused my reading to take a new direction—you introduced me to authors I might never have known if you hadn't entered my life—Jefferies, Williamson, Cloos, and oh, especially Tomlinson. The natural world began to have so much more meaning with you to share it— the joy of the interest in birds—and out of that, dear, has developed Stan's great hobby. Oh, darling, as I look back I think of all the ramifications that have resulted from some little beginning.

I scarcely need to mention the opening of the door to the edge of the sea with all the lovely experiences which grew out of that—there again you were able to bring Stan into our interests.

Do you understand that if it hadn't been for you, darling, his retirement might be an empty existence!? And of course, all the exciting and lovely events that stemmed from your dedication of *The Edge of the Sea*. And all the sharing. The delight of discovering that you were a fan of E. B. White—and Robert Frost, bringing the fun of sharing anything new that E.B. produces. Not in the same category dear, but to find that you and I could understand each other so well when the subject is Cats. Who else (except Stan) in all this world could appreciate how we feel? Oh, Lois—of course. Which brings me to another category of the way you have enriched my life. In no other way would I have ever known people like the Teales and the Bestons—and this rare relationship with Lois.

Even if I never write at all, it has been enlightening to know people who have—and above all are You! I suppose you have no conception of how much I have learned from you about the profession—in small ways and in large ways I've been admitted to the secret order. Just that afternoon last spring with your files was worth a 4-year college course. And again Stan has shared that—another common ground for him and me.

Of course, darling, all that we have shared in the field of music I'm sure I could never expect to share with anyone else. Stan will always be an outsider. Recorded music—Our Symphony, Our Concerto, Our Leonard Bernstein—I suppose that is one area that perhaps does not need a sharer to be happy, but oh, how sweet to have one. Just to look in someone's eyes to find a response which tells you the feeling is the same.

And then there are so many tangible reminders of you. Here in my room, darling, there is your picture in which I've always thought you were listening for veeries—it's always there waiting when I come up here. In my jewel case the dear golden wreath lies on the velvet speaking to me of eternal friendship. The two dear lamps shed light and warmth and on the walls the woodland portraits—my white violets and my trilliums. Downstairs in the living room more woodland portraits and did I tell you that now the pewter candelabra holds the central place over the fireplace? And records—lovely records—including one we have not yet listened to together—Bach's *St. Matthew's Passion*. I shall have to take it the next time I go to Silver Spring. It will be so glorious on the Capehart!

Even the pen I write with speaks of you as well as to you.

[8] Arthur Cleveland Bent.

But of all the tangibles, darling, of course the gifts of fine books you have showered upon us are the most enriching. I can't name them all—someday I think I shall make a list of them. But I must mention the Bent[8] volumes—not easy to come by—and to accompany them the Bird Song Record! Oh, Darling, one of the first books was *The Wind in the Willows*—remember—how I loved that. Need I say that your own creations, your brain children are everything to me.

Besides all I have mentioned, I suppose the memories of the moments, the days, the nights, the weeks, we have spent together are most to be cherished. Someday I'm going through my diaries & make a list of them.

You spoke of the moonlight shining in your room—how many happy memories that evokes. If we had only moonlight, shared, to remember, our storehouse would be unusually rich. But there are the Sea, the Shore, the Woods, the Gardens, the Marshes, Phosphorescence, Wind, Sun, Sand, Scents—oh, my Darling.

And then there is the Sadness and the Unhappiness we've shared. I wonder how I could have stood all I did in those 4½ miserable years without your sustaining and continuing love and understanding. I have tried to imagine what it would have been like if there hadn't been your letters to take to bed with me, or your dear voice on the phone so frequently. To-day I remembered one little incident—do you remember the day at Southport when I threw my back out—my children were coming and I needed to see Mother. You drove me up to Edgecomb. And I think that was the day Mother had had another shock and was so disturbed. Oh, darling, it was so good to have you along. Little either of us dreamed when you wrote in the Hyacinth letter of heartache, great weariness of mind and body, the black despair in relation to creative writing that both of us were to meet those very things in other realms. How good we couldn't know the future. How lovely, how beautiful, how comparatively free from care was that first Maytime.

For me it has meant more than I can ever tell you to have your love to enfold me—love that was your arms about me in my dark hours.

My skies are brighter. Would, my dearest, that yours were. In your dark hours now, please know that my love, like enfolding arms, is about you as yours was about me.

Your skies will be brighter, too. The time for them to reach you seems long, but how shining they will be when you are well again.

Now I've read this over. Between the lines I hope you can read what I've never been able to say, adequately—that in the going-on-eight years in which I've known you, my life has been enriched, broadened, sweetened, smoothed, softened, and enlarged beyond expressing—all because of you. You have had fame and fortune and I'm glad. But I hope my love which you've had and continue to have has made you as happy as the fame and fortune.

And I believe it has. You have shown me in so many ways.

Are you glad we met? I know even if we could have met without the intro-duction by your wonderful *The Sea Around Us*, I should have found in you ex-actly as I have, the same qualities that have endeared you to me—so that the Fame would make no difference. There is no Pedestal. You are You, my Beloved One.

WEDNESDAY MORNING

Darling, in reading this over I find I have not told you one half the thoughts I could or would. But I know you know. On the other hand, it is good to remember. I wish we could live all the lovely moments over again, together.

We are off to Norwood on a morning when it is still just zero!

This letter seems to be to serve as an anniversary remembrance of the Hyacinth letter—and that is what I wanted it to be.

With it goes the boundless love which has grown and grown over the years between.

I love you.
Dorothy

FEBRUARY 2

My darling [Dorothy],

Just a few words to you—things I've wanted to say and couldn't.

You wrote me (during the week after your return, which seems so long ago, but it was also about the time of the beginning of this siege) on the day of Dr. Dooley's[9] death, feeling you could after the conversations we had. I had been thinking so much about you all that day, darling, and hoping the news had not set up unhappy thoughts. That was Thursday, two weeks ago. I know because I decided to call you that night, not because I was anxious to pour out the tale of new ailments, but because I thought it might help if you were sad. So that was my Inauguration Eve call. (Of course, darling, we know there are no parallels to be drawn anyway—his case was quite different.)

It seemed odd to have my own concern shifted from what I would have thought would always seem the major disability to a wholly new set of disor-ders.[10] I confess I wasn't happy about the finding of staphylococcus, and I guess in my low state the memory that a "staph" had claimed Roger's "other mother" during the last days of January four years ago didn't contribute to my morale. If there is still anything so old-fashioned as a "crisis" in illness, I think I passed through it last Thurs. evening. I had slept heavily and awoke around 6 P.M. feel-ing so indescribably weak and ill that I was frightened. I just had the feeling that at that moment life had burned down to a very tiny flame, that might so easily flicker out. I didn't want Ida to know how bad I felt (we were then marooned in a blizzard) but I kept her near me on some pretext. She rubbed me with alcohol, later got me some tea, and in a few hours strength was somehow coming back—and since then the trend has been up.

[9] Dr. Thomas Dooley, who had died of cancer on January 18, 1961, was an author and widely known as a physician who practiced in primitive areas.

[10] RC was troubled by joint inflam-mation, bladder problems, and phlebitis.

Now I'm sure the infection is very nearly conquered, darling—the slowly improving temperature record proves that.

Another thing I want to say, darling—sometimes in our conversations I almost feel you are not sure I would have wanted you here—as though perhaps you wondered why I didn't ask you to come. Darling, you *know* that from a purely selfish standpoint nothing else could make me so happy. But everything has been against it. In the early days, the danger of infection, though probably not great because of its location.[11] Then the fact that you could not, and I would not let you, undertake my care while it still involves such *heavy* chores. Then the weather, plus the fact that you had just been away and needed some time to yourself.

Darling—if I reach a point where I am at least semi-ambulatory, but still limited about resuming household cares, and having a problem about going for treatment—then I might ask if you could come for most of a week, allowing me to put some of the money I would pay out to helpers, cabs, etc., into your ticket. This if you would realize you must not do it if it seems unwise at home, for I *can* always work things out somehow. You spoke in terms of *driving* down with Stan, which of course would be a joy both to Roger and to me—if only the season were different. But with these storms sweeping in one after another I would be so worried.

Well, dear, this is just a thought—but I did want you to understand my failure to ask you meant only that for your sake I couldn't. For me, the only heaven I can imagine now would be found in looking into your blue eyes—

My love—always
Rachel

SUNDAY A.M., FEBRUARY 5

Darling [Dorothy],
I'll write a note and hope someone may come in so it can get on its way. I wonder so whether you got the force of the storm. I did hear it was very bad in New York so I can hardly imagine it missed you. Well, I hope your week-end plans weren't spoiled and most of all that you have been able to keep warm and cozy whatever came.

Our snow ended early Saturday morning. Elliott came with another man and dug us out but so far as I know the snow plough has never been up Berwick. People are getting through. Poor Ida stayed through from Friday A.M. until Saturday afternoon. When her husband came for her he also brought Mrs. Tennie,[12] who is now "stuck" until tomorrow. Poor old Mary, with her faltering car, just can't make it in this weather.

A letter from Lois yesterday. She had received a note I wrote about a week ago, also a letter from "dear Dorothy." I know she is so grateful to you for keep-

[11] The infection had settled in RC's knees and ankles.

[12] A new nurse, whose name in subsequent letters RC spells "Tenney."

ing her up to date. I always marvel at the speed of mail to and from that remote place.

Yesterday I had two good trips into "outer space." Moppet settled in my lap and rode about with me, watching birds at the various windows. On the second trip I took time to hear some music—a bit of opera on FM radio, and the Bach record you gave me. It was like "discovering" the Capehart all over again—I'd forgotten how glorious it is.

The only penalty for these excursions was a considerable stiffening of the right knee (it has always been worse) and somewhat more pain in it, but the doctor thinks this to be expected and no reason for discontinuing the experiments.

Just then, darling, you called, so my questions about you are answered. How thankful I am that loss of power doesn't mean loss of heat for you. Sometime I must find out what sort of device you have. (I believe it works only with hot water heat. The hot air has to be circulated by electricity. I did inquire several years ago.) To have our power go has, of course, been a nightmare in the back of my mind during each of our snows. Were I up and able-bodied I could cope somehow but in this situation it hardly bears thinking about.

Darling, I don't see how you have kept up this wonderful flow of mail. Something practically every day. I know there is much in letters that came early in my illness that I wanted to comment on, and of course never did. Some had to do with the Inauguration. (Roger thought the "Holy Smoke" was the Cardinal's breath! I thought he was trying to make the Inaugural Address himself. But wasn't that fire threat alarming?) I liked so much what you said about Jacqueline—her poise that must come from an "inner serenity"—for that does describe her so perfectly. Although I haven't met any of the Kennedy sisters, she is such a complete contrast to what they seem to be—and I think it is a tribute to our President's taste that when he had an opportunity to choose, he turned from the brash type of female with which he had been surrounded to a being of such rare and exquisite quality as Jacqueline. I did think his address a masterpiece and I am glad you liked it, too. The *New Yorker* devotes the first part of "Talk of the Town" this week to a tribute to it.

Excuse change of color!

I thought the whole handling of the proceedings that morning was a model and something we should be proud to have the world see—the Eisenhowers' gracious invitation to coffee before going to the Capitol, the behavior of the outgoing and the incoming in relation to each other all the way down the line, the views of old and new Presidents chatting before the ceremony. But I did wish Mr. Eisenhower would wear his hat! At least Mr. Kennedy has hair—but I worried about him when he took off his coat.

Now I'm going to get this ready to go, darling, for if Robert & Vera went to church this morning they will stop in soon. I'll be writing more, and during the week there is less problem about mailing. (Our mailman was not stayed from his rounds by the storm.)

I do feel stronger each day now and the evening temperature elevation is now very slight. I had thought perhaps I'd feel quite weak when I first got up but it hasn't been too bad.

Have debated about sending this airmail but hesitate. Mail to and from Lois, who would seem to live in the very cradle of storms, always goes via air, but I fear Boston and Washington are more uncertain quantities.

You are in my mind and heart constantly. Love to Stan, and love to you.

Rachel

I loved hearing about Stan and the chick-a-dee.

For February 6

Darling [Dorothy],

The same thoughts that inspired the "hyacinth letter"—the same love and the same need of you—lead me to add once again to the hyacinth corner of your garden. Meanwhile, may their fragrance and beauty tell you that I love you.

Rachel

Tuesday, February 7, 6:15 a.m.

Darling [Rachel],

Last night I got in bed at 8:30—very unusual for me—so now I seem to be slept out. I'm glad, for I can talk to you. Yesterday the temp. went to 36°. Very balmy indeed. About 4:30 I went out to fill up the bird feeders for the pre-dark feeding. Stan was still asleep—also Willow. I wandered down the street when suddenly I felt like a real walk. I was dressed for it so off I went. Of course, from the appearance of the landscape with its mountains of snow everywhere (by climbing to the tops one can touch the power lines in some places) I felt as though I were in another world. John Greenleaf Whittier found a more poetic expression for the circumstance. Do you remember *Snow-Bound*? Somehow I felt more alive than I have since these stormy, sub zero days set in—"winter's icy grip" never has seemed more real. It was good to be outdoors, good to be walking. And, of course, darling I couldn't help thinking of you, lying helpless in bed now over two long weeks—quite a different "eternity" from a few weeks ago. As I returned the sun was just setting with that flame-like color between the trees that always calls to mind the glimpse one gets at Deep Cove from the road at that time of day. Above were the smoky plumes of clouds against a turquoise sky which foretell more beauty in the after sunset glow. And the promise was fulfilled last night exquisitely. And as always I longed for you to be sharing it.

Just then Willow pushed his way into my room (we have not been putting him in the cellar these cold nights). Instead of wanting to settle down with me, he told me very plainly he wanted me to get up. I let him out into a 10° above zero morning. This snowy world is a difficult place for little cats who are used to finding soft dirt for a bathroom. (We have Kitty Litter in the cellar, but he doesn't ever use it.) It is fun to watch him climb, what must be for him, a Matterhorn, to get over to softer snow where he digs, sits for a while and then furiously covers it up. Then he makes a dash for the house. Too cute! Now he has eaten and tried to sit on my writing paper but I pushed him off so he is cuddled beside me on the kitchen table, purring & watching for birds. Incidentally, I've been meaning to tell you that K. Grant has had a Titmouse at her house several days.

The mailman, bless his heart, came at his usual time yesterday so, I did not have to cling to the window impatiently waiting.

Your letter was there!

It was written last Thursday, dear. And much has happened since then. We've talked twice—oh, joyful! You had warned me that it was not too cheerful a letter. Actually, darling, it was not depressing—in fact, we smiled at your picture of "hospital" life wherein one has "no little privacies left"—how true and how well Stan understands what you mean. Yes, indeed, dear, I do realize that you never get out of bed, and altho' that has seldom happened to me and then only briefly I'm sure it gives one such a helpless and dependent feeling. When you spoke of being able to "look for things in your study" via the wheelchair it underlined so well the effect of having to be in bed always.

I do hope the wheelchair is continuing to give you a little sense of freedom and comfort. Don't overdo.

I'm glad, dear, that I can *do* something for you—even if it is only mail—which in itself is no sacrifice on my part!

All you wrote in the apple brought you close. I think we must have been sharing similar thoughts on the day we learned of Dr. Dooley's death. I hoped almost that perhaps you hadn't heard and yet I knew you would in time. And during the call which you had made "because I thought it might help if you were sad" we did not speak of that sadness. Once I almost did but thought it wiser to reserve it for the letter. It is so like you to be thinking that *I* might be unhappy when the event had so much poignant meaning for you.

Darling, I know and knew then that no parallels should be drawn— I knew the type of malignancy Dr. Dooley's was at the time of his operation in New York. You know he announced it on TV. If I had thought there was any parallel between his case and yours, darling, I fear, free as I feel to speak openly with you now, I might have hesitated to write you about him. By the way, did you read Norman Cousins's editorial about him in *SR* of Feb. 4?

All you wrote of the low, low tide of that Thursday evening is so vivid, darling. To have you say you were frightened speaks volumes. I'm so glad you told me for I've wondered how you could endure so much so stoically—as you have sounded on the telephone. I'm sure the returning strength after a few hours must have seemed a miracle to you.

I have no conception of what it could mean to feel that "life had burned down to a very tiny flame." But I know that Stan could know and understand what you mean. I know that he has had the same experience—not so dramatically expressed. You know, he and I did have a wonderful emotional experience together at that time.

Darling, isn't it hard to express one's thoughts simply and accurately so that the other understands? In these conversations in which you felt "you are not sure I would have wanted you here—as though perhaps you wondered why I didn't ask you to come"—I fear I did not make you understand at all what I tried to convey. I think I shall not try now but let me reassure you that those (quoted above) two thoughts never entered my head. I was trying so hard to leave you completely free.

I suppose, I *know*, that when you were so sick I could not have given you the care you needed. When the time does come that I, we can be of some use remember we have both said that *if* we can help we want to.

When the time comes, dear, we'll work something out that will be best for all concerned in all ways.

And we shall await your suggestions, dear. I do hope you are *much* better. If I write, as I did yesterday, of our activities and doings only, please don't think that we are not concerned with you and all that involves you. We are always thinking of you.

Now I must go hang the draperies which I did up yesterday. I really enjoyed doing them—my washer-drier did such a perfect job & because they were permanent finish there was no need to starch, & I ironed them damp from the drier—I started washing at 11 P.M. & at 12:45 all six were ironed! How's that? Always used to hate doing up curtains.

This morning Stan has washed the woodwork & windows!

And this must go out to the mailbox. We have to walk into it between snow walls above our shoulders!

All my love goes with this,
Dorothy

[13] The letter preceding this postscript.

Oh, My Darling [Rachel], I had just sealed the following letter to you[13] when the bell rang. There stood a man with a huge florist's wrapped package to which was attached some purple heather. I have reasons for always thinking of you when I see heather so even before the wrappings were off I had flown to you. But then, my eyes were flooded with tears as I saw the loveliness I long to share with you. Surely you would be completely happy if you could see and smell this pot of white hyacinths—the foliage is perfect, dark shining green, not too high, giving plenty of room for the waxy whiteness—ten bulbs, two at the peak of their blooming, the other eight at various stages so there will be bloom for weeks to come, I should think. And, of course, so fragrant.

Darling, with the tears came floods of memories as well. (Stan was away so I could indulge myself.) All of the indescribable glow and out-of-this world feeling which came with the hyacinth letter returned to make me almost dizzy, altho' that's not quite the word—floating on air, I guess is better.

And, of course, when I read the dear loving message accompanying the flowers, for a few moments I was completely blinded with tears. Darling, that message must have been on its way to the florist before you received my letter telling that I had re-read the hyacinth letter recently. If ever there was Stardust, there was never a better example, for your note sounds exactly as though you were replying to what I had said, making me so sure that, in spite of everything, you still need me.

You say I'm always starting tradition or customs or celebration. But who started all this precious ritual—and who carries it on so thoughtfully and so perfectly? Bless your heart.

To-day is Feb. 7. The Hyacinth letter is dated Feb. 7, 1954!![14] How *could* you remember this year when you have so much on your mind?

I'm going to Bridgewater this afternoon and am going to try to call you so that you can know your remembrance is here.

If I don't get you, this will tell you I tried. I want to be alone when I talk to you.

Our garden we shall have to name White Hyacinth Acres, thanks to your abundant contributions.

Now I must leave you. If only I could express my thanks in person! You know, I'm sure, what form it would take.

All my love, dear,
Dorothy

[14] The original hyacinth letter was written on February 6, 1954, but postmarked February 7.

WEDNESDAY MORNING, FEBRUARY 8

Darling [Dorothy],

Our storm so far hasn't been as horrendous as the predictions—sleet during the night and a little rain or sleet now but apparently little accumulation. However, practically all area schools are closed. Ida got here only about 20 minutes behind schedule.

My night was by far the best since all this happened—in fact almost normal. The knees didn't stiffen up as they always have at night and there was so little discomfort I didn't even call for compresses. Best of all, I could lie in all sorts of restful positions, comfortably. This morning my efforts to stand were far more successful than last night—I suppose the cortisone is getting in its good

[15] In subsequent letters RC spells this "Crain."

work. According to Dr. Healy, Dr. Crane[15] really does think I'll be walking by Monday, and perhaps I will. However, they all keep thinking of things they want to have done at the hospital, and it might prove easier just to take up residence for a couple of days.

Oh—another milestone—last night for the first time my temperature didn't rise above normal.

Now the mail has come and I've reveled in your letter about the storm, laughing, of course, at the way you describe some parts of it. I'm so thankful you could keep comfortable.

I told you of coming in on the last bit of the opera Saturday. You can imagine it on the Capehart. I wished that I had looked it up in advance and known what it was to be: I might have planned to hear more, but of course that was one of my first ventures in the chair, and a few minutes was all I was capable of.

There is a long, sympathetic and concerned letter from Edwin today. Thank you for writing him. They have a Fisher, which he got when *Autumn* became a best-seller. His good news is that *Summer* has been selected as a Book of the Month alternate.[16] He writes vividly and with humor about their winter— says they still hope to get to Maine "if we can get out of our own drive way!" Nellie has been "up and down" with a persistent cold. He said she would write soon.

[16] RC refers to Edwin Way Teale's *Autumn Across America* (1956) and *Journey into Summer* (1960).

The second letter from Lois was so typical, sending "as a bouquet" a sweet little story about the wolves. But oh dear, knowing some of the hair-raising things that have happened I always sense now the danger that lurks beneath the surface.

This must be gotten ready for Ida so I must stop. Snow fell for a couple of hours this afternoon. I do hope Mary makes it in time for Ida to get her bus.

All my love,
Rachel

SUNDAY NIGHT, FEBRUARY 12

IN HOSPITAL

Darling [Dorothy],

Well, I'm comfortably established, and if I find my room somewhat smaller and more utilitarian than at Doctors, that is more than balanced by a seemingly larger and perhaps more attentive staff of nurses. It looks as though care would be adequate at least for one in my state of health. (That was before I had really tried them out. Their evening bed-pan service is pretty awful. But now [Mon. A.M.] things have been moving along pretty well—*ever since 6 A.M.* [Hello, Stan!])

The ambulance trip was easy and comfortable and of course I'm vastly relieved to be here instead of having to wonder how to bridge the gap to Dr. Caulk tomorrow. This has been another good day for the knees so I can really hope the next treatment will bring a big improvement, and that I can go home Tuesday.

They have taken blood twice and say I'm to have X-rays this morning. I've called Dr. Caulk's dept. and supposedly they also will send for me this morning.

From my 5th floor window I look west toward McMillan Reservoir and—guess what?—almost every time I look out I see one or more gulls sailing over it. I suppose they are laughing gulls. I should have brought the glasses and Peterson.

Yesterday I dreaded having Roger see me taken away. He and Ida went out to the ambulance with me, carrying my luggage. He seemed cheery enough until the door was shut—then he turned away in bitter tears, such a lonely and tragic little figure. But at that moment such a fortunate thing happened. One of the ambulance men said, "Why there was a little chickadee in the snow, and the boy picked it up." As reported later by Roger, it was down in a deep footprint in the snow, fluttering. Whether it just couldn't get out, or whether it was a weather casualty I don't know. Anyway, they took it in and Ida administered whiskey, which the bird "sucked up"! Then they put it in a box on the porch and gave it seed and peanuts. Roger wanted to keep it but I explained it would be kinder to set it free, and the sooner the better. So the release was successfully made. (It was sober enough to fly!)

Roger also reported that Jeffie came out to the living room and lay under the step-table "to watch Leonard Bernstein"—then when the program was over returned to his room! Well, I'll have to ask him about it when I return—that's two Bernstein programs I've missed.

I'm wondering now whether crutches might be a temporary answer to the problem of getting around. Guess I'll ask Dr. Crane when he comes. I do so hope to find some means of getting about soon.

Word has now come from my friends in Radiology that they haven't forgotten me, but Dr. Caulk's train was late (he's just returning from Chicago) so he will see me this afternoon. They are very nice to me down there and it was thoughtful to call and not leave me wondering. Guess I'll get this on its way, darling, and just maybe you'll have it tomorrow. When I get home I'll call you.

Dearest love—

Rachel

WEDNESDAY, FEBRUARY 15

Darling [Dorothy],

This is a very cut-up day so maybe I won't have time to write enough to send. I was out for radiation from 9:30 to nearly 10, then spent 11–12 very frustratingly in Physical Therapy. After I went through the discomfort of getting into one of their gowns and getting onto a table, a doctor looked at the joints very briefly, then went off to call Dr. Crain. Finally an attendant came with a chair and said they would have to wait till this afternoon to treat me—ultrasonic, some whirlpool business, and exercise. I can see that is going to be a time-consuming operation, which it may be hard to fit in neatly with the radiation as an Out-patient. What a strange, bleak world I'm living in right now!

Jeanne is coming this afternoon, and I do hope this treatment, scheduled for 1:30, will move along and not cheat me of her visit.

Ida reported encouragingly on the kitties today and Roger seemed cheerful enough, so we will repeat last night's arrangements tonight. I just move along a day at a time, which seems best. If I can also cover tomorrow night, that will mean half the radiation behind me, and a good start on the joint therapy.

Tell Stan his valentine was delivered to me on the proper day—and a very lovely one it was. Tell him also I'm duly impressed with his plans for Southport. I'd like to see where the windows go—about the most important part to me.

Jeanne was here when I returned from therapy, so I will send this along.

All love—
Rachel

Dear One [Dorothy],

I knew almost as soon as we began to talk last night that you were concerned about something. I wish I knew the situation but of course I can imagine its general nature.

I do want to say this, dear. I know how sincerely you mean your requests to be told what you can do to help me, and I know just how badly you want to—yes, really I do. But we have to face certain facts. At 500 miles, "the companionship of letters" is about the only thing. Diminishing the distance runs into obstacles that just now seem insuperable. The uncertain weather could so easily block your swift return if you were needed there. And we have reminders—as the little anxiety I heard in your voice last night that Stan has need of you, too. So I have put all that out of my mind, darling, and you must, too. Spring is coming, the blizzards will end, and perhaps I will be well then. And perhaps you and Stan can then drive down for "Spring in Washington."

As you see, the problems here have somehow been worked out, day by day and week by week and I am sure ways will be found.

So many thoughts I would share with you if you were here—some happy, some not. But the "nots" are better not to be written, for that makes them loom larger.

By the time you read this you can think of me as at home or almost there.

All my dearest love, darling.
Rachel

Dear Ones [Dorothy and Stan],

I'll bet you never had a letter written by anyone in my situation-of-the-moment! I feel like a cartoon missionary in a cannibal's bubbling pot. The bubbling, while vigorous, is fortunately not a matter of temperature but of some physical agitation. In other words, I'm immersed in a "whirlpool" bath to the waist—my second treatment. Yesterday I was not prepared with diversion and the time seemed interminable. So here we are, a little stand drawn up beside the boiling pot, and I won't notice the time. It's supposed to be 20 minutes in this, tho they left me for 30 yesterday. Then they come with the ultrasonic machine and treat each joint (3) for 5 minutes, also underwater. Something was said yesterday about exercise but they didn't do it, for which I was glad. I was quite ready to return to my bed.

It's clear to me now that all this hauling around for treatment simply wouldn't have done while I was really sick with the infection, so I'm sure the 3 weeks in my own *good* hospital was a fortunate thing.

Details about tonight are still to be worked out, but I plan to endure this set-up through tomorrow (Friday) morning, then off for home! With ½ the radiation behind me it will no longer seem such a gamble.

Ida reports the kitties are doing well, eating and functioning normally. Robert and Vera visited them last night on their way home from church. Jeffie was lying in the wheelchair, and Moppet hurried to the kitchen to eat her chicken liver while she had company—quite typical of her—there seems to be some inhibition about eating while she is alone.

This physical therapy set-up, and the variety of victims of this and that who are here for treatment, are quite a revelation. And the pitiful wheelchair and stretcher cases in X-ray! It has all been an education, but one I'd gladly have done without. Each day I'm wheeled down there by a young colored orderly I remember the days I *walked* in at a pace matching his own brisk one, and it seems so strange.

LATER

Physical therapy and radiation are both over and I can settle down to a restful afternoon. The therapist said not to expect marked improvement until I've had 4 or 5 treatments, after which it might come quite suddenly. But they thought I did better at standing today. And my friends in Radiology thought I looked much better. The young woman doctor who seems to be serving some sort of apprenticeship there is from South Carolina, and this morning we got into an interesting conversation about Myrtle Beach, which she knows well—remembers the exact outcropping of rock where I did so much observing, and which I described in *The Edge of the Sea*. She said if I'd bring in some specimens of the odd rock and rock-like worm tubes I found there, she would do X-rays of them, which she says could be quite interesting.

I'm planning now to accept Doris Newton's invitation to have Roger spend another night there, since both he and the kitties seem to be doing all right this way. And Mrs. Tennie is available to return tomorrow night. I've asked Mary Hayes to take over the day Saturday. She can cope with the trivial amount of waiting-on I now require and she is a good cook and can get us a nice birthday dinner. From there on I guess we sort of play it by ear.

This is all about me—3 pages of it—but I hope it will assure you that things are going reasonably well.

Your letter (carbon to house) came yesterday while I was out. Jeanne was here when I returned so I saved the letter to enjoy later. It was so good to have the familiar handwriting again. Today Ida is going to visit me on her way home, and will bring the 3-day accumulation of mail. I know there is a letter there from you!

Yesterday I had to stop before I had said much about your house plans. I'm impressed with what looks like generous space as well as many rooms. I don't know how greatly the dimensions differ from the present house, but it looks so much bigger. Well, it's fun, isn't it? Now I can't remember about closets and other storage space. You know you can't possibly have too much. What is your fireplace material to be? Any place for wood storage under cover? Will your stairway be open to allow heat to rise, or do you think it better to try to concentrate it downstairs? I suppose your fireplace location is such that a Heatolator wouldn't make much difference. You see I'm thinking, hence so many questions.

Now I think I should get this on its way. There seems to be no system of mail pick-up and I just have to hope the person I ask remembers to mail letters. *My last from here!*

Dearest love, always
Rachel

Virginia says all her bulbs are coming up. Horror—won't they freeze unless there is more snow?

SUNDAY, FEBRUARY 19

Darling [Dorothy],

Just a quick report to be mailed by Ida when she leaves.

Once I was rested from Friday's strenuous program I began to feel much better. Yesterday I gave the "walker" its first real trial and am much encouraged. Taking part of the weight on my arms allows me to walk much more comfortably. Last night I ate my first meal in the dining room in honor of Roger—quite a celebration! Of course I remained in the wheelchair.

Discussions with the doctors have resulted in a decision to give up the physical therapy at least for the present. Now that I can just concentrate on the radiation, those daily trips seem much less formidable, and as I told you, the ankle wasn't reacting well to the heat.

Roger was invited to accompany our neighbors, the Rosses, to Scientists Cliffs this afternoon to hunt fossils, and went off joyfully. Frances Ross has been so kind. Before I went to the hospital she took Roger for a haircut, and later visited me in hospital and brought down things from home.

Yesterday we had rain and heavy fog as temperature rose, then practically all our snow was melted.

Jeanne sent me such a funny card—one of those modern ones with unexpected twists. A little duck is walking along, and the very suitable and reassuring inscription is "Your doctor will have you walking in no time." But inside it says "—you'll have to sell your car to pay his bill." More soon—this is just to say all is progressing, even if the pace is slow.

All love,
Rachel

P.S.—Monday—This didn't get mailed, so a brief addition.

This morning, via walker, I crossed the bedroom and looked out of the window! And not too uncomfortably, either. That is real progress, and the first sign I may soon be able to declare my independence.

Roger brought back sharks' teeth, whale's ribs, fossil coral, fossil shells of various sorts and enough enthusiasm to pep up both of us for the evening. He had a *wonderful* day.

We take off this afternoon about 1:30. More later.

Much love to you all—
Rachel

MONDAY A.M.

Darling [Dorothy]—There was a flurry of activity when Ida left—I was on the phone and Roger was just returning from his fossil digging—and as a result I didn't give her your letter. Well, now I shall add an apple.

I wish I didn't want so much to talk to you so often—Friday night was so delicious and made me feel so much better. But I realized it was the fourth call I had made to you in a week (!) and I shall simply have to cut down. With the money pouring out at the rate of literally hundreds of dollars a week, I'm frightened. It's not as though I could look forward with real assurance to long-term health in the future. Well, last night I took the first step toward shaking off my caretakers. Roger and I were alone for a couple of hours and all went well. I do hope I can soon dispense with Mrs. Tenney. Getting Roger off would be the major problem there, but he has "grown up" a great deal—gets up and dresses without even being called!

Yes, I remembered Stan's "tiredness" just before you came here, and when I realized all was not 100% last Tuesday night I guessed perhaps it was another such experience. I'm so sorry. I hope he will just do nothing until he feels a big improvement again.

And I do want you, darling, not to feel this urgency about finding a way to help actively in my situation. As I told you last week, I see so clearly that you *can't*, and we must just accept the fact. I think sometimes I really shouldn't tell you so much about my problems and so add to your distress—but I do, and I suppose I'll continue to!

Your suggestion about the book is worth thinking about—something would be better than nothing, I guess. In the occasional intervals when my mind can rise above all this and *think*, I've tried to see how I could revamp the whole concept of the book to something much shorter and simpler. That may be the answer, when I can ever be creative enough in mind and strong enough in body to do it.

Of course what I long for now is the ability to share with you so many thoughts. High on my list of Most Cherished Moments would be the occasions when we could do just that. You will remember many of the ones I mean. Now I must stop.

I love you, dear

Rachel

THURSDAY, FEBRUARY 23

Dearest [Dorothy],

Well, I prayed for no snow during my hospital trips and so far there has been none, so I guess I can't complain about the endless rain. Tuesday it was light and no great inconvenience, but yesterday (my holiday) it was heavy and so it continues today. Friday there may be "a shower," says the cautious forecaster, which probably means more of the same.

Have I told you that the song sparrows have been trying their voices for some time now—perhaps even before I went to the hospital? But I'm puzzled that I've heard no cardinal song. That should come first.

What a show your Mr. Pheasant is giving you! I loved your story about the cats and their feigned indifference—to him and to each other. I can just see them.

Dear little Moppet is so grateful for the time I spend in her quarters—hurries to settle down on my lap for every possible moment. Jeffie, of course, is serenely happy about my invalidism and the near-monopoly it gives him on my time.

I am to see Dr. Crane today. No doubt it will be well to have the knees and ankle treated again. Everything was dreadfully stiff yesterday, but seems a bit more limber this morning.

Last night I spent an hour or more in the study listening to music. Such a welcome escape from my bed! But I never get over the strangeness of some of this. For example, sitting near the Capehart my eye lights on a book on one of the upper shelves—and instantly a message flashes to my body to get up and take it from the shelf, but my body doesn't ever hear, for there is no attempt to do it, I just sit there wondering how this could be! But I suppose much of the time I really do forget. I think it is five weeks today since I went to Dr. Healy's office and it was all beginning.

The word from, or about, Beverly[17] is very bad. It certainly doesn't seem possible she would ever pull out of it, and her condition is so distressing I guess one ought to hope her time would be short. Yet, last week there was a letter she dictated to Mrs. Coffman.

Lois *does* have a tape recorder—you know I wondered—and is going to try to send me a tape containing wolf howls! I guess you and Stan will just have to get one.

Sometime soon I must send you a copy of the new *Sea*. The box has just been sitting in my study since before I went to the hospital. As I told you, I'm not very enthusiastic. This, I have just remembered, is its publication day—Feb. 23rd. I have had such a lovely note from Dr. Bigelow about the dedication.[18]

Now I must soon get dressed for the expedition. As I've told you, my days are very full! When I get home perhaps your letter will be here—you said you mailed one Tuesday.

Well! There is a cardinal whistling! What kind of avian stardust can that be? Cardinal in the distance, song sparrows nearby—winter can't last forever.

I do hope all is well with you both.

> My dearest love,
> *Rachel*

[17] Beverly Knecht.

[18] In the Oxford Press 1961 revised edition of *The Sea Around Us*. It reads: "To Henry Bryant Bigelow who by precept and example has guided all others in the exploration of the sea."

FRIDAY NIGHT, FEBRUARY 24

Darling [Dorothy],

I want to call you but am trying to hold out until Sunday, so will spend a while with you this way. Actual news will be told before you read this so perhaps I won't be very factual now. For some odd reason, though, it seems hard for me to write any way but factually during this particular "eternity." I wonder why? I keep thinking of things I want to say to you (*long* to say to you, rather). Some are tender, some rather thoughtful, some perhaps sad and I guess they are generally in the category of things I'd rather *say* when I am near enough to whisper them to you. Do you know? Then the sad things are less sad, the tender things more tender—and all in all it's the most precious kind of eternity we can find together. In fact, on my list of remembered joys, moments of that sort would rank very high.

IT'S NOW SAT. A.M.

Of course I shall tell you this tomorrow but during last night I became aware of a high, sweet, bubbling call coming from the Wildwood. The year's first frogs!

And Thursday when we got home from the hospital killdeers were chasing across the sky, calling (and that sound always belongs to the shore in my mind). Now as I write I hear song sparrows and mourning doves. So whatever blizzards March may have in store for us, spring is surely on the way. And of course I shall be so thankful to see the end of this hard, hard winter. Yet I know you can understand that I have mixed feelings, too. You know my high hopes for the goal I might reach by March—hopes I entertained last October! After that conversation with Paul Brooks when we laid out a schedule, I said to you one night on the phone, "I feel I *can* do it—if only nothing happens!" Now I look back at the complete and devastating wreckage of those plans—not only no writing for months but the nearly complete loss of any creative feeling or desire. I'm reminded of a quotation that has stuck in my mind since college days, although I no longer remember its source: "When the lamp is shattered, the light in the dust lies dead."

As I've already told you, I've been thinking lately of a completely altered plan for the book—which would probably mean that nothing I've written would be used in its present form. But the whole thing would be greatly boiled down and contain less of illustrative detail and would perhaps be more philosophic in tone. This would perhaps be less pleasing to some but is perhaps more my kind of book.

Well, during the past week I've really felt some stirrings of desire to get at it, but the hospital trips have really monopolized my days. Our departure time has averaged about 12:30, and since bathing and dressing *are* slow processes for one in my condition, there was no morning time for work. Wednesday, my "day off," I was unexpectedly weary, and dozed away much of the day. Now next week there is only Monday for the hospital, and then Thursday to Dr. Crain's office. So perhaps the wheels can begin to grind. The visits to Dr. Crain will be once a week until I'm completely well, I guess.

Now, Saturday, Mary Hayes is here and Virginia is coming for the night. I really should stop, have my bath, and take a trip to the study.

I'm glad now I didn't call you last night—I have it to look forward to tomorrow!

Darling, I do know you have suffered wanting to come to me and knowing you must not. I have understood that all along, and been sorry for you. But now, like the telephone call, we have it to look forward to! For I do hope when balmy weather comes and Stan is at his best again you can come, as we dreamed when you were here last month. (Of course it was nearly 2 months ago, but it seems so long, long ago—another world!)

Now I'll stop, darling. My love surrounds you all the time, you know, as yours does me.

Rachel

Dearest [Dorothy],

Another Saturday of fog and rain! The ground is absolutely sodden and my swamp is a Swamp now—with the roadside ditches overflowing part of the time. But on Thursday the sun came out while I was at the hospital, and on our return I sat a while in Jeanne's car and drank in the air and the pale sunshine and the bird song. You can imagine what joy that brought a prisoner-since-Jan. 19th!

Just then the mail came and what a treat it brought![19] *When* do I get the next installment?? I turned over the last page so eagerly, only to trip and fall on p. 1! Well, I can read this over and over. It really is the very next thing to being there to have read your vivid account. Yes, Tomlinson—now I must re-read that. But it is a similar atmosphere, and the houses battered by the winter storms recalled his description of the sea's encroachment on the English cottages. Well, of course I loved your waves scaled down to fairy size. No, I think I have never peopled a beach with fairies as such, although I believe in *The Edge*—I alluded to the Hippa crabs, peering out through the wet sand, in terms that suggested a comparison with gnomes or elves. About your waves, repeating in miniature all the structure and behavior of a Mile Beach wave, I'm sure you have excellent scientific support. You know much has been learned about the behavior of waves and their effect on ships or shore installations by studying artificially produced waves in model basins—all on a decidedly miniature scale.

The same mail brought a long letter from Nellie Teale. Next week they hope to go to the Jackman area of Maine to see a "deer yard." They have had a cardinal at Trail Wood. This makes the 96th species there. She says each new bird is now a big event. They have also had 2 titmice.

A *tape* has arrived from Lois but as luck would have it my recorder is out of order. From what she said of it I think it is all Cris singing his songs. I wish she would just talk—and get the wolf voices!

I plan to call you tomorrow and will give you all news on doctors and treatments then, so won't burden this letter with such items. But I do want you to know that despite Dr. Crain's cautious predictions, I can see enormous improvement since I returned from the hospital a week ago, and I imagine I'll better his schedule by several weeks.

Well, I live for the day we can all explore Mile Beach and beyond together, our infirmities forgotten! I'm so glad you and Stan could celebrate as you did, and that you have shared it with me.

All my love
Rachel

[19] DF had written RC a long description of a day trip to a beach in Duxbury, Massachusetts.

Dearest [Dorothy],

Time for only a quick note for Ida to take. She and I made the hospital trip by cab today and I'm *so* glad it's over. For one thing, I've been feeling miserably sick from radiation for a couple of days. Then I did dread Dr. Crain's treatment for it has been extremely painful last time and the knee was so sore that even a gentle touch was to be avoided. But actually it wasn't quite so bad this time as last. He feels the ankle is improving faster than he expected, while the knee is more stubborn. He got fluid from it today, hence decided I'd better have an antibiotic again. But on the whole he seems pleased with progress and pronounced my demonstration of walking "damn good." Once I'm on my feet, I can go along with very little support.

As for the radiology people, they now swear tomorrow's treatment will be the last, with a check-up two weeks later. They say I can take a heavier dose of the "anti-sickness" medicine.

And that's about all—except that there were golden crocuses blooming in someone's yard as we went down, and there was a robin in my yard a few days ago.

Your Thurs. note was here when we returned. Good for you—3 lbs. down. I discovered a way to lose 12 lbs. but I don't recommend it. Now I'm being reckless with calories! I should think Lois would need to drive to C. Springs for Stanley[20]—I imagine the road is obscure to say the least. Of course she'd love to.

Will write more soon—just a greeting for the week-end, to carry the usual message.

I love you,

R.

[20] Stanley, Jr., was to visit the Crislers and their wolves in their Colorado mountain cabin.

Darling [Dorothy],

Guess what? There were *two* letters from you yesterday! I was so delighted by the double specimen of familiar handwriting, until I saw that they were forwarded from the hospital! Imagine taking two weeks to do it! Of course they were duplicates of letters I'd had at home.

Well, yesterday really did complete this course of radiation, and the visit was especially satisfactory because Dr. Caulk had returned. He expressed complete satisfaction with my progress—thought it normal for the time involved. There has been considerable shrinkage in the past few days. I am to see him for a check-up on the 21st.

The nausea, which was quite miserable Thursday, has practically disappeared. Yesterday I was more active all day than I've been—around the house a good deal on the walker, and as a result had the best sleep in ages, and without pills.

Mrs. Meyer[21] was dismayed to hear of my adventures (she invited me to a reception for the new G. W. Univ. president, so I wrote to tell her why I wouldn't be there) and is coming out tomorrow afternoon if the weather is good to take me for a drive. So you can imagine me spinning along in style in a chauffeur-driven Lincoln!

[21] Mrs. Agnes Meyer, owner of the *Washington Post*.

On Friday Bea Riegel is coming out to give me a new permanent in the morning. Won't that be wonderful! Really, my hair—while certainly not one of my major problems—has been a great headache all the way through. It will be a joy to have it cut and some curl introduced into it. Poor Bea insists she will be all right if she brings along her adrenalin atomizer. Well, we'll work in the kitchen and banish cats, so perhaps she will.

This is the day you are going to Mr. Little's birthday party. I hope we have sent you our yesterday—a perfect spring day.

I think I see my bluebells coming up—you know the clumps of early leaves are a dark purple. Yesterday I saw my first grackles—glistening in the sun. They may have been here a while unseen by me, for usually they return in February. All these reminders that the cycles and rhythms of nature are still at work are so satisfying.

I have read more of Eiseley's *Firmament of Time* and do find myself in agreement with so much he says—and so appreciative of the way he says it.

So much of the time I'm unconscious of the calendar, so I was surprised to realize how soon Stanley will go to Colorado. That was about the time of year Lois was returning from here last year. I am sure they will still be having pretty wintry weather, with snow a real possibility. Oh, I do hope he gets to go (to Lois, I mean.)

Maybe if I stop now this can be picked up by our mailman.

All my dearest love—
Rachel

SATURDAY NIGHT, MARCH 4

Darling [Dorothy],

Well today there were two sure-enough letters (not carbon copies) for some unknown benefactor *did* find and mail your letter. It was postmarked 2 hours before the note telling of the mishap. And how grateful I am to him or her, for that was a letter that shouldn't be lost!

And the same mail brought Stan's letter with the precious enclosure, which I'm so happy to have. I do have a black and white taken the same day and place, but I like this better. In fact I think I like it as well as any picture of you I have.

Do you realize the picture includes the lovely spruce that was a hurricane casualty only 6 months later? I have few pictures that show it.

Oh, I hope you will go to Teales' sometime, but do wait for real spring with wildflowers and birds, for they will delight in sharing all that sort of thing with you.

I've had an active day—washed my hair and set it, with help from nice Mary Hayes on both. Tomorrow will reveal results—but at least it's clean. Mary cooked a little pork roast and mashed potatoes—later I cooked a vegetable and assembled our dinner, this time mostly on my feet. Now (10 P.M.) the joints are rather stiff and sore, but probably no more than if I'd stayed in bed.

[22] Clipping not preserved.

I enclose the *Star* clipping[22] that just about everybody locally seems to have seen, including all my corps of doctors! I shall try to get more, and if you really want this, keep it. I want to send this with Mrs. Tenny in the morning, so will just remind you both of my love.

Rachel

P.S. Such a sweet thing just happened. You know how Jeffie has been through all this long illness with me, adapting his ways and daily schedule to the single end of giving me constant companionship, having none of the little diversions that used to enliven his day. But now he senses the change as he begins to see me moving about, and I can see him remembering the little things we used to do together. Yesterday as I stumped through the living room on my 6 legs he hurried hopefully to the front door and, looking up into my eyes, suggested that we go out. But tonight I went into my bathroom and was aware he was moving about near the open door, but didn't realize what he was planning. Just as I was about to leave I saw, at the hinge side of the open door, a large, enquiring green eye set in a black shadow. One of our regular evening games always involved his hiding outside that crack, and suddenly poking a velvet paw through to pat at my finger, or catch a bit of paper or string. So tonight he felt we had recovered enough for a game.

I must tell Lois. She often makes such dear comments about him, seeming to understand instinctively so much in my relation with Jeffie that lies too deep for easy expression.

"His small being is full of you," she wrote recently.

Dear One [Dorothy]—Just a little goodnight word. Your "Wednesday Bedtime" letter was very precious—I'm *so* glad it wasn't lost. I suppose I *was* rather low when I called you that night. At least the need to speak to you seemed great. You would know that Monday's news that the radiation had to be continued would upset me considerably, and for a day or two I felt the treatment was doing no good and would do none (of course I know better now—the change is definite.) And then the related nausea was with me most of the week, a horrid feeling. And now I can't help feeling a positive dread of Dr. Crain's treatments, even though I know they do much good. So all that added up to the "unhappiness" you sensed—but I couldn't speak of the first and major item (or at least of my reaction to it) and perhaps that was why neither of us could say what was in our hearts. At least, darling, we know we could pour out all of it if we could be together.

About the book, I sometimes have a feeling (maybe 100% wishful thinking) that perhaps this long period away from active work will give me the perspective that was so hard to attain, the ability to see the woods in the midst of the confusing multitude of trees. But the thought of continued long work on it, and at the expense of other things I want to write, is hard to bear.

Sometimes, as I suggested recently, I want it to be a much shortened and simplified statement, doing for this subject (if this isn't too presumptuous a comparison) what Schweitzer did in his Nobel Prize address for the allied subject of radiation. Oh, the details would have to be sketched in more than he did, but that's the basic idea. Well, you see I'm thinking.

To change subjects abruptly, I wanted to tell you a small fact that will make you smile, and perhaps bring you some of my own feelings. I have been having some skin reaction to the X-ray treatment, and as a soothing application have gotten Nivea cream. I've never used it before, but I know one person who does. Do you wonder that when I use it the fragrance brings you close, and revives memories? Now I must reach for my tube, and then put out the light. It's late.

So you still like to hear me say it? Well I do, darling—I love you.

R.

MONDAY, MARCH 6

Dearest [Dorothy],

Your Friday and Saturday notes are here today. Really I feel guilty when I realize what a chore it is bound to be to get something into the mail every day, as you have so steadfastly done. You really mustn't try to do it any longer, darling. This is a season of improvement and return to (or at least *toward*) normal— beginning Friday I gave up Mary for good, I do trust, and this morning I said goodbye to Mrs. Tenney. Jeffie and Moppie take turns sitting with me in the study and J., as I told you, rediscovers games and diversions. Wednesday Jeanne is coming to work (on income tax!). I shall no doubt write less often and you must do the same for your sake, though I selfishly hate to suggest it, I admit.

Please (when you do write) don't hesitate to write of bird walks, etc. For a shut-in, cut off from all that is most enjoyed, that is a *perfect* kind of letter. Your two-parter last week, for example. And when Jeannette—the Wisconsin girl who loves the out-of-doors—learned of my long confinement, the first thing she did was write a long letter in which she took me with her on a walk through her woods. After your letters, that was one of the most enjoyable I've had. (She also taped a tiny sprig of pussy willows to the letter—they have some miniature species, the smallest I've seen.)

I had a lovely drive with Mrs. Meyer yesterday—an afternoon when thermometer reached 80, as it has today—and we found a spot I'll enjoy returning to when I can walk. Much interesting conversation, too. Some of it rather touching, as when she revealed by an occasional remark how very lonely she has been since the death of her husband nearly 2 years ago. Here is a woman who controls a fortune (and does immense good with it), and who has a vast reputation as lecturer and writer and molder of public opinion, and whose house can be filled with interesting and important people whenever she wishes, yet without the human relation that meant most to her, she comes up against that inner emptiness just as you or I would. I wished something I might say would help—indeed I felt she was groping for comfort—but it is hard to know what to say to such a person.

Tonight we are "on our own" for the first time. I'm now about to tuck myself in, and I think all the problems have been anticipated and provided for. The nights, with rare exceptions, are times of restlessness and stiffness and pain, but I can take my own medicines and even though I can't apply compresses, I *can* turn on the heating pad.

Dorothy Algire was here for lunch today. I was so active yesterday that I entertained the idea of venturing out to see the bulbs with Dorothy and Ida for support. But this was a "down" day and I had to entertain her in my wheelchair instead. However, I've managed my walker tonight.

A wonderful chorus of frogs. I wish I could identify all the voices. One sounds like chickens clucking. Now I suppose I must say goodnight.

All my love,
Rachel

TUESDAY
The night, and the getting-off-to-school, went all right and I feel encouraged. It was wonderful to have help when I so desperately needed it, but equally wonderful now to feel I can do without, except for Ida. Most of the time since Jan. 19—especially the first month of it—seems a complete nightmare as I look back on it.

Last night in my dreams I ran across the lawn—and then was so astonished I could!

[23] By Gavin Maxwell, published in 1961.

I hope you are reading *Ring of Bright Water*[23] now. Aren't the otter pictures adorable? There was a review in the *Times* last week.

I can lend Dr. Eiseley's Seminar paper to Alice if she will be sure to return it fairly soon. Since he is reworking it for publication, I doubt other copies could be gotten.

No, you hadn't told me about Stanley and the School Committee. I'm sure he has "something to offer."

I wonder sometimes about my ability to keep my "date" with him this summer, and have thought of writing to see if he would be interested in attempting to substitute Jack Berrill, I'm sure he would provide a very worthwhile and stimulating viewpoint. I think they plan to be in Maine this summer.

How did you like Ruby Carr's account of the Winslow honeymoon?[24]

Now I must see about some work!

So very much love

Rachel

MONDAY A.M., MARCH 13

[24] Eliot Winslow, captain of the Boothbay Harbor tour boat, the *Argo*, had married, as reported by Ruby Carr, a correspondent to the *Boothbay Register*.

Dearest [Dorothy]—

A very brief good morning. I had expected Jeanne today but she called early to say she and her husband both have colds, so of course we have postponed. I plan for a quiet day of solitary work instead.

This morning began (7 A.M.) with the cries of geese, and I managed to stagger to the window (shouting for Roger to share the excitement) and get it open in time to hear them better and see the dark, shifting column in the grey sky. I don't think I've heard them from this house before.

Another "first" yesterday morning—the first robin song of the year, and Saturday we had 2 fox sparrows scratching on the ground under the feeder. They are rare with us. And I thought I heard a Carolina wren.

Yesterday's *Times* has a full-page ad for *R. of B. W.*,[25] using quotes from Edwin Teale and me. Also, it appears on the Best-Seller list. I think the editor wrote me it has had that status in England for some time. (The success of this & Elsa[26] makes me want Lois to hurry.) I've been looking over Mr. Maxwell's earlier book and between the two have developed a bad case of wanderlust—my old longing to see something of the islands and coastline of Scotland!

[25] *Ring of Bright Water*.

[26] A lion in Joy Adamson's *Born Free: A Lioness of Two Worlds* (1960).

All is not onward and upward. Apparently I was on my feet too much Saturday for by bedtime I discovered my ankle was badly swollen as well as painful. I finally decided the plan to go it alone Sunday wasn't good, so called Ida to see if she could come. She did, and I stayed abed, going out by wheelchair for our evening snack. I shall do about the same today. With rest and ice the ankle has gone down to about normal size. I guess I can't force it and shall have to let time cure me.

I wish Ida could drive! The complexities of getting just ordinary errands done are sometimes enormous. Some items and some services aren't to be had by just phoning the grocer or the druggist, and I do hate to be a nuisance to people!

I wasn't going to write long and I won't.

I do hope Stan is well over his cold by now, and that he won't take chances working outside in this changing weather.

Send me Alice's address so I can send the Eiseley paper. Probably just Middlebury College, but this is precious so I want to be sure. I see he is one mentioned as a possibility for Nat'l Book Award, to be announced tomorrow.

Hope you are all right, dear. Please read between the lines all I'd say if I had time, but I'm going to *work*!

All my love
Rachel

P.S. Wait till I hear from Lois about *R. of B. W.* Since she is writing she may not want to break off from reading just now—I've asked her.

TUESDAY NIGHT, MARCH 14

Dearest [Dorothy]—

Last night, in one of the moods of loneliness and depression that comes sometimes, I picked up the phone to be near you. As you will know by now, the result was frustration. Now, after a second night of trying to overcome 500 miles of apparently tangled wires, I am super-frustrated! It's a horrid feeling, darling, suddenly to know I couldn't reach you no matter what. Of course it isn't *really* important that I talk to you tonight, and I'm more cheerful than last night anyway—it's just the idea. Well, your operator said she would report trouble and try to have all clear by morning.

I am still having to take extra care of the ankle, making most of my house trips via wheelchair and generally keeping off it. I think I'm set back at least a week as far as it is concerned—knees are doing better.

Ida told me one of my daffodils is coming into bloom and from study window I could see a cluster of yellow buds. How I long to walk out and take inventory! They are 2 weeks earlier than last year. This, and the robins' song, and the geese flying over, remind me in more pensive moments of that most poignant of Jefferies' essays, "Hours of Spring,"[27] in which, from his bed, he is aware that the buds are opening on schedule and the birds arriving and he wonders how these things can be happening without him, who had always so carefully observed them. Each spring is so precious. I wanted this one, and feel cheated.

Soon I shall send you some of the notices of *The Sea* that are appearing. I'm especially pleased that the *San Francisco Chronicle* featured the warning on atomic waste. Somebody reads prefaces!

There is a fascinating number of Audubon Field notes just out, containing much on Hurricane Donna's effect on birds. Perhaps we can share this sometime.

Speaking of birds, I wonder if your boat-tailed grackle can possibly be the purple. The boat-tailed is not "supposed" to go north of Delaware. Of course there are many extensions of range and this might be another. Take a good look. He is huge, and has a definite keel in his long tail. He is the "jackdaw" of *Under the Sea-Wind*. That is the North Carolina name for him. I used to spend hours watching them in the marshes. Were I writing now, I'd probably say "jackdaw or boat-tailed grackle" but at that tender age I liked to be cryptic.

[27] In Richard Jefferies' *Jefferies' England* (1937).

A couple of enclosures[28]—don't return.

This is now Wed. A.M. Jeanne is coming soon so I'll just conclude and have this ready for mail.

Oh—the "lost" letter bore no signs of having been anywhere except in a fastidious lady's car!

Now—so very much love, dear

Rachel

FRIDAY NIGHT, MARCH 17

Dearest [Dorothy]—

There are murmurs of possible snow tomorrow night—oh, I do hope not! But at this season the two preceding years we've had bad ones. Tonight's temperature is to be about 20°. Think of all those buds.

This was my day to visit Dr. Crain. The troubles with the ankle this week didn't seem to surprise him. On the whole, he thinks I am walking well. However, he now feels my trouble has settled down into a case of "low-grade rheumatoid arthritis." Great, isn't it? There is apparently little question that I would have to have professional care in Maine this summer—he will locate someone for me. By that time, the treatments would probably be spaced further apart than they are now.

He is talking about the possibility of "trying to speed things up" by using intra muscular injections of gold. I don't like this prospect much from what I know of it, and am not going to agree without some further investigation and maybe asking Dr. Crile. One of the possible toxic effects is depression of bone marrow, and I think my marrow has had enough abuse via radiation for the present.

As perhaps you remember, I am to see Dr. Caulk for a check-up in his field Tuesday. I'll call you after that—please have your phone in order!

Dr. Hard phoned me last night. He will be back for another meeting in three weeks. Never one to be disheartened he is proposing I come to Scripps in the fall or a year from now.

Lois writes she has almost finished the story of Alatna up to her first pups. Something vague about an "editor friend" who would try to place it for her. This bothers me not a little. If she can recover her rights from Harper, she should get an agent and be professional about it.

I'm going to enclose a happy card from Edwin, but would like it back. Isn't it wonderful they both remain well enough to do these things? Of course I'm more than ever conscious of health! Do you know what a "deer yard" is? I confess I don't.

[28] Enclosures not preserved.

Elliott is here, coping with a great outflow of springs, resulting perhaps from a stoppage of one of the drains. We have rented a "snake" and he is trying to find the trouble, amid a sea of mud and water. Mary Hayes is here and I'm keeping off my feet most of the time. She will roast a little chicken and bake a cake for us—I like to take advantage of her ability as a cook.

We are still being threatened with wet snow tonight, but it is supposed to become rain tomorrow.

I have had another dictated letter from Beverly. How she can have the strength or clearness of mind to do this I don't know. She said she was supposed to get up that day, which again seems incredible. She has not been told all the difficulties, and is hopeful still.

I imagine the mail may bring a letter from you—in fact I've just decided to wait and let this go with Mary so I can see.

P.S. Now I'm in study with typewriter on my lap so I'll dash off a quick note after receiving yours of Thursday. (Then I'll stop a while and let you get your breath and get caught up—I guess I've been deluging you relentlessly with mail.)

So you've been having fun with bird research. I wanted to believe you had boat-tails, for this would certainly be an addition to the record of southern forms invading the north, but it did seem improbable. Besides, I always think of them as being close to salt or brackish water. How I wish I could take you to those coastal marshes off Beaufort where I used to see them. I always see them in memory against a sunset sky, with rosy reflections in the still waters of the sound. They are really very large, approaching crow size I think.

I don't believe I did notice the *Sea* ad in *Saturday Review*—I'll look. There was one in *New Yorker*, *Times*, etc. Clippings continue to come in, but mostly rather routine.

The wonderful appeal of *Born Free* (Elsa) seems to me an omen of what Lois could do with Alatna. The more I think of it the more I think Alatna (not Cris!) should dominate her book.[29] The other she can do another time if she wants to.

[29] Lois Crisler's *Captive Wild* (1968) does focus on her relationship with the female wolf, Alatna.

I see Dr. Caulk on Tuesday, Crain on Friday. I have just written a long letter to Barney Crile and shall then call him one day next week. I want his opinion on the gold treatment.

Have been listening to *Tristan*. I wish you were here beside me. But then I often do.

Dearest love
Rachel

Darling [Dorothy],

I've had this card since Christmas, intending to use it for an apple. Now it is somewhat inappropriate anyway, but you will probably like the two birds visiting under their evergreen.

You say I should not hesitate to mention my negative thoughts, as you've probably had them anyway. You will know that last night I wasn't too cheerful, having learned that the arthritis isn't going to be written off as a past experience. Of course I really don't know and I suppose no one does, how much it is going to interfere with my doing the things I love to do. I wonder, for example, whether I will walk on my beach this summer or even sit under the spruce! Pemaquid—or at least the part we love best—seems as unattainable as those western islands of Scotland I've always dreamed about. But perhaps I shall surprise everyone. I do know I shall need a driver for the long trip up (down). Want the job? (Don't feel pressed by that suggestion, darling. You'd be first choice, but there are other possibilities.)

I am also feeling somewhat upset about this proposed treatment. Of course, I've already had a taste of having to submit to something I knew was dangerous and in theory undesirable (the radiation) but there the alternative left no choice. Here I feel I'd rather endure some arthritis than gamble with the bone marrow. Especially since it has already been under attack. Well, I think I shall think this over a while before submitting.

I'm sure you understand without my spelling it out how harrowing it was to be unable to get those calls through! Wed. night when that double ring began again I could have screamed—I was so sure it was wrong, and I'd get that other number again. Well, the real need to talk to you was on Monday—I forget now why I felt so solitary and forlorn, but I did. Had I reached you I was going to say "Let's not talk factually—leave that for letters—just sweet nothings and reminiscences."

Reading this over, it seems a very cheerless apple—one I shouldn't even send, for it does not reflect my general mood, darling. I'm just spilling out to my dear one the occasional thoughts of the dark hours but in general things are so much better than they might be. And I have you to love, and be loved by.

I do, you know.
R.

THURSDAY A.M., MARCH 23

Dearest [Dorothy]—

Something quickly for the week-end. Our skies are still dripping. But we are lucky. Had it not been for some warm air that moved in aloft, our inch of rain could have been 10 inches of snow, according to the morning paper. Out in Virginia they did get snow and sleet. I do hope yours (for balance of year) will be as short-lived as your recent ones.

Tell Stan I certainly feel well-informed on deer yards now. I'm tempted to send his letter to Edwin and so perhaps save him some research! I had no idea anything so extensive could be implied—thought it was just a place they had tramped down the snow and slept in!

You ask what rheumatoid arthritis is and I guess I don't know very specifically. Even Dr. Crain's book leaves many questions unanswered, but he does recognize only 2 major types—this and osteoarthritis, the kind that represents wear-and-tear and increases with age. Rheumatoid, contrary to what I said on the phone, is the type that can produce severe crippling and even deformities, but of course does not always do so. But apparently there is a very great deal that is unknown about the whole subject. My feeling, from Jeanne's conversation with the N.I.H. man and also from Dr. Crile's comments, is that there may be other things that could account for my troubles and that the diagnosis is far from definite.

Dr. Crain speaks of a group of diseases somewhat related to arthritis but which he calls "collagen diseases"—affecting the collagen fibers that bind muscles, tendons, & joint capsules together. I wondered if some of your muscular pain might come under this heading.

He also mentions that in rheumatoid arthritis there tends to be a loss of muscle tissue. I want to ask him about this. My thighs have become ridiculously thin and flabby. This was originally true of the lower part of the leg, too, but with my gain in weight the calves seem to have filled in again to some extent. I could well believe I lost those 12 pounds out of my legs.

I am now itching to get to the N.I.H. library for some reading on arthritis. When the weather improves Jeanne and I will go. I'd be up to that now, as long as I can be deposited at door.

I'm sure you will meet many new friends, if you continue to go to a birding spot such as Duxbury. As Louis Halle said, a pair of binoculars or a telescope provide the only introduction necessary. I *do* think you should go to L. L. Bean for proper clothing for these cold weather expeditions. Everyone here who takes many bird trips swears by Bean.

You really startled me when you said you might go to Southport in six weeks. In fact I had to read it twice to be sure what you meant! And suddenly I felt quite lonely—you always seem so much farther away when you are there, a difference more than just another 200 miles. Do you think I will see you before you go? Not before your Orono trip, I'm sure, but maybe later??

Peepers Pool is lovely, but that would belong to the wet woodlands below. In fact, I'm not sure you understand what area I designate my Dismal Swamp. Not my wild corner, where I welcome the trickles of water and the standing pools, so attractive to birds and frogs. I'm referring to that thorn-in-my-flesh that is supposed to be lawn, along Berwick from my drive down, and in this wet year spreading back closer and closer toward the house. Just standing water and mud and deserving no better name than I gave it! Even the frogs scorn it. I really don't know what to do with it. (Yes—Intervale is lovely—another of the words you have discovered for me.)

Well, you will be quite impressive in your brown and beige Impala! My poor old '57 needs "a bit of a paint job" too, but I'll be lucky if I don't have to sell it, as Jeanne's card said, "to pay my doctor's bill." Did I tell you of my battle with the insurance company? I think not its recent developments, which are rather disheartening for the future. Too long a story for now.

I'm sure we shall all be looking at the weather maps this week-end, hoping for the best in Colorado. As I imagine the details, it will not be a physically comfortable experience for Stanley, but I hope it makes up for that in interest and the pleasure of knowing Lois.

Now I must go. My best love to you both.

Rachel

SATURDAY, MARCH 25

Dearest [Dorothy],

I'll write only briefly (she always says) to get this out for the mailman.

First my report on the medical front. Yesterday Dr. Crain was sufficiently impressed with my improved walking that he didn't even inject the left knee, and says that after next week we may go on a schedule of alternate weeks. He also says I may try driving for very short distances, as over to the shopping center. What an emancipation that will bring! At first I shall take Ida to do the walking about in the markets, but just to be able to cope with errands will be wonderful.

In spite of all this improvement, I had to say my little piece on the gold treatment, which he actually was planning to start yesterday. Since, for the present at least, I shall have to continue with him for the more conservative treatment, I tried to leave him a face-saving "out" on the basis of my good progress with present methods. I began in rather light vein, but in the end said very seriously that in view of the previous radiation I could not consent to taking such a risk. He was agreeable enough, and of course was able to justify his concession on the grounds of improvement. But I think he knows perfectly well now that I won't have it in any event.

Besides what I've already told you, I had further and conclusive reasons for my stand. From my work at the N.I.H. library, I was familiar with the standard reference work on the pharmacology of various drugs, and knew that details were always included on any adverse effects, precautions to be taken, etc. I asked Dorothy Algire to read the section on gold for me. The whole picture of its hazards is pretty appalling, but for me the high point in the account is the specific and urgent statement that gold should not be administered to any person who has recently undergone a course of radiation! So there I had the answer to my own hunch. Yet this man, knowing perfectly well I'd just had radiation, was quite ready to give it to me. What this does to my already great cynicism about doctors you can perhaps imagine.

E. B. White has a piece in this week's *New Yorker*. I'm temporarily about out of stamps—the reason I'm sending this airmail!—but will mail this and Mr. White next week. His is an account of his trip to Alaska in 1923 ("Letter from the North, Delayed"). You will find much in it to enjoy—it was quite an extraordinary experience.

Last night I kept dreaming about Stanley's visit with the Crislers. If my dream means anything, he will get there! I'll bet Lois is in a dither of expectation about now.

Your little note written Wednesday came yesterday, dear. Yes, Southport does seem believable now. I'll admit there have been times when it didn't.

Now I must stop before the mail comes. My dearest love, always, as you know.

Rachel

TUESDAY A.M., MARCH 28

Dearest [Dorothy]—

Another 70+ day is predicted. Since yesterday morning at least half a dozen clumps of daffodils burst into bloom, and the hyacinths are showing very white. Do you have Chinodoxa? I think it is lovely—mine forms such a pool of blue out there near that cluster of rocks—quite as Tomlinson's bluebells "put the depth of the sky between the trees." And now the lovely white and blue and purple cups of crocus can be seen ringing those rocks—I was sure I'd planted some last fall and wondered what had happened. They must be late bloomers, I must get out there today.

Unfortunately, I've had some sort of intestinal upset since Sunday morning. First I thought rather hopefully it might be diverticulitis, but now I guess it's a plain old virus. I stayed in bed most of yesterday—though that was the day I'd wanted to try my first driving! Today I'll lie low, too—though I just may dress and go out to see those flowers! Ida, of course, is taking good care of me. When I'm quiet there is less pain, but the diarrhea is still a nuisance. So it's the old round of Kaopectate and paregoric, and I have quite a this-is-where-I-came-in-before feeling.

There is a great epidemic of dreadful colds around and I've been glad my exposure has been at a minimum. I suppose I'm lucky my bug has taken this form.

Of course I enjoyed all you told me about *Ring of Bright Water*. Isn't it fun to watch a best-seller being born? When *The Sea* was at that stage I was told by so many people (strangers to that point) that every Sunday morning they rushed for the *Times* to see where it was on the list. Now I do the same thing, so I can belatedly understand. (It was #8 on *Times* list this week—from #15 and #12 before.) What really sells a book, they say, is this word-of-mouth promotion, one reader telling another. I know you'll enjoy owning it. It's one of the few books I keep wanting to return to—to dip into almost daily.

I do so hope Lois will revise her plans and make her book the story of Alatna. I can just see that becoming a best-seller in the tradition of *Born Free* and *The Ring*, but if the wolf story is just hidden away in the other it might be lost. I do so covet real success for her. A letter from her yesterday. She was apparently genuinely grateful for my renewed advice. She was really about to send off some manuscript to this man, not realizing at all what trouble she was heading for. So now she will wait, will straighten out her problem with Harper, and I think will find an agent to handle her magazine rights if she can recover them. Poor dear—she wishes she "could get someone to help carry part of the load here— laundry, cleaning, etc.—It is agonizing to spend the day in worthless drudgery when I am burning to write—*my* work." I wonder how much money could really help that situation. So far from everyone—such a strange problem—where would she find a "wolf sitter"? I've wondered about her laundry problem—it must all be so primitive.

I wrote yesterday to the Nat'l Inst. of Arts and Letters to ask about their Grants—made to writers, artists, etc., on recommendation of members and ap- proval of committee. I don't know whether there is a date by which nominations must be made—they are announced at May Ceremonial. The amount is $1500. Perhaps the time is wrong, and perhaps I couldn't put it over anyway, so I won't mention it to her at present.

Paul telephoned yesterday. He had been asking Marie about my progress and so of course (!) had little idea of the facts. He wants to come to see me soon—perhaps as extension of his next New York trip. Just out of genuine con- cern, apparently. I'll really be very glad to see him.

Lois wrote recently of waking to the voices of barred owls—a wonderful sound. During last night as I listened to the swelling chorus of peepers (from Peeper Pond!) I thought how fortunate Lois and I are to live where we can hear something so remote from the prevalent artificiality of our world. One thing that fascinated me was the way all the voices would suddenly cease, and there would then be such an alert and listening silence—then finally one "peep," then two, and soon the whole chorus again. And there was a lovely moon sinking into the west. So you see my wakeful times were in part pleasant.

Now I must try to do some work. As you know, this carries a heart-full of love.

Rachel

Darling [Rachel],

Just a note to go in my Easter wish.

Your letter yesterday gave us such good news that I feel in a way Easter can be a day of resurrection for you in reality. Of course, it is hard to believe that you may soon be driving your car—and what an emancipation that will be for you!

Dearest, I have the oddest feeling about these past two months—I can't quite describe it. It concerns the complete isolation I feel. To think you have experienced probably the most difficult time of your whole life and I, who love you so, have not been able to share any of the burdens which I so well might have done if I had been nearer.

Of course, there has been wonderful communication—letters and telephone calls—and yet, even with my good imagination, I'm sure I cannot really know all you have been through—the suffering both mental and physical. And that's why I feel isolated.

Well, darling, let's hope this is the end of such a nightmare. It is so good to know you can begin to think of Southport.

There will be more letters from me before Sunday. I saw *my* first robins this morning—others have been reporting for some time.

Stanley's letter will let you know that all went well up until Saturday! I can scarcely wait to hear of his adventure.

All my love,
Dorothy

Darling [Dorothy],

Your lovely Easter card is here. I had wanted to write you something that could serve as an Easter message but there has been no time today. But perhaps this can carry the thought and the wish, at least. Perhaps I can write you on Easter morning, as you once did—a precious letter I wish I could find. In part, it was about the Lost Wood. Do you remember?

Well, I, too, have a strange feeling about these past two months, but I am glad that already I have been able to forget part of it. There is little I want to remember. April will bring a new month and a new year, for it was just a year ago I entered the hospital and started on a road I'd rather not have taken. But perhaps that detour is behind me.

I wish you could see my bulbs—such glory of yellow and white and blue—but they will be better a week from now.

By doing, I learn that I can't do. I think yesterday's driving was a little premature. I walk very stiffly and lamely as a result—and yet it seemed so easy at the time! Well, another week, perhaps. I was hoping that next week, with Roger home, we could drive out into the woods somewhere. Tomorrow I see Dr. Crain.

A brown thrasher arrived today. But this is the season of grackles and cowbirds, most of all.

I, too, can hardly wait to hear about Stanley and Lois.

This must go with Ida and Jeanne if it is to reach you by the week-end, to tell you again at Easter that I love you. Love to Stan, and Willow and you, Dorothy.

Rachel

Darling [Rachel],

I was awake before five this morning having gone to bed immediately after I said good-night to you.

I had no intention of getting up but suddenly the lovely voice of the fox sparrow spoke and I was out of bed. I dressed hurriedly and went out into the sunrise and a world of bird song I couldn't believe. It is the first time this year I've heard it—perhaps because I haven't been awake. The chorus ceased after a half hour—I suppose they greet the sun with joy. My joy, besides the fox sparrow, was the song of several white throats answering each other. I don't remember ever hearing them here at home in such profusion. Again my efficient husband had carefully packed the binoculars!

I heard a woodpecker tapping so decided to track it down. To my amazement I discovered woodpecker sounds were coming from 5 different directions & I had to choose.

Finally I discovered a downy vigorously pounding a dead branch. As he stopped he was answered from a tree across the road by the same sound. After a while a female flew into the male's tree, they recognized each other, & after a while flew off together. It appeared that the tapping was their method of attracting each other rather than by song. I wonder if that is true.

Before six o'clock I saw Stan in the pantry and when I came in breakfast was ready. Now he has gone back to bed & is asleep!

Our yard was just full of birds & as I stood still such flying around me—especially chick-a-dees who came so close and in such numbers I could have plucked them out of the air.

Once wings fluttered around me—four goldfinches lighted over my head.

It was all lovely—and without moving off our land.

Now I should begin to move about.

We didn't plan to start too early as we'd get caught in traffic in Boston.

Darling, it was good to talk with you last night again.

It is hard to believe that you are moving about after those horrible long weeks.

Darling, I can go to you for a visit later if you would want me.

And above all I can help drive you to Southport. That you must be sure to understand. I don't care if I had to return from the North Pole to do it, I want you to know I can be with you. So remember that.

I'll be thinking of you as I go north, hoping and trusting that you and I will have many happy hours there in the not-too-far-away.

All my love, dear,
Dorothy

Darling [Rachel],

Off to the hairdresser's so will get a brief note ready to mail. We hope to talk to you to-night so you will know of the successful venture into the Rockies amidst wolves—and dogs!

After we've seen Stanley we'll write a full account.

This is to put into writing our plans for next week.

Darling, I hate to be so out of touch with you as we shall be for several days.

We leave here Thurs. & will go directly to Orono. We baby-sit Fri., Sat., & Sun. & if all goes well we'll go to Boothbay on Monday and return home on Tues.—that is April 6, 7, 8, 9, 10, 11.

So probably after you receive this you shouldn't send more mail here as we'd be gone before it reached here.

Of course, I shall write to you as the days progress so at least you'll hear something.

This is a sunny day but too cold for anything less than a winter coat.

Tommy came this morning. The garage has had its spring cleaning which befits the new car.

Stan has been raking as well as Tommy so our grounds are in the best shape ever this early. The lawn is rolled & fertilized, & bulbs are everywhere.

Took some freesias to Aunt Pink yesterday & took them to ride in new car. It's been 300 miles now.

Darling, you know how well I wish you. I'm eager to learn the results of your trip to Dr. Crain today.

I love you so,
Dorothy

Dearest [Dorothy]—

It was a happy surprise to find your Thurs. A.M. letter in the mail. Of course I expected nothing more until the middle of the week!

Now I must set my alarm and see how our early morning chorus is. I'd had the impression too there was rather limited singing so far.

Bent says the drumming of the downy is part of, or preliminary to, courtship. Apparently the female seldom if ever drums.

When I tell you what I did today you will know I'm cured! This afternoon Roger had come in to tell me something and I had followed him to the kitchen door and stood there talking with the screen door incautiously ajar. Suddenly I was startled to see a black-and-white pussy slip past my feet and down the steps. With absolutely nothing in my mind but retrieving Moppet, I followed. Mary said I almost *ran* down the steps—and steps, up or down, have been forbidden for the past 11 weeks! Moppet paused to inspect the trash cans, then, as I was almost upon her, took off again. I caught her by the corner of the screened porch. It was only as I started back with her that I thought "Good heavens, I must have gone down the steps!" Perhaps it proves the triumph of mind over matter—or perhaps "love conquers all." Anyway, I seem no worse for it.

Elliott did a tremendous job today. The drain parallel to the street seemed to be stopped up. It's a long story, but after much excavating he found a large rubber ball in the pipe almost completely blocking it! He has also done other work that may make the Swamp less Dismal.

———————

Sunday A.M. postscript: The drainage project seems to have been quite successful—we shall wait and see. Maybe, if you come this spring, the Dismal Swamp will actually be lawn! You *did* say something when last we talked that gave me a lovely hope. You know that you, or both of you, would bring me so much joy if you found you could come.

Now—all my love—
Rachel

APRIL 5

———————

Darling [Rachel],

Just a note to-day so I'll be sure something is on its way before we leave to-morrow. Up to now all is going well. There is a sense of excitement for me as I am gathering up odds and ends—waffle iron, big flashlight, suitcases of linens, extra blankets, books—that can be taken to Dogfish Head to leave now.

We've had unreasonably cold weather recently but I suppose we must expect it. My flowering quince bushes look as though the buds were frozen. I shall miss that glory if they don't bloom.

The new car is really a joy and we are happy, especially, with the ease of packing the trunk. It rides beautifully too—so smoothly and so quietly.

It's been 400 miles now so by the time we get back it will be just ready for its first check-up. There is an added interest in the Orono trip with more details to hear from Stanley of the Colorado adventure.

We took a silver wedding gift to the Johnsons last night as we won't be here to help them celebrate. We were shown the colored slides of their Carribean trip (incidentally, it was their actual celebration)—some excellent ones taken with a Brownie Starflash—no settings, you know.

But reading between the lines of their commentary, I have no desire at all to do what they did. It was a very expensive trip, and I feel they got so little out of it—not to mention rough, stormy weather, heat, smells, etc.

Last night I had such a real dream. What happened seemed so natural. It was at Southport. The sea was absolutely calm—no swells, no chop but not mirror-like. The tide was the highest ever for every reef was covered with no surf breaking anywhere. Quite as a matter of course Stan, another girl (I think it was his secretary who is now a nun) and I went for a walk on the water. We started from the Head, through Ebenecook around the island so we emerged at Christmas Cove where we walked out to and over the Cat Ledges looking down on them as you can look down through clear ice when skating. But we were walking on water! We wound up back at the Head. I wish you had been there!

The envelope with *New Yorker* material arrived Monday I think. Of course, Stan had a good laugh at the Stock Holders' meeting. He is going to send it to Jim Timberlake who will also appreciate it. And of course you know I couldn't wait to read E.B. It was highly interesting in view of the place of Alaska at the moment. However, I was a little disappointed in the writing—it lacked the usual flavor that stamps it as E.B. Didn't you think so? Did I tell you, speaking of Journal or Diaries that Mil Nye loaned us a rare precious diary written by a great-uncle as he journeyed across the U.S. by train, boat, canal-boat, mule and on foot to California to search for gold—about 1859, I think? He was killed in Civil War.

It is thrilling to read a firsthand account. Have just finished Moss Hart's "Act One"—another picture of the 1920s.

Darling, I do hope there will be some mail from you to-day. I shall be anxious to know how you are before I move 300 miles farther away from you.[30] I think we are both terribly aware of the separation.

I shall write, of course, as I move North.

All my dear love,
Dorothy

[30] For a six-day trip to Orono and Southport.

APRIL 7

Darling [Dorothy],

By now I suppose, you are well launched as baby sitters. According to the weather maps, you have no snow. Here it is cold and windy and blossoms come along very slowly.

My plans worked out satisfactorily, but not quite "the way we planned them." There was a letter from Dr. Crile yesterday saying they had to leave this morning shortly after 10, and asking whether I could "have coffee" with them at his sister-in-law's in Georgetown between 9 and 10. Well, it would have taken some doing, so when he called later in the day I told him I thought we'd better just talk by phone. And really, except for the pleasure of seeing them, it was just as satisfactory. He is well pleased with all Dr. Caulk reported to him and that was about all it was necessary to know, though he did clarify a few things I was wondering about.

Had I told you Dr. Hard was also to be in town today? I decided to go ahead to lunch with him. Quite a milestone—first social engagement in *months*! I drove into Silver Spring, parked there, and took a cab. This meant driving 3 or 4 times as far as I've done before, but there seem to be no ill effects. It is just wonderful to be able to drive, get out and do an errand, and even walk a block, almost like a human being!

Dr. Hard had carried all the way from California yesterday a beautiful little Cymbidium orchid which his wife had sent me from their garden! You know they are my favorites among orchids anyway.

Ida phoned early yesterday that she had a bad cold and wouldn't be out. I encouraged her to stay off today, too, though this complicated things a little. I took Roger along to hairdresser yesterday A.M.—then had Page here from 12 to 5. Then the Newtons had Roger today—sort of an eye-for-an-eye, etc., arrangement. School again Monday.

I might have known I couldn't stay within that space!

Your Wednesday letter came today. I'm so glad the car is giving you so much satisfaction from the beginning. I don't believe you were ever entirely pleased with the last one.

I'm sure when you deposit linens, waffle iron, etc., at Dogfish Head you will really believe winter is over.

As I write I'm listening to the Library of Congress concert—the Budapest String Quartet.

I think you'll be interested in *New Yorker*'s comments on last week's Philharmonic concert. It *was* Mahler's Third you wrote about, wasn't it?

Today Dr. Hard told me such a poignant story of his return to an exquisitely beautiful trout stream in Idaho. It (his story) was an exact counterpart of "A Lost Woods"—and as it happened the stream was called Lost River. On his second visit the A.E.C.[31] had taken over!

[31] Atomic Energy Commission.

You know my thoughts are spanning the extra 300 miles, and that I'll be with you especially at Southport. But please don't try walking on the water!

All my dearest love
Rachel

WEDNESDAY P.M., APRIL 12

UNDER THE DRIER

Darling [Rachel],

It was such a treat to talk to you last night. And it is especially wonderful to be able to think of you moving about again. The little heartbreak note a while back in which you spoke of "wanting this Spring," made me sad. Now I have the feeling that you *are* having this spring after all. And it was not so long ago that Dr. Crain had told you "a matter of months"—not days or even weeks, and of course, pessimism took hold to set me wondering if it would be wise for you to try to go to Southport. But now the sun seems to be shining again for you.

Which brings me to the question of whether I should insert myself into your spring.

In one of your recent letters you said that summer was now less than three months away, and probably we could wait until then.

Of course, my thought to go down for a visit was when you were so confined & hadn't begun to work.

Now I feel that your time is precious; that you are picking up momentum in your work; you are feeling better and able to get about. So that, much as I know (shamelessly) you would enjoy having me there, I think it would be wiser and more sensible all around if I didn't interrupt the momentum. At best your time before Southport will be short for all the "catching up" you must have to do, & for me to spoil the greater part of a week for you, wouldn't be the kindest thing I could do.

Of course, when I first thought of seeing you this spring, it was with the idea of stopping off on a trip with Stan. Then when we gave that up & you were still badly off, I longed to go to comfort you. When I thought, as apparently you never did (well, perhaps that is not wholly true), that you might not make it to Southport this summer, I felt I couldn't stand not seeing you before I went up for good.

But now the gloom is dispelled, and I am confident we are to have time together this summer, I think it is kinder if I settle the uncertainty for you by deciding that I won't try to make you a visit. I almost think that the decision will give you a sense of relief for you can settle down to real work without the uncertainty of a possible interruption.

Of course, darling, if you need me I can always go, but when I think how I *might* have served you in the nightmare I doubt if you can say you need me now.

So why don't we start counting the days until July 1 and in the meantime put aside a folder to file bits of conversation & reading material away to share during the hours we can have together this summer?

And I'm sure Time will fly with all you have to do indoors, and with good days that you can enjoy out doors.

Now isn't that a very sensible way to look at it?

And now that you are so much better, and working, let's cut down on the letter writing, too. I'll try to help by not writing such volumes or so often.

If you can send me a report of progress once a week, I'm sure I can be content—and on this end, I won't promise to cut it to once a week but at least not so much.

However, there is still a volume I want to write so I won't stop just yet.

Darling, the white hyacinths which were a gift from you last year are encircling a quince bush & ready to burst into bloom, come some warm weather! I'm dry so will mail this as I go home.

With all my love.
Dorothy

THURSDAY, APRIL 13

Dearest [Dorothy],

It was such a relief to know you had reached home without incident. You can imagine my imagination had done full justice to the weather reports.

Speaking of weather—when I looked out at seven this morning there was a fine dusting of snow here and there! Nothing to last, of course. We've had heavy rain beginning yesterday. I hope it clears before tomorrow, when I go to Dr. Crain.

Of course I'm eager to hear details of your trip—what you did with the children, etc. And more about your adventure at Portland Head Light.

I spent a good while yesterday fussing with that sea essay for *Johns Hopkins Magazine*[32]—of course I always give too much time to the "little" jobs! But having written a book about the sea, it was very difficult to write 300 words about it! That, plus captions for the 6 or 7 "spreads" of photos, is my contribution.

Now today I return to the book. I'm writing with a certain amount of pleasure now, but as always, slowly.

I kept Roger home today. He complained of headache and nausea last night, but had no fever. However, I wanted to be sure no trouble was brewing, and I guess it isn't.

You will see more on Mahler in *Saturday Review* this week, a somewhat dissenting opinion.

Probably I won't try to write more before week-end, dear. I'm working most evenings now—Roger's bedtime until 11 or even 12. But Saturday looks like a gardening day if weather permits. I have plans for putting in some shrubbery (not personally, of course!). Meanwhile you are in my thoughts, you know.

My dear love—
Rachel

[32] The article, entitled "The Sea," was published in the May–June 1961 volume of the *Johns Hopkins Magazine*.

THURSDAY A.M., MAY 25

Darling [Dorothy],

The shoe box full of loveliness arrived at 8:15 this morning, about 18 hours after it left you. The flowers are as fresh as though you had cut them an hour ago—it is just amazing! And such fragrance! I have a lovely bunch in my bedroom, where I am writing, and another in the dining room. They will still be fresh and lovely on my birthday, to speak of you, dear. How can I thank you!

You will laugh to hear that for a moment I wasn't going to open it, thinking "the bad thing, she's sent another birthday present and she wasn't supposed to!" But something wasn't right about Air Mail-Special 2 days before, and suddenly it dawned on me—flowers! You darling!

If you want a business for your "retirement" years, why not try Flowers-by-Mail?

Now I want to return your letter from Lois, which arrived yesterday. You will meanwhile have had the later word in my letter. What a situation!! And my heart aches for her to have this grief with Alatna, especially while Cris is away.

Virginia and Lee are coming here Saturday for dinner. They wanted to take us out but I said (and meant) I'd rather do it this way. Mary can have the dinner ready before she leaves. Perhaps I'll have Robert & Vera too.

School May Day yesterday went off well—a beautiful day though a trifle cool for some of the costumes. I saw Mrs. Brooker Monday and am to see the public school man tomorrow. Have also had a telephone conversation with Mrs. Emery, Roger's teacher. They are most understanding and cooperative, and Mrs. B. is not pressing for a decision. However, all the suggestions and alternatives that have come out of these conversations leave me, if anything, more confused!

I must not write more now, dear. Time flies and I wish I could finish another chapter this week.

What day do you return to Maine? *Maine!* I haven't half told you how wonderful your Southport letters were, breathing the very air of the place.[33] They made me long to take off the very moment R. is out of school.

And that reminds me—Bob called last night, obviously ready to take off anytime, too. His son has a summer job in Alaska and has received permission to leave school before Commencement Day. So father Bob will go out to see "that feller" soon if he can scrape up the money. He has cleared the way with his chief for a week's vacation sometime after June 15. That was my clue to how long he plans to stay! Well, it will be fun, and he and Roger can have a fine time fishing and exploring woods. When you do return, dear, would you ask Mrs. Kenrick if her place is committed before July 1? I really do think that is the solution.

Now I *must* go. How I love these lilies-of-the-valley—and you and Stan, who grew them.

> I do really, you know—
> *Rachel*

[33] After visiting RC in Silver Spring from May 7 to 11 DF had gone to Southport from May 18 to 21 to open the Freeman cottage.

FRIDAY, JUNE 2

Darling [Rachel],

[34] DF and Stanley had arrived in Southport on May 31.

We're going to B.Bay[34] so I'll put a wee bit in the mail for you. Last eve we went birding. I heard not one hermit—I can't understand it. We rode over to Salt Pond to see what we could see—flycatcher & Red Starts.

Rode along toward beach to find rhodora and there it was along the road—more than I've ever seen there. But too near the edge for safety. We also found it in bloom in Brunswick—so lovely, in what area has been left untouched but just waiting for the bulldozer! I wish I could write like Tomlinson, I'd send a letter to someone in Brunswick to save it!

But now listen—while we stopped to look at the lavender mist, I heard—yes, I did—veeries! Just on the corner in the woods by Mrs. Kenrick's house-in-the-woods. It was so wonderful—the best, or nearest, I've ever been to the song. I was so thrilled. Mrs. K. is not here yet so I think I'll send you her home address. Then I'll also keep watching & will speak to her about the house if she arrives here.

Mrs. Harriett Kenrick
2 Rustic Rd.
Stoneham, Mass.

Cloudy yesterday & in the night heavy rain with bombarding thunder, & rain continuing all day to-day.

But knowing I have all summer ahead of me I don't mind the wet and unlike Jeffie I did *not* growl at the rain-on-the-roof. In fact, with it and my electric blanket I had a sense of well-being which only your presence could have enhanced.

> I love you,
> D.

SATURDAY MORNING, JUNE 3

Dear Heart [Rachel],

We have surf almost like Pemaquid this morning driven in by a strong southwest wind but there is a softness in the air that lets us know it is Spring even in this latitude.

And it was even so at 4:10 A.M. When I went to bed, as forecast had been for a good day, I decided to try to hear the Maine dawn chorus if I woke up without an alarm. I did. So I quietly stole out with a furry companion. Even at 4:30 it was far lighter than I could imagine. At that hour the loudest voice was a Phoebe, evidently guarding the nest on the Robinson porch. Such a raspy voice but also persistent. It went on steadily, leading up to sunrise. Of course, the multitude of White Throats were singing on all sides.

Because wind & surf were strong I knew I couldn't hear much chorus if I went down on the Head but the cloud formation in the East made me realize I'd better take in this sunrise & forego the quiet of the woods.

It was well I did—there may not be another like it all summer. Someone had opened those "gates of glory" wide and the *whole* sky flamed up for a while. It was Wagner, in sight rather than sound.

I think I shall try to capture it in words.

When the fury had faded Willow and I walked up the road as far as Chicoines'. A pair of Towhees scolded us & followed us all the way. Sometime you must have the fun of a bird walk, with a cat, with me.

Yesterday, at the junction of the Newagen Rd. & the Cross Rd., even while the car was running I heard Veeries—at 3:30 in the afternoon! Darling, oh my darling. They were just wonderful. I hope they last until you come. But no hermits. They were here when Hazel & I were here. Off to the mail to carry my love,

All of it,
Dorothy

ON WAY TO B. BAY TO MAIL

Darling [Rachel],

Just to prove your violets survived![35]

We planted freesias in your garden this morning. All is well there.

Gorgeous day—bright sun.

Much to tell you but this is merely to say good-morning.

Stan needed to get some mail out to-day hence trip to Harbor.

On way home we are going to try to transplant some rhodora! Details in letter.

Darling—veeries are singing all over Southport. I really feel satisfied at last. How I wish you were here to share the songs.

Your letter came yesterday. It sounds so happy.

Just a week ago this moment I was "walking on air"!!

We are so happy here. It seems that we are really living at last.

More to follow.

All my love,
Dorothy

[35] DF had enclosed a sprig of dried violets in this letter.

THURSDAY P.M., JUNE 8

Darling [Rachel],

Stan's napping & I'm going to P. O. with mail so will talk briefly to you.

Your Monday letter came to-day—probably it was here yesterday but we didn't get back from our Isleboro trip in time to get mail.

What a lovely thing for you to do for Lois[36]—how thrilled she will be if it goes through.

Darling, you amaze me at the nonchalance with which you say "two more chapters off to Paul." How incredibly wonderful! How do you account for this smooth "rolling along?" You must be feeling unusually well, & the creative fires burning briskly. I am so thrilled for you.

Maine temperatures are far from 92°. It was 48° last night, but electric blankets laugh at that. Our wood stove really is a joy. I talk of doing away with it when we do the house over but we may be sorry. It is, of course, a dirty thing, but lends such a dry warmth at all times—in fact we've been too hot.

[36] RC had written to the National Institute of Arts and Letters recommending Lois Crisler for one of its grants in literature.

By the time you get here I'm sure it will have warmed up. We've had some very windy days but those will not increase.

I'm so sorry Roger got sick, and oh, good heavens, I do hope you don't get whatever he had. Take good care.

You will have heard we had a delightful day on the Isleboro trip. On the ferry ride back we went topside where we could get the full benefit of the wild wind & waves of the blue Penobscot. The waves hit on the side & you should have seen the cars on the deck rock, & the spray blew over them so the car & windshield were covered with salt. Stan took car for a wash this A.M.

Found a good place for a steak dinner in Camden. We were starved.

Then came home via Rockland to inquire about the boat to Matinicus which sounds like our next project. It goes Tues., Thurs. & Sat. so if Tues. (June 13) is auspicious we plan to go. Will have to leave here at 6 A.M. Think we'll go for only the day this time & then find out about accommodations to stay over— it has to be for 2 nights—so by staying overnight get a chance to go out to see the rock where the Artic terns & puffins are. We could do that later. That would be my birthday celebration—the day trip next week, I mean.

Mad writes they will be here sometime between June 16 (when school closes) and July 4 (when Institute starts) but that interval will also include a trip to Suncook as well as a visit at Cape Elizabeth so they probably won't be here long.

It will be so much easier this year for me.

Was so interested in the gift of Mrs. Bingham's[37] to Amherst & Mr. Barnes'[38] article. It makes me long so to acquire our Lost Woods.

You'll be happy to know that hermits were singing in the parula area as we came home from the store about 5 o'clock. And we see a hermit near our camp almost every day.

I shudder at the thought of a "Silent Spring."[39]

The increase in Veeries is just amazing. Surely it isn't that I haven't tried to hear them other years—my ears have always been open for that song above all others.

No, I haven't heard an olive-back yet but I told you I saw one when I was here with Hazel.

Now it is June 8—then 9, 10, 11, 12, and on until in a few weeks you'll be here! Oh, my darling. How wonderful that will be. Every morning to greet you. Oh, pure delight!

Keep well, don't overdo, & allow yourself extra time for the last week's preparations! Do you know what I'm thinking as I listen to the ocean outside my room as I drift off to sleep?

It's lovely—and I love you,

D.

[37] Millicent Todd Bingham, author of several books about Emily Dickinson, was also a geographer. In 1961 she gave the Mabel Loomis Todd Forest to Amherst College.

[38] Irston Barnes wrote a weekly column entitled "The Naturalist" in the *Washington Post*.

[39] "Silent Spring" was originally the title of only the chapter on birds in RC's manuscript.

Dearest [Dorothy],

I think this is the day you planned another sea voyage and I wonder if you went. We are in the midst of a horrid hot spell—hot and humid. Last night it was a real ordeal to sit through the play, especially since I'd seen it before. Roger's "big" part was Saturday night, when he was one of the 7 dwarfs in *Snow White*. The dwarf scenes were really darling—in fact it was all extremely well done. But that couldn't keep me from dripping and suffering!

Paul has come and gone. It was good to see him and some helpful ideas emerged from our talk. Insofar as they involve reorganization, I shall put them aside until a complete draft is done. As you know, we have never planned for illustrations, but today we talked seriously of having them (sketches—not photographs)—partly to aid understanding, partly to break it up and make reading easier. I'm delighted.

I told you that a possible opening sentence had drifted to the surface of my mind recently. It was—"This is a book about man's war against nature, and because man is part of nature it is also and inevitably a book about man's war against himself."

Very plain and simple, but I thought perhaps it went to the heart of it. Paul agrees. Out of our discussion of that came a couple of possible book titles—*The War Against Nature*, or *At War with Nature*.

(In desperation, Marie has been calling it "Carson; Opus No. 4.")

Yesterday I had a phone call from Dr. Anshen—back from Europe, in Washington Monday, eager to see me. I couldn't say no, but oh dear, there is a day shot!

Yesterday I left the car all day at a Silver Spring place highly recommended by Lee, to get cured of stalling. Taking it home, after paying out $28.40, it stalled 9 times. I've lost count since, but it is just as bad as before. Now I shall have to go around tomorrow and lose more time. Wouldn't you know!

Thurs. I see Dr. Caulk. Sat. A.M. I shall try to take Roger & me to the clinic for blood tests. In the afternoon Bette Haney[40] is getting married and I shall have to go! It will be some sort of miracle, I guess, if we get off a week from Thurs.

Mrs. Kenrick writes she has not rented the cottage and will save it if I let her know when. I guess I'll tell her probably starting the 27th, with hope of changing to 23rd. I may ask you to negotiate the change if it is possible.

Thank you so much for measuring the drapes. And I'm glad I asked you to go, since it made you see the porcupine. I guess that is another of the rewards of being there early, before people!

Probably we will have talked before you read this. I'll try not to repeat everything I've just written.

I'm writing on the porch—past 10 P.M. and sweltering. Insects are trill-

[40] A research assistant to RC.

ing—dogs are unhappy or disturbed and barking all over the neighborhood. I'd rather be in Maine! Not many more letters, dear! But this carries all my love, as always—

Rachel

WEDNESDAY

School's out! I'm spending the afternoon on errands, CAR, etc.

At graduation exercises this morning Roger received an Award of Merit for Proficiency in Dramatic Art!! One such award is given to a boy, one to a girl.

In haste now—but with very much love—

R.

JULY 12[41]

Darling [Rachel],

The Sea's voice is growing louder below my window as I write this goodnight to you to carry you my love on the anniversary of the day we first looked into each other's eyes.

It speaks of you and a flood of memories washes over me. Has it occurred to you that, as a rule, the memories we cherish most are of the happy times? Isn't it wonderful that it is so?

To-night then, when I put out my light I shall drift off to sleep with a thousand beautiful thoughts of sweetness and loveliness and delights we have shared in these precious eight years.

As I told you the other night I can't imagine what my life would have been without you—very hollow, indeed, I fear when I realize all that has filled it for which you are responsible.

Please know how grateful I am for all you have done to enrich my life as the years have marched along.

Thank you for making me know and understand the Sea which had been such a part of my being for so long—and yet it took you to reveal it to me.

I wonder if you are as glad as I am that we were brought together.

Once again, I want to tell you

I love you,
Dorothy

SEPTEMBER 1

Dear Heart [Rachel],

It was with great relief that I knew you were safely home, for I was terribly worried about you. A two-day trip with a strenuous child, two cats, the responsibilities of the car, and all the driving would tax a strong able-bodied man. And when I saw *you* drive off, I wondered if you could stand it.

Now, if for some time you feel over tired please understand the reason why. I'm sure the heat won't help, either.

Darling, I must keep repeating what a Godsend it is for me to be able to be in this Haven of peace and quiet.[42]

[41] RC and Roger had arrived at Southport on June 23.

[42] The Freemans had begun renovations on their cottage and were making use of RC's place. She had offered it to them in an August 23, 1961, letter to Stanley, which reads in part: "It is part of loving people to give freely as well as to receive—so won't you please let me have this real happiness?
"There is no one whom I could leave in charge of the house with greater peace of mind. . . . Please do this for me.
"Because we love you both—Rachel"

You simply can't know what it means.

I love my room. The Seguin fog horn groaned in the night but a bright star was framed in the window at 1 A.M.

This morning the fog was thick, there was not a sign of a cobweb, the sun was hot as it shone through the fog over the hilltop, and now at 9:30 Five Islands is appearing across the Bay. Why should there be dewy cobwebs one morning and not another?

Last night in the deep dusk at the Head a large bird fluttered around the reef for a long while. It probably was a night heron for it lacked the long neck and legs of the Great Blue & yet it was not a gull. When it finally flew off a long trail of seaweed hung behind from its legs. We wondered if it had eaten something which had had seaweed attached to it.

Stan and I are going to Damariscotta & Boothbay this morning—for a haircut & a last lunch at Cheechako and errands. Then back to watch the children in the pool this P.M.

The sun, as it has so many times, was a ball of fire last night but sank into a cloud. But while it was hanging there, a flight of birds passed under it over the spruces, foretelling what is to come.

Darling, I love you—
Dorothy

SUNDAY, SEPTEMBER 17

Darling [Rachel],

7 P.M. and the sun has already been gone twenty minutes. The Long Night has truly begun. To-night it sank in a cloudless sky, one of few, as you know. The temperature is 53° but Stan and I, in our winter mackinaws and blankets, with Willow, deigning to sit in my lap (usually in summer he gives me the icy stare) sat in the hammock to make our nightly count of Great Blues—4 so far. Last night we were startled as 3 huge ones suddenly flew from the Head at once, within close range. Their silhouettes are so different from other birds, and their flight so deliberate and slow.

This morning I was awake at 6:15—the sunrise glistened in the Mac windows urging me out. It was 44°. I built a fire, had hot juice, toast and coffee and took to the woods. Evidently, the warblers are passing through.

Yesterday morning Stan and I were also out early to find the deciduous trees above Cutlers' road alive with tiny movements. To our joy we discovered a pair of parulas so busy combing a birch tree in the sun.

We had a wonderful show for as long as we wanted to linger. And it was much the same to-day. Of course, the fall warblers are not as easily identified as in Spring but I knew some. To-day there were parulas again, a black and white, myrtle, Maryland yellow throat, a black-throated green that I watched for 20 minutes, a redstart, and what I like to think was a kinglet. The chick-a-dees have arrived in great numbers & flew around me as though I were a dead tree—so busy and full of chick-a-dee talk. And the red-breasted Nuthatches come in swarms everywhere. A pair of white-breasted examine our trees every day along with a brown creeper. Besides all these, to-day there were towhees, catbirds, white throats, song sparrows, juncoes, flickers, downies, hairies, and even a kingfisher flew over. They are numerous along the shore, also. No purple finches now.

When I returned from my walk I found Stan, too, had been out & was full of enthusiasm for what he'd seen. But he was back in time to have bacon, scrambled eggs, toast & coffee waiting for me.

Yesterday morning Willow gave us a hard time for a few hours. Stanley spent Fri. night with us but had to be in Orono for a Freshman program at 9:30 A.M. Sat. So we were up at 5:45 to feed him & get him off at 6:30. Willow was not on the shelf at the window as is his custom. I thought perhaps 5:45 was too early for him. But we wondered why he didn't come when we went up to the car to see Stanley off.

After we had our breakfast we decided on a walk for it was a NW morning with all its sparkles. I thought if we went out on the Head Willow might be there for he brings trophies home from there. Half-way out Stan said "What's all this?" Beside the path over about an area of a square yard in the grass and low bushes was a covering of fluff—curly fluff—whitish and gray—Willow's fur! There had been some sort of fight surely, but what with? Of course, you can understand what our minds leaped to—mink, fox, dog, wild cats! It was a horrible moment. There was no sign of blood and no indication of where he'd gone—no trail of fur.

The next two hours of searching every rock crevice, every bush, and beach on the Head were agonizing. We both combed it all, getting sicker and sicker. Finally we thought we should walk up the road, and that's when we saw the warblers, but they could not distract us from the awful prospect that he was gone for good. You, I'm sure, can know what it was like. We tried to talk calmly of the possibility, and that we must be sensible, and that he'd been a wonderful pet, and that we'd been prepared, etc., etc. But by then I was crying. So many thoughts rushed through my mind. And I remember thinking that nothing mattered—if only we could have him back.

Stan went back to the Head—of course, we'd been calling "Willow" frantically all the time.

I came home & to keep busy, I began to wash the breakfast dishes. Suddenly, and I scarcely could believe my eyes, I saw the darling coming up the path from Pink's. Even before I greeted him I rushed to the porch and screamed to Stan, "He's coming home."

When I went to Willow he had a wild expression (otherwise, no sign of injury—only much loose fur) and acted so frightened. I gathered him into my arms & he did purr a bit but never relaxed. He finally ate a dish of fish but then ran upstairs to hide under the bed until afternoon.

Well, I was sure done in. I said to Stan to-day, "If we never knew before we now know what that little cat means to us."

At the moment he is curled on his back with a paw over his face asleep in a chair so peacefully.

And last night he willingly spent all night indoors.

I suppose we shall never solve the mystery.

Monday morning

I must finish this. So much to tell if time permitted. Another walk this morning, this time together. Several interesting finds—perhaps most exciting, was, I feel sure, a female scarlet tanager—we both saw it for a long time. Too big for a warbler, coloration resembles the book description—no other bird quite meets it.

Darling, you would have loved it—cobwebs, covered & glittering with dew, draping every bush, tree, rock, the smell of woods, hints of brilliant foliage to come. Only patches as yet.

Last night, oh my darling, the moon—quarter size—was more beautiful than any I recall—a half hour above the horizon, pure gold with a golden path just its width from Five Islands to our cove. I'm sure you would have caught your breath!

I must tell you of the nights of phosphorescence. The first night, a wink or two from the cove in the middle of the night; the second night, more, and on the third night, when the tide, at 2 A.M. was at its flood, below me was a field of fireflies of the sea.

Willow joined me on the porch. There was enough motion to make silver lace-edged wavelets. I thought, "If I were younger I'd like to play with it." I tossed some pebbles from the porch with such delightful results that I could no longer resist. I found an oar shaped stick (remember this was 2 A.M.) & worked my way through the bayberry & juniper to the sloping rock below the porch. Guess who rubbed my ankles. With the stick I paddled, with quicksilver dripping back into the water. I splashed the water on the rocks where twenty little cold eyes blinked at me, and on the end of my stick was a crown of stars as I waved it through the air. I felt that I had the power of a fairy godmother! But the power wasn't quite potent enough for as I waved it I said, "I wish Rachel were beside me" and waited, but you didn't come.

After this grandmother had dallied quite some time she went back to the house where Willow demanded to be fed.

Stan heard me at the refrig. & called, "If you are getting something to eat I'll be down." I said, "Want some cat food?"

But the idea turned into toast and honey and coffee which we ate at 2:30 on the porch watching the phenomenon still adding beauty to the night.

Early the next morning the sea began to murmur and by low tide the murmur had risen to a chorus, the Bay was filled with long swells with deep troughs, and a day of turbulence had begun. I tried to work but was drawn to the porch too often to accomplish much. We ate our meals there in spite of the fact that at times there were heavy rain showers.

When the tide was at the right height the rollers broke in two directions over the reef and met with a huge clash that sent flying spray high into the air. There was constant booming and grand surf all day—even in our cove combers broke half-way up. The sky was wonderful to watch, too, for occasionally the heaviness would break, showing a streak of blue with bright clouds scudding past. Then black clouds would form again & the rain would descend shutting out the far shore. Here was the proof of the old weathermen "Open and shut, sign of more wet."

I won't bother you with our numerous activities of last week, except to tell you that we were invited to the Eliot Howards' on Barter's Island for an evening of bridge. They have a lovely old house with huge lawns and gardens. They told us they get their plants from a Mr. Graffam—of course we laughed & they said "Do you know him?" And of course, you know the answer they got. Mrs. Howard said that she said to Mrs. Graffam, "Mr. G. is such an interesting man" & Mrs. G. replied, "Yes, that's why I married him." Mrs. G. is the daughter of the famous (around Boston, at least) Dean Archer of Suffolk Law School. The bridge game didn't amount to much, for we discovered, early, that Mr. Howard arrived at big Christmas Cove the summer of 1896. His father was a school-teacher & bought an old farm there. You can imagine the reminiscing that went on between bids and deals!

He got out books showing pictures of the boats & we lived again those trips from Boston.

They say the Delano development on Barter's Island is quite fine. We must ride over.

Along with our "social" life we're hard at work on house plans. Saw electrician last week & have decided on electric heat similar to yours & to do away with wood stove which solves several kitchen problems.

One evening I laid out the kitchen in detail—where to store what, work areas, outlets, etc., etc. It was quite relaxing to get it all down on paper.

Also have talked with linoleum man & looked at materials for floors & counters but the decisions will be made in the spring. A visit to Trading Post to check on beds, etc. We shall have at least 3 new ones.

Stan spent 4 mornings on pulling up the floor covering upstairs. Only he can describe the work, the mess, the variety of material, the bags of dirt he emptied from the vacuum! Wow. That I'm sure is the worst job of all.

And we are gradually nibbling away at all the packing & dismantling jobs.

Stanley will plan to stay over Fri. night & until late Sat. P.M. this week, & we can finish up jobs that require help. Then after he's gone I think we'll be ready to move over to your house until Oct. 1 when we plan to go home for a week & then back on the 8th or 9th for a final week.

I hope that is all right with you.

Darling, if only you could realize what a relaxed feeling & a sense of security it gives us to know we can move over there when it's too difficult to live here.

Bless you for wanting us to use it.

Am enclosing Lois's letter. I just think it's outrageous to think of that woman living in that spot alone with those animals. Suppose something happens to Cris & he can't get home even once a week. And according to this letter, it can happen!

Guess what. I'm at the kitchen shelf—a weasel just ran across the mossy opening between here & our camp!!

At first I thought it was a red squirrel from the coloring but suddenly it dawned on me that it wasn't at all the shape of a squirrel—long, flat, & a skinny tail stretched out behind.

How I rave on. Oh, I wish you could be here these gorgeous Sept. days—cold (41° at 7 A.M.) but oh so lovely.

Next year why not put Roger in school here for six weeks and have this season? It would be a good experience for him.

Now I must stop. So thrilled that *Silent Spring*[43] is moving well, that I don't even mind the absence of mail from you. Just to know you are working is all I ask & long for.

All my love, dear,
Dorothy

TUESDAY A.M., SEPTEMBER 26

UNDER DRIER

Dearest [Dorothy]—

Judging by the speed with which a new girl "set me up" this morning I won't have much time to write if she has any way to speed the drying process!

I try to picture what you may be doing. It is fun to think of you getting meals in my kitchen, probably eating before the picture window, having a fire. You had hurricane-born rain yesterday, if our weather man was right. Too bad—I hope you are now done with rain and fog for the year.

The Frechs from Baltimore are coming to lunch today. I don't think I've seen them for 10 years! They are lovely people.

I am working late at night most of the time now. If I can fight off the desire to go to bed around 11:30 I seem to get my second wind and be able to go on. This chapter has been very difficult but by now I understand myself and my way of working well enough to know I'm over the hump and it is now all fitting together about as it should. But with any chapter that presents difficult problems, as this one does, there is first a period when nothing moves and then it is hard not to be discouraged. What lies underneath the most important part of this

[43] The entire book had gained its title.

chapter is a whole field of the most technical and difficult biology—discoveries only recently made. How to reveal enough to give understanding of the most serious effects of the chemicals without being technical, how to simplify without error—these have been problems of rather monumental proportions.

Lois will send in her Guggenheim application this week. She has some fine backing and Marie is convinced that's what counts. Douglas wrote her as soon as he returned to Washington. I know she is happy to have his help. Her plan, at least tentatively, is to let Cris take care of the animals a while and she will go away—perhaps to Seattle—to write. This, of course, if she gets the fellowship.

Roger returned to school yesterday—seems all right. And I didn't get it. I'm quite all right except for being tired sometimes.

Our weather is autumn at its best—really warmer than fall should be but delightful to be out. Every time I look at the willow near my bedroom I see kinglets giving it a thorough going-over—several at a time. We still have catbirds, thrashers, towhees, but I suppose they will leave soon. Probably I won't write again to Maine, dear. But I'm thinking of you.

All my love,
Rachel

OCTOBER 10

EVENING ON THE SHORE OF RANGELEY LAKE

Dear One [Rachel],

The day started for me as a V formation of black birds (probably cormorants) flew by my bed!—yes, literally, so close it seemed I might have touched them. But their appearance made me realize I should be outdoors looking for something more spectacular than cormorants. You see, we kept strict watch of the western sky last evening for it was Oct. 9 and an anniversary of flights of geese. After a dismal morning (thanks to Frances) the sun came out to sink to rest in a cloudless sky. The orange yellow that lingered so long on that first eventful evening did not develop. We watched from the porch and the look-out above the beach until darkness seemed near. Then I took up my post at the picture window, luckily, for after a while & after almost giving up, suddenly the fluttering black line over Five Islands. I suppose we could never hope for the drama of that first experience. Last evening there were just 3 streamers but that was enough to satisfy us—we saw them on Oct. 9.

And so by 6:30 I was out this morning. No sign in the west but suddenly as I turned to watch some small birds over your house two V's appeared directly overhead—decided the open, barren space behind the house would make a good vantage point. From there I saw two streamers headed south—the evening ones were going north—in the west. But perhaps more wonderful than the geese this time to me were the myriads of smaller birds in the air. I called

Stan for as I searched the sky for the geese my binoculars picked up hundreds of birds—all black, for the sun hadn't risen. But when the sun began to light their under parts we had a sight to behold. Suddenly a wild flight would descend & we could see the colors—once about a hundred robins swooped over us. Then countless flickers, and again a whirlwind of juncoes—and chick-a-dees. And all the time the nuthatches & brown creepers were busy in your trees. I suppose such flocks happen every year but I have never seen anything like it.

This morning they all seemed headed for Dogfish Head.

We loved every moment.

As the sun rose we knew the day was to be fair.

Before nine o'clock Mr. Soule had called me about the deeds, and I had called Myrtle Bath & John Bath & we made real progress.[44] I tell you this because I had the charges put on our telephone number altho' I made the call from yours. (The operator said I could.) So if you get a Worcester & Shrewsbury charge (altho' you shouldn't) it will be mine. There will also be a couple of Wiscasset calls which I made before I realized I could do that. I'm to go up Thurs. to get the 3 deeds to be signed by Bath heirs, and that will be one of the first things we shall do when we get home—go after those signatures. Will I ever be glad when the whole thing is finally settled!

The day was too good to waste. We threw things into bags, got a picnic basket ready & were off by 9:30 for inland. Our goal was Eustis Ridge Outlook—years ago in our travels a man we met had told us of this view—he said "the finest in the world"—at that time it was far off the beaten path but we wrote down directions.

Perhaps if you read the West Southport column, you've read of people spending the week-end at Two-Deer Lodge. Well, it belongs to Maurice Sherman[45] & others. It is in the town of Eustis so we had asked Maurice if he knew about the view we had heard about. He did & told us how simple it was to get there.

It was a warm sunny day & as we came inland the foliage improved with every mile. From Augusta up (it's Route 27 all the way if you have a map of Maine) the colors are at their peak and no leaves have dropped—all satisfying & rewarding. The roads were excellent for it is skiing country & that brought good roads. So little traffic we'd go for miles without seeing a car.

In Eustis is a magnificent stand of red pine called Cathedral Pines which the road goes through for two miles or so. Darling, you would have loved it. As we approached the mountains, clouds began to form around them as they so often do on a warm day so that by the time we reached the Ridge the view was greatly obscured but we could still see the outline of distant mountains with countless lakes at their bases.

Next summer we (& that means you) shall dash up here some morning

[44] David Soule, Sr., a Wiscasset, Maine, lawyer, had been employed by DF to clarify questions for her and her cousins concerning ownership of her Dogfish Head property.

[45] Boothbay area house builder.

when the NW wind makes the atmosphere crystal clear for I'm sure there was no exaggeration about the view!!

Afterwards we came over here through wonderful scenery to Rangeley where I'd never been—Farmington, 40 miles away, is the nearest. And I'm now in bed in a lovely motel on the lake's edge a mile in from the highway so the silence is deep. I spent an hour just sitting beside the lake, with the glasses. Had a fine time watching 2 dear little horned grebes fishing up & down the lake, & later a merganser joined us. Also 2 *sea-gulls*. The scenery is varied—the long wide lake surrounded by mountains, its shores growing with huge, tall, white, white birches in the midst of flaming maples and dark evergreens. And it was so quiet—just the gentlest of lapping sounds.

We went in town for supper, & even in the center it was so quiet that I couldn't understand why, for there were cars—parked—but no people in sight. Then I realized there were no cars moving. I was never so aware before of how our lives are tuned to the sound of the motorcar so much that we don't hear it except when it isn't there. (If you know what I mean.)

It's early but I think I shall try to go to sleep as I'd like to get up before sunrise if it is clear in the morning. The lake should be lovely in the early light. Excuse scribbles & mistakes. All day long I *ached* for you to be sharing this loveliness.[46]

All my love,
Dorothy

FOR CHRISTMAS[47]

Dear One [Dorothy],

One of the qualities that makes you precious is your way of establishing lovely little customs. Our Christmas Eve letters are an example—you set the pattern and now we are exchanging the ninth in the series—can you believe how the time has flown?

I remember the first of your Christmas letters so clearly—and how I read it and all its enclosures in the small hours of a chilly Christmas Eve night, when at last I could give my thoughts completely to you. There was a dewy freshness and wonder and delicate beauty about the whole experience that miraculously still lingers, for I shall approach the hour of reading the Christmas letter which came today with much the same feelings. Thank you, dear, for this and all the other lovely things you have brought into my life.

I'm writing now before a fire where we have sat happily—in the room where the Capehart this afternoon brought me the glorious music you have just given me. I wish we could hear it together. I played it all and thought it magnificent. But I'll speak of that later.

This paper is not Christmasy, but can perhaps suggest the woods we love—woods where hermits and olive-backs and veeries sing. Woods where we shall wander again, before many months. The memory of the veery's song in the

[46] The Freemans left Southport on October 14, returning November 9–11 to check on the rebuilding of their cottage.

[47] RC had experienced eye trouble in mid-November, but she and Roger had been able to travel to West Bridgewater to spend three days with the Freemans at Thanksgiving.

green dusk by the little church was one of our high points for 1961. That and the fog on the beach. And we will add many more memories in '62, when my infirmities are even farther in the past.

I am so happy about the future you and Stan are building at Southport—may there be only happiness, and many good summers there.

Our ice storm has now turned to heavy rain on the roof—can you hear it with me?

This is only a token letter, but you understand why. But let it whisper in your ear, at Christmas and always, that I love you dearly.

Rachel

1 9 6 2

Darling [Dorothy],

It seems a very long time since I have written an apple—opportunities for writing at all have just been so limited that double letters have been difficult to manage. I'm sure you understand, but I miss it and perhaps you do, too.

I hope you have been safely at home today. If the news is correct, Boston is having an ice storm with very bad driving conditions. Really we haven't had anything too bad so far this year—oh, several bad nights but nothing lasting very long.

Yes I do remember that you came to me a year ago this month and that it was a precious and happy visit in spite of the "undertones." And the premonitions there might have been of what lay ahead! Yes, there is quite a story behind *Silent Spring*, isn't there? Such a catalogue of illnesses! If one were superstitious it would be easy to believe in some malevolent influence at work, determined by some means to keep the book from being finished. Some of the earlier things have been more serious, but I don't think anything has been frustrating and maddening in quite the same way as this iritis. And of course having the end in sight when it struck makes it, in a way, all the worse. I just creep along, a few hours a day. And I know that before I can happily let it go to the printer, there is a tremendous lot of work that only my eyes can do. I have always known I am visual minded, and I've certainly been reminded of it now. Having Jeanne read is of such limited help. I have to see it, and on revision I have to keep going over and over a page—with my eyes!

Of course, darling, your Christmas letter made me very happy. I'm glad that before publication you have come to understand not only why it is important to me, but to the world. And I'm glad all these other things are happening to emphasize that people are ready for the book, and need it now. I, too, think a couple of years ago would have been too soon. But now I know that there are many, many people who are eager to do something and long to be given the facts to fight with.

Last year as I flew home from Cleveland I thought rather deeply, as you might suppose, and I knew then that if my time were to be limited, the thing I wanted above all else was to finish this book. Doing so, not swiftly and easily, but draggingly with the impediments of the arthritis and now the iritis, has been rather like those dreams where one tries to run and can't, or to drive a car and it won't go. But now that it seems I shall somehow make this goal, of course I'm not satisfied—now I want time for the *Help Your Child to Wonder* book,[1] and for the big "Man and Nature"[2] book. Then I suppose I'll have others—if I live to be 90 still wanting to say something!

There is rain on the roof and now and then strong gusts of wind. A cozy night, really, and now I'm going to turn out the light.

Another day, and I'll just finish this briefly so I can mail your letter. Re-reading what I wrote last night, I'm afraid it sounds a little in a minor key. It shouldn't. Really, in spite of my complaints, I'm optimistic that the eye will let me stumble along somehow until I "come out into the light."

See the quotation from Camus in Lois's letter. I guess that's what I should strive for now.

One more thing. I'm so happy, darling, that you are feeling again the stirrings of your own urge to write. You know—or I hope you do—how much I hope you will. I hesitate to say much about it, for in this area it has always been my unhappy fate to say the wrong thing so that the effect isn't at all what I mean. Don't let that make you unhappy, dear—it's just a fact which I wish could be changed. But please know that I very much want you to set down in permanent form the lovely things that are in your heart and mind so that others may share them. It will make me deeply happy if you do.

> All my love, darling
> *Rachel*

S U N D A Y   A F T E R N O O N ,   J A N U A R Y   7

Dearest [Dorothy],

After rain and fog yesterday we have a beautiful, mild day. We seem to have been in a little oasis with perfectly horrid weather all around us in every direction. I do hope yours wasn't as bad as it sounded on the reports.

I loved hearing all about your At Home. It was so easy to picture it now I

[1] RC's working title for what was published in 1965 as *The Sense of Wonder*.

[2] RC likely refers to her contemplated book on life and its relationship to the physical environment outlined in her February 1, 1958, letter.

have seen your redecorated home. Your idea of arranging the greetings according to subject or color was such a good one—I'll have to try it next year. I, too, had a number of nice bird cards.

This will jump around over various subjects without much connection. You wondered about the approach of the city planning consultant. Really he never did say how he knew of my interest in preserving "open spaces," etc., but began by describing his own connections, various people who knew of his work, etc. At the very end of the conversation he mentioned seeing my picture in *Life*, which probably had something to do with his call. Incidentally, I haven't heard from him again as yet. Perhaps I discouraged him, though I did leave the door open a crack. But really, I don't see how I could give any time to it. Tell me sometime exactly where the rhodora was in Brunswick—I've never known exactly the place you were referring to. I did ask him about the Bowdoin pines; he said that was in the hands of the College, and that the new road would insure no further highway development through there.

As a further result of the *Life* picture, I had a letter from the U. of Rhode Island, asking me to come on their Visiting Scholars program next fall. (They had never invited a woman before!) The committee chairman who wrote said they had often talked of asking me to come, but it was only after seeing the picture that she had the courage to write. What sort of ogre do you suppose they had pictured?? And why? I should think it would work the other way around. Well, I said no, for next fall. I'm still terrified of pinning myself down to a date; besides, I don't want a lot of such things coming between me and the next book.

Your birds sound wonderful. I don't know why we never have goldfinches here—we used to other places. But no tree sparrows, evening grosbeaks, pheasants (!) and other specialties of your house. However, we do have lots of birds, and they are a joy. The new feeding area is so appreciated, and when I go out with seed there is such a rustling and whispering of soft calls in the pines and chickadees and titmice gather—always the first to come. They come so close to me that if I had persistence I think they would come to my hand.

No, you hadn't mentioned the partridge berry wreath—it sounds lovely. Jeannette, the Wisconsin girl, sent the usual box of greens. And did I tell you Jeanne and Burnet[3] gave me a lovely Chinese holly for the garden—one he had raised from a cutting? And a record of Robert Frost reading his own poetry. Speaking of records—*L'Enfance du Christ* is being performed at the Cathedral today, and is on FM radio.

Well, now you will have fun the rest of the winter picking up items for your Dream House. I know how I enjoyed it—but of course I had to start from scratch. What a wonderful gift from the Littles! (I don't think I told you about an elderly couple on the train when we were going to you; the woman reminded me of Mrs. Little. They had chairs across the aisle from us. She was so tastefully dressed. I especially remember her hat, of velvet in various shades of brown and rust. She read part of the time from one of H. L. Mencken's books, and would

[3] Jeanne Davis's husband.

often lean forward to read bits to her husband with such obvious enjoyment and amusement. Well, the funny thing was that when I was returning from New York about ten days later, there they were in my car again. I suppose the train had come through from Boston. They were from Baltimore, and of course I imagined they had been visiting "children" in Boston. But I felt as though I knew them by that time.)

I'm sending two recent letters from Lois. Please return; I haven't replied to the more recent one. Now I'm keeping my fingers crossed about the Guggenheim. If there is anything doing, she should hear something from them soon—a query for further information, which would mean, at least, that she is in the final running.

I have about decided to go to the library and "read up" on the subject of iritis. That would at least give me an idea of whether there are other approaches than the one used by Dr. Wilber. If I find there are, I might then suggest a consultation. I am, of course, much better than I've been much of the time, but a little trouble constantly, with the threat of more keeping me from working as I wish and need to do.

One further medical item. I eventually (meaning a few days ago) had to go to Dr. Caulk about the spot on my nose, which Dr. Fields had treated about a month ago. At first it had disappeared entirely, then returned and was about the same as before the treatment. I knew then what I more or less felt before—that I really should have Dr. Caulk's opinion. His experience and equipment are so far superior. He said it simply needed a heavier dose of X-ray than Dr. Fields had used. The one treatment he used Tuesday is supposed to take care of it. I'll see him the first of February, and have my other check-up then. In case you are wondering, dear, there is absolutely no connection between the two. These skin things are quite unrelated to anything else, and are just the consequence of my fair skin, I guess, plus some unknown that makes me more susceptible than some. And they are easily handled by an expert like Dr. Caulk. (This is really a very tiny spot, and the area treated probably less than ¼ inch in diameter.)

Now I must go. Robert and Vera didn't pay their usual Sunday call, so we'll probably go in for the *Times* and mail this.

> Love to Stan, Willow, and YOU.
> *Rachel*

TUESDAY, JANUARY 23

UNDER DRIER WITHOUT GLASSES

Dearest [Dorothy],

I'm going to call you tonight and will hope to find you at home. As you know already, last week was rather a momentous one, for I achieved the goal of sending the 15 chapters to Marie—like reaching the last station before the summit of Everest. I also sent her duplicate copies for Mr. Shawn, and learned on

Sunday that she had sent them along to him Friday. Last night about 9 o'clock the phone rang and a mild voice said, "This is William Shawn." If I talk to you tonight you will know what he said and I'm sure you can understand what it meant to me. *Shamelessly*, I'll repeat some of his words—"a brilliant achievement"—"you have made it literature" "full of beauty and loveliness and depth of feeling."

And with his remark about publishing in the spring I suddenly feel full of what Lois once called "a happy turbulence"—aware, of course, of how very much is to be done with last minute checking, etc., but so excited that the time is so close. Of course, this may well be June, and for Paul's sake I hope so—he will be frantic. But all the people who are so eager to have it to work with will snap up copies of the *New Yorker*—and it is needed for the spring and summer season.

I'm to see Dr. Wilber later today, but I can tell you her news tonight. The eye quieted down rapidly after the treatment last week. I have used it sparingly.

More soon. Now much love—

Rachel

Darling [Dorothy],

I longed so for you last night to share my thoughts and feelings. It was odd—I really had not been waiting breathlessly for Mr. Shawn's reaction, yet once I had it I knew how very much it meant to me. You know I have the highest regard for his judgment, and suddenly I knew from his reaction that my message would get across. After Roger was asleep I took Jeffie into the study and played the Beethoven violin concerto—one of my favorites, you know. And suddenly the tensions of four years were broken and I got down and put my arms around Jeffie and let the tears come. With his little warm, rough tongue he told me that he understood. I think I let you see last summer what my deeper feelings are about this when I said I could never again listen happily to a thrush song if I had not done all I could. And last night the thoughts of all the birds and other creatures and all the loveliness that is in nature came to me with such a surge of deep happiness, that now I *had* done what I could—I had been able to complete it—now it had its own life!

And those are the thoughts I would have shared had you been here. I wish you were!

All my love,
Rachel

A DAY TO REMEMBER

Darling [Rachel],

I've just talked to you. You must be tingling with excitement. How thoughtful of Mr. Shawn to call you so soon—even before you had time to wonder when he would. The wheels are beginning to move. It seems such a short time ago that you were saying you were wondering if you could ever finish. And even now the date is being discussed as to when *your* words will be printed in the *New Yorker*! There must be a great sense of relief for you, darling, that the great Mr. Shawn has figuratively smiled upon your creation—altho' I'm sure you had no doubts as to his acceptance of it. And truly the buoyancy that must come to you will lighten the burden of writing the last chapter. Have you comprehended what the publication of *Silent Spring* is going to do to you? Once again you will be public property, no denying that. First because a famous author has now produced another book. Secondly because of the subject matter of the book. You'll be pressed for interviews, TV appearances, panel discussions, even hearings, perhaps.

So for a long time ahead you'll be swamped with decisions to make as to what you will and won't do publicly. I'm sure you can't and won't want to deny them all. I suppose even Southport will be invaded.

More than ever I think you'll be in need of a "quiet bower." And that's what I hope I can provide for you. Will you let me, dear?

As for the letters, darling, when I finished talking to you I decided that for your peace of mind I must burn them. It seems tragic. If I start reading them I know it would be doubly hard so I think I'll just close my eyes and let them warm me for a final time. There are some which I have labelled because they relate to the creation of the book. Perhaps I'll save those to give to you for you really might want them.

Now, darling, a new era is dawning for you. You have had far more than your share of unhappiness and tragedy so I hope that what is ahead means joy and gladness with fair skies. And remember my arms will be wide open in that "quiet bower."

I love you so,
Dorothy

JANUARY 26

Darling [Rachel],

Your Apple of Joy came to-day. It made me feel warm inside and so close to you—close enough almost to do what I long terribly to do—put my arms around you and listen to what you could say.

The knowledge that you longed for me at that supreme moment is almost more than I can bear. It would have been so wonderful for me.

But, perhaps, darling, it was well that you were alone with only a mute furry friend to share your emotion for you could express your feelings fully—and I know you needed to after these four long troubled years.

I know from experience that a loving cat can fill one's need when one is stirred to the depths. When I used to come home from the hospital in those darkest of days two years ago my relief came from kneeling beside Willow, putting my face in his fur and letting my grief pour out. And like Jeffie he could express his understanding.

So as long as it was happiness with you, much as I wish I might have shared it, I know it was a lovely experience for you—alone with Jeffie. And probably you had a better chance to explore the depths of your feeling than if I had been there.

Since I know too well that there were moments when you weren't sure you would be able to finish, I understand the double thankfulness that you have been able to complete it.

Thank you, darling, for the loveliest apple ever, I think.

I am so happy for you.

The telephone call I needed. I wanted to say these things to you. My tears came without warning. I read the letter at least five times from the goldfinch paper and as I cuddled down under the puff to think of you, suddenly my face was wet. I know now why—because there have been so few times in so long when I had anything of real happiness about you to cherish in those pre-sleep thoughts.

Remember how I used to tell you that as I put out my light, I'd cuddle down with lovely thoughts of you to drift off into slumber.

But there's been so much trouble that was uppermost that I've had to reach back to some of our happy hours—the afternoon at Pemaquid—well, a recent walk on Mile Beach in the fog.

FRIDAY MORNING

Now I must get this ready for the mail before Hazel, my slave-driver, arrives. Darling, the invitation to come up for a little vacation is a permanent one, you know. It would be so wonderful to talk with you now. But, of course, I do realize that you are going to be busier than ever in the months ahead. I did, even before our conversation, so full of a different busyness, last night. In fact I think, stardustily, I had already foreseen it in a previous letter saying something of your possible need for a "quiet bower."

Come to us whenever you can. When the tears came yesterday afternoon I thought perhaps I hadn't grown up as much as I believed I had. Maybe in that respect, of being touched when something lovely happens to you, I haven't but as far as mail goes dear, I have.

So, in these busy weeks ahead let me say again I shall not be watching the mails.

I love you, darling—as always,
Dorothy

Darling [Dorothy],

You can never know what it means to be able to turn to you now.[4] Even being in the hospital here, where I could "run things" by phone, was so hard and now the added distance would make it so much worse. With you here I can feel so comfortable about Roger. It is not just a matter of my being away, but (for him) the emotional strain of another hospitalization. To be able to stay in his home with someone he loves and has fun with will make all the difference in the world. By giving me that peace of mind you are doing for me what no one else could do.

The enclosure is for your round-trip fare, and any extras there might be. I'm not going to take time to call for fares, etc.—if there is any change you can return it! This is positively the only way I'll let you come—and remember I'd have quite an outlay for "hired help" if you didn't.

I mustn't write more. Suddenly there are many little things to see to.

With this goes a whole ocean of love, and my endless gratitude to Stan for sharing you and to you for coming.

Rachel

[4] RC was to return to Cleveland to continue battling her cancer with Dr. Crile, and DF had offered to come to Silver Spring to care for Roger and the household in her absence.

M A R C H 5 , 2 : 3 0

Dearest [Dorothy],

Only a short time to go.[5] I have with me for belated answering the letter from the "girl"—also a graduate of P.C.W.[6]—who sent me the poetry books. I think you would like her closing—"As we Scottish people say: 'May the roads rise with you, and the wind be always at your back, and may the Lord hold you in the hollow of his hand.'" It seems appropriate, not only for this rather bumpy flight, but for what is ahead.

I want you to know, darling, that I am not afraid. I was yesterday, but that is all behind me. I'm perfectly calm and steady now, and I have real faith that all will be well. So—the Lord bless you and keep you, while we are absent one from another.

All my love—
Rachel

[5] RC wrote this letter while on the plane to Cleveland.

[6] Chatham College, where RC had received her undergraduate education, was named, at the time RC was there, Pennsylvania College for Women.

My Darling [Rachel],

How I dread to leave you. I'm so torn. I long to stay here, but I'm sure you understand that as long as you are in no desperate need for me now I should get back to Stan.

I am so glad I could be here. I've tried to tell you some of the reasons why I can almost call it one of the happiest times I've ever had with you.

If it were not for the shadows in the background I'm sure I could really call it the happiest.

I have done so little. But if I have given you the peace of mind you so terribly needed when you started that uncertain journey to Cleveland I can say, "Mission accomplished."

And, darling, do know that in the future if you need me you have but to ask. Let us pray, and I mean pray, that such a time may never come.

The months until Southport can't help but be strenuous and exhausting as well as exciting for you. And during them remember I shall be content with very little in the way of the written word.

If I know you are resting instead of writing to me I can be happy indeed.

Darling, it has been a sweet time—bittersweet in its way—but for me lovely and for you, I hope, happy enough to have let you forget for a few precious moments.

As I leave you, darling, I can only say you are an inspiration of bravery and courage.

And, of course, I love you more—if that is possible. I was so moved by your plane letter. Now may I say "May the Lord watch between me and thee while we are absent one from the other."

All my love, dear,
Dorothy

THURSDAY, 2 P.M. [MID-MARCH]

HOSP. COFFEE SHOP

Dearest [Dorothy],

You said not to write "for the week-end" but you are going away so I do want you to have a word first.

Another milestone—now after one more the first week will be over. Dr. Caulk came in today and we compared notes on signs of spring—crocuses, grackles, killdeer, cardinal song. He has a country place. A dear person, really.

I do hope you are resting now before your trip. I knew there would be a let-down yesterday, besides weariness from the trip, for I don't think night travel is really restful.

My routine since you left has been to spend most of the morning in bed, working. This morning I got another Chapter (X) so far along that I think another hour will finish it. So we move toward the goal.

I loved hearing about Willow—I know both your boys were happy at your return. I hope they can know how much I love them for sharing you.

And do you know how much I love you for what you have meant to me at this time—and always?

This note is tiny but it carries an immense load of love.

Rachel

Darling [Dorothy],

I do so hope the last trace of sniffles has vanished and that your day in bed did worlds of good.

I hope you weren't sad after our conversation. I shouldn't have let you see my courage had deserted me for a time. But it's all right now—all the "fight" is back in me today. This is due in large part to a call from Dr. Biskind. He had known nothing of the recent trouble, but when I told him he had such good and encouraging advice that I felt better at once. Details later, but he feels much can be done to offset the radiation effects—my concern of the moment. My mother would surely have termed his call "providential"—perhaps it was.

Off now in great haste to mail Chapter 14.

All my love—
Rachel

Dearest [Dorothy],

Your good letter of Monday A.M. came today. I'm so sorry you turned out really to have a cold, and hope by now you are completely well. Our weather has been delightful for days. The crocuses are a joy; the first daffodils have opened and a few grape hyacinths. Mertensia and bleeding hearts are pushing through the ground. Many robins every day—and fox sparrows have been regular visitors for about a week.

Dear, I want to explain what I meant about the radiation. I don't question whether it is the right thing. I know that 2-million-volt monster is my only ally in the major battle—but an awesome and terrible ally, for even while it is killing the cancer I know what it is doing to me. That is why it is so hard to subject myself to it each day. That's why I meant I would be happier if I knew less. But under the circumstances I have no choice but to accept the hazards of radiation. As to dosage and duration of treatment, of course only a radiologist can determine that and I have to believe Dr. Caulk knows. The decision as to when to stop will be made next week. At the moment I'm not feeling I can count on anything. Mornings I feel reasonably good and can work, but nausea usually develops around midday. Late afternoons and evenings I'm not worth much!

There is now considerable skin reaction, especially under the arm. Rather like a sunburn, and very sore. Nivea cream helps some.

Dr. Biskind told me heavy doses of CVP would help on the radiation sickness, and in other ways reduce the ill effects, especially by reducing destruction of capillaries. I wish I'd called him, for ideally I should have started a week before radiation. He feels, also, that faithful use of the liver compound will help in the control of the malignancy. This agrees with much experimental work I've read. I must try to stay with it. But such an array of medicines! Marie once said her answer to the question of what to take to a desert island would have to be "a pharmacist." Mine, too!

I was thinking today—if only I could set the calendar back two years. It was April 1 I entered the hospital. How differently I would handle it now—how carefully I would select the surgeon. It's hard to see how I could have given so little thought to the possibilities. But there's no use thinking of it now.

Yes, the record did come, promptly. I meant to tell you.

Here's something you will like. Shirley[7] and a geologist friend went to Rehoboth, Del., after the storm—said in many places all sand was stripped away, down to beds of clay. Somewhere out there they found remains of an old buried forest of pines—just like Tomlinson's *Turn of the Tide*.[8] The geologist took samples for dating. I'd love to go. This is a funny week-end letter, but will carry my love—

Rachel

[7] Shirley Briggs, an artist, friend, and colleague from RC's years of employment with the United States Fish and Wildlife Service.

[8] Published in 1947.

THURSDAY, AT HOSP.

Dearest [Dorothy],

I'm afraid the note I wrote last night sounded depressed and perhaps I shouldn't send it. But it tells some things I want you to know, so I will.

Dr. Caulk says today there will be three more treatments, then a week's rest, then he may want to resume for 4 or 5 more. But after that, definitely no more unless there should be further trouble.

Paul wrote about the sales conference—now I can't remember the date but it is the third week of May. Well if you are at your Dream House I just might try to act on your suggestion!

I guess my pipe dream of Texas and the Grand Canyon is only that, but I've developed a great longing to walk on one of those South Carolina beaches again, so if I feel up to it, Roger and I just might drive down during this vacation. A nice thought anyway. Your letter came just before I left. I suppose your cold has to run its course—do hope you are better now. So very much love—

R.

Dearest [Dorothy],

What a happy April Fool's Day call! Now I'm going to the mailbox shortly and want to send a word to go with you to Maine. I do hope weather will be kind and you can go. I know it will be a thrill to see your own fireplace—really the heart of your new home. Do you suppose it could be used now? That is lovely about the bricks. I know you said you wanted old bricks, but didn't understand there were enough of your own. The whole thing makes me so very happy for you—and if I can possibly join you for a housewarming day or two in May I will. The sales conference is May 21 and 22. It would be better for me to go on to you after that, because it is harder to be away over a week-end. If your house isn't ready we can use mine.

When Dr. Biskind called last week I had to cut short the call in order to go to the Hospital, so I called him today to go into further details. He has great confidence in the anti-cancer factor present somewhere in the B-complex—it isn't known exactly where so that is why he urges a whole-liver preparation. This is borne out by research I'm familiar with—animal studies, I mean. Dr. B. has had patients on such a program who have simply had no recurrences, even though the cancer had metastasized at surgery. Of course one should also make a strong effort to eliminate the chlorinated hydrocarbons from one's food, because they cause loss of the B vitamins and also damage the liver. But civilization has made it so very difficult to do that!

Anyway, once again I feel greatly encouraged after talking to him. My spirits are rather mercurial these days, but after all it is hard to be either philosophic or courageous when one is feeling sick at one's stomach! Today I'm escaping that—far enough away from the treatment, I guess. So I should soon be in position to feel a great deal better, mentally as well as otherwise.

Last night's rain has suddenly brought the lawn to life in a surge of green. And everywhere there is a mist of green from the willows and of red from the maples. The blue buds that I first took to be grape hyacinth opened into my lovely Chinodoxa. I'd love to give you some in the fall, and must plant more myself. I'm glad the daffodils I gave you are emerging. Recently I realized with a start that it was too late to plant freesias—and I had so wanted them again.

It has suddenly occurred to me to wonder whether you are having book shelves put in anywhere. I haven't heard you say. Perhaps as part of your study wall.

If you still have Ruby Carr's gem I wish you'd send it to me to pass on to Edith Oliver at the *New Yorker*.

Now we must go to the mailbox. Robins are singing now in the rain, as they do every morning. Do you know Mark Van Doren's poem "Morning Worship"? I think I heard him read it once, on television. I'd like to find it, for I remember it as very lovely.

I'll go to Maine with you in my thoughts, you know. My love to both of you goes with this, and I'm so glad you are better.

Dearest love,
Rachel

P.S. If you see the Mahards or anyone else who might ask about me, say you heard from me recently and I said I was fine. And I am.

THURSDAY, APRIL 5

Dearest [Dorothy],

I hope you are having as lovely a day as this, though far more wintry, I'm sure. Today I brought in the flowers of the red maple to marvel at as the microscope shows them. You know the two big trees off the corner of the house that intermingle so they appear as one? As one could tell only at this time of year, one is male, one female. It is the female trees that make so vivid a showing now, for the male flowers are delicate by comparison. I also brought in flowers of spice bush—so lovely, too. Yesterday I photographed the maple flowers against a blue sky. How I wish I could do it through the microscope.

Your note written yesterday A.M. is here. I marvel at you—to have preparations for your trip so in order you could write a letter at 6:20 A.M.!!

I thought you might like to read the enclosed—one of the finishing touches! Paul thinks we should use both quotations (as a sort of "motto" on one of the front pages, you know). The E. B. White is too perfect to pass up, and the Keats helps explain the title.[9] We have worked all day on the bibliography and it seems to me we hardly got started! Miss Phillips called today (H.M. editor) and said text will go to printer today or tomorrow. Galleys in 2 or 3 weeks then! It is wonderful not to be going to hosp. for a few days. But the effects of radiation linger on so I'm not quite able to forget it. I wish we had your goldfinches! Have ordered a bluebird house—how I'd love to have it occupied. I don't really *realize* the book is done—it can't be possible, it seems! This rambling note is to say welcome Home & to carry *much* love—

Rachel

TUESDAY, APRIL 10

Dearest [Dorothy],

Waiting for Dr. Caulk, so will start a note. Yesterday was fun, in spite of grey skies and drizzle. I don't know what sort of expressions I managed to present to the camera, but I do know that my hair looked its very best thanks to Bea. She combed it very little before we went down, and did a real job on it in the dressing room. I wish it could always look just like that. I'll get proofs Thurs. or Fri. and surely hope we got something fit to use.

[9] The quotations appearing in *Silent Spring* are: From E. B. White: "I am pessimistic about the human race because it is too ingenious for its own good. Our approach to nature is to beat it into submission. We would stand a better chance of survival if we accommodated ourselves to this planet and viewed it appreciatively instead of sceptically and dictatorially." And from Keats: "The sedge is withered from the lake, / And no birds sing."

I wish you could have been along when we went to investigate wigs. It's really a howl—everyone is perfectly casual and matter-of-fact about it. We spent too much time at the wrong place, but at least learned a lot about what not to get. Then we went to Eliz. Arden, but by that time we were in a hurry. However, I think that is the place. They have an enormous number of hair samples, including a perfect match for mine. Every wig is made to order, according to measurements, etc., of the purchaser. They use only real hair, of course, and in its natural state, undyed, etc. Bea knows so much about it that it was a tremendous help to have her along to ask the right questions. I'm in luck, because brown hair is cheapest! Gray is more. (I'll require a sprinkling of gray in mine, but not enough to put it above the $350 price!). It takes up to a month to get one made, so I want to order it next week. Bea had talked to a representative of another place and thought we might see theirs, but I really think I'll go ahead with E. Arden. As we left there the receptionist said to me "Aren't they lovely—I can hardly wait to get mine!"

Your second letter from Maine came yesterday, telling of your wonderful trip to Merrymeeting Bay. I wonder what it is about geese that is so deeply stirring. I don't know whether you realized it, but when you were telling me Sunday of your experience, and what the woman told you of that immense gathering and then of the abrupt departure for the north, I was almost unable to speak for emotion. It seemed as if all my longings for things I still want to see and experience were merged in the tremendous longing to see those geese—and hear them. I almost felt I must fly there quickly, before they go!

I am having a *very* long wait, as you can tell. There seems to be an unusual number of patients for consultation with the doctors. Have heard Dr. Caulk's voice in the hall, but no more!

Have you heard from Lois? I have not, and Marie said last night she had heard nothing for a very long time. I can't help being concerned, especially after sensing her desperation when she spoke from Denver.

Well, the news is somewhere between my hopes and fears—better than my fears, or some of them, but worse than my hopes. There is to be no more radiation just now, but soon I'll have to return for another course probably of two weeks' duration. I told you, I think, that there had been pain and soreness recently quite far up in the armpit, and that I thought I felt "something." And I did—there is another enlarged node. It is just about on the border line of the former treatment area—would have received some radiation but not enough to prevent its going bad. Dr. C. does not want to resume immediately, and will try to wait until after my Easter trip—if I go. I'm to see him a week from Thursday and he will see how it's developing and decide.

I was quite prepared for this, as I intimated, because the pain one night was quite definite, and something new. It has not continued, but soreness has.

There has also been soreness in the neck, and of course I was afraid of new trouble there, but Dr. says it is just the effect of treatment. So that was good news. Also, a report on the spinal X-rays showed nothing but some arthritis quite consistent with my age. I may not have told you there was some concern because my back hurt while lying on the treatment table, so Dr. C. wanted pictures. The trouble with this business is that every perfectly ordinary little ailment looks like a hobgoblin, and one lives in a little private hell until the thing is examined and found to be nothing much.

This has been a beautiful day of blue, blue skies, all green and gold with willows and forsythia. As I write in the dining room there is a late afternoon convention of grackles and cowbirds outside. Many white throats now. I think I forgot to tell you about tracking down a spring peeper, one showery evening by flashlight, as he sat on a tiny twig springing out from a pine tree beside the porch. He was well above my head—no bigger than my fingernail, the enormous bubble swelling in his throat as he sang.

It was so good to talk Sunday, dear. Now I must stop.

All my dearest love—
Rachel

Darling [Dorothy],

If you could know how truly happy I am about this joyous interlude in your life you could certainly have no "guilty" feelings about your happiness. I just can't tell you how happy I am for you—so you see it means much to me that I could know about it and, I hope, see you in the house. And you don't have to tell me, darling, that your happiness doesn't mean you feel no concern about my problem. I know you do, and I wish I could have spared you that. I can imagine my own feelings were the situation reversed. Sometimes I feel I should not spell out these various complications, but I think you do want to know. With new troubles coming along as they are, it is difficult to keep up an attitude of complete optimism, so I fear I sometimes convey too much gloom to you. I think I shall call Dr. Crile next week. I believe what he tells me and his interpretation of what has happened may help.

It is so good to have you, darling—do you know?

All my love.
Rachel

TUESDAY, MAY 20

UNDER DRIER

Dearest [Dorothy],

Another milestone (or do I mean mill stone?)—I'm mailing tax data when I leave here. Now on to speech no. 1.

An unexpected diversion last night, but very pleasant and worthwhile.

Clarence Cottam[10] phoned yesterday A.M. on arrival in Washington & invited me to a dinner of Natl. Parks Assoc. trustees, and a later meeting of the Conservation Forum to be addressed by Justice Douglas. The Justice and Mrs. D. were at the dinner. He came to me and said "Your book is tremendous."[11] She said "I'm selling it every place I go." In his talk at the Forum, which was about Potomac River dams and the Army Engineers, he digressed to speak of the havoc wrought by "experts" in other fields, and added, "Everyone should read Rachel Carson's forthcoming book, *Silent Spring*, to learn what the chemical engineers are doing to our world."

An odd feeling, darling. It's out on its own now, my fourth brainchild, and it's beginning to move.

I must hurry on. Oh—a perfectly HUGE box came from Filene's—what in the world have you sent me? I want to keep it for Sunday, but am tempted to open it before you call.

Home again—will just add a little and put out for mailman. Darling, I've been thinking about something I want to mention. You are going back to Maine soon where you'll be seeing people who know me and will perhaps ask about me—the Bennetts, Mahards, Pinkham family, etc. You know something of how I feel about this, but probably not the depth of that feeling. There is no reason even to say I have not been well. If you want or think you need give any negative report, say I had a bad time with iritis that delayed my work, but it has cleared up nicely. And that you *never saw me look better*. Please say that. If you look at my picture you will know you can say it truthfully. It is what everyone says. I know what happens when even an inkling of the other situation gets out. As last night, scraps of dinner table conversation about poor Senator Neuberger: "You know she had a cancer operation.". . . "They say she's down to 85 pounds" . . . "If you'd see her on the Senate floor you'd know she can't last." That's the sort of thing I couldn't bear, and the reason I have told so few people. Whispers about a private individual might not go far; about an author-in-the-news they go like wildfire. So let people think I am as well as I look. As to those few you have felt it necessary to tell, will you please try to impress on them how I feel about it?

Almost every day Roger says he can hardly wait to get to Maine. For me it will surely seem a haven of escape. But really, although at the end of each task I'm so exhausted I think I can never get up again, I'm fresh and all right by morning.

Last night, finishing my taxes after my return from dinner, it was one o'clock before I turned out the light. Before I slept a whippoorwill began singing so close I went to the window and looked out in the bright moonlight. Could see nothing but felt as though I could touch it. So I put on robe and slippers and went out. It was on the study roof—of course I couldn't see it, but stood right below it, hearing a funny little preliminary note one never hears at a distance. So that's my bird story.

[10] Biologist, colleague of RC's from the United States Fish and Wildlife Service, and since 1955 director of the Welder Wildlife Foundation, Sinton, Texas.

[11] Justice Douglas had read an advanced copy of *Silent Spring* and was quoted in advertising for the book.

Now my Wayside irises are a glory to behold—I never saw such thrilling ones. And the little Dutch irises are like orchids.

Perhaps you will have this before we talk. Darling, you *are* going to my house, aren't you? It would truly distress me if you didn't.

All my love
Rachel

DENVER TO L.A., MONDAY, JUNE 11

Dear Ones [Dorothy and Stan],

After this[12] I'm afraid I shall become an inveterate air traveler, jets preferred. Both flights have been thrilling, this one especially. I can scarcely take my eyes from the window. This is all, of course, so new to me.

Lois's friends have a delightful home in Denver. They were away—only housekeeper and baby there. But I could see Lois longed to take me to Crag Cabin for the day so I agreed. It was a tiring trip—to one already tired—but I'm glad we did it. Now I have the setting—have seen Alatna, and met Cris, who is really quite a dear. He returned with us and gave his morning to seeing me off, with Lois.

I may mail you a copy of the speech from L.A., though I still want to work on it—an introduction, some deletions, an addition or two.

Now I must return to it. I feel fine—and so GLAD to be away from phone. Guess this will go to Maine.

Dearest Love—
Rachel

Will call Thurs. night or Fri. night.

[12] RC was flying to Claremont, California, to deliver a commencement address at Scripps College.

JUNE 13

Dear One [Dorothy],

This, it turns out, is my birthday greeting to you, 3000 miles away. An unusual one, but I know you will want to read what I said yesterday.

The time has flown, happily and pleasantly, and in my few spare moments I have had catnaps. As you know, I brought along a considerable burden of weariness, but with these rests I have gradually "come back" and am now quite refreshed and ready for La Jolla.

I *loved* every minute of the jet flight and am anticipating tomorrow.

It has been sweet to have you with me dear, via your little messages.

You have been with me constantly, and especially as I walked in the academic procession yesterday, anticipating the Big Moment. And I guess it went off all right.

And now, darling, all my love to you on Your Day, and many happy returns.

Will talk to you soon.

Dearest love.
Rachel

Darling [Dorothy],

Although I shall almost certainly talk to you before you read this, I can't resist the urge to speak to you tonight. Indeed, only the time difference prevented my extravagantly spanning the 3000 miles by phone, but by the time I could call, you should have been tucked in bed.

You know now that what I never counted on—really never even allowed myself to hope for—has happened and *Silent Spring* will be the October Book-of-the-Month. No one could say whether total sales and income will be greater this way but what gives me deep satisfaction is the feeling that this, added to other things we know of, will give it an irresistible initial momentum. And the BOM will carry it to farms and hamlets all over the country that don't know what a bookstore looks like—much less the *New Yorker*. So it is very, very good and tonight I am deeply and quietly happy. It is perhaps not shameless to say that after three best-sellers one does not get wildly excited about such news, which is perhaps too bad, but the deep satisfaction is there.

Now I have just read your Letter from the East—I do hope you are in my dream house, with your dream house coming true to your satisfaction.

Well, I have loved your way of "keeping in touch" *more* than you know— an added glow to the end of the day or sparkle to its beginning, or a companion in lonely travel. And besides all these tangible messages, others have, I know, been flying in both directions at greater speed than that of a jet plane.

Soon I must get to bed, for I'm advised to take the 7:30 limousine in order to make the 9:00 plane.

There is so much to tell of Lois but I fear I must wait till I see you.

The *New Yorker*, faithful to its word, had proof here awaiting me. I have read most of it, begrudging time from sightseeing as I fly home.

Do you know how much I love you—and how much it means to have you to share all this? Goodnight—Happy Birthday—and my love, always.

Rachel

AT HAIRDRESSER'S

Darling [Dorothy],

A last note, which should reach you before I do. It would have been impossible to leave tomorrow, as well as unwise, but I think we can do it with reasonable ease Friday. Ida will spend Thurs. night here—always a blessing for early departure.

The letter you mentioned last night is here, and a dear one. It's been a strange interval, hasn't it, with so little communication, yet I think it must have come at a good time for you, with the stress (and fun) of moving in. For me, I have been in another world, with so little contact with "my" world. Nothing quite like it in my life.

No, darling, I don't like "I told you so" people, and besides it didn't apply. I never predicted the book would be a smashing success. I doubted it would, so this is all unexpected and wonderful to me, too. It was simply something I believed in so deeply that there was no other course; nothing that ever happened made me even consider turning back. The other day I saw a wonderful quote from Lincoln that I can't repeat verbatim, but something about "the sin of silence" when one is aware of a wrong is what "makes men cowards." I told you once that if I kept silent I could never again listen to a veery's song without overwhelming self-reproach.

Had a manicure so little time to write. Now I'm home. Elliott came & put TV, microscope, etc., in car. No suitcases ready yet, and trunk still to be packed. But tomorrow seems relatively free.

Everyone who has been involved in this terrible push seems ready to collapse. Poor Helen Phillips just called, sounding almost too tired to talk.

I hope you will either be at my house when we arrive (I shall of course have called that morning) or come over soon afterward. I don't want our first meeting to be in populous Dogfish Head. There is too much meaning, too much emotion involved—something about the end of the long, hard road, something of the undreamed of and dizzying promised success, something of Dr. Caulk's "almost a miracle."

It is just possible I'll decide to go to the Teales' Saturday, finishing the trip Sat. evening or Sun. A.M. But of course I'll call you.

Dearest love,
Rachel

The quote is "To sin by silence when they should protest makes cowards out of men."

SUNDAY AFTERNOON, SEPTEMBER 9

Dearest [Rachel],

Your reassuring telegram arrived at 4:45 P.M. Sat. bringing relief to two guilt-burdened persons for we were unhappy over your undertaking that drive alone. Altho' you said all four arrived in "good shape," nevertheless I'm sure you must have been at the point of exhaustion. I do hope all went well during the whole trip.[13]

Now we are 700 miles apart. Your days will be overflowing, and your life will be in another world from now on. My letters will be inconsequential compared to mail that will be pouring in. Why don't you save them for bedtime when you can fall asleep over the unimportant words I'll be writing and it won't be world shattering if you do?

[13] RC, Roger, and the two Carson cats had just arrived back in Silver Spring from Southport.

I fear they'll have to be mostly about us.

It seemed strange last evening not to be involved with people—to be alone in the house with no one to entertain so we both were in bed at ten o'clock. We had had a woods walk in the morning after the Childs[14] left, naps in the P.M. (I, on the porch) and about 4 P.M. the Mahards, with Steve Perry, came over to see the house. They lingered for an hour and a half, and after supper Merrill's[15] brother & his wife, Alice, came for the "guided tour," but left by 8:30. Alice is very knowledgeable about antiques and we learned several interesting bits from her—especially about our old furniture—bureaus and chairs—as well as the old dishes I have. She also is bird-minded so we enjoyed her.

It seemed strange not to put in a bed-time call to you these last two evenings. I suppose I'll get used to it.

The moon has been lovely both nights. We took the Childs on the Head after the crowd left Fri. eve.

How I longed for you, but at least we have the memory of the beauty of that last night you were here. How wonderful that we were allowed that!

As I was awake at seven to-day and the day promised fair I decided on a walk, mostly to pick some blueberries I had seen the day before so I can make muffins for the Nyes. Birds were not in evidence on Sat. A.M. altho' we sat in Parula Paradise listening and watching for some time—the sun was so good on our backs.

But to-day was different and exciting. And now I know where to go for birds—at least at this time of year. To-day I have already seen *24* kinds.

Merrill told me there were high blueberries on the Tenggren land near a clump of spruces on the ridge to the left of the road. On my way to investigate I discovered the birds. There is a wide area which stretches from the road, way through to Tenggren's buildings, quite open, with low bushes—blueberry, huckleberry, bayberry, roses, ferns, which is framed with deciduous trees on all sides. And there the birds had congregated. I saw quantities flying in and out of the trees & they would dart ahead of me out of the shrubs as I approached. There were tentative songs, too—some warbler sounds & one miraculous one. An ovenbird sang & whisperings by purple finches. Towhees in abundance—I saw 3 males in one bare bush at once. A hairy woodpecker is in my day's collection. And one sight you would have loved: As I scanned the top of a large, cone bearing fir tree with the binoculars, motion among the cones caught my eye. The cones are upright you know. There in bright sun sat 3 lady purple finches eating the seeds out of the cones, & resembling the cones in coloration & marking. I watched for a long while. Two catbirds meowed and flicked their long tails at me. Well, I won't try to list them all—warblers: myrtle, black-throated green, black and white Maryland yellow throat, immature parulas—& there might have been a fleeting kinglet—it was so tiny. A phoebe, a kingfisher & a warbling vireo.

But I doubt if you'll believe my prize. I had heard a chattering note which

[14] Stanley Freeman's sister, Gladys, and her husband, Ken.

[15] Merrill Towne, married to one of DF's cousins.

seemed familiar but I could not quite place it. Suddenly a bird landed on the top of a fir near me in the bright sunlight. Almost gold with dark wings with wing bars. It couldn't be anything but a Baltimore oriole but I could scarcely believe it. But then I remembered that noise from West Bridgewater. And soon after, out of the tall tree came the bubble of a few notes, the quality of which could only be an oriole. Thereafter I saw several at intervals with an occasional spill of liquid notes. So my belief was confirmed.

Later, on the other side of the road I saw six at once, three of whom flew to one tree where I could confirm them. There was none of the brilliant black and orange—just yellow & olive—female or immature birds.

Wasn't that a lovely experience? I suppose they are on their way South—like one of my dear friends.

To-day, suddenly I longed for some good music. I need something for my inner self when you aren't here, dear. Evidently you've been the "music I long for" all summer for I haven't felt the need.

But now it is different. And to my joy I have discovered an FM music station on my radio which will take care of those wants, I think.

I've had a rest on the porch, Stan is up from his nap, & I want to go to West Harbor for some groceries. Then I can mail this.

I shall be thinking of you all this busy week, all the things you will be doing—to-morrow is wig day, I believe & I do wish I could be sharing that with you.

In the old days I would have known where you are staying in New York & probably have sent notes, but as I didn't find out before you left, I fear there won't be any mail there from me, dear. But be sure I'll be thinking of you. I hope you don't get worn out.

Well, you've stood more than anyone I know could have stood already, so I doubt if a few more important and exciting interviews will wear you out!

Oh, the landscape this morning gave promise of the coming Fall and the mellowness in the air foretells those warm October days. The huckleberries have touches of red. If this is a year they "flame" you must come up.

Remember, in all your busy days,[16] my thoughts are never far from you.

I love you so,

Dorothy

THURSDAY, OCTOBER 4

Dearest [Dorothy],

You will find several things of interest in this issue, but most of all I want you to know about the convention.[17] I'm taking care of all arrangements. All you need do is present yourself in Silver Spring no later than Thursday.

Dr. Cottam says weather will be about as here now—in 50–70 range, but be prepared for rain or a cold snap.

[16] The impact of *Silent Spring*'s publication on September 27, 1962, and RC's related schedule of appearances are the likely reasons for the absence of RC letters for September and most of October.

[17] Perhaps a meeting of the Audubon Naturalist Society of the Central Atlantic States at which RC was to autograph copies of *Silent Spring*. Whether DF attended is not known.

What fun! Is your percolator bubbling? Wish Stan could go, too.

Tuesday evening[18] was pronounced a great success and I found it not too difficult. A very large and responsive audience. In question and answer period later, I expected the chemical lobby and agriculture would try to trip me up. But no—all questions were entirely friendly, although a number of Government men, at least, were in the audience.

Tomorrow night I'm attending the Audubon (local) dinner here, and Irston Barnes has prevailed on me to "say a few words" informally.

Last night Jane Howard of *Life* phoned to say there had been a sudden decision to use the "story" immediately—so I'll be in the next issue![19] Hope you know me, and are not unhappy with the new Me. I suspect you'll still like the Hartmann picture best—as I do. But if they've selected the ones I think they have, it's not too bad.

An important reason for letting them do it was the fact (did I tell you?) that *Reader's Digest*, dropped the plan to do a condensation. Of course, we'll never know why. Pressure? or just impossible to cut, as it may well have been. But with that "mass medium" eliminated, everyone felt I should take advantage of *Life*'s pages. Well, I hope I won't regret it.

Every mail brings more requests to speak. Declining all, except perhaps Women's Nat'l Press Club—date undecided.[20]

Before I went to New York for the party, I mailed you an early Anniversary present. I hope it has arrived by now.

Texas coast birds, Dr. Cottam says, are a mixture of eastern, western, and some Mexican species. *You'll* have to do some ornithological research before we go[21]—I won't have time.

Speaking of time, I'm writing in Dr. Wilber's office (with a "this is where I came in" feeling) to see what the situation is in my eye. There is still some inflammation. I was afraid the TV lights would blind me Tuesday, but actually it wasn't too bad. And my voice held up well, so I was doubly thankful.

Now, on to the National Council[22] speech! Hope I'm not writing it the night before I go to New York, which will be on the 10th—speech on the 11th. After those two, the others should not be too difficult.

I'm sure these October days are speeding by for you, bringing your time of departure. It will seem strange to go back to your "other world" won't it?

Now I must close. Will try to add a note after I see doctor; she is about ready.

All love—and with a glow of happy anticipation.

Rachel

It is iritis, but not too bad. Dr. W. thinks it will clear up in a few days.

———————————

This is Friday A.M. I came home in such a downpour I could hardly see, so didn't stop at P.O. then.

[18] RC had spoken at the annual meeting of the National Parks Association in Washington, D.C.

[19] In its issue of October 12, 1962, *Life* magazine published "The Gentle Storm Center," presenting a biographical sketch of RC and a review of *Silent Spring*.

[20] RC gave this speech on December 5, 1962.

[21] A trip RC and DF had planned for November 1962 to the National Audubon Society convention. The trip did not occur because of RC's and Stanley's health problems.

[22] National Council of Women of the United States.

Darling [Rachel],

If I hurry & try to be brief I can get a message into the afternoon mail.

All these lovely days I find myself talking to you inwardly, aching & longing to share every detail with you for all that I am experiencing is the world you love. Where shall I begin to try, in this brief half hour, to give you the feeling?

Sunday morning I woke before sunrise—sat up in bed (Richie's) & to my pure delight, October's full moon was still an hour high in the western sky—still making a path across the water. My mind leaped to geese but could not believe the morning could be so perfect. But it was—suddenly they began to stream by—southward, great ribbons of them. The sun came up to add brilliance. Of course the moon began to pale but before it had—a whole flock had flown across its face!! I had called Stan so he shared it all.

Such a low tide, too, but with a strong NW wind there would have been no pleasure tide-pooling. And neither did we hear geese because of the noise it made.

We decided our own spot was too lovely to spend the day away from it as we had planned—an all day trip on the Argo, lovely as it might have been—& besides there was work to be done.

So I did one of the chores facing me—gave the stove a thorough cleaning—while Stan worked to cross things off his list.

About 11 o'clock after coffee & toast, we went to West Harbor (found *SS* fifth on the *Times* list & 3rd on *Boston Herald*) & returned via Newagen.

I know I have raved over our autumn scene, but, darling, I have never seen it so breathtaking. I've talked of the flame of the huckleberry—it is racing through all the woods, starting at the roadsides—just bankings of it. And from the water it starts at the very rocks & covers all the ground as far as you can see into the woods.

Even as I sit here, the Head is ablaze with it.

We wanted a final walk at Newagen. Started at Sunset Rock at the outer point & followed the path as far as it went, skirting the rocks. You would have loved it all—one of those crystal days when the water is that deep, deep blue. The sumach, the huckleberry, the raspberry, & blueberry bushes plus rose bushes with hugh rose hips all along the path. We passed through low swampy area with beautiful grasses and finally came to the cranberry bog where we picked over a quart of cranberries (we went prepared with containers). It was rather cold but the sun was warm.

At the end of the shore path we found the ocean end of the Lichen Path to which we had never gone before, and followed it back to the Inn.

And in the depths of the woods, a hermit thrush flew silently into a tree & flicked his tail at us!

We had wild cranberry sauce with our chicken & Stan said "This is our Thanks-giving dinner." And it was—thanks-giving for a thousand reasons!

At sunset we watched from the Head—a blazing one, hoping again for geese & we were not disappointed & you know what that next half hour was like—with the turquoise and orange of the sky & the waves of geese.

This morning we were up at 6:15 for it was moonlight, & the Bay was all a sparkle! It was only 35° so we donned our winter clothes—walked to the Head, Willow skittering along. The moon was 2 hours high. It was such a cold wind that we went to Charlesworths' to view the rising. There on the reefs were any number of seals & in the trees, so close I could almost touch them, a flock of golden-crowned kinglets!

I ate oatmeal before the fire after that walk!!

We both worked at cleaning, & about 11 A.M. we took the boat by outboard to Cozy Harbor for the winter.

Oh, darling, darling—if only you could have had that ride—the shore from here to Cozy is perfectly exquisite now. Between your house & Mahards' & in front of your house is the most brilliant display of huckleberry anywhere!

And at Steeveses' & in the swamp back of Salt Pond the maples are still flaming. Oh, lovely, lovely. The tide was high, high—11'.6." So we rode into Lighthouse Beach & along the shore & through the narrow passage between David's Island & the shore all flaming & yellow against the white rocks & blue waters. We could even ride almost to the Lighthouse road & then in the little cove back of the Yacht Club. Oh, darling, how I wish you could share it. Next year you must.

More to tell but time runs short. This morning a new bird for my life list. Stan discovered it & it lingered a long time so we had time for Peterson & both to see through glasses—a yellow-bellied sapsucker! Thrilling for us. Also to-day two field sparrows. Loons, black ducks, eider ducks, a wren, hermit thrushes—!!!

[Love, *Dorothy*][23]

OCTOBER 25

Dearest [Dorothy],

Imagine—the first letter I've written to West Bridgewater this fall! What an extra-ordinary winter (fall-year-whatever!) that you should have been home a week without a letter. Yesterday I had a great desire to phone you before I left, but the morning slipped away and suddenly the cab was there and it was time to go (11:30). But I needn't have rushed—our intended plane had had to go in for service (nice they discovered this before we left) and we had to wait for another. So we were very late leaving, very late arriving, and I had to be rushed straight to the Museum.[24] Fortunately, I was wearing my green suit and was presentable, and, as it turned out, appropriately dressed for the occasion.

[23] The last page or pages of this letter not preserved.

[24] The Museum of Natural History in Cleveland had organized a reception to honor RC.

[25] Jane Crile.

Jane's[25] sister, Kay Halle, who lives in Washington, had phoned Tuesday to say she and a friend were going up on the same plane. We met at the airport and had a very pleasant time on our somewhat protracted flight. Kay is a very interesting woman, who "knows everyone" in Washington and who is now interesting herself in my "cause" in ways that promise to be productive. The friend, who lives in Cleveland, had been in Washington for the poetry meetings—a gentle, white-haired woman who was very sweet. Her doctor is a grand-nephew (perhaps an extra generation or so in there) of Richard Jefferies. There was much talk of people you and I love. Kay remembered meeting Tomlinson who used to come to the Halle store to autograph. And both are admirers of Loren Eiseley—and when another Halle sister met us at the airport, she had *The Immense Journey* under her arm!

It is a delightful, comfortable family—a Crile daughter here with her 5-week-old son—other Criles and Halles in for supper last night—the Crile cocker and a visiting, 6-month-old Newfoundland who belongs to the baby's family—this incredible wild fowl sanctuary in the back yard—a Belgian hare—and now a capy bara (sp?) that was Barney's Christmas present to Jane! A most incredible and beguiling animal, and the cause of much hilarity last night when he was briefly allowed in the house.

I am writing in a little morning interval while everyone is busy about something. Kay getting ready to speak at a luncheon, Jane seeing to various things. No invalid, I can tell you! I said goodbye to Barney last night—he is busy at the hospital and can't get to the luncheon.

All this written as though the menacing shadow did not exist, yet the day before I left it seemed as though time was standing still and there might even be no tomorrow. So many things to say, were we together!

I keep returning in my thoughts to all you have written of those early mornings at Southport, of that clear, incredible light, and then to Tomlinson's passage about the thrush, "proclaiming the only news known to him"—of a world far better than we know if only we would let it be.[26]

[26] RC refers to this from H. M. Tomlinson's "The Little Things" in *The Face of the Earth* (1950): "My thrush was unaware of the news known to me. He could only publish all the news known to him."

I'll talk to you, most likely, before you read this. I may mail this here today, or take it on to Washington and add to it on the plane.

7 P.M.

We have just stopped in Pittsburgh, after a bumpy flight from Cleveland. Wet snow here—weather here bad so our captain announced he might be unable to land. Washington weather is said to be good. They will serve dinner after we leave here; to tell the truth my stomach is a little queasy after the rough ride and I'm not sure I want any. Well, I had a busy afternoon at Halle's, who always handles things nicely. However, I'm just as happy I've decided against further autographing. Now to go home and concoct another speech.

The letter you wanted to reach me before Cleveland did so, and you know it brought much happiness in the reading. Yes, I'm glad for you to take things like the White House call[27] in stride. Strangely, it seems quite natural to me, too—in a way, that is. Now I'm running out of paper—good reason to stop.

All my love, as always, you know.

Rachel

NOVEMBER 3

To my dear ones [Dorothy and Stan],

Here are a few transfusions[28] from the only kind of bank I have ready access to. If enough real blood is supplied by others, there will still be many extras, and you know it gives me great happiness to help.

My dearest love,

Rachel

DECEMBER 6

Dear one [Dorothy],

I shall almost certainly talk with you before you read this—but here I am waiting for X-rays so I shall talk to you. I do chafe so at wasting time in this manner. I have sat here now for 40 minutes. They are "short handed" they say. Meanwhile I know it is snowing madly, my snow tires aren't on, and I'm just praying the streets remain warm enough to keep it melting there. —Now, *at last*, they've done me but I still have to wait here for the films to be developed. If there's anything wrong with me that X-rays will show they certainly must have discovered it!

I spent the early part of my waiting period writing to Nellie Lee Bok. I hadn't heard from her since the telegram telling of Curtis's death,[29] until a long letter came several weeks ago. She also sent me a copy of the book he had finished just before he died—a novel published this fall.[30] She plans to take an apartment in Philadelphia after she sells the house. Her daughter Rachel is back in Phila. now. Curtis was able to see his grandchild before he died. Gulph Mill is such a big place—she must be very lonely there with only the servants.

I loved your letter about the woods walks and about identifying the chickadee for your neighbor. It is extraordinary how inaccurate people's descriptions of birds always are. You'd think they could get *color* right.

LATER

As you will know, all is well, at least as to any serious possibilities. Now I'm home and will finish this for Ida to mail. Two enclosures,[31] one for a laugh, one you will enjoy more thoughtfully.

Our spell of 60-degree weather apparently had our roads so warm the snow couldn't accumulate, but lawns are white and the wind and driving snow were bitter. But now I'm *home*, and *no speech to write*!!

Tomorrow I'll have to do something about the mail. Often I don't even get all of one day opened—then another layer is added like new snow over old.

[27] In later years, DF recorded that the telephone call was to invite RC to the home of Interior Secretary Stewart Udall.

[28] Stanley was in the hospital for blood transfusions; RC sent some money to purchase comforts for him. She also visited DF in West Bridgewater in November.

[29] Curtis Bok had died on May 22, 1962.

[30] Entitled *Maria.*

[31] Enclosures not preserved.

A little package started on its way to you from McManuses, where you got my cake box. It is *what* I wanted but not necessarily in the style I hoped for, but I think it will blend, and be useful. DO NOT OPEN TILL CHRISTMAS!

So much love to you both
Rachel

WEDNESDAY, DECEMBER 12

Dearest [Dorothy],

The weather is under control so I came in to let Bea do my (own) hair. Roger's school was closed—two station wagons never did get back last night—although public schools are open. Poor Ida reached home at 8 last night so I urged her to wait for 10:30 bus this morning. She said her bus sat near Mrs. Kay's for an hour or more, then when they got to the transfer point for city buses there were none. (This was last night, I mean.) Jeanne didn't come. I called her last night to suggest we skip today. She wanted to wait and confer in the morning; however she never called and I guess just made her negative decision without benefit of conference. So you can see it has been a rather mixed up day, but I did stay abed until ten!

[32] Joy Adamson, author of *Born Free: A Lioness of Two Worlds* (1960).

I'm sure it is wiser all around to forego meeting Mrs. Adamson,[32] though it is a great disappointment. Suburban temperatures are to go to zero tonight so the streets, now covered with water and slush, will be hard ice again. And any but a door-to-door trip would, I'm sure, be unwise for my ailments. Too bad!

I have now reached that state of eminence where my sniffles, like the President's, are news. The morning paper explains my failure to appear at the Air Pollution Conference with a fairly conspicuous article carrying the heading "Author of *Silent Spring* Silenced by Cold." What good news in chemical circles!

[33] Ornithologist, artist, and author of several books, including *The Eye of the Wind* (1961), his autobiography.

Peter Scott,[33] who will now be the sole guest of honor at the World Wildlife Fund dinner, is coming here next Monday and will come out to see me.

The days seem full despite the no-speech interval. I have to just deliberately make stretches of time like yesterday's morning abed to get any feeling of relaxation. Well, there will be two weeks of late sleeping beginning next Thursday, with Christmas vacation.

THURSDAY P.M.

Another day. Meanwhile, the lovely surprise of your call last night. And now your letter, too. Quite like old times! I will, indeed, look up your letters soon. But I do want them returned sometime. If you copy passages on the typewriter—where such things always look different—you'll be surprised to find how much of your book is written!

We have swarms of starlings today—giving the lawn a thorough going over, and feasting on frozen apples, the last of the year's crop still on the ground. I love the starlings—their behavior is so comical, as is their rather rough and shaggy appearance compared with other birds.

Another morning in bed—guess I'm just beginning to find out how much I wanted sleep. It is delicious to give in to it. I seem to be having arthritic aches and pains all over these days—wrist, elbow, shoulder, back, etc.—and *wish* I'd remember to take aspirin on a regular schedule. There is no swelling or inflammation, however, for which I'm thankful.

I want to send this with Ida, so will stop. I want to write of Lois, and what I hear through Marie and Elizabeth Lawrence. Next time!

Now—all my love goes with this, and you know you are always in my mind and heart, in spite of the long silences.

Rachel

WEDNESDAY, DECEMBER 19

Dearest [Dorothy],

I want to write just a note to send with Ida, having had my outing for the day—the Christmas pageant at school! Roger was the "king" this year. It was fun to see the smaller ones in some of the parts *he* used to play—a reminder of how the years fly. Now we are launched into the 2-week vacation.

Your letter enclosing the exercises came today. They look simple enough and I suppose would do no harm. The joint where I hurt most (junction of last lumbar vertebra and sacrum) shows some evidence of deterioration the "wear and tear" arthritis that is normal enough. Dr. H. thinks a board in my bed may help. Virginia has one she will lend me for a trial. Dr. Alfaro thought everything looked better yesterday, and doubt I'll go back. Perhaps the antibiotic will help or *is* helping, I mean.

My first big batch of Christmas cards is in the mail, but I have so many to do! I guess I won't attempt much more shopping.

Here are various items of news: The Animal Welfare Institute (Christine Stevens) is giving me its Albert Schweitzer Medal, on Jan. 7—timed for my convenience so one New York trip will cover two events. *Silent Spring* is back in #1 place on *New York Times* list. (Somehow they printed the book review last week in spite of the strike.) Sales now 106,000. As Paul says "who would have dreamed it five years ago?"

I have now found time to read *Maria*—the book Curtis Bok finished just before his death. You will love it, I know. Full of beauty and elemental things, the sea, sailing lore, lovely descriptions, the apt phrases that seemed to come so readily from his pen. It is very revealing of the kind of man he was. It was a privilege to know him even as well as I did. It is most interesting to see how he has utilized his own trans-Atlantic crossings, told now as happening to his fictional characters. Shall I send it to you after Christmas? Poor Curtis! Nellie Lee said he hoped so much to live to see it published. But it is more important that he lived to finish it.

I must stop now—almost time for Ida to go. I will write more before Christmas—but now how speedily it approaches!

I do so hope Stan is feeling more comfortable and that the good days will come more and more often.

Oh—I wanted to tell you that Stanley wrote me such a lovely note—about my going to you in November and such things. It really touched me very much. He is a dear boy—Now goodbye, and all my love—

Rachel

Of course you saw in the *Register* about the Orchards[34] "making the *New Yorker*"!

[34] Harriet Orchard was the West Southport postmistress.

FOR CHRISTMAS EVE

Dearest [Rachel],

Nine Christmases now! What can I say to you for Christmas Eve that I have not already said a thousand times before? No matter what or how I say it, in simplest terms it is that I love you.

I like to believe that you and I, if we had met some other way, would have quickly found the bond that has tied and held us these long years. I remember so vividly the feeling which welled up in me as we walked down on the Head that September afternoon in 1953—"if only I could know her better." But it was goodbye immediately. It seemed such a pity. But you kissed me, and I knew the parting would be only because of time and space and not of the heart and spirit.

For

I come in the little things Saith the Lord: Yea, on the glancing wings of eager birds, the softly pattering feet of furred and gentle beasts.

And so

A well-worn path runs through my thoughts
with lighted lamps along the way,
that mark the memories we share
of many a happy bygone day.

And now that Christmas time is here
Those lamps are shining bright
With memories and thoughts of you
Aglow with friendship's light.

Now we are coming to the end of 1962. What memories and thoughts of you shall I carry from this momentous year? Let me think. I know that, in a way, you were prepared for the kind of thing that has happened to you, but I doubt that in your wildest imagination, you could have envisioned the colossal impact you have made. I don't need to tell you what it has meant to me. You know.

What I do need to tell you which you may not know is that with all the publicity, the acclaim, the fame, you have not changed. Above and around it all the sweet, generous you shines out.

How completely you have shared with me. The long telephone calls when you were weary and exhausted beyond belief—but still you called.

I ought also to list all the material ways which show your generosity. I am surrounded with symbols!

I must speak again of the time you gave so freely of yourself. Darling, I wish you could know fully what it meant to have you come to me when Stan was in the hospital. As I look back, I fear I accepted that gift far too casually. Now I am so aware of all it meant to you—dropping the burdens of your work (when time was so precious) which only continued to accumulate while you were gone; making the arrangements for your household (which in itself is a major problem); the travel from home to here; the weariness from weeks of work; the speeches you needed to write; all these and more—for you to come to me. Who am I that I deserve so much of yourself? Your reward must be to know that for a few days I knew a comfort and peace that I hadn't known and haven't known since.

For everything, my heart is deeply grateful and if it is possible, I love you more.

This is the year when you achieved what you had striven for so long, so wearily, so eagerly, under unbelievable difficulties. I know you are satisfied. For the coming year my wish is that the satisfactions will mount but that the burdens that have attended your achievement will be lessened with added leisure and tranquility for you. For me I hope to enjoy some of that leisure with you.

For Christmas Eve then, here is my wish

May stars shine whiter
Candles burn brighter
And troubles seem lighter.
At Christmas.
May friendships grow dearer
And life's meaning clearer.
At Christmas.

And all the blessings of having accomplished your mission be showered upon you.

A precious and blessed Christmas be yours with the knowledge that I love you always.

Good-night,
Dorothy

FOR CHRISTMAS

Dear One [Dorothy],

Early this morning the first flakes fell from a grey sky, and now it is snowing heavily, coming out of the northeast, with prospect of 4 inches or more. My plan to send this Air Mail is clearly a poor one—we shall see what Special Delivery will do. I shall speak to you over the week-end anyway. Whenever you read this, its message is the same—just a reaffirmation of the love we were discovering with such joy nine years ago—a restatement of the deep happiness of having you in my life. There is no real need to say these things again, but they are good to say and good to hear, and this is the time to repeat them once more.

There is so much in my heart, and in yours, I know, that cannot be said. But in the sharing of the spoken and unspoken, the tangible and the intangible, lies the real essence of our precious friendship. This is what matters: the things we planned that didn't work out, the things that were "not the way we planned them" are not important as long as we can share our joys and sorrows. Perhaps the sharing seems to have been broken and interrupted by these long months when I could write so little but by way of stardust and intuition and loving thoughts I know it goes on just the same.

It has been such a mixed year for us both—joy and fulfillment in the Dream House built and lived in, and in *Silent Spring* published and making its mark. And on the other hand, the shadows of ill health. For me, either would have been a solitary experience without you, and I know you feel the same.

Now, to you both, so much love and the hope that the new year will bring us all more joys than sorrows and renewed joys in being together—in belonging to each other.

My dearest love—
Rachel

Part Four: **Wonder**

ook it out to,
ng the next
ed I say —
— I love you

New Years Day, 5 p.m.

Darling [Dorothy],

It is so clear that we are in the period of lengthening days—it is hard to believe, though, that a week past the winter solstice could make so much difference. Not long ago it was almost dark at five but now there is still sunset color in the sky. But so cold! The birds look well nourished and happy, but I always wonder where they find shelter these bitter nights. We have about a dozen mourning doves and I guess an equal number of cardinals. Only a few chickadees, though—and I just realize I haven't seen a nuthatch this winter. Nor our handsome red-bellied woodpecker.

I was so glad to hear you sounding better today and to know your fever has left you—and that you will have help tomorrow clearing up after Christmas.

As I think you suspect, I have been holding out on you a little, but only until after the holidays, so you must forgive me. I could not write or tell anything that would detract from whatever happiness Christmas and the holidays might bring. And I've intended all along to confess now, dear.

The main thing concerns the back pain. You will remember that Dr. Caulk was sick the day I was in for the X-rays, and although I'd had a report that everything looked all right, I felt I wanted to discuss the back with him, since it was getting worse, and at least get his views on what kind of doctor might be able to help me. So I called him about a week before Christmas. He took another look at the X-rays, called me back, and said that although nothing shows, he felt it advisable to use some radiation. The point is that early stages of trouble in a vertebra may cause pain but changes visible on X-ray may not appear for several months, by which time it is more difficult to handle. So, given my history, he felt it wise to go ahead with treatment. He thought 5 would take care of it. I went in that day—Thursday—for the first—then a blizzard made it impossible to go Friday or Saturday! Life is never smooth is it? Then of course Sunday they are closed. I had one Monday—then there was Christmas—then by a streak of luck Wed., Thurs., & Friday we had no snow and I finished. He had hoped for some improvement by that time but says I should not be discouraged that it is slow. Barney Crile approves thoroughly of doing this, and said it might take 2 or 3 weeks to get the pain under control. However, I'm to report to Dr. Caulk at the end of this week. Sometimes I think it's a little better, but on the whole I guess there is little change.

Now there are several things I want you to understand about this, dear. The diagnosis is by no means definite, and it is possible the trouble has no relation to the malignancy. But it is much safer to assume it has—to "run scared," as the politicians say. On the other hand, if it really is a metastasis, then we have gotten it quite early, before any real damage has been done. So there is much reason for optimism.

The treatments themselves caused much less psychological distress than earlier ones—largely, I think because this time the machine was not the 2-million-volt monster but a much smaller one with a less awesome sound, in a friendlier room, etc. It did cause a good deal of nausea, though. But that is behind me.

Then I suppose I shall have to tell you of a silly incident, not because it is important, but only because we're not supposed to conceal things! About a week before Christmas I was in the Chevy Chase Woodward's buying Roger's record player, began to feel "funny," and then black clouds descended and apparently I collapsed over a table of records, etc. It was the first time in all my life I'd fainted! Anyway, it was very brief and when I opened my eyes someone was easing me into a chair and the clerk was calling the store nurse! How lucky no reporter was hanging around! Presently I went up and had a cup of coffee, then since the Clinic was only a block away, went over there and Dr. Healy saw me before he went to lunch. Nothing much was apparent except a fast heart—I guess things had just piled up too much.

However, both Drs. Caulk and Crile feel I should see a heart specialist—not because of the fainting, but the recurrent chest pain. They disagree with Dr. Healy that the cardiograms would necessarily reveal angina, and think other symptoms suggest it. Well, I may do something about it one of these days, but if it is angina certainly it's a mild case and I'm not running up any hills or anything like that!

Now—that's all I know, and nothing very terrible but of course I would ordinarily have been spilling it all out to you as it happened. But this was certainly not the time to do that!

Well, I do hope the weather will be kind for my Boston trip.[1] How awful if I got there but couldn't get to West Bridgewater! I really think I won't do the TV thing. I wish heartily I hadn't agreed to these two speeches, and beyond them I think I'm just going to be kind to myself for a while. I'm even losing enthusiasm for Europe-in-the-spring!

Now I should stop and at least outline the Garden Club talk. I have talked to Ida and she will be here tomorrow—thank goodness! The simplest household chores are painful and difficult now—as you well know because of your history of back trouble. So I'll be very glad to turn bed making, etc., back to Ida.

[1] RC was to travel to Boston to deliver a speech to the New England Wildlife Preservation Society.

Jeanne has not been here during the holidays. I knew she wanted the time, and with my days cut up by Hospital visits, etc., I felt I'd really rather let things go. And they certainly have—such a pile in the study!

Well, dear, it is wonderful to think I may be seeing you and Stan in 16 days. You know it will have to be brief, but anything is better than not seeing you. Meanwhile, this letter carries all my love.

Rachel

P.S. Wed. A.M. Ida is here—I had breakfast in bed and have spent much of the morning there. Delightful!

SUNDAY, JANUARY 6, 3 P.M.

My dearest darling [Dorothy],

Your New Year's Day letter was one of the sweetest in a series of sweet and wonderful letters, dear one. It brought you very close, dear, and eased some hard moments more than you can know.

For the moment, shall I just say that all you dreamed and imagined and wished for, I long for, too. And could things be that way even for a few hours, how much I long to pour out to you! Some I shall try to write, but as you say, it would be so much better to talk!

Meanwhile, dear one, I am mindful of your own problems and worries, and do hope things are going more smoothly now.

I love you always and allways, darling
Rachel

JANUARY 19

ON TRAIN—HOURS LATER!

Dear Ones [Dorothy and Stan],

As the miles and hours creep by the mystery deepens—Where is the fog? Where is N.E. Airline's mysterious storm? There was no real fog in New York. Now, far side of Phila. it is fairly misty but lights are plainly visible, and I'm more and more of the opinion this long journey was unnecessary. Well, we shall see.

During the first hour of the trip we managed to lose about 15 minutes and are now about 20 minutes behind schedule (although at one point 30, so I guess we are making up a little). We must have had a Diesel engine at first and as you may have noticed my car was directly behind it, and so we were treated to a strong oily aroma. By New Haven it must have grown tired, and they replaced it with another—electric, I guess. No more fumes! Then in New York the whole train got taken apart and I now have cars in front of me.

I scanned magazines a while and then slept! About 4 went in for a cup of tea. (Tolerable—of course it *helps* to make it with boiling water.) Then, although not really hungry, I went back for supper around 5:30, to get ahead of the crowd getting on at New York. Tomato soup, club sandwich, & coffee—really not too bad.

Have been reading a book borrowed from Jeanne (or Burnie, rather) *Nature and Man's Fate*[2]—quite good and well written. And have written several pages to Lois, tho I haven't finished that. So you see I've been busy—and haven't finished my new book as yet!

I keep thinking about the kitties, alone and no doubt wondering. How glad they will be!

We must be making up time or else this is just naturally a rough section of road bed!

I don't think you can ever know what it meant to me, after the session with the adoring dragons, to be carried off to that quiet bower where I could quietly collapse, get over my upset stomach and shed at least some of my weariness under the loving care of dear ones who made no demands and wanted only what was easiest and best for me. There is no adequate way to say thank you. Who else would understand as you do?

I'll call you in the morning and try not to repeat what I've written here as to the journey. I'm afraid I have no stamp to mail this at station.

The jolting is so bad I won't try to write more.

All my dearest love
Rachel

S U N D A Y

A word before I take this to the box. We now have weak sunshine, although I think there are mutterings about possible snow tomorrow. Well, let it! Though I'm supposed to see Dr. Healy in the morning about my back. According to the *Post*, fog was very bad, and both jet fields (Dulles and Friendship) closed. It sounds as though National remained open yesterday, but I'm sure it would have been a miserable landing even if achieved, so I have no regrets about our decision.

I'm now in communication with a possible week-end maid, who actually sounds promising. Her name is Adjerina![3] She has a regular Monday–Friday job, but wants to save money for a car and has been looking for week-end supplements. So I think I'll give her a try.

Jeffie has been galloping around the house in an excess of good spirits; Moppie crawls on my lap every chance she gets and curls up like a tight little caterpillar.

I still (2 P.M.) haven't looked through the mail, but I want to get this off to you and also mail the letter to Lois.

My dearest love, and my thoughts are always with you, you know.

[2] By James Hardin, published in 1959.

[3] RC subsequently spells her name "Adgerina."

Dearest [Dorothy],

Happy Week End—if the P.O. cooperates. Here is the Schweitzer Award[4] speech. When Christine wrote to thank me for hers, she said she was sending a copy immediately to the woman who is such a noted photographer of Dr. S.—I can't think of her name. Anyway, this woman is about to go to Africa to see him, and Christine thought he would like to see it. Imagine!

For some reason I got up today feeling chilly and aching, temperature 100°. Don't know whether it's a kind of grippe or my old diverticula, but there is no pain so I suspect the former. I'd also had to keep Roger home with a horrid cough, tho he has no fever. So he's staying in his room with vaporizer going and taking cough syrup. Jeanne & Ida have just been out marketing, and now Ida is cooking for our supper. I got up and dictated a while and am now back, snug abed with Jeffie.

Have just had an invitation to meet with the President's committee[5] on pesticides Saturday A.M.—not a command performance, but just come if I'd like to. I guess I should; perhaps it's a chance to straighten out some thinking.

I'm sorry I didn't have the enclosed clipping[6] last week so we could have laughed together over the company I'm in. Don't return—I have lots of them.

Now it is like a lovely dream that last week I was actually with you for 50 hours. As you say, it seems so natural at the time, as if it had always been and would always be, that it is a shock when suddenly the "guillotine" descends.

I loved your letter, darling, every word of it.

I came home feeling that Stan has really made good progress all things considered, in the two months since I saw him in the hospital. It is really wonderful.

Oh—I have an appointment with Dr. Bernard Walsh, a cardiologist, next Monday. Dr. Healy clings to his theory it is radiation-caused, but since the result is the same (insufficient blood to heart muscle) it really doesn't seem to matter much. He did blood test for rheumatoid arthritis (re back, shoulder, etc.) which was negative, but this doesn't completely rule it out. Blood pressure is a little low and so is hemoglobin (probably as result of recent radiation) and I suppose this is why I feel tired. Well, I've exercised my ability to say No on about a dozen letters today, and will continue.

Thanks for the check list! You forgot my decorating project.

I'll spend some happy time today going over your letters and finding some that will contribute to your writing project. And I keep wishing you would

[4] Rachel had received the Schweitzer Medal of the Animal Welfare Institute on January 7, 1963.

[5] The President's Science Advisory Committee.

[6] Clipping not preserved.

write up your recollections of the Boston–Maine boat trip. And hurry up! Before Mr. Weeks[7] retires! This is just the sort of thing he loves.

[7] Edward Weeks,
Atlantic Monthly
editor.

We are due for snow and very cold weather tonight, if predictions can be believed. Well, the freezer is stocked so I don't have to wonder about getting out.

Now I must stop so Ida & Jeanne can take this.

Take care of each other, please. You are very precious.

Dearest love
Rachel

TUESDAY, JANUARY 29

Dearest [Dorothy],

You will be wanting news, but today has been full and now there is time for only a note. More details later.

I like Dr. Walsh very much. He is pleasant, direct and detailed in his explanations, and no sugar-coating—all to my taste. I do have angina, "a classical case." The cardiogram taken there shows some scarring, which of course may be a recent development. But he says angina doesn't necessarily show, and that even without the cardiogram he would have known from my account of symptoms. "It couldn't be anything else."

Now, for some time, my life will be quite regimented. I am not to step out of the house, no stairs, no *anything* that can be done for me. I'm to get a hospital bed (it's ordered) and elevate head 9 inches. I'm taking peritrate (don't know how to spell it) which he says is a long lasting form of nitroglycerine. (Of course I have the regular n-g pills, too—with instructions to take at the first hint of pain.)

This rather stringent program is necessary because I have the somewhat uncommon but well-recognized type of angina in which most of the attacks come on while I'm sleeping or at other times unprovoked by exercise or something else I've done. In other words, the solution isn't so simple as just stopping running around the house!

I think the fact of the matter is that Dr. Walsh doesn't know now how long these restrictions will have to be imposed—he will have to see whether the attacks diminish under this program. I told him about New York Feb. 15—he smiled and said, "We'll see." Detroit seemed "possible." When I was talking to him I had the crazy idea Feb. 15 was a month away. Now I realize it is two weeks I'm pretty sure I can't go.

In the future, I'll always have to lead a pretty tame life. This sort of condition isn't helped by physical exercise, unfortunately. At least, that's his theory. He would like to have used an anti-coagulant, but after consultation with Dr. Healy agreed to try it without, on account of the ulcer.

Now, dear, this must go. It seems strange to be a prisoner again. But I'm thankful he doesn't want me in the hospital.

Will write more soon, dear, but I seem to have covered all essentials of the story.

I'll be looking for your Sunday letter tomorrow—I hope. Don't worry, dear ones. I'll be OK.

All my love
Rachel

JANUARY 31

Have been reading the Blue Nile[8]—*learning history I'd forgotten or never knew*

Dearest [Dorothy],

I've resolved to date my letters hereafter, and recommend you do, too! I've been going over some of your letters, and find the "Tuesdays" or "Fridays" not very informative. Of course the letters often contain clues. So far I haven't struck the real "pay dirt" on your Nature Notes but they are here, and I'm accumulating a little pile for you. Also setting aside some for me, for keeps, and regretfully discarding many. This was a good way to spend an evening and I enjoyed it.

Your good, long letter of Sunday came yesterday, with its interesting enclosures. Tell Stan I think his letter to the Senator is splendid—should make her blush! There has been so much interest in these Maine bills.[9] I hadn't heard from Muriel Parlin[10] in ages, but she *phoned* the other evening about this, and to say Mr. Hassan (sp?) is introducing a bill.

I continue to get good letters people have written the Nutrition Found., a Chem. Co., or something. I wish we had time to copy them to pass along.

There is a marvellous editorial in the Richmond paper. This, I must have photo-copied and will send you.

The Garden Club of America writes today that, altho' they have already given me their highest conservation award (Frances Hutchinson Medal) they wish to do more, and wish to present me with a "Special Commendation" at their annual dinner in Philadelphia May 9th. This is a specially created award, all for me.

And the association of Rod and Gun writers is giving me an award in New York Feb. 21. And, going from the sublime to the somewhat ridiculous, those Natural Food Assoc. want to give me *another* award—they already forced one upon me.

Yes, I wish I *had* known you when *The Sea* was published. That first round of awards was, of course, most exciting. These have their own special flavor, of course, and perhaps are more appreciated because of all the brick bats that are flying, but the first time for anything of this sort is unique. It has, as you say, a dewy freshness that can never be duplicated.

[8] By Alan Moorehead, published in 1962.

[9] The Maine Legislature was considering bills to ban pesticide spraying near waterways and to establish a pesticide regulation board. Stanley had written a letter of support to the sponsor of one of the bills.

[10] A typist who worked for RC when she was in Maine.

Dear, I have sad news. Jane Crile died last night. You will know the overtones this has for me, apart from the sadness in losing a friend. Added to the news I received Monday, this just isn't a good week and I can't help feeling depressed and 90 years old.

But yesterday I heard a cardinal singing. This, you know, is the early prelude to the spring chorus. (See *Spring in Washington*.) It should occur in January, and did. Song sparrows will be next. By the way, Louis Halle is distantly related to the Cleveland Halles. Jane's nephew, a young man doing graduate work here at Am. Univ., was the one who called me last night. I had met his mother and brother at the Criles' in October. He seems such a nice young man—so upset about Jane—but then somehow we got to talking about birds, and now we have a "date" in the Park to hear veeries in May or June.

This is all for now, darling. I am doing next to nothing these days, but should get some letters done this afternoon.

My dearest love, always—
Rachel

No in-the-night pains since I saw Dr. Walsh. Isn't that wonderful?

Titmice whistling today—Spring will not be silent here!

All love to you—
Rachel

FRIDAY MORNING, FEBRUARY 1

Dearest One [Rachel],

There were many wakeful moments in my night during which my thoughts were always with you. There is so much I want to say to you at this special time but I need to be near you to express myself adequately. But I must tell you that I know what a difficult time this is for you. I grieve for you in the loss of Jane as a friend, and as a symbol. I was deeply touched, dear, when you told me the analogy you had applied to her. Now that guiding light has gone out and what can I say to comfort you? If understanding can help, please know that I do.

To come at a time when you are trying to adjust to the knowledge you have recently learned concerning your heart must make it doubly hard. Of course, I hope that Dr. Walsh's strict orders may be to see to it that the rest you have so long needed is achieved. Please give yourself up to it as completely as you possibly can.

There is much more I want to say, but for now this is a message from my heart. If I can mail it now you might get it to-morrow to tell you how much I love you.

With so much love, dear, and understanding,
Dorothy

Dearest [Dorothy],

My routine now is to return to bed after Roger goes, have breakfast there, and linger much of the morning. In fact, for most of last week I never did dress but just "lay around" all day. As often happens, that only seemed to make me more weary for a while, but yesterday I definitely began to feel more rested. And such pains as I've had have come in the waking hours when I could cope with them quickly. So I *think* there is progress.

This is a beautiful day, but very cold. The cardinals have been whistling vigorously. Irston Barnes's column yesterday was about the song sparrow's singing on his Connecticut place. We haven't heard them, but actually we have only an occasional song sparrow—more white throats. Our joy the past two days has been a male purple finch at the feeder—the first this year. And the other night a possum visited us! We have been entertaining two rabbits nightly and try to keep apples out for them. That was the special attraction for the possum.

Your two precious letters came Saturday—wonderfully fast for the one. Airmail does help in this direction; I'm not sure about east-bound mail.

Adgerina seems too good to be true so far, at least. She really does everything very nicely, is kind and pleasant, quiet—oh, quite a list of virtues! And to think she had already been "found" when I needed her so badly.

On Sundays I'm having her get our dinner, and she has the kitchen all cleaned up before she leaves. Then we just have something light in the evening. Perhaps we'll do that Saturdays, too. It does simplify things.

Jeanne has been laid up with flu and still won't be here today. This is added inducement to me to do nothing, but I'm afraid I'll have to turn out a few letters today.

I'm sending a little packet of your letters today. There will be more to come for there are still a couple of drawers full—to say nothing of a canvas case of *old* letters downstairs. If you ever went through them you'd probably find you had your book written!

It is giving me so much pleasure to go through these letters that I'm glad I've been a hoarder. They recall so many precious things that one forgets otherwise. Please don't destroy these I'm sending you. And *please* put them to use.

Perhaps I've already asked you but didn't I send you a number of nature letters a year or two ago? Perhaps about the geese passing over when you were on the shore—the trip to Duxbury Beach, etc.? I hope you kept them! And hurry and write your book so I can read all that again!

This was interrupted by the early arrival of the mail and now, as usually happens, I have a feeling of having been swept by a tidal wave—so many new matters to cope with, added to the sea of papers in the study!

Now I'll say goodbye for now, with this, as you know, goes my dearest love, as always.

Rachel

HYACINTH-TIME

Dear One [Dorothy],

This year, instead of adding to your hyacinth garden, I have decided to call you on February 7, which you tell me is the date of The Letter. I hope you may be at home, and free, that evening.

Do you realize I have known you for a sixth of my life? Not as long or as generous a share as I could wish, but certainly a good, substantial fragment of anyone's life. And a fragment so very different from anything that preceded it, darling. Because you have brought so much happiness into my life—the joy of sharing loved and lovely things, companionship, comfort in sorrow and sickness. As I told you nine years ago, I had needed you without knowing quite what it was I needed—but when you came into my life I quickly realized something, at least, of the place you were to fill.

It seems strange, looking back over my life, that all that went before this past decade seems to have been merely preparation for it. Into that decade (with a little stretching back to 1951) have been crowded everything I shall be remembered for. And most of the sorrows, tragedies, problems, and serious illnesses, too, have been crowded into that period. You have said sometimes that you didn't know how I managed to "take" it all—but you are forgetting your role. I truly cannot imagine those years without you, darling. Because of you there has been far more joy in the happy things, and the hard spots have been more bearable. And so it will be in the time to come, I know.

Always keep a white hyacinth in your heart for me, and remember that all it meant in 1954, it means today, and always.

My dearest love
Rachel

THURSDAY NIGHT, FEBRUARY 14

Darling [Dorothy],

I suppose there was no "good" time to tell you the news, but I am sad now to think of you taking it to bed with you, having it in your mind in wakeful intervals. I had planned to write of it tonight. Then, at least, it would have reached you in daytime hours. But remember, darling, it is just another of the series of battles I knew I must face, and I am sure it is not the last. We will win this one. You know the lymph tumors are very susceptible to radiation.

These lie just above the collar bone, midway to the shoulder, on the left side. One is just under the skin, its shape visible over the bone. It developed during the week between my first conversation with Dr. Caulk and my visit yesterday. One or more lies a little higher in the neck than any I had on the other side. I expect this (the changed treatment area) may mean more difficulty in swallowing after a few treatments. You know I had some before.

Jane is a continuing inspiration even now that she is gone. Kay called me yesterday. She told me that when Jane went back to the hospital for the last time (she had been home part of this interval—I hadn't realized that) she looked at the doctors assembled in her room and said, "Now which of you is in charge of not giving up?" Let's remember that, dear.

I can't pretend that I am light-hearted about it though—you would know better. Mostly, I try not to think too directly on the subject. I suppose the renewed angina pains during the past week may well be related to this suspicion (almost a certainty) I was carrying in my mind. Their return is a little discouraging, I must admit. Short of completely giving in to an invalid's life, I scarcely know what less I could do.

This past 2½ weeks has seemed so strange. Except for feeling very tired I don't feel sick, so it's odd to be so restricted—I reach to raise a venetian blind and then realize I mustn't—hesitate about picking Jeffie up, etc. I'm almost as confined as in a hospital, but it's lonely in a different way. I've told almost no one, so everyone just thinks I'm still rushing around being busy—so there are no get well cards, inquiring calls, or any of the things that perhaps make sickness a little less solitary affair.

This isn't meant to be a depressing letter, darling. I'm just pouring out some of the thoughts that would no doubt be expressed if we could be together. I wish I could shield you from knowing any of this but I can't.

I've been writing in front of the study fire. This is a cold night, noisy with wind. Now I must go to bed. Perhaps I can add a word in the morning.

Now—I love you.

R.

FRIDAY A.M.

I came back to bed to write—find I have this wrong size paper with me. Once I'd have jumped up to get more. Now I have *learned* and I'll just use this!

There is time for just a few words while awaiting Ida and breakfast; then I'll have to dress for our trip to the hospital.

Darling, I do so wish I could have spared you all this, and knowledge of the heart condition, too. You have so many worries and heartaches as it is. If only I could have remained as a refuge for your thoughts—a quiet bower inhabited only by happy memories and happy anticipation. But now it is far otherwise. I do try to spare you some, darling—while I feel bound to tell you the facts I don't share all my thoughts as I once did. Even if we were together I wouldn't.

Some things, I've learned, one must not share. Now don't let that make you sad, dear.

This is a sunny day but the wind is still howling. Roger's riding day—but with thermal underwear and an extra sweater he doesn't mind, and doesn't seem to catch cold.

Now Ida is here so breakfast is on the way. I love you, dear. Yes, it remains the same for me, too—a wonder and a joy, always.

R.

Monday, February 18, at hospital

Dearest [Dorothy],

What better way to fill the moments of waiting, even though they are few? There was a dear letter from you this morning, with several enclosures which I saved for later—but not the letter. Well, I guess your florist *did* know I was sending a valentine, although I didn't exactly say so. I guess my description of what I wanted was enough.

Before I forget—the new De Jager bulb catalogue has the loveliest assortment of freesias—all colors. They will bloom late into the fall according to the catalogue (and our experience). I think I'll get some, but probably the best thing is for you to plant them in Maine, at your place. I'd probably see some before I leave.

This is the warmest day we've had in a long time. I told Jeanne we'd look for crocuses when we get home.

Yesterday Marie phoned and said, "I have a surprise for you—wait till I put him on." It was Barney![11] And I had just mailed him a long letter, for he had known nothing of any recent developments. I didn't want to bother him while Jane was sick. So we talked, and as usual he was reassuring. "Radiation has taken care of it before and it will again." So that is what we must believe. He also sounded optimistic about the heart. Well, I've decided to humor Dr. Walsh a while longer—give myself that good rest I know I need—but I certainly don't intend to live this kind of life forever! We'll do some, at least, of the kind of things we love in Maine this summer. Perhaps not our particular spot at Pemaquid, but we'll find another.

Tuesday

Now I'm home and it is, in fact, another day. Officially we are having "rain"; actually there has been wet snow all morning but it's melting on the streets and dripping from the eaves so I guess drivers will have no problem. And this is my day to stay at home.

There is one more medical fact I must give you. Don't get the idea I'm withholding anything, but in the initial period of mere suspicion I see no need to burden you. The fact is that there is a little trouble in the left shoulder. You know I've been murmuring about "arthritis" since December, but I had finally

[11] Dr. George "Barney" Crile, Jr.

become suspicious and tackled Dr. Caulk about it when I went in last week. The first X-ray (picture) they took last Friday left him not entirely certain; yesterday they tried a different angle and now he's sure. How is your anatomy? It's the coracoid process of the scapula, a place of attachment for various arm muscles, which I guess accounts for my difficulty about certain movements. He showed me the pictures. Of course the area involved is quite small—the edge of the process just looks irregular rather than smooth. So now they have just extended the area of treatment to include that. I think it's very tidy of me to have managed to have the two trouble spots so close together they can be treated simultaneously!

I told Barney about this Sunday and he insists the bone metastases yield to X-ray as readily as the lymph and that this will be all right, too. I guess it's just a matter of detecting them. Dr. Caulk says that hereafter we must be more alert to any pain in bones or joints. Of course my arthritic history made it easy to mistake this one, but now I think a lesson has been learned all around.

Now, dear, that is positively all in the bad news department—nothing more I know or even suspect! And on the good side the heart is behaving very well, and considering the trips, etc., I think this is encouraging. In fact, if it were not for the flu epidemic I'd ask Dr. Walsh to let me go to Detroit, but flu is something I can well do without! So I won't.

The main thing I want to say, dear, is that we are not going to get bogged down in unhappiness about all this. We are going to be happy, and go on enjoying all the lovely things that give life meaning—sunrise and sunset, moonlight on the bay, music and good books, the song of thrushes and the wild cries of geese passing over. (That, I've just realized, I might hear some night a few weeks from now. And this warm snow-rain must be seeping down to waken my frogs.) So—let's think and live happily, enjoying whatever time there is.

And by the way, I'm not so sure Myrtle Beach is out. We'd have to fly, of course, and rent a car. It would be fun, wouldn't it?

Now I must close so Ida can take this.

All my dearest love
Rachel

P.S. I've written Lois, told her about the angina but *not* about the new treatments. I suggested she come here from Detroit but don't suppose she can.

WEDNESDAY, FEBRUARY 20

Dearest [Dorothy],

Today I forgot my glasses, so can only write through a blur. But I hate to waste time so will try.

Spring arrived today in the form of a box of lovely freesias from my dear Valentines. Of course I didn't have to read the card to know whence they came! You know without my telling you how much they delighted me. You know some of the Stardust (from my letter of yesterday) but not all. A few days ago I felt a sudden hunger for freesias. I called Fishers—they expected some but flowers had been delayed by bad weather. I asked them to call me when they got some in. (I remember now this was yesterday.) They said they would—but all the time I suppose they had your order! So this morning these arrived—mostly white, a few yellow. I have the large bunch of white (with asparagus fern) in my bed-room. The yellow are a center piece for the dining room table. Thank you, my dear, for this loveliness with all the thoughts and memories it inspires.

This is now Wed. evening and I'm in bed. You have been out. I know be-cause I've tried several times to call you. I will almost certainly talk to you before you read this so I won't write two things. I want to tell you. This is just a week-end note to say, Thank you and I love you.

Rachel

Thurs. A.M.—at hospital.[12] Your 2 letters are here. But I hope to talk tonight. Love.

Dearest [Dorothy],

I wanted so much to get a letter into the mail today; however, "the best laid plans—." Adgerina telephoned about nine to say that she had started out, but felt so bad she had to turn around and go home. It sounds like flu, and of course I'm thankful she didn't come, but it will be a hard week-end. Then I thought I'd get Robert and Vera to mail the letter I hoped to write. They came before noon, instead of the usual late visit, but I'm writing this in haste while they are out doing their shopping, and some errands for me.

It could be that we'll talk before you read this anyway; I may yield to temp-tation tomorrow. It is such a joy to talk, but how the minutes speed by! I have a dear note from you this morning, written *yesterday*! I want to reply, but not, I guess, now, for the right thoughts and words do not come when one feels hurried.

These are difficult days, I must confess. Almost any movement now is painful, for both the large area over my ribs and my back protest when I rise from a chair, lean over to pick up something, or move in any way in bed. I didn't mean by that that a "large" rib area is actually involved—the spot on the rib is about the size of a pea—but the painful area is more like the size of my hand with fingers extended. All this, plus the now troublesome nausea, make it diffi-cult to concentrate on any work. Yet this H.M. pamphlet must be done, and very soon. And in the doing of that I'll accumulate enough for the *Register*. I'm inter-ested to know what you are thinking of now. Of course you realize I wouldn't ob-ject to your writing if you really want to; I just think it wouldn't carry much weight with those who know we are close friends. I imagine the Parlins are quite angry about it, too.[13]

I have some wonderful statements from a group of half a dozen profes-

[12] RC's cancer treat-ment required this and many other day trips to the hospital.

[13] RC was planning a rebuttal to Ervin G. Conley's negative article "Views on Silent Spring" that appeared in the *Boothbay Register*, and similar infor-mation for Houghton Mifflin.

sors at the U. of Wisconsin. These have never been used, and will be very effective. Also the Kettering man I told you about.

This is the day I was to have been in Detroit for the award.[14] Clarence Cottam is to accept it for me. There is now an award coming from Drexel—will tell you by phone.

Darling, please don't keep your thoughts and concern from me. It would be strange, after all, if you weren't concerned, and I think it would help us both to express more freely what we think. But don't hesitate to put in the "frivolous" things, too. It is also good for us to smile and laugh. Now goodbye, and I love you.

Rachel

[14] Conservationist of the Year award from the National Wildlife Federation.

SATURDAY NIGHT, MARCH 2

Darling [Dorothy],

There is so much stardust in the letter that came today—the note written "under the drier." It proves all over again that so often our minds are pursuing similar thoughts. This time it is the thought of somehow being unable to communicate with the other. I will tell you now that there is in my "tin box" of important papers a letter I wrote you more than a month ago. There was a night just before I saw Dr. Walsh when the pains were so frequent and so severe that I realized there might be no tomorrow, and I thought of the great emptiness there would be for you if there had been no chance for any sort of farewell. So the next evening I wrote you a letter and put it away. I don't know that it really says what is in my heart, but from time to time I may add to it, and leave it there for you to have someday.

Now that the heart is responding so well the possibility I considered is certainly remote. But I tell you this just to show you that I, too, have this great sense of wanting always to communicate with you, always to express what is in my heart. And I do want you to know the letter is there.

Please, darling, don't hesitate to speak what is in your heart. I know I have held back, even when with you, out of a desire to spare you—but really is this for the best? All that is most wonderful in our relationship has been based on that spontaneous outpouring of thoughts and feelings. We both know that my time is limited, and why shouldn't we face it together, freely and openly? I know you have dark thoughts and "hard nights"—how could it be otherwise? So why not share the thoughts—some of them at least?

Of course I long, too, to have you come but I realize you should not. Maybe you and Stan can come, but of course you will stay *here*! When did your presence in this house ever make things harder for me? You could be cook and bottle washer in the hours when there is no Ida.

Oh, I know, it would probably be unwise to think of Myrtle Beach—unwise for any of us (but Roger). The only sensible way would be to fly and rent a car. It is a *long*, tiring drive from here, and for you to add this to a drive from B.

would be too much. And we could be very happy here—if even that seemed wise for you. "Spring in Washington" is lovely, as you know. But when are you going to Maine? Well, not before April 20, I'm sure—and we'd have early shrubs and bulbs before that, anyway.

I shall feel better soon, I'm sure. The present great weariness is due to the very heavy radiation I've had, undoubtedly. And the "misery" in my side will presumably disappear. Sometimes I wish I had nothing to do, but probably it is better to keep my mind occupied. But the never dwindling piles of letters sometimes oppress me—like a treadmill—and I wonder how to get free to think about the book[15] I still hope to write.

[15] Presumably the book RC refers to as "the big 'Man and Nature' book" in her January 6, 1962, letter.

So many ironic things. Now all the "honors" have to be received for me by someone else. And all the opportunities to travel to foreign lands—all expenses paid—have to be passed up. Sweden is the latest, as I shall probably have told you before you read this. Now I really should turn out the light. I love you darling, always and forever. Never forget that.

Rachel

Dear One, In the light of day, I realize what I wrote last night has a very negative sound. I didn't mean at all that the things I wanted to say to you were unhappy; on the contrary it was mainly of the great happiness we have had that I wanted [you] to know. But I do also mean that we do not need to pretend to each other that we never have unhappy thoughts about the present situation.

But you know what I mean, I'm sure. And most of all that I love you.

R.

MARCH 6

Darling [Rachel],

I had planned to start "writing" to-day, but I'd rather talk to you.

Your apple letter was here when we got home from a quite delightful trip to Wayside Inn yesterday. Mrs. Little, at 88, got far more of a kick out of it than would have some of my contemporaries. And her companion-nurse was child-like in her enjoyment. It was a longer drive than I had realized—55 miles actually—we chose an off superhighway route, winding through countryside where the snow grew deeper in the woods and on the slopes with every mile. They both expressed such pleasure at seeing snow. It was a dull day but even without sun Flora kept pointing out the colors in the landscape.

Lunch was very good in its Colonial atmosphere. Afterwards the hostess took us on a guided tour of the rooms. Of course, Stan is especially concerned with the place for it was a seventh generation ancestor of his who built and operated it as the Red Horse Tavern.

Afterwards he guided us to a spot near the road where we saw wintering mallards and Canada Geese—a thrill really. Mrs. Gordon, in an Edwin Tealish style, announced after a short time, "There are 111 of them." There was open water which I supposed was maintained by their diligence in spite of the thick ice on the edges.

It was quite a day. Stan stood it well—he drove over but I drove back. We came home from Flora's with a bunch of pink & white snapdragons from her little greenhouse.

Of the four of us I think *I* was the most tired. I was glad to crawl into bed in the early evening. This morning we are having heavy rain; here in my room I hear it on the roof of the study. I wish you were lying on the bed beside me so we could talk.

A letter from Lib Porter yesterday enclosing a colored picture of our Southport house taken on Feb. 22. The snow is deep & the shadows blue. The house looks strong and substantial with its burden of snow on the roof. Lib said, "Of all the years we have been going up it was the first time we could not stay in the house. We ate there with all the fires going. Got water out of the well with ready made ice cubes. What ice in the old well!"

I feel quite sure that at the first warm spell Stan will say "Let's go." If we did, it would be for over only one night—& of course, we wouldn't stay at the house.

If you were here we could talk about the contents of your apple. Darling, need I tell you that I cried as I read it. And yet, dear, I have a sense of relief that you have said that it is best that we talk freely and openly.

I think, as always, you have found a way to express what is in my heart and thought, beautifully, simply and definitely. The stardust was rich this time. I suppose that as we face the future this desire to communicate would inevitably be terribly urgent—that there never will be time enough to say all we need to say. And yet, darling, in a way, we both know what the other needs to say, and if it could never be said we would still know. Nevertheless, the fact that you wrote a letter for me "if there should be no to-morrow" makes my heart almost burst. To know that in the midst of severe pain and, I'm sure, fright you could think of me and the emptiness that would follow for me, if your heart suddenly rebelled, tells me how much I mean to you! And it points up that awful thought I had in the night, "What if we could never speak to each other again."

And in relation to that, darling, I must tell you something that happened to me last night. (You said, you know, that we should not hesitate to share all our thoughts.) Suddenly, as I was lying awake in the darkness, a thought, that was so different, hit me like a revelation. To state it very simply, I have become convinced of immortality. We have talked of this, and I remember of telling you when we first knew each other that my idea of immortality was that we live afterwards in the memory of those whose lives we have touched and in our accomplishments during our life. And that has been enough for me. But now it is not. Suddenly, I believe that whichever of us goes first (and it could be me, dear) *that* one will still go on knowing about the other. Darling, this is all such a new idea I have not explored it thoroughly. And, dear, even when Stan was at his lowest the thought did not come to me. You have brought me to this belief. There is more than a memory—there is a consciousness that goes on.

If this is to get out for the mailman I must stop soon. Let me say this, darling. Subjects such as this are not easy to write about as a dialogue, especially where most of the mail has to be shared. Don't try to answer this kind of thought for I'm sure you'd feel the need of enclosing your reply as an apple. And I realize that is always difficult. We can talk about it when we are together, dear.

For the most part almost anything you write can be shared. Stan knows that we love each other to a greater depth than other friendships.

I want you to feel at ease and to be able to write freely.

Now there is more that I want to answer in yesterday's letter, but I'll save it for my next.

All my love, dear,
Dorothy

TUESDAY, MARCH 19

Dearest [Dorothy],

Very likely I'll call you before you read this, and as usual will have told you all that is in the letter! There isn't much to tell, factually. The routine of treatment goes on. I find I am in greatest pain from late afternoon until I get into (or *on* to) bed, so this morning I'm trying staying abed until lunch time. I'm sure it is better for now to keep weight off my spine. Yesterday it seemed a little easier to get on and off the treatment table, so maybe there is some kind of improvement. You speak in today's letter of the pain of walking. There is that, of course, but it isn't pain that causes me to try to be as inactive as possible—it is the fear of bringing on that dreaded collapse of the vertebra. No one will tell me precisely what that would mean—some degree of crippling, of course.

I am about to write Dr. Ivy in Chicago about Krebiozen. No doubt all the doctors connected with me would disapprove, and I should probably have to find someone who *is* using it locally. I think you said you knew nothing about it. It has been a subject of bitter controversy for more than a decade, though for reasons that reflect chiefly the bickerings, struggle for power, bigotry, etc., within the medical profession rather than any valid objection to the drug. "Drug" really is a misnomer; it is an anti-cancer substance produced by living tissues (by injecting a mold preparation into horses, then extracting this substance from the blood serum). So, instead of attacking the local manifestations of the disease, as by radiation, it really helps the whole body resist. There is no claim it is 100% effective, but about 50 percent show great improvement for considerable periods, relief from pain, return to active lives, etc. A recent article in the Journal of the AMA makes a comparison of breast cancer patients treated with Krebiozen, androgens, estrogens, removal of adrenals, pituitary, etc., and the Krebiozen patients survived longer than any other. I have just gotten this literature from Dr. Biskind, and think I shall write Dr. Ivy today. It is non-toxic and it is claimed there are no side effects. Treatment is by weekly or twice-weekly injections.

Oh dear, now I feel hurried. I must soon get up, shower, dress, and have lunch. My days are busy, my evenings are at a low ebb physically, and I get settled on this bed and read. By the way, I have recently "discovered" Forester's *Hornblower* novels and have read two with enjoyment. Do you know them? Two old salts like you and Stan should get much pleasure out of the details of handling those old sailing vessels. The fine points are lost on me, but I enjoy them.

Darling, there is so much I want to say. My tax data went off yesterday, thank goodness, and as I feel better I can talk to you more.

Oh—at long last, the first thin bubble of frog song came from the swamp Sunday night, after a warm, sunny day. And last evening I heard the first robin song. So spring is not to be silent!

My dearest love.
Rachel

THURSDAY, MARCH 21

Dearest [Dorothy]—

As when I last wrote, there is the feeling that I shall talk with you before you read the letter. Tuesday Paul Reimers came just as I was about to call. Last night I was tired! Now I shall try tonight. Perhaps you will have gone to Maine! I do hope not, for it must be wild and wintry there. I had a letter from Mrs. Washington at N. Edgecomb—she said it was the worst winter there in years. She had just had her drive ploughed that morning—"and now it's snowing heavily!" She wrote that the Bestons have stayed on the farm this winter, for Henry hasn't been up to going away. Oh, on the subject of Maine, I had a wire from Olive Stratton asking me to phone her collect if I had anyone in mind who would like to buy the Steeveses' cottage. So last year's buyer must have thought better of it quickly. Well, I didn't, so I didn't.

These days are so full. We have gone to the hospital mornings except for that blessed Tuesday when I stayed abed. Then there is lunch, and the afternoon to be divided between rest and Jeanne. Yesterday Kay Halle and her nephew drove out to see me. Today a reporter; tomorrow Dr. Cattell—well, at that point the phone rang and rang, and the wretched answering service wasn't getting it so I had to. It was Dr. Cattell himself, calling to ask if he might come next week instead. So tomorrow looks more comfortable. But I started out to say that I feel so frustrated about writing to you—I also sense somewhat the same frustration (though perhaps for different reasons) in yours to me. "This isn't the letter I wanted to write" we both say. Darling—perhaps it is in part because some of the things that we would say are difficult, requiring the right mood for expression, and I find when I am very weary or uncomfortable I can't command it. Once I could rise above it. As I look back it seems I kept pouring out my thoughts to you through all the physical miseries of the onset of the ulcer, the arthritis, etc. Well, now I am not only ill but getting older and needing my rest—could that be it?

Certainly rest helps on the back—in fact by late afternoon it simply demands rest. And I continue to appreciate this hospital bed I once scorned. As I'll tell you tonight the back is improving, though slowly. But "they" say they are encouraged.

I think I could translate all of Lois's letter for you. I know I'm sometimes baffled, but this mainly when she drops a story half told, or alludes to something she has never told. But I have the advantage of knowing her in the flesh. I think we must remember that she lives in a world almost wholly without companionship, something hard for us to conceive. There is no "small talk" in her—she has forgotten the easy chatting and exchange of not-so-important comment that makes up social intercourse. She thinks deeply—when she speaks the thoughts come from far down in the recesses of that solitude-bound mind and personality. "Like someone from another world," Jeanne said. She means, at the end, that I have begged her to give the world the story of Alatna—that she must not fail me by not doing so.

She wrote such a heartbreaking, revealing thing (if more revelation is needed) about the morning after her return—that when she awoke she lay abed for a while, moaning from time to time, and that the dog who is her special companion came and laid his muzzle across her face, trying to comfort. I could see that it was agony for her to return to that life.

Perhaps some of the comments about me puzzled you. I discussed the whole problem openly, as it seemed at that time. There was a question about how much time might remain. I told her Barney had said it was possible to live with various bone metastases for 4 or 5 years. I think that is her "Five years." She gives undue weight to the heart pains—that situation, I'm sure, is under control. I haven't told her about the back trouble and see no point writing it. If I saw her, I'd probably tell her, but that's different.

Again, "this isn't the letter"—it's not the "way I planned it." But it's been good to spend an afternoon hour visiting with you, and I do hope I'll find you at home tonight.

All my love, as always,
Rachel

The first day of spring! There was snow on the ground when we wakened, and a cold, biting wind all day.

Darling [Dorothy]—

I was wakened this morning by the cries of geese, but when I got to the windows could see or hear nothing. But I'm sure I was not deceived. Then I went back to bed to listen to the first sustained robin song—now in mid-morning the frogs dominate the un-silent spring.

Last night's call was so satisfying—I wish we could do it every evening.

Bea Riegel is coming out to do my hair this morning, bringing her shampoo tray because my back won't allow me to hang over a basin. It will be a joy to have it done. She hasn't been well so we haven't been able to get together for a while. Anyway, I may not get this finished in time to send with Ida today. Oh well, I can mail it tomorrow.

Did I tell you that I finally received the drawings for the shelf and cabinet arrangement and have given my approval—and deposit—and have a promise they will at least *try* to have them in within 3 weeks. I do so want to have that in, the hall papered, and the new rug, before you come. I want you to be able to picture the "new" house. Perhaps we could think in terms of the last week of April for your visit here, if that fits your other plans. There should still be bulbs, and maybe azaleas, and a good bird chorus. Remember our pre-sunrise recording for Lois? That must have been two years ago. Well, you know I will be supremely happy to have you here, whenever you can come. Even if I'm not up to much activity that won't matter—just to be together is the main thing.

At the moment I find it requires a considerable act of faith to believe this back of mine will ever be up to travel, or normal activity, but of course I refuse even to consider the possibility of not going to Maine. However, I suppose we have to know there *is* that possibility, or that if I get there my stay might be curtailed. But perhaps Krebiozen will change the picture. Dr. Healy has had his conference—he was able to talk directly to Dr. Durovic, the man who developed the method. A supply of Krebiozen and dosage instructions will be sent, presumably this week.

It is now bedtime. Bea was here a long time. She gave my hair an oil treatment, set it, gave me a manicure and recombed the wig. After she left I was glad to lie down—had a long nap in fact, until time to get dinner. Then back to bed quickly—several phone calls, read a little, and now I'm sleepy again!

The enclosed CBS release[16] arrived Special Delivery this A.M.! The same thing had reached me a week ago via Marie. Now that I've scanned the list carefully, I'm pretty sure I won't like the program. I've marked the names with symbols; + means at least reasonably on my side, o means neutral and if anything disposed to be negative, – means, in these cases, strongly negative. So it seems to me the show is weighted against me, and I'm rather annoyed.

I have some good material from the citizen-scientist committee recently

[16] For the April 3, 1963, "CBS Reports" television program "The Silent Spring of Rachel Carson" with Eric Sevareid reporting.

set up in Connecticut. I think you and Stan would like to read it. I'll try to send it soon but would like it back.

Now dear, I suppose I must turn in and go to sleep to a lullaby of frog song—I guess they are happy tonight because of the rain. I wish you could hear them too. I love you.

Rachel

WEDNESDAY A.M., MARCH 27

Dear One [Dorothy],

When I got up this morning and made my usual tour of the house, opening and raising blinds, etc., I uttered a loud "Oh!" when I opened the blind of the side study window. One large clump of daffodils is suddenly in full bloom— there must be 6 or 8 blossoms. Well, spring must be just about on schedule, in spite of our record cold winter. I remember that three years ago, when I entered the hospital March 31, we had our first daffodils.

Darling, there is so much I want to say to you. It is hard for me (and perhaps for you) to see why I have been unable to find time and mood to respond to some of the things you have written. But the days do seem absurdly full, especially during that week and more of daily hospital trips and trying also to keep up correspondence. Evenings in bed I'm too weary to write—just read, doze, and talk on the phone!

There are three things I want to talk about as I can, my plans for Roger, your writing, and your dear letter in which you talked about your new thoughts on immortality. Of course, darling it touched me deeply that this new conviction has come to you through me. I have never formulated my own belief and feeling in words and am not sure I can now. Of two things I am certain. One is the kind of "material immortality" of which I wrote in the concluding paragraphs of "Undersea,"[17] and which is expressed in one of Charles Alldredge's poems which I am sending you. That is purely a biologist's philosophy. For me it has great meaning and beauty—but it is not wholly satisfying. Then, the immortality through memory is real and, in a personal way, far more satisfying. It is good to know that I shall live on even in the minds of many who do not know me, and largely through association with things that are beautiful and lovely. When E. B. White wrote me last summer that he would always think of me when he heard his hermit thrushes, I told him I could think of no more lovely memorial. And I know, darling, that as between you and me, the one who goes first will always speak to the other through many things—the songs of the veeries and hermits, and a sleepy white throat at midnight—moonlight on the bay—ribbons of waterfowl in the sky. But, as you ask, is that enough? No, it isn't. For one thing, the concept of nothingness is hard to accept. How could that which is truly one's self cease to exist? And if not, then what kind of spiritual existence can there be? If we try to form a definite concept we are, of course, only guessing, but it seems to me that if we say we do not know and can't even imagine, this doesn't mean we

[17] "Undersea," in the *Atlantic Monthly* magazine of September 1937, was RC's first literary publication. The last paragraph reads in part: "Individual elements are lost to view, only to reappear again and again in different incarnations in a kind of material immortality. . . . Against this cosmic background the life span of a particular plant or animal appears not as a drama complete in itself, but only as a brief interlude in a panorama of endless change."

disbelieve in personal immortality. Because I cannot understand something doesn't mean it doesn't exist. The marvels of atomic or nuclear physics, and the mathematical concepts of astronomy are wholly beyond my ability to grasp. Yet I know these concepts deal with proven realities, so it is no more difficult to believe there is some sort of life beyond that "horizon," and to accept the fact we cannot now know what it is. Perhaps you remember what I wrote in "Help Your Child—" about the old Swedish oceanographer Otto Petterson—how, as he neared the end of his long life, he said to his son that in his last moments he would be sustained "by an infinite curiosity as to what was to follow." To me, that sort of feeling is an acceptable substitute for the old-fashioned "certainties" as to heaven and what it must be like. I know that we do not really "know" and I'm content that it should be so. At least, that is my present feeling. I'm glad, darling, that you opened up the subject and I hope we can talk about it. It is not a gloomy subject and certainly does not relate especially to my own situation, for this is something we all share—a normal part of life. Barney's comparison of the life-death relationship to rivers flowing into the sea is to me not only beautiful but somehow a source of great comfort and strength.

Now, darling, this must be all if I'm to get this mailed this morning as I want to do. When I can, I'll get to the other subjects. Meanwhile, dear, I do so deeply wish I could lift from you the burden of sadness that I know lies over your thoughts of me now. I do hope we may have a truly happy summer, full of fun and happy sharing of many of the things dearest to us both. Let us try to fill these weeks with lovely memories, darling.

Goodbye for now, and remember how much I love you, always—

Rachel

I'm so sorry about the uneasiness over Stan. I know so well how you both must have felt. I suppose, with all the surgery that has been done, some upsets are inevitable and I do hope it means no more than that.

Love, always
R.

MARCH 28, AFTERNOON

Dearest [Dorothy],

Well, I've just received my Conservationist of the Year award. Mr. Kimball of the Wildlife Federation came out with a photographer. It is handsome indeed—a large bronze plaque mounted on a walnut base. This is the first such award to be given.

This morning I had a fascinating phone call from a man on the Republican Policy Committee of the Senate. He wanted to know whether I had seen the original draft of the report of the President's pesticide committee. Of course I haven't. His group has heard that this draft was so "hot" that enormous pressure has been brought on the committee, especially by two senators, and also by industry, etc., and that in consequence they have watered it down considerably. I told him I hoped he was misinformed, but if not, I hoped they could be instrumental in bringing out the original report. I gave him the names of two of the staff associated with the committee, to assist him in his digging. Now isn't that interesting?

This is another marvelous spring day. I'm surprised to hear, via your wonderful letter, that it has been warm enough for you to sit out in the sunshine. Maybe I'll get our chaise out and try it, too. Right now I'm going to drive Ida over and let her do a little marketing—I won't go in. I haven't driven for a week, but guess it will be all right.

Here are a few odds and ends[18] you may find interesting. Thanks for the prompt return of the British clippings. A French newspaperman was here this morning for an interview—said obviously there was great interest in France or his paper would not have asked for it. Someone else said it is the leading French paper—I wouldn't have known!

So much love, to both of you—and Willow.

Rachel

Now in haste, can't find the clippings I had set aside. Please return these things.

SUNDAY MORNING, MARCH 31

Darling [Rachel],

Strangely your letter which came yesterday ended "So much love, to both of you—and Willow." Not that it is unusual for you to mention Willow but just the Stardust at this particular time was lovely!

Well, the darling is asleep[19] under the pines where he loved to wander, to spring out at us, to sleep in the leaves on a warm day. Nearby is a large clump of blooming snow drops, and the evergreen of myrtle is nearby to grow over the spot. Stan had been trying to root some pussy willow switches from Surgenses' lovely tree which has been so silvery in the moonlight. Now he thinks he'll try to plant them where Willow is buried, altho' I don't think it is sunny enough. I wonder if you ever saw the slide of Willow when he was young, sitting behind a vase of Pussy Willows on the dining table, sniffing at one as cats do. It's adorable, as his coloration is exactly that of the flowers & the vase is gray with brown.

Darling, it was wonderful that you should call just when you did. A few hours earlier I would still have been despairing.

I'm sure I don't need to tell you that a complete sense of peace and acceptance descended upon us when the mystery was solved. My grief had been spent in those agonizing days so that altho' I cried, when I saw and touched the precious creature (as one surely would) the sadness was tempered with knowledge and the assuaging of that longing to see him once again.

We both are all right now. Of course, I reach to open the cellar door each morning as I go downstairs, and this morning a shadow from a tree, moving

[18] Enclosures not preserved, but the March 31 DF letter mentions some of them.

[19] Willow had died while sleeping under the Freemans' porch; he had been missing for five days.

against the garden near the foundation of the house made me think it was Willow coming around the corner to greet us as he so often did.

Time will heal the sadness and the memories will be happy ones.

It was so good to be able to talk with you about Willow just when I did. Of all our friends no one understands as you do.

But it was also good to hear of the things that are happening to you—especially what you had to tell about the pesticide committee report.

You also sounded so happy about the Wellesley report. At least that is a practical concrete example to be held up for others who are fighting for the cause.

Well, Wednesday night will end the uncertainties about "CBS Reports." I can't believe it will be too awful.

We shall try to call you after it is over, as I suppose a hundred others will try to do, so if we don't get through to you, you will know we tried.

Apropos of nothing, yesterday morning early we had one fox sparrow (Don Surgens saw six back of his yard.)—I've been watching for them. And this morning a song—probably a purple finch.

Dearest, again a bit of stardust, or perhaps "you planned it that way"—to include the Memorial Service for Charles Alldredge with his poems in the letter you wrote with your thoughts on immortality. I found great response within me to all his poems. However, I really wish I understood more than I do about poetry. I'd like to have a course with John Ciardi on the meaning, the methods, the object of poetry as well as the art.

Now I need to know more about Charles. I didn't realize that he was a prominent figure but apparently he must have been to have such a service. Do you know the connection with Estes Kefauver?

More and more the idea of a memorial service seems to be developing. I like it so much. The service for Mr. Little was so fine, and such a happy way to remember him.

I wonder if you were able to go to Charles's—I doubt it.

How lovely to have daffodils in bloom. With your warm days things will pop. I'm glad our children can have a preview of spring before going back to their bleak country.

However, even there we have reports that the snow is disappearing. Arthur Grant is home—only about two feet left, he says.

Of course, this Apple now before me is very precious. You say, "It is hard for me (and perhaps for you) to see why I have been unable to find time and mood to respond." Darling, it is not at all hard for me to understand. The miracle for me is that you can write at all—and never a week has gone by without some satisfying communications from you, although you may not realize it.

All you wrote of your own feelings and thoughts of immortality opened up new vistas for my mind to travel along. I like all you said, and as always, you have been able to express it so beautifully. E. B. White's tribute must warm your heart. Of course, as you say, darling *we* have a wealth of material to keep alive the memory of the other. We are rich, indeed, to have shared so many experiences of loveliness. Someday let's make a list, when we are together.

Darling, please do not be disturbed about me because "of the burden of sadness that lies over me." It cannot be helped and has been so long a part of my life that I know how to live with it. I can't say to you that I'm not sad for you know me too well and you know what you mean to me.

But I do try to think of happy things, darling, and I, too, am looking forward to days of sharing much more loveliness.

And we shall see you when it is best for you. Now our time is very flexible. If you'd rather we came later than we had first spoken of—perhaps along in May—we can adjust. We don't have to go to Southport at any particular time, you know.

And I know it would please you if we saw the "new house." So don't feel pressed for time except perhaps you can use our visit as a jog to urge your workmen along. But not for us must you feel an urgency.

Time for Sunday dinner.

All my love,
Dorothy

MONDAY, APRIL 1

Dearest [Dorothy],

I'm writing in bed this morning, planning to give my bones a good rest today. I had Elliott both Saturday and Sunday and this involved a good deal of going in and out, but the weather was so lovely I'd probably have done so anyway. Jeanne will not be here today, and perhaps not for several. Her father returned early from California because he has to have surgery for a hernia, so she is taking him to a surgeon today. The break comes at a good time for me—it is wonderful not to have the hospital trip today.

I'm sure you know how I have grieved with you and for you since the news came on Saturday. I know so well how you feel. I can remember all the anguish at Muffie's sudden passing as clearly as if it had been yesterday. Now, when Jeffie speaks to me in the night my first thought is "Oh, poor Dorothy and Stan!" But I know, too, the great comfort it is to you to have the incessant questions of those four days answered, and to know that his death was a peaceful one, in his own home. I hope it might be the same for Jeffie, and under the circumstances I must hope it may happen before the time comes when I am unable to care for him. But how much people miss when they have not known the companionship of such precious creatures. And what a store of memories you have, all aided by those wonderful slides and photographs. In time the aching emptiness will be eased, and you can enjoy all those memories almost without pain. But oh darling, I'm so sorry for you both now.

A long interruption to read the mail—then lunch—now I'm sitting in the study while a mockingbird serenades me through the chimney. Outside we have a soft April rain, bringing new green into the lawn. The willows are now a green mist, against the red haze of the maples. The colors of spring are almost as varied as autumn.

I'm sending you (under separate cover, for I discover a critical shortage of stamps, and it's heavy) a copy of the House of Lords debate inspired by *Silent Spring*. You won't want to wade through all its heavy verbiage, sprinkled with "noble Lords" but it is interesting to sample and see the amount of time spent on it. In fact, it gives me an odd feeling to know I stirred it up. The Punch cartoon,[20] sent me today by Elizabeth Beston, is a gem, I think. Please return it in your next letter.

[20] Enclosure not preserved, but likely a J. W. Taylor cartoon showing a dead dog and one man saying to another: "This is the dog that bit the cat that killed the rat that ate the malt that came from the grain that Jack sprayed."

I think I'll call you immediately after the program Wednesday. I imagine there will be a deluge of calls and I want to speak to you first. Well, I just hope I don't look and sound like an utter idiot. When I remember my state of extreme exhaustion those two days, plus the huskiness of voice, I can't be too optimistic. Last night Roger had a CBS channel on and called to me there was a preview of *S.S.*—I missed most of it, but the shots of spraying were rather appalling.

Now I guess I mustn't write much longer. I still haven't written Barney about the Krebiozen, and I must. I know he won't like it and I guess that's why I keep putting it off. Dr. Healy will be out all week, the Clinic tells me, which poses a problem. I do want to get started. We have a new "test area" in the pains in the pelvic girdle, I'm sure, even though nothing shows as yet. I think I'll ask Dr. Biskind if he thinks it would be risky to let a nurse administer it. If these pains would yield to it, I would begin to recover some of the optimism I've lost.

Darling, I must tell you that the roses are still beautiful! They are of course fully out, and have been for some days, but not a petal has fallen. I think that is wonderful—a week tomorrow!

We'll be talking soon. Till then, my dearest love, always—

Rachel

SUNDAY NIGHT, APRIL 7

Darling [Dorothy],

It probably seemed silly for me to be worried because I couldn't reach you, but I was! The evenings I was just disappointed, but when there was no answer this morning a little nagging worry did set in. I tried several times between 10 and 1—then didn't want to interrupt a possible nap time. I was *so* relieved when Stan answered!

Soon after we talked Robert and Vera arrived. I was glad to see them. I'd been walking around the yard, wishing for someone to enjoy the beauty of the bulbs, the delicious scent of the spice bushes, now so numerous and so thriving, the promise of dogwood and other shrubs to come. They stayed till almost eight. Now I've done a few more notes, as I rest in bed. I'd intended to save time to "talk" to you a while but now I find I'm sleepy.

Darling, it is wonderful to know you are planning to come. I don't know when I want you most—I just want you! The bulbs are so lovely now, but there will be others later—the tulips and scillas, along with azaleas. Wouldn't it be lovely if we could return to the Arboretum? If you could see me now that would seem a ridiculous suggestion—but we can hope, can't we? Sometimes, darling, I'm almost glad you are not seeing this, much as I long for you. I could live with the pain; it is the crippling, real and prospective, that is hard to take. Sometimes I think it can't be real—that I shall awake in the morning and find it isn't so. But it is. Now I dread the getting out of bed, wondering whether I can walk at least as well as the day before. I shouldn't be saying all this, but I think I must prepare you a little. But just remember I *can* do things like driving a new Olds, and that tomorrow I'm starting a new treatment that may make all the difference! Even by the time you come it could, if I'm one of the lucky ones.

MONDAY A.M.

A new day—another beautiful one—and I got along fairly well with getting Roger off. I'm waiting for Dr. Healy's call. It came around noon and I'll go over soon. Meanwhile, a wonderful letter from Barney has come. I was afraid he'd be upset about the Krebiozen. He isn't at all, though, he isn't convinced it is the ultimate answer. But he is quite willing to have me try it now. This relieves my mind greatly.

Now I mustn't write more. Hope you enjoy the various enclosures.[21]

All my love
Rachel

[21] Enclosures not preserved.

Please return the House of Lords debate—but in a week will be time.

Darling [Dorothy],

It's a long time since you've had an apple, and this must be a tiny one. I just want to be sure, dear, you know how I'm longing to see you and how I'm looking forward to your visit. I think all my comments about it must have seemed quite restrained. I haven't wanted Stan to feel under pressure to come, if for any reason he felt hesitant about it. So that has acted as a brake on the expression of my feelings. But your heart must tell you how I'm longing to see you. January 7th may not be so long ago in time, but in all that's happened it seems years ago. And it was a tiny visit anyway.

Darling, of course I'm able to have you—actually, I'm feeling better than I have in many weeks. (Better in many ways than in January.) And you know, far from being a strain, your visit will make me so relaxed and happy. We don't *need* to go anywhere or do anything if we don't want to. (But I do hope we can go to the Arboretum.) I feel pleased with the plan about "Stan's suite" for I think it will be relaxing and restful for him to be able to retire to a quiet place of his own as much as he wants to. And I think it will be quite comfortable.

I just hope the long drive won't be too hard on either of you. But darling, *please* just plan to settle down for the week. I couldn't bear a time so short as to get you home before the week-end. There is nothing I have to do. (And to the extent anyone else's opinion matters, those who know about your visit know also that you are most precious to me and will be glad for me to have the happiness of your visit. So please, darling, put aside all constraint about what you "ought" to do.)

Now I must stop, dearest. I think Roger and I are going to eat out, and if so I'll mail this.

Do you know what? I love you—more and more as the years go by. And you fill a place no one else could possibly fill.

Always—allways—my love

Rachel

SATURDAY NIGHT, APRIL 20

TUCKED IN BED

Darling [Dorothy]—

For a few minutes before I turn out the light let's talk. This is a beautiful moonlight night—perhaps full moon, I'm not sure—but the lawn is flooded with light as I look out. The frogs are silent, I've just realized. Perhaps it is too chilly for them—we have warnings of frost.

I would love to call you tomorrow to learn whether your anxieties have been dispelled by a good report from the Clinic, but I suppose it is wiser not to. (I mean—perhaps it would overemphasize it in Stan's mind.) So I shall just hope for news in a letter Monday or Tuesday. I'm so sorry that what I take to have been a routine visit turned into something at least temporarily worrisome.

Of course I would understand, darling, if you felt you shouldn't come— but oh, I do hope that won't happen. Because I don't want you to have cause for worry and, selfishly, because I long *for your* visit!

Now it's Sunday, for I was very weary last night and my eyes wouldn't stay open. In spite of seeming (and being) so well, I find I have quite limited endurance, and something like Friday's trip downtown leaves me limp for a day or so. But that, I'm sure, is nothing surprising in view of all that lies behind.

So much I feel welling up that I want to say. If you can come it will all pour out. If you can't we shall somehow have to find hours under the real or figurative spruce in Maine.

I want to mail this today, so won't write more. Do you know how much love it carries? So much more than I can express.

Rachel

My darling [Dorothy]—

I can't tell you how happy I am that the news was good—Happy for Stan, for you, and for myself, too. I know you will both go off to Maine with lighter hearts because he has had this thorough going over.

As for Us—I haven't dared let myself think you were coming until this word came. My last note may have sounded restrained because of that—but you would understand. Now I really *can* count the days. I can scarcely believe it even now, darling. What deep happiness to look into your eyes!

Your apple caused me to laugh aloud—with no one but Moppet to hear, of course! Well, we shall see but I'm not the cripple you may expect to see, darling. Except that I'm usually stiff when I first get up, I walk spryly and am reasonably comfortable.

Now I must go. Maybe only one more letter to you!

All my love,
Rachel

Dearest [Dorothy],

Your letter was here when I returned from the hospital. You were *sweet* to make the trip to see Mrs. Snider. I never intended more than a call. And what a lovely thought to take her the flowers from your garden. I have those same little white daffodils (only I could never describe them so aptly as you) and of all the wealth of bulbs now in bloom they are perhaps my favorite. Well, it doesn't seem good, does it? Poor dear—with her so ill I don't know what you could see of what a lovely gentle woman she is. She and Jeanne had such an enjoyable time at the Richmond luncheon talking about their gardens, and England. Well, I must write her a note now I know she will at least be aware of it. Thank you, dear, so very much.

Driving the new car is so easy and pleasant—like floating! And it really is beautiful. Did I tell you I got seat belts? And a radio!! This a concession to Roger.

We are having a wild wind this afternoon which won't do blossoms any good. However, I don't think our dogwood and azaleas are far enough along to be hurt. What we need is a couple of days of gentle rain.

The wren is very busy carrying in sticks—such long ones, but he maneuvers to get them end-first, then I can hear him scratching around inside. I hope you can see some of this.

Elliott set up Stan's bed with great ease. I'm surprised to see how well the room takes a double bed. I think it's the most comfortable one in the house, provided one doesn't have a "back." There is a board for my old bed, which you will have (with or without board). I had liked it very much. I'll mail your directions tomorrow suddenly realizing I'll have to hurry! But remember a postponement is all right!

All my love—

Rachel

THURSDAY, APRIL 25

Dearest [Dorothy]—

I'm enclosing a 3-A map with the good news you can avoid the Baltimore tunnel and all the horrid traffic that precedes it for miles. The Beltway (northern half) hadn't been completed last year. You will see that this route is somewhat farther, but would be all plain sailing and *so* much easier that I strongly recommend it.

Directions on the penciled sheet will apply from the point where you leave the Beltway.

I will talk to you about New York. You probably have your preference. I guess construction on the George Washington Bridge is completed, and this may now be much improved. I have used Tappan Zee Bridge and Garden State Pky for years, and now that the Thruway across Westchester Co. is completed that is quite easy and far less congested than my old route. Either the Merritt Pky or the Conn Tpk makes connection with that road to Tarrytown (Tappan Zee) Bridge. (We used Conn Tpk last year and didn't care for scenery, tho driving is easy. But maybe you have a direct route to it.)

I'll be calling you, probably Friday night, by which time you ought to have this.

Darling, you know, I think, how I'm looking forward to having you. But nevertheless, I want to be *sure* you don't undertake the trip unless you both really feel up to it. I know it is a long drive, and a more difficult one than the Maine trip because of heavier traffic. So you must feel free to postpone or even to cancel if, at the last minute, this seems wise.

We should be due for warmer weather next week! But I've been glad for the cool spell which has held things back. I hear the azaleas at the Arboretum should be at their peak next week.

I have now had 3 treatments, and will finish tomorrow or Monday. (Isn't that neat timing?) The new car makes the trips quite easy, and I continue to walk better and better. We will *all* rest as much as we want or need to—don't worry about that.

Just now I thought I heard a catbird. They'll surely be here by next week. And the wren is so busy!

Goodbye for now, dear—will talk to you soon.

All my love, as always—

Rachel

Your letter postmarked W.B. at 3 P.M. yesterday, ordinary mail, was here this morning! How's that for service?

P.S. The Assoc. Press wants me to do a weekly column. I said no, of course, but isn't *that* something?

Darling [Dorothy],

I wanted to write last night but found I could not—it seemed anything I might say would only make you more sad. But now I do want something to reach you before the week-end. (Your letter of yesterday, miraculously, was here today.)

The dogwood and azaleas are still glorious in the suburbs, at least, and I need not tell you I look at them always with you in my heart. Spring seems to be the time we *need* to be together, and this spring above all others! I cannot—must not—say all that is in my heart. Well, we shall wait and see what develops about Stan. Perhaps if there are no complications you and I can salvage something, somewhere!

My heart has ached for you, darling! I lived through that unpacking of the car before you told me of it. And I'm so sorry for Stan, too. I can understand how unhappy this would make him for our sakes, and I know there would be disappointment for himself, too. It would have been such fun for all of us. But, remembering how sick he was a few months ago, I suppose that long car trip was never a good idea. I wonder why Dr. Bowles[22] didn't want him to fly?

The poor Riegels[23] are living through such a hard time. He has been treated for an ulcer for the past 6 weeks but grew steadily worse. Now a new doctor thinks it *may* be gall bladder, aggravated by the milk-cream ulcer diet! He is skin-and-bone, and in constant, severe pain not lessened by any narcotic. My private guess is pancreatic cancer. The dr. hinted at something else.

Darling, we'll talk again before you read this. Please always know how much you mean to me, and how I love you.

Rachel

Darling [Dorothy]—

Saturday afternoon—another beautiful day, warm for sitting and eating on the porch, with wrens and catbirds busy. This is so strange; I want to write you, yet I am hesitant about everything I would say, for to speak of all that surrounds me will only make us long all the more for what we hoped was to be. And I can't think what else to say! I know you feel the same way.

There are other things I need to say to you, but they should be said with my arms around you—so how can I write you of them? I feel I must see you,

[22] The correct spelling is "Boles." Both spellings are retained.

[23] Bea Riegel helped RC with styling her hair.

somehow, somewhere. I've even wildly thought of flying to Boston for a day, a little later, but given all the circumstances that *is* rather wild.

Now, I know even that paragraph shouldn't have been written. My heart aches for you, for I know (yes, I think I do!) how desperately you wanted to come, and how completely impossible it is at the moment. What makes me so sad for you, darling, is the fact that serious troubles beset two of those dearest to you in all the world. *One* would be more than enough.

I think we must drift for the present. If Stan makes a really good recovery before you go to Southport, just perhaps you would feel you could come here for a couple of days. The dark thought that keeps recurring is that once you have gone to Maine it would be so much harder for you to come, whatever the circumstances here.

This is hard to say, but perhaps must be said, for it is difficult for me to know how things look to you. Stubbornly determined though I am to get to Southport, I have to recognize there has been no time since mid-February when I *could* have put 600 miles and a presumable 2½ months between Dr. Caulk and me. And that situation really hasn't changed. Krebiozen is still a hope, but only that. Sometimes I wonder if I should just submit to Barney's operation. I guess I must talk to him soon.

Did I tell you Ethelyn Giles wrote, saying she understood my cottage would be available for rent, and could she (or a client) have it for July? And I know of other rumors that make me wonder just what sort of stories are going around. All this is a reason for trying hard to make an appearance or two, so if Tuesday's cardiogram isn't too discouraging I plan to go through with the Garden Club affair, at least.

Now darling, this is a poor sort of letter and won't bring you much comfort, I'm afraid. It is such a paradox that to write of the lovely things that mean so much to us both is only to worsen the ache in our hearts—but, at least, darling, we must be glad that in all this loveliness—the song of a woodthrush in a fairy world of dogwood, whippoorwills on a moonlight night, beautiful music— each of us lives for the other.

All my love,
Rachel

SUNDAY

Darling [Dorothy], Now we have talked, and I am still hesitant about sending the apple I wrote yesterday. I thought I wouldn't, but I reread it and it does contain things I want to say. What I regret is the suggestion that perhaps you yourself can still come here this spring. After talking to you both this morning I know that can't be, and I must not add to your frustration by suggesting it. We can still hope for the summer, but if that is not to be—well, nothing that is ahead can be easy for either of us. There is the past to remember, at least. I suppose it is only human to want more and more of shared happiness.

We are going in for today's *Times* and will mail this. Always remember how much I love you.

Rachel

Darling [Rachel],

I've already written one letter to you this morning to send to Philadelphia.[24] But you must have one for the week-end at home and as I have more to say I'll go on.

The enclosed note was the one you returned in yesterday's letter—just a greeting to us from Stan's cousin Florence, who is awfully fond of him—she is older & was motherly to him when his mother died. He wanted you to see what she thinks of you—how precious the "reverend"! Has anyone, in all their tributes to you, ever suggested that? We must enlighten her about the doctor.

I am eagerly awaiting the "enclosed" which is "being mailed separately." I assume it's a picture. Good!

If there are any special directions about the freesias—depth, time to plant, etc., please send along. We think if we can find enough depth that the open spot between our house and Pink's would be good—at least, it's sunny and well drained. We are taking up some soil that has been sifted from our compost heap which should be a help. Well, it will be fun to try.

At Easter time there was still ice on the place where the daffodils bloomed last year. It's quite damp there so I'm wondering if they will appear. The rhodora was still alive but I'm not sure whether it had flower buds or not.

Darling, I would not blame you if you are thinking that we started the rumor that you would be renting your cottage this summer. But please, don't. You see, before we left here at Easter we said we must be so careful about discussing you while we were there. As I told you we did not see Harriet Orchard for which I was glad, for that very reason. The others—Phyllis Cook, Mrs. Pinkham, and Mrs. Weitzel, all of whom we saw only briefly—talked only of themselves and their problems after inquiring for our healths. They did not ask for you. So, dear, I am confident that nothing we said could have inspired Ethelyn to ask to rent your house.

You say, "I know of other rumors that make me wonder just what sort of stories are going around." Do you mean in the Boothbay region or elsewhere?

Now I come to something I could not say until you had first made the suggestion that your presence at Southport this summer is still very questionable. Dear Heart, that thought comes as no shock to me. I have carried it deep within me these long weeks, when I know you have been so miserable. I've marvelled that you could go on planning, or at least considering it with what seems like insurmountable stumbling blocks: your health, the 600 miles on the road, the

[24] RC was to travel to Philadelphia to receive a special commendation at the Garden Club of America's annual meeting.

need for the right kind of help, the distance from your doctors. So, darling, in a way I am prepared. To say that I can't imagine being there without you is an understatement. You know it would not be the same place at all—I wonder what I would do. Sometimes in those wakeful hours in the night when my spirit is low I find myself picturing the possibility—but I must not allow myself to do that.

If you aren't there, I shall try to make an adjustment. But until the time that I have to, I shall go on hoping. You said last night we need to hope.

But I am steeled for whatever comes.

And now for another part of your letter: You are sad for me because "serious troubles beset two of those dearest to you in all the world." It is a terribly hard situation, darling. Here I am, trapped, because I dare not leave one of the two, while the longing and need to be with the other one is almost beyond endurance. Sometimes I cannot understand why it must be this way and I fight desperately to change it. What is that quote?—"to accept what cannot be changed." I fear I have not yet accepted it.

And yet of the three of us, darling, I know my lot and my problems are the simplest. I feel so sorry for Stan—the man who used to be so vigorous, who rebels so at being an invalid—and when I see him doubled up on the bed with pain, his body so emaciated—I know I must not leave him for he needs me. And yet when he has his good days I find myself struggling to make plans to go to you.

For darling, of the three of us yours is the most serious, the most desperate situation, we know. And although I perhaps should not say it I'm sure we must face the fact that with you the time element is so uppermost. (Of course, to-day could be the last one for any of us but that is something we don't really believe.) And as you intimated and I so well know "We *need* to be together and this spring above all others!" That is why the cancellation of our visit was such a hard blow to endure.

What you are enduring and what you are facing is something I feel cannot be shared. I try desperately to live it with you and I can feel the unbelief, the despair, the rebellion, to a degree, but I'm sure not to the degree that would make me one with you in this experience—no one could unless they have faced it themselves. But please know, darling, that I live it with you every day.

And that is why I am glad that you can have Loren Eiseley and all the other reasons for hope.

How wonderful that you have established this pleasant relationship with him.

Darling, I've written freely—do you want me to or should I try to be restrained about how I feel?

You have been very close to me in this hour. I hope you realize what you mean to me.

> All my love, dear one,
> *Dorothy*

The freesias have just arrived.

Dearest [Dorothy],

Now we both revive old customs—letters to and from the traveller! Your letter reached me in time to be read before turning out the light, but service at the Sheraton leaves something to be desired. I asked for mail on arrival (about 4:30) and was told there was none. When we returned at long last from the dinner I asked again—same reply. But on reaching my room a green signal light was burning. This meant "message or letter at desk." So I had to ask that it be brought to me. The stamp indicated it had arrived at the hotel that morning! Well, it was sweet to have and did arrive at the right moment. And your letter intended for the week-end came just before I left home, so I cheated and read that, too. But both will last, and can be reread for days!

I know now (if never before) why I have never been a club-woman! Why anyone submits to a continuing round of affairs like this I'll never know. Yet some very sensible women do! First let me say I came through the ordeal quite unscathed physically, but it *was* an ordeal. I left home in 90 degree heat and was half cooked by the time the cab reached the station. Phila. was just as hot. Of course the hotel was reasonably comfortable, but the Art Museum, where the dinner was, never heard of air conditioning. I haven't been so uncomfortable in a long while. Candelabra on the tables didn't help. Well, I'll give you details when we are together, but it was a *long*, tedious, and curiously mismanaged affair, certainly not worth enduring for the sake of the citation itself, but I still think it was good to "put in an appearance."

And there were rewarding moments. One of the medalists was Mrs. Robert Woods Bliss, a wonderful old lady who, with her late husband, presented the Dumbarton Oaks property to Harvard University. She apparently retains direction of the famous gardens, because it was for this she received her medal. She has a fine, erect figure, beautiful red hair, lovely dark, almost violet eyes, fair skin with fine, patrician features—and she is 83! She had spoken so warmly to me before the dinner, saying she believed strongly in what I had said in *S.S.* "Do you ever come to Washington?" When I told her where I lived she asked if I wouldn't come to see her—something I'd love to do. Her acceptance speech was very moving, and one sentence engraved itself on my mind, for reasons that will be obvious—yet I think it has meaning for us all, regardless of age or condition. It sounded so like poetry that I couldn't be sure whether she was quoting. I asked her later and she seemed surprised and said oh no, it was just her own thought. It was something like this: "As the years grow short we must waste no time, for the far-reaching dreams unrealized will haunt us to the end."

I had a lovely talk this A.M. with Nellie Lee Bok. She is ill with a "bug" that has produced laryngitis, but despite this we had a satisfying telephone visit. She will be in Camden for the month of August, so we hope for a reunion then. She is still living at Gulph Mill but has sold it and will be moving soon to Phila. to be near her Rachel, who is apparently very happily married and expecting her second child. Enid, several years beyond graduation from Radcliffe, is studying political science at M.I.T., working on some formidable problem about space age problems, and recently *represented* M.I.T. at some conference where she was the only woman! Her mother sounded justifiably proud. She was so pleased I liked *Maria* so much—said Curtis knew it was his valedictory, and wrote it with an oxygen tent always at his elbow. His "far-reaching dream" realized!

We are having a rough ride now nearing Washington. I won't mail this today anyway, because there is plenty of time to have it awaiting you on your return Monday. I love to think of you now in the spot you love. I'll be interested to hear Hazel's reaction. She'll be glad you preserved the bathroom—I remember how she admired it. And of course I want to hear about all the sights, sounds, and smells of Southport.

Thursday morning I had a lovely early awakening and lay for a long time listening to the continuation of what awakened me—the song of a woodthrush. It seemed all the other birds were silent, allowing that beautiful voice to give its solo concert in the still morning air. It was a priceless prelude for any day.

Now goodbye for today, with all my dearest love—

Rachel

M A Y 1 5

Darling [Rachel],

Well, I guess this is the day that will go down in history as Rachel's triumph—May 15th—for surely your whole labor of 5½ years (for the past year has been as much a part of your creation as was the actual writing of *Silent Spring*) reached its positive conclusion to-day. And I doubt if you could have summed it up any better than did Eric Sevareid—"a voice of warning and a fire under the government."[25]

You must be powerfully happy to-night. How I long to be with you to share your exultation. I have thought so often what a perfect title *Silent Spring* has been for the uses to which it has been put. And because a woman wrote it I like the feminine quality of the sound of it as compared with *Man Against the Earth*. I'm sure Rachel Carson's name will be remembered longer than will Gordon Cooper's.[26] And poor Gordon is still out in space. Surely now at least one of "your far-reaching dreams" is realized so it won't have "to haunt you to the end." I'm so glad your two Philadelphia events are behind you so you can really enjoy this triumph.

Darling, I want to put something into your mind to work on. It's only another version of what I've proposed before.

Could you possibly escape for a few days soon after we get up to Southport to come to us there? If you could make a plane trip to Portland I'd meet you there, and for a few days it would be so wonderful to take care of you by the sea.

[25] "CBS Reports" broadcast "The Verdict on the Silent Spring of Rachel Carson," again with Eric Sevareid reporting.

[26] Mercury space program astronaut, the second American to orbit the earth in a space vehicle.

Your birthday is coming up soon—couldn't you make yourself a little birthday present of a few days away?

Speaking of that, we put your birthday box in the mail to-day—a little early but we wanted to get it on its way from here.

There are two gifts—one terribly practical, and the other equally frivolous!

This morning I awoke at 4:50 A.M. The dawn chorus is in full swing here[27] now—I have been afraid it wasn't going to develop. But it is as loud and shrill as ever. At first it seemed it was only robins—but a thousand of them saying "Cheer up, Cheer up, Cheer up" with a rhythm of which I'd never been conscious before. It was hard to pick out any other voice from the din. But finally the furor subsided just as in an orchestra when the solo instrument takes over. And, darling, my solo, like yours, was a woodthrush, so clear and bell-like. It was constant for a long while until finally an oriole threw in a few bubbles and the catbirds took up the main theme. Suddenly in what I thought was the catbirds chattering I was conscious of a quality of sound that was different, and I thought "Rose-breasted grosbeak." But it was not strong enough to identify.

After breakfast, before we went to work, Stan said, "Let's sit in the garden for a while," which we did. It's quite lovely now in spite of its neglect—a symphony in blue and white. The white derives mainly from the invading white violets. The flowering crabs are so full, so beautiful, and so fragrant. It had rained in the night so all was fresh. There are baby sparrows now in our bird box. A pair of catbirds and a pair of orioles were noisy and busy. The woodthrush rang in the woods beyond & we went to see if we could find him. But altho' he was too far into the tangle we were rewarded for soon I heard my mysterious singer and there, high in the oak was our gorgeous rose-breasted. We both had a long, perfect look at him as that breast flashed in the sun. For me, the joy of that moment lay in the fact that I had sensed his presence in the dawn chorus. That has happened twice before for me this year—lying in bed and recognizing a voice, but not completely sure, and later in the day having my thought confirmed by a catbird and a towhee. Those are the "little things" that give a glow to life these days.

For I am denied the big things, the biggest of which would be to be with you in this triumphal hour. To see you last night (I am now writing at 6 A.M.) on the screen gave me a sense of frustration that I could not touch you! And how I should have enjoyed seeing you descend the curving stairs in the spotlight and hearing the applause. If you were a surprise to most of them, as you think, I can imagine what an impact it was—Rachel Carson!!! No wonder you couldn't hear the organ. But their tribute must have been sweet music.

Thank you for giving us the delightful details. It seemed like old times. For I have missed so much of the intimate events—just at a time when the events are Big Ones.

Well, I mustn't complain for I am so thrilled, so proud, so humble to know that I am near you in your thoughts during all these momentous happenings.

And I am quite overcome knowing that I am so close to a national figure. I almost wish at times I had the old sense of awe I had when there was that abyss between that separated me from the famous author. But there isn't, and I think perhaps you are glad. Of course, you are still on a pedestal but that position is for what you've accomplished—my worship is for what you are, darling, in spite of all your fame.

A thought struck me last night, that suddenly the dear old *Sea Around Us* has been displaced. I never dreamed that it could ever happen—that now I think your fame will rest on *Silent Spring*—when people talk about you they'll say "Oh yes, the author of *Silent Spring*," for I suppose there are people who never heard of *The Sea Around Us*, strange as that may seem to us, but surely, I doubt if there is a household in this country where your name is unknown. How could it be from "Peanuts" to "CBS Reports"—not to mention all the lawns which have become a major concern now—what to do for crabgrass because Rachel Carson says—!

Oh, Darling, the woodthrushes and orioles have been sounding your praises while I've been writing. This spring is far from silent, and because of you there is a chance now that future springs need not be! Bless your heart. I don't suppose you can put into words how you feel about all this so I shall just try to feel *with* you.

By the time this reaches you we will be well packed for Southport. Stan is so anxious to get there. And I do hope he is going to be better after we get there. He has developed a fear complex about eating now and perhaps the change of environment will help. Of course, you must know there is a great sadness for me to be moving farther away from you. But my great hope is that you will join me there some way.

Remember my invitation to stay with us for as long as you can, if you can't be there long enough to make it worthwhile to open your house.

Darling, if only I could fly to you to-day—just to hold you in my arms for a few moments.

LATER

More excitement to our morning, including *you* but that must wait as we've decided to go to Norwood to cemetery, & a call on Pink.

One parting thought: Stan has just volunteered to take care of Roger & Jeffie while you and I go to Sweden!

A mountain of love,
Dorothy

Darling [Dorothy],

This should reach you on your birthday. I hope you were not disappointed by the early call. I felt it would be hard to know when to call on Saturday, having no idea what the birthday activities would be, and besides we have always found conversations in the midst of company—even family—not too satisfactory. Now I want to talk with you this way, but am finding myself greatly distracted by the radio in the dentist's office, where I'm waiting for Roger. A very modern, attractive office, but I could do without the entertainment.

I *know* you understand, but I've been unhappy at not writing you since our visit.[28] I haven't, have I? It has been a whirl reminiscent of last year—oh, not quite such intolerable pressures, but I feel I'm in a bad dream, trying to reach that goal of readiness to go, and always finding new obstacles. It is a great disappointment not to leave next week, but I honestly don't see how I could have been ready. And now I know it would have been a sacrifice for Jeanne, I'm glad the reasons for delay aren't one-sided.

When Mrs. Pinkham gets the key, will you tell her we are delayed? I had asked her to come Saturday and help unpack & now I won't want her until Wednesday. I'll try to write her and tell her this, and precisely what I want done before we come, but just in case I don't you'd better mention the change of plans.

I've put off taking poor Roger to the dentist shamefully and now there is much more work than I realized. We have two more appointments next week.

I'm having a time finding a dress[29]—this is the wrong time of year. The "Proms" have cleaned them out and the new lot isn't in. So far I have found only two possibilities, both too expensive for the limited use I make of them. But it takes *time* to hunt!

Roger and I are at the moment having dinner at the Hot Shoppe—time has moved on—and we've just spent $69 on camp equipment. It makes a *dent* in the list, but there is still a lot to get!

Now I must stop so this can be mailed as we leave. I *wanted* to be there on the first day of summer! Mark the spot of the sunset for me and tell the baby squirrels not to grow up too fast.

I'm so glad you are *there* for your birthday. And I hope the crowds won't have arrived. You know I'll be with you in spirit, all day—as I always am anyway.

My dearest love
Rachel

Darling,

I want to try to explain my feelings about the summer. In the first place, I suppose we must remember that so easily—with just a tiny change in any of several conditions—I wouldn't have gotten to Maine at all. So I hope you and I can

[28] RC and Roger had flown to Maine on May 29 for a five-day visit at Southport with the Freemans, who had arrived there on May 19.

[29] For a dinner at which RC was to receive a conservation award from the Isaak Walton League of America.

let our thankfulness that there is to *be* another summer outweigh any disappointment that perhaps I will have to make special arrangements. But first let me try to make you understand why I can't accept your generous offer to spend nights at your house as any sort of routine practice. It's precisely because I love you so much that I can't let any compulsion exist—any situation where you could possibly feel, "Oh dear, it isn't convenient but we have to do this." Your other activities mustn't be interfered with. (The only parallel I can think of is that one shouldn't borrow money from friends—not an apt comparison but you know what I mean.) This doesn't mean, of course, that I won't ever come, but occasional visits for a special treat are very different. And you know how welcome you'll be whenever you can come to me!

As to my staying alone for the seven weeks, it would probably be quite all right. I dislike very much the thought of joining the category of those who need caretakers! There are two reasons why the doctors—and Virginia, Marie, etc.—don't like the idea. One is the heart condition. I needn't explain that; you have the same thoughts about Stan. The other is the back! The condition existing there now is known as a compression fracture. A fall, I have been warned, could have extremely serious results. This I mostly choose to forget, and probably never mentioned. But the other day, walking along the street with Roger, I turned my ankle and came close enough to falling that it scared me. (As it was, I suffered nothing worse than a bad backache for several days.) It would be wiser, I suppose, to have someone around much of the time so that such a thing would at least be discovered soon.

If I have any hesitation about having Lois, darling, it stems entirely from the wish—the determination, rather—that *nothing* must in any way marr our happiness this summer. There must be long days when we can go off together alone. There must be many opportunities for us to do together the things we love to do. But I feel this can be, even when Lois is there. She is used to being alone, and will expect and want to be alone a great deal. I think this is one of the difficulties she is finding in adjusting to the new life. She said, "I wish I could crawl into a hole." I think it will mean much to her to be with people who understand and respect her wish. I know you and Stan will love her, and will find her a wonderful person. All of us together can do much for her, I know.

If I *did* have to go off for treatment, I thought Lois could take care of the cats, with counsel from you! But I don't expect to, so that isn't a factor. I thought I'd have her come about mid-July, for perhaps 3 weeks. Then if I want to I can urge her to stay and I'm sure she would. Now this must be all. A queer sort of birthday letter, but let me just add—I love you.

R.

Waiting at dentist's

Dearest [Dorothy],

I shouldn't give you a blow by blow account of this mid-summer night's dream (nightmare?) but it seems it might help. Don't be alarmed; everything will straighten out in time, but today it just seems everything is coming apart at the seams. The day started early. I dropped Roger at school (for rehearsal) at 8:35 and proceeded on to Pohanka's to leave the car. Then I took a bus to Chevy Chase Circle, where Jeanne picked me up. Then she told *her* (true) nightmares. Perhaps I've mentioned that her 80 + -year-old father came east from California in May expecting to have surgery for a hernia. However, the surgeon he consulted here preferred to avoid an operation if possible. Well, he became very uncomfortable last Friday, and the doctor decided he'd have to operate after all. At first Jeanne thought this was going to cut out her trip to Maine, but now it has been set up for July 1 or 2, I think. Anyway, she can go as planned—provided, of course, there isn't a further emergency!

Then, calamity #2, she has to take him for a complete physical—several appointments—this week, so she won't be able to help me any more this week.

#3—Ida told me when I got home that an aunt had died in Richmond, so she has to go to the funeral *Wednesday*, the day of my dinner—and so I'll be without help *and* without my Roger-sitter. I'd asked her to stay that night. Virginia is in bed with some strange and probably infectious ailment, so he can't go there. Well, if we ever get out of this dentist's office I'll call Adgerina and see if she can come. (P.S. later: Adgerina is coming to the rescue.)

You are probably aching all over by now—but I guess that's about all, except I'm bushed! I left with Jeanne at 4, took a cab from Silver Spring to Pohanka's, drove out in heavy traffic to the school, waited half an hour for rehearsal to end, started for home, had to return from halfway for Roger's glasses—got home for a snack which I ate in bed, and came over here.

Now the bra is the monumental problem awaiting solution. I tried by telephone—two places out of my size or anything near it, in the low back kind—"because of vacation time!"

Oh well, *I knew*—

Now it's Tuesday and I don't know what I knew, except that I shouldn't have told you all this tale of woe. A good night's sleep made it all seem more possible to cope with.

Poor Bea has given me a permanent this morning. I'm under the drier now. And the wig is cleaned and re-set. I have to pick up my dress this afternoon and must deliver the White Rabbit to school by 6 P.M. And I'm thinking in terms of getting Roger's foot locker and duffle bag off to camp by Friday, but I doubt my trunk can be ready to go then. Harvey will work both Sat. and Sun. and can pack the car.

Tomorrow I go for my last injection (here) and will take Roger to be vaccinated. Henrietta Poynter (Marie's cousin) has offered me the use of her apartment to dress for dinner. This will be a great help if it is either hot or raining, because there I could get into a cab without getting wet. However, if it is a fine night I guess I'll just taxi from home.

I was glad to have the list of your Bent volumes. I think I'll pack up the others, or at least those I think we might want, and ship them direct to you. Perhaps you'll want to read up on some of the birds you are going to talk about to the Garden Club. A day or so after you told me about that, I had a letter from the president. They had voted to make me an honorary member, and she also said she hoped I was coming to the luncheon. (I can't remember receiving an earlier invitation but she seemed to think I had.) So I immediately wrote yes, to both propositions. Don't be silly—of course you are a good speaker, and you are the very one to open their eyes to the birds around us, to paraphrase a certain book title. Seriously, I've been so impressed for a number of years with the wonderful birding experiences you've had, and also with your persistence in tracking down voices and identifying what you see. And remember, I let you hear me speak—now it's my turn to be in the audience.

Now I must stop—almost dry, and besides I haven't yet thought about what I'm going to say tomorrow night.

A week from today I'll see you.[30]

All my love
Rachel

[30] RC, Roger, and Jeanne Davis arrived in Southport on June 25. Roger spent July at a nearby camp.

[SUMMER 1963]

[Dear Dorothy,]

Would you help me search for a fairy cave on an August moon and a low, low tide? I would love to try once more, for the memories are precious.

[Love, *Rachel*]

SEPTEMBER 10

Dear One [Dorothy],

This is a postscript to our morning at Newagen, something I think I can write better than say. For me it was one of the loveliest of the summer's hours, and all the details will remain in my memory: that blue September sky, the sounds of wind in the spruces and surf on the rocks, the gulls busy with their foraging, alighting with deliberate grace, the distant views of Griffiths Head and Todd Point, today so clearly etched, though once half seen in swirling fog. But most of all I shall remember the Monarchs, that unhurried westward drift of one small winged form after another, each drawn by some invisible force. We talked a little about their migration, their life history. Did they return? We thought not; for most, at least, this was the closing journey of their lives.

But it occurred to me this afternoon, remembering, that it had been a happy spectacle, that we had felt no sadness when we spoke of the fact that there would be no return. And rightly—for when any living thing has come to the end of its life cycle we accept that end as natural.

For the Monarch, that cycle is measured in a known span of months. For ourselves, the measure is something else, the span of which we cannot know. But the thought is the same: when that intangible cycle has run its course it is a natural and not unhappy thing that a life comes to its end.

That is what those brightly fluttering bits of life taught me this morning. I found a deep happiness in it—so, I hope, may you. Thank you for this morning.

Rachel

SEPTEMBER *12, EARLY MORNING*

Dearest [Rachel],

How wonderful that against the backdrop of sadness of our coming separation we have found a sweet happiness: two lovely crystal days of blue skies, Maine air and the joy in little things. Little things such as a soaring osprey, the sound and sight of kinglets in a bush and Monarch butterflies! All shared at the end of this our tenth summer of sharing. What fragrant memories will always arise as we live again those ten exquisite summers, dear.

I am so grateful to the Butterflies for bringing to me the precious thoughts you captured tangibly. Please know this message before me now is one of the loveliest possessions I shall cherish always.

And so in these last days I remember a passage I once quoted to you: "In the dew of little things the heart finds its morning and is refreshed." I hope your heart has found a morning. Mine has.

Darling, I love you—allways.
Dorothy

MONDAY, SEPTEMBER *16*

Dearest [Dorothy],

It seems strange to be back in the land of mockingbirds, cardinals, and numerous mourning doves—a different world, indeed, in all ways! It always seems as though a curtain had fallen, separating one "Act" from the next.

Your letter arrived this morning as you hoped—now I'm curious about the Bath postmark. Some pleasant expedition, I hope. I'm sad I missed the Northern Lights, but as always you described them in a way that makes me see them. I'm glad we did see some of that tumult on the bay—and hear the wind and surf.

Yes, what a leave-taking! I suppose there were compensations, but that day I couldn't see them. I wanted a last, quiet look at the bay, from the deck. I wanted to say goodbye at Moppet's grave.[31] Instead, to have all the last moments occupied with the purely physical problem of whether I could or could not get to the car! As far as our own leave-taking was concerned, perhaps it was the best.

This is just to report that with rest the pain and difficulties are gradually subsiding. I am to see Dr. Caulk tomorrow afternoon, so shall know a great deal more 24 hours from now. I shall take Ida along, for I'll need a chair. Yes, it is wonderful to have her again.

Roger got off to school this morning, looking very fine in his dress-up clothes. I'll write tomorrow or Wednesday.

All my love

Rachel

A note from Anne says "I'll bet Moppet is the cutest little black cat in cat heaven." Strangely, Jeffie doesn't seem to search for her, though obviously enjoying his new freedom. But he has settled into the old routine of long naps in my closet, head on a shoe.

WEDNESDAY A.M., SEPTEMBER 18

Dearest [Dorothy],

I'm wondering what kind of weather you are having. We have scarcely seen the sun since our return. However, it has by now warmed up to Maine-like temperatures (60's in the morning) and this morning I had coffee on the porch before calling Roger. My rewards were a bright-eyed titmouse and a wren, singing lustily while hunting his breakfast.

Most of yesterday afternoon was spent at the hospital—I've been X-rayed practically from chin to ankles! I'm not going to make a long story of it, but as I was well aware there is new trouble. All of the pelvic bones on the left side are involved, and there is ample explanation for the pain and lameness I've experienced most of the summer. In fact, I feel very fortunate, knowing how things are, to have gotten back from that precious country of rocks and root-crossed paths without a fall that would have spelled disaster.

Dr. Caulk would like to try the testosterone phosphorous treatment, but wants to talk to Barney first. (He returns this week-end.) However, this would not preclude Barney's treatment later. The phosphorous business will take about two weeks, and by the time I go to California[32] should have me in less pain, and walking better. Dr. Caulk is a dear—says he will gladly come to the house to give the treatments, to save me the now difficult trip there. However, he may want to give me a few X-ray treatments first, directed to the worst area. I am quite willing to go along with his recommendations, and trust Barney will be, too. I suspect before many months pass I shall try both treatments. This, of course, is for the bones only, while the pituitary implantation, if successful, might get the whole situation under better control.

[31] RC's cat, Moppet, had died at Southport on September 9.

[32] The trip, planned for mid-October, was to deliver a lecture in San Francisco at the Kaiser Medical Center.

[33] By Sterling
North, published
in 1963.

Dr. Caulk showed me pictures of that darling little raccoon they are raising. When I get a little better I do want to go and see her. He had read *Rascal*[33]
at my suggestion this summer, and says theirs is quite like Rascal—"a female
counterpart."

Ida went with me yesterday and was such a help—did grocery shopping
while I sat in car, took me down in a wheelchair, etc. I could drive only partway
and then take a cab, because of course I couldn't walk in from the parking lot.

I hear Ida coming now. Breakfast in bed—what a luxury!

Now I want to send this out for the mailman, so will hurry.

So you may go to Merrymeeting Bay again! It should be even more interesting as the fall advances. Remember all the details to tell me.

Thank you for going back to check on the house. Betty does do a good job,
and without us there to get in the way I'm sure she sped right along. I forgot to
mention to her again the possibility of borrowing your buffer to do a better job
on those floors. No matter, it can be done next spring.

I almost forgot to tell you—Dr. Murphy phoned yesterday to say that the
American Geographical Society (in which he has long been active) wish to give
me an award at their dinner Dec. 5th. It will be at the St. Regis in N.Y. This is not
to be mentioned—actually the committee doesn't meet to confirm it until Oct.
but I guess he wanted to be sure I'd save the date. This means I'll just settle down
in N.Y. for several days so come along!

Now I really must stop. You know I'm with you in spirit, still drinking in
with you the loveliness of the Maine fall, always remembering all the kind, loving, and thoughtful things you both did to help and to bring happiness to our
days there.

All my love
Rachel

I will remember to send check for laundry soon or will you tell me what it is &
then I'll pay you.

TUESDAY A.M., SEPTEMBER 24

Dearest [Dorothy],

You don't mind, do you, if I use some obsolete stationery for you? This is
the interval between Roger's departure and Ida's arrival—now only a half hour
or less, since Roger isn't picked up until about 8:35. He looks very fine and
young-gentlemanish in his school "uniform" this year.

Interruptions for telephone and breakfast; meanwhile, Jeffie got his
work in on this sheet, but I know you won't mind his trademarks.

Jeanne came yesterday, and high time—the study is a shambles. All
first-class mail had been opened but was reposing unsorted (and of course unanswered) in the big canvas bag. A lot of the other mail had never been

opened. I dictated until lunch time, then left her to cope with the mess while I went to the hospital. I've worked out a system so I can go without involving my helpers. I drive to the Langley shopping center (where you bought my cake box). There is a cab stand there, and I take a cab down to the hospital. Once there, I telephone Dr. Caulk's department and they send an orderly with a chair. Yesterday I went down under my own power, but Dr. Caulk gave orders I was not to do so again.

He plans to talk to Barney this morning—feeling the first day back (yesterday) would not be good. So a decision may be reached this afternoon about the new treatment. Meanwhile I'm receiving radiation over two rather large areas, one over the pelvic bones on the left, one over the ribs on the left. Not surprisingly, I feel weak and at times nauseated. It is too soon to feel any relief from the discomfort.

Darling, I couldn't help laughing when I read of your afterthought—that somehow the lot of you could have carried me to the car in a chair! As if I'd let you! To hear you, one would suppose you and Stan are as young and husky as the junior Freemans!

Well, I wouldn't want to live that day over. I'll admit now that some rather frantic thoughts were racing through my mind, and I couldn't imagine enduring that long trip, and yet I knew I had to. There is a pubic fracture in such a location that it probably is what happened that morning. It would probably have happened sometime, anyway, (there are others) but it wasn't the best timing, I must say.

Did you have an aurora Sunday night? We did—the best display here in many years, according to the paper. Not daring to walk out in the dark, I got in the car and drove just to the end of our drive, where the northwestern sky is all open and unobstructed. Many pulsating white streamers, but no color.

The moon has been lovely, and of course I've seen it in imagination as it must have peeped into my tide pool and set the moonfish to swimming across the bay.

Your letters[34] have been precious, dear. Of course I especially loved the one about your walk at Newagen—all the lovely details. When you named all the different shrubs I could see each one. And the cross bills! I remember the thrill of seeing a flock of them feeding in pine trees once years ago. And I saw them in the W. Virginia mountains, too. I hope you can see them again and get a good look at those extraordinary bills.

Well, I must stop, but not until I tell you briefly that there was another call from Lois, 48 hours after the one I reported. I won't attempt details, which are the usual confused tangle, but she is at another motel in the Boulder area, has seen Cris again, and even met with him, and a lawyer. She seems about to do a complete flip and go back to Cris—I *guess* to Crag Cabin, though I don't know. Anyway, I am quite discouraged with the whole mess. I guess one might as well try to stop the lemmings from running into the sea. So from here on I'll be an

[34] Preserved are eleven letters DF wrote to RC from Southport after RC's departure. Each describes in detail the plants, animals, birds, weather, dawns, or night skies of autumn on the Maine coast.

observer and keep my advice to myself. I wanted so much for that book to get written, but now I don't think it ever will. I gather Lake George will remain an address that will eventually reach her, whatever she does. I told her you had written and she was thrilled. She had already arranged for the Boulder mail to be sent to Lake George, but was going to try to intercept it.

Please keep telling me the details of your walks and trips—through you I can see and hear what I can't experience myself. Darling, you do know that my return is only a dream—a lovely dream.

All my love always
Rachel

Will be eager to hear how Dr. Andrews found Stan. I do hope he is feeling better now that peace & quiet have returned.[35] Love to him, too.

SUNDAY NIGHT, SEPTEMBER 29

Dearest [Dorothy],

This notepaper was sent me by some schoolchildren in Cincinnati. I understand they made it. Isn't it attractive?

Again your long letter[36] was a treat, sharing another of your post-season trips. How fortunate you have been in these experiences—and I in hearing about them!

This is just to report that, as you know, I'm starting the phosphorous tomorrow. Bea Riegel is going to drive me down. I was hesitant about the rather difficult trip as I've been making it, especially since walking has been rather more difficult the past few days. She had urged me to call if I needed help, so I did. I shall have to go only tomorrow, Wed. & Sat.

Poor Mark's[37] situation is very bad, at least as to the future. I guess he has withstood the operation itself well. But lymph nodes also were involved, and you know what that means. The growth went behind trachea, surrounded nerves to vocal cords, etc. It is certainly a pitiful situation.

Lois called Friday night. She has gone back to that "Ox Yoke" motel where she had been just before coming east.[38] This is what Cris wants at the moment, at least. So I guess it isn't to be Crag Cabin. He *says* he will pay her rent, but he also announced a plan to attack her Harper royalties. Quite a bargain!! I told her I had learned Colorado does *not* have a community property law and he has no claim on her money. She said, "Oh, what a fool I have been!" At some point the lawyer said to her that if she didn't "take" Cris now she might never have "another chance"!!! After considering this she said, "I'll go."

Her present address is Ox Yoke, Sedalia Rt. 2, Colo. I suppose there would be a certain danger that Cris might sample her mail, but it would surely be a great kindness to write her of such things as Maine in autumn—reports from the world she glimpsed. She did get your letter, by the way, and was thrilled to have it.

[35] Stanley had spent the first week of August in the hospital after experiencing chest pains and nausea.

[36] DF had described Acadia National Park.

[37] Son of RC's neighbors, Paul and Betsy Reimer.

[38] During the last week of August, Lois Crisler had visited RC at Southport.

Rain on the roof—but not hard enough to discourage the crickets from their nocturnal chant.

I do hope to hear that the X-rays *and* tooth-pulling were not too much and that you are both fit. Thank you for taking care of the laundry. I'm broke tonight and don't want to bother you with a check, so will put the money in my next.

You know you are always in the background of my thoughts. Now this carries my deepest love.

Rachel

WEDNESDAY EVE, OCTOBER 2

Darling [Rachel],

You and I have been walking on the Head in the moonlight. Do you remember the night we lay there in that lovely light? I told you you looked like alabaster. You did. How happy we were then.

Last night at 3:40 A.M. moonlight shining through the leaves of Pink's birch tree awakened me. I sat up in bed. A path of molten silver as wide as my whole window led from the dark rocks below across the Bay to Georgetown. And the moon fishes were swimming from shore to shore.

A noise outside sent me to Martha's room to the window overlooking our garbage pail. There was our mysterious invader. It was not a skunk for it was light colored in the moonlight and it was much too large.

I rushed to waken Stan, and when we both looked out the brightness of the moon revealed dark rings around its tail. And so we have a Rascal. He was struggling so with the pail which he already had on its side, but as you know the cover has to be lifted in just one spot.

Eventually, he stood on his hind feet & with front feet rolled it almost to the freesia bed.

And then more struggle until he finally gave up & began to move away. As he did so I pursed my lips to make a kissing sound whereupon he looked up at us, his eyes bright and the moonlight revealing the dear little face with its mask. He was so appealing we both uttered a delighted long-drawn out "Oh-oh-oh."

Then he went under the house. Several times I went back to look for he finally managed to get the pail around the washing machine & close to the house, where eventually he must have found the clue to opening it. His feet marks were all over it. Poor dear—all it contained were two grapefruit skins, egg shells and some lamb chop bones—I fear he didn't find the reward worth the effort. I wanted terribly to throw him a sandwich. He was larger than a spaniel dog & so fat & fluffy!

The episode ended when the moon left a red path across the water—I went to sleep and it went to bed.

That was the conclusion of a remarkable 24 hours[39] which I shall try to write about in my next letter.

[39] Spent on the sea and outdoors at Southport.

At 5:30 the moon was so glorious on the water I couldn't go back to sleep. At 6:30 Stan said, "Let's get up." We saw the full moon set and the sunrise from Charlesworths' at precisely the same moment. Now we have just returned from a long soul satisfying walk—through our path to Parula Paradise & back via Tenggrens' ridge.

I remembered what you said of wanting to experience Beauty and then share it. Surely I am experiencing it these days past understanding. If only I could share it. I want so badly to make you see it.

Your letter came yesterday along with two from Lois—one for Stan, who had sent her a topographical map of the region which she had expressed a wish for, and one for me. Both from Ox Yoke Motel—with about the same story you wrote with these added details: "My cabin has its drawbacks—cold, dark, barn-like, no bath or shower. But—Blondie can chase rabbits!"

As for yourself, darling, my heart aches for you. I think I don't need to tell you that I am living all these hours with you in spirit, and praying that the new treatment will bring relief. I was shocked when you said that walking was even more difficult.

I feel so guilty writing you of what joys I am having and which you would revel in. But you asked me to.

Stan is going to P. O. now so I'll end with

All my deep love,
Dorothy

<hr>

THURSDAY MORNING, OCTOBER 3

Dearest [Dorothy],

This is the day you expect Stanley—I gather the others aren't coming. I hope the weather will be just right for what I suppose will be the final visit of the season.

I am so relieved that Stan's X-rays went off without incident, and I hope the report is a good one. What a wretched experience that was about the chimney! It makes me feel I'd like to have mine cleaned on general principles. I didn't understand what you meant about creosote? What was that from? You were certainly fortunate, not only to have Mr. Lewis, but to have a helper provided for him by chance. I hope all the unpleasant smoky odors are gone by now.

Our trunks have only just come—3 weeks on the way! I feel the REA express, like most other "services," gets worse by the day. I don't know how they managed it, but the tray in Roger's was damaged. Also, the lock was jammed so the key wouldn't work. I had a casualty—I had decided to bring home those four Rowantree mugs and felt I packed them with great care. But two were broken. Well, Mr. Cable would be happy to send me more.

I enjoyed hearing about the children's piano lessons—that must make Grandma happy. I don't think I reported I am about to have a flutist in my family. The school has brought in a man to teach various instruments in the hope of someday having a little orchestra. After his first visit to demonstrate the various instruments Roger came home with a surprisingly strong desire to take up the flute. Actually, I'd had no thought of his going into it at all. But one can rent the instruments for 3 months, and by that time we can see if he is serious about it. He got to try out for it Tuesday, and reported that of those interested in the flute he did best, so he will be the "first flutist." He said "when I can make the noise at all it sounds pretty good."

Well, I've just had my phosphorous cocktail. Only two more to go—one at home tomorrow, and then I go down Saturday so I can have the last injection, too. This *has* to work! Actually things have been pretty rough for the past week, with increased pain skipping around from one area to another. Some days walking has been all but impossible. Now a medicine for the pain has my stomach so upset that I could keep nothing down all day yesterday. So I guess for a while I'll just tolerate the pain. They don't seem able to find anything my stomach will accept.

After the week-end I was discouraged to the point that I told Dr. Caulk I really had to know whether he had any confidence I could go to California— that I should tell the Kaiser people *now* if there is real doubt. He still feels I'll be enough better after this treatment, so I'm trying to have faith, but I must say it is hard to believe there can be such a change within two weeks.

Have I told you that I am planning to return via Claremont for a little visit with the Hards? I feel a great desire to see them once more, in their lovely home. If things work out, I will stay over a night or two with them before returning. We have corresponded about this, and now Fred is in Washington for a couple of days and we have just had a long telephone conversation.

A letter from Lois, written from that Oxbow place, but there is talk about a "dark cabin" somewhere that she may take ($35 a month). Cris will try to fix it up a little—suggests she get skis for winter travel!!! I notice she gives the Lake George address on the envelope so (not for the first time) I am confused.

Now if this is to go out for the mailman I must stop. It is not easy to write you these days, dear. I think of that little paradise you are inhabiting—the autumn loveliness, the birds, the seals, the sunsets and I don't want details of my very different days to break in upon the peace and contentment of this time. But give me your "good thoughts" that somehow this ally I now have in my bones will be able to win this battle for me—your thoughts and your prayers, too.

> And now, all my love goes with this—
> *Rachel*

Dearest [Dorothy],

All your letters are being marked with an identifying label on the envelope so they can be picked out for re-reading easily—"Raccoon," "Walk at Newagen," etc. They really are precious. If only you would write up this spectacle of fall migration that you are being privileged to witness. It should be shared with others! You don't need to consider whether it would be part of a book—just do it for itself. The birds in the bushes like notes on a musical score—what a touch!! Do you really know how fortunate you are to be seeing and experiencing all this? I know you do in a way, but perhaps only one who has lost all such things can really know.

I think these migrations follow coastlines wherever possible—down from Nova Scotia and along the Maine coast, then from some point across to the Cape. So some backtracking (as to the islands) rather than a direct southerly course is not surprising. The Head must be a wonderful point of convergence—I think you have many more migrants than I ever had at my place.

I'm so sorry your last days have to be shadowed by the news of Stan's X-rays[40] (one reason I regretted his having them there.) But do keep in mind the fact that Dr. Bowles[41] may have entirely different ideas and might even interpret the films differently.

By the way, I have a reprint Betsy Reimers gave me for Stan, which I'll send soon, and hope he will show it to Dr. B. It concerns some new work showing that people who have had a gastrectomy & related surgery often have trouble digesting certain carbohydrates—having lost the tissues that produce the proper enzyme. This is why they stay thin and have various troubles. A simple change in the *kind* of starches and sugars eaten corrects the difficulty. This has done wonders for Paul.

I'm enclosing $5 for laundry, but please tell me whether this is right. The bill itself says $4.90, but on the back several figures are totaled to $9.10. I know he was paid up when I left, but tell me if he collected more.

I have moments of optimism about next week, but hours when the thought of going seems absurd!

Now back to my writing. All my dearest love.

Rachel

UNDER THE DRIER

Darling [Rachel],

Time to talk to you again. First, to tell you that your letter enclosing the $5.00 bill arrived safely. Your laundry was, as the bill showed, $4.90. The other figuring on the back was the total I owed that day for mine and yours. So that answers your question.

[40] Showing gallstones.

[41] Correct spelling is "Boles."

This A.M. we saw Dr. Andrews & I hasten to tell you that my fears have been allayed somewhat—this is in reference to what I wrote recently that I was worried about Stan but didn't burden you with detail. One reassuring bit—he has gained almost 4 pounds in the three weeks since we saw Dr. D. & that includes the period of enemas, castor oil and fasting. Of the other items I'll write more when there is more time.

Dr. D. feels that surgery is the only safe solution to the gallstones, but I think Dr. Boles may be inclined to let well enough alone if we can keep him comfortable with diet. Well, we shall see. For once I am not worrying on the operation score & Stan *says* he is not either.

So we're going to try to live one day at a time.

I think of you constantly knowing these are crucial days for you. Oh, how I wish your San Francisco trip could have been accomplished without question or uncertainty. At best it can't be easy for you.

Now in what time is left to write I'll attempt to mention some Little Things on my list—things of no consequence except that they are for you and me.

The lovely lavenderish blue asters have been breath-takingly lovely (emphasis by repetition). In our travels they have banked the roadside only growing about two feet tall, offset by the yellow of the goldenrod—but for me the loveliest spot of all I discovered in the pre-dawn light on the Head. As the light intensified, the color deepened—there they were, as I saw them growing out of a long fissure in the granite exactly marking the spot beneath which is Our Cave. That morning the tide was right for the muffled booming sound which had, years ago, told me there was a cave below.

As I stood there all the memories flooded over me of the thrill of our first discovery; of the morning you and Stan and I bobbed around in the skiff; and of the morning you and I were able to enjoy it with a calm sea. No need to list all we saw.

Probably we may never see it again—but I am content, just as I am about the Fairy Cave. I'm sure nothing could ever quite equal those first experiences—we might even be disappointed. And so I'm happy with the memories. And how rich I feel to have the blue aster as a reminder—such brave flowers, apparently just growing out of the rock.

To compliment the blue of the asters is the golden yellow of an amazing growth I found in Parula Paradise. A huge mound of gold in the late afternoon sunshine, the yellow leaves so large the trunk & limbs were completely hidden. The shape resembled maple leaves but so large? But for once I got some help from the books—striped maple, more a shrub than a tree. And recently I found a companion piece over on Tenggrens' ridge. I was so glad I could name it. In the summer it would have been just a part of the general greenery—but now transformed to golden glory. There, more on the list but I'm dry & want to mail this on the way home.

We plan to go to Orono to-morrow. Will stay at Link View Lodge over one night.

Days continue glorious & in spite of anxiety I think both Stan and I consider this one of our happiest intervals.

> More to come, dear
> I love you *so*!
> Dorothy

MONDAY EVENING, OCTOBER 14

Dear Heart [Rachel],

Late this afternoon you and I strolled about your beloved spot for a last look for 1963. As I drove in, the maple tree directly ahead as you start down the little rise on your road was yellow gold—the leaves still intact, with a westering sun gleaming through them. The earlier coloring maples have dropped all their leaves. As I started down the steps beside the garden a Monarch butterfly gave a lingering kiss to this clover. I wonder if he is on his way to California, too. Moppet's little grave is still green—some brave yellow Marigolds are blooming nearby. The masses of scarlet huckleberry never fail to amaze me and your ledges from shore to house are all afire—juniper and bayberry mingled their greens with it. The sun was warm so I lingered in it on the porch for a while but then decided I wanted to see that banking from the shore, with my back to the sun. The shutters on the door and window hurt me as I went down the path, and a thousand memories rose up to clutch my heart—memories of you and me happily moving through the bushes.

And of course, I never go over those rocks from the spruce to the beach without that remembrance of that dark night of phosphorescence. What delight. I went out to the second ridge of dry rocks to lean against them for a long while drinking in the beauty. The white birches with their yellow dresses shone brightly but of course the huckleberry dominated the scene. And can you imagine the thoughts that possessed me as I looked—all the lovely, sweet times together?

Then, later, as the tide was low enough I skirted the waxy sloping rocks on the seaweed to go over to the salt pond, stopping to pick a few garnets out of the old boulder, quite crumbly now.

The maples around the pond still have their leaves in many variegated colors so that seems to be the last of the glory. Roger's raft is high so I doubt that any storms will move it. I broke into your woods from the road, to cut up across the wooded area to the look-out spot above Steeveses'. I think that is one of my favorites—to look down on that sea of spruces, so lush, so green. And remembrances of warm afternoons when we sat there watching the blue sky with whatever creatures passed over us. And the dear little warblers in the spruces. Today only one chick-a-dee was about but he sang a lively song. Reindeer moss is dry and crisp underfoot while the checkerberry leaves have turned a dark, dark shiny green with red berries peaking from beneath. And thus I said good-bye, and I'll confess I couldn't see too well as I walked back to the car.

To-day has been warm with less wind so that the stillness is almost audible. In this lovely hush a noise of a human is almost unbearable. I sat on the Head when I came back & was startled to hear a door shut. I couldn't imagine—then I realized someone was at Cutlers'. But it wasn't right to intrude on the peace. Without the wind I am even conscious of the stillness of the trees and I realize that we have had an unusual amount of wind.

About a half hour before sundown we wandered up to Waneceks' where we had a broad view. It was warm enough so we sat on the rocks capturing all we can against the winter. Even before the sun set, streamers of ducks began crossing the western sky. They seem to take a course over the Kennebec now so they are barely discernible with the naked eye. But what fun with the glasses. As the flocks wavered and changed position Stan talked to them—"Come on, don't hang behind," "Get together fellows," etc. How wonderful that on the 14th of Oct. on the coast of Maine we were perfectly comfortable out on the rocks until it grew too dark to see the birds.

This is going to meet you in California. I do hope all goes well and right with you. Again let me say how glad I am that you are there. Please be awfully careful, dear. I think back to those early days when, if you went away, I had to know where you were every hour. This will be quite different—but I'm hoping that whatever you are doing you will find wonderful new experiences.

Stan says you must try to find the shop in the Fairmont that specializes in the most scrumptious sundaes. At least there was such a one in 1952 for we'd walk over from the Mark Hopkins to have one.

I wonder what 11 years have done to San Francisco—many changes, I'm sure but I trust it has retained its special flavor.

Darling, please know that although my body is separated from you by far too many miles, my thoughts are there—thinking of this really momentous occasion—are you sure such a famous celebrity is the same dear person I folded in my arms a month ago? It is hard to believe. Oh,—the bunchberry leaves have all turned the color of dogwood leaves in the fall—can't you picture what a gorgeous ground cover they make? If all goes well, we shall be in West Bridgewater when you return. Please read between these lines!

                                                              I love you so,
                                                              Dorothy

TUESDAY, OCTOBER 15

Dearest [Dorothy],

Now, like the birds, you are about to migrate. This little note is to greet you at the end of your flight. I know how reluctantly you will have left, as the summer and autumn pass into memories. But how many wonderful ones you have from Southport, 1963.

When you read this, if all goes as planned, there will be more miles between us than ever but once. The talk is done and I'm trying to relax and rest today. Just a few details still to see to. When we talk tonight I'll give you the new developments.

I loved your letter about the asters on the Head, marking the site of the hidden cave. And all the memories they stirred! What a thrill that expedition was. Of course you remember how we made an unplanned collection of young anemones! But probably you are right—there can be only one perfect experience of a kind.

There are few signs of migration here—at least in the limited areas I can observe. But on Sunday a kinglet appeared several times, searching the leaves for insects. There are still towhees, but suddenly I realize the catbirds must be gone, and the thrashers. There is the usual evidence the robins are preparing to go—morning and evening conferences in rather urgent voices. Our sunset, by the way, is a little after 6:30. You gave your time as 6:00 recently. But we must be 500 miles farther west.

Now this must go out. It's just to say Welcome Home, and to carry my deep love.

Rachel

THURSDAY, OCTOBER 17

---

6 MILES HIGH

Dear [Dorothy],

Well I have seen the Grand Canyon—if not the way I most want to, at least I've had a wonderful view of it. We skirted the south rim and then followed the river. I should think most of the way to Lake Meade before clouds cut out the view. There were scattered clouds over the canyon but not enough to seriously obstruct the view. The red walls of the canyon were so impressive and several places we could see the tree clad plateaus forming the rim.

Over Colorado, in an otherwise brown and arid landscape, all the stream valleys were flicked with a gold that could only have been the aspens. Then a long stretch was obscured by clouds, and we were so afraid the Grand Canyon would be beneath a veil. One thing I enjoyed over the deserts was the way the clouds, seen as one looked back toward the east, took on the tints of the sand reflected from below!

Our trip otherwise has not gone quite "the way we planned it." I'm afraid it is typical modern travel. (We are making a bumpy descent toward L.A.— hence scrawls.) First the taxi ride to Dulles Airport. I had never been there and had only vague ideas about how to get there. So I specifically requested a driver who knew the route. When he came I asked him and was assured he did. It turned out he knew even less than I did. He had said he would go by Cabin John Bridge. We drove and DROVE, getting into always narrower country roads, and

I finally decided we were going straight to Great Falls! So I called a halt and got an admission that the driver had never been to Dulles and really didn't even know where the bridge was! We had to backtrack at least 5 miles, and ask directions at a firehouse. Well, I had allowed 2 hours for the trip instead of the cab company's recommended one, so it really wasn't too serious. But the driver continued to demonstrate stupidity, as by starting to take (on airport grounds) the turn for "motels" instead of the plainly marked "Terminal" until Marie and I screamed "Left!" in unison.

But you can see how little it mattered when I tell you that we were greeted with the announcement of a delay in the flight of at least 45 minutes. The plane had developed engine trouble after leaving the Newark Terminal and had to return for repairs. The 45 minutes lengthened to THREE HOURS! They had finally (and to my relief) decided to send a new plane.

Meanwhile, we were receiving VIP treatment. The flight manager met me at the cab with "Good Morning Miss Carson," then offered a private "lounge" (really a fancy office, with magazines and a bar) for the wait. There were numerous solicitous offers and inquiries as to our comfort, apologies about delay, progress bulletins, etc. It was really funny. Then my chair was wheeled to the mobile lounge at about 12:15, and finally at nearly 1 o'clock we were airborne. Scheduled departure was 9:45! I guess we are maintaining about the 3 hour lag. We are now sitting in L.A., and presumably will arrive in S.F. about 4:15 coast time.

We have thought wistfully how we could have lingered in bed until 9, instead of staggering out in the dark at 6!

Adgerina came to the rescue yesterday (you know Ida couldn't come). She came out about 6, made beds, served dinner, cleared up afterward, got up this morning and got breakfast. It was a life saver.

Jeanne is taking Roger Friday night & Saturday. He will sleep at Virginia's Sat night and at home again Sunday. I think I'll return on Monday. I wonder if you might possibly have this Saturday—I'll mail it at S.F. airport.

You know you have been traveling with me. Now I will close, with all my love.

Rachel

MONDAY, OCTOBER 21

RETURN VOYAGE OF THE VICTORY CHIMES[42]

Dear One [Dorothy],

Now we are over Ohio and considering the speed of jet flight I haven't long to write. But until we are east of Denver I can't bear to do anything but *look.* Then there was lunch and now we are nearly home, with the prospect of being only about 10 minutes late due to unexpected headwinds.

We flew over Yosemite, or rather just to the north, but from our altitude it

[42] A windjammer that sailed from Boothbay Harbor.

wasn't possible to form any conception of it. I can tell you its peaks were snow clad as were the mountains west of Denver. Lake Tahoe was in sight from the opposite side of the plane as we passed Yosemite.

Strange how absolutely alien and uninhabitable the west appears from the air—it might easily be the interior of Asia, so little relation does it seem to have to the world I know. I guess one should drive across it by several routes to know it. But I have been so impressed, thinking about water in relation to the landscape—or especially the lack of it!

No doubt I'll talk to you tonight and repeat anything I may say here, but for the record I'll say I fell quite in love with San Francisco and if I had another life to live would like to spend at least a few years of it there. Between the Browers[43] (Sierra Club) and Marie's friends we saw so much that ordinary sightseeing wouldn't cover. Of course one of the highlights was Muir Woods. There was a wheelchair there and a most obliging ranger took the "controls" and gave me a good long ride along the paths. Such a wonderful freshness in the air there!

[43] David Brower, executive director of the Sierra Club, and his wife, Anne.

As you know, I had wanted so much to get to Pacific Grove to see the butterflies and to Carmel. I could have had two chances to go—Sunday with the Browers or today, if I could have stayed over, with Marie's friends, but I decided the drive was too long for me and that it just wouldn't be wise to undertake it. But I did see something of the Monarchs. Yesterday Llewellyn and Carolyn picked us up at 10 o'clock, drove us around the city a while, through Golden Gate Park to the ocean and to the Cliff House for lunch. (Four sea lions asleep on rocks.) Then we went to their house in Belvedere—just a heavenly outlook over the water—and I went to bed. But all the time I lay there, Monarchs were flying past the window, headed south toward Pacific Grove. I counted for a while and I'm sure a couple of hundred must have passed while I watched, for about two hours.

It proved to be quite a chore to get to the Ballroom where the symposium was held. Besides, I stole Sat. A.M. for Muir Woods. So actually I heard none of the Saturday sessions except the last talk, by Medawar.[44] The chairs were terribly uncomfortable and an all-day session must have been pure torture. My hosts were most attentive. Dr. Sheain's secretary, an attractive little Oriental, was waiting at the hotel with a very handsome wheelchair. Then flowers began to arrive—tiny red roses from Dr. Sheain, bronze & yellow chrysanthemum from Dr. Keene, beautiful long-stemmed red roses from Paul, and later a corsage of my favorite tiny orchids from a local admirer, an old gentleman I've had some correspondence with. Very lovely, but it seemed such a waste this morning to walk out and leave them.

[44] Peter Medawar, 1960 co-recipient of the Nobel Prize in medicine and physiology.

It was wonderful that Marie could time her own trip this way, for I couldn't possibly have gone without her or someone in her place! I was far more dependent than I expected to be—indeed, I guess I was about at my worst physically. I'm not sorry I went, but am slightly appalled at my temerity in crossing the country in this condition. But now I'm almost back, and apparently am going to beat the hurricane to Washington! The captain tells us the overcast and rain are scheduled for later this evening.

My internal time clock never did get adjusted to S.F.—I always woke between 5 and 6. Now I've just pushed my watch on 3 hours.

Your *wonderful* farewell to Maine letter was waiting at the Fairmont. Getting it revived memories; reading and re-reading it have been pure delight. Now we are coasting down toward Dulles!

All my love
Rachel

WEDNESDAY, OCTOBER 23

Dearest [Dorothy],

Your good, long letter came today, to my delight. I was so glad to know Hazel had been on hand to ease the physical burdens of unpacking and settling in.[45] I know how hard it must have been to leave Maine while the lovely Indian summer lingered, but then there may be a sudden change to stormy weather. After cool cloudiness here, all is warm sunshine again today. We really need rain so badly, but none seems to be in sight. But this is good for Jeffie's outings—and how he does enjoy them!

[45] The Freemans had returned to West Bridgewater from Southport on October 18.

I've spent much of the time since my return sleeping! Now that I can afford to be dopey, I've tried again the medicine I used a few times in Maine. A dose Mon. night and again Tues. night, have produced many hours of sleep and at least some relief from pain. I have talked to Dr. Caulk, who feels there is still a chance the phosphorous may begin to work—perhaps in another week. So I guess in this interval I'll just take my pills and sleep. It is really extremely difficult to walk at all now, and with the trouble in the upper back affecting my arms I don't use the walker quite as well as I did. In retrospect, it seems a rather crazy thing to have gone gadding across the country in this condition. But I'm glad I did though I probably wouldn't do it again—if that makes any sense!

Darling, I know exactly how it is about the New York dinners,[46] for of course it may well be I can't attend them myself! When the Amer. Geog. invitation comes, why not accept—then cancel later if you have to? I can't remember that Carl Buchheister[47] has asked about friends I want invited, but if he doesn't soon, I'll mention it to him!

[46] RC was to receive two awards: on December 3, 1963, the Audubon Medal of the National Audubon Society; and, on December 5, 1963, the Cullam Medal of the American Geographical Society.

Jeanne and Burnet have gone to Bryn Mawr today and she leaves for Nebraska Thurs. night. I don't know yet how long she will be gone. Of course it is a good time, when I really don't want to work much anyway. I'll probably have a substitute in one or two days for letters.

[47] President of the National Audubon Society.

There is some difficulty writing just now because of numbness (presumably due to nerve pressure) in my right arm, so I'll save the rest for another time. My mind is still filled with vivid pictures of that dream-like drift across the continents—what a privilege we have to be able to see it that way. I'm full of thoughts about water cycles and the role of water in sculpturing those strange canyon lands of the west. Wish you were here to talk about it!

Of course I'll be most anxious to hear Dr. Bowles's thoughts. I do so hope he was able to give Stan reassurance, and that the verdict may be "No surgery"—at least for the present.

A white throat is singing dreamily outside the window, in warm sunshine made all the more golden by the maples in their fall glory. And the mockingbird fills the days with song.

Goodbye for now, dear one.

So very much love—
Rachel

Tell Stan I'm keeping my fingers crossed on the slides. Wouldn't it be fun if something happened?[48]

[48] Stanley had submitted some of his slides to the Audubon International Exhibition of Nature Photography for judging. He did not win an award.

SATURDAY AFTERNOON, OCTOBER 26

Darling [Dorothy],

Your Thursday letter was such a joy to have—I had hoped for some word but didn't expect such a good, full letter. Now of course I'm eager for the sequel to "As though the swans weren't enough—." It was as though you had planned to end this installment in a tantalizing mid-sentence!

That was a wonderful experience—more swans (Yes, they must have been whistlers; the trumpeters are only in the West.) than I ever saw, even at Mattamuskeet. But it made me long to return there, to hear the music of the thousands of Canada geese. How about a trip there in January?

I'm so happy about the outcome of Thursday's visit to your doctor, and I do hope nothing further will be necessary.

You ask about the redwoods. Of course this brief, tantalizing visit only served to answer some of the major questions in my mind and to make me eager to return, under other conditions. I longed to wander off, *alone*, into the heart of the woods, where I could really get the feeling of the place, instead of being surrounded by people! And confined to a wheelchair! I was so grateful to the Browers for taking me, and to the ranger for his hospitality and his fund of information, but the thing that would have made my enjoyment complete I couldn't have.

The setting is interesting and quite different from the way I imagined it. Once over the Golden Gate Bridge one climbs up and up into those smooth, brown hills, so much of the road lined with eucalyptus trees. (Ansel Adams refuses to photograph them, we learned, because they aren't native!) Then a long winding descent, one hairpin curve after another, into the canyon where the redwoods are. It is deep enough that despite their height they don't present good targets for lightning—this is one reason why fires, at least from natural causes, are no great hazards. Nevertheless, one sees great, burned out stumps here and there, looking fresh enough to have resulted from a fire last year; yet the ranger said there had been no fire in Muir Woods for at least 150 years. It was fascinating to see the circles of young trees surrounding the old ones. There is very little reproduction from seed in these coastal redwoods (but otherwise, I understood, in the "big trees" of the Sierra country) but instead young trees sprout up around the base of a mature tree. There was a marvelous freshness in the air, though I couldn't detect a distinctive odor. The under story of these woods is chiefly the California laurel—a huge tree. When an old tree falls, a long line of young ones grows up from the trunk, so - - - - - - - - -.[49] Then if one of these topples over the same process ensues. The ranger pointed out three generations in one place—the "grandmother" being a very old tree. Perfectly huge oxalic is a predominant ground cover and there are marvelous ferns, sword especially.

[49] RC sketched a line of seedlings at this place in her letter.

It is now Monday, and if I'm to send this on its way today I must hurry along. (Slept all morning, as usual!) The Scotts from Pittsburgh were here yesterday afternoon—they are in town for some conservation meetings.

Do you realize how many perfectly wonderful bird experiences you have had in recent years? I know, because you have been so generous in sharing them with me. How I long to get out somewhere to get the feeling of these fall migrations! I think you will enjoy Irston Barnes's column—don't return it. Everyone speaks of the great abundance of grackles, blackbirds, and the like but no one seems sure of the reason.

This morning's mail brought a copy of Sec. Udall's book on conservation, *The Quiet Crisis*. I thought it was just a publisher's copy but when I opened it there was an inscription in a bold, decisive hand: "For Rachel—An educator-crusader for conservation whose stones have wide ripples! Sincerely, Stewart." Now I want to read this book, which seems to be a history of the conservation movement. Not surprisingly, my reading this past week has a western flavor— John Muir, the Teale anthology,[50] the American Heritage book I mentioned. George Stewart did the section on the Great Basin, which has led me to a re-reading of *Storm*. Now there is much I want to learn about winds, clouds, air movements and, of course, rain.

[50] *Green Treasury: A Journey Through the World's Great Nature Writing* (1952).

Did I send you the reprint Betsy Reimers supplied? I meant to just before I left for Calif. but am not sure I did. I really wish you would ask Dr. B. to read it—there is nothing quackish about it—it seems to be important new work. It seems to have provided the answer to various troubles Paul had, including the several times he passed out completely. I believe the remedy is as simple as substituting mono-saccharide for poly.

Our leaves are going fast now, but one of the big maples is still a blaze of color—gold and scarlet—and the dogwoods are a rich wine red.

This piece of paper is smudged but they are Jeffie's tracks, so you won't mind, I'm sure. That reminds me to say that Dr. Monahan finally sent me his bill and the pathologists' report, which confirmed the diagnosis of pancreatitis. As to the bill, I had been prepared for at least $100, knowing how much time he had given little Moppet, for 10 days, to say nothing of the expensive medication. He wrote a note saying he was charging only for the food and medicines—"to include time would make the bill entirely too high." The result: $42! Of course I won't let him do it, but where except in Maine could that happen?

Now I must stop, dear. Your letters keep me feeling so close to you. Yes, Saturday's did come today, as you would know, I guess, from my comment about the blackbirds.

All my dearest love goes with this—now and always—

Rachel

P.S. The Dutch *Silent Spring* arrived today, the title no doubt a literal translation but sounding considerably less attractive—*Dode Lenten*! There has been a terrible uproar there, with Dr. Briejer[51] probably my only defender.

[51] C. J. Briejer, a Dutch biologist, director of the Plant Protection Service in Holland.

THURSDAY, OCTOBER 31

Darling [Dorothy],

Time for a week-end word to you. I guess our Indian summer has blown away on high winds, but still not rain. I'm wondering how much of Maine got the snow and whether you felt the swish of Ginny's passing. There was something on TV news about an earthquake tremor somewhere near Boston but nothing in the *Post* this morning. (They seldom recognize that there is any world east of New York.)

And now today's mail has answered some of my wondering about your storm. I envy you the rain. I'm expecting at any time they will shut off water for the gardens, and the evergreens need it badly to prepare for winter. Elliott didn't come last week, and Ida has been trying to water them a little at a time.

Vera seems to be doing very well except for soreness deep in her throat, presumably from that wretched tube.[52] She is to see the surgeon tomorrow. You know her mother has been in a hospital and then a nursing home since last spring, when she broke her hip. Now she has had another fall and this time broke the femur—so is back in the hospital, in traction, and just having a wretched time.

[52] Vera Carson had developed breathing problems during her recovery from an operation.

The routine here is about the same from day to day. Tuesday I talked (by phone) with Dr. Caulk and we were both rather discouraged. Yesterday, however, I almost felt there was a tiny bit of improvement. I woke feeling better than I usually do, and got out of bed with less difficulty. During the day I got about with a cane (instead of walker) and once or twice even took a few steps with no aids. It seemed like just a tiny bit of a thaw during a long winter's night—but whether it really means anything I'm not sure. Both Drs. Caulk and Healy brightened up greatly when I told them, willing to hope, at least, it may be a portent of better days to come. They had just come to a decision to try Prednisone (a cortisone dermative, which I took for iritis) but now will wait a few days to see what happens. Barney had recommended Prednisone as an alternative to the pituitary implant—the idea is to suppress adrenal function. As I may have told you, he is speaking at a medical meeting here in mid-November, and the three doctors will get together then.

Our birds are for the most part just the usual lot for this time of year, but at lunch today I saw the unmistakable yellow flag of the myrtle warbler, and then, from the porch, saw a *red*-breasted nuthatch trying to reach the water in the birdbath. They seemed like friends from Maine! Then I looked at the wren house and wondered where those particular little birds are today—maybe in Central America—who knows? Now I have just been out—the W. D. nuthatches are busy back and front, carrying on quite a feud with the titmice around the feeder.

People—besides you and me—seem to be especially conscious of the monarchs this fall. I have heard more comments about them than I can remember in other years. I'm glad, dear, that you still find pleasure in those thoughts I set down about them after our lovely morning at Newagen.

I guess you will be happy to know that I have been thinking of trying to do the Wonder book instead of the other.[53] I had always planned for it a section on the cycle of water, and my thoughts about the nearly waterless western lands have been geared to the book. Just how I don't know but something seems to be stirring in my mind—conscious or subconscious!

You ask about listening to the Capehart. Very little, now. My mornings are usually spent in bed (mostly asleep!) As a rule I go out to the kitchen for lunch, and usually return to lie on that funny bed after Ida has made it. In the evening, after I've gotten supper for Roger and me I'm ready to lie down again, so I really don't spend much time in the study. Obviously, I'm letting correspondence slide. I miss Jeanne greatly for the many little errands she attends to.

I'm going to send a copy of *Dode Lente* to your Dutch friend. Don't worry, I have a great surplus. It was good of her to send the clipping.

Now I'll close so Ida can get this on its way to you. You know you are always somewhere in my thoughts, wanting to share with you the birds and other lovely things, thinking of you when I waken in the night. But it has been white, white moonlight here, instead of rain-on-the-roof.

Dearest love
Rachel

[53] Presumably the "other" is the book RC had envisioned on life and its relationship to the physical world, sometimes referred to as "Man and Nature."

SUNDAY NIGHT, NOVEMBER 3

Dearest [Dorothy],

I thought I had some proper stationery at hand when I crawled into bed. I haven't, but perhaps this pad of scrap paper will do. Today I've been up longer and been more active than on any other since California, I believe. No nap at all—isn't that extraordinary?

I have been reluctant to call on the secretarial service for help because I
dreaded having someone underfoot all day, with the necessity of several hours
dictation. It just seemed more than I'm up to. So this afternoon I had a bright
idea that I could use Muriel[54] at long distance by sending her letters with scribbled replies. I called her and she was delighted. They have found a winter home
in W. Boothbay—just at the foot of the hill (as one goes out from BB Hbr) before one goes up to the store, right on the water and, of course, looking across
to Juniper Point. She said there have been many herons around. Also that they
had quite a blow and rain from Ginny, with snow the next day.

Well, I spent most of the evening doing letters for her, quickly finding that
it isn't a perfect idea on account of my hand. It would have to be my right! But I
find if I just ignore it and go ahead it doesn't seem to get worse, at least.

Your last letter was a joy—but which of them isn't? But your descriptions
of surf and stormy seas were like Shelton's[55] in words. I had just *felt* you and Stan
would be drawn by the lure of what would surely be spectacular seas running
out ahead of that prolonged upheaval off the Carolinas, even if the disturbance
itself hadn't moved your way.

You ask where Mattamuskeet is. In North Carolina, inland a bit from Pam-
lico Sound—a large, shallow, fresh water lake. Somewhere I ought to have some
copies of the gov't bulletin I wrote about it. If I can find any I'll send you one. The
thing I always remember about it is the constant, haunting music of the geese—
thousands and thousands of them. I think M. is the largest wintering ground for
the Canadas. Snow geese go to Pea Island, above Hatteras. Also at M., I remember the huge flocks of myrtle warblers, most appropriate in the numerous myrtle bushes, along with many other small birds. When Kay and I went (probably
late 40's) it was a good day's drive from here. Now with many new highways, and
bypasses around Richmond, etc., it would be much less. Want to go?

Irston Barnes's home is in Connecticut, not far from New Haven. Wall-
ingford, I think. Today he wrote about his skunk problem! He tries to trap rabbits and woodchucks (in live traps, of course) and release them a good distance
from his garden. Then once he caught a skunk.

I'm sending you a leaflet on Muir Woods. I thought I'd brought an extra
one for you, but alas, I seem not to have done so. Therefore, I'd like this back. It
will tell you about size. As you will see, the tallest known example of this species
is not in Muir Woods. I think the tallest there is about 200 ft. But the coastal redwoods do exceed the Sierra trees in height, tho not in girth.

Yes, Muir's essay about watching the storm from a tree is wonderful. I
think you would like all the parts about the Yosemite area.

Roger *does* have a bulletin board, tho it was not replaced the last time his
room was painted. But it could be.

I did enjoy Mad's description of the big day at the University. It was nice
for the children to have the experience of seeing a President[56] (even a Democrat!). I noticed her comment on his "blondness." That seems not quite the

54 Muriel Parlin,
RC's Maine
secretary.

55 Paintings of the
sea by Alphonse
Shelton, the
Maine artist RC
and DF admired.

56 President Ken-
nedy had spoken
at the Univer-
sity of Maine in
Orono on Octo-
ber 19, 1963.

word, but his hair is a very reddish brown, which surprised me when I saw him because it looks darker on TV. And I enjoyed reading of his visit to Schraft's—and of the woman who wanted her chocolate cake regardless! Doubtless she needed the calories badly.

Speaking of that (diets) I'm finding it difficult, after all, to think what I can eat without running into sodium in some form. I guess most of my lunch foods are out—tuna, welsh rarebit, peanut butter, etc. And no ham or bacon for breakfast—or prepared cereals! Any ideas? (I still weigh 125–127—3 cheers!)

Darling, please don't think of me as being in constant pain. It is often possible to find a position in which there is none, provided I don't have to move. It almost seems to me, as I think about it, that this has been happening more often lately, so that I wonder if, after all, a very gradual improvement is setting in. I think I mind the difficulty in my arms most. When I drop something it is almost impossible to pick it up. And now I guess my hand really doesn't want to write anymore tonight. Besides, I'm getting sleepy. See you in dreamland.

I interrupted a while back to listen to news and weather, and heard the silly forecast, "Slightly sunny." And our sunset is now 5:08. Yours must be well before 5.

Now it's Monday A.M. I've been busy with more letters for Muriel, because I wanted her envelope to go with the mailman, so I guess I'll let yours wait for Ida.

It was so good to hear your voice. That helps so much to bridge the gap of time and distance. Oh, about the dinners, dear. You know, I'm sure, that I feel firmly committed to go to both, so I'm just trusting I'll be enough better. Any negative decision would be a last minute one. If I don't soon hear something from Carl Buchheister I'll write him. Now goodbye for today, with all my love.

Rachel

P.S. Such a miscellany of enclosures.[57] And I'm afraid I want them all back—sometime. I thought you would like the letter from Lois, especially to know she really is writing—and to know that now *I* know what it's like to have someone planning to dedicate a book to you! I sent the last page to Marie. The "confession" was that she couldn't get the motel room (Lynnhaven, CT) after all, so is going to wait it out there until the "dream house" is ready about Christmas. That she doesn't fully trust the turn-about by Cris and will be watchful and ready to fly if necessary, but that meanwhile Cris has been rather a help. So her address remains Lake George.

Have now read the *Register*. Oh, I *hope* our trees are all right. My thoughts always fly to The Spruce.

Love, again, to you both
R.

Don't let the S.F. pictures scare you: one with such a sinister leer, the other surely retouched.

[57] Enclosures not preserved.

Dear One [Dorothy],

I don't think you have had an Apple since I left Maine! You say you don't need them; maybe I'm the one who does.

You have been very close to me through all these rather dark days, darling—a closeness helped, of course, by all your wonderful letters. There is the same surge of delight as in the early days when the familiar handwriting appears in the mail. But in other ways, too, you are especially close now. When I am wakeful in the night it is good to think of you. And I remember that you are often wakeful and perhaps at the very moment, in your far-away bed, are thinking of me!

I believe, darling, that for the most part I do manage to be "matter of fact" in my own thinking about the situation. Oh, I don't deny there are periods of depression and of dark thoughts. There is still so much I want to *do*, and it is hard to accept that in all probability, I must leave most of it undone. And just when I have attained the power to achieve so much I feel is important! Strange, isn't it? And there are times when I get so tired of the pain and especially the crippling that if it were not for those I love most, I'd want it to end soon. But I seldom feel that way.

I want very much to do the Wonder book. That would be Heaven to achieve. And if the other[58] could be added it would be "all this and Heaven too!"

[58] RC likely refers to her contemplated book "Man and Nature" mentioned in her January 6, 1962, letter.

Darling, I don't wonder you were especially disturbed about Stan just before you left Maine—those spells of almost fainting. But again it does remind me of Paul R. (several times he passed out completely) and I'll try to get another reprint and also diet details from Betsy very soon.

I'm so thankful for the respite about the surgery, and hopeful that by keeping down the fats there might never be a recurrence of serious trouble. Oh, if only this can be a really good winter for you!

And of course you know I hope you will very soon now set apart some time that will be kept inviolate for writing. You are not alone in finding it much easier to find always "another pencil" & sharpener before you begin—we all have such tendencies. But you will have to be stern with yourself and say "On such and such mornings I am going to *write*, and nothing except a real emergency is going to stop me." Oh, darling,—I'll gladly settle for fewer and shorter letters if only you would! *Please do* the boat piece *now*!!!

I love you, dear, and I love to remember all the times we have been happy together. Perhaps—oh perhaps there can be more of them. This is to carry a very special message—more special than I can express—and I hope it does. With it, my dearest love—

Rachel

Darling [Dorothy],

Yesterday I made one of my rare visits downstairs (via outdoor route) and with Ida's help dug out much material on *Under the Sea-Wind* and *The Sea Around Us*, in preparation for Marie's visit.[59] Then I started going over it, starting with *Sea-Wind*. I found one notebook in which I was planning it all—laying out the chapters, deciding on impression and moods I would be striving for. Then there is a manilla envelope for each chapter containing sometimes notes and always one or more early drafts, though not always completed. Then, of course, the printer's mss. itself, and the Simon and Schuster correspondence. It was quite an experience going over it, dear—unexpectedly wonderful. How I wished you might be beside me! It recreated the whole thing so vividly in my mind—that first real act of literary creation. And there was about it a sort of dewy freshness and innocence and wonder—quite similar to our feelings when we remember the precious beginnings, of love and friendship in 1953–54. I'm sure you can understand how it is, but I long to *share* it with you. It is an odd feeling to be preparing it for the world, but also a privilege to be able to do it personally. I hope I can see the whole job through—on all four, I mean.

Mail service is beyond reproach when it brings me, as it did today, a letter scarcely 24 hours out of your hands. Well, the long talk did me good too (though I can't say it was soporific—I think that was the night I lay awake from 3 to 5—finally went out for toast & coffee and a book and read myself to sleep! No reason known.) But it was wonderful to talk so long, almost as if we were together.

Of course, it seems too good to be true that I may be seeing you within three weeks. But it does seem it will be tantalizing, especially if you don't come down till the 5th. I believe, dear, you ought to make your hotel reservation. New York in December can be pretty full.

Last year I was going to you in January—remember?

Would you please send me once more the address of your Dutch friend? When I was ready to send the book I couldn't find it. I *know* the letter containing it is here, but it will save a search if you'll repeat.

Another letter from Lois, "up" this time. Cris is apparently behaving himself for the moment. She seems to have set herself to finish the book in another four months (!!)—says she is sending me some mss. soon. Oh, about her earlier reference to writing you instead of calling me—I think she pictures me as feeling worse than I usually do, and thinks perhaps I don't feel able to talk. That was all I could make out of it.

Well, I must say I was shocked at Barney's news, too. He is not a conventional person, but in view of his undoubtedly deep devotion to Jane, I don't see how he can rush into this so soon. And to be married Christmas Eve!!! Well, I'll know more after Saturday.

[59] Marie Rodell was to help Rachel prepare manuscripts of her books for donation to Yale University.

Now I must finish. Jeanne & Ida are out shopping, and this must go with them on their return. And my hand is giving out.

Yes—I'm glad to share Elizabeth's letter—just return sometime. She and Lois both have a gift of speaking as they write—a gift I don't have.

More soon, dear one. Or maybe not till after this busy week-end. But now this carries a heart full of love—

Rachel

NOVEMBER 17

JORDAN'S—WAITING FOR A HOT-BOILED LOBSTER

Dear [Rachel],

Can't waste time *not* talking to you—so many things to tell. I'm sure you were surprised to know we were here.

We are not sorry we came for I suppose we would have wondered all winter.

Really I am greatly saddened by the loss—3 of those big spruces at the east corner of the house where the chickadees and purple finches fed their babies with all the dear little accompanying sounds. We could look right into those branches from the guest room. Oh, dear. At the moment all the lawn, the paths, and the feeding grounds are man-deep in spruce boughs, tree trunks and branches. It looks awful!

The checkerberries are from your "Titania's Bower"—that's what I call the mossy spot, where we lay one of those last precious afternoons. Remember?—the day I watched you struggle to get up. From there I surveyed all the trees below—each one was as straight as ever.

The tides must have been awesome to see—imagine that bay so full of water! I would have loved to have seen them.

We drove up to Charlesworths' when we left. There, in a bare birch tree— a small one—were 8 pine siskin busily eating the seeds from the birch catkins. It was a marvel to behold their procedure—so rapid that the hulls rejected made a snow storm vertically. Dear little things—they will undoubtedly spend the winter here.

While we were on the porch talking with Eleanor Weitzel & Mrs. Kelley, a monstrous hairy woodpecker worked on the trees nearest us apparently not disturbed by us at all. I never saw one so large—so fat.

Another bird we saw, on the "short cut" was a partridge. And on your "Sandpiper Corner" a Great Blue Heron rose up from a low branch so close he almost hit the car. And there were seals in Ebenecook—clusters of them.

But the sorriest report of the day was the fact that we counted 97 deer on cars heading out of Maine. Imagine! Can you believe it? Think of the men who glory in such killing! Beside the deer there were also 2 bears. And the toll of hunters killed is 7.

Marguerites are still blooming in Christine's garden so I have gathered a bunch to take home.

Eleanor Weitzel is wondering if you would speak to the annual meeting of the Hospital Auxiliary next June.

I did not discuss your health with her at all. I did tell her you had addressed a meeting in San Francisco.

From all reports the storms were wild—Ginny, followed by a three-day northeaster, full of rain and much wind.

We are glad we came. I'm all ready for bed—Stan is trying to telephone Mr. Delano now so I'll wait until he returns to end this. We are at Mid-Town.

Now we have seen our place in every month of the year except January— so, come the January Thaw, don't be surprised to hear we are back—just to say we know it the year around.

The streets of Boothbay Harbor are literally a mess with the work underway for the sewer. In several places there are stretches, one car wide, where someone has to give—to back up. I'd have to back up around Mill Cove, for instance!

Stan got Mr. Delano. It so happened he had been over to your place today & knew of the broken cable. He will repair it at once. He said the winds were freakish—seemed to hit in pockets—that's what happened at our place. His property came through undamaged.

Stan also talked with Elbridge.[60] He has done a fine job so far—even had to take down our telephone wire & got Central Maine to come over to take care of the cable. The wires to the camp had to be cut so that will mean a whole new set! Guess this will be expensive. Elbridge will cart all debris away & cut up what is good wood for fireplace.

[60] Elbridge Plummer.

I told Stan to call Betty Pinkham[61] to inquire if she had got her deer yet (inquiring for fun, for she told us she always goes deer hunting—"loves to get out in the woods alone." I suppose she never would think of going into the woods in a less dangerous season.)

[61] Another member of the West Southport Pinkham family.

He talked with her daughter for Betty is in bed—has been in the hospital—Stan didn't hear well enough to know exactly what for—some kind of "emia" he said. I think I may look in on her to-morrow morning.

Now I'm going to send Christine a Marguerite from her garden, and some checkerberries to Lois. And so to bed.

This is an extra dividend for you for I mailed a letter in W. B. this morning.

Good-night, my dearest. For some reason—understandable I'm sure— you are very close to me to-night.

I love you,
Dorothy

Dearest [Dorothy],

I'm planning to call you tonight for more news of your trip, so will make this short. I'm spending the morning in bed—was quite weary after the weekend. Marie and I put in quite a lot of time on the manuscripts, and that sort of work is tiring. Now I've learned how it has to be done I can continue myself. (However, *Under the Sea-Wind* is almost ready for the appraiser.) It is unfortunate that now I am so uncertain of Jeanne's help. Of course the situation is something she can't control. They brought her father home from Omaha yesterday—her brother flew out to bring him via wheelchair and plane. But Jeanne will have him at home, and with all the uncertainties about his condition, I feel I won't know from day to day whether I'll see her or not. She thinks her once-weekly maid can come two days, and perhaps her sister-in-law would help out the third, but that seems a big perhaps. And as you know too well, situations like this with her father can suddenly change and create tremendous problems. I suppose I could get someone from the agency once a week for letters, and hope Jeanne can somehow stay with me on this mss. work—it would be twice as hard breaking in a new person.

It seems unreal that I may be seeing you in New York in a little more than two weeks. And I am trying to think how to make it yield some satisfaction in terms of being with you. At least I can join you for breakfast and stay with you until I have to go home on the 6th. But oh dear, that isn't enough!

I haven't yet decided how I'm going to travel. I guess I'm about up to coping with steps to a plane, and if the improvement continues I may "shuttle" there and back, tho I may call for wheelchair service at the airports.

The hand is troublesome, and I'm not going to write more now. Perhaps I'll add a little after your letter comes, as I hope it will today. (The one you mentioned Sunday.)

WEDNESDAY

Meanwhile we have talked. It only made me want more than ever to be with you!

Now I have a 2 o'clock appointment today with the neurologist, so I won't attempt to write more. Jeanne is here and I will ask her to drive me down. And I've made a tentative appointment with Dr. Caulk tomorrow, assuming Dr. Hustead will be ready to report, so we can get right along with whatever has to be done.

I do hope your back is better! All my love goes with this, as you know.

Rachel

Dearest [Dorothy]—

A quick report on the consultation today. Dr. Hustead proved pleasingly conservative—he recommends *no* treatment at present for he wants more time to observe the condition and be sure what and where it is. In other words, he is not convinced the trouble in my hand & arms is related to what has been going on in my bones—says it could perhaps be arthritic. And the upper vertebra that has been giving some trouble is definitely *not* the cause, for it would not affect the right nerves. This proves the wisdom of consulting someone who really knows the anatomy, etc. I'm sure Dr. Caulk would just have gone ahead and treated that vertebra. So once again I'm indebted to Barney for sensible advice. Dr. Hustead wants to see me again in a month.

Can you imagine what a relief it is not to have to start with that wretched grind of treatments again? And they always make me feel (and look) so weak and sick. A fine prelude to New York, I'd been thinking.

One angle that had made me wonder if this was something else was this: with the great improvement from the prednisone, why was the hand getting no better?

Your BB Hbr letter came today, with the precious checkerberry. It is good to know the view from Titania's Bower is unmarred by storms, but oh, I'm so sorry about your trees. Do you mean it's the ones just off the corner of your porch? I had thought at first you meant they were to the right of the path going up to Amblers'. But such a loss, whichever.

Please thank Stan for calling Mr. Delano for me. I'm glad he apparently feels he can secure the tree again. It's surprising Mr. Plummer hadn't told him about it—but maybe he wouldn't take a leaning tree very seriously.

Jeanne's father seems to bounce back from these crises in a remarkable way—he is getting around the house again so I guess for the present, at least, she will be able to come. In fact, he is counting on going to California after Christmas!

I want to send you a copy of the current *Atlantic Naturalist*. Perhaps Stan will want to try out the "bird-taming" methods. And I think you both will enjoy several other articles, including Irston Barnes's remarks on presenting the Bartsch award to me (in absentia, of course). Also, "that name" you like to see crops up in several places.

Now I guess it's time to put out the light, dear. I wish I could say goodnight in person.

> With all my love—*Rachel*

Darling [Dorothy],

It was sweet to talk to you last night, but so hard to say goodbye! You sounded sort of wistful, darling, and I felt that way, too. We ought to be so happy at the thought of meeting in New York (and believe me, dear, it would be sweet to have you there for even one of those Occasions) but I know we both feel the same way about the frustrations of having to share it all with others! I guess it is better to recognize this in advance. But please, dear one, don't feel I don't want you to come. You have said before that it would mean something to you to be part of one of these affairs, and if it can be done without strain and sacrifice I want you there, at least for the Geographic. (It does seem a great expense and perhaps too wearing on Stan to attempt both, and I definitely feel the Geographic is the *one*.) And we shall have a few hours together, some way!

But that isn't enough—I have to have a visit with you before the long winter's night settles down! In those dark weeks after San Francisco, it didn't seem possible I should ever travel again—really, dear, it didn't. Now I can be, and am, so much more optimistic. But of course no one knows how long this will last, so I have not lost the feeling of urgency about those things I want to do.

I had even entertained fleeting thoughts of asking you if you would like Thanksgiving visitors, but common sense tells me it would not be the best time for either of us. Too close to New York, for one thing. But it was a happy idea to play with.

Now this is Thursday A.M. and I want this to go out to the mail, so I'll stop. All my dearest love goes with it.

Rachel

TUESDAY MORNING, NOVEMBER 26

Dearest [Rachel],

I hope this is not too late to bring you my message of love for the coming Thanks-giving Day. It is not to be a happy Thanks-giving for anyone I'm sure. And it will be hard for many people to find any blessings to count. But I do hope that you may find some comfort in the meaning of the day.

In these past days I think we have all felt apart from the world—in time and space, living within our homes and yet so close to world-shaking events.[62]

Let me tell you three things that had meaning for us yesterday—all in a happy vein. When the services at Arlington were over we began to move about to attend to such mundane cares as washing dishes. Stan called, "There's a cardinal in our yard." And sure enough under our pine tree was the gay creature we have been looking for. It was our longest and best view of him. When he flew toward our wild wood, I rushed to the study to try to follow him. Although he had disappeared what was my astonishment to see what appeared to be an Easter lily in bloom in a tangle of now withered chrysanthemums. I was full of disbelief. But when I went to the garden it was true—an Easter lily, symbol of the resurrection, in my garden on Nov. 25! I cut it to bring into the house.

The third moving event for us was a telephone call from Stanley in the evening. He has always been tender-hearted (I think I have told you of some instances when he was a little boy). He, it seemed, *needed* to talk to us, to express

[62] President Kennedy had been assassinated on November 22, 1963.

his grief, his feelings, his thoughts. He said, "When there is a funeral in the family, the family is together and can talk it over, but in this case, the ones you want to talk with aren't with you." I suppose he is only one of millions who have been stirred to dedicate themselves to do something positive to help make a better world. When we are together, I shall try to remember some of the things he said. It was a very moving experience for us. We talked a half hour. And so, beside the memory of the tragedy of the day, I have some Little Things in which my "heart finds its morning and is refreshed"—a cardinal, an Easter Lily and a son's voice.

> And always the thoughts of you.
> All my love,
> *Dorothy*

WEDNESDAY, NOVEMBER 27

Dearest [Dorothy],

Two sweet notes from you today—increasing, in a way, my regret that I didn't achieve my aim of getting a Thanksgiving note to you. For the 3½ days when we all lived so close to the tragedy I was numb and dazed—could think of nothing else. Yesterday I turned to writing my Audubon Medal acceptance because I must, but still my mind would not function. By sitting up very late last night I was able to get something under way, which I finished this morning for Jeanne to copy. So now I shall at least mail a note tonight, and perhaps I'll call you tomorrow.

Besides the feeling of personal sorrow and loss, which for me could scarcely be greater if it were a member of the family, there are the feelings of shock, dismay, and revulsion at the black aspects of our national life so strongly underlined—the bigotry, intolerance and hatred preached by so many. The only ray of light I can see is that perhaps, because of his martyrdom, the noble ideals and aspirations that John Kennedy stood for will be understood as never before.

I have meant to tell you my own "Easter lily story" and though it lacks some of the symbolism of yours, and the timing, I think you will like it. About ten days ago I noticed a spot of white in the garden. Investigating, I discovered a pot of hyacinths, forgotten there since last spring. Green spears were pushing up from each bulb and, in the midst of several, buds could be seen. I brought the pot in to my bedroom, and now I have "white hyacinths for my soul."

I'm glad your cardinal is staying with you—probably he will become a permanent guest.

You don't tell me about your eye so I am wondering. At least you were able to write on Tuesday. And how about your back?

It is good to hear you are "thinking positively" about New York. Do you plan to stay more than one night? If so why don't you come on the 4th? Then we could have that "evening together" and part of the next day. I might even transfer to your hotel on the 5th, assuming a room is available. Are you making reservations? I do think you should.

As I think I told you, Robert and Vera are in Canada. I am having Virginia, Lee, and Tommy (Lee's son) here tomorrow. The turkey is cooked, pumpkin pie ready to bake tomorrow, salad made, some of the vegetables ready, so there will be little for us to do tomorrow. It seemed too cheerless for Roger and me to be alone.

Friday I am going to see Dr. Caulk and have some X-rays of the neck vertebrae. I'm considerably troubled with a painful neck; besides, my hand is no better, to say the least. So I think we had probably better get on with some treatment, after all. Of course I won't start till after New York, unless he considers it urgent.

I am going to try to carry the manuscripts, etc., of *Under the Sea-Wind* and *The Sea Around Us* to New York, having a horror of committing them to the mail. Every package I get nowadays is terribly mutilated. I shall of course be dependent on red caps anyway, and on a wheelchair if I go by train, so I suppose I can manage an extra suitcase weighing a ton!

Now I have to think what to say to the Geographers—especially since I hope I'll be talking to you!

I know it was satisfying to have that good talk with Stanley. And how glad they must be now for that Presidential visit to Orono!

Now I must go, dear, and take this to the box. You see, I am driving a little now. And although it is late, this letter carries a special share of love for Thanksgiving. In spite of the nearly universal sadness, I'm sure we can all find much to be thankful for. For myself, just to be here with the hope of accomplishing some of those "dreams unrealized." And as always, dear one, thankfulness that I have you.

> All my love
> *Rachel*

SUNDAY NIGHT, DECEMBER 8

Dearest [Dorothy]—

Just a note to go with the requested material—for my Press Agent!

A heavy rain started this afternoon and is due to continue through the night. Apparently conditions to the west are quite stormy, so perhaps there will be some Weather. Well, if so, I'll just wait a day or two longer to start my treatments.

I dipped into the Stearns box only enough to discover that there was no gift-wrapped inner box, and that if I went further there would be no surprise for Christmas. I really imagine everything is all right, for it is heavily packed with the shredded paper and the damage seems to have been confined to the outer wrappings.

It hardly seems possible Christmas is so close. I am by no means ready and perhaps never will be.

Jeanne called and reported that things are little changed. Her father has some days when he is himself, others when he isn't. He cannot be left alone, so a lot depends on what she can work out with her maid, which at best would probably be only two days a week for me. She said she felt she ought to give up and let me get someone I could depend on, but I told her I wanted any time she could give, now or later, even though I might have to supplement. I guess my hospital trips will be by cab, though I may be able to ~~walk~~!! drive part of the way sometimes.

In those short few hours we were together[63] it seemed so "natural" that it was easy to forget how long it has been and how precious such time is. But it was all such fun, and such a delight. And it meant much to me to have you part of one of these occasions. Now you can imagine the others.

I meant to tell you that in Mrs. Owing's[64] little speech following her Audubon citation, she used a wonderful quotation from Laurens van der Post. I think I must write and ask her for it. The general thought was that each of us must do what we can, even though the contribution is small. It was from a book I haven't read—*A Bar of Shadow*, I think she told me. She also said—here I must turn "shameless," but I think you will like this—that no other author's writing had ever meant so much to [her] as mine—that once in a dark period of her life, when she was ill and (I gathered) had other troubles, the only book she wanted to have read to her was *The Sea Around Us*.

This reminds me of something I had meant to talk about—rather an odd thing to tell, but you will understand so I can tell you. In those first awful days after the assassination, I found myself so distraught on going to bed that I felt I must read myself to sleep—but what to read? I went over one bookshelf after another, but nothing appealed. Finally I picked up *Under the Sea-Wind*! And somehow it was right. A chapter or two a night relaxed me and let me sleep. I haven't read it for many years. Of course it is the elemental nature of the subject matter, its timelessness, beside which human problems and even human tragedy fall into perspective. But out of this experience I understood for the first time what various people have told me about reading that, or *The Sea*, (or you "The Enduring Sea"[65]) in time of trouble.

I want to go on but my writing is getting bad and my hand wants to stop. So I guess I'll save other thoughts for a later day. All my love and happiest memories of the 19 hours!

Rachel

N o w A. M.

The speeches are for your files not the *Register*!

Jeanne can't come today—no maid. I've decided to wait for tomorrow to start treatments. Will wash my hair today!

[63] The Freemans had attended a December 5 dinner in New York City where RC had received the Cullam Medal of the American Geographical Society.

[64] Margaret Wentworth Owings, conservationist, artist, and Commissioner of California Parks.

[65] A chapter in *The Edge of the Sea*.

Dear Heart [Rachel],

Now it is all a memory—such a lovely one. Yesterday I tried to put my thoughts in order to express how I feel that the longed for experience was accomplished. But my heart is so full, I find it hard to find the right words.

I'm sure you know how much it meant to me to be present at one of the many events where you have been so highly honored. This was all so different from the Publication Day party for *The Edge of the Sea*. That was fun and exciting and I'm glad I could be present then. That was a tribute to the successful accomplishment of the completion of a book.

The tributes from Audubon and the Geographical have added more stature—you are a gifted writer—so was Willa Cather—but you are also a master of a great field of scientific knowledge. So your honors are for two reasons.

If you had received only one of the three awards[66] this past week, any one would have been breath-taking. How does it feel to have had three? Does the quantity in any way detract from the value, the honor, the significance of each? Surely this must be a case of a cup running over. Somehow I wish we had talked more about all that it meant to you.

When we parted in September, honestly, darling, I could only look forward to your becoming bed-ridden. That last morning was agonizing to my spirit as yours was to the flesh. San Francisco helped lift my spirit somewhat but afterwards I was again sure you wouldn't be able to keep these dates.

So, darling, to see you moving about with comparative ease, to hold you close without seeing you wince, and at last, to see you on that dais, looking so fresh and lovely, with no indication of all your suffering, was all I needed to find the tears of joy and thankfulness welling up in my eyes. When you looked down and smiled it was all I could do not to put my head down on the table and sob.

For me, then, I came home with a complete sense of satisfaction and fulfillment. I have done what I wanted to.

For Stan the trip was in a sense a triumph for him. He was so happy to share your fortunes and honors. I'm sure he loved every minute of the intimacies we could enjoy by having the rooms arrangement. Wasn't that quite a perfect touch?

But beyond those facts, there was for him a ridding of a sense of guilt caused by his "spoiling," as he puts it, of more than one occasion for you and me. Poor dear, he had the burden of the Texas trip and last spring's cancelled trip on his shoulders. Those three days in New York helped ease that burden, I'm sure.

A thousand things more to write. There was no time yesterday after we talked—many telephone calls as well as two sets of callers. No naps so we went

[66] In addition to the Audubon and Geographical Society honors, RC had been elected to the American Academy of Arts and Letters.

to bed early. But I couldn't sleep. I wanted to write but I was too tired. Now this must go out to the mailbox.

I hope somehow I've been able to tell you what our trip meant to me.

So much love,
Dorothy

P.S. I think you would want to read the *Sat. Eve Post* for Dec. 14—the tribute to Kennedy. Ours came by mail but it's on newsstands later.

THURSDAY MORNING, DECEMBER 12

Dearest [Dorothy],

This is a red-letter day—our first evening grosbeaks, the first for several years! There was a light snow in the night, bringing crowds of hungry birds. Among them, just before Roger left for school, were four grosbeaks, all females. We've put out extra sunflower, and hope to see more of them.

Weather predictions have been quite alarming but I guess it is to be rain today instead of threatened snow—thank heaven. I'm making daily trips to the hospital and don't want the complication of slippery streets. I have been driving partway, then taking a cab. This lets me do little errands, as well as cutting the expense. (Or I *could* hire a limousine!) Dr. Caulk says there will be seven treatments, but I always know he may extend it. He is taking in a rather long area, beginning about the base of my skull, all the cervical vertebrae, and I guess a few of the dorsal. On further study he found one of them has undergone compression, so my troubles are easily understood. Applying hindsight, it would seem all this might have been deduced from the symptoms in my hands and the treatment started weeks ago. But I guess then there was still faith in the phosphorous; no doubt it is hard to know. Anyway he thinks that in time my hands will improve. My chief concern about the treatments is that they may affect swallowing and voice. Oh, it would be temporary, of course, but unpleasant. They are using the big machine and going through from the back, instead of lateral treatment with the small one, as he first said.

Dear, I'd like to think, at least, about the possibility of our spending a couple of days with you during Roger's holidays, if there would be a convenient time for you, *and* we are all four well, *and* the weather permits!! I think he has two full weeks. It would be after Christmas, of course. And because of Jeffie, I'd rather it avoided the week-end, so Ida would be with him at least during the daytime. We could perhaps travel Sunday night. But you probably have New Year's Eve plans so perhaps we should instead travel Wed. night and have Thurs. & Friday with you. Well, as you know, this is all most tentative. But it is so difficult for me to arrange for Roger if I go away alone that I know this would be our last chance until spring vacation—and that looks far off. But you must tell me, really, if it would not be good for you.

I was fascinated, and rather appalled, by all the details of the storm in the *Register*. We must have been relatively sheltered, compared with the Harbor. But imagine people driving around in it, as they apparently did! And the good old *John J. Nagle* sank at its pier—shocking news to Roger.

I've been trying, with some success, to do my Christmas shopping by phone and mail. But there are still gaps that can't be filled that way. Once I could have turned to Jeanne, but she is all but lost to me for the present, at least. She was here yesterday, but I doubt I'll see her again this week. I suppose I really should look for a temporary replacement until her problem is resolved, but it is hard to give up her experience with the material.

A week ago today I was counting minutes until I could find you at the St. Regis! It seems a lovely dream. And one enlivened by so much fun. I loved your dear letter about what it meant to you to be present at the dinner. I hope you know how greatly enriched the whole thing was for me by having you and Stan there—being able to look down and see you, and catch your eye. (I'm glad you didn't cry!)

Now, darling, mundane affairs are calling. Some phone calls, take Ida marketing, go to hospital. I've been reclining comfortably on my electric bed while talking to you—a cozy way to spend this gray morning.

My dearest love—*Rachel*

TUESDAY AFTERNOON, DECEMBER *17*

Dear One [Dorothy],

I've spent the morning having my permanent; now, after lunch, I'll talk to you while I rest. I guess I still have nearly 50 cards to go if I complete the list, but unlike you, I am *not* writing letters. However, at times my hands rebel furiously, so it is a chore. It seems the picking up and handling of cards, envelopes, stamps, etc., is much worse than just settling down to write a letter, which really isn't too bad.

We had a fox sparrow on Sunday. I was so surprised, for as I told you we have only had them in spring migration, about March and April. It was with a little group of white throats, and in late afternoon I saw them all getting settled in the rose bush together. That same afternoon I had watched our covey of quail running down from Reimers'—10 of them. It was nice to know they were still around.

I have two more treatments—tomorrow and Thursday. It will be good to have that well behind me before Christmas. It seems to me that last year I went right up to Christmas Eve, for my back.

It was such fun to plan with you about the possibility of our visit. I feel I must mention now that Jeffie is another uncertain factor in our complicated equation. Last night I felt so worried about him I almost wept. He just lies under the bed or in my closet and won't eat. I made up a concoction of egg and milk spiced with a little whiskey and poured it down. Presently he got up and went into the study and ate a small bit of lamb chop. This morning he got more eggnog and eventually ate less than a teaspoon of scraped beef. Tomorrow we'll take him for another shot. But unless he is eating again, normally, I just couldn't leave him. However, I've made up my mind that if we do have to postpone, I'll just take Roger out of school and make the trip when we can. Other people do!

Have you heard from Lois? I told you of my two confusing letters—then a few days later Marie had one, saying she had gone to the mine!! I really wonder sometimes if the whole thing has affected her mind. One baffling thing was this: she told me her Social Security had gone through and she would get about $800 back money and around $50 or $55 a month thereafter. But when she wrote Marie just a few days later she said her Social Security had been turned down! How could they have given all that detail and then reversed themselves? Did she imagine one or the other? After all she told me of that dreadful mine, the road to it, etc., I don't see how she could do this. In Maine she swore she never would. Well, I long ago decided to stop worrying or trying to plan for her.

Dear, I'm enclosing a few clippings[67] about awards, etc. Please save them for me.

The card[68] goes with the gift you had to carry home from New York. Don't look at it until you are ready to open the package.

Roger has ordered a little gift for you but I very much doubt it will arrive before Christmas—it has a long way to travel. However, it is something that can be used at any time!

His notice about the magazine came a few days ago, but I held it back to give him on Christmas.

You and Stan will laugh at this story. The other day Woodward & Lothrop delivered a package. Instead of thrusting it into my hands and running, as the delivery men usually do, the rather thin, pale young man stood very politely at the kitchen door, holding the box, and asked "Are you Miss Carson?" Reassured, he went on, "Are you the Miss Carson who wrote *The Sea Around Us?*" "Yes, I am." "Well, I just wondered if I could shake your hand." He has *The Sea* and *The Edge*, but hasn't yet read the latter.

The poor Reimers are having a worrisome Christmas. Mark is having more trouble—enlarged lymph nodes under both arms. I have urged Betsy to take him out to consult Barney, and I think perhaps she will.

This letter seems to omit all I most want to say. Another will be on its way soon. Meanwhile, this carries my dearest love.

Rachel

[67] Clippings not preserved.

[68] Card not preserved.

Dearest [Dorothy],

Perhaps I shouldn't write you in a minor key so close to Christmas but my heart is so burdened about Jeffie that I need to talk to you. He is slipping so fast that I feel he will surely have left us by Christmas—so much weaker each day, and now eating nothing at all but what I give him with a spoon. I was to have taken him down for a shot today but snow kept me in (I skipped my treatment, too), and besides I would have hesitated about taking him out in the raw, windy cold. But if driving is possible tomorrow I guess I'll have to take him, even though I now have very little hope that anything can be done. It reminds me so much of our Tippy's last days. He was six years older than Jeffie, but I guess calendar age doesn't mean much.

You will know that deep in my heart I feel I ought to be willing and even thankful to let him go, for it would be so much easier for him to go while I am still here to care for him. You know that his fate has been one of my concerns. But it is so very hard to think of doing without him. His little life has been so intertwined with mine all these ten years. And how strange it would be if the three darling kitties that have meant so much to you and to us should all die within the year!

Now it is Thursday morning and my precious little companion is gone. I imagine I shall have talked to you before this reaches you and you will know. I sat up late with him in the living room, then carried him into the bedroom and closed the door so I could check on him more easily during the night. About 3:30 I was wakened by the sound of his difficult breathing, with little moans, and found him lying at the door. I sat on the floor beside him for some time, stroking him and talking to him. Finally he got up and went under the bed. That is where he died this morning, I think just before Roger left for school. We both heard him cry just as we finished breakfast. We came in and Roger reported he was under the bed. I could not see him well, but after Roger left I got down with a flashlight and then I knew. In a few minutes Ida came, and she moved the bed so I could lift him out and hold him in my arms. Then we curled him up in the little battered oval basket he loved so well. I will have Elliott bury him out under the pine trees by the study, a place that I should think would never be disturbed.

So many sad and somber thoughts, which I should not even try to express. For exactly three years, since I flew to Cleveland in December and first understood my own situation, I have worried about my little family. I knew no one could take care of Jeffie, and I felt it unlikely that whoever takes Roger would want to adopt a cat, too, so even Moppet was a problem. Last September when she died I felt that the inevitable dissolution of my little circle had begun. Now I have lived to witness another step. But oh, I should be glad for Jeffie, and soon I know I can be, for it would have been awful for him, and so frightening, if he had survived me. Now that problem exists no more.

Darling, I suppose I oughtn't to send you such thoughts, but it seems I have to express them.

Now this means Roger and I can come to you, leaving, and returning to, such a strangely empty house. I'll discuss with you the best time. Now that it makes no difference here, I am wondering whether morning or evening is the easiest time for you to meet the train, in terms of weather. Of course we won't go at a time we *know* the weather will be bad.

I have to go down for a treatment this afternoon. It's cold and windy, but bright, and I guess most of the snow is off the roads. I'll be talking to you tonight if you're home, dear. Meanwhile, all my love.

Rachel

FRIDAY MORNING, DECEMBER 20

Dearest [Rachel],

How I long to be near you to give you what comfort an understanding heart can give. The loss of Jeffie, I know, will be harder on you than on most who lose a beloved pet, for you were Jeffie's all, making the loss *all* yours and thus more poignant.

He was so close to you. As I said this morning, the time will be long before you will go into your room without expecting him to be there.

Even now there are moments when the thought of Willow opens the flood gates.

No time is ever right for grief but somehow when it comes near holidays it seems to cut a little deeper.

It will be good to be together soon, dear, (at least, I remember how I longed to be with you when Willow died—one reason why the disappointment was so keen that we didn't go to you in April as I had counted on—) to talk about Jeffie.

Remember the dear Valentine you sent me that February after you had him?

In spite of what might have been a premonition in your letter yesterday, I really was unprepared this morning.

As you said, one of your great anxieties has now been lifted. But I know that will not help the sadness.

Oh, darling, I'm sure you must know how completely I understand.

And how I ache for you.

And how I love you,
Dorothy

Dear One [Dorothy],

I have never been so late writing your Christmas letter, but you know some of the reasons. Now I can only hope it will reach you in time to carry its special message of love for Christmas.

Ten years ago there was the first Christmas letter from you—a fat envelope, full of delights and surprises and lovely thoughts. Then, as now, there was the expectation of being together within a few days. That was a precious time—our 13 hours—and one never to be duplicated, but I think no more precious than that to which we now look forward.

I can only hope you know, darling, that even in spite of the miles that separate us, you are and have been my main comfort and support in these sometimes difficult days. Just what they would be without the knowledge of your constant devotion and concern is something I can't imagine. So it has been, of course, through all of this eventful and often troubled decade, but never more than now. I've been thinking recently how wonderful it is for me that, if I couldn't have known you all my life, it is *now* that I do have you.

It makes me happy to feel that, with Stan's improving health, your own outlook is brighter than it was. May 1964 bring only good health and the shared enjoyment of lovely things to both of you.

I am sitting before a fire in my study; Roger has gone to bed and the house is quiet. But I need you beside me. So much I would like to say—and to hear you say. Perhaps we would reminisce about sitting before other fires—as in Maytime, remember? Or about talking until the dawn came. Perhaps we would remember the fairy cave, the Pemaquid surf, or the ribbons of water fowl across October skies. So many lovely memories dear, and you in the center of all of them. Wonderful to live over on a winter evening, before the fire.

Tomorrow the days will begin to lengthen and once more, even though winter will seem to be deepening, we shall be moving toward summer and Southport. I had not, until recently, allowed my thoughts to range so far into the future. Now I do. We shall yet build more happy memories.

It is lovely to think that, in little more than a week, I may look into your eyes. In the meantime, dear one, may all the joy and the deep meaning of Christmas be with you, and bring you happiness and peace.

My love, always, for all time—

Rachel

CHRISTMAS 1963 AC

Dearest [Rachel],

Ten years,[69] dear, since that first Christmas message. What can I say now, ten years later, that I didn't say in 1953? The words may be different but the theme—I need you, I love you—is the same. As I needed you then for under-

[69] Presumably, the AC in the date signifies "After Carson," meaning ten years since the first Christmas message.

standing, and for the kind of companionship that no one else has been able to give, I need you now as much, and even more. As I loved you then, for yourself, and for all you represent, I love you now—with warmth and earnestness and longing.

And so I give my Christmas thanks for this ten years—years that have enriched, yes, and even changed my life. Such years—of joy and sorrow for us both. As we shared the joys, no less have we shared the sorrows. Sometimes I wonder how I could have endured the depths without your sustaining love. Without you, in those shadowy days I know life would not have been worth living.

But I must not remember the darkness to-night. What I remember is the loveliness that has been mine because of you: the shared beauties of Nature in all its forms; the world of books and the people in that world; the companionship in music; but above all the living inspiration of you. For all this and so much more that words cannot express, my gratefulness knows no bounds. I can always reach into my memory for a lovely moment—if I tried to catalogue them I should never stop.

Yesterday at twilight the cloudless western sky was aglow with the burning orange which is at its best when seen through the dark silhouette of the spruces of our Maine forest. The diamond brilliance of the evening star was still an hour high. Below it was the first faint shimmering crescent of the young moon which is to be the Christmas moon—and which (oh, joy to be) we may share. At its tip a star punctuated the scene! No need to tell you of what happened in my eyes. There is promise in that moon for it reaches its full on Dec. 30.

I hope the enclosures may be some pleasant surprises.

Whatever time it is when you read this, please know my arms are figuratively about you. So close your eyes and know that you are loved.

May your Christmas be a blessed one.

With all my love always,
Dorothy

When I read this[70] I felt that here, in black and white, is the stated accomplishment of your crusade.

The world already acknowledges it, but how wonderful to have the triumph proclaimed.

Here, then, is my Christmas Eve present to you from your own world of books.

THURSDAY, DECEMBER 26

Dearest [Rachel],

Hoping to reach you before Sunday—just a wee note.

We did talk as though we were in the same town last night didn't we?

I can remember that first call from you ten years ago the day you were

[70] DF had clipped a column from the December 21, 1963, *Saturday Review* entitled "Trade Winds" by Jerome Beatty, Jr. In part, the column reads: "How many of the thousands of books published . . . actually move or change the course of civilization? . . . Offhand, I can think of *Silent Spring* as another example of the effect of a book on more than just bookseller and reader."

leaving for Boston. Other than when Stanley was in the service I had never had a call from so far away. The children were here and I remember how excited I was, my cheeks were so hot as I told them, "She called all the way from Maryland!" What a change in attitude over ten years—you've conditioned me, I almost believe, to receiving a call from the moon with complete calmness. Such wonderful conversations as we've had. But even as I accept the fact with composure, nevertheless the sound of the telephone bell when I'm expecting to hear your dear voice quickens my pulses even as it did ten years ago.

Oh, darling—hasn't it all been a strange and moving experience?

But I felt so inadequate when I tried to express our feelings about your exquisite gift.[71] From the fact that you wanted us to have it, I'm sure you know what it means to us. It is going to be sweet to be able to share it with you so soon.

Your two precious letters, in spite of the sadness in one, sent warmth through my heart at this season, dear. They are beside my bed where I can read them just before I put my light out.

I'm so excited about Dec. 30th as I was ten years ago—and it will be more than 13 hours! Oh, lovely thought.

All my love,
Dorothy

[71] RC had given DF a page from the original draft manuscript of *Under the Sea-Wind* on which she had sketched the head of the cat that was her pet at the time.

1964

JANUARY 2

Dear One [Dorothy],

I want to leave a little note behind for you to have under your pillow tonight—but it must be brief for I don't want to be away from you long enough to write it!

No visit could ever be long enough, but it has been wonderful to have the sense of leisure created by four days and nights unbroken by diversions. It has been a precious oasis in time, darling, to be cherished and returned to in memory always. As you, with your great gifts, always do, you have adorned the hours with love and tenderness, and with fun and laughter, too. It was especially precious to share the music with you, another thing you have given me.

I hope I have not spoken too much of the lurking shadows, especially since they may after all prove to be nothing—but it seemed better to speak of them rather than to have to write.

Now it is 6 P.M., and since I wrote this morning we have had our precious afternoon, which seems to leave nothing that needs to be said. I am so glad we had these hours, for wonderful as all the rest of the visit has been, I think we were closest this afternoon.

You reminded me of my letter after the 13 hours, and I think it was in that letter that I quoted: "A thing of beauty is a joy forever—its loveliness increases . . ." That has proved to be supremely true, darling, through all the ten years since I quoted it. And as long as either of us lives, I know our love "will never pass into nothingness" but will keep a quiet bower stored with peace and with precious memories of all that we have shared.

I need not say it again but I shall—I love you, now and always.

Rachel

FROM A QUIET BOWER

Dearest [Rachel],

I've been lying where you lay Thursday afternoon, listening to some of the most exquisite love music of all opera—Faust—drowsy and half dreaming all through the music—dreaming of you and that lovely afternoon. As you wrote in your dear farewell note "the afternoon seems to leave nothing that needs to be said." I, too, am so glad for those last wonderful hours. The memory of them will be with me always.

I have listened to so much glorious music in that particular spot—opera, symphonies—quietly, alone—and in the past ten years you have always been with me in spirit, as you well know.

So we had 100 hours! Actually, I suppose our Maytime was some longer than that but there has been nothing to equal this in many years. Every moment was satisfying. Again, darling, thank you for coming.

Now we must return to the normal pattern—letters, telephones and longings. You have much on your mind, dear. I know you were worried while you were here, but from your appearance of complete serenity no one would suspect.

And these coming days will be full of anxiety. I'm sure you are aware that I share it.

As always it was good to talk last night for I was anxious to know you were safely home. Also I was glad to know of your talk with Dr. Caulk.

The two mornings since you left have been given over to "putting Christmas away" for another year. To-day I washed the tablecloths, cleaned the silver,—even cleaned the kitchen and sink room windows. I was ashamed of them when you were here but—9° is no weather in which to wash windows. To-day again we've had 44°.

We both had long naps yesterday.

Now to-night we go to Grants. Then next Tues. we go to Duxbury for dinner with Delphine, the woman who stuck around last year at Wildflower meeting to meet you.

To-morrow I hope to go over the Xmas cards, write some thank you notes and thereby "clear the decks." I suppose unless I open up that box I'll never get started on *my* piece. I always find something else to be done first. I wish I had a big room to spread out in. It is hard to work when one has to clean up after each session so one can go to bed.

I do hope you are going to be free soon, in all ways, so that you can get to work—and I mean free in the sense of peace of mind!

Oh, Darling, it is hard to settle down—the hours with you are so vivid. It was fun dipping into the old letters, wasn't it? We could spend hours with them.

Of course, there were many things I've thought of I wish I had talked about with you. Well, I'm going to believe that we shall have more 100 hours or their equivalent in the coming year—the year which we welcomed *together* happily.

All my love, dear one,
Dorothy

SATURDAY, JANUARY 4, 2 P.M.

Dearest [Dorothy],

I'm sitting in the study, my back to a warm sun pouring in through the picture window. It will dry my hair, which I washed and Ida pinned up for me this morning. Roger has gone to a movie with his classmate Naseem, so the house is silent. And empty—that strange emptiness that again and again hits like a blow! I don't know anyone but you and Stan who can really understand what that means.

Well, our dreamed of visit is over, but the dream lingers on, and will, something to return to with a happy glow of memory. It was all so relaxed and cozy and heart-warming. I know I was *too* relaxed, but I'm also sure you didn't misinterpret my lethargy. You know how happy I was every minute of the time.

It was so dear of Stan to give Roger that wonderful day in Boston—"a day I'll never forget in my whole life" and to play games with him. He didn't want to leave; he whispered to me several times a suggestion that we stay longer.

By the way, Our Symphony is becoming a favorite of his, only of course *his* movement is the march. He asked me to play it for him last night.

And that brings me to comment on the *Tannhäuser* overture. Part of it—the "Pilgrim's March"—was so familiar, but the rest was not. (As so often before, it takes *you* to make me really hear and understand.)

But last night I searched through my records, so many of which I haven't played for years. And sure enough, there was a Music Appreciation record, the overtures to *Tannhäuser* and *Die Meistersinger*, with an analysis of each. I played the analysis first, and it brought out many of the interpretations contained in your book, or which you supplied. Then the performance. But I'm puzzled. I didn't hear all I heard with you (maybe I have to have you beside me.) And I don't think this is the same as your record—was it combined with something else? This is played by the London Symphony, and is record MAR 124B. It is quite lovely, anyway, and I shall play it often until I really know it. (Have played it again, and am sure it is incomplete.)

In quite a different vein, I must comment briefly on Aldous Huxley's *Island* which, as I told you, was a gift from Lois. (She wrote, you know, that she had ordered it for you some time ago, but the store mislaid the order. Fortunately, I'd say!) Well I picked it up last night and just began rapidly leafing through it. What poor Lois sees in either of the Huxleys is quite beyond me. But her choice of this book for me is really—if you will pardon the expression—the damnedest thing! Running through what appears to be a completely confused and sort of nightmarish narrative, are stories of two women who were victims of breast cancer, including the deathbed scene of one of them!! Instead of being depressed, it made me so mad, I threw the book on the floor! Don't worry I shan't read another word of it—and don't you, either. But can you imagine it? And how can I write to her about it? I guess I can just say it was here when we returned yesterday, and not mention that I have read any of it.

The more I think of Lois and her background, especially as revealed in that "hate passage" you read me, the more I realize the futility of all efforts that have been made to help her. I think her life has conditioned her to accept (and even to choose) the way of unhappiness, hardship, and suffering. She seems incapable of creating in her mind a vision of what her life could be and so of working her way out of this mess. And yet how grateful she has always been for such things as the Maine visit, or letters such as yours that are "like food when she is starving."

I'll write her today, and will tell her of Jeffie, and of our visit. Please, dear, don't give her any new details about my health problem. The last she knew the curve was up, and I'd rather keep her thinking that as long as possible. This is now for *my* protection more than hers!

Fortunately, the other books waiting in the mail were quite different— one about African animals and the urgent conservation problems which fits in nicely with my current passion for Africa. (The mail also brought a letter from London asking me to become a sponsor of Mrs. Adamson's "Elsa Appeal." You know she is devoting all her royalties, as well as her time, to efforts to save the African animals.) Others were *The Sky Beyond*,[1] which is about flying, and proofs of *Science, The Glorious Entertainment*, by Jacques Barzun.

There was an interesting piece in last Sunday's *Post* about Andrew Wyeth and his work. I'm afraid it got sent downstairs, but, I'll try to rescue it for you. It seems he lives as quite a recluse in his eastern Penna. home, sometimes dressing like his Amish neighbors. Apparently fame—and fortune—have sought him out, somewhat against his will.

[1] Published in 1963 and authored by Sir Patrick Taylor.

This has turned into quite a rambling letter and I must stop and write some necessary, and less inviting letters. Writing to you is next to visiting before the fire, and so I want to go on and on.

Please, dear, plan to go to the clinic sometime this month, at least. That will give you time to take off a few pounds, which may well be part of the treatment, but far more important, I think, is getting expert evaluation of the whole problem. Please!

Now dear, again my thanks for all the aura of love and thoughtfulness you wove around those four blessed days. And remember always how much I love you.

Rachel

Sunday A.M.—A titmouse whistling its clear "Peter, Peter."

MONDAY P.M., JANUARY 6

Dearest [Dorothy],

Just a quick note for Ida to take—an interim report to say that there will probably be no really definite information until the end of the week or the first of next. Dr. Hustead takes a rather optimistic view on the whole but thinks it wise to have an encephalogram—but what he means by that is a relatively simple procedure, comparable to a cardiogram. (Dr. Caulk was thinking of a *pneumo*-encephalogram when he said I'd have to be hospitalized.) So this will be done Wednesday, but results won't be in for several days. Dr. Hustead thinks the taste abnormality may be a temporary effect of radiation. He seems a little more concerned about the sense of smell, but even that may have a simple explanation. My "sore head" is less so now, but I'll have the skull X-rays Wednesday, too.

Dr. H. has a better picture of what is causing the hand symptoms as a result of today's examination. He has ruled out local arthritis, but says it is an *indirect* effect of the trouble in the neck vertebrae. This is causing considerable muscle spasms in the area above the collar bone, which in turn disturbs the nerves of the brachial plexus. Hot compresses and simple exercise may help, or he suggests some physical therapy at the hospital, but I don't want to get into that if it can be helped.

Well, that's about all on the medical front just now, dear. I think it may well be that nothing too bad is developing, so we'll just keep our fingers crossed.

A near-spring day yesterday—cloudy today and colder.

The package came this A.M. Sorry you had to bother.

More soon—meanwhile, as you know, all my love.

Rachel

Dearest [Rachel],

Going to hairdresser's so I'll get a short note ready to mail so that you'll know my thoughts are with you during these anxious days. In spite of diversions there is always a little corner of thought where you are constantly.

To-day is mild with warm rain which is reducing our snow to the point where large patches of green grass show through—green, in January! And I did tell you a Robin appeared on the 5th. And this morning very early—too dark to distinguish a bird—I thought I heard a cardinal whistle. Wishful thinking probably—instead that valve on the radiator.

Yesterday Stan and I jaunted off to Boston looking for bargains—and found them. We got in at 10:15 and before noon we had bought stationery, towels, slacks for me (my Wardrobe Maker brand, $9.00 instead of $13.00) a sport jacket for Stan, and a lovely sheer wool dress for me, sample enclosed ($35 marked down from $50). Then lunch at one of Stan's old haunts. He kept saying, "This is so good." Dear, can you understand what a relief it is for me to watch him enjoying food? There apparently is no fear that formerly obsessed him. Consequently, he's putting on weight—for two days now he has weighed 149. That's more than he's weighed since his 1962 operation! On the way home we bought jewelry for my new dress—necklace & earrings in that lightweight metal—silver or aluminum. And also three African violets—pink, purple and white which give a lift to the winter drabness. Furthermore the poinsettia is in as good condition as it was two weeks ago—almost as good as an artificial one. So we are quite festive. It was quite a gay morning for us and Stan seemed to get an especial kick out of it.

Darling, you know I'm anxious for news but I do understand it may take some time for tests and reports. I hope they are all on the positive, good side, but you won't hold anything back, will you? I have to know.

> All my love,
> *Dorothy*

Dearest [Dorothy],

As I begin to write, nine cardinals are hopping about under the willows outside my bedroom window. At least nine—they are so busy it's hard to keep count! The bare ground has apparently opened up a feast now that rain has cleared away most of our snow.

I forgot to mention your robin last night. That would be a thrill. I suppose it's a winter robin who has found a sheltered spot to wait for spring. There is now much whistling of cardinals and titmice these mornings—such a welcome sound.

Of course, I'm wondering if you made it to the Adamson talk—hoping you could, but also hoping you wouldn't in bad weather.

I'd love to see your new dress—from the sample I can imagine how becoming the color must be, setting off your blue eyes!

The other night cleaning out a drawer, I found a couple of pictures I thought you might like to have—relics of the long ago! Once you gave me such a picture of you, holding a kitty with the same type of grip. I'm practicing on the dog. Remember?

Darling, your long letter yesterday was such a feast for my soul (like a white hyacinth!) Finding it here when I returned from the hospital was wonderful.

I loved all you wrote about the music and the Opera intermission. It bears out what I said about your own gift for musical interpretation. You can always make things so much more meaningful for me. I wonder why we haven't done more listening—and talking about what we hear—at Southport. Of course, transporting many records is a problem.

Another thing I'd like to share with you is going through the manuscripts. Perhaps *when* (not if) you come to Silver Spring we can do some on *The Edge*. Not the making of inventories which is time-consuming and exhausting—just discovering what is there. But as I told you, on the recent books I was much less mindful of the possible interest of posterity, and threw away lots of early drafts! But I'm sure the field notes for *The Edge* exist and they are fun.

I want to send this along with Jeanne and Ida, so won't write more today. It has been a grey, rainy day, and I imagine there will be fog tonight. But clear tomorrow, they say.

My dearest love—
Rachel

Dear One [Dorothy]—

A little apple, just because it is sweet to talk to you alone—to talk as several times we had opportunities to do during the wonderful Hundred Hours.

And I want to urge you, dear, not to hold back expressions of the dark thoughts. It is really a relief to me to have you share whatever is in your mind about all this. And then I can feel I can do the same. You know you are really the only one to whom I could or would. Of course I tell the facts to the family, but I keep it objective—as I do to Marie or Jeanne. And you would know that my feelings are not all objective.

Yes, I realized I had dealt you a blow with my statement about the five years, and I had some regrets. But then I felt perhaps it was better in the long run that you should know. Not that there is anything definite about it. But we do have to realize there has been a great deal of activity in my case, especially in the past year, and that the disease is now widely disseminated. Dr. Caulk, who is a very kind-hearted man, said yesterday, "I do hate to be the purveyor of so much bad news to you." Then he added, "But you know, it is three years since you first came to me, and you had very serious problems then." I felt that he left unsaid, "Don't expect too much more time."

But in spite of the blow yesterday, darling, I am able to feel that another reprieve can perhaps be won. As perhaps you realized, when I left Southport I didn't expect to return. Now it really seems possible there might be yet another summer. But we do know that now every month, every day, is precious.

And you would know, too, that this latest makes it so much easier for me to accept the fact that darling Jeffie is asleep out under the pines. What agonies of indecision would be mine now, wondering at what point I must decide to let him go. For I always felt I must not, if it could be helped, leave this to strangers, for his sake.

Well, dear, this is all certainly in minor key, and I wish I had time to balance it with other thoughts, of which there are many. But if this is to go this afternoon I must stop.

As an antidote, live again all the fun and laughter and sweetness of the Hundred Hours, and dream of the things we can yet do together.

With this goes a heart full of love that is always for you, as you know.

Rachel

TUESDAY AFTERNOON, JANUARY 14

My darling [Dorothy],

My impulse, my longing, is to fly to you immediately—today![2] But I shall do whatever you wish, and I imagine that may be to wait a few days. I know there will be no lack of kind friends to do for you whatever can be done in these first days. And Stanley will be with you, and of course the Norwood family standing by. So it may well be that it would mean more to you if I came a few days later. I know dear Stan would put first, not my presence at his services, but whatever would give *you* the greatest comfort.

I am still stunned and unbelieving, as I am sure you will be for days and weeks to come. But of course one could never be ready to accept such news. And remembering the long hospital ordeals, I know you have felt that if there could be a choice, something like this would be so much better. How really wonderful for him! No apprehension, no pain, just sudden oblivion shutting down while he was in the midst of one of his happiest occupations. Certainly it is what we would all choose if we had choice.

So, darling, my sadness is not for Stan but for you. Knowing you and your great inner strength I know you will survive not only this time of anguish but the readjustment to come. Please don't try to make decisions too quickly.

In some of his crises over recent years, when recovery seemed so uncer-

[2] Stanley had died of a heart attack on January 14 as he sat at the kitchen table watching birds eat the seed he had just placed in their feeders.

tain, I used to wonder what you would do and how I could help. Then, despite some ups and downs since his surgery last year, I really felt great optimism that he would be spared to you for many years.

I want to say briefly, dear one, that I regret the premature sharing with you of what seemed at the time to be ominous new clouds on my own horizon. They are dissipated now, and all is as it was before. I am going to be around quite a while, dear, and my greatest happiness will be in doing whatever I can for you, and in sharing with you all that we can of the lovely things that mean so much — that bring peace and acceptance of the necessities of living.

The other day I came across Kay Halle's letter with Barney's words about Jane. I know you copied them but you may not have them at hand, so I am sending them now.

This must go with Ida so I can't write more. Remember, darling, you have only to tell me when you most want me and I will be there. Later, I hope you will come to me for as long as you will.

Love, love — now and always.
Rachel

I will tell Lois.

———————————

"Life has been given and life has been taken away. Life and death are one, even as the river and the sea are one. Life is eternal. Life is immortal and death is only a horizon, as the horizon is but the limit of our sight."

JANUARY 18[3]

[3] This note was written when RC was still in West Bridgewater for Stanley's funeral.

Dear One [Dorothy],

You know that in the days and weeks to come you will seldom be out of my mind and never out of my heart. It has never been so hard to leave you as it is now. I am so deeply thankful I could be with you during these days, and could witness at first hand the wonderful outpouring of love for Stan by so many people. But of course now I long to remain by your side, to do any, little things that are possible to ease the days ahead.

But I know you will come through, darling — your wonderful qualities will sustain you. You have been an inspiration and a source of strength to everyone during these days.

Leaving you now, it helps me to know that you have so many kind friends who, I know, will not forget you and will always be ready to help. And remember, whenever you need to speak to me, a few turns of the dial will bring us together. And beyond that, when and if you need me, I will come if it is humanly possible. And I am really definitely counting on our doing some lovely things together in the precious months ahead.

Now let me leave you with the words I once wrote you at another time of separation—"The Lord watch between me and thee while we are absent one from another." And this: "The Lord bless you and keep you. The Lord lift up the light of his countenance upon you and give you peace." You are very precious to me, darling.

Rachel

JANUARY 18

12,000 FEET ABOVE THE EARTH

Dear One [Dorothy],

The habit of talking to you is strong and so I'll write a little note to mail at the airport. Thanks to you I've had a satisfying lunch, with an assist from Eastern in the form of a cup of coffee. The first half of the trip was above a solid cloud floor but now the landscape has emerged. However, the sun is so dazzling that I have to keep the curtains drawn. The plane isn't crowded so I have two seats to myself. I've been reading *The Incomparable Valley*.[4] It would be easier going if I'd already seen Yosemite, but it's fascinating anyway and will make it more meaningful *when* we go. I wish I'd ever studied geology.

One of the many wonderful things about being with you now was getting to know Stanley and Mad better. They are so dear. I was so impressed with the fact that all of Stan's sweetness and gentleness has been preserved in Stanley— as I believe it may be in dear little Richie, too. Just before Stanley put me on the plane he said, "Whenever there is anything Dad would have done for you that I can do, I want you to call on me." And then he kissed me goodbye and called me "sweetheart." I am so deeply happy for you, darling, that you have such a dear son. I hope that sometime, one way or another, you can live closer to them.

Did I tell you about this notepaper? It is made by some schoolchildren in Ohio—a class composed of youngsters who are all handicapped or retarded in some way. Their teacher is related to a friend of Marie's, and sent me a package some time ago. When I thanked them I asked if they had it for sale. They do, so I bought several.

Many thoughts came to me while I was with you—thoughts I want to explore with you sometime, but this, of course, was not the time. I'll try to develop them more and I'll remember.

I do look forward to being with you more in the future, darling, now that in strange and sad ways the ties that held us both more or less immobilized have been broken. Almost ever since I have known you there have been reasons why it was usually so difficult to plan to be together except at Southport. Now, except for taking care of Roger, and my occasional inability to travel, this is changed. And when all goes well, as it has Wednesday and today, the miles are spanned so quickly and easily. Now, dear one, we are nearly in Washington so once more I shall say goodbye. You know how constantly I shall be thinking of you. *Please* do

[4] *The Incomparable Valley: A Geologic Interpretation of the Yosemite* (1950), edited by Fritiof Fryxell.

be careful of your dear self—about driving in bad weather, about icy steps and walks, about those stairs and little rugs! You know you can't help drive up the California coast if your arm is in a cast!

All my dearest love, precious one.

Rachel

MONDAY NIGHT, JANUARY 20

Darling [Dorothy],

Wasn't it sweet that we both felt the need to say Goodnight? I had just hung up the study phone after getting your busy signal when the other phone rang. I suppose you were involved with that other Maryland town while I was trying to get you.

The wind is now howling with a very wintry sounding voice, though the temperature is said to be 43°. "Still raining in Boston," said the 11 o'clock weatherman. I do hope it will have cleared by morning, for your comfort and Stanley's.

I'm sorry, darling, that you are feeling any concern about the financial picture. I can't help believing, however, that once you have all the facts assembled you will find the necessary security. But how in the world does one know what one will really need? I'm in that sort of quandary myself now—not so much about myself as in trying to spell out provisions for Roger in the new will. I had recently given Mr. Huhn the best estimate I could put together on the size of the estate. *Silent Spring* has made quite a difference since the last had such figures, and the change obviously scared him on the score of estate taxes. I think I'll get Maurice[5] in on it before we complete the will. His advice is expensive but the very best, I'm convinced.

[5] Maurice Greenbaum, an attorney.

Darling, I don't know what your thoughts are about where you would really want to go once you have sold your home there. I didn't want to ask you for the reason that I think it is much too soon for you to know or try to decide. But I do want to say what I hope you know—that as long as I live my home is yours at any time, for as long as you want or need to share it. If, for example, you did sell the house there before you had decided where you wanted to go, how happy I'd be to have you come here! So please don't let that transition worry you, at least.

I used to think, when I let myself consider the possibility that you might be left alone, how wonderful it would be if you could then be close to me, somehow, somewhere. Now, with the uncertainties as to my own future, I know you should not build any long-range or permanent plans around me.

But darling, let's resolve that we are going to make use of every possible bit of time to be together. For all of us, not just for me, time is a precious gift, and it is one that can't be hoarded, but must be used well and joyously as it slips through our fingers.

Now it is Tuesday and I'll finish this so Ida can mail it. Our mail has suddenly begun coming about 10 o'clock, so there was no chance to get it out as I'd hoped.

Jeanne arrived a little late and still rather breathless from her exertions of the morning—last night's winds blew down a big pine against their house and across the little patio where we had the Chemex coffee, doing considerable damage to that lovely stand of rhododendron and other shrubs. So she was involved in seeing that removal of the tree didn't do worse damage. Roger heard on TV that wind gusts reached 63 mph. Today is sunny but still rather windy. I hope things aren't wild up there.

Darling, I'm mailing you a *Silent Spring* paperback—thought you'd like to see its format and add it to your collection.

Also, I'm enclosing two clippings which may entertain you for different reasons. I thought the little hippo irresistible (though ugly as he can be!). Don't return it, but you might send the other back sometime.[6]

All day, each of these days, I want to talk to you, to be with you. When we telephone, it is so hard to hang up; now as I write it is hard to stop. I shall be calling you either Thurs. or Friday evening. Maybe about 9:30 is a good time—late enough that evening callers might be gone, early enough to let you go to sleep in good time!

Darling, as much as another person can, I am living these days with you. Because I love you so dearly.

Rachel

[6] The hippo clipping shows a newborn at the Washington Zoo. Second clipping not preserved.

JANUARY 22

Darling [Rachel],

I feel so guilty not having something in the mail for you every day. But we have talked—and will.

Yesterday the let down began. I was terribly tired. Only to-day have I begun on the thank-you notes and it looks like a monumental task, as well as a sad one.

Then there are all the decisions to make and it seems as though there will be so much to do. I know I don't want to keep this house—I shall not hurry and yet I have the feeling that I shall not rest until all that it involves is behind me.

Lois called last night. She had just received our letters—yours, about Stan, and mine about our happy times with pictures of New York. Her comment of the one of you and me together—"Dorothy, you looked like a loved woman!" Her address is P. O. Box 1604, Boulder.

Dear, there is something that has bothered me. When we were speaking about the possibility of going to Bull Island, I said, "Do you think you could arrange to leave Roger?" You know we had just been talking of that fantastic plan of going to California which would mean keeping Roger out of school. My thought was that if we should also go to Bull Island that you might feel you couldn't keep him out again—not that I wouldn't want to have him included. I am afraid you might have misunderstood.

It's a lovely day. Stanley had a bumpy ride up from Long Island, but all is fair for to-day & to-morrow. He hasn't reached any decision about going there, but I doubt if he does. For myself, I think it would be a mistake, but I am trying not to influence his thinking.

He's going to P. O. now.

All my love, dear,
Dorothy

AT HOSP.—FRI. P.M., JANUARY 24

Darling [Dorothy],

I want to put this in the mail, though I'm afraid you won't get it tomorrow. I had a *long* conference with Mr. Huhn this morning, so no time to write as I'd hoped. Nothing special to say (after our *hour* last night) but just that I don't want the familiar handwriting to drop out of your mail too long. And *dear*, please don't feel any compulsion to keep frequent letters coming to me—not with the mountain of notes hanging over you—many of which will turn into letters, I'm sure. We'll be talking often and really I'm not expecting mail. I'd rather you'd rest when you can. Do take some time every day to lie down, even if you just read instead of sleeping.

I'm enclosing the *Register*'s notice about Stan to add to those you have.

Dear, I knew what you meant about Roger & the southern trip. Well those are lovely plans and we must begin to think seriously about carrying out what we can. To this end, will you soon see some doctor, and get busy on whatever toning up you may need? Meanwhile I'll be faithful to my pills and injections, for I want a little more energy.

Darling, I'll talk to you very soon—perhaps Saturday night. Meanwhile, you know you are loved and thought about—so very much.

Rachel

SATURDAY, JANUARY 25

Dear One [Dorothy],

We shall have talked before you read this and no doubt shall have said everything there is to say—but still I want to send a note. Our rain has cleared but I'm not going out, and will ask Robert to mail this. I do have a little cough—not as bad as Roger's was, but I suppose I have a little piece of his cold. It's hard to take care of someone without getting infected, especially with one's resistance low, as I suppose mine is.

Four field sparrows together on the ground under the feeder today! I've seen them only singly before. They are such dainty little mites. And the goldfinches continue to come to my delight. Our mocking-bird has become so cantankerous; he tries to chase everything else away.

Darling, do you know how constantly I think about you? Especially I think of your awakening each morning (in the night, too) to realization. I know, because I've done it, too, in other situations. I wish so very much I could really help.

I do so hope you will soon go to the doctor, darling. You know it is easier to deal with trouble of any kind in its early stages—as witness my present "tired blood." *You* have to be well and stay well!

I wanted to tell you what Lois said Tuesday night when I called her soon after she had talked to you. "When I left that phone booth, in spite of my sadness I felt I was being borne along on a great tide of love." I hope you will send her the minister's words. I think I won't even try to keep you up to date with her affairs. (I know nothing since Tuesday.) It changes constantly and in such confusing ways. Apparently she will stay on at this James Hotel, and, amazingly, she is writing there.

A week ago at this time I was just getting home, having left you only a few hours earlier. I keep thinking how fortunate it was not this week—Roger's cold for one thing, and I'm not walking quite as well. But we'll get straightened out again.

No Ida today—she had to go to Charlottesville for an aunt's funeral. I trust Adgerina will appear tomorrow.

I plan to call you tonight, dear. I like the days when I can say—"Tonight I'll talk to her!"

With this go all my love and tender thoughts of you, dearest.

Rachel

SUNDAY

Darling [Dorothy], Since the other letter didn't go yesterday I'll tuck in another note before Adgerina mails it. I loved our talk last night, dear. Do you have any idea how wonderful you are? It would be so easy to give way to your feelings, but by being so brave you make it easier for others.

I had many reasons to be happy after our talk. One is your plan to put your precious self in Dr. Bowles's hands. (For stardust, see the other letter. Though I didn't mention him, I have long wished you would do this very thing.) Another was your speaking in rather definite terms of coming here for a visit. I can think of nothing in the world that would make me happier—you know that, don't you? Well, you get your most urgent business matters attended to (and I will, too), go to Dr. Bowles, and meanwhile I will discover what the next step in my medical program may be. Then we'll make our plans.

I have no fever but am staying abed today. This rather loose cough and a husky throat are really my only symptoms, but I have a call in for Dr. Healy to see if he wants to order any medicine in view of the whole situation.

I picked up several paperbacks at a bookstore near the Clinic the other day—one of them R. M. Lockley's *Shearwaters*. You know he is a British naturalist who lives on an island (off the coast of Wales, I think) where he has made many studies of birds. It is quite interesting, and besides the details on the birds contains bits of description and glimpses, of migration, etc., that I immediately find myself wanting to share with you. For example, on one of his evening vigils, waiting for the shearwaters to come in from the sea: "It was darker now. The scent of the blue-bells came to me in a gust of wind. They are nearly perfect at this hour of May, leaping up in the recent rains, thick and strong of stem, sun and wind kissed, deep purple, heavy with bells.—Suddenly I heard the first cry of the shearwater on the wing, afar off on the edge of the wind. A wild cry, but softened by distance—. The voice faded—In the interval before the next I heard a whistling, a rippling note—whimbrel flying north to the Shetlands, the Faroes, and Iceland. And then the gaggling of a skein of geese.—I could hear the hiss of wings coming up from the south louder and louder, then slowly dying away north of me. But it was too dark to see anything, perhaps they were white-fronted geese bound for the ice-covered tundra of the far north."

How would you like to share an experience like that? If I could create my own Heaven, I know what it would be.

You asked about Jeanne—I wondered later whether the question had any relation to your visit. We are on the most flexible and informal of schedules, dear. I no longer feel "guilty" when I have her only infrequently. I used to depend on her for a lot of extras but this is now much less true. Besides, if *you* were here, who better could attend to little shopping trips, driving me to hospital, etc. Oh darling, how wonderful it would be to have you!

Dr. Healy has now called. He does want to put me on an antibiotic. This is because I'm taking Prednisone. I forget just what the complication is, but I think the cortisone drugs mask some of the ordinary symptoms of infection so special precautions are in order. So be assured I'll be very careful, dear, and there is nothing to take me out until it is safe to go.

Well, Adgerina is about to bring my dinner tray so I'd better stop rambling. I hope she'll remember to mail this. I must write some other letters this afternoon, but I'd rather talk to you. A. has fixed a salad for our supper so I won't have much to do.

I'll be visiting you by phone Monday or Tuesday night, dear one, so perhaps before you have this. I'll *want* to call Mon., but will wait until the doctors have had their conference. Now, darling, I wish I could put my arms around you. But you know how much love this carries.

Rachel

Darling [Rachel],

I wish you could be here to share this spring-like day. But you aren't and I am wondering how you are. I was so sorry about your cold, dear, for you can do without. You did not sound discouraged last night, dear, but you truly have reason to be. Let's hope the new medication will work quickly.

If we don't do anything else this spring, just watching it arrive, together, will be a joyous way of "letting Time slip through our fingers," as you said.

So after "my hills flatten out a bit" here, I am planning to go to you for a long visit.

I've just been out to feed the birds who only got fed on the shelves yesterday. Did I tell you that we had a male purple finch briefly one morning? I miss them so.

All the bulbs are poking through, and the grass is green. Suddenly, as I walked around the garden (the snow is all gone except for the piles which the plough pushed up at the garage door) a new thought came to me. Perhaps it might not be too bad to keep this house for a while. There might be a possibility I could rent it in the summer to supplement the income. And now that we have found Michael to help as yard boy I feel more secure for I know with my infirmities I cannot garden to any extent.

The rental idea stems from the possibility of the summer schools at the Universities around Boston. And, of course, if need be I could always rent the Southport place for as much time as necessary to take care of the expenses.

Queer, how I vacillate. But I guess everyone does at such a time. I still marvel at how I get through the days when I'm alone. It is really harder when people come. Of course my mind has much to occupy it. I'll be glad when these coming interviews are behind me and I'll have a clearer view of where I stand.

Well, dear, not much of a letter but I did want to write a wee bit to you.

Be very sure you are in my mind and close beside me every minute of the day. If you are going to need more X-ray treatments wouldn't you like me to come down to drive you?

All my love, dear,
Dorothy

WEDNESDAY, JANUARY 29

Darling [Dorothy]—

Only a tiny note. I guess I'm tired of having a cold and don't feel too spry today. The cough is more bothersome—guess I'll confer with Dr. Healy this afternoon.

These bedtime conversations are so sweet, dear. It could easily become an addiction, couldn't it?

I'm so glad you saw Dr. Douglas and got some immediate treatment for the blood pressure, because of course it is most important to control it. For long range care, though, I do hope you will see Dr. Bowles. I want the very best for you!

And I do hope, dear, that now you have surely seen to the most urgent matters, you will slow down. There is time for everything, and all that is *really* important is for you to relax and let that blood pressure drop!

It was good to hear you say you want to do some writing. Won't you plan that as a project while you are here? From 8:30 to 3:45 each day the house will be quiet. You can go into the study and close the door. Ida will serve you lunch whenever you want it, and will make advance preparations for dinner if you ask her to. I would love to feel you were doing that.

It warmed my heart to have you say how you felt about coming, darling— that it gave you a purpose again. I hope you know how wonderful it is for me to know that the major problem is solved in advance. There is no one else, dear, who could solve it so perfectly for me.

Having heard nothing from Barney, I guess the 10th is definite. I *want* to talk to you every night, but shall try to wait till Friday night. If I don't call then you'll know I have no voice.

My dearest love, and constant thoughts of you.

Rachel

S U N D A Y P . M . , F E B R U A R Y 2
***

Darling [Rachel],

My heart aches so for you! And you are so full of courage. Always looking up, instead of being discouraged.

I would like nothing better than to drop everything and rush to you. But I shall feel easier while I'm there if I clean up several things now, and besides you said you didn't want me.

But I am aiming at Thurs. now. My hair will be *awful* but that I shall not fret about. Now *I* wish *I* had a wig. Perhaps you'll loan me Betty.

Oh, Darling, from all I've heard shingles can be perfectly *awful*. Oh, I hope they can help you *quickly* some way.

However I have my doubts that you'll be going to Cleveland immediately. Well, I want to be with you anytime, anywhere.

My thank-you notes are DONE! Now I can breathe.

Hastily as Kay & Harry are coming over & I'll send this by them.

All my love,
Dorothy

[Dear Dorothy,]

For the dearest, most precious friend in all the world, needed in those first hyacinth days of delicate beauty, needed in all the days since then, but never so much as now.

Darling, my love for you is so deep, so boundless. I hope you know.

Rachel

TUESDAY MORNING, FEBRUARY 25

Dearest [Rachel],

I am writing this with the Sheaffer pen you gave me a number of years ago. I still prefer it to ballpoints for its writing quality as well as for its association. Yesterday when I had one of those foolish insurance claims notarized the young notary looked at it curiously, "That will soon be a museum piece"!

Oh, so much red tape—it seems that nothing can be simple any longer. I get quite nervous over it all, and yet I know it will all work out eventually. For instance our stocks are all joint. Of course they have to be changed over. That means sending them away. I have decided to let the bank take care of that (at a price). But each stock has to have a Death Certificate sent with it. That meant going to the Town Hall for the copies (at a dollar apiece) & then getting them all back to the bank in Brockton.

I only tell you this as one example of red tape. One of the forms for the Insurance required the names and addresses of all the doctors Stan had in the last five years and what they treated him for! As though certified proof of death wasn't enough. I hope the poor doctors now don't have to fill in forms.

Sunday afternoon I found the precious letter you left for me when you went home after our New Year's visit. The letter is so beautiful, dear. In its way it crystallized all the joys of our ten years together in a manner that only Rachel Carson could write. I shall cherish it always.

In all that has gone between I had forgotten the loveliness and happiness of those days. In spite of the shadows we were relatively happy—at least I was. It was like an Oasis in Time, and I'm sure it will be very precious to us both.

It seems impossible to believe that you were as well as you were then. All your present afflictions make it hard to remember.

I am so sorry that you have to be unhappy over me. Try to believe this will all work out. You have your own problems and I must not be a burden. That is why I came home and yet now I feel I'm more of a burden than if I'd stayed.

I had a good night last night—I slept until 5 A.M. & woke with hardly a vestige of the mysterious ache—or pain. And went back to sleep. So, you see, that was good—for me.

I know you didn't listen to Bernstein's Young People's Concert. I am so disappointed in him. The program was all Hindemith—he tried so hard to impress people with Hindemith's "beautiful music." It was awful. The shots showing glimpses of the children revealed how either bored or restless they were.

Well, I'd like to be here 100 years from now to see if any of the music of these modern composers including Bernstein, has lived. Such a pity that the promising talent he had has been so misplaced, at least in this oldster's judgment. He could do so much—as he started out to do—in educating young and old in appreciation of music. All he seems to want to get them to appreciate is modern music—at least anything I've seen this year has been that way.

My TV was awful—rolling & clicking—last night so I finally called the repairman. As I thought, the difficulty seems to be the antenna—it was blowing hard in the evening—so he suggests trying a pair of rabbit ears which he will bring up tonight. Hope they work.

The letters about Stan continue to pour in. Yesterday came the one from New Zealand which dissolved me in tears. Such an outpouring of love and devotion to Stan—and to me. The years when they lived next door were a sweet interval in our lives. We adored the children and I know we were a source of strength to Shirley in her difficulties in adjusting.

Now she proposes that I go to them for a visit. It sounds fantastic but you know that that had entered my thoughts—that sometime I just might go—if my finances would allow it. Oh, not yet—but in the years ahead after I have adjusted to this lonely life. For it is lonely, dear. Even when I wake at night I find myself trying not to make a sound that might waken Stan. I know now why TV holds such a place for people living alone. Mrs. Winslow says she keeps it on just to hear some sound in the house.

Well, I'm not that bad, but I do find myself planning to eat my dinner while the evening news is on. I just can't eat at the kitchen table anymore—Stan & I always had breakfast there in the sun.

Oh why do I pour this out to you? I have thought since I came home that I let my own unhappiness invade our days together far too much. I should have left it all behind me.

Well, dear one, in spite of everything, those days brought some precious hours—not enough, of course. I wish we had done more with the box of *Under the Sea-Wind* for what little we did was so revealing. Remember how many questions I raised?

Then I'm glad we talked about my writing. At the moment it seems as though I could never put my mind to it, but I hope when I straighten things out & the pressures are off I can really be in earnest about it.

My next step is to tackle the Income Taxes—I am going up to the offices of Int. Revenue and State Income Taxes. That will take a morning each. With those behind me I think the pressure will be off. Now I have to go up to the bank with the stocks, etc.

It is cold. And I get so nervous about the possibility of more snow for my driveway is narrow enough with high solid walls on either side that I wonder what will happen with more.

Next winter I think I'll really close the house and flee to a warmer clime—

Now, dear, I must get dressed and off. Dearest, I know too well how difficult it is for you to write—the physical effort as well as the feeling of depression. You know I know so please don't try.

I think I know more than you think I do of what all your present difficulties mean. I can't talk about it but I realize that this is a terribly sad and trying time for you—physically and mentally. And my heart aches so!

I love you deeply,
Dorothy

Dearest [Rachel],

I've been ironing and listening to the "Venusberg" music. No need to tell you where my thoughts have been. Back to the lovely day we listened to it together when we were relatively happy.

I'm glad we shared that particular music. The exquisite quiet section at the end brings such a feeling of peace. I've played it more than once.

Last night I got in bed at 7:30 P.M. Somehow I can endure the loneliness that way more easily, especially if I read. But sleep took over before 8 o'clock & I didn't wake up until 10:45 P.M. when I got up, ate an orange, cleaned up for the night, took my little capsule and was off again until 5:45 A.M. And although I did not sleep again I was relaxed enough to stay there until 6:45. Every other morning this week I've had reason to go uptown. To-day I'm doing the household chores—I've washed & ironed & changed my bed. I've decided to give up sending to the laundry—with my good washer-drier it seems silly just to send for my own bed linen. And I'll save a little bit thereby.

Darling, there is something I want to talk about. In retrospect, I am wondering if I disappointed you that lovely afternoon when you told me about the books you wanted me to have. I fear I could not express myself as you might have hoped I would.

If I didn't it was because my heart was too full and I was too deeply moved. You see, dear, it is so hard for me to talk about or even comprehend the reason by which the books would become mine. Do you remember the little passage I read you from your collection of Great Books?—that people don't believe in death.

But now I must tell you that it will be a great joy for me to own the particular collection you mentioned—not just to have them, but because they are the symbol of the doors that you opened to me, of the joys that we shared. They could not have so much meaning to anyone else I'm sure.

So, dear, if I left you unsatisfied by my response that afternoon, please let this tell you what I couldn't seem to find adequate words for then.

Again it is a sunny morning with prospects of above 32° to help melt the snow.

If you should try to call me evenings & I don't answer don't worry. The Grants with Betsy have asked me to play Bridge. I thought it would be so hard without Stan, but we did play one night and as we say, I shut my mind and got on well. I know I need to get out of myself. I've even invited the Johnsons for Sunday dinner. That will keep me busy, and I do need to make some gesture to thank them for their many kindnesses. It will be good for me.

While I've been ironing I've been comparing mine with the perfection of Ida's. Nothing quite like hers. She is a dear. Please remember me to her and thank her again for me. I gave her some money when I left which in no way re-paid her.

The envelope with more mail from S.S. arrived yesterday. One was a let-ter from Myron Murray describing watching a flock of 100 cedar waxwings de-vour every berry on some Pyrocanthus trees in a park in Orlando.

Now I've heard from the two Christian Scientists. Bud Hatch, the former camper when Stan was at Medomak (you know he visited Stan that last week) wrote "It was wonderful to have the brief human visit. Now all my visits can be in Spirit as they have been these many years." He wants to take me out to lunch when he is working in this area.

Now I must get this out to the mailbox. I don't plan to go out to-day until I go to Grants' this evening. In fact, I feel a nap coming on.

You are never out of my mind, dear. I wish the news from you could be that you are improving. So much love goes with every word I write.

Dorothy

SATURDAY, FEBRUARY 29, 8:30 A.M.

Dearest [Rachel],

It *was* snowing when I said good-night to you last night. Afterwards I stayed up to catch the late news and weather so it was 11:30 before I crawled into bed again with a pill. And I did well. It was 6:15 when I awoke. Fortunately the snow had ceased, but there is enough to require shovelling. Our town plough had already done its usual excellent job. We are fortunate. Everyone says you can know when you cross the line into West Bridgewater by the condition of the streets.

Of course, we have all kinds of heavy equipment which goes all night dur-ing a major storm.

Now we shall see if my snow shoveller shows up. I won't press him yet as I am not planning to go out to-day.

I think I told you I had invited the Johnsons for Sunday dinner. Yesterday

I did all the grocery shopping fortunately. It seems so strange not to be considering diets as I shop. The only consideration for the Johnsons—and me—should be calories! Even in my own diet I am so in the habit of following Stan's limitations that it comes sometimes as a shock to realize that I can eat things that weren't on his list.

The sun is out—the birds are hungry. I've filled 3 shelves & thrown out much bread etc. but birdseed thrown on the snow would just sink in.

I'm enclosing the bit about hospitals, some of which I'm sure you'll appreciate! And the Big Sur article.

I can't tell you how distressed I am that things seem to grow progressively worse. As though you didn't have enough trouble without a case of Chicken Pox! I do hope the restrictions on returning to school are not as stringent as when Stanley had it. Then you couldn't go back until every scab had disappeared. It was a matter of well over two weeks, I remember. Poor Roger has missed a lot of school.

Dearest, since I came home that bag of letters has been constantly on my mind. I wish very earnestly that you would just let Ida take them into the study and burn them quietly. I wish now I had. I'm sure I do not want them back, honestly. It was fun finding that letter about Martha but I know that I would never wade through them all even if I had them.

There are such quantities of yours that I do want to go through carefully. And there are so many other things I need to do in the line of going through things—I never did finish the task of my mother's accumulation. Now there is all Stan's desk to go over. I also want to go through all the colored slides to reduce them. There are Stan's files, there are my files on our trips, and files of letters from other people. All these I want to attend to before I think about selling the house which I continue to feel I want to do if only some solution presents itself as to where I should go.

The Freemans want me for a visit but as I contemplate it I don't see how I could stand it for long—no room of my own, and sleeping on a sofa bed in the living room.

If I could hire a room nearby, but I can't afford a motel at $10 a night. Perhaps they'll know of someone who has a room.

Well, to go back to the letters—for all these reasons, I'm sure I wouldn't have time to read my own letters. True they might give me some ideas about my book, I suppose, but already I have enough material in my head to have to discard!

So darling, please take the step NOW. I really am uneasy about them. In the *Sat. Review* I read about Dorothy Thompson's correspondence that went to Syracuse and there was one statement that really frightened me—I don't want to put it in writing but I'll just say that the same implication could be implied about our correspondence.

So, dear, please, please use the Strong Box quickly. We know even such volume could have its meanings to people who were looking for ideas.

Having someone return them to me leaves possibility of miscarriage of your intentions and I really don't want them.

I am very much in earnest about this.

Dearest, I long so for you to feel better. The miserable nausea must be awful. I saw Stan suffer with it so much, and altho' I am not afflicted often, I know it is a sensation that makes me wish I could get down on the floor and forget.

Well, I hope leaving off the Stilbestrol will help. I do hope you like the new doctor—perhaps it will be well to have someone to size up the whole situation. Sometimes I wonder if it would be possible to drop every drug for a while and start over again. It does seem as the variety of kinds could make anyone ill. Who knows what the interaction could be.

Now it's drawing near time for the mailman so I'll get this into the box— will have to wade a bit but it's not too deep.

Remember I think of you constantly. And, dear, because you caught me asleep last night please don't think you mustn't call me at that time. If I am asleep then, I have not actually settled down for the night. I would always be getting up sometime. And you might as well make it after nine—it is less expensive.

You could just as well find me asleep between 6 and 9. It is strange to be so unfettered by time—it is all my own so meals can be anytime—very irregular—like breakfast at 6:15 A.M.

Now I must cease but not without telling you I love you dearly, all my love.

Dorothy

S ATURDAY EVENING , F EBRUARY 29

Dearest [Rachel],

The mail was unusually wonderful to-day. I saved your letter for the last. In it were checks from two insurance companies in full payment. Also there was a notice from the Vet. Adminis. that the claim had been allowed and would be paid in a while. That's the first I've heard from it. So all that was nice to have. Then there were precious letters from Gratia, Helen Lanning, and my dear Nellie Droms, my Scotia landlady, who has known more tragedy than happiness in her lifetime. She sent a little poem which I'm copying for you.

And then I could open your dear letter. What an effort it must have been for you to write so much. What can I say about Stan's letter? It is indeed quite wonderful, isn't it? Of course, it made me cry but that is all right. It helped me to know that he was aware of the seriousness of the blood situation—more than I was sure he knew. I didn't want to alarm him and I suppose it was the same with him.

Helen Lanning wrote "we have known how fulfilling and complete in every way a *happy* marriage *can* be! Lots of people never have that privilege. Mine wasn't as long as I could wish but it was so rich while it lasted." It still is hard for me to comprehend unhappy marriages, just as it was such a revelation that Lois found love in a home to be a *rare* thing!

I am truly fortunate in the long years of giving and receiving love. Thank you, dear, for letting me have the letter.

As for the time I was with you, dear, please don't feel guilty on the score that I was nervous about all the unfinished chores. Actually, dear, it probably was a good time for me to be away. I really wasn't nervous for I had started the ball rolling and knew it was to be a waiting period anyway. And if I'd been home watching the mails, I might have gotten nervous. And it was good for me to have something to do—something that I hoped was helpful.

But it was a poor time for me to be with you as far as my own spirits went. I was not the companion I should have been—you needed to be lifted, and about all I could offer was depression and periods of sadness.

But we did harvest some worthwhile moments—at least, I feel we did. Yes I surely remember, "The time is beginning to seem precious."

I wish we might have talked about the things you "greatly wanted to talk about." Our trouble has always been that we don't start talking soon enough. "We thought we had more time."

Let's profit by this and the next time we are together, let's begin talking at once. Dear, I can't tell you how my heart aches for you with all your tribulations. Especially, I hope the nausea disappears—it's such an awful sensation.

I shall be interested in how you liked the new doctor.

S U N. A. M.

This is March first and guess what, a song sparrow or sparrows sang for the first time! Was I thrilled!

Now I must get to work preparing dinner. I have decided that having company for Sun. dinner is a good idea. It keeps me busy and from being lonely—I think I've told you that Sundays are the hardest days for me.

My Michael showed up yesterday morning to shovel me out completely—bless his heart.

Now to-day they predict "in the fifties"—wonderful, for that should reduce the snowbanks considerably.

The opera yesterday was *Eugene Onegin* by Tchaikovsky—I had only heard it once before—so its beauty was fresh and lovely—exquisite melodies with beautiful decorative accompaniments twining in and around and over. I couldn't help comparing it with the awful stuff Bernstein presented last week.

Dear, you know how much I love you. I'm sure, but do you mind my telling you once more?

I love you,
Dorothy

HAVING A PERMANENT

Dearest [Rachel],

Under the drier now. It will seem good to have my hair shorter and staying up. It has been so droopey lately it has made me feel weary just to look at myself.

I was so glad I called you yesterday morning for I felt so frustrated Sun. night, especially where you had been so miserable when we talked on Fri. night. Oh, dearest, I am so sorry for the continuation of the nausea. I do wish you could get some relief from that.

I am relieved that you now have someone living in. Oh, I'm sure it has its drawbacks and irritations and frustrations. It would be hard to find anyone that could be perfect. But you will try to keep her for a while, won't you, dear, until you really begin to feel up to doing things for yourself?

Also, I'm glad that you were pleased with the new doctor. There is so much at stake that it's good to have another judgment in on the case. Well, I think it is wonderful if it can be worked out for you to go for the operation to N.I.H. I always dreaded the thought of you going off to Cleveland. If need be you could go there in an ambulance. So let's hope you improve enough so you can have it done—if that is the consensus of opinion, to have it done.

Yesterday proved to be a pleasant afternoon. My cousin Jessie is a remarkable woman—she's 99% blind, has had 3 serious heart attacks—one recently—and has had an ileostomy so she wears a bag. With it all she is so cheerful and full of wit and humor. She had us in gales of laughter over her latest heart attack—she was unconscious when they got her to the hospital & as they didn't know her religion they called a priest—just to be sure—and as she described it—"I've had something none of you have had—the last rites of the Catholic Church." Her two daughters brought her to Norwood—Lois and Avis. Jessie was the first grandchild in the Whitney family—was a child bridesmaid at my mother's wedding. She's one of the Baths. Aunt Pink looks very well but, of course, can't use her arms & hands the way she wishes.

We told Jessie that at 76 we thought she was pretty lucky to have an *aunt*. Pink is 87.

Lois had brought a cake and Mildred had made one so the calories held sway—delicious cherry ice-cream, two kinds of cake and coffee!

I got home just after sunset. To-morrow I see Dr. Boles. I think the pain has diminished considerably—I no longer lie awake nights turning from side to side trying to get comfortable. However, there is a definite sore spot on the ribs which may have some meaning.

This morning Brookie called to ask me to ride to Fall River to see Marj. Of course I couldn't because of my permanent so she is going to stop off for a visit this P.M. on her way home. And so the days fill up. You are never out of my thoughts.

That was a strange visit, dear. And yet I'm glad I could be with you. I do hope the next time you will be feeling so much better.

About dry, so I'll get ready to mail this on the way.

All my love, dear,
Dorothy

MARCH 5

Dearest [Rachel],

A blustery south wind eating into the snowbanks ravenously. Oh, what a wonderful feeling to look out upon lawns again. I think I have never felt the chains and bars of winter so completely as since I came home from you.

It is also misting and quite foggy—a poor day for flying. I am thinking of you having transfusions—I hope you are satisfied with the way it works out.

Oh, darling, my heart is in anguish over your condition and what can I say? I long so for you to be free from that miserable nausea.

I hope my news last night was good for you. I had decided I ought to have a check-up so when Dr. Boles suggested it I went right along with him. I had thought of going, probably, to the Lahey Clinic as all my records are there. But this is a much happier solution. It will be good to be in the hospital & of course, so reassuring to have that tower of strength in charge of it all.

My hyacinths at the back door are showing buds and song sparrows are singing. I hope you hear your frogs!

Only a brief note, dear, for it is time for the mailman.

All my love,
Dorothy

SATURDAY MORNING, MARCH 7

Dearest [Rachel],

Just a wee note before Michael comes to start our spring projects. I'm not going to work, of course, but I'll get him started on odds and ends. First we are going to take the lawn mower up for sharpening. Then I want him to uncover the snowdrops that are crying to be free and he can start trimming the yews.

As the weeks widen between January 14 and now I am coming to realize that perhaps I shall be happier to stay in this area. My roots are here, my friends are here, my doctors, and dentist, oculist are here—also some relatives. If I can find people to depend on for help on chores, grounds, etc., that should give me a sense of security. Well, at least, I'll try it out for a year to determine if I can afford to keep this house. Where the rub will come will be when it needs major repairs—such as painting—and it soon will.

There, enough of me. Dear, I can't tell you how differently you sounded last night—your voice was so much stronger, even with hope in it.

It was like a transfusion for me, and I'm sure you know now the full meaning of that! Of course, it is hard for me to understand that in a little over a week you might be headed for Cleveland, but I hope that will work out. Will Mrs. Patterson[7] stay on to care for Roger?

It was good to nestle into my pillow with a lifted heart and I fell asleep quickly.

I was disappointed that you didn't tell me some flowers had arrived from me, so I surely trust they'll reach you to-day.

Isn't this painting sweet? I bought them at the Joy Adamson meeting—just 4 days before Stan went.

I do hope your sense of well being continues. I hope I shall hear that the Strong Box was used to-day!

All my love,
Dorothy

[7] A live-in caretaker.

MONDAY MORNING, MARCH 9

Dearest [Rachel],

A rainy day but I rather enjoy it. The last vestige of snow has gone. Snowdrops are popping in my garden. The brave hyacinths continue to grow. Yesterday two male red-wings, and a grackle, and this morning a male purple finch on the tray—the first one in weeks.

Your letter came Saturday with the dear miniatures in almost perfect condition—perfect enough so I could appreciate how lovely they must be in the garden. I love miniatures—I always think of that line from *Mrs. Miniver* of "smallness squared."

I wonder how you are. You surely amazed me when last we talked. I do hope the improvement continues.

Sunday went off well. The Grants came at 1:30 for dinner. I know that it is good for me to do something like that. I had a hard moment when I opened the last can of B.C. Cocktail (orange & apricot) which Stan had bought. You know he consumed large quantities of it with crackers & cottage cheese between meals in those last months. It is little experiences like that that seem harder now. I walked in the wildwood Sat. & wept at Willow's grave where Stan had planted pussy willows. Oh, dear, I shouldn't write like this to you. Just as the Grants left Dorothy & Eldon Egger dropped in to invite me to go with them for a snack. That was thoughtful. And I did go.

I have been writing furiously meanwhile to clean up sending the letter I had mimeographed about Stan. I've been through his address card catalogue & my own Christmas card list & now I am almost done. I have solved the Thank-You note mystery. Am on way to P.O. now.

Hastily but with so much love,
Dorothy

Dearest [Dorothy],

Well, I can at least get off a letter of "Welcome" today! By the time it arrives you will no doubt be cozily installed in your quarters, getting ready for engagements before X-ray cameras the next day. I hope and really believe, dear, that you won't find it too bad. The "G.I." X-rays have been made so much simpler and easier in recent years. And I'm confident your mind will be relieved when all the reports are in.

This morning was bright and windy, 75° and full of bird song. Now "a low" is bearing down upon us, with rain and thunderstorms along its border, and much colder air.

Yesterday Jeanne brought me her copy of Lawrence Durrell's *Bitter Lemons*—an account of several years he spent on Cyprus. I find it perfectly delightful. It is beautifully written—such beautiful descriptions. And entertaining, too. I've no doubt it will provide an excellent background for understanding what is going on now. I'm going to try to have a copy sent you there. If you have it you can save it for me.

Have managed to pick up a copy of another of Helen MacInnis's spy stories, but am going to try to save it for Cleveland.

Dr. Caulk is going to stop in some afternoon on his way home. "Just a social call." He, too, thoroughly approves of going to Cleveland.

Have discussed plans with Mrs. Patterson and she is quite willing to stay on. Roger is pleased with the idea—"I want you to keep her a long time." Now I'm waiting to hear when Barney can have me.

Darling, I was of course saddened to hear you sound so depressed last night, though I can understand the reasons. My dearest hope for you is that the strength to bear and surmount your troubles and your anguish of spirit may come quickly—I know it will in time.

I feel there are things—about your problems and mine—which we should have talked about, but no time when you were here seemed right, and I doubt this is either. Perhaps when next we meet, whenever that may be. Meanwhile, we have only to remember the joys we have shared, the love each has felt for the other; all this is enough for a lifetime.

Now, darling, I must say goodbye. Ida will soon be going. You know this carries a heartfull of love—

Rachel

Rachel, dear,

When you open your eyes I want you to have a message from me. I do hope you are improving every day.

Spring is coming although there is hoarfrost on the landscape every morning here, and my poor bulbs are struggling hard. •

A letter from Eleanor Engelbrekt yesterday said the geese had been arriving in the past week altho' the cold and snow had slowed them up. It was just about this time two years ago that Stan and I had such an exciting view of them on Merrymeeting Bay. I know how you love the sound of them. Remember my thoughts are with you constantly.

If you reach the point where you would want me to come out to Cleveland, just say the word and I will fly to be with you.

As always, my dear love,
Dorothy

Dearest Rachel,

As each day goes by I am always hoping and praying that you will have added strength and comfort.

I long to be near you to talk with you about the memories of the loveliness we have shared. I am thinking now especially of the morning we rose before dawn in Silver Spring to make the tape of all those bird voices to send to Lois. How they sang, even in the very dim light and how lovely as each new voice came in to swell the symphony.

I shall never forget the joy of that morning hour.

Remember how Lois even heard our voices talking, in the background?

Incidentally, Lois called me two evenings ago to get the latest bulletin from you.

We are all thinking of you, be sure.

May Easter Day bring you its blessings.

With so much love,
Dorothy

Dearest [Rachel],

It's raining here but I heard on a weather forecast of snow in Cleveland! Well, probably that won't bother you for I know you are tucked away in a hospital where you are receiving "good care" according to the precious letter I had from you yesterday. How happy I am to have heard from you, even altho' it was a dictated letter. Please, please understand that I did not expect mail from you, dear, while you are there. I'm glad you liked the flowers—of course, as we both know, one can never be sure if telegraphed flowers are satisfactory.

Well, this has been a rare morning for me, and one that you will appreciate.

First, I discovered a flock of fox sparrows, at least eleven of them, scratching in the back garden. How the oak leaves flew. It was so funny. And while I was enjoying them in flew Mr. Cardinal! I believe I told you he had reappeared, for the first time since you saw him on Dec. 31, last Sunday.

And to my great joy later in came Mrs. Cardinal. So now I can hope for some babies! Wouldn't it be wonderful if they founded a colony here?

Then while I was doing the dishes, I heard a new song—a lovely sweet song reminiscent of the purple finch, but I knew it wasn't. I put the window up to listen. Then I remembered you had said your fox sparrows had sung so sweetly. Thanks to you I was able to corroborate my thought that it was a fox sparrow singing by playing the Bird Song Record.

And then I was sure! This is the first time I've heard a fox sparrow sing to know it.

Wasn't that a lovely morning?

I know I don't need to tell you that my thoughts are with you constantly.

This goes with so much love,
Dorothy

FRIDAY MORNING, MARCH 27

Dearest [Rachel],

It was good to talk with Vera last night to learn about your condition. Although I realize you are very weak and have been very sick, what she told me was reassuring. Perhaps I may even hear your voice within a few days.

Yesterday was "misty, moisty." So when I started for bed I was surprised to see moonlight lying on the hall floor. As I looked out the upstairs window, there in a large puddle on the driveway was the reflection of the full moon.

Do I need to tell you how my thoughts leaped to your tide pool where we have watched, together, in it the reflection of more than one moon? And so for some time my thoughts dwelt on the lovely nights we have watched the moon descend in the western sky over Sheepscot Bay, with all the changes in its path—and the little moon fishes that swam and swam—and how the path finally disappeared as the huge red crescent or oval dropped behind the dark spruces. Lovely memories.

Last night Madeleine called. She said she was taking Martha and Richie to see & hear Joy Adamson and the film of Elsa. I am so glad. Stanley stayed a day longer than he planned in San Francisco—I may be able to see him for a few hours at the Boston airport this evening.

My thoughts are with you, dear.

And I send my love,
Dorothy

Dearest [Rachel],

Need I tell you that the sound of your voice Saturday evening was the sweetest music that I have heard for weeks. To know that you were better, that the operation had helped you made yesterday the "Happy Easter" that everyone was wishing me.

I know that the way back will be long for you have been so sick, but you did win! Oh, Darling.

I trust that every day will bring you added strength. It was not a pleasant Easter Morn here so the sunrise services were cold, misty and raw. But it brought the cardinal to my garden again! That was a good start.

Then I went to the 9 o'clock service at our church. The flowers were lovely, and there was good music. And I tried hard not to be sad this first Easter without Stan—I did as we know we must—I shut my mind to it.

Out of the whole service I gleaned this thought from the responsive reading to carry in my heart. "In the memory of virtues lies immortality."

Stan's virtues have surely brought him immortality for he is living in the memory of so many. Dearest, the letters continue to pour in all with the theme of the fine man he was. I wish I could share them all with you.

After church I went to Gladys's where in the general excitement and confusion I could forget. Little Jimmy, the 4-year-old who is "retarded" from spinal meningitis is such a problem. He is never quiet for a moment and requires someone to watch over him constantly. The whole family takes turns.

Gladys had a delicious dinner which represented so much work that it left me exhausted just thinking about it. She's got a tough spot somewhere.

Kennie's family with his mother-in-law and her sister left about six, so altho' I had planned to come home early, I lingered on to help with the work. Glad. has a dishwasher which did overtime yesterday. But there were still plenty of utensils that couldn't go in it.

But I got home in time to watch the "Breakthrough" program so I had a wonderful opportunity to observe your "Barney" Crile—John Chancellor said in introducing him as Dr. George Crile, Jr., "He is better known as Barney."

Like Dr. Boles he could inspire confidence. I was so glad to see him.

To-day is sunny but cold. I hear there is snow in Washington! No school for Roger, I'll bet.

I'm going to Norwood for lunch—I haven't seen them for some time. And this is one of my "low" moments for some reason, so I need to get away from myself.

Thank goodness you are not the reason to-day.

Oh, darling, Saturday night was so wonderful for me as I knew the day had been for you. I'm sure you will have much to tell me of your Resurrection.

All my love,
Dorothy

P.S. I wrote the good news to Lois at once.

TUESDAY MORNING, MARCH 31

Dearest [Rachel],

What joyous news when Vera called last night! I couldn't believe my ears when she said the subject of your going home had been mentioned. Somehow I was prepared for you to have to stay there for several weeks.

Of course, I shall be anxious about you whenever you go home for being The Head of a Household again is going to mean carrying burdens that I hope you have put aside while there in Cleveland.

I do hope you'll have plenty of competent help and care when you do return.

I try to put myself in your place to imagine how you must feel to know that you are going to be able to go home feeling better. I'm sure no one can quite understand what it means. What a lovely time of year to have this happen.

You will be going home into the glory of spring—bird song, blossoms, and returning warmth. Perhaps, if you want me, I can share some of it with you.

Please, please, please try not to be too ambitious—don't overdo.

After all you've been very sick!

I send you all my love,
Dorothy

APRIL 12

AIRBORNE

Darling [Rachel],

Looking down on the long sandy beach of the outer shore of Long Island with its fringe of white foam which means breakers. How I wish you and I might be walking along some such beach, for the sounds and smells and the feel of the air.

I loved the fact that in your recent experience of another world you remembered and were at Todd Point. That place has so much meaning for me, too.

Looking down on these islands with their lagoons with marinas and boats, I try to imagine how the people down there feel about their own spot. Is it beloved, like ours?

To-day the clouds are still high above us so I can see continuously below—even knew the Chesapeake Bay Bridge & remembered the day Stan and I went home that way. On my flight down the clouds were below us so I only had occasional glimpses. Well, flying is a wonderful way to travel and I'm glad that at last I have accepted it, if only for the fact that it gives me the feeling that I can get to you quickly.

You know how glad I am that I had these past hours with you and why, so I shall not list the reasons.

Wasn't it wonderful to have so much time to be together? And I do hope you could give way to the drowsiness once I had gone.

The cherry trees I should judge are at their height and although I should have liked to walk around the basin, nevertheless I enjoyed the long range view of them.

I was at the airport at 10:45, in plenty of time.

Now we are about to descend so I'll get this in an envelope to mail at the airport. It is only 1 P.M. & we've been told we are approaching Boston —

All my love,
Dorothy

MONDAY A.M., APRIL 13

Darling [Rachel],

Promise of a spring-like day to-day. My birds seem to have deserted me but, of course, I'm sure they felt I had deserted them in spite of the whole pail full of seed I put out before I went to see you. I suppose they ate it all the first day.

I am so glad I had my visit with you. Now I can picture your routine in my mind, even to the delicious massage!

This morning I went to the drawer, where I have letters from you, to find the one about the Monarch Butterflies. Dear, it is one of the loveliest bits you ever wrote, and I'm wondering if you would like a copy of it. Ask Jeanne to tell me if you would. I can't let the original out of my hands for it is far too precious.

When you are stronger and begin to look for the part in *Under the Sea-Wind* you told me about will you ask Jeanne to tell me the page numbers.

I was so sorry that now you are having the discomfort of the drainage — I know how miserable it can make you feel.

It was good to talk with you last evening. You know my thoughts are there with you constantly.

With so much love
Dorothy

Good-morning, Darling [Rachel],

My waking thought is always "How did Rachel sleep?" I can be sure you wake up to bird song which I enjoyed so much in my snug little apartment beneath you. Yesterday a male purple finch feasted at my tray for at least a half hour. I wish he would bring a wife!

Yesterday my new car was delivered—I suppose I should be thrilled. My only feeling is one of a bit more security. It is so-called Meadow Green but to my way of thinking not nearly as pretty as the more blue green of yours.

Dearest, I want you to know that yesterday I realized I had come home with a great sense of peace about you—not about your health—but about the fact that at last I know you are being cared for as I have wanted you to be for so long—someone to be with you at night and to give you loving tenderness during the day.

I have just now opened my desk drawer to find the letter dated Jan. 2 which you left after that visit. You called it "a precious oasis in time, to be cherished and returned to in memory always." It was just that, dear. "Four days in a quiet bower stored with peace and precious memories of all that we have shared." How wonderful that we could have them before the storms broke.

And although my visit with you just now could not have the same tranquility, nevertheless there were very special moments when I felt we were in a "quiet bower."

> Again, I say—All my love, *allways*
> Dorothy

JANUARY 24, 1963[8]

Darling [Dorothy],

I have been coming to the realization that suddenly there might be no chance to speak to you again and it seems I must leave a word of goodbye. Perhaps you will never read this, for in time—if there is time—I may destroy it. But last night the pains were bad and came so often that I was frightened. No, that isn't quite the word, but I realized there might come a time when I wouldn't rouse from sleep in time to reach for the pills. And it seemed it might be a little easier for you if there were some message.

Perhaps I shall write this letter a little at a time, as I can and I shall leave it in an envelope addressed to you.

When I think back to the many farewells that have marked the decade (almost) of our friendship, I realize they have almost been inarticulate. I remember chiefly the great welling up of thoughts that somehow didn't get put into words—the silences heavy with things unsaid. But then, we knew or hoped, there was always to be another chance—and always the letters to fill the gaps.

I have felt, darling, that it is better for you that in this past year, the tempo

[8] RC died on April 14, 1964. This letter with notes dated April 11 and 30, 1963, was delivered posthumously as the envelope containing it had directed in RC's script: "For Dorothy Freeman."

of our correspondence has slowed down so greatly—to the point where I'm sure you no longer watch for the mailman. When there can be no more letters the wrench won't be quite so great.

What do I most want to say? I think that you must have no regrets in my behalf. I have had a rich life, full of rewards and satisfactions that come to few, and if it must end now, I can feel that I have achieved most of what I wished to do. That wouldn't have been true two years ago, when I first realized my time was short, and I am so grateful to have had this extra time.

My regrets, darling, are for your sadness, for leaving Roger, when I so wanted to see him through to manhood, for dear Jeffie whose life is linked to mine.

Perhaps there is more time than I think. But for the past year I have been able to feel much less optimism. And now this new development! But as to the angina, in a way it is almost like a secret weapon against the grimmer foe—so if it should take me quickly, darling, remember this is the easier way for me.

But enough of that. What I want to write of is the joy and fun and gladness we have shared—for these are the things I want you to remember—I want to live on in your memories of happiness. I shall write more of those things. But tonight I'm weary and must put out the light. Meanwhile, there is this word— and my love that will always live.

Rachel

APRIL 11, 1963

My darling, For all these weeks I have written no more, but I have said so much in the letters that went to you that there has seemed to be no need. And now you know of the existence of this last little message to be left for you.

My sadness for you increases, darling. One by one, those you love are being taken from you, for now dear Willow is gone, and you must know I haven't long. And I know that both Willow and I, in our different ways, represented comfort for you in time of trouble, as well as companionship in happy moments! May there be new sources of strength, dear one.

APRIL 30, 1963

My darling, You are starting on your way to me in the morning, but I have such a strange feeling that I may not be here when you come—so this is just an extra little note of farewell, should that happen. There have been many pains (heart) in the past few days, and I'm weary in every bone. And tonight there is something strange about my vision, which may mean nothing. But of course I thought, what if I can't write—can't *see* to write—tomorrow? So, a word before I turn out the light.

I have wanted so terribly to have you here. I've been afraid you wouldn't come if you knew how ill I feel, for you seem to think your being here would make it harder for me, while of course it is just the reverse. And of course I've felt this might be the last time I'd see you.

Darling—if the heart does take me off suddenly, just know how much easier it would be for me that way. But I do grieve to leave my dear ones. As for me, however, it is quite all right. Not long ago I sat late in my study and played Beethoven, and achieved a feeling of real peace and even happiness.

Never forget, dear one, how deeply I have loved you all these years.

Rachel

In a codicil to her will, dated February 13, 1964, Rachel Carson named four persons as possible guardians for her adopted son, Roger: Mr. and Mrs. Paul Brooks and Mr. and Mrs. Stanley Freeman, Jr. The codicil states:

My choices are dictated in part by my conviction that Roger's best interests will be served if his guardianship or custodianship can be undertaken by friends who are parents of children of somewhat comparable age and who would undertake to rear him with affectionate care in the companionship of their own children. I therefore make the following nominations, with the request that at the time of my death my executors discuss the matter with these persons, finding among them, if possible, with due regard to the circumstances then prevailing, a person willing and able to act . . .

Neither the Brookses nor the Freemans had known of Rachel's wishes concerning Roger prior to her death. Paul and Susie Brooks became Roger's guardians.

Dorothy Freeman lived in her home in West Bridgewater, Massachusetts, until 1968. In September of 1968 she married a retired Coast Guard commander, Southport native, and friend of hers and Stanley's. Dorothy and her new husband made their home in a new house they built on Southport, two miles from the Freeman cottage. In 1970, Dorothy's second husband died. For the remainder of her life, Dorothy resided on Southport, spending the colder months in the house she had moved to with her second husband and the warmer months in the Freeman cottage. She traveled to Europe on birding tours and to New York for the opera, and made new friends and correspondents. Dorothy died on Southport of a heart attack at age eighty on August 6, 1978.

In the early 1970s, the owners of Dogfish Head, the small headland near the Freeman cottage, and of the land between and near the Carson and Freeman cottages that Rachel and Dorothy called the Lost Woods, began to sell parcels. Today, a house sits on Dogfish Head. A dirt road circles through the Lost Woods between the Carson and Freeman cottages, and houses have been built on several wooded lots. Much of Southport, and of the land in the vicinity of the Carson and Freeman cottages, appears as it did when Rachel and Dorothy resided there, however. The Carson and Freeman cottages remain essentially as they were in the 1960s. The rocky beach before Rachel's house, the cove with its sandy beach beside Dorothy's house, and the view of sunsets from the shore have not changed perceptibly.

BOOKS BY RACHEL CARSON

UNDER THE SEA-WIND

Simon and Schuster, New York, 1941
Buchergilde, Gutenberg, Switzerland, 1945
Oxford University Press, New York, 1952
Staples Press, London, 1952
Amiot-Dumont, Paris, 1952
Garden City Books, New York, 1953
Uitgeverij Born, Assen, The Netherlands, 1953
J. H. Schultz Forlag, Copenhagen, 1953
Tidens förlag, Stockholm, 1953
Edizione Casini, Florence, 1954
New American Library, New York, 1955
New Asia Trading Company, Colombo, Ceylon, 1956
Albert Bonniers, Stockholm, 1963
Panther Books, London, 1966
Vuk Karadzic, Belgrade, Yugoslavia, 1966

THE SEA AROUND US

Oxford University Press, New York, 1951
Staples Press, London, 1952
Tidens förlag, Stockholm, 1952
Editions Stock, Paris, 1952
J. H. Schultz Forlag, Copenhagen, 1952
Editorial Atlante, Mexico City, 1952
H. Aschehoug and Company, Oslo, 1952
Edizioni Casini, Rome, 1952
Uitgeverij Born, Assen, The Netherlands, 1952
Bungai Shunju Shinsha, Tokyo, 1952
Biederstein Verlag, Munich, 1952
Biederstein Verlag (illustrated edition), Munich, 1953
Tammi, Helsinki, 1953
Mal og Menning, Reykjavik, 1953
Technichka Kniga, Belgrade, Yugoslavia, 1953

The Sea Around Us (cont.)

Lipa, Koper, Yugoslavia, 1953
New American Library, New York, 1954
Tauchnitz Verlag, Stuttgart, 1954
Ikaros, Athens, 1954
Shumawa Publishing House, Rangoon, Burma, 1954
Udom Publishing Company, Bangkok, Thailand, 1954
New Asia Trading Company, Colombo, Ceylon, 1955
Penguin Books, London, 1956
N. Tversky and Company, Tel Aviv, 1956
Editora Nacional, São Paulo, 1956
Kuo Publishing Company, Taipei, Taiwan, 1956
Ulyu Moonhwa Sa, Seoul, Korea, 1956
Sahitya, Prevartaka Co-op Society, Madras, India, 1956
Franklin Publications, Lahore, West Pakistan, 1956
Harsha Printing and Publications, Puttur, Madras, 1957
Egyptian Ministry of Education, Cairo, 1957
Allied Publishers, New Delhi, India, 1958
Rajpal and Sons, Delhi, India, 1959
Franklin Publications, Tehran, Iran, 1959
Oxford University Press (revised edition), New York, 1961
Prisma, Stockholm, 1962
Editions Stock (abridged for Africa and Indo-China), Paris, 1962
Wydawniczy, Warsaw, 1962
Em. Quirido Utgeverij, Amsterdam, 1963
Hayakawa Shabo, Tokyo, 1964
Current Books, Madras, India, 1965
Higginbothams, Tamil, India, 1966
Gon-Yaung Press, Rangoon, Burma, 1967
Panther Books, London, 1969
J. H. Schultz Forlag, Copenhagen, 1969
Guilio Einaudi Editore, Turin, 1971

THE SEA AROUND US

Junior Editions

Golden Press, New York, 1958
William Collins & Sons, London, 1959
Folket I Bild, Stockholm, 1959
Casa Editrice Giuseppe Principato, Milan, 1960
Cocorico, Paris, 1961
Forleget Fremad, Copenhagen, 1961
Zuid-Nederlandse, Antwerp, 1963
Editorial Novaro S.A., México D.F., 1966
Otto Maier Verlag, Ravensburg, Germany, 1968

THE EDGE OF THE SEA

with illustrations by Robert Hines

> Houghton Mifflin Company, Boston, 1955
> Staples Press, London, 1956
> Amiot-Dumont, Paris, 1956
> Biederstein Verlag, Munich, 1957
> New American Library, New York, 1959
> Cadmus Books, Eau Claire, Wisconsin, 1965
> Panther Books, London, 1965
> New American Library, New York, 1971

THE ROCKY COAST

from The Edge of the Sea, *with photographs by Charles Pratt and drawings by Robert Hines*

> McCall Publishing Company, New York, 1971

THE SEA

the three sea books in one volume

> McGibbon and Kee, London, 1964
> Panther Books, London, 1967
> McGibbon and Kee, London, 1968

SILENT SPRING

> Houghton Mifflin Company, Boston, 1962
> Hamish Hamilton, Ltd., London, 1963
> Penguin Books, London, 1963
> Plon, Paris, 1963
> Biederstein Verlag, Munich, 1963
> Feltrinelli Editore, Milan, 1963
> Gyldendalske Boghandel, Copenhagen, 1963
> Tidens förlag, Stockholm, 1963
> Tiden Norsk Forlag, Norway, 1963
> Tammi, Helsinki, 1963
> H. J. W. Becht's Uitgeversmaatschappij N.V., Amsterdam, 1963
> Fawcett Publications, New York, 1964
> Luis de Caralt, Barcelona, 1964
> Companhia Melhoramentos, São Paulo, 1964
> Shincho Sha, Tokyo, 1964
> Bokforidget Prisma, Stockholm, 1965
> Almenna Bokafelagid, Reykjavik, 1965
> Tiden Norsk Forlag, Norway, 1966
> Editorial Portico, Lisbon, 1966
> Teva-Ubriuth, Petah Tikvah, Israel, 1966

Silent Spring (cont.)
 Livre de Poche, Paris, 1967
 Tammi (reprint), Helsinki, 1970
 Drzavna Zalozba Slovenije, Ljubljana, Yugoslavia, 1971

THE SENSE OF WONDER

with photographs by Charles Pratt and others

 Harper and Row, New York, 1965
 Harper and Row, New York, 1967

MAGAZINE ARTICLES BY RACHEL CARSON

"Undersea" in *The Atlantic Monthly*, September 1937

"How About Citizen Papers for the Starling?" in *Nature Magazine*, June–July 1939

"The Bat Knew It First" in *Collier's*, November 18, 1944

"Ocean Wonderland" in *Transatlantic*, April 1945

"The Bat Knew It First" (condensation) in *Reader's Digest*, August 1945

"The Great Red Tide Mystery" in *Field and Stream*, February 1948

"Lost Worlds: The Challenge of the Islands" in *The Wood Thrush*, May–June, 1949

"Birth of an Island" in *Yale Review*, September 1950

"Wealth from the Salt Seas" in *Science Digest*, October 1950

"The Shape of Ancient Seas" in *Nature Magazine*, May 1951

"The Sea" in "Profiles," *The New Yorker*, June 2, 9, 16, 1951

"Why Our Winters Are Getting Warmer" (excerpt from *The Sea Around Us*) in *Popular Science*, November 1951

"The Edge of the Sea" (excerpt from *Under the Sea-Wind*) in *Life*, April 14, 1952

"The Edge of the Sea" (excerpt) in "Profiles," *The New Yorker*, August 20 and 27, 1955

"The Mystery of Life at the Seashore" (condensation of *The Edge of the Sea*) in *Reader's Digest*, February 1956

"Help Your Child to Wonder" in *Woman's Home Companion*, July 1956

"Help Your Child to Wonder" (condensation) in *Reader's Digest*, September 1956

"Our Ever-Changing Shore" in *Holiday*, July 1958

Silent Spring (excerpts) in "Reporter at Large," *The New Yorker*, June 16, 23, 30, 1962

"Poisoned Waters Kill Our Fish and Wildlife" (excerpt from *Silent Spring*) in *Audubon Magazine*, September 1962

"Beyond the Dreams of the Borgias" (excerpt from *Silent Spring*) in *National Parks Magazine*, October 1962

"Beetle Scare, Spray Planes and Dead Wildlife" (excerpt from *Silent Spring*) in *Audubon Magazine*, November 1962

"Moving Tides" (excerpt from *The Sea Around Us*) in *Motor Boating*, July 1963

"Rachel Carson Answers Her Critics" in *Audubon Magazine*, September 1963

"Miss Carson Goes to Congress" in *American Forests*, October 1963

... ...
... ...

Beaufort, North Carolina, xxv
Beebe, William, 131, 132, 199
Bennett, Christine, 122, 267, 429
Bent, Arthur Cleveland, 101, 336
Bernstein, Leonard, 163, 287, 345;
   Maria Carson's fondness for, 269–70,
   271–73; concerts, 161, 197, 208, 212,
   217, 219, 251, 269–70, 525–26
Bernstein, Morey, 154, 156
Berrill, Jack, 133, 140, 359
Berrill, Jacquelyn, 154
Berrill, Norman John, 50
Beston, Elizabeth, 451
Beston, Henry, xxiv; DF's desire to
   write to, 26; RC and DF's visit to,
   41n.20; RC's correspondence with,
   54; review of *Under the Sea-Wind*, 23,
   24, 26, 28, 29; *The Saint Lawrence*, 46
Bigelow, Henry B., 12, 27, 35, 172,
   351
Bingham, Millicent Todd, 379
Biological oxidations, 291, 292
Biology of the Spirit (Sinnott), 126
Birds and birdwatching: barred owls,
   228, 367; black birds, 387, 388; blue-
   jays, 175, 266; boat-tailed grackles,
   360, 362; brown creepers, 191, 388;
   brown thrasher, 369; cardinals, 351,
   425, 432, 433, 468, 496, 513, 537;
   catbirds, 179, 283, 383, 387, 409,
   462; chickadees, 42, 285, 289, 345,
   369, 382–83, 388, 425, 478; cormorants, 387; cowbirds, 369; cuckoos,
   49; downies, 383; Easter lily, 496;
   finches, 523; flickers, 383; flycatchers, 42, 376; fox sparrows, 399, 449,
   537; geese, 359, 440, 445, 488; goldfinches, 298, 520–21; grackles, 355,
   360, 362, 369; grosbeaks, 501; gulls,
   56, 345, 389; hairies, 383; hermit
   thrushes, 70, 116, 117, 120, 283, 379;
   herons, 42, 488, 492; juncoes, 266,
   383, 388; killdeers, 279, 352; king-
   fishers, 383, 409; kinglets, 289, 290,
   409, 480; mallards, 440; mockingbirds, 311, 451, 468, 484; mourning

doves, 352, 425, 468; myrtle warblers, 487, 488; nuthatches, 383, 388,
   487; olive backs, 120, 228; orioles,
   462; ovenbirds, 42, 43; owls, 367;
   partridges, 492; parulas, 382, 409;
   phoebe, 409; on Pratt's Island, 267;
   red starts, 376; robins, 359, 368, 399,
   401, 443, 445, 513; scarlet tanager,
   384; sparrows, 175, 266, 289, 352,
   359, 383, 399, 449, 462, 520, 537;
   starlings, 289, 416; swans, 484; Texas
   coast birds, 411; thrashers, 369, 387;
   titmice, 341, 353, 432, 513; towhees,
   377, 383, 387, 409; veeries, 17, 42,
   43, 50, 110, 115, 116, 117, 228, 378,
   379; warblers, 382, 409, 478; waterfowl flights, 285–86; water thrushes,
   42, 43; whippoorwill, 405; white
   throats, 116, 117, 289, 290, 300, 377,
   383, 404, 484; woodpeckers, 293,
   369, 492; wood thrushes, 43, 49, 179,
   462; wrens, 179, 454; yellowlegs, 191
Birds Over America (Peterson), 41
Bishop, Isabel, 131
Biskind, Dr., 399, 400, 401, 442, 451
Bitter Lemons (Durrell), 535
Blake, William, 328
Bliss, Mrs. Robert Wood, 460
Blue Nile (Moorehead), 431
Bok, Curtis, 213, 278; death of, 415; illness, 183–84; *Maria*, 415, 417, 461;
   RC's correspondence with, 141, 149–
   50, 152, 155, 159, 171, 177, 188, 192,
   204; RC's dream about, 168–69; and
   RC's election to Board of the Ameri-
   can Foundation, 193, 196; RC's week-
   end with the Boks, 159, 179, 180–81
Bok, Enid, 181, 461
Bok, Nellie Lee, 196; Curtis Bok's last
   book and, 414, 415; RC's correspondence with, 183–84, 215, 460–61;
   RC's weekend with the Boks, 159,
   180, 181
Boles, Dr., DF's visits and consultations
   with, 456, 476, 477, 484, 521, 532,
   533

Book-of-the-Month, 109, 407

Book of the Sea, The (Spectorsky), 144

Books Abridged, version of *The Edge of the Sea*, 128, 133, 159

Bookstores, 126, 129

Boothbay Register, 6, 82, 222, 297, 418, 438, 489, 502, 520

Born Free: A Lioness of Two Worlds (Adamson), 362, 367, 416

Boston Herald, xxvii

Boston Museum of Science, 128, 129n.54

Bowen, Elizabeth, 99, 100, 135

"Bread from the Sea," article in *Collier's*, 43

Briejer, C. J., 486

Briggs, Shirley, xix, xxx, 400

British Petroleum Exploration Co., 237

Brockman, Sallie, 129

Bronx Zoo, 132

Brooker, Mrs., 376

Brookings Institution, 287

Brooks, Charles, 172, 181

Brooks, Paul, xiii, xviii, xix, 199; editor for *The Edge of the Sea*, 27, 60, 93, 94, 100, 102, 109, 128, 133, 143, 156; editor for *Silent Spring*, 352, 367, 378, 380, 400, 402, 417; guardianship of RC's adopted son, 545; and *New Yorker* proposal, 48; party for the publication of *The Edge of the Sea*, 122

Brooks, Susie, 51, 93–94, 545

Brower, David, 482, 484

Brown, Francis, 160

Brown, John Mason, 41

Browning, Mortimer, 62

Buchheister, Carl, 483

Buck, Pearl S., 39, 199

Burgoon, Mrs., 100

Burrage, Miss, 112

Burt, Maxwell Struthers, 293

Burton, Maurice, 61

Caine Mutiny, The (Wouk), 154

Cancer: anti-cancer factor, 401; cancer chapter in *Silent Spring*, 295; Kre-

biozen, 442, 445, 451, 452, 457; RC's hospitalization for breast cancer, 302–4; RC's radiation treatments/therapy for, 313–14, 324, 326, 327, 345–46, 347, 354, 356, 393, 399–400, 403–4, 425–26, 434–35, 436–37, 438, 442, 452, 455, 467, 469, 471, 475, 483, 501; spread of RC's, 313, 319

Cancer and Common Sense (Crile), 125

Canfield, Cass, 133, 150, 151, 255, 276–77, 292

Canfield, Katherine, 150

Cape Cod Compass, 232, 235, 236

Captive Wild (L. Crisler), 362, 367, 376, 444

Carnegie Foundation Building, 199

Carr, Ruby, 359, 401

Carroll, Lewis, 83, 288

Carson, Emily (sister), 226

Carson, Maria (mother), xv, xxvi, 101, 169; death of, 271–73; illnesses, 54, 184, 185, 188, 192–93, 194, 234–35, 237, 269, 270; RC on death of, xxvii; reaction to WHC article, 170

Carson, Rachel: awards, xxx, 37, 38–39, 177, 179, 184–85, 196–97, 198–99, 417, 429, 431, 439, 447, 458, 464, 483, 495, 499, 500; beach visits, 9, 54; biographical account, xxiii–xxiv; biographical sketch of, 411; Bronx Zoo visit, 132; car trouble, 262–63; "catalogue of illnesses," xxvii, 390; cats. *See* Jeffie; Moppet; Muffie; comparison of writing *The Sea Around Us* and *The Edge of the Sea*, 127; concerns for Jeffie's care, 450; concerns for Roger's welfare, 219, 332; concerns regarding her impending death, 439–40, 515, 541–43; considers new home, 172, 173–74, 179, 182–83, 191; construction of new home in Silver Spring, 217–18, 220, 221, 222, 225, 228; death of, xxx, 541–45; on DF's writing abilities, 88, 95–96, 105, 113; Distinguished Democrat inaugural reception, 326, 328; "Dream" of financial freedom, 203–5, 206–7, 208, 210, 212–14; earrings gift to DF, 189; efforts to establish a foundation, 204, 208–10, 212–14; "famous author" concept, 23, 28, 130, 334; fan mail, 79–80, 160, 185–86; fears of DF dying, 223, 224; first meeting with DF, xiii, xxv–xxvi, 3; first night in new home, 229; hospitalization, 302–4, 344–45, 397; illnesses, 57–58, 130, 131, 138, 211–12, 213, 232, 234, 237, 254, 277, 295–96, 297, 299, 302–4, 313, 319, 327, 337–38, 339, 343–44, 360, 361, 362, 363, 364, 365–66, 403–4, 416, 426, 429, 465, 520, 521, 522, 523–24. *See also* Angina; Cancer; Iritis; lectures and symposiums, 9, 12, 27, 33, 35, 36, 39, 61, 62, 63, 109, 112, 142, 285, 286–87, 411, 469, 482; on loneliness and writing, 28–29; on material immortality, 446–47; *Nature Notes* to DF, 289–90; new car, 50, 454, 455; physical therapy treatments, 345–46, 347; preoccupation with night, 166–67; purchase of television, 171, 172; purple snail incident, 165–66; tide pool explorations, 3–4, 5–6, 109–10; visits to DF, 15, 26, 28, 32, 35, 75, 94, 109, 117, 129, 154, 186, 310, 389, 415, 464; wig purchase, 403; will and estate, 257, 518, 545; writes *The Edge of the Sea*, 6, 7–8, 9–10, 27, 32–33, 35, 46, 48–49, 53, 60, 81, 85, 86, 88, 89, 92, 93; writes *Silent Spring*, 251, 252, 255, 258–59, 260, 268–69, 287, 289, 291–92, 294, 295, 296–97, 314, 352, 357, 378, 380, 390–91, 393–94, 399, 402, 461

Carson, Robert (brother), xv, 135–36, 172, 181, 230; house hunting, 277; illness, 105, 109, 110; visits to RC household, 347, 451–52

Carson, Vera (sister-in-law), 98, 230,

255, 269, 277, 347, 451–52, 486, 537, 539

Cash McCall (Hawley), 133

Cather, Willa, 113, 500

Cattell, Dr., 443

Caulk, Dr., RC's visits to, 326, 327, 344, 345, 354, 361, 362, 380, 393, 398, 399, 400, 402, 403, 425, 426, 435, 437, 469, 471, 475, 483, 486, 494, 501, 514–15, 535

Cave pool, 99

"CBS Reports" (television program): "The Silent Spring of Rachel Carson," 445, 451; "The Verdict on the Silent Spring of Rachel Carson," 461

Cerf, Bennett, 249

Chancellor, John, 538

Chas. M. Cox Company, 106, 230

Chatham College, xxiii, 179, 397

Chessie (stuffed toy cat), 60, 65

Child from Five to Ten, The (Gesell), 219

Childs, Gladys and Ken, 409

Christie, Roger (grandnephew), xv, xxvi, 7; accidental fall, 86; beach visits, 8, 54; bird walks, 110, 267; birthday celebration, 101; childhood antics, 60–61, 112, 129, 153, 160, 162, 174, 186, 324, 332–33; education, 194, 228, 233–34, 268, 470; excitement over new car, 50; guardianship of, 545; illnesses, 171, 214, 216–17, 239–40, 256, 269, 379, 429, 464, 529; mother's death, 216, 248; music lessons, 475; RC's adoption of, 216; and RC's hospitalizations, 345, 346, 348, 349; receives school award, 381; relationship with Stanley Freeman, Sr., xviii, 54, 56, 188, 230, 510; school plays, 380, 417; summer camp, 466–67; trips to Boothbay Harbor, 54, 56; visit to Virginia and Lee King, 287

Chute, Beatrice Joy, 199

Ciardi, John, 449

Clark, Eugenie, 80
Clarke, Winnie, 206
Cloos, Hans, 10, 16, 335
Coates, Christopher, 132
Coatsworth, Elizabeth, 41n.20
"Collagen diseases," 364
Collected Impressions (Bowen), 99
Collier's, 43
Conley, Ervin G., 438n.13
Conley, Mr. (landscaper), 32
Connelly, Marc, 132
Conrad, Joseph, xxiv, 249
Conservation Forum, 405
Conservation Foundation, 200
Consumer's Union, 291
Conversations with the Earth (Cloos), 10, 132
Cook, Mr., 159, 161
Cook, Phyllis, 458
Cooke, Alistair, 270
Cooper, Gordon, 461
Cooper, Margaret, 10
Cottam, Clarence, 405, 410, 411, 439
Cousins, Norman, 342
Cox, Sidney, 254
Cranberries, 290
Cranbrook Institute of Science, RC's lecture at, 27, 33, 35, 39
Crane, Dr.: book on rheumatoid arthritis, 364; RC's visits to, 344, 345–46, 350, 352, 356, 361, 362, 365, 368, 375
Crile, George "Barney," Jr., 331, 414, 447, 491, 538; *Cancer and Common Sense*, 125; RC's consultations with, 317, 325, 327, 361, 362, 364, 372–73, 397, 404, 425, 426, 436, 444, 452, 487
Crile, Jane, 331, 414, 432, 435
Crisler, Cris, 276, 293, 471, 472, 475, 489, 491
Crisler, Lois, 276, 288, 335, 386, 387, 393, 465; *Captive Wild*, 362, 367, 376, 444; DF's correspondence with, 282;

gift to RC, 511; RC's correspondence with, 293, 338–39, 344, 351, 353, 361, 367, 437, 444, 471–72, 474, 475, 489, 491, 503, 519, 521; RC's recommendation for NIAL grant for, 378; RC's visit to, 406; Stanley Freeman, Jr.'s planned visit to, 354, 355, 366, 371
Cruel Sea (Monsarrat), 154
Culbeath, Jack, 87

Daly, R. A., 11
Darwin, Charles, 41
David and the Seagulls (Downer), 166
Davis, Burnet, 392, 483
Davis, Jeanne (RC's assistant), xix, 282, 288, 291, 292, 294, 328, 346, 348, 349, 357, 359, 390, 392, 416, 427, 444, 464, 470, 483, 519, 522; father's illness, 450, 466, 494, 495, 499; illness, 433
DDT, xxvii, xxviii, 265n.24
Deer, 56, 492
Deer yards, 361, 364
Delaney, Mr., 161
Delano, Mr. (building contractor), 38, 134, 155, 191, 192, 260, 493, 495; and construction of RC's new home, 218, 220
Demerol, 192
Dennewitz, Dr. (veterinarian), 179, 180, 263
Dermont, Maria, 283
Diamond, Mr., 252
Dick, Dr., 168, 318
Dickson, Elizabeth, 158, 196, 261, 263, 304
Dinosaur Monument, dam recommendation in, 16
Dodd, Mead and Co., 155
Dooley, Thomas, 337, 341–42
Douglas, Justice William O., 314, 387, 405
Dove, Joan, 257
Dow Chemical Co., 287

Jeffie (RC's cat): antics, 18, 29, 30, 35, 87, 134, 171, 191, 345, 347, 356, 357, 428, 485; birthday cards to, 57; death of, 504, 505; favorite foods, 48; first valentine, 22; illnesses, 179, 180, 263, 502–3; injuries, 36–37, 39, 41, 44, 50–51, 61; as kitten, 14, 33; Moppet's death and, 469; steps designed for, 58

John J. Nagle (fishing trawler), 56, 502

Johns Hopkins Magazine, RC's "The Sea" article in, 375

Johnson, Mary, 196, 208, 237, 239, 260, 300

Johnson, Mrs. (nurse), 184, 185, 192, 194

Journal of Researches into the Natural History and Geology of the Countries Visited during the Voyage of H.M.S. "Beagle" Round the World under the Command of Capt. Fitz Roy R.N. (Darwin), 41

Journey into Summer (E. W. Teale), 344

Kaiser Medical Center, 469

Kamala, Markandaya, 199

Keats, John, 15, 402

Keene, Dr., 482

Kefauver, Estes, 449

Kennedy, Jacqueline, 312, 339

Kennedy, John F.: appointment of pesticides committee, xxviii–xxix; assassination of, 496, 497; Inauguration, 328, 339; Science Advisory Committee, 429, 447; speech at the University of Maine, 488–89

Kenrick, Harriet, 321, 376, 377, 380

Kimball, Mr., 447

Kimbrough, Mrs., 196

King, Lee, 287, 376, 498

King, Virginia (niece), xv, 10, 61, 101, 348, 417; illnesses, 261, 277, 466; Roger's visits to, 287, 481; visits to RC, 352, 376, 498

Kipling, Rudyard, 207

Kirkus, Virginia, 127, 128

Kitty (A. Mullen's sister), 161, 222–23

Knecht, Beverly, 288, 292, 306, 351, 362

Krebiozen, 442, 445, 451, 452, 457

Kubly, Herbert, 149n.6, 154, 155

Ladies Home Journal, 174

Lake Mattamuskeet, North Carolina, 286

Lake Meade, 480

Laminarias, 5

Lanning, Helen, 530–31

Lawrence, Elizabeth, 258, 276

Le Corbeiller, Mr., 252

Lee, Mrs., 287

Leggett, Jack, 199

Leventhal, Al, 199

Lieper, Maria, 10, 132, 200, 209

Life Histories of North American Shore Birds (Bent), 101

Life magazine: "The Gentle Storm Center," 411; RC's picture in, 392; RC's proposed jet stream article for, 62, 165, 167, 171, 172–73, 177, 181

Limited Editions Club, RC's award from, 37, 38–39

Lincoln, Abraham, 408

Lincoln County Cultural and Historical Association (Maine), 109n.31

Lindbergh, Anne Morrow, 108, 113, 120, 137, 140, 150, 154, 156, 196–97

Lioness of Two Worlds, A (Adamson), 359n.26

Little, Walter and Flora, 144, 175, 318, 355, 392, 440, 449

"Little Things, The" (Tomlinson), 414

Living Philosophies (Einstein), 67–68, 69

Living Wilderness, The (magazine), 16

L. L. Bean, 364

Lockley, R. M., 522

"Locksley Hall" (Tennyson), 59

London Symphony, 511

Loons, 6

"Lost Woods, A" (Tomlinson), 36, 202, 224, 253, 373

Lost World of the Kalahari, The (Van der Post), 280

the *Birds* (recording), 197; *Tannhäuser* overture (Wagner), 510; *Tristan and Isolde* (Wagner), 28, 362; Violin Concerto in E minor (Mendelssohn), 159, 203, 206, 211

"My Life Is a Bowl" (Ripley), 324

Nash, Ogden, 132

National Agricultural Chemicals Association, xxviii

National Audubon Society: Michigan Audubon Society, 287; RC's award from, xxx, 483; RC's lecture to, 61, 62, 63; RC's talk to Audubon Society of the District of Columbia, 285

National Book Award, 149n.6

National Council of Women of the United States: RC's award from, 196–97, 198–99; RC's speech to, 411

National Gallery of Art, 328

National Institute of Arts and Letters, 367, 378n.36

National Institutes of Health, 289, 364, 532

National Parks Association, 405, 411

National Press Club, 234

National Wildlife Federation, RC's award from, 439, 447

Natural Food Association, 431

Nature and Man's Fate (Hardin), 428

Nature Conservancy, 204

Nectar in the Sieve (Kamala), 199

New England Wildlife Preservation Society, 426

Newman, James, 200, 203, 204, 213

Newton, Doris, 318, 348, 373

New Yorker, The, 125, 208, 339, 366; ad for *The Sea Around Us* in, 362; first installment of *Silent Spring* in, xxviii, 407; proposal for serial rights to *The Edge of the Sea*, 46, 47, 48, 102, 109, 111; RC's proposed pesticide article for, 252, 255, 256

New York Herald Tribune, 13, 122; *The Edge of the Sea* on best-seller list, 133, 135, 137, 145, 154, 156, 182

New York Times, 29, 44, 122, 129, 358; ad for *The Sea Around Us* in, 362; *The Edge of the Sea* on best-seller list, 133, 135, 143; Maxwell's *Ring of Bright Water* on best-seller list, 359, 366–67; *Silent Spring* on best-seller list, 417

New York Zoological Society, 81, 144, 199

Nobel Prize: for literature, Pearl S. Buck, 39; for medicine and physiology, Peter Medawar, 482; for peace, Albert Schweitzer, 62; for physiology, John F. Enders, 143

Nobleboro, Maine, 26, 41

No Room in the Ark (Moorehead), 292

North, Sterling, 470

Northern Farm (Beston), 26, 41

Northern lights, 276, 468

North with the Spring (E. W. Teale), 41n.23

Norwood, Massachusetts, 90

Nye, Mil, 372

Oakley, Walter, 199

Ocean Floor (Pettersson), 61

Octopus, 9

"Ode to Joy" (Schiller), 272–73

Oliver, Edith, 401

Olivier, Sir Lawrence, 161

"Omnibus" television program, 217; RC's "Clouds" script for, 145, 146–47, 148, 150, 152, 153, 155, 158, 159, 161, 165

Open Heart, The (Weeks), 123, 124

Orchard, Harriet, 418, 458

Osborn, Fairfield, 132, 200, 257

Osteoarthritis, 364

Our Changing Earth (Daly), 11

"Our Ever-Changing Shore" (Carson), article for *Holiday* magazine, 231, 232, 236, 238, 240, 241

Outermost House, The (Beston), xxiv, 23

Out of Soundings (Tomlinson), 36, 202

Owings, Margaret Wentworth, 499

Oxford University Press, 129, 198, 199, 202, 351

38, 103, 129, 136, 193, 242, 403, 482; Bronx Zoo visit with RC, 132; manuscript preparation for RC, 491, 494; at National Council of Women of the United States awards dinner, 196; and "Omnibus" project, 152; and *Reader's Digest* proposal for *The Edge of the Sea*, 48; and *Woman's Home Companion* project, 149, 171

Rose, Mrs., 265

Ross, Frances, 349

Rutledge, Archibald, 10, 46–47, 66

St. Lawrence, The (Beston), 46, 54

St. Nicholas (magazine), xxiii

Salar the Salmon (Williamson), 11

Sandburg, Carl, 292

Sanderson, Dr., 313

San Francisco Chronicle, 360

Saturday Evening Post, 255, 501

Saturday Review, 125, 133, 362, 375, 507n.70, 529

Saudek, Robert, 270

Schaefer, Vincent, 152, 159, 161, 165, 191, 237, 257

Schiller, Johann Christoph Friedrich von, 272–73

Schultz, Mr., 144

Schweitzer, Albert, 62, 154, 357; Albert Schweitzer Medal to RC, 417, 429

Science, The Glorious Entertainment (Barzun), 511

Scientists Cliffs, 349

Scott, Peter, 416

Scripps College, 40, 146n.80, 330, 332, 361, 406, 482

Scytosiphon, 109

Sea and Earth: The Life of Rachel Carson (Sterling), xviii

Sea and the Jungle, The (Tomlinson), 9

Sea Around Us, The (Carson), xiii, 237, 304, 360, 463, 499; on best-seller lists, xxiv; film based on, 4, 6, 9; first edition of, 59; fog passage in, 11; "Island" chapter in, 81; junior edition of, 199, 202, 252; manuscript donation, 491, 498; publication of, xxiv, xxv; revised edition of, 351; Yugoslavian translation of, 42

Sea Beach at Ebb Tide, The (Arnold), 47

Seals, 6, 492

Search for Bridey Murphy, The (M. Bernstein), 154, 156

Sears, Paul B., 290

"Sea, The" (Carson), 375

Sea Shore, The (Yonge), 109

Seaweed, 109, 115

Secrets of Life (film), 196, 201

Seguin Island, 140, 141, 320, 382

Sense of Wonder, The, xiii, 149n.5, 170, 277n.5, 391n.1

Sevareid, Eric, 237, 445n.16, 461

"Shallow Waters" (Carson), 232, 235, 236

Shaw, Mrs. (nurse), 214–15

Shawn, William, xxviii, 46, 48, 100, 109, 200, 295, 393–94; and RC's proposed pesticide article for *The New Yorker*, 252, 255, 257

Sheain, Dr., 482

Shearwaters (Lockley), 522

Shelton, Alphonse, 77, 80, 488

Sheraton-Park Hotel, Washington, D.C., 184n.49

Sherman, Maurice, 284, 388

Sherman, Mr. (building contractor), 134

Shingles, 524

Shoemaker, Mary, 260, 265, 266, 276

Sierra Club, 482

Silent Spring (Carson), xix, 463, 518; advertising for, 405; article on, 438; on best-seller lists, 417; on the Book-of-the-Month, 407; Dutch translation of, 486; House of Lords debate on, 451; Keats quotation in, 402; paperback edition, 519; pesticide research for, xiii, xxvii; publication of, xxix, xxx, 410n.16; research for, 145, 251; reviews of, 411; E. B. White quotations in, 402; working titles for, xxviii, 286, 379, 380, 386

Simon and Schuster, 10, 154, 198, 199; RC and *World of Nature* project, 200, 201, 203, 204, 209, 210–11, 213

Simpson, Mr., 173, 174, 179

Since Silent Spring (F. Graham), xxix

Sky Beyond, The (P. Taylor), 511

Smiling Cow (gift shop), 57, 60, 101

Smulders, Francis, 199

Snider, Mrs., 454

Snow-Bound (Whittier), 340

Snows of Helicon, The (Tomlinson), 254

Soule, David, Sr., 388

Southport Island, Maine, xiii, xx–xxi, 3

Spectorsky, A. C., 144

Spock, Marjorie, 265

Spring in Washington (Halle), 42, 45, 99, 432

Sprow, Ida (housekeeper), 208, 209, 212, 232, 260, 269, 282, 317, 318, 338, 345, 346, 347, 348, 359, 407, 416, 466, 470

Sputnik I and II, 233

Stardust, significance of the term, 26

Star-Points (Mrs. Waldo Richards), 293, 324

Sterling, Philip, xviii

Stevens, Christine, 417, 429

Stewart, George, 485

Stilbestrol, 530

Storer, Mr. and Mrs. John, 286–87

Storm (Muir), 485

Strange Nurseries: Another Wonder Book (Jacquelyn Berrill), 154n.12

Stratton, Olive, 443

Ström, Else, 129

"Strong box," significance of, xvi, 19

Suncook, New Hampshire, 65

Surgens, Don, 449

"Sussex" (Kipling), 207

Swinger of Birches, A (Cox), 254

Tarka the Otter (Williamson), 11

Taylor, Deems, 132

Taylor, Norman, 255

Taylor, Sir Patrick, 511

Teale, Edwin Way, 41, 103, 138, 188, 199, 257, 359, 361, 364; *Autumn Across America*, 344; *Green Treasury: A Journey Through the World's Great Nature Writing*, 485; "guest author," 155; *Journey into Summer*, 344; RC's foundation efforts and, 208–9; visit to RC, 255

Teale, Nellie, 188, 255, 344, 353

Teasdale, Sara, 123–24, 303

Tenggren property, 200, 202, 205, 213, 409, 477

Tennie, Mrs. (nurse), 338, 348, 349, 356, 357

Tennyson, Alfred, Lord, 59

Theta Sigma Phi, 36

Thomas, Elizabeth Marshall, 280

Thompson, Dorothy, 529

Thomson, Virgil, 132

Thoreau, Henry David, 177, 266

Tidemarks (Tomlinson), 44

Tidens förlag, Stockholm, 129

Tides, 29, 57, 99, 186–87, 385; tide calendars, 80; tide pool explorations, 3–4, 5–6, 109–10, 115; tide race, 281

Timberlake, Jim, 372

Tomlinson, Henry Major, 37, 42, 88, 150, 151, 233, 241, 335, 353; *The Face of the Earth*, 44, 235, 414; "The Little Things," 414; "A Lost Woods," 36, 202, 224, 253, 373; RC's misplaced letter in a Tomlinson book, 134; *The Sea and the Jungle*, 9; *The Snows of Helicon*, 254; *Turn of the Tide*, 400

Tornadoes, 221

Toscanini, Arturo, 43

Towne, Merrill, 409

Toynbee, Arnold Joseph, 21–22

"Trade Winds" (Beatty), 507n.70

Train note, significance of term, 41

Turn of the Tide (Tomlinson), 400

TV Guide, 217

Udall, Stewart L., xxix, 415, 485

Ulcers: RC's duodenal ulcer, 295–96,

COLOPHON

Always, Rachel was set by Wilsted & Taylor in Baskerville, Helvetica, and Bulmer types. The text was designed by Diane Jaroch. The book was manufactured in Harrisonburg, Virginia, by R. R. Donnelley & Sons.

The paper on which the text was printed is 50-pound Nature's Offset by P. H. Glatfelter. It contains 100 percent recovered fibers, including a minimum of 20 percent postconsumer content. The photo insert was printed on 70-pound Westvaco American Eagle coated, which contains 50 percent recovered fibers including 10 percent postconsumer content.

The cloth used for binding is Rainbow Imperial, a pyroxylin-free, recyclable material. It and all other binding materials were manufactured by Ecological Fibers, Inc., using processes that contributed no solids or emissions to the waste stream.